HISTORY OF THE MONGOLIAN PEOPLE'S REPUBLIC

University Press of the Pacific
Honolulu, Hawaii

History of Mongolian People's Republic

by
USSR Academy of Sciences
MPR Academy of Sciences

ISBN 0-89875-035-0

Copyright © 2000 by University Press of the Pacific
Reprinted from the 1973 edition

University Press of the Pacific
Honolulu, Hawaii
http://www.UniversityPressofthePacific.com

All rights reserved, including the right to reproduce this book, or portions threof, in any form.

CONTENTS

Preface 9
Introduction 12
Brief Survey of the Sources for, and Basic Literature on, the History of the Mongolian People 23

PART I

Section One. *The Primitive Commune*

Chapter I. Age of Stone Tools 57
Chapter II. Age of Bronze Tools 63
Chapter III. Introduction of Iron Tools 69

Section Two. *Decay of the Primitive Commune System and Formation of Feudal Relations in Mongolia*

Chapter 1. Decay of the Primitive Commune System, First Tribal Alliances and Formations of States in Mongolia 71
    The Hun Power 71
    The State of Syan'pi 77
Chapter II. Early Feudal States in Mongolia 81
    The Zhuzhan Kaganate 81
    The Turkic Kaganate 83
    The Uighur Khanate 87
    The Khitan Empire 89

Section Three. *Mongolia as a Feudal State*

Chapter I. The Social Structure of Mongolia at the End of the XIIth—the Beginning of the XIIIth Century. Formation of the Mongolian State 98
    The Mongolian Tribes at the End of the XIIth—the Beginning of the XIIIth Century 98
    Stratification of Classes in Mongolian Society at the Outset of the XIIIth Century and Growth of Feudal Relations . . 102
    The Struggle for Power between the Mongol Khans . . . 106
    Formation of the Mongolian State and Its Class Character 108

Chapter II. The Campaigns of Conquest of Genghis Khan and His Successors. Formation of the Mongolian Empire 110
    Military Campaigns of Genghis Khan 110
    The Mongolian Empire under Genghis Khan's Successors (1227-1259) 113

Chapter III. The Yuan Mongolian Empire (1260-1368) 124
Chapter IV. The Culture of the Mongols in the XIII-XIVth Centuries 132

Section Four. *Mongolia in the XIV-XVIIth Centuries (the Feudal Disintegration of the Country)*

Chapter I. The Social Structure of Mongolia in the XIV-XVIIth Centuries 143
Chapter II. Feudal Disintegration and Attempts to Overcome It . 153
Chapter III. The Spread of Lamaism in Mongolia 163
Chapter IV. The Beginning of the Manchu Invasion 169
Chapter V. Relations Between Russia and Mongolia in the XVIIth Century 176
Chapter VI. The Culture of the Mongols in the XV-XVIIth Centuries 179

Section Five. *Mongolia Under the Rule of the Manchu Conquerors (1691-1911)*

Chapter I. Mongolia Becomes a Borderland of the Manchu Empire 185
  Popular Anti-Manchu Revolts in Outer Mongolia 190
  The Lamaist Church Subservient to the Manchu Usurpers 192
Chapter II. The *Arats* Increasingly Exploited as Feudal Serfs Under Manchu Rule 195
Chapter III. Mongolia at the Time of the Penetration of Foreign Capital into China. Growth of the Liberation Movement among the Mongol *Arats* 206
Chapter IV. Development of Russo-Mongolian Relations (the XIXth—the Beginning of the XXth Century) 217
Chapter V. The Culture of the Mongols in the XVIII-XIXth Centuries 221

Section Six. *The National-Liberation Movement of the Mongolian People (1911-1912). Declaration of Mongolian State Autonomy*

Chapter I. The Movement for National Liberation, 1911-1912 . . 228
Chapter II. The Overthrow of Manchu Rule and the Formation of a Feudal-Theocratic Mongolian State 232
Chapter III. Social and State Structure of the Feudal-Theocratic Monarchy 250
Chapter IV. Culture During the Period of the Mongolian Monarchy (1911-1919) 261

PART II

Section One. *The Mongolian People's Revolution and the Proclamation of the Mongolian People's Republic*

Chapter I. Universal Historical Importance of the Great October Socialist Revolution in Russia and Its Influence on Mongolia 269
  Influence of the October Socialist Revolution on Mongolia 269
  Establishment in Mongolia of a Regime of Occupation by the Chinese Militarists and Aggravation of the External and Internal Situation of the Country 275
  Emergence of Revolutionary Groups in Urga and Establishment by Them of Links with the Comintern and Soviet Russia 277

Chapter II. The Mongolian People's Revolution of 1921 283
    Further Aggravation of the Situation of the *Arats* as a Result of the Irruption of White Guard Bands 283
    First Congress of the Mongolian People's Party. Formation of a Provisional People's Government. Triumph of the Nation-Wide Armed Uprising in Kyakhta Maimachen . . 288
    The Spread and the Triumph of the People's Revolution . 295
    Complete Destruction of the Ungern Bands and Agreement on Friendship Between People's Mongolia and Soviet Russia. Start Made on Solving Social Problems 300
Chapter III. Democratic Changes and Proclamation of the MPR (1922-1924) 310
    Democratic Changes in the Country 310
    Intensification of the Class Struggle and General Line of the Party Aimed at Non-Capitalist Development of the Country 313
    The Grand People's Hural and the Proclamation of the MPR 315

Section Two. *The Mongolian People in the Fight for Development on Non-Capitalist Lines (1925-1940)*

Chapter I. Struggle for the Liquidation of the Economic Positions of the Feudal Class and the Liberation of the Country from the Influence of Foreign Capital (1925-1932) 320
    Consolidation of the External and Internal Position of the MPR 320
    Socio-Economic and Political Measures and Their Significance 322
    Defeat of the Right Deviationists 325
    Decisive Attack on the Economic Positions of the Feudal Class 328
    Left Deviation Overcome 330
Chapter II. The MPR During the Completion of the Stage of General Democratic Revolution (1932-1940) ....
    The Mongolian People's Fight to Implement the "New Course" Policy. Ninth Congress of the MPRP 337
    Increase of the Menace Constituted by Japanese Imperialism. Intensification of the Class Struggle Inside the Country. Defeat of the Japanese Aggressors in the Khalkhin-Gol Region 343
    Completion of the General Democratic Stage of the Revolution. Tenth Congress of the MPRP. New Constitution of the MPR 351

Section Three. *The Fight to Build the Basis for Socialism in the MPR (1940-1952)*

Chapter I. The MPR During the Years of the Second World War (1939-1945) 361
    The MPR During the Years of the Great Patriotic War of the Soviet Union 366
    The MPR's Part in the Defeat of the Armed Forces of Imperialist Japan 374
Chapter II. MPR's Transition to Peaceful Planned Economic Development (1946-1952) 381
    Consolidation of the International Status of the MPR in the Post-War Years 381
    Transition to Peaceful Construction. First Five-Year Plan for Economic and Cultural Development 387

Results of the First Five-Year Plan and Further Democratization of the Electoral System 394

Section Four. *The Fight of the Mongolian People for the Victory. of Socialism*

Chapter I. The Socialist Transformation of the Economy of the MPR 404
    Prerequisites for the Socialist Transformation of the Economy 404
    The Completion of *Arat* Husbandries' Cooperation . . . 420
    Ratification of the New Constitution 433

Chapter II. The MPR in the Fight to Complete the Construction of the Material and Technical Basis of Socialism 437
    The Tasks of Creating the Material and Technical Basis of Socialism in the MPR. Fourteenth MPRP Congress . . . 437
    The Mongolian People in the Campaign to Fulfil the Third Five-Year Plan for Developing the National Economy and Culture 442

Section Five. *Cultural Construction in the MPR*

    Public Education 458
    Cultural and Educational Activities 462
    Science 467
    Literature 474
    Theatre, Films, Circus 480
    Music 487
    Fine Arts 489
    Afterword 497
    Basic Dates in the History of the Mongolian People's Republic 506
    Bibliography 514

PREFACE

The *History of the Mongolian People's Republic* was issued in one volume in 1954, in the Mongolian and Russian languages, in Ulan Bator and Moscow, the result of collaboration between Mongolian and Soviet historians. This first joint Marxist work of scholars of the MPR and the USSR covering the whole history of the Mongolian people over many centuries, served during the 12 years after its publication as a valuable teaching manual in secondary schools and higher educational institutions in the MPR, as well as for a wide circle of readers interested in the history of the MPR.

During this period, however, big changes have taken place both in international affairs and in the internal and external situation of the MPR. Over these years the Mongolian people, with the fraternal assistance of the USSR and the other socialist countries, have made great progress in economic and cultural construction; co-operation has been fully introduced in the agriculture of MPR; socialist principles have now been fully adopted in the country's national economy and the basic objective before it is to complete the construction of socialism and develop and consolidate its material and technical base. The international standing of the MPR and its authority in foreign politics have also been immeasurably consolidated. In these circumstances it became abundantly clear that it would be necessary to re-issue the single-volume work and to supplement it with material on the history of the MPR for the years that have since elapsed.

The re-issue appeared appropriate also in the light of the fact that the first edition in one volume was issued before the historic XX Congress of the Communist Party of the Soviet Union (CPSU), the decisions of which were of exceptional importance not only for the CPSU but also for all the other Communist and Workers' Parties. Other considerations taken into account were the decisions of the XIIIth, XIVth, XVth and

XVIth Congresses of the Mongolian People's Revolutionary Party (MPRP). In this connexion steps were taken to eliminate from the second edition of the one-volume work defects and errors contained in the first.

It has further to be borne in mind that in the last 12 years a large number of monographs by Mongolian and Soviet scholars have appeared dealing with very important problems in the history, economy and culture of the MPR. These works, reflecting as they do the achievements of Mongolian historical science and Soviet-Mongolian studies have been taken into account in this second issue of the volume, new sources have been utilized, as well as very important facts and data, and greater precision introduced into certain postulates and conclusions on basic stages in the history of the MPR.

In view of the fact that the English edition of this book is being published six years after the Mongolian and Russian edition, some minor points in the text have been somewhat amplified in accordance with the present level of development of historical science in the country, and a new paragraph has been added to Chapter II, Section Two, dealing with such important events as the XVIth Congress of the Mongolian People's Revolutionary Party, the celebration of the 50th anniversary of the foundation of the MPR and the victory of the people's revolution.

In the group of authors of the first and the present, second edition of the *History of the MPR*, representing the collective effort of Mongolian and Soviet scholars, the following writers participated:

Mongolian representatives — B. Shirendyb, Sh. Natzagdorzh, B. Tseden;

Soviet representatives — A. Yu. Yakubowski, S. V. Kiselev, L. I. Duman, S. D. Dylykov, I. Ya. Zlatkin, G. I. Mikhailov, B. I. Pankratov, P. P. Staritsina, I. N. Ustyuzhaninov, N. P. Shastina, A. T. Yakimov.

The following chapters and paragraphs were written afresh for the second edition: Introduction — N. Ishzhamts; Chapters I, II, III of Section One, Part II and a new paragraph in Chapter II, Section Four—B. Shirendyb; Chapter IV of Section Three, Chapter IV of Section Four, and Chapter V of Section Five of Part I—Sh. Bira; Chapter I of Section Four of Part II—Sh. Sandag, M. Sanzhdorzh, D. Dugar, B. Tudev; Chapter II of Section Four of Part II—D. Dashzhamts. The following passages were redrafted and amplified: Section One of Part I and paragraphs 1 and 3 of Chapter II of Section Two—N. Ser-Odzhav; Paragraphs 1 and 2 of Chapter I of Section Two—T. D. Dorzhsuren; Paragraphs 1 and 4 of Chapter II of Section Two—Kh. Perle; Chapter III of Section Three—N. Ishzhamts; Chapters I and II of Section Three and Section Four — Sh. Natsagdorzh, Section Five of Part I—Sh. Natsagdorzh and D. Gongor; Section Six of Part I—Sh. Sandag; Chapter I of Section Two of Part II—M. Sanzhdorzh; Chapter II of Section Two of Part II—B. Tseden; Chapters I and II of Section Three of Part II—B. Tudev; Section Five of Part II—G. Tserendorzh and Sh. Bira.

In editing the one-volume edition in Mongolian the following contributors participated: N. Ishzhamts, D. Gongor, Ts. Puntsagnorov, N. Ser-Odzhav, B. Tudev.

In editing this edition in Russian the following contributors participated: L. I. Duman, L. Ya. Zlatkin, L. A. Yevtyukhova, G. D. Sanzheev, P. P. Staritsina, S. K. Roshchin, N. P. Shastina, A. T. Yakimov, L. M. Gataullina, G. S. Matveeva.

The editorial board of the English edition express their sincere gratitude to all Mongolian and Soviet colleagues who took part in reviewing the text and contributing new material and afterword.

INTRODUCTION

The one-volume *History of the Mongolian People's Republic* encompasses the history of Mongolia from the very earliest times up to our day.

It consists of two parts: the first part narrates the history of Mongolia up to the people's revolution, while the second is the history of the people's revolution and the Mongolian People's Republic.

Section One of Part I of the book covers the period of the primitive commune system: the Stone Age, the era when tools were made from bronze, and the beginning of iron tools. Archaeological investigations by Mongolian and Soviet scholars have in recent years brought to light on the territory of the MPR artifacts of the Middle and Lower Palaeolithic periods which make it possible to move the chronology of Mongolian history back 200,000 years before our era. Like other very ancient peoples, the remote ancestors of the Mongols passed, in the course of their development, from the stage of the primitive horde to a primitive commune system and thereafter also to a class society.

Section Two is devoted to the decay of the primitive commune system and the emergence of class societies and early feudal states on the territory of Mongolia. In Central Asia a class society and a state structure first emerged in Mongolia with the Huns in the third century before our era as a consequence of the decay of the primitive commune system. The first state of an early feudal type to emerge on Mongolian territory among the Mongol-speaking tribes was, in our opinion, the Kaganate of Zhuzhan, which existed in the IV-VIth centuries A. D. The Turkic Kaganate (VI-VIIIth centuries) and the Uighur Khanate (IX-Xth centuries) were also early feudal states but more developed as compared with the Kaganate of Zhuzhan. The process of feudalization becomes further developed in the Khitan Empire which existed in the X-XIIth centuries on the territory of South-Eastern Mongolia and Northern China and which, in respect of social-economic and cultural development, stood higher than the Turkic and Uighur Khanates.

Sections Three to Six describe the completion of the process of the formation of feudalism and its further development.

Section Three shows the process of consolidation of the Mongolian nation and the strengthening of feudal relationships in connexion with the formation of a Mongolian feudal state.

The foundation of a Mongolian feudal state at the outset of the XIIIth century stimulated the growth of productive forces and the consolidation of the internal unity of the Mongolian people and is considered by us to be a progressive factor in their history.

The political unification of Mongolia in a single state could have helped towards a further advance in the country's productive resources and its economic and cultural progress. The obstacle to this, however, was the aggressive policy of the Mongol feudal leaders headed by Genghis Khan, who turned the people into warriors and the country into a military camp. The aggressive campaigns of Genghis Khan and his successors against the peoples of China, Iran, Russia and other countries were a supreme disaster, since they held up for a long time the progressive development of those peoples. During these campaigns enormous material and cultural assets were destroyed and tens of thousands of people were wiped out. The aggressive wars of the Mongol feudal leaders also had the effect of halting the growth of the productive forces and culture of Mongolia itself and brought the Mongolian people nothing but sufferings.

Created by fire and sword from the blood of peoples, the Mongolian Empire which was rent by internal contradictions and, without one common economic basis, fell under the attacks of the peoples of the countries the Mongols had conquered.

Section Four is devoted to a description of the period of feudal disintegration (XIV to beginning of XVIIth century). At this time, even on the territory of Mongolia itself, all trace of the former centralization disappeared and in place of a single Khan wielding dictatorial powers there were individual Khans warring among themselves, "petty Khans" as the Mongolian chroniclers called them.

From the end of the XIVth and beginning of the XVth centuries protracted warfare began to be waged between the West Mongolian and East Mongolian feudal chieftains. The reasons for these wars should be sought primarily in the feudal nature of production relations in Mongolia and in the state of crisis in which the Mongolian economy found itself after the collapse of the Empire. The grievous consequences of the campaigns of conquest, the predominance of a natural economy, the lack of domestic markets, etc. were serious obstacles in the way of unifying the country and creating a centralized state.

However, even in such difficult times, the Mongolian state not only managed to survive intact; it also succeeded for a long time in maintaining its political independence too. It was during this period that numerous attempts were made to re-establish the political unity of the country and to cope with feudal disintegration under Esenkhan, Mandukhai-tsetsen khatun, Dayan Khan, Tumen Zasagtu Khan and, finally, under Legden Khan. Furthermore, Mongolia, as a sovereign state, plays at that time the part of an active international entity which had political, economic and cultural relations with China, Tibet, Russia, and other countries.

One of the phenomena characterizing the end of this period was the spread of Lamaism in Mongolia; later it became the predominant religion of the country.

By the beginning of the XVIIth century alien aggressors from Manchuria were threatening Mongolia. As it had not yet overcome the fragmentation of feudalism, Mongolia, despite the heroic resistance of its people and as a result of the treachery of a reactionary section of the higher priesthood and the bigger feudal lords, succumbed to the Manchu yoke. The period of Manchu domination (Section Five) lasted for more than two hundred years, during which Mongolia lost its political independence and became an oppressed borderland of the Manchu Empire.

In order to retain Mongolia under their authority the Manchu emperors pursued a policy of maintaining and strengthening feudalism as a decisive factor and also of keeping the country isolated from the outside world. The lay and religious feudal leaders formed the social support of the aliens who ruled over the Mongol people.

Thus, the people of Mongolia found themselves under a twofold yoke—that of the Manchu conquerors and Chinese merchants, on the one hand, and of their own feudal lords on the other. The natural result was a further worsening of the situation of the *arats* (peasants) and protracted stagnation in the expansion of the country's productive forces.

The Manchu yoke, the protracted isolation of the country from the outside world and the domination of reactionary Lamaism were the reasons for the economic and cultural backwardness of the Mongolian people.

Imperialist expansion into Mongolia from the end of the XIXth century onwards had an especially serious effect on the country's economy and culture, accompanied as it was by an ever-increasing intensification of the oppression exercised by the foreign agents of capitalist merchants and usurers over the country's economy.

Notwithstanding the grievous alien and feudal oppression suffered and the baleful influence of Lamaism, the freedom-loving spirit of the Mongolian people was not stifled. The Mongolian *arats* more than once rose up in arms against the Manchu yoke. The biggest of these uprisings before the early years of the XXth century was the anti-Manchu revolt of the Mongolian people for their independence in the years 1755-1758 under the leadership of the Oirat Prince Amursana and the Khalkha Prince Chingunzhav, who were joined by many influential representatives of the ruling class of Khalkha and Western and Inner Mongolia. But at that time the liberation movement of the *arats* bore a spontaneous and unorganized charater and the *arats* did not have their own political class organization. In these circumstances the feudal lords took over the leadership of the movement for their own narrow class interests and often betrayed the insurgent *arats* by acting in collusion with the Manchu authorities. Despite this, the spontaneous *arat* uprisings weakened and undermined both the alien rule and the feudal structure in Mongolia itself and gave the *arats* a wealth of experience in class warfare.

The Russian Revolution of 1905 helped to promote the political awakening of Mongolia, increased the activity of the *arat* liberation movement and widened the friendly links between the Mongolian labouring classes and the Russian people. Isolated anti-Manchu outbreaks by *arats* in 1911 developed into a major armed uprising which led to the re-establishment of Mongolian statehood in the form of a feudal-theocratic monarchy (1911-1919), the history of which is described in Section VI of Part I of the book. After the overthrow of the Manchu yoke in 1911 the Mongolian Government proclaimed the independence of its country. Inner Mongolia announced its reunion with Khalkha in a single Mongolian State.

As, however, imperialism was completely dominant all over the world, there could be no possibility of this desire of the Mongolians being implemented.

In 1915, under the so-called "Tripartite agreement" Russia and China forced Mongolia to accept the status of an autonomous State within the borders of China.

Nevertheless, the re-establishment of Mongolian statehood after a long experience of alien rule did unquestionably represent progress and the period of feudal-theocratic rule or autonomy was an advance on the preceding period, since during the period in question certain political, economic and cultural reforms were carried through. But the *arat* population still enjoyed no political rights and were socially oppressed. The feudal-theocratic clique, as the rulers of the country, increased their exploitation of the *arats*, who from personal experience became more and more convinced that genuine, complete emancipation could only be achieved by a struggle not only against foreign aggressors but also against their own feudal lords.

The subsequent periods in the history of Mongolia, covering the most recent events in its history, starting after the October Revolution, are narrated in Part II of the present volume.

The triumph of the Great October Socialist Revolution of 1917 in Russia, which was a turning point in the history of mankind, opened up before the people of Mongolia the way to complete freedom from oppression of any kind—the way to socialism.

The great Lenin pointed out that "... with the aid of the proletariat of the advanced countries, backward countries can go over to the Soviet system and, through certain stages of development, to communism without having to pass through the capitalist stage."[1] In these words of Lenin the Mongolian *arats* found their supreme source of inspiration and derived their belief in the ultimate victory over the forces of reaction. The fraternal alliance between the Mongolian *arats* and the Russian working class played a decisive role in the victory of the peoples' revolution of 1921 and in the whole subsequent struggle of the Mongolian people to consolidate their national independence, to secure the triumph of the non-capitalist path of development and build socialism.

The contemporary history of the Mongolian people can be divided basically into two stages, namely, the first stage from 1921 to 1940, when the anti-imperialist and anti-feudal revolution was completed and a firm foundation laid for non-capitalist development, and the second stage from 1940 up to the present day, when socialism is being built up. Each stage in turn consists of several periods which are dealt with in separate Sections.

Section One, Part II of the book covers the history of the Mongolian nation from 1918 to 1924.

The early years of this period are notable for the gradual intensification of the process leading to the stagnation of the feudal system and to acute deterioration in the conditions of the mass of the population. Furthermore, in 1919 Mongolia was occupied by the Chinese militarists and its autonomy abolished; a year later the country was occupied by Russian White Guard troops thrown out of Russia by the October Revolution. Both the White Guards and the Chinese militarists, acting as the hirelings of foreign imperialism, turned Mongolia into a military bridgehead against Soviet Russia. At this difficult moment the ruling feudal-theocratic clique in Mongolia decided on a policy of betraying their own country.

The patience of the Mongolian people was strained beyond limits and in 1921 they rose determined to fight it out with the foreign aggressors and native reactionaries. Under the leadership of the Mongolian People's Revolutionary Party, and with the help of Soviet Russia, the insurgent people swept away the foreign occupation and won political power in the country, overthrowing the government of the Bogdo-gegen.

On July 11, 1921, the victory of the people's revolution was proclaimed in the capital of Mongolia.

The Mongolian people's revolution represents an anti-imperialist and anti-feudal revolution.

As a result of the triumph of the people's revolution Mongolia was the first of the nations of the East to drop out of the colonial regime of the imperialist plunderers.

After the victory of the people's revolution and up to 1924, the country's old machinery of government broke down and local people's assemblies (*hurals*) were set up as organs of the new ruling power. Steps were also taken to revoke the rights of the feudal class to the ownership of land and of serfs; all debts of any kind to foreign firms, merchants and moneylenders were annulled and feudal servitudes and levies abolished.

With the help of the Soviet Union *arat* co-operative consumers' and marketing associations were formed and a Mongolian trade and industrial bank, schools and new cultural, scientific and medical institutions founded.

The Third Congress of the Mongolian People's Revolutionary Party, held in August 1924, after discussing the prospects for the further development of the country, defined the general Party line to be the non-capitalist path of development as laid down by Lenin.

On November 26, 1924, the Grand People's Hural proclaimed Mongolia a People's Republic and adopted the first constitution. The Mongolian People's Republic became the first country of national democracy.

Section Two covers the period from 1925 to 1940, during which the anti-imperialist and anti-feudal stage of the revolution was finally accomplished and the foundations laid for the non-capitalist path of development.

During this period a national currency was put into circulation, a uniform state finance system was approved, co-operative trade was expanded and intensified, and state trading organized. The policy governing customs duties and taxation was directed towards restricting and ousting foreign firms. In 1930 the state set up a foreign trade monopoly and closed down big foreign trading firms, as a result of which the problem of ousting foreign capital was solved.

Between 1929 and 1939, on the initiative and with the active participation of the poorer and middle-class elements of the *arats* the holdings in property and livestock of the wealthy feudal lay and public officials were confiscated, which dealt a decisive blow to the economic power of feudalism. By the end of the thirties the feudal class, both lay and religious, was virtually liquidated and the anti-feudal revolution gained a total victory.

At the same time, under the leadership of the Mongolian People's Revolutionary Party and with the help of the USSR, a huge campaign of creative activity was carried out: in agriculture a network of machine-harvester stations was set up, the first *arat* production associations were formed, new industrial enterprises were set up, roads and railways laid down, state motor transport developed and a state socialist sector established in the national economy.

A new social force was being born and trained—the young Mongolian working class, which was destined in future to take over the leadership of the country's socialist construction.

In the field of popular education, culture and the arts brilliant successes have been achieved. A people's working class intelligentsia has emerged, possessing modern education and armed with the ideas of Marxism-Leninism.

In 1940 the Eighth Grand People's Hural adopted the New Constitution which reflected the successes and achievements of the Mongolian people in the development of their own country.

The general democratic stage of the revolution has been successfully terminated and has created the preliminary conditions for a gradual transition to socialist construction, by-passing capitalism.

Sections Three and Four of Part II deal with the history of the Mongolian people's fight to build up the bases of socialism and with the triumph of socialist producton relations in the national economy between 1940 and 1970.

In 1940 the MPR, steadfastly pursuing the non-capitalist path of development, immediately moved on towards socialist construction. However, the perfidious assault of the German fascists on the USSR and the threat from Japanese imperialism interrupted the peaceful, creative activities of the Mongolian people and obliged them to find big material resources, forces and time to meet the country's defence requirements and extend what assistance it could to the Soviet Army.

The historic victory of the Soviet Union over German fascism and the rout of Japanese imperialism achieved by the Soviet Army with the participation of Mongolian troops and the formation of the socialist camp headed by the Soviet Union created exceptionally favourable conditions for socialist construction in the MPR. The Soviet Union and the other socialist countries, by constantly extending brotherly aid to the Mongolian people, speeded up the tempo of socialist construction in the MPR.

Starting in 1948, the MPR introduced long-term planning for the development of the national economy and culture. Previously, plans were adopted for each year. In the years of the First and Second Five-Year Plans and a Three-Year Plan for the development of the national economy, the Mongolian people, together with other nations, in the fight to strengthen peace and reinforce international friendship, gained more and more new victories in developing the national economy, more especially in industry and transport. Industrial output in 1960 was 7.4 times the 1940 figure and the share of industrial production relating to group "A" rose from 25% in 1952 to 53% in 1959.

As a consequence of the successes achieved in the industrial sphere the MPR has been transformed from an agricultural to an agricultural-industrial country.

In agriculture a new branch has made its appearance alongside livestock-breeding—socialist land cultivation, which is being quickly developed on the basis of advanced technology. As a result of the successful development of grain farming the problem of supplying the country with home-grown seed and flour had by 1960 already been solved. The basic branch of the national economy—cattle-breeding—is being steadily expanded and meets the main requirements of both consumers and manufacturers, as well as of foreign trade.

The most complicated and difficult matter was the campaign for the socialist transformation of agriculture. The general successes achieved in the development of industry, transport, culture, the increase in personnel and the creative application of the experience obtained in collective farming in the USSR—all these factors had a favourable effect, leading to the correct and successful solution of the problems involved in the socialist reconstruction of the country's agriculture. The voluntary transition of the *arats* from individual ownership to socialist tenure proceeded at a particularly rapid rate from 1955 onwards and was completely achieved in 1959. The victory won by socialist co-operation in the *arat* economy meant the permanent establishment throughout the national economy of socialist production relations.

Thanks to the sagacious policy of the Mongolian People's Revolutionary Party, which was guided in its activities by the invincible teaching of Marxism-Leninism, the task of building the foundations of socialism in the MPR was successfully accomplished.

Section Four covers the period from 1961 to 1971, during which the Mongolian people were fighting to create the material and technological basis for socialism.

After socialist production principles had won supremacy in the whole national economy, the MPR found itself faced with the new and immense task of finally completing socialist construction by creating a material and technological basis for it. The XIVth Congress of the MPRP, held in 1961, confronted the country with the problem of finalizing the creation of a material and technological basis for socialism; this meant fully equipping the national economy with modern means of production, with up-to-date technology, above all, and transforming the MPR in the immediate future from an agrarian-industrial country into an industrial-agrarian one. The Mongolian people successfully carried out the Third Five-Year Plan for economic and cultural development for the years 1961-1965 and this achievement constituted a considerable step forward in the direction of creating a material and technological basis for socialism and transforming the MPR into an industrial-agrarian country.

During the years of the Third Five-Year Plan the number of cattle increased by 15.4%, the area under cultivation by 81% and the volume of industrial output by 70%.

Agriculture is becoming mechanized at a rapid rate, modern technological methods are being introduced into industry and transport, new industrial enterprises and power stations are being built. The first section of the Darkhan-Sharyngolsk industrial project has been brought into operation and will form the second major industrial centre of the country after the capital.

In connexion with effective realization of the task of creating a material and technological basis for socialism special attention has been paid to training engineers and technicians. During the years of revolution, and more especially in recent times, there has emerged a very large body of engineering and technical personnel trained in the higher educational institutions of the Soviet Union, the German Democratic Republic, Czechoslovakia, Poland and other socialist countries as well as in the state university, polytechnical college and other technical schools and training courses of the MPR.

In order to solve the problem of finally establishing a material and technological basis for socialism in the MPR, it is exceptionally important to maintain the closest collaboration with the Soviet Union and the other socialist countries. The accession in 1962 of the MPR to the Council for Mutual Economic Assistance of socialist countries constituted a major event in the history of Mongolia. The collaboration of People's Mongolia with the other socialist countries on the principle of international socialist division of labour will enable the MPR to complete socialist construction at the earliest possible moment and with the least expenditure of effort and of material and financial resources. It is a firm guarantee of the fact that in a short time the MPR will be able to succeed in overcoming its relative backwardness as compared with the leading socialist countries in its level of economic development and to establish the preliminary requisites for a more or less simultaneous move forward, together with the other socialist countries, to communism.

As a result of the brilliant successes achieved in the matter of non-capitalist development and socialist construction and also of following a peaceful foreign policy, and thanks to the heroic struggles of the Mongolian people, the international standing of the MPR is being steadily consolidated. The MPR has established diplomatic relations with all the socialist countries and with many other states. Its admission in 1961 to membership of the United Nations was a complete triumph for the MPR's fight for national independence, the result of, and a proof of, the victory of the whole socialist camp in the fight for peace, democracy and socialism over imperialism and reaction.

The MPR as an independent, sovereign socialist state has won rightful recognition all over the world.

Section Five of Part II of this book is devoted to cultural construction in the MPR during the years 1921-1970.

From the early days of the people's revolution in Mongolia the country was faced with the problem of developing the national culture as one of the most important tasks in building up its new existence. Nevertheless, in the course of accomplishing this task the Mongolian people were confronted with incredible difficulties, due mainly to the extreme backwardness of the country. A major obstacle was Lamaism—the predominant ideology of pre-revolutionary Mongolia, which, as the basic religion of the country, for a long time wielded enormous influence over the masses, even after the revolution.

However, following the guidance of Marxist-Leninist teaching, the MPRP succeeded in organizing its people for victory in this sphere, too, overcoming difficulties and obstacles.

The specific feature of the cultural revolution in Mongolia was that, in the course of its development, it passed through two stages, namely, the revolutionary-democratic stage (1921-1940) and the socialist stage, beginning in the forties.

In the first stage of the revolution the basic tasks were to end illiteracy among the population, lay the foundations for a system of public education, new literature and art, based on the principles of revolutionary idealism and also train a national intelligentsia. During this stage the Mongolian people achieved major successes in the sphere of public education; the country was covered with a network of primary and secondary schools and secondary technical schools.

During the second stage of the revolution an enormous transformation occurred in the cultural development of the MPR, qualitatively changing the face of the country. A new alphabet, intelligible to the people, was created, illiteracy was wiped out completely and a state university and other higher educational establishments were opened. Increasing numbers of Mongolian teachers, doctors, veterinary surgeons, zootechnicians, agronomists, engineers and technicians are coming forward—graduates of local institutes of higher education and technical colleges or trained in other socialist countries.

The ranks of Mongolian scholars and literary and artistic workers are filling up.

An MPR Academy of Sciences has been established—a noteworthy event in the history of Mongolia and one that is enormously important for the further development of the country. Although it is a young institution, the Academy of Sciences of the MPR is making no small contribution to the cause of building socialism.

Socialist literature and art are developing successfully in Mongolia; they are socialist in content and national in form.

The MPR has gone through a cultural revolution, the final stage of which will bring it abreast of the other socialist countries in the cultural sphere.

Thus, in a matter of some 50 years the MPR has succeeded in moving forward from feudalism to socialism, by-passing the capitalist stage of development, and is successfully accomplishing the task of creating a material and technological basis for socialism.

Under the leadership of the MPRP and with the help of the Soviet Union, the Mongolian people, as a member of the socialist commonwealth of nations, are achieving new successes in creating a material and technological basis for socialism in their own country and in the fight for peace and friendship between all nations.

BRIEF SURVEY OF THE SOURCES FOR,
AND BASIC LITERATURE ON, THE HISTORY
OF THE MONGOLIAN PEOPLE

The sources for the history of the Mongolian people may be divided into material sources and documentary sources.

I

Material sources will comprise different kinds of archaeological materials such as: domiciliary memorials, i.e. sites occupied by primitive man, ancient town sites, ruins of towns; funerary monuments, casual finds of hoards and individual articles.

On the basis of archaeological materials an approximate picture can be built up of life in past centuries and some kind of idea obtained of the cultural and economic development of earlier generations of people. Burial grounds supply materials connected not only with a narrow range of customs and beliefs, on the basis of which a judgment can be formed of the ideological superstructure of a given society, but also materials characterizing the mode of life of a nation, its economy and social relations. Materials of this kind which have been found in the MPR are of great scientific value in studying the ancient and medieval history of Mongolia.

From the very earliest times Mongolia was a cultural centre of the nomadic tribes and nationalities in Central Asia.

This is proved by the profusion of monuments of material culture found on the territory of Mongolia. The archaeological study of Mongolia began comparatively recently, and may be considered to have started with the discovery by N. M. Yadrintsev in 1889[1] of the ruins of the ancient capital of Mongolia, Karakorum.

Of great importance for the study of the earliest period of Mongolian history are the archaeological finds made in recent years by the Soviet-Mongolian archaeological expedition under the scientific leadership of A. P. Okladnikov, corresponding member of the USSR Academy of Sciences. The most important result of the expedition was the discovery of a series of sites of primitive peoples of the Lower and Middle Palaeolithic periods.[2]

The Bronze Age in Mongolia has received less study. We have available some material from 50-60 tiled tombs excavated on the territory of the Mongolian People's Republic and also various finds kept in museum collections in Ulan Bator and in *aimak* centres.

In describing the originality of the bronze articles in the National Museum collections, S. V. Kiselev, writing an article "Mongolia in Ancient Times," was the first to express an opinion on the archaeological knowledge about the Bronze Age in Mongolia and defined its basic features and stages. Recently, individual studies have been appearing on the Bronze Age in Mongolia.[3]

The excavations made by P. K. Kozlov in the Noin-ula Mts. in 1924[4] constitute a major contribution to the study of Hun memorials. This was one of the biggest archaeological discoveres of the XXth century.

For a study of the history of the Huns the archaeological excavations carried out by Mongolian archaeologists are of quite considerable importance. In 1954 Ts. Dorzhsuren resumed the excavation of the Hun tombs in the Noin-ula and it was he who discovered the previously unknown centers of Hun monuments and a large number of tombs on the territory of Mongolia.[5]

On the history of the Turkic peoples, that inhabited of Mongolia, there are quite a number of material memorials and runic inscriptions, known as "Orkhon-Yenisei." These inscriptions contain valuable information on the history of the Turks, Kirghiz, Uighurs and ancient Mongol tribes. Russian and Soviet Turkologists and archaeologists have played an important part in discovering and deciphering the inscriptions.[6]

In the years 1957-1959 Mongolian archaeologists conducted excavations and investigations of Turkic tombs and excavations were also made by a Mongolian-Czechoslovak expedition.

In 1957 N. Ser-Odzhav and Ts. Dorzhsuren excavated the tomb of Tonyukuk, an adviser to the Turk Kagan, in the valley of Bayan-Tsogt, not far from the Nalaikh mine, 50 kilometres south-east of Ulan Bator. During the excavations runic (Turkic) wall inscriptions were discovered, scratched on the plaster of the burial structure and on other structural materials.[7] In 1958-1959 a Mongolian-Czechoslovak expedition excavated the burial edifice of the Turkic Prince Kul-Tegin in Khosho-Tsaidam in the basin of the River Orkhon and discovered formerly unknown fragments of runic (Turkic) inscriptions, a stone image of the head of Kul-Tegin and fragments of ceramic ware of the VIIIth century.[8]

In addition, finds are still being made in Mongolia of new Turkic inscriptions on stones and individual items—seals, coins, etc.

The excavations made on USSR territory, particularly in the Buryat ASSR and in Khakassia, are also quite important for studying the history of the Huns and Turks. The excavations carried out by S. V. Kiselev and A. P. Okladnikov have provided a lot of data throwing light on the economy and the social system of these ancient states, whose centre was situated on the territory of the Mongolian People's Republic. The most important archaeological exploration work done in Mongolia has been the excavation of towns and settlements of ancient and mediaeval Mongolia. The results of the excavations at Karakorum and other towns, carried out by Soviet archaeologists headed by S. V. Kiselev, corresponding member of the USSR Academy of Sciences, in collaboration with Mongolian scholars, have been described in an interesting, comprehensive work which appeared after the death of the leader of the expedition, S. V. Kiselev.[9]

As a result of the scientific expeditions carried out by Mongolian archaeologists, traces of hundreds of towns and sites on the territory of the Mongolian People's Republic have been discovered.[10]

In the light of the new material discovered, the role played by settled communities in the history of nomadism in Mongolia becomes more significant than was at first thought.

The above is a brief survey of the studies carried out on archaeological memorials in the Mongolian People's Republic.

Recent archaeological discoveries have made it possible to throw light on many problems bearing on the ancient and mediaeval history of the Mongolian People's Republic.

II

Written memorials containing information regarding a particular historical event, the notes made by direct participants or witnesses, the texts of laws and regulations, publications of treaties or state instruments and similar documents are valuable historical sources.

There are a considerable number of written sources for the study of the history of the Mongols. Mongolian chronicles which appeared at an early stage in the development of writing among the Mongols are especially important. Only one Mongolian historical chronicle compiled in 1240 has come down to us—*Mongolyn nuuts tovchoo* ("The Sacred Legend"). According to the indications, however, of various authors it can confidently be averred that, before the XIIIth century, the Mongols had historical chronicles and legends which formed the basis of the above-mentioned historical work, the only one that has come down to us. The complete Mongolian text of this chronicle has been preserved in Chinese hieroglyph writing and in a Chinese translation entitled *Yuań-chao-pi-shik*. It is, for instance, known that there existed a secret history of the family of Genghis and his descendants entitled *Altan debter* ("Golden Book", i.e. regal book), preserved in the Khan's treasure house and accessible only to a few people. This chronicle has been examined by many specialists in Mongolian studies. The text and translations of it have been published in several languages. The distinction of discovering this chronicle and bringing it into scientific circulation, and also the first translation made of it into Russian from the Chinese condensed translation, belongs to the eminent Russian Sinologist Palladiy Kafarov, who published his translation in 1866 under the title *The Ancient Mongol Legend of Genghis Khan*.[11]

In the study of *Mongolyn nuuts tovchoo* a great deal of work has been done by Mongolian and Soviet scholars, by specialists in Mongolian studies from the fraternal socialist countries and by Orientalists in capitalist countries.[12] Academician S. A. Kozin published the Mongolian text, a translation into Russian and a study of the work in 1940. A translation into modern Mongolian of the chronicle *Mongolyn nuuts tovchoo* has been made by Academician Ts. Damdinsuren. The chronicle is extremely important for the study of early mediaeval Mongolia.

During the time of the Mongol Empire a legal work was also compiled—*Tsagan-teukhe*, which has survived in a XVIth century text. Although it is small in size, it contains a wealth of factual material about the political structure of Mongolia in the XIVth century.[13]

The campaigns of conquest waged by Genghis Khan and his immediate successors could not fail to attract the attention of XIIIth century writers and chroniclers in other countries. The devastating raids and conquests, accompanied as they were by the destruction of prosperous cities and the extermination or mass enslavement of their population were reflected in the writings of contemporary authors.

These writings supply a critical assessment of the actions of the Mongol conquerors. The early sources of Mongolian history contain not only a description of the course of historical events but also cite a great deal of contemporary evidence illuminating the events from the standpoint of the vanquished peoples.

There are many such sources, but we will note only the most important of them. Prominent among these sources is the

Collection of Chronicles, written in the years 1300, 1301, 1310 and 1311 by the distinguished mediaeval Iranian historian, Rashid ad-Din, on the orders of Ghazan-khan. This comprehensive historical work constitutes a codex of universal history in which the author has included events which he himself witnessed, i.e. up to the reform of Ghazan-khan at the beginning of the XIVth century. Rashid ad-Din considered that, in writing the history of peoples of Moslem origin, one should take as a basis the sources and literary traditions of those peoples. Such a view on the writing of history was a step forward for Iranian historians, who had previously ignored the history of non-Moslem peoples. Rashid ad-Din took as a basis for his work on the Mongol tribes, Genghis Khan and his successors, the original Mongolian chronicles *(Altan debter)* etc., and oral traditions. This circumstance enabled Rashid ad-Din, Academician B. Ya. Vladimirtsov says, "to give a remarkably detailed picture of the nomad existence of the Mongolian tribes."[14] Rashid ad-Din also made use of written Iranian and Arab sources. His work is one of the detailed sources for the early mediaeval period of Mongolia, and has been translated into various languages, the most important translation being that executed by a group of associates of the Institute of Oriental Studies of the USSR Academy of Sciences.[15]

Among other Iranian sources mention should be made of the chronicle of Ibn al-Asira who wrote about the Mongolian invasion of Turkestan immediately after it ended. The chronicle gives very vivid impressions of the destruction of Bokhara, the capture of Samarqand and other events. Part of Ibn al-Asira's chronicle telling the story of the Mongol invasion has been translated into Russian.[16]

Another extremely interesting work is the full and detailed review of the Mongol campaigns given by the Iranian historian Juvaini, who, although he was not a direct witness of the conquest of Turkestan, wrote his account shortly after the events occurred. He had occasion to travel a great deal over the immense territory of the Mongolian Empire and visited not only Turkestan but also Uighuria and Mongolia itself. His chronicle contains much valuable information on the history of the Mongol campaigns and has appeared in English translation in two volumes.[17]

The testimony of European travellers like Plano Carpini, Rubruk and Marco Polo, who visited Mongolia in the XIII-XIVth centuries, is also extremely important for producing a history of early mediaeval Mongolia. The first two were envoys sent, one on the heels of the other, by the Pope of Rome and the French King Louis IX to conduct negotiations with the Mongol Khans.

Plano Carpini travelled through the western part of the Mongol Empire and visited Karakorum in 1246. He gave a detailed description of this capital city of the Mongol Khans, as well as much information about the Mongols and their pattern of life.

Eight years later Guillaume Rubruk visited Karakorum and his account is even more exact and detailed. Both of them supply details of the military and economic conditions and the political life of the country. Our information about the city of Karakorum is based mainly on the material supplied by these two travellers. Plano Carpini, in particular, reports on the work of the Russian goldsmith Kuzma, who lived in Karakorum and who made a throne for the Khan and also the state seal; Rubruk tells about another goldsmith, the Frenchman Guillaume Bouchier, who constructed a wonderful fountain for the Khan's beautiful palace.

Both Plano Carpini and Rubruk spent relatively little time in Mongolia and in their writings could convey only general impressions of the country. Their books have been published in various languages of the world and some have appeared in Mongolian. Complete Mongolian translations of the writings of Plano Carpini and Rubruk are preserved in manuscript form in the Mongolian collection of the State Library.

Marco Polo was more fortunate; he was the son of a Venetian merchant who lived 17 years in the Mongol Empire and was in the service of Kublai Khan, on whose orders he made several journeys to different places in the Mongol state. Marco Polo wrote, or, to be more correct, dictated his book several years after returning from China.

The book contains detailed information on the administrative structure of the Empire, the organization of government, the cultural level of life in China, the Mongol troops, postal highways, etc., and also much historical information. Marco Polo's book is well known to Orientalists and is important not only for the history of Oriental studies but also for the history of world culture. It has become a subject for research work and has been published and republished, along with extensive commentaries.

Among recent works in European languages may be mentioned a historical and linguistic commentary on Marco Polo's book compiled by Pelliot and Hambis.[18]

Marco Polo's book has been translated into Mongolian three times.[19]

Armenian sources on the Mongols are very important for studying the early history of the Mongolian state. Among these sources are the writings of Grigor Aknertsi Magakiy,[20] Vardan Vardanet,[21] Mkhitar Airivanetsi,[22] Stepanos Orbelyan, Smbat Sparapet,[23] Kirakos Gandzaketsi,[24] Bishop Stepanos, the Bezimyanny Sebastasi, Getum II and Nerses Palients.[25] In addition to the works of the above mentioned authors there exist also inscriptions and notes which contain valuable information on the history of XIIIth century Mongolia.

The value of the Armenian sources, as has been noted by K. Patkanov, lies in the fact that "Armenian writers enjoy the favourable distinction, as compared with others, especially Moslem and Byzantine writers, of being sober-minded and truthful in reporting the events of which they themselves were contemporary eye-witnesses."[26]

Chinese sources are very important for the study of the ancient history of Mongolia. According to tradition, Chinese historians always compiled a detailed official history of each dynasty after it ceased to exist. Dynastic histories of this kind contain much factual material but it is usually narrated from the standpoint of the Chinese feudal bureaucracy, extolling rulers and idolizing emperors.

When they complied the dynastic histories and chronicles of China the court historians usually gave information about the numerous nomadic people living in the lands to the north of China. Separate "chapters" or "notes" were devoted to the commercial, political and cultural links with the nomadic tribes and these "chapters" and "notes" contain much factual material about the ancient tribes and peoples such as Huns, Syan'pi, Zhuzhans, Turks, Uighurs, Kirghiz, Khitans, ancient Mongols and others.[27]

In recent years collections have been published in the Chinese People's Republic of Chinese texts of dynastic and historical accounts, chronicles and other writings of Chinese travellers and other documents.[28] Some of them have also been issued in separate volumes.

Among the most important sources on the problems of the ancient history of Central and Eastern Asia are the translations done by Russian and European Sinologists, who have collected and systematized a number of texts taken from Chinese histories.[29]

Most of these works have withstood protracted scrutiny over the years and have lost none of their importance even in our day, although they were published more than 100 years ago.

Mongolian historians have done a great deal of work in studying Chinese sources on questions of the early and middle periods of the history of Mongolia. For example, the well-known authorities on Mongolia, Ch. Bat-Ochir, L. Dendeb and other Members of the Science Committee of the Mongolian People's Republic have worked on producing translations from Manchu and Chinese texts of the dynastic histories and chronicles of China dealing with the ancient inhabitants of Central and Eastern Asia.[30]

Among the principal sources in Chinese for the history of mediaeval Mongolia should be noted *Sheng wu Tsin Ch'en lu* ("Story of a Campaign") and *Yuan shih* ("History of the Mongol Yuan Dynasty"). The former work has been translated into Russian, French and Mongolian.[31]

Pelliot and Hambis consider that this Mongolian chronicle, which has survived in a Chinese translation, was compiled in the second half of the XIIIth century.

Yuan-shih was compiled during the era of the Ming dynasty in the XIVth century. It is an extensive work of 210 volumes and was completely translated from Chinese into Mongolian in the 1920s by Danda-Syan-sand, Member of the Science Committee of the MPR. Wide use has been made of this dynastic history by Chinese, Japanese and also some West European scholars. It was drawn upon by N. Ya. Bichurin for his *History of the First Four Khans of the House of Genghis* published in St. Petersburg in 1829, a work which has still not lost its importance for specialists in Mongolian studies.

Among other Chinese works of indubitable interest are the following descriptions of travellers who journeyed to different corners of the Mongol Empire:

1. *Si-yu-lu* ("Notes on the Mongols' Western Campaign, 1219") written by Genghis Khan's counsellor Yelyui Chu-tsai.[32]

2. *Bei-shih-chi* ("Notes of the Journeys to the North Made by Chinese Ambassadors Who Travelled to Mongolia in 1220-1221").[33]

3. Description of the journey of the taoist Chang Chun, who travelled from China when summoned to visit Genghis Khan at his staff headquarters. Chang Chun travelled through Mongolia and Turkestan to the borders of India, where Genghis Khan's camp was at that time located. One of his companions kept a diary of the journey which contains detailed information about the Mongols. It has been translated into European languages.[34]

4. *Men-da-bey-lu* ("Full Description of the Mongolian Tartars") was written by the Sung ambassador Ch'ao Hun, who travelled to Peking in 1221 to visit Mukhul who at that time was the viceroy of the Mongol Khan in Northern China.[35]

The Mongolian translation of this work, made by Yendonzhamtso, with a preface and notes by Chinese researchers is preserved in manuscript form in the Mongolian collection of the Institute of History of the MPR Academy of Sciences. A Russian translation is being published in the USSR.[36]

5. *Men-da-bey-lu* and *Khey-da-shi-lyue* ("Notes of Chinese Travellers of the XIIIth Century on the Ancient Mongols"). These sources were recently partially translated into Russian.[37]

6. *Si-yui-chi* ("Travel Notes") of Ch'an-de-khoi, who travelled from China to Kublai, resident on one of the slopes of Khangai, contains interesting observations and information about the life of the Mongols.[38] For example, Ch'an-de-khoi mentions the existence in Mongolia of several settlements of craftsmen.

In addition to the above-mentioned works there are several other Chinese sources relating to the same period. Of a certain importance for the study of early mediaeval Mongolia are epigraphic materials, such as wall inscriptions, *paidze*, khan tags or labels and inscriptions in square script. Not many of them have survived but in many cases they have formed the subject of research.[39]

For the study of the Middle and later Middle Ages in Mongolia the most important sources are the actual Mongolian historic works, including, more especially, the feudal chronicles and annals. After the expulsion of the Mongol conquerors from China the tradition of writing annals apparently was not interrupted but only those compiled in the XVIIth century have come down to us. Earlier chronicles have not so far been discovered and it is only on the strength of isolated indications that we can assume that the tradition of annal-writing continued to persist in the XIV-XVIth centuries. All the Mongolian chronicles of the XVIIth century which have come down to us are of the feudal type and are from the pens of authors belonging to the feudal khan or priestly class. In all of them basic attention is accorded to the events connected with the life of the princely families, beginning with the history of the family of Genghis Khan, from whom many Mongol feudal princes were descended. Thus, these chronicles are, primarily, histories of princes. In them little space is given to the history of the Mongolian people proper but it is still possible from them to gather some information about the situation of the *arats*. These chronicles are valuable sources for studying the historical process that occurred in Mongolia in the period of feudal disintegration.

The view has long been firmly held in the literature devoted to Mongolian studies that the most important of the chronicles of the XVIIth century are *Erdeniin tobchi* from the pen of the Ordos Prince Sagan-Setsen, and *Altan tobchi*, written by an unknown author at the beginning of the XVIIth century. The chronicle *Erdeniin tobchi*, completed by the author in 1663, contains a wealth of factual material, especially as regards events of the XV-XVIth centuries, for the study of which it constitutes the basic source. It has been frequently studied, and translated into Chinese, Manchu, Russian, German and Japanese and republished in Mongolia and also in foreign countries in different versions. When utilizing the chronicle of Sagan-Setsen, however, it must not be forgotten that he himself belonged to the "golden family" of Genghis Khan, that he wrote at a time when Buddhism had spread to Mongolia and when the Manchu dynasty had subjugated the whole of Southern Mongolia—circumstances which could not fail to affect the character of his work. In utilizing the chronicle of Sagan-Setsen, as well as of other Mongolian chroniclers, it is essential to adopt a critical approach to the material—or, more exactly, to the peculiar way in which the material is communicated and explained by the feudal chroniclers and annalists.

Altan tobchi is a shorter work than Sagan-Setsen's. The information contained in both chronicles is in many respects similar, but *Altan tobchi* contains a number of details not found in Sagan-Setsen.

Besides these two chronicles, mention should also be made for the XVIIth century of *Shara-tudzhi*, *Altan tobchi*, written by the lama Lubsan Danzan and *Asragchi nertiiyn tuukh*, composed by the Khalkha Prince Zhamba (published by Kh. Perle in 1959). *Shara-tudzhi* (published by N. Shastina in 1957) was evidently the work not of one but of several authors and was added to cover a rather long period. It served as one of the sources for Sagan-Setsen, as he himself mentioned in his chronicle. In the genealogical tables which constitute part of *Shara-tudzhi* mention is also made of the names of princes who lived at the very end of the XVIIth century. The value of *Shara-tudzhi* and *Asragchi-nertiiyn-tuukh* lies in the information they contain about the Mongolian tribes and in the detailed genealogical tables of princely families.

The principal remarkable feature of the chronicle of Lubsan Dandzan is that it contained a large part of the short version of the *Sacred Legend*. Before this chronicle was discovered the *Sacred Legend* was known only in a phonetic writing in Chinese characters. Furthermore, the chronicle contains much information from other ancient chronicles which have not come down to us. The only extant copy of this chronicle was discovered by the First President of the Science Committee of the MPR, Zhamyan, in what is now the Eastern *aimak*. The *Altan tobchi* of Lubsan Danzan has been published several times in Mongolia and foreign countries.[40]

Recently there has been discovered in Inner Mongolia an interesting chronicle written in verse form—the biography of Altan Khan and of the Tumet nationality. The manuscript contains information not only about the activities of Altan Khan but also some material on the history of the XVIth century Mongols. Some extracts from it are preserved in the manuscript collection of the Institute of History of the Academy of Sciences of the Mongolian People's Republic.

Among other Mongolian sources of the XVIIth century

mention should be made of a law collection, representing a code of laws drawn up at a meeting of princes held in 1640. Until recently scholars have only known the Oirat text of this collection. It was studied and translated into Russian by K. F. Holstunsky.[41] The collection of Mongolian laws is extremely important for studying the social system of the Mongols, and it supplies graphic illustrations of the class differences in a feudal society.

Among other historical works of the XVIIth century in Mongolian may be mentioned the biographies of very important representatives of the Buddhist church. These contain a considerable amount of information on the life of the Mongols but a strictly critical approach has to be adopted in utilizing "biographies".

Apart from Mongolian sources, the Chinese dynastic history *Ming shih* ("History of the Ming Dynasty"), and the several volumes of the code of the secret archives of the Ming emperors, published in Japan, are very important for the study of the XIV-XVIth centuries. *Ming shih* was extensively utilized by D. Pokotilov in compiling his work on the history of Mongolia.[42] However, when utilizing material out of *Ming shih* it should be borne in mind that it reflects the point of view of Chinese ruling circles of that period on events that occurred beyond the Great Wall of China. A great deal of attention is devoted in *Ming shih* to describing Mongolian external affairs, principally, the wars waged by the Mongol feudal leaders with China, and between themselves, and the economic situation of the Mongols; little is said—and that scrappily—about the social system.

Among other sources should be mentioned the works of Chinese authors: the *Bey lu iyn su* of Syao Ta-syan and *Wen li i gun lu*. The first work has been translated into Mongolian.[43]

In the first quarter of the XVIIth century a further type of source appears which contains data on the history of the Mongols during the later Middle Ages—these are documents from Russian archives, the importance of which has already been frequently mentioned in scientific circles. Recently Soviet experts on Mongolian studies have been making wide use of the materials in Russian archives and have produced comprehensive works on the history of the Mongols in the XVII-XVIIIth centuries.[44]

Among the sources of Mongolian history during the Manchu rule, mention should primarily be made of the sources in the Manchu language, the most important of which are the *Bodogon-i-bitkhe* of the Manchu emperors (219 volumes) and *Iletun-ulabun* (120 books). *Bodogon-i-bitkhe* is an extensive work and represents a collection of materials on the relations between the Manchu emperors and the Mongol (Khalkha and Oirat) princes and the conquest of Mongolian territory by the Manchu conquerors from the 1630s to the 1760s. Both sources have been translated into Mongolian. *Iletun-ulabun* is a collection of special genealogical tables, with information on all the numerous Mongol princes and short biographies of them. Its compilation was organized by the Manchu government in the first half of the XVIIth century and it was published in parallel series in three languages—Mongolian, Chinese and Manchu. The compilation was based on the genealogical records kept in Mongolian princely families. Two editions were published in Mongolian—in 1776 and 1803, and copies of the book were distributed to the *khoshun* administrations, where they were completed with records of current events. Although the official entries are rather brief, *Iletun-ulabun*, nevertheless, gives a fairly full view of the history of the Mongolian princedoms which, after 1691, were under the rule of the Manchus.

L. Dendeb, B. Buyanchuulgan and other Mongolian experts on Manchurian history have done a great deal for the study and systematization of sources in the Mongolian language. They have produced translations which are kept in the collection of the Institute of History of the Academy of Sciences of the Mongolian People's Republic, in the State archives and in the State Library in Ulan Bator.

Two publications of Japanese Orientalists: *Manchu and yargiyan kouli* ("Notes on the Ancestors of the Manchus") and *Man'-wen-lao-dan* ("Archive Material of the Manchu period") are of considerable importance for studying the history of Mongolia in the Manchu era.

Very important too are the legal sources of the period under consideration, i. e. the collections of laws and the *Mongol Code*. The most important of the codes of laws for the Manchu period is the *Khalkha Dzhirum*, which is the title under which the collection of laws of three Khalkha *khoshuns* is known; it was issued in 1709 and subsequently supplemented on several occasions.[45] The code has been fairly well studied from the legal angle[46] and translated into Russian.[47] Among other legal collections mention should be made of the collection of court decisions or rulings of the *shabin* department, entitled *Shav yamny ulaan khatsartaas khulsan duram*. This collection contains a record of court decisions from 1820 to 1913 and reflects the reactionary role played by the Lamaist church, which mercilessly exploited its serfs or *shabinars*. *Ulaan-khatsart* has been studied and published by Academician Sh. Natsagdorzh in Ulan Bator in 1959.[48]

The *Mongol Code* has been published by the Foreign Relations Chamber of the Manchu Empire in three parallel texts—Mongolian, Chinese and Manchu, and was intended for use in administering subject Mongolia. It was compiled for the firs time in the reign of Chien Lung and published in 1789, re-issued a second time in 1817 and for a third time, considerably augmented, in 1826. The *Mongol Code* has twice been translated into Russian.[49] There are many details in this source which reflect the feudal conditions prevailing in Mongolia, not only during the Manchu period but also in earlier times.

All the collections mentioned above contain a wealth of material for explaining the social system of structure of the Mongols and they illustrate the arbitrary conditions under which the *arats* lived. Material on these problems is also to be found in the documents, correspondence and various orders and regulations of the Manchu government and the Mongol princes, but not all of these have been sufficiently studied.

One cannot ignore the very rich collection of archival documents for the period of Manchu rule in Mongolia which are preserved in the state archives of the Mongolian People's Republic. The State Central Historical Archives in Ulan Bator is systematically publishing the more valuable materials on the history of the Mongolian people in the XVIII-XIXth centuries.[50]

The Institute of History of the Academy of Sciences of the Mongolian People's Republic has published several interesting documents on the economy and social structure of the Manchu period.[51]

The tradition of compiling historical chronicles continued even during the rule of the Manchu dynasty and the style of chronicle writing was maintained. The authors of the Mongolian chronicles, just as they had done previously, failed to draw a clear distinction between legend and genuine fact. Furthermore, the later-dated chronicles exhibited in greater degree the influence of Lamaist ideology, as well as the pro-Manchu feelings of the feudal princes. Nevertheless, the importance of these chronicles cannot be underrated, since there can be found in them, some—if only, occasional—indications of the oppressed situation of the masses of the people. Among such may be mentioned the 3-volume chronicle *Bolor Toli* compiled by the lama Zhambadorzh and which begins, like most works of this kind, with an account of Buddhist conceptions of the earth's origins. In *Bolor Toli* the history of the Mongols has been brought up to 1820. There are also such Mongol chronicles as *Bolor Erikhe* compiled by Rashi-Puntsag, *Erdeniyin Erikhe* of the Khalkh *taidzhi* Galdan (in the fifties of the XIXth century). Galdan devotes a lot of attention in his chronicle to biographies of the *Bogdo-gegens* and to descriptions of their "miraculous" deeds. This chronicle must be viewed with a critical eye, since it clearly reflects the feudal ideology of the higher-ranking lamas.

There are important sources for the history of Buddhism in Mongolia, most of them compiled by Mongolian lamas in the Tibetan tongue. These Mongolian sources in Tibetan contain much factual material on the problems of the history, culture and religion of mediaeval Mongolia.[52]

There are quite a number of sources for studying the period of modern history; among them may also be included some of the Mongol chronicles mentioned above, which were compiled in the XIXth century, such as *Bolor Toli*. Mongol chronicles of the period of modern history differ little in their style and narrative form from the earlier chronicles.

The writings of Russian travellers who journeyed to China through Mongolia in the XVIII-XIXth centuries contain considerable material on the modern history of the Mongols. The most important of these are the writings of N. Ya. Bichurin,[53] who collected a lot of information from Chinese sources on the situation of Mongolia in his day. His own personal observations greatly amplify the material he collected and make his work more valuable.

The same applies to the book written by E. E. Timkovsky,[54] who travelled to China via Mongolia in 1820 and 1821.

The second half of the XIXth century is covered in numerous accounts of travels in Mongolia undertaken by the most eminent Russian explorers of Central Asia. In the majority of cases the studies were carried out, not by specialists in Oriental studies, but mainly by geographers, whose writings also reflect the situation of the Mongolian people at the time in question. The well-known travels of I. M. Przhevalsky opened up a new and brilliant page in the history of exploration of Central Asia in general and Mongolia, in particular. Following his first journey, others were made by G. N. Potanin, who collected an immense amount of material on the ethnography and folklore of the Mongols. The books of Przhevalsky[55], Potanin,[56] Pyevtsov[57] and Kozlov[58] furnish a great deal of material on the situation of Mongolia and on particular events which came under their observation during their journeys. The works of A. M. Pozdneev[59] who made several journeys in Mongolia are especially important for the study of the last 50 years of Manchu rule in Mongolia. His great work *Mongolia and the Mongols* represents the diaries of the journeys he made in 1892-1893, in which he gives a detailed picture of Mongolia at that time. He also collected a great amount of material on the economy of Mongolia but did not publish it; of the seven volumes of *Mongolia and the Mongols*, which he intended publishing only two volumes of diaries have appeared.

Valuable sources for the study of the economic state of Mongolia at the end of the XIXth and beginning of the XXth century are materials published from consular reports, which contain much statistical information, in particular about Mongolia's trade with Russia and China.

The sources for the period of the Mongolian feudal-theocratic state are the collections of treaties and diplomatic documents dealing with the relations between Mongolia and China, which were published in 1912-1915. After the Great October Socialist Revolution in the USSR several volumes were published of a series of documents dealing with international relations before the Revolution. In the volumes of this series, under the general title *International Relations in the Imperialist Epoch*, there have been published many documents, protocols, reports and diplomatic correspondence on the so-called Mongolian problem. This documentation throws fairly full light on the political situation of autonomous Mongolia.

There are valuable sources available for the period of the Mongolian feudal-theocratic state in the years 1911-1919.

There is an uncompleted chronicle in Mongolian on the history of Mongolia at the beginning of the XXth century, compiled on the orders of the Mongolian Government. It does not differ in character from the histories of the preceding period and recounts always the same story of princes.

Among the legal sources mention should be made of the *New Mongolian Code*, compiled in 1914, and also the records of the *khoshun* regulations and court decisions which exist in every *khoshun*. These contain numerous details describing the grievous and oppressed situation of the masses in the Mongolia of that time.

The Mongolian sources of the time of the 1921 revolution differ basically in character from the old feudal materials. From the earliest days of the Mongolian People's Republic steps were taken to lay the foundations for a scientific study of sources.

In 1921 a Science Committee was set up to organize scientific work in the country. Gradually, the Committee began organizing the scientific study of the history of the Mongolian people on the basis of Marxist-Leninist methodology and drawing upon the experience and friendly assistance of Soviet scholars. The Science Committee conducts the study of the history of the Mongolian people along two lines: collecting and publishing documents and old sources and initiating historical investigations and preparing manuals for the study of the contemporary period. The Mongolian People's Revolutionary Party attaches great importance to the problems of formulating the history of the revolution and of the Mongolian People's Revolutionary Party. The most important sources for the history of the Mongolian revolution and the Mongolian People's Revolutionary Party are the minutes or records of the Party congresses, Party conferences and plenary meetings of the Central Committee, and other Party documents. Specially important are such documents as the programme and rules of procedure of the Mongolian People's Revolutionary Party.

The most important sources for the history of the Mongolian

People's Republic are the official records published in the MPR of the Grand People's Hural, the sessions of the Little Hural, the texts of the Constitutions of the Mongolian People's Republic, and the collections of laws and regulations of the Presidium of the Grand People's Hural and also of the Council of Ministers of the Mongolian People's Republic. The texts of the first and of the currently operative Constitution of the Mongolian People's Republic vividly demonstrate the successes achieved in the development of the Mongolian People's Republic.

The basic documents for the first period of the contemporary history of the Mongolian People's Republic have been published by the History Cabinet of the Science Committee under the title: *Documents on the History of the Popular Revolution of 1921* (1917-1924), *Revolutionary Measures of the People's Government (1921-1924)*, *Formation of Popular Democratic Local Self-Government in the MPR* (1921-1925) and others.[60]

From the 1940s onwards the Science Committee was very active in collecting the reminiscences of people who took a direct part in the revolution as partisans. In 1961 there appeared a collection of the reminiscences of Mongolian partisans—people who had taken part in the 1921 revolution.[61]

The documents and materials published by the Party and Government show the experience gained by the people's revolution and throw light on the non-capitalist development of the Mongolian People's Republic.

The documents and materials dealing with the history of the non-capitalist path of development followed by the MPR have been collected and edited by Ts. Nasanbalzhir under the title *Mongolian People's Republic's Path of Non-Capitalist Development (1925-1940)*. Two collections have been issued on the history of the war period of the MPR: *The Mongolian People's Republic in the Years of the Great Patriotic War of the Soviet Union* and *Letters Sent to Front-Line Fighters from Mongolia*.

In recent years numerous collections of documents have been published dealing with the history of the political structure of the MPR, its national economy, foreign relations, culture, education, etc.[62]

Due to the intensification of work on the publication of documents it is essential to point out certain serious shortcomings and mistakes deriving from an incorrect attitude towards prime sources which developed during the personality-cult period, and also from insufficient acquaintance with the scientific principles governing the study of texts and sources.

The biographical material dealing with the Mongolian popular leader, Sukhe Bator, is very valuable, as, in addition to the biographical data it gives a broad picture of the struggle of the Mongolian People's Revolutionary Party for the people's freedom and for the building of a new and happy existence.

The documents relating to the biography of Sukhe Bator have been published in four volumes. The first volume was published by the Science Committee in 1943; the second, containing additional material, in 1948; the third, in 1952 and the fourth in 1954; a fifth and more complete volume appeared in 1965.

This last volume contains valuable reminiscences of veterans of the people's revolution about Sukhe Bator and extensive notes, as well as several separate articles, by active members of the MPRP and the MRP about Sukhe Bator—in these lies the value of the volume.

In addition to sources in the Mongolian language, material in Russian is of great importance for studying the pre-revolutionary and post-revolutionary history of Mongolia; it includes publications of treaties and agreements between the MPR and the Soviet Union, the socialist countries and other world states.

III

The science of historiography has at its disposal a vast amount of literature illustrative of different periods in the history of the Mongolian people and historical studies of the latter exist in various world languages.

The roots of Mongolian historiography go back deep into the past. The Mongolian chronicles mentioned in Part I of this survey and dealing with different epochs represent not only sources; they also reflect the complex process of the growth of a world concept in the science of history.

Genuine scientific study of national history in Mongolia began after the victory of the people's revolution in 1921, which was a turning point also in the spiritual life of Mongolian society. People began to re-think and re-assess the historiographical patrimony of the Mongolian people in the light of Marxist-Leninist ideas, the ideas of the Great October Socialist Revolution and of the Mongolian people's revolution. In the first decisions and resolutions adopted by the Party and the Government Mongolian historians found practical guidance for their scientific work.

Gradually but surely Marxist-Leninist methodology took firm root in the field of historical science, displacing the long-standing traditions of feudal historiography.

The affirmation of this, the only scientific type of methodology, was not achieved without resistance from the representatives of feudal historiography. The situation was further complicated by the fact that there were no personnel with a revolutionary outlook on the world. Nevertheless, all these difficulties, complicated though they appeared, were overcome and history has been put at the service of the people.

In the early years of the revolution individual works of Mongolian historians[63] began appearing, such as those of Ch. Bat-Ochir, Kh. Nagsarzhav, L. Dendev, A. Amor, Navannamzhil and others. Although these historians of an older generation were not Marxists, they had moved a long way away from the representatives of feudal historiography. Their work, reflecting as it does the revolutionary changes that had occurred in the country, bears witness to the fact that a thousand-year-old domestic tradition of writing history in the form of a genealogy only of khans and religious leaders had given way to a more or less objective narration of history; and this constituted a definite landmark on the road to the dialectical comprehension of historical processes. Nevertheless, the studies of the above-mentioned authors, which display an objectivist standpoint that at times alternates with idealistic concepts, have the appearance of a logical account of events bereft of any kind of socio-economic analysis; this is what constitutes their general inadequacy. Another defect common to them may be considered to be the way they underestimate and ignore the part played by the masses in the historical process; as a result they treat history as a kaleidoscope of "heroes", "strong personalities," etc., replacing one another in turn. The lack of a system of footnotes in these works diminishes their scientific value. Generally speaking, however, despite their defects, they represent a positive move forward in Mongolian historiography and are useful manuals for students of Mongolian history.

The further development of Marxist historiography was very considerably influenced by the Mongol historians becoming acquainted with translations into Mongolian, made in the 1920s and 1930s, of historical and general theoretical works of the classical writers on Marxism-Leninism.[64]

In this connexion the work of Kh. Choibalsan, D. Losol and D. Demid[65] on the history of the Mongolian people's revolution, describing its origin, development and progress, should be singled out for special mention. These writers showed that the motive force in the 1921 revolution was the masses of the people, who had imbibed the ideas of the Great October Revolution in Russia in 1917 and rose in the determination to combat feudalism and imperialism. The authors' conclusion is that, as a general rule, the Mongolian people, backed by the support and assistance of the Soviet state, and under the leadership of the Mongolian People's Revolutionary Party, won a complete victory over the internal and external enemies—the feudal lords and the imperialist enslavers.

Later on, approximately from the 1940s onwards, Mongolian historiography was enriched by a series of new studies, devoted to the heroic past of the Mongolian people and the prominent figures in the liberation struggle and the people's revolution. Studies were published, dealing with the difficult situation of Mongolia under the yoke of the Manchus and the growing popular resistance to the alien conquerors,[66] and also biographies of active workers in the liberation struggle—Damdinsuren,[67] Togtokh and others.[68]

In these works attempts were made to give a correct assessment of the role played by popular heroes in history against the background of contemporary events. G. Navannamzhil's book, however, gives an incorrect description of the personality of Togtokh, one that bears no relation to real facts.

In the years that followed, more intensified studies continued to be made of past and present-day Mongolia on different subjects of current scientific importance. It is common knowledge that the history of the Mongolian feudal-theocratic state of Bogdo-gegen has until recently never been examined from the Marxist angle. Yet this period is an extremely important turning-point in the history of Mongolia when, as a result of a new upsurge in the broad-based anti-Manchu national liberation movement of the Mongolian people, Mongolian statehood was reborn, after having disappeared for 200 years, and the Manchu-Chinese colonial hegemony in Mongolia was swept away. In contrast to previous works, the book of Ts. Puntsagnorov represents a monographic study of history—the history of the Mongolian theocratic state.[69] The author supplies a correct evaluation of the economic basis and political structure of the Mongolian feudal-theocratic state, emphasizes the decisive role of the masses in the national liberation movement of 1911-1912 and exposes the colonialist policy of imperialism in Mongolia.

Interesting studies are also contributed on the history of the liberation movement of the *arats* during the imperialist period, demonstrating on the basis of concrete historical evidence the anti-Manchu and anti-feudal actions of the *arat* masses, their specific features and at the same time their identity whith peasant uprisings.

Following the principles of Marxist-Leninist methodology, Mongolian historians have produced several monographs on the history of the period of Manchu rule in Mongolia.

On the basis of extensive archival material and manuscript sources, Academician Sh. Natsagdorzh has made a detailed analysis of the feudal structure of Khalkha-Mongolia from the XVIIth to the beginning of the XXth century. He describes the situation of the masses, the forms and extent of the exploitation by their Manchu-Chinese and Mongolian feudal nobles and by merchants and usurers and tells of the liberation struggle of the Mongolian people against alien oppression.[70]

He has also written, on the basis of archival evidence, the history of the *arat* movements which sprang up in Mongolia in the second half of the XIXth and beginning of the XXth century. The author rightly considers that these local uprisings paved the way for the national liberation movement of 1911, which overthrew the 200-year old Manchu regime.[71]

By making use of Manchu and other sources Ts. Nasanbalzhir studied the workings of the Manchu military-bureaucratic administration and its taxation system in Mongolia.[72] He showed how the national-colonialist oppression of the alien conquerors lay like a grievous burden on the shoulders of the Mongolian workers who more than once rose in rebellion against their enslavers.

The anti-Manchu liberation movement headed by Amursana and Chingunzhav is the subject of works by Ishzhamts, M. Sanzhdorzh, Ts. Sodnomdagva, S. Purevzhav, D. Tsedev,[73] while other writers have made studies of various aspects of the history of Mongolia under the Manchus, e.g. the penetration of Chinese capitalist merchants and usurers into Khalkha-Mongolia, questions of religion and the priesthood, organization of the Mongolian administration, etc.

The contemporary period—that of the creation, growth and development of the Mongolian People's Republic has been described in a number of works by Mongolian and Soviet historians. The approach to, and elaboration of, the problems of the contemporary history of the MPR and of its political structure and economic development constitute fresh achievements in the field of Mongolian studies. The study of the problems of this period of history is being conducted on the principles of Marxist-Leninist methodology.

A number of writers, working as a team, have produced a volume entitled *The Great October Socialist Revolution and the Mongolian People's Revolutionary Party*,[74] published in the 1950s. It narrates how the latter Party, the avant-garde of the Mongolian people, having accomplished the people's revolution in 1921, hold aloft the banner of Marxism-Leninism and proletarian internationalism.

Among the more generalized studies of the revolutionary period of the history of the Mongolian People's Republic special mention should be made of the works of a number of Mongolian historians. The monograph of B. Shirendyb, *The People's Revolution in Mongolia and the Formation of the Mongolian People's Republic*,[75] is an important study of the history of the people's revolution in Mongolia.

Another work by Academician B. Shirendyb *Mongolia on the Frontier of the XIXth and XXth Centuries*, published in 1963,[76] is a major work on the contemporary history of the Mongolian People's Republic. The third work of B. Shirendyb

The History of the Mongolian People's Revolution is a new research work which generalizes a vast amount of material. Basing himself on a large number of primary sources and other documents, the author has retraced the historical path followed by the progressive development of Mongolian society throughout an extremely important period of world history—the junction of the imperialist epoch and the new era that was opened by the Great October Socialist Revolution. The author makes a detailed scientific analysis of the class contradictions in feudal Mongolia, showing them to be closely linked with the intensification of national-colonialist oppression, and shows the objective causes of the national liberation and revolutionary movement among the Mongolian people.

The social and economic situation of Mongolia in the imperialist era, the influence of the Great October Socialist Revolution on the destinies of the Mongolian people, the Mongolian people's revolution as a new type of revolution, its internal and external factors and the transition of a backward, feudal Mongolia towards socialism, by-passing capitalism—all these key problems in the most recent history of the MPR are clearly and lucidly answered in the book mentioned above.

The author devotes a great deal of attention to a comprehensive study of the Mongolian experience in non-capitalist development, which is a realization in practical life of Lenin's well known theory.

The historian L. Tudev has devoted his work to an extremely topical subject—the process of the formation of a working class in the MPR and its transformation into a major social and political force in new Mongolia.[77]

Diplomacy, foreign policy and international relations in pre- and post-revolutionary Mongolia are accorded the space properly due to them in the historical studies produced. This is the direction in which Mongolian international historians are working. Arrangements are in train to publish monographs dealing, more especially, with the foreign policy of the Mongolian People's Republic in the post-war period and also with the diplomatic activities and the international position of the Mongolian feudal-theocratic state (1911-1919).

The first attempt to produce a comprehensive Marxist study of the history of the Mongolian People's Republic was *The History of the MPR*, published in 1954. This work, produced by creative collaboration between Mongolian and Soviet scholars, played a major role in its day in equipping young Mongolian cadres with historical knowledge. The first edition, however,[78] reflected the state of contemporary historical science and has now become obsolete and contains quite a number of defects and mistakes.

A valuable generalized Marxist work on the contemporary

history of the Mongolian People's Republic is *Short Outline History of the Mongolian People's Revolutionary Party*.[79] In it is traced the glorious path of the Mongolian People's Revolutionary Party as a Marxist-Leninist party, from its foundation up to our time, a party on which devolved the historic mission of guiding the revolutionary transition fo Mongolian society from feudalism to socialism, by-passing capitalism. It shows how the Mongolian People's Revolutionary Party, by creatively applying the theory of Marx, Engels and Lenin, in the concrete, actual situation of Mongolia, not only succeeded in carrying the people's revolution through to the end but also coped creditably with the historical task of transforming it into a socialist revolution. The Mongolian People's Revolutionary Party followed a heroic path from the first revolutionary group to its establishment as the ruling Marxist party, acting as the staunch vanguard of the Mongolian people and reaching maturity in relentless struggle with right opportunists, left ultra-revolutionaries and other anti-Party elements of all kinds, always firmly upholding the purity of Marxism-Leninism and the mighty banner of proletarian internationalism.

The incorrect views on different problems of Party history, disseminated in the field of historical science in Mongolia during the personality-cult period of Kh. Choibalsan, have been eliminated and the most important stages in the history of the Mongolian People's Revolutionary Party have been interpreted on sound lines.

In their scientific studies Mongolian historians constantly follow the guidance of Marxist-Leninist theory and the directives of the Mongolian People's Revolutionary Party as contained in the proceedings and decisions of plenary meetings of the Central Committee and Party congresses, as well as in the speeches and statements made by Yu. Tsedenbal,[80] First Secretary of the Central Committee of the Mongolian People's Revolutionary Party and President of the Council of Ministers of the Mongolian People's Republic, which help the historians to present a correct, Marxist interpretation of various problems of the history of the Mongolian people, more especially, in the contemporary period.

The works of Marx, Engels and Lenin contain a number of most important theoretical postulates which indicate to historians the correct way of solving historical problems and furnish them with an understanding of the historical process. The works of Karl Marx contain numerous expressions of views connected with the history of Mongolia.[81] Lenin's works contain a number of very important statements bearing directly on Mongolia. Of special interest are the materials dealing with Lenin's interviews with Sukhe Bator and other members of the Mongolian delegation. [82] The decisions taken at the time by the Comintern and relating directly to the Mongolian People's Revolutionary Party, which was a "sympathizing" member of the Comintern, constitute important material for the history of the Mongolian People's Revolutionary Party.

Study of the classical works of Marxism-Leninism is exceptionally important for studying the laws governing the historical development of society and for solving the problems of the non-capitalist development of backward countries in moving from feudalism to socialism.

Mongolian scholars, in fruitful collaboration with their Soviet colleagues, have laid a firm foundation for the scientific study of the Mongolian revolution. Mongolian historians are working on problems of different stages of the revolution and of the economic and cultural development of the Mongolian People's Republic, in doing so applying Marxist-Leninist methodology and conducting their studies in accordance with the principles laid down in the classical works of Karl Marx, Frederick Engels and V. I. Lenin.

The Central Committee of the Mongolian People's Revolutionary Party attaches immense importance to the Marxist interpretation of the history of the Mongolian people. Scientific books on history, written from Marxist-Leninist standpoints, help the Mongolian Party to carry out ideological work successfully, as they help to educate the workers in the spirit of socialist patriotism and proletarian internationalism, expose the efforts of bourgeois ideologists and all kinds of nationalistic and anti-Party elements to distort the history of the Mongolian people.

Of the vast literature in various world languages on Mongolian studies only a few basic works are listed in this survey, those which represent a certain stage in the development of the historiography of Mongolia.

From approximately the end of the XVIIIth century, Russian scholars have been systematically studying the history of Mongolia and its people.

We may regard as the first stage in the historical work done in studying Mongolia the works of members of the Academy expeditions for the study of Siberia, undertaken in the 1770s, in which there can also be found information about the part of Mongolia bordering on Siberia. Basically, the character of these works was determined by Russian archival material, and so, in the well-known books of Academicians I. E. Fisher[83] and G. F. Miller[84] most of the attention is devoted to relations between Russia and Mongolia. The books also contain a good deal of information on the history of the Mongol-speaking peoples who lived on Russian territory—the Buryats and Oirats. The book by Academician Pallas,[85] published in German, is mainly devoted to the history of the Oirats, but at the present time its importance is purely historiographical. It should be noted that this work is based on Oirat materials which have been very badly vitiated by poorly-qualified translators, on whom Pallas was completely dependent, as he was unacquainted with the Mongolian language. Basically, the importance of the works mentioned lies in the way they treat the problem of the history of the Mongols as the history of a people which played a notable part in the history of Central Asia. Almost simultaneously with the works of Russian academicians in the XVIIIth century there appeared works by French Sinologists on the history of the Mongols.

These include the works of De Guignes, Visdelou and Mailla.[86] Little attention was paid in them to the history of the Mongolian people; they described mainly the life and actions of Genghis Khan and his conquests. In the overwhelming majority of cases they treated their subject without an adequately critical approach to Chinese sources. The best of these works is that of Mailla, who devoted the greater part of the ninth, tenth and eleventh volumes of his work to the history of Mongolia.

Mailla and the other authors agree in certain aspects with the views of Chinese official history as regards the Mongols. For instance, Mailla fully justifies Kansi's invasion of Mongolia. The importance of his work lies in the systematic and detailed way in which he narrates the history of the Mongols. Another work, written by De Guignes, discusses the question of the origin of the Turks and the Mongols, an approach which was a step forward for its time.

The most notable, however, of the works connected with the problems of the ethnic origin of the Mongols is that of the eminent Russian Sinologist, N. Ya. Bichurin,[87] a work that rates considerably higher than those of West European scholars. In one of his works Bichurin justly wrote: "Many scholars in Europe are now engaged in studying the origin of the peoples who, they believe, settled Mongolia but, having no fundamental knowledge either of the people or of its history they adopt, in making this investigation, the fallacious principle that they must pass judgment on everything solely in a superficial way by guesswork, and finally find themselves at a loss".[88]

In discussing the works of West European students of the Orient it must be pointed out that they reflect the colonialist approach to the questions of studying the historical destinies of Eastern peoples. This approach, typical of Oriental studies in the West began to be reflected especially clearly in works written in the second half of the XIXth century, when Oriental studies became subservient to the aggressive policy of capitalism, which it was called upon to justify.

The work of D'Ohsson is the most considerable of the works written by bourgeois historians of the mid-XIXth century.[89]

D'Ohsson had an excellent knowledge of Iranian and Arabic sources in the original tongues and made wide use of them. He also succeeded in making a correct assessment of the results of the Mongol conquests which brought destruction and ruin to many of the countries of Central Asia, Iran and Eastern Europe.

Nevertheless, there are a number of serious gaps in D'Ohsson's work. Thus, when narrating the campaigns of Batu against old Russia and further West, D'Ohsson underestimates the part played by the Russian people in holding up by their heroic resistance the westward advance of the conquering Mongol armies. At the same time he exaggerates the importance of the Teutonic Orders, whose resistance to the Mongol armies constituted, in his opinion, the decisive reason why Batu's advance on the West was arrested. He did not take sufficient account of the information contained in Hungarian, Polish and German chronicles and the evidence of Russian annals which give much information on the Mongol invasion of Russia. All this diminishes the value of this extensive study.

After the end of the XIXth century West European historians tried to produce comprehensive works on the history of the Mongols. One such work is the composition of H. Howorth[90] who wrote four bulky volumes on the *History of the Mongols,* an extensive compilation of previously published works. Howorth did not know a single Oriental language and was entirely dependent on translations, which were not always of the best.

The work done on Mongolian studies at this time by Russian scholars was distinctly superior to Western work, as it produced a number of major works of real value. The appearance of A. M. Pozdneev's *View of the Condition of Khalkha in the Second Half of the XVIth and Beginning of the XVIIth Century*[91] constituted a fresh contribution to Mongolian studies. It represents an extensive commentary on a translation of several chapters of the chronicle *Erdeniyn Erikhe.* The value of this work lies in its wealth of factual material but it contains a number of fallacious postulates by the author. Thus, he considers that the Mongols, as early as the XVIIth century, were still living under tribal conditions and that the tribal system prevailed among the Mongols.[92] Accordingly a critical view must be taken of the work of Pozdneev.

Among the comprehensive works on the pre-revolutionary period of Mongolian history special pre-eminence attaches to that of V. V. Bartold, *Turkestan at the Time of the Mongol Invasion.*[93] In this fundamental study devoted to the history of pre-Mongolian Turkestan, the last chapter deals with the question of the formation of the Mongol Empire. Bartold was the first to raise the matter in a scientific historical study of the social system of the Mongols and the way in which the empire of Genghis Khan was organized. To the latter problem he devoted the above-mentioned work, small in size but important in content.

Bartold adduced new Moslem sources which no one had utilized before him. On the basis of numerous sources, very thoroughly scrutinized, he described the character of the Mongols' military organization, defined the importance of Genghis's personal guards and drew a picture of the state structure of the Mongol Empire. Bartold, however, overestimated the significance of the role of Genghis Khan as the organizer of the Mongol state, as he left out of account the previously existing states of the Khitans and others, much of the structure of which Genghis Khan had borrowed.

Bartold, while right in believing that the Mongol state bore a class character, is wrong in assuming that only Genghis Khan represented the interests of the steppe aristocracy and that his rival Jamukha represented the movement of the masses against these aristocrats. In point of fact Jamukha was the leader of a particular group of feudal Mongol nobles and his struggle with Genghis Khan was a struggle for power.

The book by the well-known traveller in Mongolia, G. E. Grumm-Grzhimailo,[94] although published in 1926, was nevertheless written from an idealistic standpoint. It gives, for instance, an incorrect assessment of the personality of Genghis Khan and of the empire he created; the book presents him as a mighty general and organizer—a strong personality and maker of history. Such a claim by Grumm-Grzhimailo is inconsistent with the actual facts and with the Marxist evaluation of the Khan's conquests. Further, he exaggerates the importance of the geographical factor in his explanation of the historical role of the Mongols. The positive aspect of Grumm-Grzhimailo's book is its wealth of factual material and the carefully compiled references.

In 1934 Academician B. Ya. Vladimirtsov's books *Social System of the Mongols*[95] was published posthumously. It proved to be a most valuable contribution to the study not only of the history of the Mongols, but also of the history of all the nomadic peoples. Its basic distinction is that it throws light on the history of Mongol society from the materialist standpoint. With the help of numerous examples and a profound analysis of terminological data Vladimirtsov convincingly demonstrated that nomadic society did not by-pass the phase of feudal development, which acquired a special character under a system of nomadic pastoral economy. In discussing three phases of the development of feudalism among the Mongols, Vladimirtsov took the view that the period of Mongol history from the XIth to the XIIth centuries represents the beginning of feudalism, the XIV-XVIIth centuries, its zenith, and the XVIII-XIXth and the early part of the XXth century, its disintegration. Vladimirtsov's work is of great importance for studying the problems of feudal society in Mongolia.

The work of A. Yu. Yakubovsky on the Golden Horde, which he wrote in collaboration with Academician B. D. Grekov (published in 1937),[96] is important for the history of the Mongols. It is the first book which adopts a Marxist-Leninist approach to the problems of the creation, development and collapse of the Golden Horde, a phenomenon closely bound up with the history of the Russian people.

The second chapter of the book, *The Golden Horde and Its Downfall*, gives a brief description of the Mongol state of Genghis Khan and reveals the predatory nature of its campaigns of conquest. Starting basically from the view put forward by B. Ya. Vladimirtsov on the feudal character of the Mongol state, A. Yu. Yakubovsky defines certain postulates more closely, and, in particular, stresses the part played by the *noyons* and *nukers* in forming the Mongol state. In the course of compiling his book he introduced new material from sources in the Arabic and Persian languages. He had a high opinion also of the material in Russian chronicles and pointed out that they were still not being sufficiently used in studying facts from the life of the Mongols in the XIII-XVth centuries.

The book by Soviet Academician I. M. Maisky, *Contemporary Mongolia*, re-issued in 1962, can be regarded as a most valuable work dealing with the history of Mongolia from 1911 to 1919. The first edition was published in Irkutsk in 1921. In 1919 the author, as a member of an expedition equipped by the Irkutsk office of the All-Russian Central Union of Co-operative Societies, visited Mongolia and spent a year and a half in the country. The book is based on the author's direct personal impressions and contains much valuable factual material, especially of an economic nature.

In the new revised edition of his book Academician I. M. Maisky[97] subjects all these data to a strict, scientific analysis and reveals the causes of the profound political and economic crisis of the Bogdo-gegen monarchy which proved to be the precursor of the people's revolution of 1921. The Mongolian people, ground down under an incredible social and national yoke, quickly imbibed the liberating ideas of the October Revolution and, under the leadership of the Mongolian People's Revolutionary Party, rose to overthrow the stronghold of feudalism and set out on the path of anti-feudal and anti-imperialist revolution.

The book of I. Ya. Zlatkin *The Mongolian People's Republic— Country of People's Democracy*,[98] published in 1950 with another edition in 1957, is an attempt to present in concise form a complete and comprehensive picture of the present-day development of socialist Mongolia in the light of Marxist-Leninist teaching and is to this day the best Soviet scientific work in the field of Mongolian studies on this problem.

Following the guidance supplied by the works of Marxist-Leninist classical writers, Soviet historians and economists have, especially in recent years, worked on a number of questions relating to the history of the Mongolian revolution, the Party structure and the MPR's economic development. Their works[99] sum up the results of the economic and cultural development of the MPR and supply brief information on the historical development of the Mongolian people during the years of revolution, from 1921 onwards. Two interesting books by B. Tsybikov[100] and A. Kislov[101] deal with a narrower problem. On the basis of a large amount of archive material the writers examine the hardships and difficulties experienced in the struggle of the Mongolian people against the White Guard bands and the Chinese militarists.

A number of popular scientific writings also deal with the problems of the contemporary history of the MPR.[102]

Separate problems of the contemporary history and economic development of the MPR are discussed in a number of monographs by other Soviet scholars, specialists in Mongolian studies, who on the basis of new data show the road followed in the socialist development of Mongolia.[103]

In the people's democracies increasing interest is being shown by specialists in Mongolian studies in the history of the MPR and, in particular, its archaeology, ethnography, politics, economics, etc. Scientific collaboration between Mongolian scholars and their colleagues across the frontier is constantly increasing. It is worth drawing attention to the joint expeditions recently carried out by Mongolian, Soviet, Hungarian and German archaeologists and ethnographers which have produced positive results in the study of the antiquities of the Mongolian people. In Czechoslovakia there has appeared a book by I. Poukh which is a historical-philological study of the well-known XIIIth century Mongolian chronicle *The Sacred Legend*. After the People's Republic of China was proclaimed a number of studies appeared on the history of the Mongols, among which may be mentioned the works *Northern Di and Hunnu* in 1962 and *Ukhuan and Syan Pi* of Ma Chansu, and the *Social-Economic History of the Khitans* of Chen-su, published in 1963, *et alia*.

In this brief survey it is difficult to include all the literature produced by bourgeois specialists in Mongolian studies, as represented by numerous monographs, publications and newspaper and magazine articles; we shall, accordingly, note only their most general features.

The first thing to be noted is the actual development of Mongolian studies in the West. Whereas, before the Second

World War, Mongolian studies in the West were the occupation of individual scholars—Professors B. Laufer and F. Lessing in the USA, Professor Ramstedt in Finland, Professor E. Hainisch in Germany, Professor P. Pelliot in France and others,—it is now represented by a large company of scholars and is in the process of becoming an independent scientific discipline, designed to furnish the ruling circles and the society of the capitalist countries with a volume of information on the historical past, the present-day situation and the language and culture of the Mongolian people. This is primarily due to the radical change in the balance of power and the growth in the general interest taken in the world of socialism, of which the MPR constitutes an integral part and in which it enjoys equality of rights.

In post-war years there has been a special revival in bourgeois Mongolian studies, for many reasons. The economic and cultural successes achieved by the MPR in socialist construction, the special features of its development from feudalism to socialism, by-passing capitalism, and also the special nature of its historical past, the expansion of the international relations of the MPR and its entry into the United Nations—all this evokes a keen interest in Mongolia on the part of the public in Western countries. This sincere aspiration of wide circles of society in the West to ascertain more and more about Mongolia has nothing in common with the self-seeking interest displayed by the reactionary circles in the West. They are interested in Mongolia to the extent that it coincides with their provocatory schemes and the interests of their aggressive policy; they seek to place Mongolian studies at the service of diplomacy and militarism. In this connexion the advance in Mongolian studies is bound up with the intensified development and re-orientation of the whole system of social studies, including Oriental studies, for the struggle with Communism, which is carried on particularly extensively and energetically in the USA.

One quite important reason for the growth of Mongolian studies since the war is the output of Soviet and Mongolian literature and also the knowledge of the country gained by many observers and specialists from Western Europe and the USA as a result of the consistent way in which the Mongolian Government pursues a policy of peaceful co-existence and expansion of international contacts.

As a result of the operation of all these factors Western interest in Mongolian studies has not only mounted speedily, has not only firmly established itself in bourgeois scholarship but, having widened the research front, has begun to spread out in fresh directions and passed beyond the framework of a traditional enthusiasm solely for antiquinty, linguistics and source studies.

A systematic study of the contemporary history, the economy, the state structure and the present situation of the MPR is the new and most characteristic feature of bourgeois Mongolian studies, and stems from the colossal changes that have occurred in the world since the war. It is here that one can most clearly discern two trends that to a certain extent characterize the bourgeois West's interest in Mongolian studies as a whole and which reflect, on the one hand, the growing interest of the public in socialist Mongolia and, on the other hand, the contradictory attitudes of official circles in the West towards the MPR. One trend is exemplified by the impartial and conscientious students and publicists from whose works Western readers can extract more or less trustworthy information about Mongolia while the other is represented by people who are far removed from science and truth, the reactionary ideologists of militarism who disseminate pseudo-scientific and anti-communist views regarding the MPR.

Many of the authors representing the first trend hold, in the main, sober views about the history of Mongolia, seek to acquaint themselves with, and try to understand, its present and its past, its achievements and its plans for the future.

This is the case, above all, with the works of Owen Lattimore on the present-day situation and the history of the national liberation movement and the 1921 revolution,[104] of Phillips,[105] Tang[106] and Friberg[107] on the position in international law of the foreign policy of the MPR, and of G. Murphy[108] on general problems, etc.

Among the works of Japanese authors devoted to various problems of Mongolian history mention should be made of Tayama's *Social Structure of the Mongols during the Period of the ching Empire, Finds from Noin-ula in Mongolia,* S. Ume's Hara's *Study of the Sacred Legend,* K. Kobayasi *et alia.*[109]

Among the representatives of the reactionary trend may be mentioned the essays and "scientific-research" articles of R. Rupen,[110] W. Ballis[111] and others, which bear an overtly tendentious character in the picture they give of the policy and internal situation of the MPR. These "scholars", incapable of passing sober judgment because of their arch-reactionary concepts, regard the MPR as nothing but a "satellite state", a view which does not stand up to criticism. Their works, written on the basis of extremely scanty materials, abound in pre-conceived judgments that have nothing at all in common with science and serve the ends of anti-communism.

The most glaring inconsistencies characterizing the new trend in bourgeois Mongolistics dealing with contemporary Mongolia have manifested themselves in the last two very voluminous works: Lattimore's book *Nomads and Commissars.*

Mongolia Revisited[112] and Rupen's monograph *The Mongols of the XXth Century*.[113]

In his work which is, virtually, a sketch of the contemporary history of the MPR, Lattimore, in differentiation from the point of view that predominates in bourgeois historiography and in modification of his own personal views—the result of acquaintance with Mongolian facts of life—gives priority to internal factors and not to external actions in discussing the key problems of the development of the MPR from 1911 up to the present day and in evaluating the revolutionary changes in the MPR and the successes won in improving its economy and culture. Lattimore's book may serve as an example of the objective approach to a study of the history of the MPR.

In contrast to the favourable and serious attitude adopted by the author of *Nomads and Commissars*, Robert Rupen tries in every possible way to lay emphasis on the "shady" phases of past history and utilizes his knowledge of the subject to group facts together so as to cast aspersions on the mutual relations between the MPR and the USSR and on the achievements of the non-capitalist form of development. In this respect his work aligns itself in its tendentious treatment of facts with the frankly anti-MPR interpretations of such scholars and servants of imperialism as A. Park[114] and D. Knutson.[115]

Little attention is paid to the hackneyed hostile assertions of ill-intentioned writers even by the very representatives of the bourgeois school of Mongolian historians, who have taken and are taking their stand on realistic grounds. They are beginning to evaluate realistically the basic problems of Mongolian history. This fact speaks for the continuation of positive trends in bourgeois Mongolistics.

While the study of the contemporary history of Mongolia constitutes a new phenomenon in the field of Western Mongolistics, their study of sources is a traditional branch which even nowadays remains one of the basic trends in bourgeois Mongolian studies. The novelty here lies in the serial publication of sources which has assumed quite considerable proportions since the war, especially in the USA and West Germany.

Progressively-minded Western public figures, such as the recipient of the international Lenin Peace Award, Ivor Montagu,[116] and others who have visited the MPR, paint in their books and articles a truthful picture of present-day Mongolia and its political, economic and cultural achievements and give an objective and correct description of the historical past of Mongolia. Their writings and statements help in consolidating correct impressions of the MPR in the West and form a worthy reply to the bourgeois writers of all types who falsify the history of the Mongolian people.

One of the characteristic features of the bourgeois historiography of Mongol feudalism is the attempt to set on a pedestal the conquerors, to extol in every possible way their bloodthirsty exploits, etc.

In his book *The Mongols and Russia*,[117] the American historian G. Vernadsky, waxes lyrical in praise of Genghis Khan, belauding his predatory campaings in foreign countries as essential stages in the formation of a Mongol state. He explains the unification of the Mongol lands under the rule of Genghis Khan as the realization of some kind of "imperial idea", which, as he puts it, gave him no peace.

A similar spirit of idealism also pervades the book of another American historian, H. D. Martin *The Rise of Genghis Khan and His Conquest of North China.*[118]

It is to be regretted that certain historians of the Chinese People's Republic, in flagrant transgression of the truth, have recently begun to put forward in their works reactionary views borrowed from the bourgeois ideological arsenal. They endeavour, in particular, to depict the history of the MPR as no more than an appendix to the history of China, which is a gross distortion of historical reality.

They also assume the role of apologists for Genghis Khan and his bloodthirsty deeds. Strange though it may seem, they attribute a progressive function to the campaigns of conquest waged by Genghis Khan, from which the Chinese people also suffered severely.[119]

The work done by Genghis Khan in uniting the disparate lands of Mongolia into a single organic state answered the nascent requirements for social and economic development of the Mongolia of that day and so did have, objectively regarded, a progressive significance. Nevertheless, while stressing the positive function of the formation of a Mongol state, attention must be drawn to the quite obviously ruinous effects of the Genghis Khan conquests both on the peoples who were subdued and on Mongolia itself, the population of which was reduced and its productive forces dispersed over foreign lands.[120]

The publication of the present enlarged and revised second edition of the single volume *History of the MPR* will undoubtedly prove an important contribution to the study of the history of Mongolia viewed from the standpoint of Marxism-Leninism.

PART I

SECTION ONE

THE PRIMITIVE COMMUNE

CHAPTER I

AGE OF STONE TOOLS

It has been established by Marxist historical science that all the peoples and nations presently existing have been formed from different ethnical elements in a process of prolonged and complicated historical development. The ancestors of the present-day Mongolian people also have, naturally, passed through this complex historical process. The past history of the Mongolian people cannot, therefore, be studied merely from the particular moment when the first references to it appeared on the pages of written history.

The history of the predecessors of the Mongolian people goes far back into the remote ages—to the era of the primitive commune system.

The most recent evidence shows that the territory of Mongolia was inhabited by very early man about 100,000-200,000 years ago. The earliest traces of man's activity on the territory of Mongolia relate to the end of the lower Palaeolithic period—the Acheulian-Mousterian period.[1]

The first traces of human activity in this remote period have been discovered: at Odon-mant in the *aimak* of the Southern Gobi, on the mountain of Ikh gazar (Bogd *somon*) in the Uburkhangai *aimak* and at the Moiltynam declivity opposite Erdeni-Tszu on the Orkhon.

Among the large number of stone artifacts collected in these places may be mentioned the disc-like and rectangular-shaped nuclei, a chipped weapon of the so-called Levallois[2] type, roughly-shaped pebbles and numerous chips struck off nuclei. In the large river valleys there are not infrequently found rough stone chips and equally primitive chopper tools; the latter are made from well-rounded river pebbles, one end of which is chopped off and smoothed with a few skilfully directed blows. They could be successfully used for chopping and cutting.

The people who owned these weapons were obviously the Ordos man type[3], and, according to scholars, the Ordos man closely resembled the Neanderthal man in physical appearance.

During the lifetime of the Ordos man the climate was more temperate: conifers and deciduous trees grew in the mountain forests while on the lower levels there were stretches of marshy ground in which lived mammoths and steppe foxes which were accustomed to a cool climate, and warmth-loving antelopes and ostriches.

The transition from the Lower to the Middle Palaeolithic periods (100,000-40,000 years ago) coincided with glaciation, considerable changes ensued not only in plant and animal life, but also in the physical appearance of man himself. Improvements were made in tools and their uses widened. Pointed artifacts were used for knives and spearheads and scrapers for working skins and wood. More widespread use was made of disc-shaped blades made from nuclei, a characteristic feature in the technique of Middle Palaeolithic industry. Tools of this type have been found in Moiltynam on the Orkhon, in the localities of Dukh Baatsagaan *somon* in the *aimak* of Bayankhongor and Bogd *somon* in the Uburkhangai *aimak*.

One of the greatest achievements of the Middle Palaeolithic period was the artificial production of fire. Fire enabled people to warm themselves when cold, to protect themselves against wild beasts and to use food in other than raw form.

The people of this period abandoned their open dwellings and began to live in caves under overhanging rocks and to wear treated skins as clothing. This was when the primitive commune—the first human collective—began to take shape.

The next stage of palaeolithic development is the Upper Palaeolithic (40,000-12,000 years ago).

Human sites of this period have been discovered: in the valley of the River Selenga, near the town of Sukhe Bator, and on the River Tola in the vicinity of the city of Ulan Bator; on the Orkhon in the region of Erdeni-Tszu; in the Khalkhin-Gol basin—in the east, and in the Gobi—on the slopes of the Mongolian Altai Mts., near Kobdo *somon* in the *Uburkhangai aimak*.

The remote antiquity of these settlements is proved by the circumstance that their traces are usually found in specific geological conditions—on high river terraces, often at a distance from the beds of present-day rivers which, in the thousands of years that have since elapsed, have become considerably deeper.

Judging by some of the finds made the animal life which surrounded the man of that period was very different from that of today. The primitive people lived in the valleys of the Tola and Selenga when they were inhabited by mammoths, the Siberian woolly rhinoceros, large-antlered reindeer, bison, wild asses and *saiga*.

The Upper Palaeolithic inhabitants of Mongolia were familiar also with animals of more southern origin—a now extinct type of antelope with spiral horns, similar to the African species, and a special kind of ostrich, also very similar to the present-day African.

It was at this stage of Palaeolithic development that the present-day physical type of man (*Homo sapiens*) appeared. The Upper Palaeolith is related to the end of the glacial period which preceded our contemporary geological epoch and so a brief word should be said about the glacial period on the territory of the MPR.

Scholars have established that a glacial period succeeded the warm Tertiary period[4] on the earth's surface, i.e. a time when the climate became suddenly cooler and huge masses of ice formed over a considerable part of Europe, Asia and America, and left its mark also on Mongolia.

It is true that, because of the continental character of the climate of Central Asia, the ice or glacier cover was restricted in extent only to the tract of mountains and foothills, more especially the Khantei and Altai Mountains.[5] Here the ice cover was not continuous as in Europe but the proximity of glaciers, nevertheless, had a severe effect on the climate, animal life and vegetation and on the living conditions of primitive man.

In the Upper Palaeolithic period the basic means of human existence was hunting which had now become a more accomplished pursuit than in the case of the people who lived in the earlier periods of the Stone Age. It was at this time, for instance, in the Upper Palaeolith that special hunting equipment began to appear—especially, missile darts, the use of which considerably simplified hunting and made it more productive. It is a characteristic fact that an Upper Palaeolithic bone dart-head with slots along the sides for securing flint blades has been found on one of the most interesting sites in the MPR, at the 125-kilometre mark on the highway between Sukhe Bator and Ulan Bator.

It can be assumed that the Palaeolithic hunters as distinct from people of earlier times, were then using corrals and all kinds of snares or traps. More productive hunting conduced to a more settled existence, as the hunters no longer needed to be constantly moving around and could now cover their needs in smaller hunting grounds. This is proved also by the character of the Upper Palaeolithic sites in Mongolia. The inhabitants of these sites lived on them for lengthy periods, as is evidenced by the remains of household utensils discovered in excavations of these sites.

Important changes in the social organization of people of this period are also closely linked up with the progress made in hunting. People of the Upper Palaeolithic period lived in primitive communes at the stage characterized by the development of a primitive gentile commune.

Lenin described the earliest stage in the history of mankind as the era of the primitive horde; having survived this era, mankind emerged into the era of the primitive gentile commune. Archaeological evidence goes to show that this was precisely what took place in the Upper Palaeolithic period. It is true that we possess no direct evidence of the nature of the social system of the Palaeolithic inhabitants of Mongolia. But evidence of this kind has been found not far away from Mongolia, in Palaeolithic remains in neighbouring Siberia. Since there is a great similarity between the finds made on Palaeolithic sites in Mongolia and Siberia and it can be assumed there were certain links between their inhabitants, it is permissible to conclude that the most important features peculiar to the mode of life on Siberian sites would be equally characteristic of the Palaeolithic hunters of Mongolia.

In this connexion it should be borne in mind that, during excavations of two Palaeolithic sites in Transbaikalia at Malta and Buret, near Irkutsk, numerous small statuettes of a female figure were found. They evidently served to express specific ideas connected obviously with the special status of women in the Upper Palaeolithic period. Women occupied this position at an early stage in the gens system when the gens of hunters were relatively settled. At that time the woman was the basis of the unity of the gens, since kinship was reckoned in the female line. As she remained at home, looked after the storing of produce, prepared food and clothing and brought up the children, she was the real ruler of the household.

Matriarchy constituted at that time the basic feature of the gentile system and the predominant role in the social life of the gens devolved on women. It is, therefore, natural to find statuettes of women appearing in Palaeolithic sites. They were used by Palaeolithic man to convey the image of woman as the head of the gens and the guardian of the domestic hearth.

All that has been said above enables us to conclude with every confidence that both the ancient hunters of Siberia and the closely related—both as regards level and type of culture—population of the Transbaikalian sites and sites in Mongolia were already living under a matriarchal gentile system in the Upper Palaeolithic period.

In their further development from the Palaeolithic to the Neolithic period the ancient dwellers of Mongolia passed through a period of transition—the Mesolithic period (about 12,000-7,000 years ago). The distinguishing feature of this period is the appearance of bows, arrows and sheath weapons. Approximately from this date choppers, sharp-pointed tools, Siberian-type scrapers began to be replaced by tools made from knife-like flakes struck off from prismatic nuclei. Such weapons—bifaced blades shaped on both sides—have been found on the River Yero in the Selenga *aimak* and on Mt. Dulan in the Eastern Gobi. In forms of economy and social relationships the Mesolithic period was closer to the Palaeolithic period, which is why archaeologists sometimes call the Mesolithic period epi-Palaeolithic.[6]

As a result of investigations made from the 1920s up to the present time Neolithic settlements have been found to be widely distributed over almost the whole territory of the MPR. In the majority of cases these settlements were located near ancient rivers, springs or lakes, which have for the most part vanished.

Among these the Neolithic sites discovered in the Gobi at Baindzak and Dzun-Khairkhan ula are very interesting. Here were found remains of stone-built hearths, around which were strewn masses of flint pebbles (conical nuclei) of the usual Neolithic type, chippings, narrow knife-like flakes, miniature disc-like scrapers and arrow-heads.

Neolithic people inhabiting the territory of Mongolia had an excellent command of the technique of working stone whether by drilling or grinding; as evidence may be mentioned large polished axes made from fine crystalline types of stone. Numerous stone pestles and primitive corn-mills testify to the growing importance of collecting wild edible cereals, and possibly to rudimentary land cultivation.

Along with these stone artifacts there have been found in the Gobi the oldest Neolithic clay vessels in Central Asia, shaped like half eggs and covered on the outside with the characteristic imprints of fine wicker network. Such vessels and stone weapons of a similar type are characteristic of the early stages of Neolithic life in the neighbouring areas of Eastern Siberia—first and foremost, of Transbaikalia. This is evidence of the fact that the cultural links between the tribes of Mongolia and those of Eastern Siberia were not interrupted even after the Old Stone Age and that the earliest history of Siberia and Central Asia had a good deal in common in the New Stone Age (Neolithic), approximately 5,000-4,000 years B. C. Archaeologists have also found that cultural links existed between the Neolithic tribes inhabiting the Pri-Amur territory and the ancient tribes of Eastern Mongolia in the region of Tamtsak-Bulak and Khalkhin-Gol.

The Neolithic period saw the development and consummation of what had sprung up in the late Palaeolithic period as the first clear-cut form of social organization—matriarchy. The gens was the sole owner of all the implements of production and, as society continued to develop, a social conscience developed and primitive ideas of religion became more complicated. These are reflected in the numerous rock drawings depicting mountain goats, horses, miniature human figures, snakes, etc.

Apparently by the end of the Neolithic period differences became observable in the quality and quantity of the weapons and ornaments buried along with the dead. In a Neolithic burial excavated at Ustai-Burgastai in the Munke-khan *somon* of the Sukhe Bator *aimak* there were found a miniature arrowhead, a pin, knife-like flakes and a prismatic nucleus. The interesting feature of the burial artifacts is that they were made, possibly specially for the dead, out of a single lovely piece of green flint.

It was at this time that individual gentes started trading between themselves, though still in a casual way. As examples of such trade may be mentioned the nephrite articles, such as axes and adzes found in southern and northern regions of Mongolia, the raw material for whose manufacture is located in other places hundreds of kilometres distant.

In this way we see that the stone artifacts found in different localities of the Mongolian People's Republic prove that this part of Central Asia was settled during the Neolithic period and are evidence of the gradual transition of the population from the Stone Age to the era of weapons made from metal: copper and bronze.

CHAPTER II

AGE OF BRONZE TOOLS

After the end of the Neolithic period the tribes inhabiting the territory of Mongolia, while perfecting still further their working tools, gradually turned to producing metal implements made from bronze. It was the existence of copper and tin deposits in different areas of Mongolia that enabled the working of bronze to be developed in that period.

In Mongolia ancient methods of bronze working developed to their highest pitch at the end of the second and beginning of the first millennium B. C. In this Bronze Age, simultaneously with the steppe tribes in Europe they changed over to cattle-raising.

A considerable number of finds relating to the Bronze Age are known to have been made in the Mongolian People's Republic.

The earliest of these relate to the so-called Karasuk stage,[1] memorials of which were first studied by archaeologists in Southern Siberia (in the territory of Minusinsk).

The large number of bronze tools found in different places in Mongolia and now kept in museums in the MPR, can be attributed to this period.

Here mention should, first of all, be made of a series of massive bronze knives; the same group of finds also includes an exceptionally well-finished war axe, discovered in the Southern Gobi, and double and triple-bladed pendants, which may at that time have been plaited into a woman's tresses.

On the Uldzun post-road in the Khentei aimak at the foot of Delula, 10 kilometres from Bayan-ul, bones, chippings of flint and shards of "eggshell-walled" clay vessels were picked up. Similar shards have been found also in the Gobi and in the basin of the River Selenga; in technical finish and shape they resemble the Karasuk pottery of the Yenisei and Altai.

Examinations made have shown that an analogous similarity can be established in the anthropological type of the ancient population of Southern Siberia, on the one hand, and Southern Mongolia, on the other.

The specific type of culture of the Karasuk period in the Central Yenisei and Altai arose in connexion with the penetration into those areas of considerable groups of people from Southern Mongolia. These were apparently cattle-breeding tribes living between the Gobi and Hwang Ho.

The level of social development attained by the inhabitants of Mongolia during the troubled times when the ancient Bronze Age tribes were moving northwards can be gathered mainly from the fact that, even in the era that followed, the ancient unity of the gens was still maintained for a very long time, although, obviously, the family, headed by the man, was becoming more and more independent inside the gens.

The patriarchal type of family became more rapidly entrenched with the growth of an economy in which cattle-breeding gained more and more ground.

In Mongolian territory we know of rock drawings dating back to the Bronze Age which were done with red paint. The principal subjects depicted are rectangular and circular "yards" with lots of dots inside. They also show stylized animals, small human figures (usually two or three), standing hand-in-hand in rows, and, lastly, an eagle with wings outstretched over the whole composition. These drawings were found at a place called Khachurt, 40 kilometres beyond Ulan Bator, and a place called Tolzhgiy Boom in the *aimak* of Khubsugulsk, etc.

In these drawings primitive people sought to express their hopes and yearnings for the well-being of members of the gens, success in hunting, the preservation and augmentation of their herds of cattle—their basic wealth. Some of the drawings found also show nomad tents, and the bronze articles include miniature reproductions of a harness yoke.

The next period (VII-IIIrd centuries B. C.) in the history of the culture of the tribes inhabiting the steppe belt of Europe and Asia is usually termed the Scythian period, as this culture was most clearly expressed among the Scythians inhabiting the territories bordering on the Black Sea.

Among both the Scythians and all the other tribes who no doubt spoke different languages, and differed ethnically and culturally in the steppe zone (Urals and Kazakhstan, Western and Southern Siberia, Transbaikalia and Mongolia), numerous similarly-shaped articles were at the time in everyday use. This applies especially to weapons, horse harness and ornaments. Everywhere in these areas, just as in European Scythia too, the predominant items in weaponry were, to begin with, bronze bushed arrow-heads with a flat oval- or rhomb-shaped feather (striking end); later on they were everywhere replaced by triple-edged bushed pyramid-shaped arrow-heads.

Changes were also made in the shape of daggers. At first, they had a hilt in the form of a bee's outspread wings, typical of the short Scythian sword *(akinak)*. Later on, the hilt is straight and is more like the Sarmatian sword found in the lands bordering the Black Sea.

A clear resemblance is discernible also in the construction of horses' bits. At first, the type most commonly used was a bit with loops at the end like a small stirrup, specially characteristic of the Scythians of the VII-VIth centuries B. C. Later on the late-Scythian bits with round rings came into use all over the Eurasian steppes.

There is a similarity also in the productions of pictorial art. Drawings of a beast of prey curled into a ring, executed in the typically Scythian "wild beast style," are constantly met with everywhere, as are ornaments in the form of a vulture's head and figures of a leaping reindeer, alongside representations of local fauna.

The reply to the question why there should be such a wide and almost simultaneous dissemination over enormous areas of identical forms of ornament lies apparently in the change in modes of communication between the different nomad tribes.

The sharp increase in mutual intercourse between the nomad tribes made it essential to use horse-riding for long-distance travel and this could only be done by adopting bridles and metal bits or curbs. This was finally achieved in the European steppes in the VIII-VIIth centuries B.C. and helped to strengthen the economic and cultural links between far-distant territories.

Natural conditions made it particularly advantageous for the population of Mongolia to keep cattle. In the steppes of Mongolia, especially in the basin of the Orkhon, the Kerulen and the Tola, the flocks and herds were amply provided with excellent pastures and watering-places. The foothills of the Sayan and the Altai on the north, of the Greater Khingan on the east and of the Khangai range in the centre of Mongolia were also suitable places for nomad camps. In addition, the forests in these mountainous areas abounded in wild animals and wildfowl. Hunting could be carried on there with success and meat and valuable furs obtained.

It should, further, be noted that there is direct evidence of the existence of agriculture in many places in Northern and Southern Mongolia as far back as the VII-Vth centuries B.C. This is proved, primarily, by finds of corn-mills. For example, in the sites along the Tola river these corn-mills have been discovered in the same places as arrows typical of the VII-VIIIth centuries.

In the nature of their culture the ancient tribes of Mongolia were in Scythian times close to the neighbouring steppe tribes of Southern Siberia and Transbaikalia. With the tribes of Southern Siberia they were closely associated culturally by the general character of their art, their buildings and to some extent their household utensils; among the latter, for example, are the characteristic "Scythian" cauldrons on a high conical base.

Evidence of the mode of existence of the population of Mongolia in the VIII-IIIrd centuries B.C. and of their close links with Transbaikalia is supplied by the so-called flagged burial graves, which were given this appellation because they were framed on the surface of the ground with rectangular borders composed of ribbed stone flags. There are large numbers of such graves in the central and north-eastern part of the MPR, in the Khentei *aimak* and in the basin of the Kerulen, and also south of Ulan Bator in the Gobi *aimaks*. In the northern areas of the MPR stone-flagged graves have been noted on the shores of Lake Kosogol and in the Selenga valley. In the west they are met with in the interior of the Kobdo *aimak*.

In addition to the large number of such graves there are, scattered all over the territory of Mongolia, the so-called "reindeer stones," stone pillars decorated with pictures of leaping reindeer. In some cases these stones form the pillars standing at the corners of a fence surrounding stone-flagged graves.

It may be mentioned that among the "reindeer stones" recently discovered are the very interesting "Kosogol stones" with drawings of a man and horses. Excavations of stone-flagged graves in the MPR have been made in a number of places along the Tola and Kerulen rivers and near the health resort, Khudzhirt, on the River Orkhon.

The dead bodies found in these graves were laid face upwards, head pointing to the east, with different articles alongside. Sometimes, under the head or heel of the deceased was laid a flat stone "cushion".

The items most frequently met with in graves are necklaces of bronze and cornelian beads and also flat and cylindrical beads made from white and red paste. In addition to beads, flat bronze plates turn up occasionally in the form of round buttons with a little hook at the back. Similar ornaments are met with in Transbaikalian stone-flagged graves and in Scythian *kurgans* (burial mounds) on the Sayan-Altai range, as well as in earlier VIII-VIIth century B.C. burials. Bone arrow-heads found near Khudzhirt in the *aimak* of Uburkhangai are entirely similar to those found in Transbaikalia and Minusinsk.

Potterly is represented by two kinds of articles. The first are vessels of reddish clay, with handles and very similar to the jugs that are found on sites dating to the VIII-IIIrd centuries B.C. in Ordos and Zhekha; the second are vessels made from coarser brownish-grey clay, covered with scorings and interesting because they remind one of the rough clay ware so characteristic of the following stage—the tombs of Mongolia and Transbaikalia.

In all the features described above the Mongolian stone-flagged graves resemble the Transbaikalian, in which there have been discovered a certain number of finds supplementing those listed above.

For example, in the stone-flagged graves in the Selenga valley finds include celts—bronze arrows and axes, a bronze dagger, ornamented with a figure of a bear, a bronze mirror with handle shaped like an animal, a needle-case with bone needle, a fragment of a "Scythian" cauldron and *psalii* (snaffles) from bronze bits, as well as ornaments already familiar from Mongolia—beads and plagues. Furthermore, in one of the stone-flagged graves in Transbaikalia bridle bits turned up—made from iron. On the strength of the finds made in graves it was possible to conclude that some graves were constructed in the VII-IVth centuries B.C. and others in the III-IInd centuries B.C. It was precisely in these latter that the first iron articles were found.

This is all extremely important, as it enables us to draw inferences about the social structure of the population which has left us these stone-flagged graves. There can be no doubt that, notwithstanding certain advances made in developing productive forces and transport (emergence of agriculture and improvements in the technique of smelting bronze, the use of horses for riding) the gens system as a basis was still fully preserved.

The monotonous appearance of the exteriors of burial mounds and the uniformity in the composition of their contents approximate the stone-flagged graves to the burials of more ancient eras. One innovation only may be noted—the way the graves inside the burial ground are laid out in a series of rows—chain-wise. From this it may be inferred that the burial ground represented the cemetery of a gens and each chain of graves was the burial place of a family, of close kin. Apparently this reflects a process constituting one of the most characteristic aspects of the development of the gens system—based now on patriarchal principles when "the monogamian family became a power and rose threateningly against the gens."[2]

Very great changes ensued at this time in the economy and the culture of the ancient inhabitants of Central Asia. It was precisely in the Bronze Age that, simultaneously with the steppe tribes in Europe, they changed over to rearing cattle.

Frederick Engels attached immense importance to this fact, as he considered that, in consequence of the growth of cattle-breeding, "pastoral tribes singled themselves out of the rest of the barbarians: first great social division of labour."[3]

Not only did the pastoral tribes produce more than the hunters or fishermen but the means of livelihood produced by them were different. They had "not only milk, products and meat in greater abundance than the others, but also skins, wool, goat's hair and the spun and woven fabrics which the abundance of raw material brought into commoner use. This, for the first time, made a regular exchange of products possible."[4]

At the beginning of the Bronze Age cattle-breeding was becoming widespread not only in the areas of Siberia and Transbaikalia, favourable for stock-breeding, that bordered on Mongolia but even in the Lake Baikal region, contiguous with the taiga, where in a number of sites and burying grounds, which still remained very archaic in character; bones of the domestic ox and sheep have been found in excavations.

The first major social division of labour had a further, even more important consequence: the thousand-year old foundations of the ancient matriarchal clan system were shattered. As Engels pointed out:

"The herds and the other new objects of wealth brought about a revolution in the family. Procuring the means of subsistence had always been the business of the man; he produced and owned the tools of production. The herds were the new tools of production, and their original taming and subsequent tending was his work. Hence, he owned the cattle, and the commodities and slaves obtained in exchange for them. All the surplus now resulting from production fell to the man; the woman shared in consuming it, but she had no share in owning it. The 'savage' warrior and hunter had been content to occupy second place in the house and give precedence to the woman. The 'gentler' shepherd, presuming upon his wealth, pushed forward to first place and forced the woman into second place."[5]

CHAPTER III

INTRODUCTION OF IRON TOOLS

In tracing the changes in the material culture of ancient Mongolia we have already mentioned the appearance of iron.

It is more than likely that iron articles first began to be produced locally towards the IIIrd century B.C. The production of iron, iron weapons and implements constitued a most important achievement in the process of developing productive resources.

Much greater specialization was required for working iron ore and forging even the very simplest articles than for casting richly ornamented bronze daggers. This raises the question of the division of labour in the handicraft sphere. The specialist—the craftsman—the communal blacksmith makes an appearance. As time goes on, the division of labour in the handicraft sphere becomes intensified and more complicated among the Central Asian tribes. In a Chinese chronicle, for instance, there are records of artisans producing arrows in Mongolia and of specialists in the making of bows used in war.

All this indicates that craftsmanship was gradually becoming more and more specialized and this could not fail to encourage the further development of labour inside gentile societies. The resultant growth in trade proved to be the most important cause of the unequal concentration of family property.

The ways in which this accumulation came about and the sources from which it was derived are testified to by a report on the endless raids that were carried out from the north on Chinese possessions in the late Chou period. As early as the IIIrd century B.C. Chinese princes were compelled to begin building "long walls" to form a barrier protecting them against northern nomads. But plundered property was not the only source of the wealth acquired by the steppe warriors; among their booty, slaves—prisoners of war—are constantly mentioned.

The use of slaves for production must have greatly augmented the quantity of goods produced and helped to develop trade with the neighbouring countries. Indirect evidence of the existence of such trade is provided by the finds of Chou knives, and various metal objects, chiefly weapons, in the north. It is also known that the tribes in the north used to obtain salt from Chou-ruled China.

All the above goes to show that the old gentile organization of the tribes inhabiting Mongolia was already being shattered in the IIIrd century B.C. by the force of private ownership that had grown up on the basis of new forms of distribution of labour by slavery and the intensification of trade exchange. Furthermore, the leaders of military raids, the heads of tribes and the tribal elders were becoming more and more important. From their ranks a strong and wealthy steppe aristocracy was being built up.

Even in its funeral rites this aristocracy sought to single itself out from the remaining mass of the population. It is worthy of remark that it was precisely at the time of the introduction of iron, the growth of trade and the use of slave labour that burial structures came to be divided into two types. One type preserves in the main the traditional forms, while the other, more complex, is much less often met with and belongs to the tribal aristocracy.

It was not merely the raids for plunder that strengthened the patriarchal-gens nobility. Their representatives also acquired real power because they began to own ever larger amounts of private property and slaves whose labour they used to augment their own household economy. Thus private property began undermining the very roots of the primitive commune system—collective ownership of production and acquisition.

Here, too, the primitive commune system had outlived its day and was falling into decline.

SECTION TWO

DECAY OF THE PRIMITIVE COMMUNE SYSTEM AND FORMATION OF FEUDAL RELATIONS IN MONGOLIA

CHAPTER I

DECAY OF THE PRIMITIVE COMMUNE SYSTEM, FIRST TRIBAL ALLIANCES AND FORMATION OF STATES IN MONGOLIA

The Hun Power

Chinese sources contain brief references to the various tribes who inhabited the territory of Mongolia in the second millennium B.C. Fuller information relates to the V-IVth centuries B.C. by which time two tribal alliances had been formed in Central Asia—the Huns and the Tungus. Until recently there has been no final solution of the problem of the ethnic origin or derivation of these two groups of tribes. Controversial views have been expressed about this problem, the biggest differences being about the Huns.

An eminent Russian scholar, an Orientalist of the first half of the XIXth century—I. Ya. Bichurin, was the first to propound the theory of the Mongolian origin both of the Huns and the Tungus. He pointed to their common customs, similarity of language and to the fact that both tribal groups belonged to the *peidi* ("Northern di") tribe, which was the name used by ancient sources to describe the various proto-Mongolian tribes, which, long before the Huns, had roamed as nomads over the territory of Southern Mongolia.[1] In later times other scholars, some of them Soviet, proffered the view that the Huns were an ethnologically Turkic tribe and that Turkic elements predominated in their language. As for the Tungus and the various tribes which later emerged from them, West-European scholars considered them to be Tungus or Turkic tribes.

Archaeological and linguistic research done in recent years enables us to draw a conclusion which basically confirms the view of I. Ya. Bichurin. The Tungus tribal group and its offshoots, the Uhuan, Syan'pi and Zhuzhan tribes and branches of the Syan'pi—Muyun, Toba, Yuven, Kumosi, Shipei and Khitan tribes, are according to source data, interconnected by their

71

general ethnic origin, similarity of customs, language and culture and basically similar (save in the case of the Muyun, Toba and Khitan) level of social development. This group of tribes, as the latest research studies show, is probably of Mongolian origin and multi-lingual. The Turkic and Tungus elements met with in their language can be fully explained by the fact of the close political, economic and cultural association of the proto-Mongolian tribes with the Turkic and Tungus tribes.

In the case of the Huns the problem of their ethnic derivation calls for still further investigation. One point, however, is beyond doubt: in level of social development, customs and culture the Huns were very close to the proto-Mongolian tribes of the Tungus group. It is quite possible that the Huns were of Mongolian origin but that subsequently, after they seized the "Western Territory" (Eastern Turkestan, Central Asia), they were largely assimilated by Turkic tribes. On the other hand, some of the Huns in the first century A.D., after being crushed by the Syan'pi tribe merged with the latter and were assimilated by them and this was reflected in the Syan'pi language.

Chinese sources sometimes use the term "Hu"—"barbarian" to designate the Huns. This term has a broader meaning—it was used to designate all the northern non-Chinese tribes. The appellation Tungus means "Eastern hu", i.e. tribes living to the east of the Hu tribe (Huns).

Both the Huns and the Tungus were pastoral tribes. By the IIIrd century B.C. the Huns had become the strongest of them. The Huns and other tribes exchanged the products of livestock-breeding and furs for the agricultural produce and handicrafts of neighbouring countries. The Huns led a nomadic type of life. Each tribe was allocated a specific territory for migratory purposes, as described by the sources: "Each possessed a separate strip of land and migrated from place to place, in untrammelled search for grazing and water." The Huns had cattle and goats and at times bred camels, asses and horses of different breeds.

Their needs in food and clothing were basically met from the products of livestock breeding. Cereals, handicraft articles and luxury items for the tribal nobles were obtained through trade with neighbouring settlers, principally from China.

From the Ist century B.C. onwards, however, the Huns took up agriculture, too. Written evidence exists of crop failures due to drought, frost and the appearance of locusts; and of granaries and cereal storehouses. In excavations of Hun graves we come across grain and vessels for storing grain with an opening in the base. Similar vessels for storing grain are commonly found even to this day in different parts of Mongolia. Iron ploughshares and traces of canals have been found in archaeological excavations.

Craftsmanship played an important part in the Hun economy; the Huns built town sites in which handicrafts were practised and iron was worked. In the Ivolga town site in the basin of the Selenga river slag—industrial waste—was found and in Hun graves at Noin-Ul remains of cast-iron were and a cast-iron bell.

The Huns were skilful in making clay vessels—by hand or on the potter's wheel. Pottery made by the latter method had smooth sides and a square-shaped imprint on the base.

Pottery vessels were used for different purposes: saucers, cups, large jars for storing grain and making cheese, etc. The Huns also made ornaments from silver, gold and precious stones. Craftsmen wove and spun yarn. Woven woollen cloth and skeins of woollen thread have been found in the Noin-Ul excavations.

In the last decade of the IIIrd century B.C. the Hun tribal alliance was considerably strengthened, helped partly by the weakening of its neighbour China, where popular uprisings had occurred and aristocratic cliques were battling for power.

The social system which the Huns had by this time developed was in the stage of transition from the primitive commune to class society. The political form of tribal organization was a military democracy.

The system of "military democracy" directly precedes the formation of a state, i.e. a class society. The term "military democracy" was interpreted by Engels as meaning the kind of social organization in which gentile rule begins to disintegrate and the hereditary authority of a gentile aristocracy emerges, military leaders become prominent and predatory wars become a regular industry. Such a system, however, still retains the elements of a primitive gentile democracy—a council, a people's assembly. This is what distinguishes it from "public authority," from the instrument of class oppression—the state.

The following is what Engels says about military democracy: "The military commander, the council of chiefs, and the popular assembly formed the organs of the military democracy that had grown out of gentile society. Military democracy because war and organization for war were now regular functions of national life."[2]

Among the Huns authority was a hereditary function, invested in a specific gens and passed on from father to son. At the head of the tribal alliance stood the ruler—*shangyu*, who in the IIIrd century B.C. was no longer elected by the tribe or the council of elders. The tribal nobility, the princes, came into prominence. The council of elders still existed but did not play a decisive role. Although he asked advice from the elders, the Hun *shangyu*, Modêh, who seized power in 209 B.C. after killing his father Tuman, often not only paid them no attention but even ordered that their "heads be chopped off," if he disagreed with their opinion.

The reforms introduced by *shangyu* Modêh after he seized the throne strengthened the hereditary authority of the Hun aristocracy. Lands in subjection to the Huns were divided into three parts. One part was used by the nomad horde of *shangyu* Modêh, the other two—eastern and western—were headed by "princes": Prince Chuki and Prince Luli. The eastern or left side was regarded as the senior. Usually the heir to the *shangyu* throne was the eastern Prince Chuki.

The hereditary elders—*tyemniks*—were subordinate to the princes and held different titles. For admininstrative purposes *tyemniks* nominated officers commanding 10,000 horsemen. The most distinguished families among the Huns were the Huang, Lang and later the Shuibu. Hereditary princes and important war leaders were appointed from their ranks.

The existence among the Huns of a ruling hereditary aristocracy denoted the collapse of gentile or tribal relationships, the transition to a class society and the emergence of the foundations of an organized state. The continuous and frequent wars waged by the Huns played a major part in the emergence of a hereditary aristocracy, in its usurpation of power and in the stand taken by the whole tribe against the clan nobility.

The brilliant description given by Engels of the process of creating hereditary rule and of the emergence of a hereditary nobility in the ancient world is equally applicable to other peoples and tribes: "The robber wars increased the power of the supreme military commander, as well as of the subcommanders. The customary election of successors from one family, especially after the introduction of the father right, was gradually transformed into hereditary succession, first tolerated, then claimed and finally usurped; the foundation of hereditary royalty and hereditary nobility was laid."[3]

Survivals of primitive commune relationships were retained in the social structure of the Huns; polygamy (levirate) was prevalent. According to Chinese sources "on the death of a father or brothers they take to themselves the wives for fear the family should die out; and so, though there is incest among the Huns, families do not die out."

The constant warfare waged by the Huns with other tribes and neighbouring peoples led to the capture of property and slaves. Written sources state: "caputured men and women are taken into slavery...", "whoever brings back a dead man from a battle will receive all his property..." As well as making their captives slaves, the Huns also practised local slavery, as can be gathered from the fact that members of criminals' families were enslaved: "For theft the family is confiscated." The emergence of slavery resulted in the appearance of a stratum of socially oppressed persons. Nevertheless, the Huns did not make wide use of household slavery; the practice did not exceed the limits of patriarchal slavery and did not develop to the point of a slave-owning society.

For the Huns at the stage of social development where the transition was being made from the primitive commune to a class society, war was a permanent occupation.

This was a typical feature not only of the Huns but also of the other tribes at this stage of their development. "War, once waged simply to avenge aggression or as a means of enlarging territory that had become inadequate, was now waged for the sake of plunder alone, and became a regular profession."[4]

Like his successors, the Hun *shangyu* Modêh was continuously at war with his neighbours. In 209 B.C. he suddenly attacked the Tungus tribe, defeated them and seized the lands, cattle and property of the vanquished. Some of the Tungus became vassals of Modêh and began to pay him tribute in the products of livestock-breeding and of hunting. Another section of the Tungus, refusing to submit, fled northwards and occupied lands along the Onon, Kerulen and Argun rivers. The bulk of the Tungus population, however, emigrated to the upper reaches of the River Liao.

Later on, Modêh defeated the Yüch-chi tribe in the west, subdued in the south the tribes living as nomads on the Ordos, recovered the lands taken from the Huns by the Chinese general Meng Chan, during the reign of the Ching dynasty (221-207 B.C.) and then subdued a number of northern tribes.

Under Modêh the Hun power attained its greatest might and occupied a wide stretch of territory. In the west the frontier of Hun possessions was formed by the cities of the State of East Turkestan and on the east by the River Liao, in the upper reaches of which Tungus tribes lived in nomad tents; on the south by China (the territory of present-day Shansi province of China), the border with which passed along the Great Wall, and on the north the possessions of the Huns reached Baikal.

The Huns' success in predatory warfare and in expanding their territory can be explained by specific circumstances—the relative weakness of the other nomad tribes and the civil warfare in China. On the other hand, they were helped to this success by the use they made of heavily-armed cavalry, borrowed by the Huns from the ancient people of Khwarezm and by their own military and administrative organization. The new departure in armament was the use of heavy armour—coat-of-mail for the horse and rider and also a long assault-lance attached by a chain to the horse. Military-administrative organization consisted, as mentioned above, in splitting up the force into military units—of ten, a hundred, a thousand and tens of thousands—so as to ensure constant military training. This kind of organization made it possible to train troop reserves and transformed all the male population into a permanent army.

Chinese sources also tell of the annual journey made by the elders to the seat of the *shangyu* to offer sacrifices to ancestors, to the heavens, the earth and the spirits. In addition, every autumn the elders assembled to hold a battue-hunt at which a check was made of the number of people and cattle, i.e. a kind of population census was taken and the amount of taxes payable determined. As statehood began to take shape, the Huns found that they needed writing in order to keep records of population and livestock and to communicate with the outside world. At first the Huns used Chinese hieroglyphs for official correspondence and, in addition, attempts were made to devise their own written language, as is proved by archaeological finds made at Noin-Ul and other places in Mongolia in the form of various marks scratched on everyday household objects. At the present time 14 such signs (excluding duplicates) have been counted and they are identical with the letters on the monoliths (steles) of Kosho-Tsaidam on the River Orkhon.

The effect of the conquests of *shangyu* Modêh was that the Huns came to absorb ethnically different tribes of Mongol, Tungus and Turkic origin. In the south a small part of the Chinese population also became subject to the Huns.

The Chinese Han Empire, which had suffered from constant raids by the Huns, was obliged to ransom itself with gifts—a special type of tribute—and to acknowledge the independence of the Hun power.

In 162 B.C. the Han Emperor Siao Wen-di, in a message sent to the Hun *shangyu*, Liaoshan-Giyiu, the son of Modêh, officially declared that "...the nomadic possessions which lie to the north of the Long Wall must obey the behests of the *shangyu*. I am the ruler of those who dwell inside the Long Wall..." In the same message it is further stated that "the Han and Hun countries are two contiguous and equal states".

Despite the fact that from 198 B.C. China more than once renewed the treaties concluded on peace and kinship, sent Chinese princesses to become the wives of Hun rulers and paid tribute, the Huns did not cease making raids on China's territory. These irruptions resulted in towns being devastated and crops destroyed. For a long time China's trade with the West was stopped because the Huns were seizing the territory formerly traversed by the "Great Silk Road," which linked China with the Western territory.

Under successive *shangyu* rulers, and over a period of more than a hundred years, fighting went on both inside the Hun power between individual tribes and also between the Huns and China. In the course of the struggle Chinese troops frequently defeated the Huns (in 127, 124-123, 121 and 119 B.C.) and this prompted some of the Hun nobles to seek reconciliation with China.

The struggle inside the Hun power between tribes and also among the top-level rulers, resulted in the Huns being split up between southerners and northerners (57-55 B.C.) and in the southern Huns under *shangyu* K'u K'anyeh becoming subjects of the Han Empire. Some of the northern Huns under the *shangyu* Chichi, a brother of K'u K'anyeh, made an alliance with the Central Asiatic tribes of Kanguts and wandered off to the West.

Those of the northern Huns who moved out of Mongolia made an alliance with tribes living on the borders of the Caspian Sea and advanced deep into the West.

In the Vth century they formed an important state on the Danube under the leadership of Attila, which after the latter's death (453 B.C.) ceased to exist as a single state.

The western Huns became assimilated with many of the peoples who inhabited the territory between Central Asia and the Danube.

The southern Huns continued to remain on the territory of Mongolia as subjects of China and became weakened by fighting with the Uhuan and Syan'pi tribes of the Tungus group.

In 85 and 87 A.D. the Syan'pi tribe twice defeated the northern Huns who had remained in Mongolia, defeats from which the latter were unable to recover. The southern Huns, jointly with Chinese troops, finished them off in a series of battles (A.D. 89, 90, 91 and 93).

In the year 93 the northern Huns ceased to exist as an independent state. A large number of them had been physically annihilated and those who remained alive—some 100,000 tents— merged with the Syan'pi and assumed their tribal name.

The southern Huns, who were ruled by China, rose up in rebellion in the first century A.D., recovered their statehood and at the beginning of the IVth century conquered part of Northern China, where they founded two states in succession called Han and Chao. Southern Hun states existed in Northern China until the end of the IVth century. After their fall most of the southern Huns returned to Mongolia.

During the period of Hun supremacy in Central Asia the transition from the primitive commune system to a class society was effected. The Huns founded their first early state on the territory of Mongolia by uniting its numerous tribes.

The State of Syan'pi

As already mentioned, the Tungus tribes, when they were defeated by the *shangyu* Modêh in 209 B.C., dispersed over the territory of present-day Inner Mongolia and North-East China

(Dunpei). According to Chinese chroniclers the Tungus tribes continued to call themselves by the names of the mountains where they settled, i.e. Huang and Syan'pi. While the Huns wielded power, the Tungus did not play a big political role in history; they were tributaries of the Huns and served in their armies. But shortly before the Huns split up into northerners and southerners, the Tungus (Huang and Syan'pi) began to grow stronger. They figure in the pages of Chinese chronicles and are looked upon as a force capable of standing up to the Huns.

The Syan'pi tribe, which got its name from the Syan'pi Mts. to which it had migrated, begins to play a considerable political role in the history of Central Asia in the first century B.C. They lived further north than the Huangs and, as distinct from the latter, were less exposed to pressure from China. From the middle to the end of the first century the Syan'pi were used by China to wage war chiefly with the northern Huns with whom their lands bordered on the west.

In 54 A.D. the Syan'pi elders were given princely titles by the Chinese court and, as time went on, were paid annually quite substantial rewards for their military services.

The Syan'pi, like their Huang neighbours also, were nomadic herdsmen and hunters. Agriculture, too, held an important place in their economy and handicrafts were also considerably developed; they made bows from horn and glue, arrows, saddles and horse harness, gold and iron articles.

In social development the Syan'pi lagged behind the Huns.

In the second century A.D., for instance, they still continued to elect their rulers. The wars which they waged with their neighbours (Huns, Huangs and China) gradually resulted in wealth being accumuluated in the hands of tribal leaders which destroyed the gentile commune. The Syan'pi tribal nobles apparently owned slaves, taken chiefly from prisoners of war. Only at the end of the IInd century A.D. does hereditary rule emerge among the Syan'pi and the II-IIIrd centuries witnessed their transition from pre-class society to a class society.

After the defeat in 93 A.D. of the Northern Huns and the fusion of their remnants with the Syan'pi tribe, the ethnic composition of the latter changed. Thenceforward, the name "Syan'pi" has to be understood as comprising not only the Tungus but also the Hun, i.e. the Syan'pi became ethnically a heterogeneous tribe and this merging of two tribes was reflected also in the language.

The merging and crossing in this fashion of ethnically different tribes and language groups on the territory of Mongolia continued but it resulted not so much in the formation of a new language as in the enrichment of one of the hybrid languages, namely, old Mongolian, which was preserved, and developed and supplemented its vocabulary from other languages—Turkic and Tungus-Manchu.

In the middle of the IInd century A. D. a member of the Syan'pi tribal nobility, Tanshihuai (141-181), comes into prominence as the founder of the Syan'pi state. He was himself elected and did not inherit ruling office. "Tanshihuai laid down the laws for settling disputes and no one dared to disobey them." The sources go on to point out that he "built a palace at Danhan mountain on the River Chocheu ... he had a large number of horsemen. All the elders east and west were his subjects."

Tanshihuai occupied all the territory subject to the Huns at the time they held sway. After the Suan'pi had strengthened their position in Central Asia a series of raids began on the northern provinces of China. The Han dynasty (25-220 A.D.), disturbed by the devastation wreaked on their border regions, offered Tanshihuai the title of prince and the conclusion of a treaty of "peace and kinship" but he refused to agree. During his reign order was brought into the administration of the conquered lands. They were divided, as they had also been during the rule of the Hun *shangyu* Modèh, into three *aimaks*, placed under elders appointed by Tanshihuai.

A factor which contributed to the success of Tanshihuai's conquests was the considerable weakening suffered by the Han Empire, which from the end of the Ist century A.D. was collapsing as a consequence of a peasant uprising and the increasing bitterness of feudal internecine strife. In its weakened condition the Han Empire was incapable of repelling the raids of the nomads on its territory.

On the other hand, the state organization of the Syan'pi grew stronger, partly as a result of the subjection of other nomad tribes. A Chinese source, describing the power of the Syan'pi under Tanshihuai, remarks: "they have 100,000 troops. Their weapons are sharp and their horses faster than those of the Huns. Their gentes are numerous, no fewer than in earlier times."

The Chinese borderlands were constantly being laid waste by Syan'pi raids. This is how a Chinese source explains the reasons for these raids: "The crowds of nomads grew more numerous daily. Cattle-breeding and game-hunting were not sufficient to give them a livelihood".

The Chinese troops sent out to protect the frontiers were frequently defeated. But internal struggles among the Syan'pi, especially the struggle for power among the aristocracy, weakened the Syan'pi.

Under the rule of Kebinyn, the son of Tanshihuai, the Syan'pi power was re-established but, after his death (in 285), the princes who had already won independence during his lifetime finally broke away, and in the middle of the IIIrd century

A.D. the state of Syan'pi ceased to exist as a single whole and split up into a number of separate tribes, prominent among them being the Muyun and Toba tribes.

In the IVth century A.D., as the process of class formation intensified, early-feudal states made their appearance among the Muyun and Toba tribes on the territory of Southern Mongolia but, as conquests continued, the centres of these states moved over into China. Despite this, the early feudal states of Muyun and Toba directly influenced the formation of elements of feudal relationships among the nomadic tribes left behind in the homeland.

CHAPTER II

EARLY FEUDAL STATES IN MONGOLIA

The Zhuzhan Kaganate

Historical sources of the IVth century A.D. are the first to contain mentions of nomads called Zhuzhans who lived south of the Gobi. The Zhuzhans were apparently Mongolians by language and were ethnically closer to the Syan'pi.

Originally, they were vassal dependents of the early Toba state (Tai, 310-376) and paid tribute in products of stock-breeding and hunting. Under the leadership of Gyuiluhoi, son of Mugului, a former bondsman of the Khan of Toba, the Zhuzhans fought with the Toba Khans for their independence and, as a result, the Zhuzhan tribes were united and given the name "Zhuzhan."

At the beginning of the Vth century the rulers of the Zhuzhans, in order to emphasize their superiority, began to assume the new title of *Kagan*, in distinction to the titles *shangyu* and khan.

Thenceforward, the Turkic and Mongolian rulers rejoiced in the resounding title of *Kagan*.

Under Khan Shelun the Zhuzhan Kaganate considerably strengthened its position at the expense of new tribes they had subdued. In 402 Shelun assumed the title of Kagan, adding the style "Most Mighty."

Shelun took a number of steps to strengthen his Kaganate. He divided the Kaganate into two sectors: western and eastern, headed by *seliphs*.

He enacted military laws. Under his new military system a thousand men made up a regiment headed by a commander, while a hundred men formed a "banner" under a chief. He who attacked first was given prisoners as a reward and a large share of the booty, but anyone who retreated from cowardice was beaten on the head with stones or done to death with staves.

The political centre of the Zhuzhans and the Kagan's headquarters were situated near the Khangai mountains. The Zhuzhan Kaganate comprised Mongolia, West Manchuria and the eastern part of what is now Sinkiang in the Uighur Autonomous Region. In the Vth century the possessions of the Zhuzhans extended on the south to the Gobi, on the north to Baikal, on the west to Kharashar and on the east to Korea.

The Zhuzhans led a nomadic type of life; they reared cattle, goats, sheep and horses. Besides livestock-breeding and hunting they began in the VIth century to practise agriculture, too. For living quarters they used felt tents (*yurts*). Although often at war with Toba-Pei, the Zhuzhans maintained economic relations with it, importing thence rice, millet, cloth, lacquer, weapons, etc.

They exploited their vassals, the Altai Turks, as artisans for making weapons and other metal articles.

The Zhuzhans had a relatively highly developed culture, as can be seen from the archaeological excavations carried out on MPR territory.

The Zhuzhans did not know how to write but they used wooden tallies for reckoning, and later they began to use Chinese writing in official correspondence.

There were well-educated people among the Zhuzhan nobility. For example, the Kagan Shelun had a good command of Chinese and was interested in astronomy and mathematics. According to Chinese sources, the Zhuzhans used to bring in from North-Western China doctors, blacksmiths and weavers and they imported medicines, seismic instruments, etc.

The administrative structure of the Kaganate consisted of the Kagan, the *seliphs* (heads of the western and eastern sectors) and the regimental and company commanders. They constituted the ruling class of the Zhuzhan Kaganate. Under their authority came the ordinary nomads who lapsed more and more into dependence on them, and the slaves, mostly prisoners of war. Among the Zhuzhans slavery did not play any considerable part in social production. The Zhuzhan Kaganate was the first state of an early-feudal type in Mongolia, if we disregard the Muyun and Toba state formations which extended their conquests into Chinese territory; the Zhuzhans represented a great menace to settled states and tribes, primarily to the state of Toba-Pei in North-West China.

The history of the Zhuzhan Kaganate is a succession of uninterrupted wars and of constant fighting against the Toba emperors who sought to bring the Zhuzhans into subjection.

It was precisely the struggle against the pretensions of the state of Toba-Pei that gave birth to and strengthened the Zhuzhan Kaganate. Economic and political motives were, primarily, the basic cause of the fighting that lasted almost half a century between the Zhuzhans and the Tobas, since the Toba emperors, who held in their grasp all the economic keys to Northern China, made skilful use of their superiority in the fight against their unruly neighbours—the Zhuzhans—and prevented the latter from establishing economic links with China.

The Zhuzhan Kagans refused to submit to this state of affairs and sought to extend their rule and influence westwards to eastern Turkestan in order to satisfy the acute needs of their economy and also to acquire that country as an ally in the struggle against the Toba state.

In the Vth century internecine dissension became still more intense in the Zhuzhan Kaganate. In the short period from 402 to 445 six Kagans succeeded one another in the Kaganate and there was an intensification of separatist movements among the Gaoguis and other vassal tribes. The aggressive policy of the emperors of Toba-Pei, directed against the Zhuzhan Kaganate, and the constant warring attacks all helped to weaken the Zhuzhan Kaganate.

The Turkic tribes, especially in the Altai, who were vassal dependents of the Zhuzhans, often rose in rebellion and these uprisings assumed specially wide dimensions in the VIth century. In the middle of the VIth century the Zhuzhan state was defeated in the steppes of Mongolia by a coalition of Turkic tribes headed by the Altai Turks. In 552 the Zhuzhan Kagan Anahuan committed suicide after being defeated by the Turks and in 555 the Turks finally annihilated the Zhuzhan power and seized all its possessions. The Zhuzhans ceased to play any kind of political role in the further history of Mongolia, ceding their place to other tribes.

The bulk of the Zhuzhan population became part of the Turkic Kaganate, while some of them—about 30,000 tents (probably 130,000 people), not wishing to submit to the Altai Turks, emigrated to the West where the Zhuzhans became known under the name of Avars ("obory" in Slavonic chronicles).

The Turkic Kaganate

After the Zhuzhan Kaganate was defeated in 552 by Turkic tribes a new political association was formed in Mongolia—the Turkic Kaganate, headed by the leader of the Altai Turks, Buman (Tumen). Tumen assumed the title of the Zhuzhan ruler—Kagan, which is why his state was called a Kaganate.

The descendants of Tumen (who died in 553) continued the conquests begun by their predecessor and greatly enlarged the possessions of the Turkic Kaganate.

This aggressive policy of the Turkic Kaganate was directed to seizing fresh territory, obtaining the products of handicrafts and agriculture and establishing control over the great trade route leading from the east through Mongolia to the west.

Command of the trade route gave the Turkic nobles the possibility of wider association with the outer world and enabled them to augment their profits from customs duties.

By the eighties of the VIth century the Turkic Kaganate had attained enormous dimensions, as it comprised a large number of different tribes and peoples within its borders. In the west the Turks defeated the Eftalits and in the north the Yenisei Kirghiz. North China, too, felt the weight of Turkic armour when the kingdoms of North Tsi and North Chou, which then existed there, were obliged in the seventies of the VIth century to pay tribute to the Turkic Kaganate. North Chou alone, for instance, paid an annual tribute of up to 100,000 pieces of silk tissue. As a result of their conquests, the possessions of the Turks extended from east to west from the Gulf of Korea to Semirechye, from north to south from the Great Wall to the northern regions of Lake Baikal. The centre of the Kaganate at that time was situated in the basin of the River Orkhon and so the Turks are designated in literature as the Orkhon people. The successes achieved by the Turks in their conquering career over a short period of time were to a certain extent attributable to the weakening of their neighbours.

The political history of the Turkic Kaganate was extraordinarily stormy, as there were constant fights between the individual tribes forming part of the Kaganate, between the elders of the gentes and also between the free members of the communes and the nobles. As a consequence of the acute domestic strife the Turkic Kaganate split up at the end of the VIth century into an eastern and a western sector, which were known as Tolis and Tardush. The East-Turkic Kaganates interfered in the internal affairs of China, taking an active part in the struggle of feudal cliques in China and they contributed to the defeat of the Sui dynasty and to the Tang dynasty's accession to power in 618.

However, Tang China soon began to follow an aggressive policy towards its recent ally and strove to subdue the Turks by coercion using armed force. With this aim in view the rulers of China traduced one set of neighbours against the other, taking advantage of the constant discords inside the Kaganate itself. In the end China dealt the Kaganate a decisive blow in 630, as a result of which the Turkic Kaganate in ac- actual fact lost its independence.

But in the eighties of the VIIth century the Turkic tribes rebelled against the Tang Empire. The rebellion was headed by one of the influential representatives of the Turkic nobility, Kutulug, and his counsellor Tonyukuk. Prior to the revolt, Kutulug bore the title "Tudun" and resided in the environs of the present day city Khukhekhoto in the locality "Black Sands". After a series of successful battles they managed to re-establish the Turkic Kaganate, though in nothing like its former dimensions. As an honour for having reestablished the Turkic Kaganate, Kutulug was given the name of Elteres, which means "the assembler of people".

After the death of Elteres in 691 the Kaganate throne devolved on his brother Mocho (Kapegan). Under him (691-716), despite the economic blockade and the aggressive policy of the Tang dynasty, the Turkic Kaganate succeeded in regaining its former possessions. Mocho carried through a number of reforms directed towards improving the economy and the political position of the country, as well as a series of important measures for developing agriculture, creating a permanent army, etc. Although not all of these reforms were implemented, they helped to a certain extent to strengthen the restored Turkic Kaganate. Mocho adopted a harsh policy towards the conquered tribes. He was killed in one of the campaigns against the rebel Baiyrku.

After Mocho's death in 716 and a short-lived struggle for the throne, in the same year the son of Elteres, Bilge-Mogilyan (684-734) became Kagan with the assistance of his brother, Prince Kyulb-Tegin (685-731), a great commander and statesman.

Bilge-kagan adopted a number of measures aimed at improving the economic and political situation of the country but they failed to save the now decadent Turkic Kaganate. As time went on the East-Turkic Kagans had to battle both with China and with a whole series of tribes who had formally submitted to the East-Turkic Kaganate but were continually rebelling against the policy of enslavement followed by the Kagans.

On the other hand, as a result of the growing process of feudalization, social conflicts became accentuated among the Turkic tribes and these led to frequent revolts by the free commune members against the nobles. The Uighur tribes included in the Kaganate took advantage of the internal strife and raised a revolt, following which in 745, the East-Turkic Kaganate was crushed.

The Turkic Kaganate was replaced by the Uighur khanate. The Turkic Kaganate was an early feudal state, although the social system of the Turks still retained gentile tribal survivals. The supreme sovereign was the Kagan; the Kagan's family bore the title *Tegin*, while his nearest relatives had the titles of *yabogu* or *shad*. The latter governed the vassal tribes. The tribal nobles, *begs* and *buyuruks*, were the head of their tribes and gentes which formed the Kaganate. The main bulk of the free nomads were known as *kharabudun* ("benighted" or "dark" people) while, as distinct from them, the Kagan family and the nobles were called *konturk*. The free nomads often became dependents of the feudalized nobility. They were calle *tati*. On Orkhon monuments one often comes across the expression: "you can't have Turks without *tati*." The *tati* worked for the nobles and served in their armies and paid dues in the form of produce.

The Turkic rulers levied dues on the sedentary peoples under their rule in kind, or sometimes in cash. The oppressive way in which the nobles treated the *kharabudun* was the usual cause of the revolts. A striking instance of the acute class conflicts in Turkic society was the large-scale rebellion of nomad paupers (583-586) headed by Prince Abo, the son of a female slave.

The property and wealth of the ruling upper class consisted of pasture-lands, livestock and slaves. In most cases slaves were employed as artisans, tillers of the soil, herdsmen and domestic servants.

The chief occupation of the Turks was nomadic livestock-rearing and hunting. They had a mainly natural economy but trade, too, was beginning to develop.

In agriculture iron ploughshares and other agricultural implements were used. They were also well acquainted with the smelting of iron ore—during the rule of the Zhuzhans the Altai Turks were their tributaries and smelted iron for them.

Handicrafts were more developed among the Turks than among the other nomads. They were especially skilled in making jewellery, as is proved by the ornaments made from silver and gold which have been found in archaeological excavations.

For food they used: meat, milk, *kumiss* and other milk products. They lived in felt-lined tents *(yurts)*.

The weapons used by the Turks were: bows, arrows, lances, curved sabres and battle-axes. In addition, Turkic warriors wore chain mail and helmets. The armour was manufactured mainly by local artisans.

Architecture began to develop under the Turks, who were skilful stonemasons. Their favourite subject was the human figure, carved in different kinds of stone and vividly reflecting the style of the individual artist. Historical chronicles contain information about towns, road-building and post-stations built by the Turks. In 647, 68 post-stations were built connecting the north with the south.

The Turks worshipped spirits which personified the forces of nature. The spirits of the earth, of water and of ancestors were revered. But there is also evidence that Buddhism was beginning to spread among the Turks, although it did not develop further.

Phonetic writing—the first major cultural achievement—emerged among the Turks earlier than with other nomadic peoples. Specimens of this writing were first found in Mongolia in the valley of the River Orkhon. Hence its name—Orkhon writing. As examples of this may be cited the funeral monoliths of Kyultegin, Bilge Kagan in Kosho-Tsaidam on the River Orkhon and of Tonyukuk near Nalaikha, etc. Inscriptions telling about major political events that occurred in Turkic society are, together with other data, a valuable source for studying the history of nomad peoples in the VI-VIIth centuries.

The Uighur Khanate

After the fall of the East-Turkic Kaganate in the forties of the VIIIth century, the Uighurs formed a strong nomad power on the territory of the former Turkic Kaganate, with its centre in Mongolia. The capital of the Khanate was Karabalgasun on the left bank of the River Orkhon 50 kilometres north of Erdeni-tzu.

After the death of the first Uighur Khan Peilo (745), his successor was Prince Moyun-chur (745-759), under whom the Uighurs attained their greatest power.

Pursuing the policy of his predecessor, Moyun-chur organized a series of successful campaigns against the Kirghiz on the north and the Khitans on the east. This enabled him to expand his possessions considerably. By the middle of the VIIIth century the Uighurs already occupied the territory from the Altai mountains in the west to the Khingan in the east, on the south up to the Gobi and on the north up to the Sayan mountains.

On more than one occasion the Uighurs intervened in the feudal wars that were going on in China. Observing the weakening of the Tang Empire, the Uighurs more and more often violated its frontiers and behaved inside the country like conquerors. It was a difficult job to cope with them even in the capital itself—Changyang, where they settled down in large numbers and terrorized the population. The Uighurs controlled the caravan and trade route leading from China to Central Asia.

From the end of the VIIIth century the power of the Uighur Khanate began to decline gradually in consequence of the internecine strife that broke out among the Uighur nobility, on the one hand, and the struggle of vassal tribes, particularly the Yenisei Kirghiz, against Uighur rule, on the other.

The son of Moyun-chur, heir to the throne, fell a victim to internal strife and other Uighur Khans also met a similar fate.

In 832 Khan Chao-Li was killed by his subordinates; his successor committed suicide (839) after one of his retainers rose in rebellion against him.

In 840 the Uighur Khanate fell under the assault of the Yenisei Kirghiz. Some of the Uighurs emigrated to Eastern Turkestan and Djungaria and formed a Khanate there. The Uighur gentes, however, who remained in their old lands and mingled with the other Turkic and Mongol tribes became part and parcel of the newly-created Kirghiz Kaganate. The creators of the new Kaganate, Kirghiz tribes living in the Minusinsk basin on the Yenisei, were agriculturists and pastoralists.

By the IXth century they had formed a feudal state with a Kagan at the head but shortly afterwards the Kirghiz were driven out of Mongolia by Mongol tribes—the Khitans.

In spite of its short existence the Uighur Khanate played a big part in the further intensification of the process of feudalizing nomad society in Central Asia.

In the Uighur state the Khan held surpreme power, and subordinate to him were the *tutuks*, viceroys of the subject regions and the *begs*, local feudal magnates in the service of the Khanate. The *begs* had military bodyguards who not only escorted them in their military campaigns organized by the Khan but also helped to exploit the population who depended on the *begs*. Internally, the Uighur Khanate was organized on a system of independent principalities, which inevitably gave rise to separatist trends and feudal quarrels and as a result the whole political history of the Uighur Khanate abounded in feudal wars.

The most important branches of the Uighur economy were, as before, nomadic livestock-breeding and, to some extent, agriculture. They also engaged in hunting, the produce of which went mainly in payment of tribute or into trading. The basic means of production—land (pasture and arable land) and livestock were already owned by virtue of feudal rights.

In Moyun-chur's time the Uighurs began to engage in large-scale construction work (towns, settlements, forts, etc.). One work of great interest is the Uighur capital city of Karabalgasun built by Moyun-chur, the remains of which were excavated in 1949. It is a quadrangular erection of walls that have now become ramparts, built at the time from raw bricks or else from clay. These walls are fairly stout and in many places well preserved. There are remains of defence bastions at the corners. In the citadel, which is in the middle of the town, a building has been found, roofed with tiles, which was evidently the Khan's headquarters. On the outside all the forts were surrounded by deep moats that were formerly filled with water. According to archaeologists towns like Karabalgasun and other settlements were inhabited by traders or artisans and by farming people. Life in the towns was to a certain extent bound up with the caravan trade but, in the main, the towns and the nomad population lived from exchanges of goods. The nomads brought to market the products of their economy—livestock, leather, wool, while the inhabitants of residential settlements supplied the nomads with woven goods, articles made from leather, wood, pottery, metal, grain and other goods in demand among the nomads.

In addition, the towns served, when there was a danger of

war, as a refuge for the nomads living in tents (*yurts*) nearby. The Uighurs had developed craftsmanship to a considerable level: there were specialists in metallurgy and foundry work, potters, smiths and jewellers. There were, undoubtedly, stonemasons, sculptors, bone-carvers and builders, and also weavers.

In the Uighur period there was a wide expansion of the applied arts. Numerous ornamented gold, silver and bronze articles have come down to us which testify not only to the extreme skill of the artisans but also to the formation of an artistic tradition and taste.

The great cultural achievement of the Uighurs was the emergence of a native Uighur writing, based on an alphabet of Syrian origin.

As regards religion we know that some of the Uighurs professed Buddhism. In the middle of the VIIIth century Manichaeism penetrated into their midst. In the Xth century some of the Uighurs adopted the Nestorian form of Christianity but the greater number continued to adhere to Shamanism.

The Khitan Empire

The first mention of the Khitans appears in the IVth century.

Chinese sources relate the Khitans to the Tungus, so they have a common ethnic origin with the Mongolian tribes of Huangs, Syan'pi, Muyuñ, Toba, Zhuzhan and others. According to *Liao-shi* ("History of Liao"), in the IIIrd century A. D. the Khitans, together with the Yuiben and Kumo-si tribes, separated from the Syan'pi tribal group after the latter had been defeated by the Muyun tribe. There are also vague reports that the Shipei tribe originated from the Syan'pi. Among the Shipei tribal groups was the Mengu-shivei tribe (ancestors of the real Mongols).

Most of the Khitan words and terms, as transcribed into Chinese, are Mongolian; for instance, the Khitan sociological expressions *bouli*, Mongolian *bogul*, *boul* ("slave"); *sunde*, Mongolian *sulde* ("emblem"); *neben*, Mongolian *negun*, *neun* ("nomadic camping").

Chinese chronicles say that there was no special difference between the customs of the Khitans and the Shipei. In works by Japanese archaeologists published in the first quarter of the present century it is pointed out that archaeological monuments of the ancient Tungus have much in common with those of the Khitans, which indicates a similarity in material culture of the Tungus and the Khitans. This and other data strengthen once again the inference that the Khitans and the Mongols have a common origin.

At the beginning the Khitan nomads inhabited the region of the river Shara-Muren (Huanshui). In the IVth century the Khitans still preserved primitive relationships; they lived in gentes and *aimaks.*

During the IV-VIIIth centuries the Khitans fought uninterruptedly with the Muyuns, Tobas, Turks, Uighurs and other tribes and also with China. During this period they became vassals of the tribe which held sway in Central Asia and in North-East China and paid it tribute. In the VII-IXth centuries they had close links with the Tang Empire and at times were its vassals. As they became stronger, however, they frequently rose in rebellion against China and refused to pay tribute.

In the seventies and eighties of the IXth century, after subduing the neighbouring Turkic-Mongol and Tungus tribes, the Khitans gained considerably in strength. After the collapse of the Tang Empire at the beginning of the Xth century as a result of peasant uprisings, the Khitans became the ruling power in Central Asia. By this time great changes had occurred in their social development.

As early as the end of the VIth century the Khitans had made changes in the procedure for electing the elders and chief of eight tribes—they started choosing them from one particular gens which for a specific period of time, became the ruling gens. For example from the eighties of the VIth century A. D. up to 718 the ruling gentes were the Dakhe gens, then the Yaonyan gens and from the beginning of the Xth century the Yelyui gens.

The transfer of supreme power to a single gens helped to strengthen the latter, enabled it to accumulate wealth and in the final count helped to single it out from all the others.

In the VIIth century nomadic livestock-breeding acquired decisive importance among the Khitans to the exclusion of hunting. At the end of the VIIIth and beginning of the IXth centuries the Khitans developed, in the region bordering on China and the southern part of their territory agriculture, crafts such as weaving, silkworm culture and even the smelting of metals; finally towns appeared.

The emergence of property differentiation and of antagonistic social groups, accompanied by changes in economic life, contributed to the formation of a state organization among the Khitans.

In the middle of the VIIIth century the union of eight Khitan tribes assumed the character of statehood with a Khan at the head. Laws appeared relating to government officials and prisons, evidence of an accentuation of social conflicts. From the middle of the IXth century military and administrative appointments were instituted under the authority of the khan:

ili-jin (el-ezen), yui-yuei, tamazui, sali, evidence of the further complication of the state organization.

At the beginning of the Xth century Ambagyan, a scion of the ruling Slyui gens, was chief of the Khitans for nine instead of the usual three years, because he felt strong enough not to permit new elections. Reinforcing his position, Ambagyan destroyed once and for all the obsolete forms of the tribal organization and by uniting eight tribes shaped a Khitan state of early feudal type. He began to expand the territory of the Khitans by seizing the lands of other tribes and nationalities. He annexed to his own possessions a number of neighbouring tribes: on the North the "black waggon" tribes, Shipei, on the West the Si (Kumo-si) and others. He drove the Kirghiz out of Mongolia and expanded his possessions at the expense of the lands of the Uighurs, the Tungus tribes Mokhe and Nuchens (Churchens), the Bokhai state and part of North and North-East China. By the middle of the Xth century the Khitan state had been finally built up—the Liao Empire (this name was adopted, according to some sources, in 937, according to other sources, in 947). The Yelyui Ambagyan established a hereditary monarchy and declared himself Emperor in 916.

As a result of internal development, and also under Chinese influence, the Khitans moved forward from a system of primitive communes to a feudal system, bypassing the stage of a slave-owning society. The patriarchal form of slavery that existed under the Khitans did not develop further; after the emergence and development of feudal social forms, it continued to exist merely as a social stage.

Both ethnically and in the social and economic sense, the Liao Empire was heterogeneous. The numerous tribes and races of which it was composed were in different stages of social development—from gentile structure to mature feudal relationships. The Liao Empire comprised nomadic and semi-nomadic tribes in the north and a sedentary population in the south.

Nomadic livestock-breeding played a leading role in the economy of the Liao Empire, especially in its northern sector.

Land cultivation was a principal feature of the economy of the southern regions of the Liao Empire, inhabited by Khitan and Chinese settlers, and to some extent in the north. The basic crop of the Khitans was Mongolian millet but they also grew rice and musk in some parts.

The Liao Empire developed such crafts as weaving, silkworm culture and the smelting of metals. A Xth century Chinese traveller in a description of Shan-tsin (Upper Capital of the Khitans) remarked: "...Here can be found craftsmen making silk tissues, public officials, learned doctors of occult sciences, schools, athletic games, Confucians, Buddhists and Taoists..."

The Khitan feudal nobles owned enormous herds of livestock. The *Liao History* mentions that among the Khitans there were people who "... own 10,000 horses."

At the same time Chinese sources report that ordinary Khitans had less than ten head of livestock, including a few sheep and maybe 1 or 2 horses. These figures show what vast differences in possessions there were in Khitan society.

There was a lively trade carried on in the Liao Empire. In the Upper Capital Northern and Southern Chambers of Commerce were established. The Northern Chamber of Commerce was in charge of trade with the nomadic tribes and nationalities, while the Southern traded with the sedentary population. In addition, several urban and local markets operated.

Although barter trade was very widespread in Khitan commerce, in the X-XIth centuries bronze coinage began to play a prominent part in commodity turnover.

Although the indigenous Khitan pastoral population was exempt from a number of the servitudes imposed on the conquered tribes and nationalities it still rendered servitudes to some extent. For example, Khitan herdsmen or livestock-breeders, unless they were of noble family, were obliged to serve as postal couriers, to graze the cattle of the Emperor's family located on pastures in areas inhabited by Khitan population, to transport grain and other produce and provide for that purpose means of transport (horses, carts).

Furthermore, the nomads were obliged to serve in frontier army garrisons. A very burdensome servitude was the obligatory participation of nomads in Imperial hunting parties.

The Chinese working population performed official servitudes in the building of towns, palaces, temples, roads, irrigation canals and in repairing dams and other works.

In the Liao Empire there were basically two forms of feudal land ownership—state and private. According to Chinese sources state or official land ownership applied to land in military settlements and land handed over for use by the peasants.

Private land ownership covered such classes of land as the lands of the Khitan nobility and of other Khitan and Chinese feudal lords and also monastery lands.

Private land ownership was not uniform as regards the area owned or the type of farming. Some land was owned by small- and middle-income landowners, who did not represent the aristocracy or the service nobility. Such land was accountable to the state for the levy of tax or rent but could be mortgaged and sold.

Large landed properties were owned by the Khitan aristocrats and bureaucrats who were in the service of the Khitan emperors or, in some cases also, of Chinese feudal nobles. As a rule, land was tilled by" "leaseholders" or tenants who paid the landowners up to 50% of the crop. "Tenants" were the same feudal dependents whose exploitation was disguised as rent, which in this case took the form of payment in kind.

In the Liao Empire ownership of land by the church, in the majority of cases by Buddhist monasteries, was a major factor. Buddhism became very widespread among the Khitans, especially at the outset of the Xth century. In 942 there were 50,000 monks in the Khitan state and in 1078—360,000. The Khitan rulers paid great respect to Buddhist and also to Taoist temples, often giving them donations of land, serfs, money and grain.

The temples, particularly those of the Buddhists (they were the more numerous in the country), owned a considerable amount of landed property and large numbers of serfs.

Monastery lands were cultivated by serfs bound over (donated) to the monasteries and were also "rented out" to the local peasants. The forms of exploitation practised in ecclesiastical ownership of land were *corvée* and rent paid in kind. This related to the territory inhabited by the settled Khitans and to the Chinese. No information is yet available about land use and ownership on the territory of the nomad Khitan population.

After the formation of the Liao Empire great changes took place in the class structure of Khitan society. The exploiting class included, in addition to the feudal laity, headed by the Emperor, the feudal clergy also. The exploited class comprised the official feudal vassal "taxpayers", the serfs and the feudal dependents of different grades who were in subjection to the feudal lords and also the new serfs—"alien speakers" ("non-Khitan nomads") and "captive families" ("captive Chinese"), who had been forced to settle in different corners of the Liao Empire. The section of the exploited class with the least rights were the slaves. They were predominantly prisoners of war from various ethnic groups. Some of those sentenced for serious crimes were also made slaves. Slaves were employed on different kinds of work by the Khitan imperial family and also by the court nobility and by the higher officials and clergy.

A bitter class struggle was waged between the exploited feudal dependents and the feudal lords—a struggle that assumed differing forms. At the same time a struggle was proceeding between the masses of the conquered and dependent countries against the Khitan feudal lords, a struggle which was sapping the foundations of the Empire. A persistent struggle was conducted by the masses of the Mongol Zu-bu tribes and the Tungus tribes of Churchens and Kore.

Such in general outline was the economic system of the Liao Empire, which was unquestionably feudal, though there were at the same time considerable remnants of slavery gentile relations.

At the time when its might was at a peak the Liao Empire covered a territory extending over South-East and Central Mongolia (Inner and Outer Mongolia), a large part of North-East China (present-day Tunbei) and the northern provinces of China proper (present-day Hepei, Shansi and part of Hunan).

The state apparatus of oppression in the Liao Empire was composed at its higher levels of the Khitan nobility, representatives of the Imperial clan, relatives of the Empresses and also of other noble families. The nobility representatives comprised the hereditary aristocracy and the military serving nobles. Most Government appointments were hereditary and were filled by representatives of the nobles of one and the same gens or several gentes.

In the Khitan Empire state administration was, because of the heterogeneous composition of the population, divided into two parts. A Northern Horde was formed to administer the affairs of the nomads and a Southern Horde to govern the settled population.

The political history of the Liao Empire in the X-XIIth centuries was marked by endless wars with its neighbours, in particular with China, Korea, etc., as well as by internal struggles both among the Khitan ruling circles—noble gentes, as well as between the ruling class of feudal lords, on the one hand, and the exploited classes of serfs, slaves and freemen of the communes, on the other. This struggle was supplemented by constant uprisings of the subjugated tribes who formed part of the Khitan Liao Empire.

One of the major political events to be noted is the war with China, which was waged almost throughout the whole of the Xth century but became very bitter after the creation of the Sung Empire (960-1279).

In 1004 the Khitans concluded a peace treaty with China under which they received an annual tribute of 100,000 *lan* in silver and 200,000 pieces of silk material. In the XIth century the Liao Empire waged war with Korea and the Tangut Empire Si Sia ("Western Sia"). Later on the Liao Empire again exerted pressure on China, securing an increase in the tribute, and in 1074-1075 getting the Sung Empire to cede some territory.

Inside the Liao Empire various vassal tribes were constantly rising in rebellion. On the other hand, the struggle among the nobles burst out into an open onslaught by Yelyui Jun-yuan against his nephew, the Khitan Emperor (1063). When this rebellion was suppressed the fight for the throne still went on. It reinforced separatist trends among the leaders of the tribes composing the Liao Empire.

Weakened by the internal strife within the ruling class and by the rebellions of the different tribes, the Liao Empire was unable to resist the combined forces of Sung China and the Churchen state of Ching which had been formed in the north (1115). The last five years of its existence were the years of its death throes, of the collapse and loss of its territories. In 1125 the Churchens captured the last Khitan Emperor and this put an end to the existence of the Liao Empire.

Some Khitans merged with the new state formed in Manchuria and North China—the Churchen Empire of China. Another section did not submit to the Churchens and under the army leader Yelyui Ta-shi, moved off westwards and set up in Central Asia the State of Si-Liao—"Western Liao", better known under the name of "Kara-Khitan."

A wealth of archaeological material, discovered in Inner Mongolia and testifying to the considerable cultural development of the Khitans, has been published by Japanese and Chinese archaeologists.

In the opinion of some scholars a characteristic feature of Khitan culture is the combination of indigenous nomad traditions with those of a settled, agricultural people. As an example, Khitan clay or pottery dishes are a literal copy of the flask-shaped vessels, sewn from leather and embroidered that were very widely used by the nomads.

According to written sources, in the VIIIth-Xth centuries some branches of knowledge, closely connected with cattle-breeding, agriculture and handicrafts, were developed by the Khitans, such as: veterinary science, the training of weavers, agronomy, seri-culture, etc.

The Khitans who inhabited the central, southern and south-eastern parts of the Empire had developed the building of towns, large-size religious structures, bridges, etc., arts which they had obviously assimilated under the influence of the Chinese population.

After the Liao Empire was formed Khitan scholars produced two kinds of writing. One was created in 920 by the Khitans Tulyuibu and Yulyui Lubugu (a nephew of Ambagyan) on the model of Chinese hieroglyphic writing (the so-called "great writing").

A second kind of writing, which was really a Khitan invention, was created by the son of Yelyui Ambagyan, Yelyui Tela (Junduhun) ("little writing").

Several specimens of Khitan writing were discovered by scholars in 1922 and Khitan hieroglyphs have been partially deciphered by scholars from China, the USSR, Hungary and other countries.

A knowledge of Khitan writing was widespread also among the Churchens. It is also vaguely known that the Mongols themselves used Khitan writing.

The ruling classes, and especially the Khitan nobility, also used Chinese characters in writing.

The Khitans had their own literature written in their native language and they also wrote werses in Chinese. Yelyui Ambagyan's grandson Lungyan compiled a literary collection *Park*.

The Emperor Shenchun (983-1080) wrote more than 500 poems and translated from Chinese into the Khitan tongue the *Satirical Collection* of the famous Chinese poet Po-Chui-i.

The Khitan scholars Siao Hang-chianu, Yelyui Yang, and Yelyui Shu-chen were in their day (the end of the Xth and the middle of the XIth centuries) widely renowned as historians. Hang-chianu with Yelyui Shu-chen wrote the history of the Khitans from the time of the Kagan Yaonan (VIIIth century) up to 1032. He also wrote a book *On Ethics* and translations were also made into the Khitan tongue of the history of the U-tai period (907-970) and other Chinese works.

The Khitans also developed a certain knowledge of geography, medicine, painting, sculpture, wood-carving, and music—all showing traces of Chinese influence.

In their religious beliefs the Khitans were basically Shamanists. The Khitan nomad tribes believed in the worship of ancestors, heaven and earth. They made images of spirits out of wood (wooden figures of spirits have been found by Mongolian archaeologists when excavating Khitan towns). After the formation of the Liao Empire Buddhism, Confucianism and Taoism were strongly supported and disseminated by the feudal upper classes. The state religion, though, was declared to be Confucianism but in the Liao Empire Buddhism was the religion with the greatest influence.

The Liao Empire, in an existence of more than two hundred years greatly influenced the social and cultural development of the Mongol, Tungus and other tribes and peoples of Central and Eastern Asia. By creating on the territory of the south-eastern part of Mongolia and of North-West China a mainly feudal state, the Khitans helped to accelerate the process of forming a class society among the indigenous Mongol tribes and races. In fact, the Mongols proper, the Mongolian Tartars, the Kereits, the Naimans and other Mongolian tribes began, after the collapse of the Liao Empire, to play a considerable part in the history of Central Asia.

The reason for the slow process of decay of the primitive commune system in Mongolia was, primarily, the extensive method of production—nomad cattle-breeding.

This process was further complicated by the fact that the territory of Mongolia was inhabited by heterogeneous ethnic groups (Mongol, Turkic and Tungus tribes), which in their turn were subdivided into a number of sub-groups. Accordingly, the fight for usurpation of power by the tribal nobles was closely interwoven with the struggle of individual tribes and tribal unions which had no desire to be ethnic vassals of alien tribes.

The process of decay in the primitive commune system began in the second half of the last millennium B.C. in the central and southern regions of Mongolia. It resulted in the further decay of the gentile commune, an intensification of inequalities in property-holding and also of class antagonisms.

SECTION THREE

MONGOLIA AS A FEUDAL STATE

CHAPTER I

THE SOCIAL STRUCTURE OF MONGOLIA
AT THE END OF THE XIIth—
THE BEGINNING OF THE XIIIth CENTURY.
FORMATION OF THE MONGOLIAN STATE

*The Mongolian Tribes at the End of the XIIth—
the Beginning of the XIIIth Century*

The formation of a Mongolian state and the fusion of the Mongols into a nation occurred at the beginning of the XIIIth century. Until that time the Mongols lived as separate tribes or tribal unions. Each tribe had its own leader, the Khan. The Mongol tribes led a nomadic existence as pastoralists and at the end of the XIIth century were beginning to develop a feudal system of production.

In their social development the Mongol tribes did not represent a unity. B. Ya. Vladimirtsov was fully justified, following the example of Rashid ad-Din, in dividing them into "forest" and "steppe" nomads. They were on different levels of social development inasmuch as the "forest" tribes still caught fish and hunted wild animals, whereas the "steppe" nomads reared livestock. The pastoral nomadic tribes, however, formed the majority of Mongolian society and played the leading part in its life.

Source evidence shows that in the XIIth century Mongol tribes populated the territory from the Great Wall of China to Lake Baikal. The southern section of the Mongols living as nomads by Lake Buir-Nor along the borders of the Ching Empire (North China) were called "white Tartars". Some authors identify the "black Tartars" with the tribes constituting the core of the tribal union which at the outset of the XIIIth century was given the general designation "Mongol".

Historical science has so far not produced a uniform interpretation of the actual word "Mongol" or "Mongols". According to Chinese and other sources the Mongols were one of the ancient tribes on the territory of Mongolia. The more probable assumption is that the expression "Mongol" which, to begin with, meant one of the tribes became a collective term to mean the whole Mongolian nationality taken together. The most important Mongolian tribes at that time were the Khamag Mongols, the Jalairs, Taichiuts, Keraits, Merkits, Naimans, etc.

The Khamag Mongols lived in the basin of the Onon, Kerulen and Tola rivers. The Jalairs who lived in nomad camps in the River Onon valley were numerous and powerful. The valley of the Onon and Selenga rivers was inhabited by the nomad tribe of Taichiuts. The smallest of the nomad tribes was the Onguts, who humbered altogether only 4,000 families. They lived a segregated existence and were in the service of the Ching emperors, guarding the frontiers of China.

The Keraits were numerically a large tribe and highly important. They dwelt mainly between the Hangai and Hentei ranges, in the valleys of the Orkhon and Tola rivers. On the west the Keraits had as neighbours the Naiman tribe and on the north the "forest" tribes. Association with the Naimans with whom, in fact, they were at enmity over grazing grounds, and with the Uighurs also, who were the most cultured of the Turkic peoples, helped the spread of cultural habits among the Keraits.

Places to the west of the Kerait camping grounds, in the areas between the Hangai and Altai mountain ranges, were occupied by the Naimans. According to Rashid ad-Din some of these nomads dwelt in mountainous places (foothills) and some in the plains. The nomad camp sites of the Naimans reached as far as the River Orkhon to the places where the first capital of the Mongol Empire was subsequently founded—Karakorum. The Naimans were the most cultured of all the Mongol tribes. Naiman nobles, for instance, made use of the services of Uighur scribes, though there were few Naimans with a knowledge of Uighur writing.

Another of the important tribes was that of the Merkits (Merget). They lived in the basin of the Selenga river and in the north they bordered directly on the "forest" tribes. They were distinguished from the other Mongol tribes by their warlike character and they had a powerful army.

The "forest" Mongol tribes—catching fish and hunting wild animals—lived in the forests on the banks of rivers, principally in the Lake Baikal region, in the taiga areas of Eastern Sayan-Tannu Ola and Southern Altai. North and north-west of Lake Baikal and in present-day Trans-Baikal lived the Chori, Bargut, Tumet, Bulagachin, Keremuchin, Uryankhat, Urasut and Telengut tribes. The Oirats dwelt in the Sekizmuren (Vosmirechiye)[1] province. These were the principal tribes in Mongolia in the XII-XIIIth centuries.

The Mongol tribes of the period we are describing were living at different levels of social development.

According to Rashid ad-Din the "forest" tribes lived in huts and shelters made of branches. Their principal occupation was hunting, and the tribes often fought between themselves over hunting grounds. The *Sacred Legend* often mentions this fighting as an everyday occurrence. Like the livestock breeders, they lived as nomads, using yaks to transport their chattels when they moved camp.

The sources known to us afford no evidence that throws sufficient light on the nature of the social relationships among the "forest" tribes. Nevertheless, it would not be wrong to say that, on the whole, they had only just begun to emerge from the stage of primitive-commune relations. The religion of these tribes was Shamanism, which sanctified the relationships and supported the authority of the gentile and tribal elders. Incidentally, the religion of the pastoral tribes was also Shamanism which, in a somewhat modified and more complicated form, served also as an ideological basis for early feudalism.

As productive forces developed and the influence of more cultured neighbours—nomad pastoral tribes—made itself felt, the process of the decay of the primitive-commune structure began among the "forest" tribes. But there was still no very clearly marked differentiation of classes among the "forest" tribes at the end of the XIIth—beginning of XIIIth century.

Cattle, sheep and horses represented the basic wealth of the Mongol pastoral tribes. There were few camels. Only the Naimans had large numbers of the latter. Sheep played a role of paramount importance in the Mongol economy. Their meat, hides, wool and milk—were all used both for personal consumption and for trading on the markets of their settled neighbours, and, primarily, of North China. Talking about the role of the horse in the life of the nomads, the Chinese historian Chao-Hun writes: "The Tartars are born and grow up in the saddle and on horseback; they learn by themselves how to fight because their whole life, all the year round, is spent in the hunt." The horse was a means of locomotion, their faithful friend on the march, in battle and in hunting down game and finally, the mare supplied milk from which the Mongols prepared *kumiss*. The nomad Mongols and pastoral Mongols could make a livelihood only by moving from place to place, with camping grounds strictly apportioned between the summer and the winter campers. The direction followed in moving camp was determined by the make-up of the herd: a site that suited the sheep was no good for horses. The Mongols moved camp by *kurens* (ring-formation).

According to Rashid ad-Din one *kuren* comprised about a thousand tents (kibitkas)—families. As long as the pastoral nomads lived as a primitive commune, the *kuren* was the definite form of nomad camp. No matter where the tribe arrived it had to form up in the shape of a ring consisting of about 1,000 tents. In the centre of this ring was the *kibitka* of the head of the tribe and from it he ruled his *kuren*. With the decay of the primitive-commune system, i.e. as class distinctions emerged, the importance of individual families of wealthy people in the tribe became greater. The limits of the *kuren* cramped the wealthy and they began to graze their cattle separately and to keep servants and slaves. The rich pastoralists strove to strengthen their influence over the ordinary members of the *kuren*, the simple nomads who reared cattle, utilizing for the purpose clan or tribal ties, economic or non-economic pressure, relying on their economic power and their armed force of *nukers* from whom, as time went on, they formed squads of personal bodyguards. In this manner the *kuren* or communal system of practising a pastoral economy gradually broke down.

In its place it became more and more customary to form camp by *ails*, i.e. by individual families and not by gentes. The new system of semi-patriarchal, semi-feudal relations that had emerged among the Mongols, became a more practical way of conducting a nomad economy than the *kuren* system. Yet, though it had lost its economic significance, the *kuren* still continued to conserve its defensive importance. It is noteworthy that, when a tribe moved from camp to camp, as it settled into a new site, it tried to protect itself from sudden attack by forming a *kuren*. This occurred even more often during hunting or military expeditions.

The transition from the *kuren* to the *ail* form of economic organization went on by stages over a long period.

At the beginning of the XIIIth century, when the Mongol state was still only in the process of formation, the *ail* became established as the type of economy, even though the *kuren* continued as before to be the method followed in changing camping grounds. The triumph of the *ail* system was finally achieved under a feudal society regime.

In a time of transition to a class society, more especially in a nomadic economy gentile institutions do not disappear very easily. In the case of the Mongols gentile organizations, customs and beliefs were retained as survivals long after the emergence of feudalism. The old system acquired at the same time a new class content. The remnants of the communal gentile structure, in particular customs and beliefs (Shamanism), survived among the Mongols over a period of several centuries after the feudal system of production had become predominant.

The reason for the persistence of gentile or tribal survivals was partly that, in the case of the Mongol tribes, unity of the gens was associated with a special reverence for the "eldest" in the gens. On this point a passage in the *Sacred Legend* says that a descendant of the eldest in a clan was elevated to the special rank of "beki" and figured also as the high priest or shaman of the clan.

In an *ail*, by gentile custom, great importance was attached to the household hearth, the guardianship of which was vested in the youngest son. For this reason the youngest son could not leave the home when there was a division of property: he inherited the parents' *yurta*. These and similar gentile customs were taken advantage of by the feudal aristocracy that was taking shape and the feudal lords usurped the rights and titles of the elders of the gentes and tribes.

The protracted existence of survivals of the communal-gentile system left its mark on the development of feudalism in Mongolia.

Stratification of Classes in Mongolian Society at the Outset of the XIIIth Century and Growth of Feudal Relations

In the process of building up a class society among nomad pastoralists household slavery played a considerable part. It helped to promote the relatively rapid segregation of the wealthy and economically powerful *ails*. Slaves were acquired by the tribal nobles in wars. They were usually prisoners of war. In the *Sacred Legend* and in Rashid ad-Din's work there are frequent references to the existence of slaves among the Mongol aristocracy. Slaves were household servants but they often functioned as herdsmen. Ownership of slaves was not so extensive in Mongolia as to become a basic slaveowning form of the social economy but it existed as a factor in feudal society in Mongolia at an early state of its development.

Rashid ad-Din and the *Sacred Legend* cite many facts confirming that in the second half of the XIIIth century the nomad Mongols had in almost all their tribes wealthy cattle-breeders, a steppe pastoral nobility—*noyons*. These held different titles, such as: *batur*—hero, *sechen*—wise, *mergen*—sharpshooter, *bilge*—wise, *buke*—strong man. Often they bore titles borrowed from peoples of other nationalities.

In the circumstances of nomad life the tribes often quarrelled about grazing and trapping grounds. These quarrels were sometimes very brutal and resulted in the defeated and weakened tribe becoming completely subservient to the victorious tribe.

The Mongols used the term *unagan-bogol* to denote this subservience. In describing the subservience of the *unagan-bogols*—Academician B. Ya. Vladimirtsov points out that "service to a ruling clan consisted, principally, in the fact that the *unagan-bogols* had to move round together with their owners or form *kurens* and *ails* on their orders, thus enabling their masters to operate conveniently a large pastoral economy. During battue hunts they would be the beaters and flush game. The relations between masters and *unagan-bogols* often evened out to such an extent that they began to be reminiscent of those between two allied gentes."

At the beginning of the XIIIth century, in the course of the struggle for the formation of the Mongol state, noticeable changes occurred in the condition of the mass of ordinary nomads. The former social and economic equality had already disappeared, though it could still not be said that the whole mass of nomads had completely lost their personal freedom.

The process of further stratification of classes and intensification of feudal dependence was accelerated by the formation of the Mongol state at the beginning of the XIIIth century. In this the *nukers* played a leading part. *Nukers*—"friends", or more correctly, bodyguards,—were the close collaborators or servants of the *noyon*.

The institution of *nukers* emerges when classes start forming and irreconcilable class antagonisms make their appearance. In such circumstances the ruling class—the *noyons*—in order to protect their own interests, form squads of armed men—*nukers*. This is also confirmed by the historical sources mentioned. The *nukers* played an enormous role in the position of their *noyons*. Only the *noyon* who was able to gather a powerful gang of *nukers* could acquire influence in his tribe and with his neighbours.

Wealthy *noyons* who could rely on their nukers subordinated to themselves whole groups of people of a tribe, sometimes an entire gens in their efforts to establish their rule over the whole tribe. A typical feature of the Mongolia of that day was the struggle of *noyons* both within and without the tribe to expand their rule.

The Mongol army was organized on the system of groups of ten (tens, hundreds, thousands and a myriad, i.e. ten thousand). It was connected primarily with the *kuren* and it is not a mere accident that sources, when referring to the *kuren*, remark on the division into tens, hundreds and thousands. Remember—the *kuren* contained a thousand nomad tents (*kibitkas*)—*ails*. Except for the *keshik*, i.e. the personal bodyguard instituted by Genghis Khan, the whole organization of the Mongol army was taken over by him as a legacy from the preceding period.

The facts narrated about the Mongols of the period described afford justification for the following conclusions.

In spite of the way the tribes were dispersed on the borders of the XIIth and XIIIth centuries the Mongols had much in common—language, type of economy and method of operating it, customs and culture.

In consequence, however, of the low level of development of productive forces in Mongolia no economic relationships had yet been created to any wide extent. The process of class differentiation in the tribes had already reached the stage where a powerful class—the *noyons*—had come to the fore, a class which, in order to reinforce its commanding position in a nomad society, could not be satisfied with the old gentile-tribal organizational forms and needed a powerful instrument of coercion in the shape of the state. The beginning of the XIIIth century in Mongolia was a period of intense struggle to build up such a state, whose essential achievement was the unification of all the disunited tribes into a single Mongol nationality. Thus, the formation of the Mongolian nationality occurs at the time when a feudal society was being formed.

Feudalism in Mongolia contains certain specific peculiarities which distinguish it from feudal society in many other countries. Its decisive peculiarity is that it arose and developed not on a basis of agriculture, as was the case in the overwhelming majority of other countries, but on the basis of an extensive nomad pastoral economy. This circumstance could not fail to leave its impress on many features of the social system of the Mongols. Another important peculiarity of the growth of feudalism in Mongolia is that, as stated above, it was formed not in the process of a collapsing slave-owning organization but, by-passing the latter, in the process of decay of a primitive-commune system. This was the reason for the simultaneous initiation and irregular growth of the feudal method of production among the different Mongol tribes. The Mongol tribes which populated the forest regions around Lake Baikal and the upper reaches of the Yenisei and Irtysh, whose material production was essentially based on trapping wild animals and hunting, grew away from the gentile or tribal relationships and made the transition to feudalism later and more slowly than the other Mongolian tribes inhabiting the steppe regions of Central Asia whose productive activities derived basically from nomad livestock-rearing.

Under the regime of primitive communes both the grazing grounds and the livestock were the property of the Mongol clan. With the decay of the primitive commune when livestock had already become the property of the patriarchal family, the grazing grounds were still owned for a long time by the gens. As time went on, gentile ownership of land (pastures) gave way in ever larger measure to private family ownership.

This is precisely what Karl Marx is referring to when he says that "...among pastoral peoples ownership of the natural produce of the soil—sheep, for instance,—means at the same time ownership of the meadows across which they move."[2] Traces of this form of ownership of the land have been preserved among many peoples.

The feudalization of Mongolia was essentially based on the usurpation of communal ownership of the land and grazing grounds by the feudal aristocracy that was being formed, the conversion of the direct producers—the free *arats*—into a class of feudal vassals—*albatas*—and the enslavement of the *arats* by binding them to pasture grounds which had become the monopoly of the class of feudal lords. This process developed earliest of all and to the most intensive degree in the steppe regions and considerably later and less intensively in the forest areas of the Yenisei and around Lake Baikal. Among the Buryats, the feudalization of society began in the XVI-XVIIth centuries.

In monopolizing for themselves the ownership of land or pasture grounds, the Mongol feudal lords, once they had formed themselves into a class in the XIIIth century, made allotments of the land to the direct producers, the *arats*, thus enabling them to carry on their own private economy as nomad pastoralists but requiring them in return to perform a number of servitudes. Sources show that, by the end of the XIIth century the *arats* were already furnishing the *noyons* with fuel, milking their cattle, preparing milk products for them, shearing their sheep, etc. Subsequently, as the size of the *noyons'* herds increased, it became more and more the principal task of the *arats* to pasture these herds. This was how *corvée* or statute labour arose and developed so widely in Mongolia.

Specific forms of large-scale nomad pastoral economy led to feudal ownership of land assuming such a peculiar form as the right of regulating nomad migration movements and, in general, of controlling nomad camp sites. As Academician Vladimirtsov remarks: "He who is able at his own discretion to dispose of the grazing grounds is considered by the nomads as the owner *(ejen)* of the lands *(nytug)*."

As in all countries feudalism in Mongolia was based on a natural economy in which artisan production existed alongside a pastoral economy. Every Mongol *ail*, in addition to the basic occupation of looking after cattle, was busied in preparing for its own needs felt, carts, harness, household utensils, weapons, etc. As its own production covered its own requirements in household equipment and everyday domestic items and weapons, a nomad household had few economic links with other similar households. The natural character of its economy turned the holding of a feudal prince into a closed, self-contained unit which had either no economic, or very weak economic, links with other similar holdings. This does not mean, however, that the Mongol society of the time knew nothing of commodity production or commodity exchanges.

The Mongol nomads naturally needed agricultural produce, textile manufactures and the metal articles produced in neighbouring countries. From their contacts with the population of China and the sedentary peoples of Central Asia the Mongols acquired the goods they needed in exchange for horses and other domestic animals. This kind of trade, however, did not, and in the circumstances of the time could not, disturb the stability of the natural economy which continued to be absolutely predominant within Mongol society.

Such were the basic peculiarities of the development of feudal relationships in Mongolia in their initial phase. The feudal form of exploitation and the consequent loss by the *arats* of personal freedom gained its full triumph later as a result of the conquests made during the period of the Mongol Empire. Even during that period, however, numerous and highly significant survivals of patriarchal relationships continued to persist.

The Struggle for Power between the Mongol Khans

The tribal alliances that arose as a result of the decay of the gentile system at the beginning of the XIth century in the process of their further social development, assumed the form of state confederations of a primitive type. One such state confederation is the *Khamug mongol ulus* state which emerged in the basin of the rivers Onon and Kerulen. A state of the *Khamug mongol* type also existed among the Keraits and Naimans but there was a stubborn struggle between them for power.

The formation and development of early feudal states undoubtedly paved the way for the subsequent creation of a single Mongol state at the beginning of the XIIIth century.

Among the representatives of the steppe aristocrats who were battling with one another for power one was preeminent—the young Temuchin, son of Yesukai Bator, grandson of Khabul, the first Khan of *Khamug mongol ulus*.

Temuchin was born in 1162 at Delyun Boldog on the River Onon. His father, Yesukai Bator, was the most powerful and influential of Khabul Khan's successors. He owned numerous herds and had a bodyguard of *nukers*. Under his command he had the Taichiuts, the most numerous tribe of the *Khamug mongol*.

In 1166 Yesukai was poisoned by the Tartars who had been feuding with him and died. After his death the *nukers* deserted his family and soon the Yesukai *ulus* disintegrated.

Yesukai's wife and children lived in poverty but not for long. The eldest son, Temuchin, now a grown man, made an alliance with his father's *anda* or friend, the influential Kerain khan, Togoril, and his own *anda*, Jamugha, and began successfully to reassemble and take command over the former vassals of his father. Temuchin, Togoril and Jamugha together attacked and defeated the Merkits and divided the spoils of war between themselves. However, the alliance between the three of them did not last long because of disagreements and enmity between Temuchin and Jamugha, both laying claim to rule over the *Khamug mongol ulus*, which still had no khan. In battles with Jamugha at Dalan Baljut Temuchin was defeated, but Jamugha was unable, despite his victory, to take advantage of it to strengthen his position. By giving generous rewards and promises Temuchin succeeded in winning over to his side most of the tribes subject to Jamugha, and with the active support of the *noyons* and *nukers* in 1190 he mounted the throne of *Khamug mongol ulus*.

In order to rally round himself the *noyons* and *nukers*, Temuchin gave them various privileges and, in particular, he established the privileged class or estate of *darkhans*. The *darkhans* were exempted from all taxes, had the right not to divide their booty with others, had permanent free access to the Great Khan, and went unpunished for the first nine offences. Temuchin started organizing his troops on the system of "tens". He appointed the *noyons* loyal to him at the head of every thousand and he also selected captains for hundreds and tens.

A *keshik* (bodyguard) was organized, divided into two sections: "80 *kebteuls*—as night watchmen and 70 *turkhauds*— as daytime bodyguards."

In accordance with the *Sacred Legend* the *keshik* included mainly sons and brothers of *noyons*, chiliarchs and centurions.

Temuchin's position was also strengthened by his taking part in the campaign against the Tartar tribe organized by Altan-khan (the Ching Emperor).

Temuchin readily accepted Altan-khan's invitation, as he regarded it as a suitable moment for taking vengeance on the Tartars. He also won over to his side the Kerait khan Togoril. The campaign was successful and Temuchin and Togoril shared between themselves the booty seized, including prisoners. The Ching state, to mark their services in subduing the Tartars, awarded the title of *Wang* to Togoril and that of *Jautkhori* to Temuchin. Thenceforward, Togoril became known under the name Wang-Khan.

The above events occurred on the borderline between the XIIth and XIIIth centuries, apparently in the year 1200. While Temuchin was engaged in the campaign against the Tartars, Jamugha managed to strengthen his ties with a number of groups of gentes and tribes. He was joined on this occasion by the Tartars and Taichiuts, the Hatagins, Saldjeuts, Hungerats, Merkits, Oirats and others, who decided to proclaim Jamugha their Khan. Jamugha resumed the armed struggle with Temuchin but was defeated.

In 1202 Temuchin came to an agreement with Wang-Khan to wage war jointly against the Merkits and Tartars. Wang-Khan was to fight the Merkits and Temuchin the Tartars. In the autumn of 1202 Temuchin took the field against the Tartars and the campaign ended in the almost complete destruction of the latter.

At the same time Wang-Khan took up the struggle against the Merkits, some of whom were defeated and made prisoners while the rest fled towards Bargudji-Tokum—on the territory of present-day Pribaikalye. On completing these campaigns the forces of Temuchin and Wang-Khan moved towards the Altai to attack the Naimans. This campaign was also successful but soon afterwards a struggle for power over the defeated tribes began between Temuchin and Wang-Khan. The latter allied himself with Temuchin's old rival, Jamugha. Temuchin again emerged from the struggle victorious and, taking advantage of the victory, strengthened his position.

In 1204-1205, having subdued the Naimans and the Merkits, Temuchin completed the unification of all the principal tribes of Mongolia under his own rule.

*Formation of the Mongolian State
and Its Class Character*

At the *kuriltai* convened on the River Onon in 1206 the Mongol *noyons* proclaimed Temuchin Genghis Khan, i.e. Great Khan. Compared with the previous early feudal states the Mongol state bore the very distinct character of a feudal state. It was based on a military administrative organization. Genghis Khan divided the population of Mongolia into two wings: a right wing *(barun gar)* and a left wing *(djun gar)*. The wings were composed of *tumen*. A *tma* (myriad) was made up of ten thousand men, a chiliad of ten "hundreds", a "hundred", in turn, of ten "tens". Thus, the smallest military administrative unit in Mongolia was a group of *ails* which had to supply ten warriors, while the biggest unit was a holding that enabled the Khan to mobilize 10,000 men. Genghis Khan could turn out 95,000.

The *nukers*, the armed bodyguards of Genghis Khan, were appointed chiliarchs—a military-administrative rank. They ruled over the *arat* families of their chiliads together with all their territory. The chiliarchs and centurions received *hubi* (portion from the Kagan as a reward for services rendered). Thus, the former *nukers* became vassals of the Kagan and the formation of the chiliad, as a military administrative unit with paid officers, was a decisive blow dealt to the gentile system which had outlived its day. In peace time all the nomads had to perform various duties for the khan and the *noyons* and in time of war everyone fit for war service was called up to join the ranks of the army which, as indicated above, was organized on a system of "tens".

Troops were called up not only for campaigns but also for trapping and hunting. The latter activities were pursued not merely for economic purposes but as a form of military training.

After the *kuriltai* in 1206 Genghis Khan increased the size of his personal bodyguard—*keshik*—to 10,000 men. Bodyguards guilty of breaches of discipline were given severe punishments, as set out in detail in the *Sacred Legend*. Nevertheless, however strict the discipline maintained in the *keshik*, it was regarded as a great privilege to serve in the latter.

The *keshik* was not only the protection and bodyguard of Genghis Khan, it was also the basic force with whose help he maintained the rule of the *noyons* over the rank and file nomad pastoralists and the forest people who trapped wild beasts and caught fish.

The *Sacred Legend* contains particulars of the first steps taken by Genghis Khan to organize the administration of the widespread territories of Mongolia. In order to strengthen the status of the ruling dynasty and centralize the country, Genghis Khan assigned separate *uluses* to his mother, his sons and younger brothers: to his mother, jointly with Otchigin, he assigned 10,000 families; to Juchi—9,000 families; to Chagatai—8,000; to Ugadei—5,000; to Khasar—4,000; to Alchidai—2,000 and to Belgutai—1,500. He enacted a law aimed at binding the *arats* to the *noyons*. According to the *yasa* of Genghis Khan *arats* were forbidden to transfer without permission from one "ten" to another or from one "hundred" to another.

Genghis Khan also instituted the office of state judge—*zarguchi*, whose function it was to review and give a verdict in accordance with the *yasa*. *Arats* were cruelly punished for the least signs of resistance.

The setting up of the new administrative organization, the creation of the chiliad system, the introduction of a corps of bodyguards, the generous distribution of *ulus* allotments to relatives of the khan and to individual feudal nobles—all this was directed against the gentile or tribal forms of organization and the separatist tendencies of individual feudal nobles.

This clearly reflected an intention to strengthen the new class or feudal relationships. The very act of establishing a single Mongol state was unquestionably a progressive step in the history of Mongolia in the sense that it once and for all consolidated feudal relationships. It contributed towards the formation of the Mongol nationality.

The elimination of tribal divisions and the political unification of Mongolia into a single state could have helped to augment the productive forces of the country and promote its cultural growth but this was hindered by the campaigns of conquest undertaken by the steppe feudal aristocracy under the leadership of Genghis Khan.

CHAPTER II

THE CAMPAIGNS OF CONQUEST OF GENGHIS
KHAN AND HIS SUCCESSORS. FORMATION
OF THE MONGOLIAN EMPIRE

Military Campaigns of Genghis Khan

Side by side with the exploitation of the *arat* Mongols, spoliation of alien peoples became the chief aim and object of Genghis Khan on seizing power, of the *noyon* nobles and of their *nuker* bodyguards.

With such a limited economic basis of their own as nomad cattle-breeding there was no possibility of satisfying the ever-increasing demands of the feudal nobles and their men-at-arms. Headed by Genghis Khan, the Mongol feudal lords saw that their main source of enriching themselves lay in the conquest of agricultural countries. They were also forced to engage in predatory wars by the aggravated form that class antagonisms had assumed within Mongol society. The success that attended their campaigns of plunder was mainly attributable to the well-organized Mongol cavalry and the employment of what was at that time a high degree of military technique—the skilful way in which wars were waged by the Mongol military leaders. One of the chief reasons for the successes of the campaigns of conquest also was the fact that the countries of Europe and Asia which were invaded had been greatly weakened by being split up between feudal regimes and by domestic quarrels between the feudal nobles.

In 1211 Genghis Khan began his military operations against Northern China on the pretext of liberating the Mongol tribes from the yoke of the China state which, over a number of years, had been pursuing a policy of sowing discord and enmity among the nomads and was forcing them to pay tribute.

After a series of battles the troops of Genghis Khan advanced far into the interior of the country and in 1215 captured Peking (Chundu). The success of the campaign was due to the situation that had developed in Northern China. The country was ruled by the Ching ("golden") dynasty of Churchen conquerors, alien to, and hated by, the Chinese people. For almost 100 years this dynasty had oppressed the Chinese people.

Frequent peasant uprisings and internal dissensions made the situation of the Ching state extremely unstable, a factor which predetermined the defeat of its troops in battles with the troops of Genghis Khan. This campaign, however, did not result in seizure of the territory of China. After capturing enormous booty and a large number of prisoners, the hordes of Genghis Khan left China. News of Genghis Khan's Chinese campaign and his capture of Peking gave rise to a mass of rumours in Central Asia. In order to verify these rumours and gain an authentic impression of his potential adversary, the head of the Khwarezmian state, Khwarezmshah Muhammed despatched two embassies in succession to Mongolia. After a certain time Genghis Khan, on his part, sent an embassy in return, which was headed by a Khwarezmian merchant, Mahmud Yalavach, who was in the service of Genghis Khan. This embassy met the Khwarezmshah in Bokhara and was received by him there.

In 1218 Genghis Khan despatched to the capital of the Khwarezmian state, Urgench, a new ambassadorial caravan for diplomatic and trading purposes. Subsequently, relations between Genghis Khan and the Khwarezmshah became tense and deteriorated into armed fighting.

In 1218 the Mongol troops occupied Eastern Turkestan and Semirechye. The technical equipment of Genghis Khan's army was, for its time, rather superior. In addition to cavalry and infantry, siege weapons in the form of battering rams and stone-throwers played a big part in the Mongol forces. Genghis Khan had many missiles which projected clay vessels containing burning liquid made from petroleum.

Genghis Khan also employed in Central Asia the tactics he had tried out in the war with China of exterminating the peaceful population of towns and villages if they made the slightest attempt to resist; he also made slaves of the artisans.

In the winter of 1219-1220, at the head of his main forces, Genghis Khan advanced into the interior of Maveraannahr towards Bokhara and, after capturing the latter, handed over this rich and cultured city to be sacked by his soldiers.

In March 1220 the Mongol armies occupied the ancient and wealthy city of Central Asia—Samarkand.

After its capture by the Mongols, Samarkand became as desolate of population as Bokhara. Now came the turn for the march on the Khwarezmian capital, Urgench. The siege of the city began at the very end of 1220 or the beginning of 1221. The inhabitants displayed a genuine affection for their native city and defended it stubbornly and with heroism against the aggressors. It was only after losing many thousands of their men and after a siege of 4-5 months that the troops of Genghis Khan were able to capture the capital of the Khwarezmian state. The enraged conquerors slaughtered an immense number of the townspeople. Artisans were deported for labour in the rear of the Mongol army.

The last of the large cities of Central Asia whose labouring population put up a heroic resistance against the Mongol armies was Merv. It was captured in 1221. What had, not so long before, been a prosperous and cultured country was now depopulated. Most of the cities lay in ruins. The news of Genghis Khan's invasion of Central Asia spread far and wide all over the Near East.

In 1221 the Mongols (Tartars in Russian chronicles) burst into Azerbaijan and then into the land of Georgia. After seizing the town of Shemakha, the Mongols crossed over the mountains into the Northern Caucasus and from there reached the Crimea, where they captured Sudak.

In 1223, on the bank of the River Kalka, the Mongols defeated the army of the Russian princes. The cause of the defeat of the Russian troops was that the Russian princes, at the moment of the greatest danger, were unable to put aside their domestic differences. The Mongols, however, did not linger in the steppes of South Russia but moved on towards the Middle Volga to the mouth of the River Kama, heading for the Bulgar princedom. This advance did not meet with success. The Bulgars laid an ambush, heavily defeated the Mongol armies and forced them to stop advancing further. This defeat was due not only to the strength and courage of the Bulgar troops but also to the fact that the aggressors had been considerably weakened by the fight on the River Kalka.

In the autumn of 1225 Genghis Khan returned home and spent the last one-and-a-half years of his life warring against the Tangut state. The Tanguts were defeated and their towns pillaged and burnt. This campaign was Genghis Khan's last military enterprise. At the very height of the Tangut expedition he died, in 1227.

Genghis Khan played a definite and positive role in bringing the disunited tribes together into one state and in establishing a single Mongol state. But he and the feudal clique he had welded together directed all the energies of the state that had just been formed into wars of aggression and into enslaving other peoples.

The Mongol conquerors barbarously devastated the prosperous centres of the then civilized world and the yoke of the Genghis hordes hindered for many centuries the economic, political and cultural development of a whole series of countries in Asia and Europe. The predatory wars waged by the Mongol feudal nobles not only caused the peoples of the conquered countries incalculable suffering but also had a baneful effect on the mass of the simple *arat* population and on Mongolia itself. They helped to promote disunity among the Mongol nationality, exhausted the manpower resources of Mongolia and resulted in its protracted political, economic and cultural decay in the centuries that followed.

The empire of Genghis Khan had no common economic basis and represented a conglomeration of tribes and peoples which had fallen under the heavy yoke of the Mongol feudal nobles and suffered the oppressive weight of the military-administrative government of the conquerors. In the final count there could be, and there was, only one result: the collapse of a power that was as unstable as it was extensive.

The Mongolian Empire under Genghis Khan's Successors (1227-1259)

Even during the lifetime of Genghis Khan the extensive territories included in the Mongol Empire were divided up between his four sons. The lands distributed by Genghis Khan are customarily termed allotments or *ulus*.

The older the son the farther away from Mongolia did his *ulus* lie. Juchi, the eldest son, was given the lands west of the River Irtysh as far as those remote borders "which the hoofs of the Mongol horses had reached"; the Central Asian possessions forming the *ulus* of Juchi comprised the lower reaches of the Amu-Darya, i.e. Northern Khwarezm and its capital Urgench and also the lower reaches of the Syr-Darya. Juchi's headquarters was located in the valley of the Irtysh.

Genghis Khan's second son, Chagadai, received Kashgar, Semirechye and Maveraannahr with headquarters in the Ili valley.

To Ugadei Genghis Khan transferred Western Mongolia and Tarbagatai. He had his headquarters at Chuguchak. The fourth son of Genghis Khan, Tului, inherited the indigenous *ulus* of his father.

During Genghis Khan's lifetime the sons were entirely subordinate to him and cannot in any sense be regarded as his vassals. Properly speaking, they were his viceroys. There was an abrupt change in the situation after Genghis Khan died: his heirs were inclined to regard their *ulus* as semi-independent possessions.

Most of the *noyons* who held posts of command in the army of Genghis Khan as centurions, chiliarchs and myriarchs had become wealthy as a result of the spoils of war. Many of them became *darugachi*, and *tamgachi*, i.e governors and deputy governors, in individual towns and provinces of the conquered countries. This enabled the representatives of the *noyon* class to despoil the population almost at will.

Even during Genghis Khan's lifetime his third son Ugadei was marked out to succeed him. But within a year after the death of Genghis Khan the real power was held by Tului who, as his youngest son, was almost always by his father's side, as the guardian of the family hearth.

After the relevant negotiations had been held, the home *yurta* of the Genghis gens in the Kerulen river region was chosen as the site for the *kuriltai*. Thither, in 1228, came representatives from every *ulus*. From Desht-i-Kipchak came the sons of Juchi Khan—Batu, Shaiban, Berke and Berkechor. From Semirechye and Kashghar arrived Chagadai with his sons and grandsons. Ugadei with sons and grandsons also appeared, and other kin and near relatives.

The *kuriltai* of the emperor's sons and of the nomad nobility elected Ugadei as Khan. After the election a ceremonial feast was held in honour of the new Khan and 40 beautiful maidens of the families of the Mongol nobility were then offered up as a sacrifice to the "spirit" of Genghis Khan.

Ugadei ruled from 1228 until 1241. In the year when he ascended the throne the dimensions of the Mongol Empire were extraordinarily vast.

Besides Mongolia, it comprised Northern China, Eastern Turkestan, Central Asia, the steppes from the Irtysh to the Volga, the greater part of Iran and the Caucasus, although in the two latter countries the authority of the Mongol feudal nobles was not sufficiently secure. Under Ugadei it became the custom to administer the conquered countries by appointing special commissioners—*darugachi* and *tamgachi,* and this system was maintained until the collapse of the Empire.

The ruling class in the conquered countries, in the persons of the big landowners and higher-ranking clergy, and also the important merchants—for the sake of preserving their wealth and privileges—took service with the conquerors. The Mongol conquerors left in a number of provinces even local officeholders, making them obedient tools in their hands and placing them under the supervision of *baskaks.*

The *kuriltai* held in 1235 is linked with the name of Ugadei, and it was at it that, according to Rashid ad-Din, it was decided to levy a *kopchur*[1] on cattle at the rate of one head per hundred. Furthermore, Ugadei gave orders that from every 10 *tugars* of grain crops 1 *tugar,* i.e. a tenth, should be paid to the treasury.

The *Sacred Legend* too, tells of similar regulations issued by Ugadei: "The payment to be made to the state food supply fund—*shulen*—shall henceforward be made at the rate of one two-year-old sheep per flock. ... Everywhere let a mare be taken out of every thousand and arrangements made for them to be milked. Milkers to be appointed to the herds; grazing grounds to be placed under managers who will continuously succeed one another—*nutukchins* who will at the same time be *unguchins* also, in charge of the younger horses". This last passage quoted offers interesting information about the milking servitude designed to supply the feudal nobles with *kumiss*. In reality, this was now a feudal servitude devolving on every group of a thousand nomads. In the three decades since the formation of the state the process of feudalizing the Mongol society had been considerably intensified. As a result of the rapacity of government officials and the excesses wreaked by the Mongol military detachments and also of the abuses connected with the system of farming out taxes and servitudes, mainly to Moslem merchants, the burden of these latter had become several times heavier. Moreover, the actual rates levied locally were on various pretexts considerably higher than what had been decreed by the central government.

A grievous servitude imposed on the masses of the working people in the nomad and agricultural population was the postal service, organized in 1235. This postal service had to serve the whole administrative system of the Mongol Empire, i.e. convey messengers, runners and government officials. Ugadei laid it down that "every *yam* must have 20 *ulachins*", a specific number of horses, sheep for provisions, milch mares, draught oxen and carts.

Much harm was done to the inhabitants of villages and towns by the so-called *paidzy*. These were gold, silver, bronze or even wooden plaques which gave the holder the right to impose on the working population various kinds of servitudes. This worsened still further the situation of the peasants and artisans and undermined the potential revenues of the treasury.

The different dues and servitudes levied in the countries subdued by the Mongol feudal nobility assumed enormous dimensions. Under Munke Khan, i.e. by the fifties of the XIIIth century, the economic situation had taken an acute turn for the worse. The Khan himself was obliged to admit in one of his *yarliks* (orders) that "the acts of violence and oppression had reached an extremely high level and the cultivators especially had been reduced to such extremities by the multitude of different kinds of burdens—exactions and impositions of extraordinary taxes—that the advantages they derived were not equal to one half of the exactions (in the form of servitudes)..."

A heavy burden laid on the backs of the working people, especially the captive artisans, was the erection of the Mongol capital of Karakorum, begun already in the lifetime of Genghis Khan and completed in 1235.

The capital city was built on the bank of the River Orkhon. Chinese, Tadjik, Turkic, Persian and other skilled workers and artisans helped in the construction of the city and the palace of the Khan.

The testimony of the monk Rubruck, ambassador of the French King Louis IX, is interesting; he personally visited the capital of Mongolia under Munke Khan and reported as follows:

"The city is surrounded by a clay wall and has four gates. At the eastern gates wheat and other grains are sold, which, however, are rarely brought in; at the western gates they sell sheep and goats; at the southern they sell oxen and carts; at the northern they sell horses." This indicates that Karakorum was a big trading centre.

The peoples under Mongol rule were not willing to live under the yoke of foreigners, and in 1238 the peasants and artisans of Maveraannahr rebelled. At the head of the uprising was Mahmud Tarabi, an artisan and native of the village of Tarab near Bokhara.

Mahmud and his followers succeeded in driving the Mongols out of Bokhara, seizing power there and defeating at Kermin, with the help of the peasants, a large Mongol army and detachments of the local nobility. The forces, however, were not evenly matched and some months later, after the death of Mahmud Tarabi, the Mongols succeeded in suppressing the popular revolt.

The campaigns of conquest of the Mongol armies did not end with the death of Genghis Khan. Mongol feudal leaders ruled over Eastern Turkestan, Semirechye, Central Asia and the Asiatic part of Desht-i Kipchak. Iran was not completely conquered. And even in the conquered regions the authority of the conquerors was not firmly anchored. In 1253 Hulagu Khan made the final conquest of Iran.

As regards Transcaucasia—Azerbaijan, Armenia and Georgia—these countries were conquered only in the thirties of the XIIIth century. From the forties of the XIIIth century until 1257 Georgia and Armenia were under the rule of the *ulus* of Juchi and after 1257 of the Mongol *ilkhans* of the Hulaguid dynasty.

The principal events in the march of the Mongol armies into South-East Europe and the conquest of the lands of ancient Rus took place in the last years of the reign of Ugadei. The question of marching into the Volga area and further west was raised twice at the *kuriltais* held in 1228 and 1235. The campaign was led by Batu, son of Juchi.

Batu spent the years 1236-1238 in campaigns for the conquest of the princedoms of Ryazan and Vladimir. The Grand Dukes Yuri Igorevich of Ryazan and Yuri Vsevolodovich of Vladimir were defeated as they fought the Mongols separately because of the internecine fighting that prevailed. In March 1238, at the end of the winter, the Mongols advanced on Novgorod but, weakened by the earlier battles, were unable to reach it. On the way back the Mongols encountered heroic resistance from the small town of Kozielsk. Brave Russian patriots held up the Mongol army for nearly two months.

In 1239 Batu made a second advance into Russian territory. This time he directed his main attacks southwards to the lands lying in the basin of the Dnieper and its tributaries. He took and pillaged Pereyaslavl, Chernigov and in 1240 Kiev. From there the roads lay open to Volhynia and Galicia. By 1241-1242 the Mongol armies made their appearance in Poland, Hungary and Moravia.

But when Batu heard the news of the death of Ugadei, he decided not to advance any further west as he wanted to take part in the election of the new Khan, in which Batu played a very prominent part. As, in addition, they had been weakened by the courageous resistance put up by the Russians and other peoples, the Mongol conquerors were obliged to return to their homes.

The result of Batu's march and the subjugation of extensive territories was a considerable expansion of Juchi's *ulus* and the formation of a state which was given the name of the "Golden Horde"; to begin with, this state still formed part of the Mongolian Empire as its *ulus*, but later, after the 1360s, it separated off into an independent possession.

Ugadei died in 1241 and Chagadai died in the same year. The situation in the Mongol Empire suddenly became complicated. It was very difficult to come to quick agreement on a candidate for Khan; there were too many contradictory opinions on the point in the different families of the Genghis clan. Ugadei's widow, Turakina, was left to act as regent. The interregnum dragged on for five years. A *kuriltai* was at last held in 1246, at which the son of Ugadei, Guyuk, was elected Khan.

At the time when Guyuk was being elected, there arrived at the headquarters a Franciscan monk, Plano Carpini, who had been sent to Mongolia by Pope Innocent IV, nominally for the purpose of converting to Christianity the head of the Empire and his family and establishing enduring peaceful relations with the Mongols. In actual fact, though, his mission was to find out all he could about the strength and power of the Mongol Empire. Plano Carpini was present at the election of Guyuk and recorded quite a number of valuable observations. At the Khan's headquarters he found the Russian Prince Yaroslav, the father of Alexander Nevsky, two sons of the Georgian tsar, the ambassador of the last Abbasid Caliph Mustasim, several Moslem sultans, Chinese dignitaries, etc.

At Guyuk's headquarters Plano Carpini met a remarkable goldsmith, the Russian Kuzma (Kosma), who was working for the Khan. Plano Carpini refers in very warm terms to the assistance, both material and moral, which Kuzma gave to the Franciscan monk-ambassador in the difficult days when he was staying at Guyuk's court.

Although Guyuk had been put on the throne by the *kuriltai*, he was still not accorded general recognition. Batu, with whom he had been quarrelling ever since the time of Ugadei, did not recognize Guyuk and did not swear fealty. According to the sources, armed hostilities were even being prepared between them. Guyuk set out to march against Batu but, on the way, while still inside the borders of Mongolia, he died in 1248.

As Batu was at enmity with the family of Ugadei, he made energetic efforts to have Munke, the son of Tului, elected.

Two families—Juchi and Tului—united against the two families of Ugadei and Chagadai.

In 1251 the *kuriltai* assembled in Mongolia. It was attended, in the main, by representatives of the Juchi and Tului families. Hadan and Munke arrived as representing the princes of the Ugadei family and the princes of the Chagadai family, those who had suffered at the hands of Khan Guyuk.

Thus, the 1251 *kuriltai* did not represent all the descendants of Genghis Khan. Nevertheless, it considered itself competent to act and elected Munke as Khan. This was a kind of coup, carried out by the descendants of Juchi and Tului. Munke's accession to power (1251-1259), occurring as it did against a background of struggle, led to a succession of repressive actions by the new Khan against his enemies.

Munke despatched special troops to carry out a massacre in the *ulus* areas of Ugadei and Chagadai. The result of the hostile policy pursued by Batu and Munke against the families of Ugadei and Chagadai was that the previous role and importance of the latter completely disappeared. They ceased to exist as large *uluchi*. The Mongol Empire split up virtually at this time into two parts—the possessions of Munke, who held the title of Khan, and the possessions of Batu. The whole of Maveraannahr became the property of the latter and the frontier of Juchi's *ulus* was now not on the Amu-Darya but in Semirechye, somewhere not far from the River Chu.

By the beginning of the reign of Khan Munke the position of the Mongol Empire was extremely shaky. The subjugated peoples in Northern China, Eastern Turkestan, Semirechye, Maveraannahr, Iran, Transcaucasia and Eastern Europe groaned under the intolerable taxes, tributes and servitudes and also the abuses of government officials. There was always the possibility of a repetition of popular uprisings similar to that of Mahmud Tarabi in 1238.

Khan Munke immediately set about strengthening the central apparatus of government. He made Bulgai his principal dignitary and secretary and instructed him to compile the Khan's orders—*yarliks* (*zarliks*). He appointed persons whose job it was to issue the scarlet *tamga* (seal), to manufacture *paidzy* from gold, silver and bronze, to administer the Khan's arsenal, etc.

The court officials were carefully selected. Two Moslem *bitikchis* were specially nominated by the Khan to issue *paidzy* to merchants.

He invited specialist merchants to assess the value of the various precious stones, furs, decorative textiles, etc. bought by the Khan's court. He also gathered together a large number of scribes, with a good knowledge of the Persian, Chinese, Uighur, Mongolian, Tibetan and other languages.

Munke appointed a number of persons to posts as viceroys both in Central Asia and in Asia Minor. The conquered countries and provinces of Iran and Transcaucasia were governed directly under the control of Munke Khan.

As regards the situation of the ruling class in subjugated countries, the Mongol authorities established contact everywhere with the big local landowners and the higher-ranking clergy, i.e. with the secular and religious feudal nobility. The Mongol Khans treated the rich merchant class, too, with consideration. The great majority of the ruling class was quick to take sides with the Mongol Khans. In addition, all the Mongol Khans—Ugadei, Guyuk, Munke and the owners of individual *ulus* domains, i.e. the Khans of the Genghis family, took an active part in the caravan trade, seeking to extract from it the greatest possible profits. Attached to the courts of the Khans were *urtaks*, i.e. Moslem merchants who carried on the Khan's trade and earned big personal profits from these transactions. According to Rashid ad-Din, Ugadei himself paid for a shareholding in the trade turnover 200 gold *balyshes*—an enormous amount for those times.

The understanding between the conquerors and the ruling classes of the subjugated countries cost the people—the peasants and artisans—dearly.

In most cases the Mongol authorities took over everything or nearly everything produced by the artisans and paid them the barest subsistence. "Each one is given a daily ration of bread by weight, but very little, and also they issue them nothing else save a small portio nof meat three times a week".

Under Munke Khan two fresh large-scale campaigns of conquest were launched. One, under the command of Kublai, Munke's brother, was begun for the final subjugation of the whole of China; the other, under the command of Hulagu, another brother of Munke, was conducted to secure the complete conquest of Iran and, more particularly, to destroy the Ismailite state.

Having finally, in 1256, defeated the Ismailite state, which was the last stronghold of Iranian independence, Hulagu Khan sent his troops to attack Bagdad and the lands belonging to the Abbasid Caliph Mustasim (1242-1258). The Mongol conquerors marched to Bagdad hoping for huge booty. The view widely held in those days of Bagdad was of a place of untold treasures accumulated over the 508 years of the existence of the Abbasid dynasty. Mustasim, the last Abbasid Caliph, and also his immediate associates, were worthless individuals, without even a rudimentary understanding of the military and political situation. The Bagdad rulers were incapable of making any use whatever of their capacity for resistance, and Hulagu captured Bagdad without difficulty. On February 15, 1258, he rode into the famous capital, looted the enormous treasures of the Caliph, killed Mustasim and finished off the Abbasid dynasty once and for all. Hulagu continued his advance further to the West. In 1259, however, the Mameluke Emperor of Egypt, Kutuz (1259-1260) dealt the Mongol army a heavy defeat, expelled the Mongol conquerors from Syria and put an end to their further advance.

The vast state of the Juchi family, known in Russian chronicles as the "Golden Horde", had a history peculiar to itself.

On the west the borders of the Golden Horde reached as far as the Dniester and embraced the Crimea and on the east—up to the Irtysh, on the north-east the borders of the Golden Horde encompassed the princedom of the Bulgars, on the south—the Northern Caucasus as far as Derbent, on the south-east—Northern Khwarezm with Urgench and the lower course of the Syr-Darya. Tributaries to the Golden Horde were the Russian princedoms which, however, retained their own princes and their internal way of life.

The Golden Horde represented a state which had been formed artificially by the forcible seizure of foreign territories and the forcible unification into one whole of different peoples, speaking different languages and professing different religions.

In the persons of its first two rulers, Batu Khan (1236-1255) and Berke Khan (1256-1266), the Golden Horde instituted on the territory above defined the same regime of looting and violence as had been set up in Central Asia, Azerbaijan, Georgia, Armenia and Iran.

The Mongols who arrived along with Batu did not adopt a sedentary way of life but continued to live as nomads within the borders of Desht-e Kipchak. The huge expanses of the latter had long since been settled by the nomad Turkic people—the Polovets (Kipchaks), Kangli and others. As the nomad Mongols were fewer than the Kipchaks and, in addition, had a higher level of culture, by the XIVth century the process had already begun of assimilating the Mongols, who gradually began to master the Kipchak language.

The Mongol khans and the Golden Horde khans levied huge tribute from the Russian people. The situation was especially burdensome for the Russian peasants and the Russian towns which were forced to tolerate the Mongol or, as they were called in Russia, the Tartar *darugaches* and *baskaks*.

In the subjugated countries the Mongol khans of the Golden Horde relied on strong military garrisons and they possessed a rich treasury formed by levying large taxes and tribute from the subjugated peoples.

Somewhat later than the Golden Horde, a Hulagu state was set up in Iran and Transcaucasia, sometimes called the Ilkhan state. As pointed out above, this state was the result of the final conquest by Hulagu Khan of Iran. Hulagu Khan included in the new state, besides Iran, the territories of Azerbaijan, Armenia and Georgia, in which, incidentally, the local dynasties remained in the role of dependent and tributary rulers.

In the 1360s these states, for all practical purposes, broke away from the single Mongol centre headed by the Khan, and in the second half of the XIIIth century each of these *ulus* areas actually pursued an independent policy and paid little attention to the Mongol khan.

The reasons why the Mongol Empire broke up into separate parts were the lack of sound economic links, for which the caravan trade was no substitute, and the fact that the Mongol khans of the various *ulus* areas had become more and more dependent on the local feudal lords and wealthy merchants, on whom they relied for oppressing and exploiting the subjugated peoples. Local politics isolated these khans more and more—both in the Golden Horde and in the Hulagu state—from the distant khan who was increasingly more preoccupied with the affairs of China and Mongolia proper than with the *ulus* which had branched off. Links between the *ulus* khans soon became purely nominal.

A large number of Mongol tribes left Mongolia and dispersed themselves in the newly formed *ulus* areas on the territory of the subjugated countries. There were relatively few Mongols in each of the separate subjugated provinces, because nomad Turks (Kipchaks, Kanglys and others) made up the bulk of the Mongol military units. The fact that a considerable proportion of Mongols took their cattle and property and left their homeland and never returned is evidence of the weakened condition of Mongolia's economy. As regards the immense booty obtained by the Mongol soldiery from the predatory wars of Genghis Khan and his sons and grandsons, all this plundered wealth enriched not the Mongolian people but the higher ranks of the military commanders, the Mongol *darugaches* and *baskaks*. Moreover, only a small part of these stolen riches reached Mongolia itself, and what did arrive did not raise—in fact could not raise—the productive forces of the economy. Mongolia still remained, as before, a backward pastoral country.

It is characteristic that feudal relations developed faster among the Mongols who had during the wars been scattered over remote and more cultured countries in Iran, Maveraannahr, the Golden Horde Empire and Northern China than in their homeland. The population of Mongolia proper became more and more backward, both economically and culturally. The less cultured nomads, even though they had conquered the countries of cultured people, succumbed later to their influence. In this connection we cannot but recall the remarkable words of Frederick Engels: "Every conquest by a more barbarian people naturally disturbs the economic development and destroys numerous productive forces. But in the immense majority of cases where the conquest is permanent, the more barbarian conqueror has to adapt himself to the higher 'economic order' as it emerges from the conquest; he is assimilated by the vanquished and in most cases he even has to adopt their language."[2] This was the phenomenon that was observed also in the countries conquered by the Mongol feudal lords.

The *yasa* of Genghis Khan constitutes a very valuable source for the history of the social life of the Mongols of the period of the Mongol Empire. To judge by the record of it preserved in Juveini's account, the *yasa* was compiled during the conquests, since it reflected also the conditions of the agricultural population among the subjugated peoples.

The *yasa* specifically declares that peasants liable to servitudes and taxes (in the form of *kopchur, avarizit*, i. e. the additional tax for upkeep of runners, post stations, etc.) must be called up to the army when this appears necessary. Thus, according to the *yasa*, the agriculturists of the subjugated countries also formed a militia force in the same way as the Mongol nomads. It should be emphasized that, if an agriculturist became a soldier, this did not exempt him from paying the taxes and servitudes due to the Mongol authorities; these had now to be paid by the remaining members of the family—men and women. This militia force was organized on the "tens" system, i. e. it was divided into tens, hundreds, thousands and *tumens* (myriads), in the same way as the army formed from the Mongol nomads.

According to the *yasa* a man who had been assigned to a particular thousand, hundred or ten could not leave it and transfer to any other sub-unit. In such case it was forbidden to retain such a man. Anyone leaving his unit was sentenced to severe punishment (death) and the person who took him over was also punished.

In this way the agricultural population and the nomads were formally attached or bound as soldiers to the tens, hundreds or thousands, i. e. to the land owned by the chiefs of the hundreds, thousands and myriads. This attachment was based on the feudal regime that existed in the conquered countries where the peasants were already in fact tied to the land.

We have seen above that feudal dependence had already begun to appear during Genghis Khan's lifetime and was specially clearly expressed in the regulations issued by Ugadei, as related in the *Sacred Legend*, by Rashid ad-Din, in the *yasa* and in Chinese sources. During the time of the Mongol Empire Mongol society had become feudal, notwithstanding the presence of considerable survivals of primitive-commune relations. During several decades of the Mongol Empire's existence the Mongol *noyons* had grown into a powerful military feudal class which held sway both in its own country and in the extensive territories of the countries subjugated.

During their numerous forays the Mongol conquerors took large numbers of prisoners who in reality became slaves. The Mongol feudal nobles employed them on heavy labour tasks and also in war, sending the prisoners, when towns were under siege, into the most dangerous spots; many of the captive artisans too, whom the Mongol troops removed in tens of thousands from the towns they captured and looted, really became slaves. In the nomad economy, however, slave labour was not widely used.

During the half century or so from 1206 to the 1260s great changes occurred in the situation of the ordinary Mongolian people. At the very beginning of the XIIIth century most of the nomad pastoral Mongols were still basically free, although signs were beginning to appear in Mongol society of the growth of feudal relations; in the middle of the XIIIth century, however, class differences had intensified to such an extent that the mass of simple nomads had lost personal freedom and became the serfs of the ruling class of Mongol feudal nobles.

In the XIIIth century, when the most important expeditions for purposes of conquest and pillage had ended, the Mongol military aristocracy of *noyons* tried to corrupt the rank-and-file soldiery by forcing them to plunder the peaceful population of the agricultural countries. But when the period of wars of conquest was over, the nomad Mongols in their great majority took up pastoral occupations and went over from being soldiers to peaceful labourers.

In the subsequent periods of their history the Mongolian people more than once demonstrated both their natural bent for peaceful labour and also their love of liberty. By standing up for their independence and fighting against alien aggressors and local feudal nobles the Mongol people displayed their staunchness and their fervent love for their country.

CHAPTER III

THE YUAN MONGOLIAN EMPIRE
(1260-1368)

The Mongol conquerors were gradually seizing the territory of China. Genghis Khan and his first successors conquered the Churchen state of Ching which occupied Northern China. But they succeeded in gaining final possession of the whole of China only subsequently.

To gain firm possession of Northern China the centre of government had to be brought nearer to it and for this purpose Munke Khan had ordered his brother Kublai in 1255 to set up his headquarters not far away from the present-day town of Dolon Nor. In the following year Kublai built in this region a town which he called Kaipin.

While he was marching against China, Munke Khan temporarily left his youngest brother Arig-Buga in command of the headquarters in Karakorum. The latter, after Munke's death in 1259, wanted to take advantage of a fortunate concurrence of circumstances in order to seize power as Khan. He decided to convene a *kuriltai* in Karakorum in the hope that he himself would be elected Khan. He had the support of Munke Khan's senior wife and sons. When he heard of this, Kublai did not hesitate to infringe the traditional methods of electing a khan and dispensed with summoning the Genghis princes to a *kuriltai*. Instead, he convened only his own loyal partisans and was proclaimed by them Mongol Khan in Kaipin in 1260. By taking this step in the struggle with Arig-Buga, Kublai was setting up Kaipin as the new administrative centre of the Empire in opposition to Karakorum.

After ascending the imperial throne Kublai continued with the conquest of Southern China, already begun under Munke. The Mongol conquerors met with stubborn resistance from the Chinese in the area of the central course of the River Yangtze and it was only after occupying the town of Uchang, which was the key defence point of a large area, that they were able to advance further eastwards and then south. The Sung dynasty failed to organize the people for a country-wide fight against the enemy and in 1276 the Mongol troops seized the capital, Hangchow. Individual Chinese detachments continued the struggle for some time further but without success and in 1279 China was completely taken over by the Mongol conquerors.

Even before Southern China had been completely conquered, Kublai set out in 1267 to build a new capital in Chundu, the former residence of the Ching dynasty. The town was called Daidu—the "Great Capital", to distinguish it from Kaipin, which had been named Shandu, meaning "Upper Capital". Later on, Daidu was re-named Peking.

In 1271 Kublai adopted for his dynasty the Chinese appellation Yuan.

As time went on the Mongol military feudal nobility in China assimilated a series of methods new to them of exploiting the subject population, methods that had been practised by Chinese feudal landowners, and enormous wealth soon began to accumulate in their hands.

To reinforce their domination in China and safeguard their interests the Mongol feudal lords utilized the Chinese feudal administrative machine that had existed before them.

As the Mongol Khans relied in the main on the Mongol military feudal nobility, they could do no other than make use of the large numbers of Chinese government officials, seeing that the Mongol feudal nobles themselves had no experience of governing such a country as China.

Kublai continued the old system of examinations for training candidates for government service and a historiographical committee was set up with the participation of Chinese scholars. As a rule, the directors of central bodies were representatives of the Mongol military feudal nobility and, in some cases, natives of Central Asia; the Chinese were employed in posts of secondary importance.

The country was divided up into 10 "roads" (*lu*) or provinces, headed mostly by Mongol governors. The provinces were divided into prefectures, districts and departments, with the appropriate chiefs at their head. The latter had under their orders the local administrative machinery, the basic function of which was to squeeze taxes out of the population.

In order to put down opposition from the Chinese people, Mongol military garrisons were quartered in a number of provinces and military farm settlements created in which the soldiers performed military duties and worked as tillers of the land. The Mongol soldiers quartered in China lived along with their families, with all their cattle and other property.

The church, especially the Buddhist church, played a prominent part in the system of oppression operated by the Mongol feudal nobles. The Mongol Khans, and Kublai in particular, tolerated the simultaneous existence in the Empire of different religions: Buddhism, Confucianism, Islam and Christianity. However, the only religion of importance throughout the state generally was Buddhism and, to some extent, Confucianism. Kublai supported the Buddhist priesthood, especially after he sent a military expedition into Tibet and made it a dependent vassal. Large numbers of lamas began arriving in China from Tibet; they preached Buddhism and gained the support of Kublai and, later on, of his successors.

The Buddhist clergy were given landholdings and exempted from taxes and servitudes.

On Kublai's nomination Pagda-lama was placed at the head of the Buddhist church with the title "emperor of the faith in three countries", i.e. Tibet, Mongolia and China. It was really Pagda-lama who compiled the Mongol alphabet (square letters) on the basis of Tibetan writing, since, after Mongolian became the official language in China, all official correspondence was conducted in it.

When they conquered China, the Mongol feudal lords encountered a developed feudal syste, the foundations of which they could not alter; they made use of it, however, for their own purposes. The Mongol Khans confiscated the lands which belonged, in the north, to the Churchen and, in the south, to the Chinese feudal nobles. A large part of these lands became the hereditary property of the Khans themselves and their relatives, the remaining lands were distributed "to nourish the Mongol army leaders and senior-ranking officials." According to Rashid ad-Din they received "innumerable places for summer and winter nomad camping..." The dimensions of the landholdings granted were considerable, especially in the south of China, which was economically more developed and where the Mongol feudal lords were glad to go to serve as there was more possibility there to loot the population. Some Mongol feudal nobles received tens and hundreds of thousands of *mu* of land and several hundreds of thousands of tax-paying peasants each. To Kublai's son, for instance, were transferred 105,000 tax-paying families, the revenue from which was put at his personal disposal. General Bayan received 6,000 families, and so on. Many peasants were made slaves by the Mongol military feudal nobles.

In numerous cases the Mongol feudal nobles, in addition to what was granted to them, took forcible possession of the land of Chinese landowners and often turned tilled fields into pastures for cattle and into hunting grounds.

The rule of the Mongol feudal lords led to the Chinese peasantry being still more closely tied to the land and impoverished. The basic form of exploitation was, as previously, rent payable in kind; simultaneously, there also existed the system of corvée-labour rent. The peasants were obliged to pay taxes to the state, though these differed from locality to locality. The taxes levied by the central government and the local authorities were a grievous burden and resulted in the impoverishment of the peasantry. The burden of taxation was further aggravated by the abuses practised by local authorities who introduced new levies additional to the taxes fixed by the central government.

The population suffered also from the financial policy of the Mongol Khans—excessive issues of paper money. The Mongol Khans made a wide practice of this method of levying taxes, taking advantage of the experience of issuing paper money that had been gained during the Tang and Sung dynasties. During the rule of the Yuan dynasty seven different kinds of assignations were put into circulation, one after another. Special mints were built for exchanging gold and silver into paper money. Twenty bundles of paper money were issued in exchange for one *lan* of gold. As they had been proclaimed the sole means of payment, the population was obliged to surrender silver in exchange for pieces of paper that cost nothing and quickly depreciated.

The land and fiscal policies of the Mongol feudal nobles produced an abrupt deterioration in the situation of the peasantry—landlessness, impoverishment, increased vagrancy and mass starvation. This resulted ultimately in the decay and devastation of the once fertile and better developed provinces of Southern China.

Immense riches became concentrated in the hands of the Mongol feudal nobility—riches which were not utilized for the further development of the productive forces of the country but were squandered on satisfying the caprices of the feudal nobles, on luxuries and carousing and also on the upkeep of the large number of troops.

After his seizure of power Kublai found he had to wage a struggle with hostile groups of Mongolian princes who contested his throne.

His own brother, Arig-Buga, contested his right to the throne; in the warfare that developed Arig-Buga was defeated in battle and in 1264 surrendered to Kublai. Two years later he died.

In 1266 Kublai was confronted with a fresh coalition of Mongol princes headed by Haidu, grandson of Ugadei. Haidu had possession of the lands along the Emil river and had extended his rule to Eastern Turkestan and the southern part of Siberia. The enmity between him and Kublai began when the latter was elected Khan. Haidu backed Arig-Buga in his claims to the imperial throne and then later began to assert his own claim to it.

The struggle between Haidu and Kublai continued right up to the death of the latter in 1294. Haidu organized a rather powerful and stable union of princes against Kublai; it included the descendants of Ugadei and Chagadai, and subsequently they were joined also by Shirke, the son of Munke, who, when sent by Kublai with troops to advance against Haidu, broke faith and went over to Haidu's side. It was only after Bayan was given command of the military operations that Kublai succeeded in driving the enemy back and temporarily triumphing over them. Haidu, nevertheless, continued gathering coalition forces together and, after 10 years, again formed an alliance of princes against Kublai. He was joined by the princes Nayan, Hadan and Sintur who owned property on the territory of the Churchens. Nayan was the most influential of these princes.

In 1289 Nayan and the other princes advanced with their troops against Kublai. The princes' rebellion, however, was put down and Nayan was taken prisoner and executed. He was rolled up in a piece of felt and suffocated in it.

The struggle of Arig-Buga and Haidu against Kublai was, in reality, a struggle for power but, objectively considered, its aim was to keep the political centre of the state in Mongolia itself and to prevent it from becoming a borderland of the Empire and save the Mongols from falling under Chinese influence.

The struggle with these princes rather restricted the scale of Kublai's warring campaigns. Many of his campaigns of conquest beyond the borders of China were unsuccessful. After seizing Southern China Kublai undertook a series of campaigns against Burma, Cambodia and Annam. Although there were temporary successes, these campaigns, nevertheless, ended in failure because of the stubborn resistance of the peoples of these countries and the difficulties encountered by the Mongol armies in waging war in a tropical climate. After two campaigns Kublai had to abandon his attempts to subjugate the ruler of Chancheng (Tyampa). Finally, however, Burma and Annam acknowledged Kublai as sovereign and paid him tribute. The rulers of the Zond Islands also acknowledged themselves vassals of the Yuan Empire.

Kublai also undertook two large-scale expeditions by sea against Japan—the first in October 1274 and the second in 1281. Both were unsuccessful.

The extensive connections which China had built up with the outside world before the Mongol regime and the encouragement given by the Mongols to trade contributed towards the penetration of Europeans into China.

Under the Mongol dynasty many foreigners arrived in China, attracted there mainly by an interest in trade. The Mongol rulers willingly maintained trading relations with more than 20 countries, as they saw this as an important source of state revenue. The most important of early European journeys to Kublai's Empire, from the scientific point of view, was that made by the Italian, Marco Polo. He arrived in Peking in 1275, lived 17 years in China and became an intimate of the Yuan Emperor. After he returned to his native Venice, Marco Polo dictated a book which for a long time served Europeans as the most important source of their information about China. Marco Polo's book contains a wealth of factual material about the reign of Kublai and the system he created for ruling the Yuan Empire.

It was Kublai who gave expression to the interests of the feudal nobles who were the ruling class in Mongol society. He died in 1294. While still alive he had appointed to succeed him his son Chinkim who, however, died before his father during an expedition to Tibet of which he was in command. Kublai nominated a new successor to himself, his grandson Timur, son of Chinkim.

Timur (born in 1265, reigned 1295-1307) had been given the title of Uldzeitu Khan, had previonsly been victory in the city of Karakorum and had led military operations against Haidu. When he became emperor, he concluded peace with Annam and established links with India. Under him the protracted feudal struggle with Haidu and other Mongol princes came to an end. During his reign a large-scale popular rebellion broke out in Yunnan and was brutally suppressed.

After Timur the throne was seized by his nephew Haisan, who reigned from 1308 to 1311 and was given the nickname Kulugkhan. On his election as Khan the court intrigues began which were a feature of the whole subsequent short-lived history of the Yuan dynasty. These intrigues reflected the struggle for power between the various groups of the Mongol military feudal nobility.

Between 1295 and 1333 there was a succession of eight emperors, most of whom did not survive to adult age and were, more often than not, helpless marionettes in the hands of one or other grouping of Mongol feudal nobles.

The policy of the Yuan Emperors was aimed at firmly establishing and reinforcing the domination of the Mongol conquerors in the subjugated countries. To this end they utilized not only the state authority and military forces but they also pursued a rather subtle policy towards the subjugated peoples. In order to maintain these latter in subjection the Mongol Emperors divided all the nationalities in the Empire into four categories: the first category included the Mongols themselves, the second—the Central Asian and other peoples of the Western region, the third—the Khitans, Churchens and Northern Chinese and the last or fourth—the Southern Chinese, who had formerly been Sung subjects. The purpose of this division was, primarily, to sow dissension among the nationalities. It is reminiscent of the traditional method employed by the ruling classes of the slave owning and feudal empires of Asia and

Europe in order to govern the subject countries on the principle: *"Divide et impera."*

During the rule of the Yuan dynasty Mongolia proper was always a vice-regency for the heir to the throne. It was then called Davaani aryn-muzh, i.e. the province lying to the north of the Changhsia-kou range.

The Yuan Emperors used Mongolia as an important nomad pastoral area where they could graze their herds for the army and the imperial herd. But, in addition to stock-breeding, agriculture, handicrafts and trade developed in Mongolia to a certain extent under the Yuan dynasty. Some of the traders, too, were Mongols.

A big detachment of Mongol troops was kept in Karakorum. In the early days steps were taken to enlarge the city, to rebuild the palaces and erect new buildings, but under the Yuan Emperors Karakorum gradually fell into decay and lost its importance as the centre of the Empire.

For Mongolia itself and the Mongol people the rule of the Yuan dynasty brought neither further growth in productive resources nor an increase in the prosperity of the people. On the contrary, as B. Ya. Vladimirtsov has rightly remarked, "the prosperity of Mongolia and the Mongols greatly deteriorated." The Mongolian people remained, as before, in political and economic bondage to the feudal nobles. The reason for the economic decay of Mongolia was the feudal wars which erupted constantly in Mongolia during the whole period of the dynasty's rule. Most of them were actually fought on Mongol territory and had a grievous effect on the population. The maintenance of a large contingent of Mongol troops for the defence of the Empire also exhausted the country's resources and cut off a large part of the population from productive labour.

The rule of the Yuan dynasty ended with the lengthy reign of Togon-Timur (born in 1320, reigned 1333-1368) and was notable for the intensified exploitation of the Chinese population, the increased lawlessness and arbitrariness of Mongol administration and the severe deterioration in the situation of the masses. More than once during his reign famine broke out in the country and large numbers of people perished. In 1337 rebellions began in China. In the south the rebels tried to proclaim a descendant of the Sung dynasty Chinese Emperor and in the south-west and north other pretenders appeared. In Mongolia, too, a pretender to the throne of the Khan was produced—one of the descendants of Ugadei. The war with the Chinese people in revolt ended with the fall of the Yuan dynasty. In 1368 Togon-Timur fled from his capital of Daidu, which was occupied by the rebels practically without resistance.

The fall of the Yuan dynasty accelerated the process of the collapse of the Mongol conquerors that had already begun earlier. A powerful blow had been dealt them by the Russian troops at the historic battle of Kulikovo in 1380. This battle predetermined the further weakening and the overthrow of the Mongol yoke in Russia. In his book *Secret Diplomacy in the XVIIIth Century* Karl Marx gave an extremely apt description of the Mongol rule in Russia. He emphasized that the Tartar-Mongol yoke not only suppressed, it corrupted and drained the very soul of any people that had fallen victim to it. The Tartars established a regime of systematic terror by means of pillage and mass murder.

The colossal military feudal empire created by the Mongol conquerors was uncompromisingly opposed to the fundamental interests of the subjugated peoples, most of whom had a higher economic and cultural level of development than the Mongols. With their regime for oppressing and pillaging the population of the vassal countries, the Mongol feudal conquerors were unable to create a firmly-based empire. The peoples of the Mongol dominions rose in rebellion one atfer another and gradually emancipated themselves. The working people of Mongolia itself were also exposed in ever greater measure to cruel exploitation at the hands of their feudal aristocracy. Eventually the Mongol Empire, rent by internal disputes, collapsed completely under the attacks of the peoples of Europe and Asia battling against the yoke of the conquerors.

CHAPTER IV

THE CULTURE OF THE MONGOLS
IN THE XIIIth-XIVth CENTURIES

The XIIIth century saw big advances in the cultural development of the Mongols as a result of the further extension of feudal relationships in Mongolia. The formation of a single Mongol state, consequent on the unification of the scattered Mongol tribes, gave a powerful stimulus to the development of the national culture of the Mongols.

As the formation of a single state in Mongolia proceeded, the process of spiritual and material rapprochement among the Mongol tribes became greatly intensified. The Mongols as a whole adopted a pastoral system of life, although retaining quite a number of the features of a hunter's life. The pastoral Mongols satisfied their every day economic requirements by processing the products of stock-breeding. Their basic nourishment was derived from meat and dairy produce. The poorer people and the slaves, however, often had to be content with occasionally trapping smaller game such as ptarmigan and the like. More often than not they were content to fill their stomachs even with dirty water at a time when the important gentry had estates in the south from which they were sent supplies of millet and flour for the winter. Source information such as this illustrates vividly the sharp contrast in the levels of existence of the Mongols of that time.

The sources available clearly show that in those days the Mongols prepared meat and milk products in virtually the same way as they do today. Among such milk products may be mentioned *chige* (mare's milk), *tsagan tos* (butter), *agarul* and *khurut* (dried curd).

The standard type of housing used by Mongols in the XIIIth-XIVth centuries was the felt-covered *yurt (ger)*. Plano Carpini wrote about the Mongolian *yurts* of that period: "Their *stavni* are round and made to resemble tents, formed of withies and thin sticks, on the top of which in the middle there is a round window to let in the light and also let out the smoke, because in the centre of the tent there is always a lighted fire. The sides and roof are covered with felt and the doors also are made of felt. Some *stavni* are large but some are small depending on the wealth or poverty of the people." Thus, in the XIIIth century the *yurts* differed very little from present-day *yurts*. They had been considerably improved and were much more comfortable, as compared with the original type of construction. The *jurts* of the steppe aristocrats, the khans and *noyons*, the so-called *ger-ord at* (palace-*yurta*) were particularly distinguishable from the others not only by their size but also by their rich decoration. Their *Altan ord, Altan terme,* as described in the sources, accommodated hundreds, sometimes even thousands of people. There were *yurts* which, as they were permanently fixed on waggons, could not be dismantled like ordinary *yurts.* Such *yurts* were called *ger-gereg,* i.e. waggon-*yurt.* They varied in size: for transporting on a waggon a smaller *yurt* one ox would be sufficient, for large *yurts*—three, four or even more. The khans and *noyons* had special waggon-*yurts,* which were called *ordger-tereg,* i.e. "palace waggon-*yurt.*" According to eyewitness evidence, living quarters of this type were made so big that they were sometimes thirty feet wide and drawn by 22 oxen. The axle of such a waggon was as big as the mast of a boat. In addition to the waggon-*yurts* the Mongols made wide use also of so-called *kharagutai tereg* (covered waggons).

By the XIIIth century there was a marked difference in the dress of the rich and the poor as regards finish, cut and also quality of material. "The rich wore clothing made from silk and woollen materials, expensive furs brought from different parts of the world. They lined their dress *(deli)* with silk padding which was extremely soft, light and warm. The poorer people made outer fur coats from the skins of dogs or goats and lined their dresses with cotton fabric." "From felt they made cloaks, *shabracks* and hats to protect themselves against rain." Mongol robes *(deli)* of that time were quite different from present day types. They had no collar, were open from top to bottom, and drawn in at the breast; on the left side they were fastened with one, and on the right, with three buckles. On the left side the cloaks were also cut to the sleeve. Married women wore a special type of *caftan (nomrog),* very wide and open all the way down the front. On the head they wore the so-called *bogtag.*

The ancient Mongols organized all kinds of feasts and celebrations. Most of all they delighted in and quite often conducted the so-called "three competitions for men" *(Eriin gurvan naadam),* i.e. wrestling, archery and horse races. In addition to various religious celebrations connected with Shamanism, the Mongols often had purely family festivals also—weddings, birthdays, etc. Holidays were celebrated with singing, music and dancing.

By the XIIIth century considerable improvements had been made in the working implements and household articles of the Mongols. This in turn helped to encourage the further development among the Mongols of new technical and artisan skills. Lacking these, they could not possibly have perfected the art of erecting a *yurt* of large dimensions or making the waggon-*yurt* described above. The development of the blacksmith's art, the extraction of iron ore and the smelting of it by using a blacksmith's leather bellows, augmented the Mongols' knowledge of practical and applied physics and also their information about the rudiments of geology. The manufacture by the Mongols of the XIIIth century of high quality felt and their skill in processing wool, leather and other kinds of raw animal products, in preparing milk and meat products would have been impossible of achievement without a knowledge of practical chemistry.

The techniques and methods of animal husbandry reached quite a high level of development among the Mongols. They had a good command of practical veterinary and zootechnical skills.

Popular medicine developed among the Mongols in the XIII-XIVth centuries. They had an understanding of the curative properties of certain plants and made use of them for treatment purposes. Rashid ad-Din wrote that "the forest tribes, like the Mongols, were well acquainted with Mongol medicines and made good cures after Mongol fashion" and that "there exist certain Mongol medicines which at present are called *kadzhir*, but in olden times were known as *kadir*, i.e. strong medicine". Mongol and Chinese sources report separately on different methods of treatment: cauterizing a wound with a hot iron, wrapping up a wounded person in the warm hide of an ox, sheep or other kind of beast that had just been killed, using a poultice made from the entrails of slaughtered animals to treat ailments of the joints, etc.

Historical knowledge was widely developed among the Mongols. Rashid ad-Din wrote that all Mongol tribes had "a clear and precise family tree, for the custom of the Mongols is such that they preserve the pedigree of each child that is born into the world and for this reason there is not one man among them who does not know his own tribe and origin."

After the appearance of writing the Mongols created a written history based on oral historical tridition and so Mongolian national historiography was born.

At the beginning of its development Mongolian historiography was created at a time when feudal relationships in Mongolia were intensifying and a single Mongol state was being formed as the result of the unification of the dispersed Mongolian tribes. Quite naturally, therefore, it reflected the social changes which were occurring at that time in Mongol society. The *Sacred Legend* compiled in the XIIIth century is a great historical memorial of that period.

The appearance of such a major historical and literary work as the *Sacred Legend* at the dawn of Mongolian historiography testifies to the considerable advance in historical knowledge achieved by the Mongols of that time. The *Sacred Legend* is not just an ordinary annual register; it bears the creative mark of an original composition written by a historian who could wield a skilful pen.

B. Ya. Vladimirtsov has written that "the *Sacred Legend* can be described not as the production of a heroic epic but as a history-chronicle transmitted in epic style and redolent of the aroma of the steppe."

We are sometimes astonished by the ability of the author of the *Sacred Legend* to discern the basic trends in the development of historical events and to solve some of the most important historical problems in the spirit of the time. The most characteristic feature of this work is that it is imbued with the idea of the single kinship of the different Mongol tribes and their union around a single Mongol state headed by a powerful Khan.

A remarkable point to note is that the author of the *Sacred Legend* casually expressed his suppressed anxiety for the future of the Mongol state when Genghis Khan took the decision to set out on a campaign against Khwarezm (Sartaul).

The Sacred Legend is written on a rather high level of mature feudal ideology which leads the author to seek justification for the concept of the inviolability of the authority and the person of the Khan and the loyalty of subjects to the lord. According to the *Sacred Legend* the motto of Genghis Khan was "he who raises a hand against his own Khan must be punished," or "the serf who has once raised a hand against his own Khan cannot be loyal to another Khan."

The author of the *Sacred Legend* had an excellent command of the method of working pictorially and artistically on the emotions of the reader. In his elucidation of historical events he makes more use of devices that provide an artistic knowledge of history than of logical or theoretical analysis.

By the XIIIth-XIVth centuries there existed, in addition to the *Sacred Legend*, other historical compositions which, unfortunately, have not come down to us. We learn about these works only from several foreign sources. The authors of such works as *History of the Conqueror of the World* (Juveini), the *Collection of Chronicles* (Rashid ad-Din) and *Yuan-shi*, made use, in the main, of Mongolian sources in writing the history of the ancient Mongols. Rashid ad-Din, for instance, made wide use, as he himself writes, of "that which is contained in the Mongolian lists and chronicles year by year" and is contained in the history which "was written in the Mongolian language and in Mongolian script but was not collected together and put in order..." Among his Mongolian sources the one to which the Persian historian refers most frequently is the *Golden Book*

("Alten debter"), which was always kept in the treasure-house of the Khans. Judging by the information borrowed by Rashid ad-Din from the *Golden Book*, it can be inferred that it was the official history of the "Golden Clan" of the Genghis gens, composed in the ancient Mongolian language. It must be considered that one of Rashid ad-Din's books dealing with the history of the Mongols is in reality the work of the Persian scholar's Mongol colleagues.

It can be assumed that the history of the Mongols in the *Collection of Chronicles* by Rashid ad-Din was originally written not in Persian but in Mongolian by Bulad-chinsan and other Mongol chroniclers, and that the basis of this part of the work was the *Mongolian Book* written by Bulad who, as the person "without an equal" (in being acquainted with different art forms and in his knowledge of the origin of the Turkic tribes and their history, especially the history of the Mongols), was the head of a commission for the compilation of a universal history.

Some scholars consider that the well-known work called the *History of the Campaign of Genghis Khan* is a Mongolian chronicle which has been preserved in a Chinese translation made in the second half of the XIIIth century.

From a Tibetan source, the *Red Book*, compiled by Gungadorzhe in 1346, we learn of the existence in the XIII-XIVth centuries of another Mongolian historical work entitled *Ikh tobchiyan*.

Thus, the opening period of development of Mongolian historiography is marked by the appearance of a number of important works. For the period of the Mongol Empire we have only one small historico-juridical composition the *White History* ("Tsagan tukh"), which has been preserved in a XVIth century version. The interesting point about the *White History* is that it constitutes evidence of the initial penetration of Indo-Tibetan Buddhist ideology into Mongolian historical literature. It is the first book to produce a table showing the three Buddhist monarchies (India, Tibet, Mongolia), which was later taken over and used by Mongol historiographers.

The *White History* provided the basic arguments for the well-known concept of Buddhist thinking about the state, according to which the essential basis of state administration is to ensure a close link or even a fusion between the state and the church. The author is interested in history only in so far as it is necessary for illustrating this concept.

The basic principles governing the writing of the *White History* were, we can presume, borrowed from the work *The State Teacher of the Mongol Empire of Pagda-lama (1235-1280)* ("Clearest understanding").

In the XIII-XIVth centuries there was a considerable expansion of legal knowledge, as is shown by the appearance at the beginning of the XIIIth century of the first code of Mongol laws, the *Great Jasa*. Although this has not come down to us in the original, the sources that have survived provide us with a definite idea about it. The *Great Jasa* was a code of laws containing the basic elements of the state, administrative, military, criminal, civil and common law of the Mongols. Being the fundamental law of the Mongol feudal state, it was designed to reinforce feudal institutions in Mongolia and to enslave the masses.

The first Supreme Judge of the Mongol State, the most eminent legal thinker of his time, Shikhi-Hutag (1180-1262), played a leading role in compiling the *Great Jasa* and also in the forensic practice of the Mongol Empire.

An event of major importance in the development of religious culture among the Mongols was the appearance at the beginning of the XIIIth century of an official all-Mongolian form of writing, based on the Uighur script which derived from the Soghdian and ancient Aramaic alphabets. The adoption of writing by the Mongols greatly stimulated the development of Mongol literature and the spread of enlightenment and knowledge. The Mongol state needed literate and educated people and for this purpose steps were taken to organize the systematic education of Mongols in reading and writing.

Writing enabled the Mongols to formulate and establish a written Mongolian literary language. The original of Mongolian written literature can conventionally be dated from the XIIIth century but it is not excluded that the Mongols may have literary memorials that existed even before the XIIIth century.

At the outset of the XIVth century a new period began in the development of written Mongolian, connected with the activities involved in producing translations for Mongols. Final shape was given to written Mongolian, neologisms which had arisen as a result of the influence of vigorous popular dialects were finally established, correct spelling—sometimes imitative of Uighur models but sometimes deliberately digressing from them—was laid down.

In the XIVth century the first indications of scientific knowledge became discernible among the Mongols. Under the influence of the ancient Indian and Tibetan languages school linguistics developed in specially marked fashion. The Mongols made a study of the grammatical treatises of Panini (Vth century B.C.), Tomisambata (VIIth century A.D.), Sazh-pandit Gungazhaltsan and others, and they also wrote independent works on the model of the said treatises. Their principal interest lay in working out problems of Mongolian writing, orthography and grammar and also literary translation problems. The most famous linguist of that time is Choizhi-Odsor, a Mongolized

Uighur. Scholars know little about him. According to the evidence of some sources it can be concluded that he worked under Khans Ulauitu (1295-1307) an dKhansan-Khulug (1308-1311) and continued productive work right up until 1321. Choizhi-Odsor was an outstanding scholar of his time and left after his death a number of important linguistic, philosophical and literary works. He wrote the first grammar of the Mongolian language *Zurkhmiy tolt* ("Cover of the Heart"), which has not come down to us in its original version but about which a judgment can be formed from some later notes on it which include the basic contents of the main text (commentaries by Danzandagva, Bilgiin-Dalai). In his work Choizhi-Odsor laid down a number of very important rules of Mongolian phonology and orthography such as the harmonization of the vowels in Mongolian, the definition of vowels and consonants and the classification of sounds on the principles of the five *makhbodi*.

During the Yuan Empire Kublai Khan took steps to carry out a reform of Mongolian writing; in 1269 he introduced the so-called square script, modelled on the Tibetan alphabet of Pagvalama Lodoizhantsan. As B. Ya. Vladimirtsov has pointed out, Kublai Khan proposed the creation of an international alphabet which his multi-tribal subjects—Mongols, Chinese, Turks, Tibetans and others—could use for writing their own languages. The Mongol Khan made great efforts to achieve his purpose. He issued numerous edicts aimed at disseminating the new alphabet in his Empire. The use of Uighur writing was banned, numerous schools were opened, etc. A great deal of work was done in translating and publishing, for the most part, Buddhist literature in the new alphabet. All these efforts, however, yielded no effective results. The literary language of the Mongol world continued to be the old written language of the Mongols with its Uighur script.

Oral artistic creativeness among the Mongols was widely represented in legends, traditions, heroic epics, folk songs, proverbs and sayings. The ancient Mongols loved making vivid poetical speeches, skilfully rhymed and containing many maxims, exhortations, proverbs and sayings. They had a habit of conveying most oral messages in skilfully rhymed and allegorical speech. Such messages were called in those days *duu bariulakh*, i. e. "trust the voice." The result of all this was that the Mongols developed an oral poetry which was one of the special forms of ancient Mongolian oral literature. Many examples of such poetry can be found in the sources *(Nuus tovchoo, Collection of Chronicles* of Rashid ad-Din, etc.) Most of the verse fragments in the *Sacred Legend* are in reality the best specimens of ancient Mongolian oral poetry consigned to writing. Among the Mongols of that time there were quite a number of talented popular poets, skilful storytellers and improvisors. Rashid ad-Din notes that Mongol poets composed many poems in praise of Kutul-kaan (*Hotol haan*), describing his daring and courage. He goes on to cite typical examples of how the Mongol poets sang the praises of their heroes, in this case Kutul-haan. "They say that his voice was so loud that his shout was heard across seven hills and was like an echo which resounds in another mountain, that his hands were like the paws of a bear; he gripped with both hands a man whom none was stouter or stronger and, without (any) difficulty bent him in half, as if he were a wooden arrow, and cracked his spine. They relate how on wintry nights he threw into the campfire (whole) trees and lay down near it; the red hot ashes from the burning fire fell on his body and burnt him but he paid no attention to it. Each of his meals consisted of a (whole) big three-year old ram and a huge bowl of *kumiss*, yet his hunger was not stilled."

Mongolian written literature, deriving its sources from oral poetical invention, had by the XIIIth century achieved considerable development. This is proved by the appearance of the *Sacred Legend*, which is not only a unique historical monument but also a masterpiece of the literary art of the Mongols in the XIIIth century.

It is not only the poetical fragments of the *Sacred Legend* which are of great interest, but the whole book in general. The language and the style serve to prove that the art of words and the literary language of the Mongols, even in the XIIIth century had attained a quite high level. The author of the *Sacred Legend*, by skilfully using the wealth of spoken popular poetical invention, wrote a history of Mongolia, as Professor Ts. Damdinsuren has remarked, not by cataloguing facts but by artistically depicting actual historical facts.

Among the productions of the same (Yuan) or adjacent epoch, the *Tale of the Two Trotting Horses of Genghis*, the *Instructions of Genghis Khan to His Younger Brothers and Sons* and several others of a similar type are well-known. In all these compositions, as can be seen even from their titles, Genghis plays a prominent part. They reflect the ideology of the Mongol feudal lords and hymn the praises of Genghis Khan.

The end of the Yuan period (XIVth century) was marked by the characteristic work entitled *The Tears of Togon-Timur*. In this composition, the feudal writers express their grief concerning the fall of the Yuan dynasty and the loss of rule over China.

Alongside feudal literature, there existed in the period described works of Mongol popular literature. These include, for example, *The Tale of the Wise Discourses of the Orphan Boy with the Nine Comrades of Genghis*. In this work, the role of hero is played by an orphan boy who quarrels with the all-powerful followers of Genghis. Through the lips of this boy, the people sought to contest views held on life by the Mongol feudal aristocracy.

Another work is a unique example of a lyrical popular song, inscribed on birch bark in the Mongolian language in Uighur letters. It was found by Soviet explorers in the area of the River Volga which once formed part of the Golden Horde.

The inscription relates to the end of the XIIIth or beginning of the XIVth century and the following is a summary of the contents. A mother is escorting her son who has been called up for military service by some governor or other. In this popular song, the mother and son appear in the roles of labouring people. In poetical dialogue they express their love for each other. The mother is worried about the fate of her son who is setting off to serve a master. The son is also not attracted by this service and his thoughts turn towards the coming spring and the camping season that has begun. In this composition also is reflected the difference of interests between the feudal aristocracy and the ordinary people. The ideals of the simple nomad are contrasted with the interests of the steppe aristocracy. If the thoughts of the feudal lords were directed towards carrying out predatory raids, as reflected in feudal literature, the thoughts of the ordinary people were turned towards peaceful labour, the breeding of stock, etc. This difference in outlook on the world determined also the diametrically opposed aspirations of feudal and popular literature in the period in question.

By the XIVth century, there had been an unusual intensification of work on translating the art, and, particularly the Buddhist, literature of India, China and Tibet into Mongolian. Only a small number of the literary works has come down to our times. There are for instance, *Bodicharya-avatary*, the ancient Indian philosophical and literary work translated by Choizhi-Odsor; *Banzaragch, Altangerel* translated by Sharav-Senge; *Doloon ovgoniy sudar*, the *Subashid* of Gungazhaltsan translated by Sonom-Gar; *Achlalt nom*, a Confucian composition translated and published in 1307, etc.

An outstanding representative of Mongolian literature of the XIVth century was Choizhi-Odsor, to whom we have already referred. He was a talented poet who wrote a number of interesting literary works, such as the commentaries to chapter X of *Bodicharya avatary*, an epilogue in verse to *Banzaragch*, *Song of Praise to Makhagala* and others.

Architecture and art. The towns which sprang up in the XIIIth century in Mongolia and, above all, Karakorum served as a basis for the development of the art of building. According to Rashid ad-Din, the people who worked in Karakorum were mostly foreign master builders, the majority of whom had been deported from the subjugated countries. A special site in the capital was occupied by the Palace of Ugadei, built on a lofty foundation, each side being an arrow's flight in length. In the middle of the palace a throne room was built which gleamed with artistic ornamentation, especially paintings. Alongside the Khan's palace stood the rich and beautiful houses of the nearest relatives of Ugadei, his sons and other imperial heirs. On Ugadei's order, many beautiful utensils and dishes were made from gold and silver in the shape of elephants, lions, horses and other animals.

In 1948-1949 large-scale excavations were made of the ruins of Karakorum. The imperial palace was found in the south-western part of the city. There, behind a clay wall, were found the remains of six buildings and a stone pedestal in the shape of a tortoise with a triumphal inscription in honour of the Khan. The principal building of the palace stood on a high plinth and consisted of an enormous hall with 64 columns. The floor of the hall was paved with green glazed tiles. All the palace buildings were covered with green and red tiles and decorated with different representations in relief. Particularly prominent among these are heads of women, executed very realistically in the style typical of Uighur art of the XII-XIIIth centuries.

The excavations of houses in the town, especially the house at the cross-road of two central streets, showed that Karakorum was an important centre of various handicrafts. Workshops have been discovered for making all kinds of vessels—Chinese, Tangut and ware similar to Tadjik and Persian, often decorated with the most delicate patterns. The Karakorum smiths and iron founders manufactured enormous quantities of agricultural implements—ploughs with moulding boards, ploughshares, billhooks and scythes, various weapons and helmets. They cast iron cauldrons and bushes for the wheels of carts on which were transported army-trains. The high level of development and large volume of production of the blacksmiths' shops and the iron-casting and bronze-casting foundries of Karakorum justify the assumption that it was, in particular, a very important centre for the equipment of the Mongol armies.

A study of the finds made in Karakorum leads to the conclusion that in its construction and in its culture, especially in the early period, the traditions of the old culture of the Uighur towns of the IX-XIIIth centuries played a considerable part. Nevertheless, from the very beginning, the Karakorum culture is distinguished by the fact that it is composed of differing elements taken from the countries conquered by the Mongols.

The Mongols themselves did not, in the first half of the XIIth century, yet possess their own artisans and master-builders who could have erected urban buildings; for this reason a national Mongolian urban style could not have emerged in Karakorum.

In the details of the buildings and in their decoration, however, can be discerned local techniques and traditions which had existed in Mongolia long before Genghis Khan and which have been embodied in the architectural monuments of the IX-XIth centuries (for example, in the architecture of the town of Kharabalgas on the River Orkhon).

The sources mentioned supply information on the applied arts of the Mongols of that period and refer more particularly to the patterns on the chimney breasts and the representations of berries, trees, birds and animals drawn on the felt which covered the entrance to the *yurt*.

There is a brief description in the *Sacred Legend* of the ornaments on clothing and household objects of the Mongols. Mongol warriors apparently also decorated their weapons (bows, lances, swords, shields, chain-armour, etc.). Epic compositions give a vivid and colourful description of the appearance and of the decorations on the armour of the heroes sung in these epics. Some specimens of such decorations which have been found in the Karakorum excavations confirm the high level of workmanship of the Mongol artists.

The art of jewellery-making had long been known to the Mongols and was very widespread among them. Rashid ad-Din mentions that, among other trophies, the company of Temuchin captured from the Tartars a silver cradle. In another place he states that the Dayan-Khan of Naiman ordered the skull of the Van-Khan at Kerait to be mounted in silver. Archeological finds have yielded specimens of delicately chased designs on metal articles. Musical instruments were in wide use. According to the sources, the Mongols before going into battle sang songs and played on musical instruments. Mention is made of war-drums covered with ox-hide. The Mongols also had ritual tambourines which were used by the Shaman priests. Another musical instrument mentioned is the *khuur* (a string instrument). This instrument is referred to in the *Sacred Legend* in connection with an account of a funeral procession. Reports by travellers mention the trumpets which were used in court ceremonies.

SECTION FOUR

MONGOLIA IN THE XIV-XVIIth CENTURIES
(THE FEUDAL DISINTEGRATION OF THE COUNTRY)

CHAPTER I

THE SOCIAL STRUCTURE OF MONGOLIA
IN THE XIV-XVIIth CENTURIES

The policy of conquest pursued by the Mongol feudal nobles had extremely negative consequences not only for the countries they conquered but also for the Mongol people themselves.

Under the leadership of Genghis Khan and his successors the Mongol feudal nobles regarded forcible seizure of the wealth accumulated by other peoples as the basic source of their enrichment. In addition, Genghis Khan and his successors not only legalized the enslavement of the *arat* population who were forced to contribute their labour to maintain the class of Mongol feudal lords but they transformed the overwhelming majority of the *arats* into soldiers, the shedding of whose blood made it possible for the khans and princes to enrich themselves from the loot of more and more new countries.

As a result of the wars of conquest Mongolia lost a large proportion of its productive population which was permanently cut off from the home country, was left in strange lands and absorbed by other peoples. The looted valuables, on the other hand, enriched only the parasitic class of *noyons*, without in any degree stimulating the growth of the country's productive forces and culture. The era of conquests disturbed the normal socio-economic and cultural development of Mongolia and doomed it to backwardness. The country retrograded and an extensive nomadic pastoral economy retained its importance as the basic form of productive activity among the Mongols.

The economic weakness of Mongolia was revealed in all its acuteness immediately after the Yuan dynasty of Mongol feudal nobles had been overthrown by the Chinese people and ejected from their country. Mongolia found itself cut off from the Chinese market which at that time was the only one where the Mongols could dispose of the products of their economy and where they could procure the agricultural and handicraft products they needed. The Mongolian economy found itself in an impasse. Restoration of economic links with China was a vital necessity for Mongolia. But a solution of this problem was hampered by the fact that the Ming dynasty was not interested in wide barter trade with Mongolia, especially in the early days of its rule.

The critical situation of the Mongol economy was intensified and made more acute by the circumstance that, on the one hand, the Mongol feudal caste were not, immediately after being expelled from China, willing to forego their ambitions to re-establish their domination and for a number of decades, therefore, waged endless wars across the borders of China, while, on the other hand, the Ming dynasty, having displaced the Mongol feudal lords in China, frequently invaded Mongolian territory with their armed forces, in an effort to weaken the Mongols and subjugate Mongolia.

The above were the circumstances governing relations between Mongolia and China during the rule of the Ming dynasty. They make it easier for us to understand the internal history of Mongolia at this time and enable us to determine, more especially, the reasons for the internecine struggle between the Oirats and the feudal nobles of Eastern Mongolia.

As we have already said, the basic occupation of the Mongol people was extensive nomad stock-breeding. The wealth of the country consisted in the herds of cattle, camels and horses, and flocks of sheep. The *arats* moved around in small groups of *ails*, changing from one place to another according to the time of the year, in search of pasture for the livestock. Each group of *arats* moved about within the boundaries of a strictly defined area which constituted the possession of the feudal lord to whose land such *arats* were bonded and from which they had no right to stray.

As Academician Vladimirtsov says: "The simple Mongol had to roam as a nomad in accordance with the orders of his seignior and was obliged to halt wherever he was told and move away to fresh grazing grounds also at the will of his master." The basic unit of production continued to be the *ail*—one or a small group of individual households or separate families. Both in summer and in winter the Mongols lived in *yurts*. These were of two types: old-fashioned *yurts*, erected on ox-carts, and a lighter type, similar to present-day *yurts*.

Hunting continued at this time to play an important role in the country's economy. "As the Mongol grows up, hunting becomes his usual occupation. He leaves in the morning and comes back in the evening. The flesh of the wild animal killed is used for food and the skins are slept on"—thus writes one of the sources of the end of the XVIth century. In summertime the *arats* hunted in small groups or singly in order to satisfy their personal needs. In the autumn thousands of them were enlisted by the feudal lords to take part in large battles which lasted two or three months at a time or longer.

In their domestic life the *arats* produced only those household items which satisfied the most urgent requirements of nomad existence. Sheep's wool was used for making felt, the hides of domestic animals were used for making straps, harness, vessels and also for sewing garments, headgear and footwear. From wood they made vessels, carts and framework for *yurts*. In addition, every *arat* had to make and keep ready to hand a specific quantity of arrows, but bows and armour were articles that had to be specially produced and for this purpose special artisans were maintained at the princes' headquarters. Bows were made out of mulberry and elm and thin thongs were used for bow-strings. The shafts for arrows were made from willow and the arrow-heads of different shapes from forged iron.

The return to Mongolia of the khans and princes expelled from China following the popular uprising considerably changed the situation in the country. Whereas, previously, Mongolia had been, for more than a hundred years, merely one of the border provinces of a feudal empire, the remote patrimony of the Yuan emperors, it had now become once more an independent political and economic organism. The fortunes of the country now depended principally on domestic factors, on the level of development of its own productive forces. It was in this context that the further development of feudal relationships in the country proceeded.

In the period we are now considering two classes are clearly distinguishable in Mongol society: the ruling class of feudal lords, on the one hand, and the oppressed class of *arat* serfs, on the other.

The class of feudal lords included the descendants of Genghis: the khan himself and the princely heirs *(taiji)*, who stood on the topmost step of the hierarchic ladder of the ruling class and who bore the title *tsagan yasun* ("white bone"). The khan was the head of all the feudal lords. One step below stood the prince-heirs of Genghis stock *(taiji)*. The latter in turn had as vassals the minor feudal lords—the service aristocracy, descendants of former *tyemniks* and chiliarchs. The important feudal lords had their hereditary estates *(hubi)*. In addition to exercising supreme rule over all Mongolia and administering his *ulus*, the khan had special charge of the so-called left wing *(dzun gar)*, i.e. the eastern part of the country, while the right wing *(barun gar)*, i.e. the western part of the country, was handed over to be ruled by the heir to the khan's throne *(huntaiji)* with the title of prince-co-ruler *(jinon)*. The important feudal nobles were the hereditary owners of *otoks* or *aimaks* and were dependent vassals of the khan.

The duties of a Mongol feudal lord in his capacity as vassal were defined by the word *alba*—service, servitude. This service was constituted by the fact that the feudal lord was bound to take part in gatherings for deciding on administrative or military matters, in courts of law and in government. At the same time he was obliged, on the demand of his suzerain, to take part in campaigns by putting into the field a specific number of fully-armed soldiers and giving material aid to his master. Nevertheless, the mutual relations between feudal nobles were governed not by established rules of any kind but by brute force. Our sources provide no materials which would enable us to trace the process by which conditional grants *(hubi)* became converted into absolute or hereditary fiefs or *umchi*. But there can be no doubt that in the period described the typical form of land-tenure throughout Mongolia was not *hubi* but *umchi*. With their *umchi* to rely upon the vassals strove to be independent, often refused to comply with the orders of the suzerain and sometimes even usurped the khan's authority themselves. All of this led to endless internecine wars and to internal fragmentation which was characteristic of Mongolia in the XIVth-XVIIth centuries.

The *arats*, cattle tenders were feudal dependents of their princely rulers *(edzen)*. This dependence was based on the fact that the class of feudal nobles had monopoly ownership of the basic means of production—the land, i.e. the grazing grounds *(nutug)*, of which they disposed as they liked. This enabled them to dispose also of the *albatu* themselves, move them over to new places, fix on a place for them to graze the cattle. "As in the old days of the Empire," writes Academician Vladimirtsov, "the seignior owned the people *(ulus)* and the place, the grazing grounds where they could live as nomads *(nutug)*.

The basic features of feudal dependence and feudal exploitation of the *arat* population, which had become noticeable at a still earlier stage of feudalism in Mongolia had now been strengthened and been further developed. The Mongol feudal nobles, by assigning to the *arats* appropriate grazing grounds made it possible for them to operate their own small-scale pastoral economy, based on personal *arat* labour. The *arats* were owners of a certain number of cattle and they also possessed simple working tools. The existence of an individual *arat* economy was a most important condition for the feudal system of production in Mongolia. The small-scale *arat* economy was essential to the existence of the large-scale feudal economy. "The peasants' 'own' farming of their allotments," Lenin wrote of the Russian countryside before the agrarian reform, "was a condition of the landlord economy, and its purpose was to 'provide' not the peasant with means of livelihood but the landlord with hands."[1] This was precisely the situation in Mongolia where the *arat's* "own" holding was designed not so much to provide the *arat* and his family with means for a livelihood as to provide the feudal lord with a labour force without which the latter's large-scale pastoral economy could not exist.

The economic system in Mongolia at the time we are describing had a good deal in common with the corvée system of economy of settled or sedentary peoples in the feudal era. Lenin found that for such an economic system to prevail the following four conditions were essential:

"... firstly, the predominance of natural economy. The feudal estate had to constitute a self-sufficing, self-contained entity, in very slight contact with the outside world... Secondly, such an economy required that the direct producer be allotted the means of production in general, and land in particular; moreover, that he be tied to the land, since otherwise the landlord was not assured of hands... Thirdly, a condition for such a system of economy was the personal dependence of the peasant on the landlord... Fourthly, and finally, a condition and a consequence of the system of economy described was the extremely low and stagnant condition of technique, for farming was in the hands of small peasants, crushed by poverty and degraded by personal dependence and by ignorance."[2]

Lenin's analysis of the corvée economic system can, with certain limitations consequent on the pastoral type of economy, be applied to mediaeval Mongolia. The fact that handicraft was not separated from agriculture, did not become an independent form of production but went on existing jointly with agriculture, converted the feudal landholdings in Mongolia into serf-owning estates, self-sufficing, closed units, very weakly linked with the rest of the world. The direct producer in Mongolia, the *arat*, was supplied, as we have seen, with the basic means of production—land, i.e. grazing grounds, but he was at the same time tied to that land. He was also personally dependent on the feudal serf-owners. The low, backward level of technical development of the nomad pastoral economy in Mongolia was, on the one hand, the condition and, on the other hand, the result of the corvée system of economy that prevailed in the country.

Relying on their economic power and taking advantage of extra-economic compulsion, the feudal nobles kept the economic activities of the *arats* subject to their control and arbitrarily restricted their freedom of economic initiative.

The *arats* could not without their lords' permission assign property to their children, marry off their sons, give their daughters in marriage, borrow or lend money. Such limitations on the economic initiative of the *arats* reflected the extent of the exploitation and personal dependence of the *arats* but it did not extinguish their property rights in the cattle and working tools they owned personally.

During the time we are describing the most widespread form taken by the feudal exploitation of the *arats* was corvée rent, the clearest expression of which was the handing over of cattle by the feudal lords to the *arats* to be grazed or the enlistment of *arats* to work directly for the feudal lords as shepherds, milkers, shearers, etc. As well as corvée rent, it was a very common practice, as a form of feudal exploitation, to levy rent in kind. Every *arat* household was obliged to give the feudal proprietor free of charge a definite proportion of its herd. According to the sources, every *arat* household which had forty sheep or more and two or more head of large cattle gave the lord three sheep per year. Furthermore, according to later sources, the *arats* had to defray the costs involved in such events in the feudal lord's family as births, weddings, funerals, removals to other camping or grazing sites, etc. In such cases the feudal lords received one horse and one ox-harnessed cart each from every ten *arat* households, as well as a specific amount of milk, fermented milk, felt, etc., depending on the size of the *arats*' herds and flocks.

It should be noted that rent payable in kind was not a substitute for corvée rent, did not take its place or supplant it. The historical development of Mongolia furnishes convincing proof of Marx's theory that "To whatever extent rent in kind is the prevailing and dominant form of ground-rent, it is furthermore always more or less accompanied by survivals of the earlier form, i.e., of rent paid directly in labour, corvée-labour..."[3] Rent payable in kind in Mongolia existed side by side and parallel with corvée rent, which retained the importance of being the decisive condition for the existence of the large-scale pastoral economy of the feudal nobles.

In addition to the ordinary forms of corvée rent and rent in kind the Mongol *arats* bore the burden of many other servitudes. They were obliged to pay up in cattle for their prince if a fine was imposed on him or if the prince found he had to make a present to a more senior feudal noble, etc. They had, in addition, to carry out, on their lords' orders, any menial work required at their headquarters, to serve in the feudal militia, keep their arms in good repair, set out on a campaign, go into battle, fight and die in the cause of the feudal lord. One of the most onerous servitudes that devolved on the *arats* was the *urton* (transport) servitude under which they were obliged to give their labour, their cattle and their funds to provide a postal service in the country and to supply provisions to government officials and feudal nobles passing along the roads.

In a large-scale pastoral economy rent payable in kind, being the natural result of backward forms of natural economy, became in its turn a factor that contributed to the preservation of such backward forms. This is where the trend finds expression in a law which was discovered by Marx, namely, that, as a result of rent paid in kind, "...through its indispensable combination of agriculture and domestic industry, through its almost complete self-sufficiency whereby the peasant family supports itself through its independence from the market and the movement of production and history of that section of society lying outside of its sphere, in short owing to the character of natural economy in general, this form is quite adapted to furnishing the basis for stationary social conditions as we see, e. g., in Asia."[4]

This can be applied *in toto* to medieval Mongol society, in spite of the fact, that, as distinct from the agricultural commune in India and China, it vitally needed barter trade with settled agricultural countries. But trade with neighbours during the period described left the natural character of the internal economy of Mongol society quite unaffected; such trade did not contribute to the development of social division of labour on the basis of which local markets could have been established in the country. This is to a certain extent explained by the specific nature of the trade between Mongolia and China.

Only members of the embassies which periodically turned up at court had the right to trade with China. These envoys brought with them, in addition to the so-called tribute, i.e. gifts to the emperor, goods for sale. These goods were usually bought by the treasury at fixed prices, either for cash or in exchange for Chinese products. If some of the goods had not been bought by the treasury, then special markets, lasting 3-4 days, were opened in the courtyards of the embassies where barter deals were conducted under strict governmental supervision. In addition to the trade transacted with embassies, China sometimes opened horse fairs in the border districts for the neighbouring nomad peoples. To these horse fairs the nomads drove in not only horses but also cattle and they brought along furs to exhange for Chinese goods.

Under the Ming dynasty a special feature of border trading was strict state control and even partial government monopoly.

On the other hand, the principal suppliers at these markets were the Mongol feudal nobles who drove in cattle for sale and brought along the products of stock-breeding and hunting collected both from their own property and those they received from the *arats* in the form of various levies in kind and servitudes. While the barter trade was strictly regulated in their own interests by the authorities of the Ming dynasty, it was equally strictly regulated too by the Mongol feudal nobles in their own interests.

The horse fairs organized in the border strip were usually opened once or twice a month and trading went on for three to five days depending on the amount of goods brought in. The Mongols had to appear unarmed and immediately trading was over leave Chinese territory, keeping not less than 50 kilometres distant from the frontier. Deals were basically of the barter type but the use of silver was not excluded. The goods offered by the Chinese included cotton and silk fabrics, iron articles, cauldrons for cooking food, agricultural implements, grain products, tea, etc. in exchange for Mongolian horses, cattle, hides and furs. There was a strict ban on selling the nomads' weapons.

In the context of the increasingly intensified disintegration of Mongol feudalism and the interminable fighting of prince against prince, trade between Mongolia and China transacted on such official and strictly controlled conditions restricted the development of the social division of labour, the growth of handicrafts and commodity production.

The *arats* who were the basic productive class which by its toil maintained the whole of Mongol society were not a united force. Processes of differentiation were operating among them. In the leading place were the so-called *sain humun* ("better people"), which comprised the wealthy, office-holding families (*yambutu*), next came the *dunda humun* ("middle-class people") composed of well-to-do people who were not office-holders *(yambu ugei);* the last group consisted of paupers—*hara humun* ("black people").

The lowest class of all was that of the slaves *(bogol).* Slave-owning, a last survival of the pre-feudal era, took the form of household slavery. The slaves performed principally the duties of servants. They could own property but did not hold full rights of title to property. Slavery was, as a rule, a life-long and hereditary status.

A privileged position in the social structure of that day was held by the class of *darkhans.* Generated in the early stage of feudalization of society, the institution of *darkhans* became very widespread under Genghis Khan and his successors. Sometimes even people who had emerged from the common people were enrolled as *darkhans* for having specially distinguished themselves in the service of a feudal noble and been exempted by him from servitudes, punishments for certain offences, etc.

Such was the economic situation of Mongolia in the XIV-XVIIIth centuries and such was the structure of its society. The political organization of the country corresponded to its social structure.

Traditions relate that in the times of the Yuan dynasty the Mongol army consisted of 40 *tmas* (*tumens*—myriads) but this figure did not include the Oirats who made up another four *tmas*. From this is derived the expression long current in Mongolia—*duchin durben hoyar* ("forty and four"), i.e. forty eastern and four western *tmas* of Mongols—used to designate all Mongols.

When the Yuan dynasty fell, only remnants of the formerly numerous army returned to Mongolia. In the post-Yuan epoch both Mongolian and Chinese sources talk only of the six *tmas (tumens)* into which all eastern Mongols were divided. Of these three belonged to the left wing and the other three to the right wing of the Mongolian people. As for the Oirats they continued as before to make up four independent *tmas*.

In the XIV-XVIIth centuries the expression *tumen* (literally 10,000) ceased to be used to designate the component part of "wing", becoming a synonym to designate the large domains—*uluchi* into which the eastern and western Mongols were at that time divided. Moreover, quantitatively the *ulus* was not equal to the *tumen* of the era of conquests and of the Yuan dynasty. Even during the Genghis Khan era the *tmas* were magnitudes of a more changeable size than the chiliads, and after his successors had been thrown out of China the *tmas* bore no relation at all to their name, i.e. areas which had to muster 10,000 warriors each. Accordingly, in the post-Yuan period the expression *tumen*, like *ulus*, was employed as the name for a large property irrespective of the number of troops it had to put in the field.

Each *ulus* was subdivided into large groups of *ails*, united with one another by the fact that their grazing grounds occupied common territory and had at their head one common hereditary landlord *(edzen)*, who owned the territory in question and was directly answerable to his suzerain, the owner of the *ulus*. Such united properties were in the post-Yuan period called *otoks*. From the military point of view an *otok* also represented a specific unit, as its militia made up a special military detachment, known as *hoshun (hoshigun)*; in the Mongol sources of the XVIIth century the terms *otok* and *hoshun* are often used interchangeably.

Otoks were composed not only of kindred groups; they could also include, and they included, as with the "chiliads", representatives of different gentile associations. The determining factor for an *otok* was the sharing of a common territory and the consequential feudal dependence of all inhabitants of an *otok* on a particular *edzen*. Wars and the allocation of new grants of land reduced the number of *ails* composing an *otok*.

Besides the division into *otoks* Mongolia also had a division into *aimaks*. As distinct from the *otok*, an *aimak* represented an association of related families which derived their origin from one common ancestor. *Aimaks* differed greatly in size;

sometimes several *aimaks* made up one *otok* but sometimes an *aimak* did not differ in size from an *otok*.

The apparatus of feudal authority and of the feudal oppression and exploitation of the workers was at the time under review quite uncomplicated. In each feudal estate there sat its hereditary suzerain who personally administered all the business of his estate. He commanded its troops, pronounced judgment and meted out punishment; he fixed all kinds of taxes and servitudes; the whole amplitude of military, administrative and juridical authority was wielded by him; for the vassal *arats* he was the single and all-powerful sovereign. If he needed an adviser on any kind of complicated problems he found one in the circle of his relatives; if he needed an envoy for a diplomatic mission it was also easy for him to find one from the circle of his near relations. In reliance on his troops, on his near relations and kinsmen who held the most important posts in the army and in the civil administration, the prince-proprietor in Mongolia felt himself very assured. Such an organization of feudal authority found more or less successful solutions for the problems both of the domestic and the foreign policy of the feudal nobility.

In conclusion it should be noted that the description given in this chapter of the economy, social structure and political organization relates in the main to those regions of Mongolia inhabited by the basic pastoral population of the country. In the case of the forest regions in the north and north-west of the country where the Buryats and other ethnic groups lived and among whom the vestiges of the gentile-tribal structure still survived to a very great extent, in those areas feudal relationships did not attain the same degree of maturity and this was correspondingly reflected in their social structure and political organization.

CHAPTER II

FEUDAL DISINTEGRATION AND ATTEMPTS
TO OVERCOME IT

At a certain level of the development of the feudal system of production a feudal society begins to break down into a more or less considerable number of independent feudal domains. The economic and political strengthening of fiefs derives basically from this process. Having managed to convert their conditional grants—benefices—into unconditional hereditary fiefs, the owners of these latter gradually strengthened their economic and political might, both by brutally exploiting their own serfs and also by seizing the domains of their weaker neighbours. As time went on, as the economic independence of the fiefs increased and as the vassal lords became economically more and more independent of their suzerains, there was a weakening of the ties which had at one time bound vassals and suzerains together and kept the former in a state of dependency on the latter. The era of feudal disintegration had begun.

In Mongolia the period of feudal disintegration began at the end of the XIVth century. The unusually long-drawn-out process of feudal disintegration, which led to the country losing its political independence and to the establishment of the yoke of the Manchus, was one of the reasons that decisively conduced to the socio-economic and cultural backwardness of Mongolia.

The end of the XIVth and beginning of the XVth centuries found the Mongols living in scattered settlements over a huge territory from Baikal and the Khingan foothills in the east to the Tien Shan in the west, from the upper reaches of the Irtysh and the Yenisei on the North to the Great Chinese Wall on the south. Separated from one another by vast spaces, and often by almost impassable natural obstacles (the Gobi Desert, the Altai Mts.), vitally dependent to an equal extent on economic links with China but economically quite independent of one another, the feudal princedoms of Mongolia, after the overthrow of the Yuan dynasty, quickly became transformed into independent petty feudal despotisms unwilling to submit to anyone. The authority and effective power of the Khan of All Mongolia over the feudal nobles began to decline. The imperial throne became increasingly a tool in the group struggle between the different feudal cliques which dethroned and killed some khans in order to place on the throne other khans more acceptable to them. Chinese sources testify that the Mongol feudal nobles did not immediately give up the hope of regaining their power over the Chinese people, who had expelled them in 1368. After fleeing from Peking, Togon-Temur stationed himself with his troops at Inchang (near Lake Dalainor), maintaining contact with his general, Kuku Temur, operating in the north-west of China, and also with Nagachu, whose forces were located in the mountains of Tsin-shang to the north-east of Peking. Backed by these forces, Togon-Temur got ready to fight for the restoration of the Yuan dynasty. But in 1370 the Inchang group was defeated by the Chinese troops which captured the whole camp of Togon-Temur with a numerous suite and with Togon-Temur's wives. Only Ayushridara, Togon-Temur's son, escaped and fled to Karakorum, where Kuku-Temur also arrived shortly afterwards, his army also having been defeated. Karakorum again became the political centre of Mongolia and there in 1370 Ayushridara was proclaimed Khan with the title of Biliktu-khan; a military force began to be formed there with whose help Biliktu-khan counted on returning to power in China.

In 1372, however, troops of the Ming dynasty invaded Mongolia and in battles with them the troops of Biliktu-khan were defeated. A year later, however, the Mongol feudal nobles themselves carried out a number of raids on the border provinces of China.

Desirous of negotiating peace terms with the Mongol Khan, the government of the Ming dynasty in 1374 released from captivity Biliktu-khan's son, Maidaripal, and sent with him an offer of peace. The peace was kept until 1378 when Biliktu-khan died. His successor, Togus-Temur (1378-1388), resumed military operations against China. In the spring of 1380 the Chinese army again invaded Mongolia, occupied Karakorum and razed it. Fighting continued with varying success until 1388 when Togus-Temur was decisively defeated and was killed.

Chinese sources testify that during a period of 12 years from 1388 five khans succeeded one another in Mongolia; each of them was dethroned as a result of a palace coup d'état and destroyed by his opponents. Vassals no longer obeyed their suzerains. They pursued an independent foreign policy, guided exclusively by their own interests and allying themselves with one set of feudal nobles against another; yesterday's ally could today easily become an enemy and an enemy an ally.

The border feudal nobles gravitated towards China and some of them changed over to become subjects of the Ming dynasty. Prince Nagachu, for example, whose nomad encampments stretched along the Great Wall from Kalgan to Kaiyuan was the first of the Mongol feudal nobles to acknowledge himself a vassal of the Ming Emperor. On the orders of the Emperor of China the domain owned by Nagachu which, according to the evidence of sources, was reckoned to have a population of about 200,000, was reorganized in 1389 and given the appellation "Three districts of Uryankha". The Ming dynasty was very much interested in playing off its new vassal against the other Mongol princes with whom armed struggle still continued. The links between the princes of the three districts of Uryankha and the Ming dynasty became increasingly close. They gave armed support to one of the claimants to the Ming throne who in 1403 became Emperor of China under the name of Yun-lo and generously rewarded the Uryankha princes.

At the beginning of the XVth century protracted internecine warfare began between the western and eastern feudal nobles of Mongolia. The indigenous population of the western part of Mongolia consisted of Oirats, who are first mentioned in the sources in 1204, when, in alliance with the Naimans, they fought against Genghis Khan. In 1208, however, they accepted allegiance to him. At that time the Oirats inhabited the extreme northwest of the country, the upper reaches of the Yenisei and were a semi-nomadic, semi-hunter people. Because of the unequal development of feudalism in Mongolia the Oirat tribes at the beginning of the XIIIth century had still not emerged from the decadent stage of the primitive-commune system. At the time we are describing, however, they had already settled in the stretches of steppe mainly to the west of the Altai mountains and had taken up livestock-breeding; feudal relationships had become predominant, although survivals of the gens-tribal system were more noticeable among the Oirats than among the eastern Mongols.

At the end of the XIVth century the feudal chief of the Oirats was Munke-Temur, after whose death his domain was divided between three successors—Mahmud, Taipin and Batu-Bolod.

One of the decisive causes of the struggle between the eastern and the western feudal princes of Mongolia was the cessation of trade links between the Mongol princedoms and China. This deprived the Oirat feudal nobles of the advantages and profits accruing to them from the fact that their camping grounds were situated along the trade routes connecting China with the countries of the West. With the objective of restoring economic ties with China, the Oirat feudal princes began a struggle for mastery over the trade routes into China through Mongolia. In the course of this struggle the Oirat feudal princedoms relinquished their allegiance to the Khan of all Mongolia whose main headquarters were in the east. To begin with, the Ming dynasty was very much in favour of the aspirations of the Oirat princes to closer relations with China; it calculated on making use of them for the fight against the feudal nobles of Eastern Mongolia who at that time were its principal enemies. To encourage his probable allies, Yun-lo presented the three Oirat princes mentioned above with honorary titles and various valuable gifts. Abetted by the Ming authorities, the Oirat princes in 1409 embarked on a first major campaign against their eastern neighbours and dealt them a serious defeat. The country in actual fact broke up into two parts, each governed by its own ruler.

Fearing, however, that the Oirat feudal princes might become too strong, the Ming dynasty soon began to support the eastern Mongol princes and in 1413-1414 sent to their aid a large army which defeated the Oirat troops.

At this time the life of the country and the people was marked, on the one hand, by an incessant struggle between the feudal nobles of the west and east and, on the other hand, by systematic armed raids by the Mongol feudal nobles on the Chinese borderlands. The endless wars ruined the *arat* peasantry, accentuated their impoverishment and impelled them to struggle against their oppressors. An indication of the class war of those days is contained in a report from a Chinese source of a complaint submitted in the 1440s by one of the Mongol princes to the Ming Emperor. The complainant asserts that 1,500 *arat* families have wilfully left him and that he is unable to bring them back with his own forces. The Ming Emperor, of course, granted the request of the Mongol feudal noble and gave orders for the return of the fugitives "to their lawful owner".

In the course of almost the whole of the first half of the XVth century—notwithstanding efforts to the contrary made by the Ming dynasty—there was a continued strengthening of the Oirat feudal nobles at the cost of weakening the eastern Mongolian princes. Wars between these two groups of feudal classes ended, as a rule, in victory for the Oirats, attributable to the superiority of their organization as compared with that of the eastern Mongol feudal princes, whose forces were weakened by the extreme disintegration that prevailed. The successes of the Oirat princes were also helped by the fact that they had at their head an energetic ruler, Togon, son of Mahmud, who was formally only the prime minister *(taishi)* of the Mongol Daisun-khan but in actual fact functioned as dictatorial ruler of Mongolia. After bringing under his rule all the Oirat princedoms, Togon advanced to attack the numerous feudal princes of Eastern Mongolia, systematically subduing them, one after another, to his rule and compelling the recalcitrants to move away further and further beyond the borders of the country. By 1434 the whole of Western and Eastern Mongolia was already under his rule except for the part of it which was subject to the eastern Mongol Adaikhan and his prime minister, Aruktai. In 1434 the decisive battle took place between Togon and Aruktai and ended with the complete defeat and death of the latter. Thanks to his prime minister Daisun-khan found himself the sole and sovereign ruler of a united Mongolia. His first task was to regularize economic and political mutual relations with the Ming dynasty of China. Togon began active preparations for a march on China with the intention, by use of force, to compel the rulers of China to agree to a system of economic and political ties which would correspond to the interests of the Mongol feudal nobles. In 1439 Togon died and his son Esen (1440-1455/6) was appointed to the post of *taishi* under Daisun-khan.

Continuing the policy of his father, Esen won over to his side the feudal rulers of the three districts of Uryankha and thus consummated the unification of the Mongol lands.

The relations between Daisun-khan and Esen and China at this time continued on the surface to remain friendly. Both Daisun-khan and his *taishi*, as well as other Mongol feudal princes, regularly sent embassies to Peking with presents and goods for sale and the Ming court regularly sent the Khan and his prime minister embassies with gifts in return.

Soon, however, Esen, feeling that he had become sufficiently strong, changed his tactics. He began systematically to disregard the traditional procedure under which embassies could be sent to Peking only once a year and should not number more than a few dozen in strength. In breach of this procedure Esen would send several embassies a year and increase their numbers to 2,000-3,000 men. He also demanded that the Chinese authorities provide Mongolia with supplies of foodstuffs, and made the refusal of the Ming Emperor to comply with one such demand a pretext for war.

In the autumn of 1449 Esen opened the campaign. The Chinese army sent to meet him, under the command of the Emperor, met with severe defeats. Unprepared, badly equipped and led by mediocre commanders, it was driven back to a place called Tuma[1], where a full-scale battle was fought in which the army of the Emperor In-tszun was destroyed. The trophies that fell into the hands of the victors were enormous; they captured large numbers of prisoners, including In-tszun. Thereafter, Esen offered peace terms which were apparently unacceptable to the ruling circles of China who, after proclaiming a new emperor, reinforced the defences of Peking and hastily formed a new army to fight against Esen. The peace negotiations dragged on. According to the sources, during one of the meetings with the representatives of the Ming dynasty, Esen, wishing to justify his attack on China, declared: "Why did you lower the prices for horses and often deliver poor quality and damaged silk?"

This reproach, however, the Chinese representatives rebutted by saying: "It is not our fault if we had to give you less than should have been paid for horses; after all, you yourselves every year brought over more and more of them." The conversation quoted between Esen and the representatives of China constitutes important evidence as to the nature of the economic relations between Mongolia and China at the time we are describing and on the economic background to the wars waged between them.

Peace between Mongolia and China was concluded only in the autumn of 1450.

Soon afterwards the mutual relations between Esen and Daisun-khan became severely strained. In 1451 military operations began between the Khan and his prime minister. Daisun-khan was defeated and killed. After suppressing the resistance of a number of local feudal nobles, Esen in 1451 found himself the sovereign and sole ruler of the country from Liaodun to Khama. In the same year, Esen, having proclaimed himself Khan of all Mongolia, sent a special embassy to Peking to inform the Chinese that he had ascended the throne and was assuming the title of the "Great Yuan Khan."

Esen, however, did not long remain Khan of a united Mongolia.

In 1455 a series of mutinies broke out, fomented by local feudal nobles from whom Esen had demanded unconditional allegiance but who were determined opponents of centralized authority. In the struggle that began between the local princes and Esen-khan the latter was defeated and killed.

With the death of Esen the authority and real strength of the khan's rule declined still further and the country again became for practical purposes divided between a number of independent despots. The sovereign princes of Mongolia again began to take independent decisions on the foreign and domestic policy problems of their princedoms.

While continuing to be economically dependent on trade with China the sovereign princes of disintegrated Mongolia sought to regulate separately their mutual relations with the Ming dynasty, sometimes by making armed raids on China's territory, sometimes by concluding peace with her government. The opening of markets was the basic price invariably demanded by the Mongol feudal princes for not making raids on the towns and villages of China and keeping the peace.

In 1479 the khan's throne was occupied by Batu-Munke (born 1460, died 1543), known in history as Dayan-khan. During his rule a second attempt was made to overcome disintegration and unite the country under the rule of a khan for the whole of Mongolia. By 1488 Dayan-khan had brought under his authority most of the sovereign princes of the country. In credentials forwarded with an embassy in 1488 to the Ming Emperor Dayan-khan again calls himself the "Great Yuan Khan." His embassy established peaceful relations with the house of Ming and as a consequence the government of the Ming dynasty in the same year of 1488 enacted a law laying down the procedure for trading with the nomads. The law decreed that markets for barter trade would be opened in the frontier regions three times a year. The peace terms of 1488 were adhered to over a number of years by both parties. At the appointed time markets were opened along the frontier to which the Mongols brought horses, cattle, furs, horse hair, etc., while the Chinese merchants brought cotton and silk fabrics, cooking pots and other goods for the household and personal needs of the Mongols.

By 1500, however, peaceful trading relations with China had been broken off. The sources do not relate the reasons for the breach. All that is known is that, from 1500 onwards, Dayan-khan, having transferred his headquarters to Ordos, held the power in Mongolia firmly in his hands, that he often took part in organizing large-scale armed raids on China and returned from them with booty that enriched the Khan and other feudal nobles.

The sources offer no materials which would enable us to judge of the domestic life of the country during the years of Dayan-khan's rule, the situation of the masses of the people or of their struggle against feudal oppression, against the raids on China which brought suffering to the Chinese working people and were ruining the working people of Mongolia. It is, however, well known that Dayan-khan had to use armed force time and again to subjugate to his authority individual sovereign feudal princes who tried to recover their former independence. The biggest feudal mutiny occurred when Ibiri-taishi and Mandulai Agulkhu killed Dayan-khan's son, who had been assigned to them to act as the Khan's viceroy, and rose in rebellion. Very typical as illustrating the mutual relations existing at the time in question between the khan and his vassals are the words attributed to these rebels in the chronicle of Sagan-Setsen: "Why do we have to accept a master over us?" said one of them to the other." After all, we can use our own heads ourselves. We'll kill this hereditary prince."

Dayan-khan sent a punitive expedition against the rebels, inflicted a defeat on them and forced them to flee.

Dayan-khan died in 1543. He was the last Khan of All Mongolia. After his death Mongolia again fell apart—this time, finally—into a number of independent domains.

The internal and external circumstances of the time were not favourable to efforts to unify the country on a sound basis. The economic backwardness of Mongolia, its predominantly natural economy, the absence of internal markets and towns as centres for crafts and trade, hindered the formation of social forces which could have constituted support in the struggle to overcome the feudal disintegration and to create a centralized state. Another serious obstacle to unification of the country was the policy of the Ming dynasty, which did its utmost to prevent the unification of Mongolia and to keep it in a state of disintegration and endless disputes between princes, calculating that such a policy would guarantee the safety of the frontiers of its empire.

The eldest sons of Dayan-khan were given apanages in the south of Mongolia and became the first founders of the princedoms of Aokhan, Naiman, Barin, Jarud, Keshikten, Utszumchin, Khuchit, Sunit, and Ordos. The youngest son of Dayan-khan, Geresendze, inherited the ancestral *ulus* in the north of Mongolia and became the progenitor of the sovereign princes of Khalkha-Mongolia.

After the death of Dayan-khan he was succeeded on the throne in turn by: Bodi-Alag (1505-1549), Draisun (1549-1557) and Tumen (1553-1593). Among these successors of Dayan-khan Tumen occupies a special place. More than any of his predecessors, Tumen persistently tried to put an end to feudal separatism. In order to maintain the unity of the country he set up a central government of Mongolia consisting of representatives of the Mongol princedoms of the left and right wings. But these efforts, too, had a short-lived success. The feudal princes of the right wing, having grown in strength, ceased to recognize the supreme authority of the Mongol Khan. The ruler of the right wing, one of the grandsons of Dayan-khan, Altan (born 1507, died 1582), began entitling himself khan, even during the reign of Bodis-Alag, and he also refused to recognize the supreme authority of the Khan. Altan followed a policy aimed at bringing the whole of Mongolia under his rule. He subdued the Oirats in the north, in the west he occupied Kukho-nur and tried to extend his influence to Tibet; in the east he competed with Tumen-khan in a struggle for mastery over the whole of Mongolia.

The rule of Altan-khan was notable primarily for his persistent endeavours to organize normal trade with China; in the sphere of domestic policy may be noted Altan-khan's attempt to set up in Mongolia centres for agriculture and handicrafts. Altan-khan was the first of the Mongol feudal princes to declare "yellow cap" Lamaism the official religion and to begin disseminating Lamaism in the country.

For a long time Altan-khan's peace overtures were rejected by the ruling circles of Ming China who, in 1541, promised a large money reward to anyone who would deliver his head to Peking, and in 1542 and 1546 they executed his envoys. In

1548 Altan-khan again sent a message to Peking in which he asked for peace and trading rights, declaring his readiness to punish severely violators of the peace and also announcing that, if peace prevailed, the Chinese could without hindrance engage in agriculture and the Mongols in stock-breeding. The Chinese feudal princes once again rejected Altan-khan's offer. Having failed in his objective, Altan-khan organized a series of armed raids.

In 1550 Altan-khan with his troops reached the environs of Peking and from there again made an offer of peace. As a preliminary condition the government of the Ming dynasty put forward the demand that Altan-khan should immediately leave Chinese territory. Altan-khan accepted the condition and returned to Mongolia. In 1551 peace was concluded. Markets were opened in Datun and Sianfu. The peace, however, proved an unstable one and the markets were shut down; a new wave of armed attacks by Altan-khan on Chinese towns and villages began. As the Chinese sources point out, the main purpose of Altan-khan's wars was to force the Ming Emperor to open up markets.

This state of affairs continued until 1570 when several eminent Chinese dignitaries came out in support of Altan-khan's proposals. Peace was concluded and barter markets were opened in a number of border towns. Some idea of the turnover in trade between Mongolia and China at that time is afforded by the reports given by one Chinese source to the effect that in 1571 in four markets (Datun, Kalgan, Sinin, Khukhe-khoto) operating on an average for 12 to 14 days, the Mongols sold more than 28,000 horses of a total value of about 20,000 *lan*.

Until the very day of his death Altan-khan strictly observed the terms of peace and thwarted the attempts of his vassals to violate the peace and revert to the system of armed raids.

The construction by Altan-khan of the city of Khukhe-khoto reflected the substantial improvements made in the country's economy.

According to the evidence of Chinese sources Altan-khan decided to build the city on the suggestion of the Chinese who formed the bulk of the population of his domains. The princely headquarters camp of Altan-khan became a city which began rather rapidly to turn into a centre of handicrafts and trade; in the city environs agriculture was developed and engaged in not only by Chinese but also by Mongols. The construction of this centre of agriculture and handicrafts is undoubtedly linked up with the general desire of Altan-khan to normalize peaceful trading relations with China. Thus, we can discern in the foreign and domestic policy of Altan-khan certain new features distinguishing it from the policy of his predecessors.

There can be no doubt that these changes were conditioned by changes in the socio-economic life of the country, some evidence of which is furnished by the fact that, during the period described, armed irruptions by Mongol feudal nobles into China became more and more rare and were replaced by lengthy periods of peaceful trading. Another fact which bears this out is that it was just at this time that Lamaism became the official religion of Mongolia, and that it was Altan-khan himself who was, after the overthrow of the Yuan dynasty, the first Mongol feudal prince to adopt Lamaism and take the first steps towards spreading its message.

The sources available do not, unfortunately, enable us to make an exhaustive study of the changes which led up to this policy on the part of Altan-khan.

Altan-khan ruled over the wide stretch of territory to the South of the Gobi and North of the Great Wall; the western border of his possessions was Kukunor to which Altan-khan appointed as governor his son Bintu. According to a Chinese source, at the beginning of the 1570s Bintu carried out an armed raid on the province of Szechwan. The Ming dynasty's government appealed to Altan-khan to exert the necessary influence on his son. Altan-khan replied that Bintu had acted only from urgent necessity because in the neighbourhood, at Gan'su, he had no open market for trading and it was a long way and inconvenient to go to Ningsia; accordingly, even if Altan-khan had ordered Bintu to keep quiet, he would not have been listened to. The Ming dynasty was obliged to make concessions and in 1574 a market was opened in Gan'su for barter trading with the local Mongols.

When Altan-khan died his empire broke up into a large number of petty princedoms between which fresh struggle flared up for predominance.

CHAPTER III

THE SPREAD OF LAMAISM
IN MONGOLIA

Karl Marx gave a graphic and remarkably accurate definition of the essence and role of religion when he called it the opiate of the people. In his article "Socialism and Religion" Lenin pointed out that "... impotence of the exploited classes in their struggle against the exploiters just as inevitably gives rise to the belief in a better life after death as impotence of the savage in his battle with nature gives rise to belief in gods, devils, miracles, and the like."[1]

By poisoning and beclouding the minds of the working classes, religion has always, in the hands of the governing and exploiting classes, served as a weapon for stupefying the masses and diverting them from the class struggle. Religion serves the interests of the exploiters, it is profoundly hostile to the interests of the working classes, it preaches a metaphysical, idealistic, and anti-scientific outlook on the world.

The anti-scientific essence of religious teachings is utterly characteristic of Buddhism in all its forms and trends. Emerging in India in the 6th century B. C., Buddhism in the 7th century A.D. penetrated into Tibet and soon became very widespread there. While it remained unchanged in its basic dogmas, Buddhism in Tibet, nevertheless, underwent considerable changes in the ritual and ecclesiastical sense and in the organization of church institutions. These changes were directed towards adapting Buddhism to the greatest possible extent to the interests of the governing class of Tibetan feudal society. Buddhism assumed the form of Lamaism. The founder of Lamaism in its present-day form was the Tibetan monk, Dzonhava (1357-1419), who founded the sect of "yellow caps". Up to then, the teaching of the "red caps" sect had been dominant in Tibet.

Dzonhava instituted a complicated system of ecclesiastical hierarchy, drew up a statute for Lamaist monasteries, established celibacy for lamas and allowed lamas to own property. With a view to exercising more effective influence on the masses, he introduced an elaborate ritual for religious services, accompanied by music, and arranged feast days and mysteries in honour of various Buddhist divinities. The "yellow caps" sect was the fullest expression of the interests of the feudal classes and as time went on displaced almost entirely the other sects.

In conformity with the basic dogmas of Buddhism, Lamaism teaches that life is suffering, that it consists in a change from one form of existence of living beings to another, that in this change of forms there is an order of succession. Accordingly, Lamaism teaches that a human being in his present life carries responsibility ("Karma") for the form of life followed in his previous "reincarnations." Thus, according to the teaching of Lamaism, khans, *noyons*, and in general all rich and famous people must have earned the right to authority and wealth by a life of well-doing in their previous "incarnations" while the working *arats* suffer privations and are oppressed because this is their punishment for a sinful life in their previous "incarnations".

This was the way in which Lamaism interpreted the domination of the feudal lords and the oppression and exploitation by them of the working people. To the working masses, Lamaism preached the gospel of submission and renunciation of struggle for a better life, and impressed on them that they themselves were to blame for their impoverished and deprived situation. The Lamaism of feudal Mongolia can be described as reminiscent of the reactionary role of Christianity cited by Karl Marx, who pointed out that the social principles of Christianity that served the interests of the Prussian monarchy proclaimed the oppression of the labouring classes as "... a just punishment for inherited and other sins or a suffering which God, in his great wisdom, bestows on the people He has redeemed."[2]

In appealing to the mass of the working people to be patient and submissive and to suffer without murmuring the unhappiness and privations of this life, Lamaism promised them "salvation" in the life to come and in future reincarnations. In order, however, to attain this "salvation," Lamaism teaches that a man must have the assistance of a "good teacher-friend"—a lama, and be supported by the *Chubil Khans*—the "living gods" or embodiments of the *bodhisattvas* who come down to earth for the "salvation" of men.

It was in Lamaism that the teaching about *Chubil Khans*—"living gods"—and about lamas being the "good teacher-friends" found its fullest and widest expression.

Lamaism teaches that the *bodhisattvas*, i.e. beings which have come close to the condition of *nirvana*, come down from heaven to earth, taking the form of a human being, and help people along the path to "salvation." In Tibet, and later in Mongolia, there was a large number of such *Chubil Khans* or "living gods." Persons who had been proclaimed by the Lamaist church to be *Chubil Khans* held leading positions in monasteries, were surrounded by an aura of sanctity and sinlessness and they constituted the uppermost stratum in feudal church circles. Along with them there was the enormous mass of ordinary lamas or monks who acted as the direct teachers or "good friends" of every person individually. Lamaism preached that, without the help of a teacher-lama, no man could attain "salvation" and it demanded that every layman should have such a teacher and should be strictly guided by his "good counsels and teachings." The Lamaist church instilled into its followers the belief that a man who had assumed the title of lama and had devoted himself to the service of Buddha stood incomparably higher than the ordinary layman and that his instructions were infallible.

The Lamaist church had at its disposal in the lamas a very numerous body of propagandists who kept on, day in day out, instilling into the minds of the population a reactionary ideology and preaching submission to the feudal nobles, religious and secular.

Buddhism had been known in Mongolia for a long time. As early as the XIIIth century Kublai Khan had been strenuously sponsoring Buddhism in Tibet and had tried to encourage its dissemination in Mongolia also by declaring it the official religion; nevertheless, at that time Buddhism had not spread very widely in Mongolia.

Buddhism in its Lamaist form began to spread more widely in Mongolia at the end of the XVIth century. By then Mongolia had been broken up into feudal apanages and had no economic or political unity. The internecine feudal wars which went on for over two hundred years brought the country's economy to the point of extreme exhaustion and contributed to the impoverishment of the masses. This naturally intensified the discontent of the masses with feudal exploitation and sharpened the class struggle. The feudal classes realized more and more acutely the need to strengthen their influence and their domination over the mass of the population. One of the most important weapons in the hands of the feudal princes for the spiritual enslavement and exploitation of the *arats* was religion. Shamanism, however, which had sprung up in the pre-class era could no longer, because of its primitiveness, satisfy the feudal nobles as a means of exerting pressure on the *arats*. In order to strengthen their domination the feudal nobles needed more sophisticated methods of ideologically enslaving the *arat* masses.

The experience of the feudal nobles of Tibet was appreciated by the Mongol feudal nobles who considered that they could use Lamaism as an effective weapon for subjugating wide sections of the population and strengthening their rule over the *arats*.

At the same time as they adopted Lamaism the Mongol princes sought also to establish political links with Tibet. For instance, Altan-khan, while accepting Lamaism, carried on political negotiations with the head of the Lamaists in Tibet, the lama Sodnomzhanmts, who had come from Tibet to Mongolia for the ceremonial celebration of the adoption of the new religion. Altan-khan officially recognized Sodnomzhanmts as the spiritual head of the Lamaist religion and attributed to him the title of Dalai Lama and Sodnomzhanmts in his turn recognized Altan-khan as the Great Khan.

The most important influential princes of Mongolia—the Khalkha prince Abatai-khan, the Chahar prince Ligdan-khan and the Tumet prince Altan-khan—as well as the Oirat princes, accepted Lamaism almost simultaneously (Abatai-khan, in particular, in 1580) and began actively to disseminate it among the *arats*. Hundreds of lamas were invited from Tibet to preach the religion; arrangements were made to translate Lamaist church literature into Mongolian from Tibetan, and partly from Chinese (special zeal in this connection was evinced by Ligdan-khan, who organized a translation of the *Ganchura*—a collection of Buddhist canonical books in one hundred and eight volumes). Lamaist monasteries were turned into feudal domains of their abbots and other higher-ranking lamas. Feudal nobles themselves or their sons usually became heads of monasteries and the Lamaist church proclaimed some of them *Chubil Khans* which heightened their spiritual authority.

The first Lamaist monastery in Khalkha was built in 1586 by Abatai-khan. The feudal nobles allotted the monasteries landed estates and *arat* serfs, who, after they had been registered with the monasteries, were designated *shabinars*, i.e. pupils.

In order to induce the *arats* to adopt Lamaism and become lamas, the feudal princes even introduced a number of inducements—lamas were exempted from military service, from taxes and other feudal servitudes; cases are also known of *arats* who adopted Lamaism being allotted a certain number of cattle.

When the Mongol princes invited Tibetan lamas to come and preach, they did not at first scrutinize too closely whether they belonged to any one particular sect. When, however, it became obvious that by that time the "yellow cap" sect was gaining predominance in Tibet, Lamaism in the form taught by the "yellow cap" became the established form of religion all over Mongolia.

Shamanism offered a certain amount of opposition to the spread of Lamaism but was not in a position to block its path, inasmuch as the ruling class of feudal princes, whose interests Shamanism really served, preferred Lamaism to Shamanism. It is to be noted that Lamaism followed a rather subtle policy in its struggle with Shamanism; it included in its ceremonies a number of Shamanist rites and retained in particular the veneration paid to the so-called *obos* who were particularly popular with the people at that time, although it also gave this veneration ceremony a Lamaist character.

In Mongolia, as also, incidentally, in Tibet, Lamaism greatly simplified and even mechanized the procedure of "communication" between believers and the gods—the procedure of praying. The custom became very widespread, for instance, of using *khurde*—revolving cylinders (praying-wheels). A large number of small bits of paper with printed prayers were inserted into the *khurde* which was an empty cylinder. All the worshipper had to do was to revolve the *khurde* and it was then considered that he had read a prayer.

Having adopted Lamaism as their ideological armoury, the Mongol feudal lords naturally tried to strengthen the position of the Lamaist church, to create authority for the higher-ranking lamas and to extend various privileges to lamas in general.

In particular, Altan-khan enacted laws which gave lamas of varying ranks equality with the feudal rankings. For instance, a *tsorji* was ranked the equal of a *khuntaiji* (a princely title).

In the course of time the position of the Lamaist monasteries as feudal domains grew stronger and stronger. The area of their landed estates grew larger and the number of serfs or *shabinars* bonded to them was augmented. With the growth of the economic power of the monasteries, the political influence of the higher-ranking lamas—feudal princes of the church—rose also.

It would, however, be wrong to treat all lamas as belonging to the class of feudal nobles. Only the higher-ranking lamas belonged to this exploiter-class, of which most of them were members by birth. The great majority of monastery lamas were by origin members of the class of pastoral *arats* and by virtue of their property-owning and legal status did not belong to the class of feudal nobles.

Of course, these ordinary lamas, too, were propagators of feudal ideology. In exchange for this they were given certain privileges as compared with the *arats* and to a certain extent they benefited by the results of the feudal exploitation operated by the monasteries and the upper governing class of lama clergy. This does not, however, imply that, while in many cases they constituted forty or more per cent of the male population of the Mongol *khoshuns*, they belonged to the feudal nobility class.

The ordinary, lower-ranking lamas formed part of the class of *arats*, constituting a special stratum in it. As Academician B. Ya. Vladimirtsov has correctly pointed out, lamas can be subdivided into two groups. "One group comprises the re-incarnated Great Lamas, all closely connected with the class of the Mongol feudal aristocracy, though they did not always necessarily belong to it by birth. The second group includes monks from the ordinary people, the *albatu* and *shabi;* they, of course, do belong to the class of simple, ordinary people."

In an analysis of the problem of the class composition of the clergy in Germany during the Peasant War, Engels wrote: "The clergy was divided into two distinct groups. The feudal hierarchy of the clergy formed the aristocratic group—bishops and archbishops, abbots, priors and other prelates... They not only exploited their subjects as recklessly as the knighthood and the princes, but they practised this in an even more shameful manner." With regard to the plebeian section of the clergy consisting of rural and urban preachers, Engels said that they "were outside the feudal hierarchy of the church and participated in none of its riches... Being of a middle class or plebeian origin, they were nearer to the life of the masses, thus being able to retain middle-class and plebeian sympathies, in spite of their status as clergy."[3]

This definition of the class composition of the clergy can to a certain extent be applied also to the Lamaist priesthood.

As the ideological buttress of the feudal regime, Lamaism played a reactionary role in the history of the Mongol people. It helped to reinforce social oppression and contributed to the loss by Mongolia of its independence.

CHAPTER IV

THE BEGINNING OF THE MANCHU
INVASION

At the end of the XIVth century a Manchu military-feudal state began to take shape in Eastern Asia which, as time went on, played an exclusively negative, reactionary role in the history of the peoples of China, Mongolia, Korea and other countries in Asia which fell victims to the aggressive policy of the Manchu feudal nobles.

The Manchurians or Manchu are one of the numerous southern-Tungus tribes inhabiting the territory of present-day north-eastern China. At the time described the economic activity of these tribes was based on hunting, primitive agriculture and livestock breeding. They were in the initial stage of forming a feudal system of production. The tribal leaders had already become hereditary princes *(beile)*, who fought with one another for predominance, for wild game hunting grounds and pastures and for better conditions of trading. According to the evidence of Chinese sources, there were more than 60 petty Tungus feudal domains inside the borders of Manchuria in the second half of the XVIth century. They were all interested in trading with China to which they sold furs, ginseng root and horses in exchange for the products of Chinese agriculture and handicrafts.

The Manchu tribe dwelt in the southern part of Manchuria. The residence of its prince was situated 135 km east of Mukden at a place called Khetualua. In 1575 Nurkhatsi became prince of the Manchu. Taking advantage of the convenient geographical situation of his princedom, through the territory of which passed the trade routes to China, Nurkhatsi gradually began to subjugate to himself one princedom after another. In 1616 he compelled the princes he had subjugated to acknowledge him as Khan of the Manchu state. This had been preceded by a bitter armed struggle over many years between the rulers of the Tungus princedoms which did not want to be subject to a central Khan authority—to Nurkhatsi—who had secured the throne of the Khan. Mongol feudal nobles whose domains were located in the neighbourhood of the Manchu princedoms also took part in the struggle against Nurkhatsi. According to the sources, in 1598 the Khorchin prince Ongudai, in alliance with the Tungus princedoms of Ula, Deda, Khoifa and others, took up arms against Nurkhatsi but was defeated. Thereafter he abandoned the struggle, entered into an alliance with Nurkhatsi and was the first of the Mongol feudal princes to become related to the family of Nurkhatsi.

The era of Manchu wars of conquest began in 1618 with a campaign against Korea. The formation of a Manchu military-feudal state and its expansionist policy had a most direct bearing on the interests of the Mongol feudal nobles. The Manchu feudal nobles understood that their military successes would not be durable as long as independent Mongol princedoms with a freedom-loving population existed on their right flank. This is why one of the most important tasks of the Manchu feudal lords was to destroy Mongolia's independence.

As regards the Mongol feudal nobles, the overwhelming majority of them could have no interest in supporting the plans of Nurkhatsi and his successors. These plans were even more alien to the masses of Mongolia who could expect from the Manchu state only additional oppression. This is precisely why the final subjection of Mongolia demanded from the Manchu feudal princes an enormous extra effort, more than one and a half centuries of severe struggle and a series of bloody wars.

Taking skilful advantage of feudal disintegration, bribing some Mongol princes, crushing others by force of arms, the Manchu conquerors gradually broke down the resistance of the Mongol people and in the first decades of the XVIIth century subjugated one princedom of southern Mongolia after another. Determined resistance to the aggressive plans of the Manchus was shown by the last Mongol Kagan, Ligdan—the great-grandson of Dayan Khan's eldest son. Ligdan-khan (1604-1634), by showing determined resistance to the aggressive plans of the Manchus, was seeking to centralize in his own hands real authority over the princes subject to him and to create a united independent Mongolia under his own rule. In 1625 he despatched a punitive expedition against the princes of Khorchin, Derbet, Jalat and Gorlos who had been disloyal to him, had betrayed their homeland and gone over to the side of the Manchu conquerors. This punitive expedition did not bring success to Ligdan-khan. The result of his defeat was that a number of south-Mongol princes acknowledged themselves subjects of the Manchus.

Thus, between 1624 and 1635 the princes Aokhan, Naiman, Barin, Jarud, Khorchin, Onnyut, Gorlos, Keshikten and others went over to the side of the Manchu conquerors.

Although the defection of these princedoms greatly weakened Ligdan-khan, he still had considerable forces at his disposal. The Manchu Khan Abakhai (1626-1643), who had replaced the deceased Nurkhatsi, more than once suggested that Ligdan cross over to the side of the Manchu feudal princes and promised him all kinds of benefits in exchange. Ligdan-khan, however, firmly rejected all these proposals.

Entering into alliance with the Ming dynasty of China, Ligdan continued to struggle for the independence of Mongolia against the conquerors. In 1634 a decisive battle was fought between the forces of the Manchu conquerors and the considerably weaker forces of Ligdan-khan, which ended in the latter's defeat. The victors meted out drastic punishment to the recalcitrant enemy: they destroyed the Chakhar khanate, splitting it up into small sections and distributing them to their obedient vassals. Ligdan-khan, with the remnants of his forces, withdrew to Kukunor, where he died shortly afterwards. His son Echzhe carried on the struggle against the conquerors but was soon afterwards captured by them and killed.

The victory over Ligdan-khan brought Abakhai the throne of the Mongol Khan. In 1636, on his orders, all the subject princes of Southern Mongolia were convened and they proclaimed him Khan of Mongolia.

This was basically the end of the first stage in the conquest of Mongolia by the Manchu feudal princes.

It was now the turn of Northern Mongolia, which had been divided up into seven independent princedoms and was consequently called "Khalkain dolon khoshun" (seven *khoshuns* of Khalkha). By the end of the XVIth century three powerful feudal princes had come to the fore in Khalkha—Tushetu Khan, Dzasaitu Khan and Tsetsen Khan; they had made the remaining sovereign princes their subjects and played an important role in the subsequent history of Northern Mongolia.

The feudal nobles of Khalkha took no part in the struggle of the Southern Mongol princedoms against the Manchu conquerors and offered them no help.

Giving no thought to the fate of the country and caring only for their own personal interests they looked on passively while Southern Mongolia was turned into a province of the Manchu Empire. Only one of them, known in history as Tsokto-taiji, entered into an alliance with Ligdan-khan and together with him fought actively against the conquerors.

Tsokto (1580-1637), the youngest son of Bagarai-khoshuchi, the grandson of Gersendze, was a gifted man, a poet, and one of the active partisans of the dissemination of "red cap" Lamaism in Khalkha and of the unification of the country. After being expelled from Khalkha for supporting Ligdan-khan's policy of unifying Mongolia, Tsokto-taiji occupied the region of Kukunor and for a short time became extremely strong but Tsokto-taiji and Ligdan did not succeed in combining their forces because the latter died soon afterwards.

After the death of Ligdan, Tsokto-taiji had the intention of occupying Tibet but was defeated and killed in the region of

Kukunor by the combined forces of the feudal princes of Tibet and Kukunor, who had not become reconciled to the idea of Tsokto-taiji growing stronger.

But after the Manchu feudal princes had meted out severe punishment to the Chakhar khanate and after Abakhai was proclaimed Khan of Mongolia the feudal princes of Khalkha made an attempt to secure their future by establishing "friendly" relations with the conquerors. According to the testimony of the Mongol chronicle *Erdeniin Erikhe,* in the winter of 1636 three Khalkha Khans sent their envoys to Abakhai with an offer of alliance and friendship, in token of which they sent him tribute in the form of eight white horses and one camel. That was still far from an act of submission; the Khalkha feudal lords were acting as independent rulers, voluntarily offering their friendship. Very soon, however, the Manchu conquerors made a categoric demand on the Khalkha Khans to cease supplying the Ming army with horses, threatening, if they disobeyed, to do the same to them as they had done to Ligdan-khan. The Khalkha feudal lords did not risk disobeying and stopped the trading links with China. As time went on, the Manchu rulers intensified still further their interference in the domestic affairs of Khalkha.

In 1640 the Khalkha Khans took part in a congress in Djungaria of Mongol and Oirat sovereign princes, convened on the initiative of the Oirat Batur-Khuntaiji. The purpose of this congress was to regulate the internal mutual relations between the Mongol feudal princes and to create conditions for a united struggle against the Manchu threats.

The death of Abkhai in 1643 and the ascent to the throne of the young Shun Chih (1644-1661) were taken advantage of by Tushetu Khan and Tsetsen Khan with a view to completely liberating themselves from Manchu control. They supported the anti-Manchu action of the Sunnite prince Tengis and sent their troops to help him. This attempt, however, was unsuccessful. Tengis was smashed by the Manchus, and the troops of the Khalkha Khans also suffered defeat.

In 1644 the Manchu conquerors, as a result of the treachery of Chinese feudal nobles, captured Peking, which was the beginning of their domination of China. The position of the Mongol princedoms of Khalkha worsened very considerably as a result. In 1655 the Khans of Khalkha capitulated to the government of the Manchus on the question of the hostages demanded by the Manchus and whom the Khalkha princes for a number of years stubbornly refused to send. In 1655 the hostages demanded were sent to the Bogdikhan Shun Chih.

The Manchu conquerors could not at the time solve the problem of Northern Mongolia by direct military invasion. Their positions in China itself were far from being firmly held and there was no cessation in the active struggle waged by the mass of the Chinese people against the aggressors. Compelled to direct their main forces to overcoming the resistance of the Chinese people, the government of the Manchus temporarily refrained from invading Northern Mongolia, as they calculated they could gain possession of the country by "peaceful" methods.

As a result of the provocative policy followed by the conquerors, the agreement between the Mongol feudal princes concluded in 1640 at the congress in Djungaria was rescinded. Disputes and conflicts broke out again between the Oirat and the Khalkha feudal princes, in the course of which the parties turned for help to the Manchu Bogdikhan, thus intensifying their dependence on the latter. In 1688 warfare broke out again, provoked by the Manchus, between the Oirat feudal princes and the feudal princes of Khalkha. The latter were severely defeated and most of them fled to the South, to the Great Wall, where, at a special congress and on the proposal of the head of the Lamaist church, Undurgegen, a member of the family of Tushetu Khan, they resolved to become subjects of the Manchu (Ching) dynasty. In 1691, at a meeting of all the princes of Southern and Northern Mongolia and in the presence of the Manchu Emperor Kansi, the feudal princedoms of Khalkha were formally included in the Empire of the Manchus. Thus ended the second stage in the conquest of Mongolia by the Manchu feudal princes. The third and last stage of this struggle began and was directed against the Oirat khanate, which had retained its independence.

Little is known of the history of the Oirats from the death of Esen Khan to the end of the XVth- beginning of the XVIth centuries, a period extending over 100-150 years. Of one thing there can be no doubt that, at the time described, this part of Mongolia did not constitute a single unit, but was split up into a large number of independent feudal princedoms, sometimes fighting one another and sometimes uniting together to make attacks on neighbours. The economic and political links between the Oirat feudal princes and China were, during this period, extremely irregular, which explains the absence of information about them in Chinese chronicles. It can be presumed that, as a result of a series of unfavourable cricumstances, the Oirat territories found themselves in a state of protracted crisis which seriously weakened them.

At the end of the XVIth century the process began of uniting the Oirat territories under the rule of the princely house of Choiros. In the course of a prolonged domestic struggle there was a considerable regrouping of the Oirat feudal princes, some of whom left their native camping grounds and emigrated to other places beyond the reach of the Choiros rulers.

At the beginning of the 1620s Kho-Urlyuk, prince of the

Turgouts, left the places that had long been settled and headed towards Russian territory. He took with him more than 50,000 tents, i.e. 200-250,000 people, and with these settled ultimately in the lower reaches of the Volga. In 1635 his example was followed by the princes of the *khoshuns*, headed by Turu-Baikhu (subsequently known as Gushikhan), who also did not wish to be subject to the house of Choiros, whose head Batur-khuntaiji, in 1635 declared himself Khan of all the Oirats. Turu-Baikhu moved his camping grounds south-west to Kukunor. The sites of those who left were occupied by the Oirat feudal nobles who remained behind and who used them to extend their domains.

Batur-khuntaiji became the all-powerful sovereign of the Oirat state. The real strength of his authority is testified to by the fact that from the end of the 1630s the government and local authorities of Russia began to refer to him on all matters, whereas previously they had dealt with individual Oirat princes.

Having consolidated his authority over the Oirat princedoms, Batur-khuntaiji (1634-1654) began to think of extending his influence to the whole of Mongolia. In 1640, on his initiative an all-Mongolian congress of sovereign princes was held which discussed and approved a collection of laws—*Tsaadjin bichig*— the object of which was to put an end to the internecine domestic fighting between the princes, to regulate the mutual relations between them and to unite their efforts to repel the Manchu threat.

After the death of Batur-khuntaiji a struggle arose between his sons for the throne, which in the final count was seized by Galdan (1671-1697). He continued his father's policy in seeking to consolidate and expand peaceful economic and political relations with Russia. Galdan also tried to organize trade links with China. For this purpose he used to dispatch every year to China numerous embassies and trading caravans composed of as many as 3,000 persons. These embassies and caravans carried on extensive trade in China from which they brought out commodities needed by the population, especially tea. But in 1683 Kansi forbade the admission to China of embassies and caravans which exceeded in number 200 persons. Galdan made frequent applications to Kansi requesting him to re-establish trading but Kansi invariably turned down these requests. Relations between the Manchu rulers and Galdan began to become strained. Galdan began to regard as enemies not only the Manchu conquerors but also the Mongol princes who pursued a policy of capitulating to the Manchu court and, betraying their homeland, submitted to the conquerors and went over into their service.

Realizing that in the person of Galdan he had a serious opponent, the Manchu Emperor Kansi made numerous efforts to set the other Mongol feudal nobles against Galdan. In the knowledge that relations between Galdan and Tushetu Khan were unfriendly, Kansi in 1682 sent them both rich gifts and in 1687 awarded Galdan the title of Khan. Ultimately the Manchu conquerors succeeded in provoking a war between the Oirat and Khalkha states in 1688, which ended with the defeat of the Khalkha princes and their becoming subjects of the Manchus.

After defeating his Khalkha enemies, Galdan, at the end of the same year 1688, again sent envoys to Kansi with an offer of peace. His peace terms were, first, the establishment of normal trading relations, second, the surrender to him of Tushetu Khan and Undurgegen whom he considered to bear the blame for the war and to be his principal enemies. But the Manchu dynasty was not interested in peace with Galdan. Kansi felt that the circumstances were favourable enough for him to capture with one blow both Khalkha and the Oirat khanate. Accordingly, Galdan's efforts to negotiate peace were not crowned with success.

The military operations continued. A large and well-armed Manchu army took the field against Galdan. Under the pressure of the enemy's superior forces Galdan was forced to begin a retreat. In 1696 he suffered a defeat and within a year died.

The consequence of Galdan's defeat was the final subjection of Khalkha to the Manchu dynasty.

CHAPTER V

RELATIONS BETWEEN RUSSIA AND MONGOLIA
IN THE XVIIth CENTURY

At the end of the XVIth century large numbers of Russian migrants moved into the spacious territories of Siberia and the Far East, which at that time were inhabited by a great many petty tribes and nationalities at various states of the process of decay of the primitive-commune structure and the formation of feudalism, and were engaged in hunting, primitive agriculture and nomadic livestock-breeding. The migration of Russians to Siberia and the Far East coincided in time with the formation of the Manchu military-feudal state. But, whereas the policy of the Manchu rulers towards Mongolia and China was highly aggressive and predatory, the policy of the Russian state, by virtue of the special characteristics of its international and domestic situation at that time, was a policy of peace and peaceful trade vis-à-vis those countries.

Situated between the empire of the Manchus and tsarist Russia, Mongolia could not help being affected by the conflicting policies pursued by Russia and the Manchus. The existence of these conflicts lightened the weight on the Mongol people of the struggle for its independence against the Manchu conquerors, since this struggle, objectively speaking, met with support from Russia, which had no interest in seeing Mongolia annexed by the Manchus.

In this way conditions began to form for the development of friendship between the Mongol and Russian peoples, and the reinforcement and development of these conditions could not, as we shall see below, be blocked either by the corrupt and mercenary Mongol feudal nobles or by Russian tsarism with its avaricious officials and rapacious merchants.

According to the evidence of sources, Russian settlers first encountered the Mongol nomads in 1605-1606. From then onwards relations between the Mongol princedoms and the Russian state began to assume a more and more regular character. In 1608 the first Russian embassy went to Mongolia and in the same year an embassy from Mongolia arrived in Moscow. As time went on, exchanges of embassies between the Mongol princedoms and Russia became more and more frequent, reflecting the growth in economic and political links between them.

The first people to come into contact with Russia were the

Oirat feudal nobles, as well as the feudal princedom of Khalkha, ruled by Shola Ubashi-khuntaiji, which was located in the area of Lake Ubsa-nur and known in Russian sources as the state of Altan Khan.

The problems which were raided by the parties during negotiations boiled down, in the main, to the following. The Mongol feudal princes appealed for assistance in the struggle against one or other Mongol prince who had become the appellant's enemy, they wanted trading privileges, they insisted on their right to collect tribute from the tribes and nationalities of Southern Siberia and the Altai which had previously been their subjects, they asked for specialists in one trade or another to be sent to them and they complained of insults from local Siberian governors and the Russian Cossacks. In their turn, the Russian authorities took up with the sovereign princes of Mongolia the questions of improving conditions for transit into China, expanding Russo-Mongolian trade, ending the practice of illegally collecting tribute from subjects of the Russian state, punishing those Mongol princes who breached the peace in the frontier region and made attacks on peaceful Russian towns and villages.

While the Manchu conquerors were interested in intensifying the feudal disintegration of Mongolia, which would have made it easier for them to conquer the country, the Russian state, on the other hand, was interested in strengthening a central Mongol authority capable of preventing the armed raids on the Russian lands which were from time to time undertaken by individual local princelings, and also capable of resisting Manchu aggression.

The desires of the Mongol feudal nobles to develop trade with Russia met with support from the latter. This explains the almost complete absence in the sources of references to disputes or conflicts in matters of trade. In 1647 Batur-khuntaiji received from the Russian Tsar Alexei Mikhailovich a charter granting his subjects the right to trade without payment of duty in the towns of Siberia. The Mongol princedoms successfully sold to Russia horses, cattle, sheep, furs, rhubarb, etc., receiving from the Russian merchants in exchange for their goods different kinds of fabrics, leather, articles made from metal, etc. Sources state that in the course of 1653 alone five caravans of Oirat merchants arrived in Tomsk; a special site was allocated in the town area for trading with the Oirat merchants. Later on, the Oirat khanate was permitted to drive horses through Astrakhan for sale to Moscow.

According to the evidence of the Russian envoy, Spafari, who travelled in the 1670s through Mongolia to China, lively trading was going on in the region of Lake Yamishev. He wrote that "hither come many thousands of people, Kalmyks and

Bokharans and Tartars and they trade with the Russian people." A similar picture was observed in other towns of Siberia whither Mongol caravans of several hundreds of camels often came.

In the 1640s Russian migrants appeared for the first time in Transbaikalia where they entered into relations with the Mongols. Here, as in other frontier regions also, peaceful trading relations were formed between Mongols and Russians and began to grow stronger. Spafari testifies that in the Selenginsk region "the Mongols wander around everywhere and trade with the Cossacks: they sell horses and camels and cattle, as well as all kinds of Chinese goods and buy from them sables and many other Russian goods".

The same picture could also be observed in other towns of Siberia where Mongol caravans of several hundred camels often came.

As they were finding themselves more and more exposed to pressure from the Manchu dynasty, the feudal lords of Khalkha more than once raised with Moscow the question of assuming Russian citizenship. Negotiations on the subject were conducted in Urga in 1665 by the Russian envoy V. Bubennoy and in 1666 by P. Kulivinsky; in 1675 the same question was brought up in Moscow by the envoys of Khalkha.

The Manchu dynasty was alarmed at the development of Russo-Mongolian relations, regarding them as a serious threat to its aggressive plans. It increased pressure on the Khalkha feudal nobles, inciting them to intrigues, provoking conflicts between them, egging them on against the Russians and encouraging them to make attacks on Russian villages and towns.

In the 1680s Tushetu Khan, at the instigation of the Manchus, twice carried out armed attacks on the Russian town of Selenginsk which had been founded in 1666.

Such conflicts, however, were not characteristic of the relations between Russia and Mongolia. The basic feature of these relations was the expansion of peaceful trading in the interests of both countries.

Good neighbourly relations between Russia and Mongolia were a factor which made it easier for the Mongol people to struggle against Manchu aggression.

The Khalkha feudal nobles wavered between the Manchu conquerors and Russia. The government of Russia, however, was not anxious to intervene actively either in the internal struggles of Mongolia or its relations with the Manchu dynasty; the Russian government did not have adequate forces in Siberia and the Far East for an active policy of this kind. The Khalkha feudal lords, incapable of coping with the domestic struggle which was weakening them, slipped into capitulation to the Manchus.

CHAPTER VI

THE CULTURE OF THE MONGOLS
IN THE XV-XVIIth CENTURIES

The aggressive policy of the Mongol Empire exercised a baneful influence on the condition of the country's culture. The feudal disintegration and the internecine warfare which followed upon the collapse of the Yuan dynasty seriously disturbed the normal course of cultural development among the Mongols. As a result, however, of the efforts and the creative energy of the Mongol people the cultural development of the country was not arrested even during this period.

In the period under description oral works of folk art continued to develop: many epic compositions were created which reflected the ideals of the simple nomads. Heroes of the epic tales fought against characters personifying the evil element. The enemies of the heroes appear either as mythical *manguses* or as quite real khans. The *manguses* and the khans, moreover, are endowed with many undesirable characteristics. They are distinguished by their malice, their brutality and their predilection for predatory and devastating warfare. The epics invariably end with the victory of the positive heroes and the defeat and destruction of the forces hostile to the people.

The tradition of literacy was not interrupted even during the period of feudal disintegration and was jealously guarded mainly by the masses of the people. Private schools were operated in the homes of individual scholars, and these played an important part in maintaining and spreading literacy amongst the population. Information on private schools is supplied by Syao Da-syan, who at the beginning of the XVIIth century visited the southern part of Mongolia: "...the man who knows how to read and write is called *bagsh* (teacher) and he who is learning to read and write is called a *shav* (pupil). When a pupil begins to learn reading and writing with a teacher, he makes him a bow and brings him as a present a sheep and *arkhi* (a kind of drink). After (he) has learnt the lesson, he expresses his gratitude to the teacher by offering him as a present one horse and a white *deli* (cloak). The *deli* may be of linen or silk. It depends on whether the (pupil) is rich or poor and the number of gifts is not fixed."[1]

Literary work among the Mongols begins to be pursued more actively towards the end of the XVIth and the beginning of the XVIIth century. This coincided with the approach of a period when feudal warfare in Mongolia slackened and also when the Mongols adopted the new religion of Lamaism. This is also the period when such literary compositions appeared as *the History of Ubashi-khuntaiji and His Wars with the Oirats*, the verses of Tsogtutaiji, the Oirat epic *Jangar, The Legend of Mandukhaisetsen khatun* and the *Ode in Praise of the Six Tumens of the Mongols of Dayan Khan*. The last two works have come down to us in the form in which they were recorded in the chronicles of the XVIIth century (*Sharatudji*), *Erdniin Erkh* of Sagan-Setsen *(Altan tovch)*. The *History of Ubashi-khuntaiji* is not a production of feudal literature but represents the record and literary elaboration of an oral legend and it marked the rebirth of a literature and the continuation of traditions which had been lost in the post-Yuan period.

The poetry of Tsokto-taiji, an eminent political figure, scholar and poet of the first half of the XVIIth century, was a continuation and development of traditions. The verses of Tsokto-taiji, carved on a cliff by his comrades Guen-bator and Daichin-khia, represent an example of Mongolian lyricism of the XVIIth century.

It is interesting to note that the *History of Ubashi-khuntaiji*, which comes from the popular sphere, shows no traces whatever of the influence of Lamaism, which had by that time become the ideology of the Mongol feudal nobles. In the poetry, however, of Tsokto-taiji, who came from the class of feudal nobles, the influence of Buddhism is obvious.

Notable changes also occurred in the XVIIth century in Mongolian historigraphy. Mongol historians compiled a number of important works. The most interesting are *Altan tovch* ("The Golden Button") by an anonymous author, *Shar tuuj* ("The Yellow History"), *Altan tovch* of Luvsandanzan, *Erdniin tovch* ("The Precious Button") of Sagan-Setsen (born in 1604). The authors of these chronicles follow, in the main, the ancient Mongolian historical tradition which can be called the tradition of the *Sacred Legend*.

The basic data about the ancient history of Mongolia contained in these works recall in many respects the early Mongolian historical works. The XVIIth century chronicles, more especially the *Altan tovch* of Luvsandanzan and the *Erdniin tovch* of Sagan-Setsen, are couched in an epic style. The authors of these compositions often resorted to the devices of reproducing a historical picture in artistic and emotional terms. The other distinguishing feature of the historical compositions of the XVIIth century, testifying to a new period in Mongolian historiography, is the strengthening of the Buddhist influence. In spite of the Buddhist veneer, the Mongolian chronicles of the XVIIth century are valuable sources containing a very rich store of factual material on the history of the Mongol people.

In addition, they are very fine specimens of literary memorials testifying to the artistic mastery of their authors. At that time, in particular, no distinction was made between the historical and the fictional. In writing history the Mongolian authors attached great importance to describing historical events in an artistic and epic form and in their works of fiction they were attracted by subjects of a historical and legendary nature. In these circumstances many of the historical compositions of this period contained valuable examples of the artistic creativeness of the Mongolian authors. The chroniclers of this period were, at one and the same time, also fine writers and poets. One example is Sagan-Setsen from Ordos. He came from an old Mongol aristocratic family tracing back its descent to the "golden family" of the Genghis gens. His greatgrandfather was the famous Khutaktai-Setsen Khuntaiji (1540-1586), who was not only an important politician but also one of the cultured people of his time famed as a connoisseur of literature. In 1570 Khutaktai-Setsen edited the *Tsagaan Tuukh* ("White History"). Sagan-Setsen inherited from his greatgrandfather not only his title of Setsen khun-taiji but he was also able to obtain a good education. He was not only a great historian but also a talented poet. His extensive colophon *Erdniin tovch* contains poems consisting, as he himself says of 79 stanzas (*shuleg*), in 316 lines (*badag*) *(guchin arvany deer derev derven badag, doolon arvan gurvan shuleg)*. These poems of Sagan-Setsen are of great interest for the study of Mongolian verse composition in the XVIIth century. It should be noted that he wrote his colophon under the noticeable influence of the poetical devices used by Sazha-pandit Gunga-Zhaltsan, taken from his well-known composition *Subashid*, translated into Mongolian as early as the XVIth century.

At the end of the XVIth and the beginning of the XVIIth centuries considerable changes occur in written Mongolian in connexion with the revival in cultural life, changes which tell of a new period in its development. The feature of this new period of the written Mongolian language is that "old words and forms that have become unintelligible are descarded, wide access is opened up to popular dialect elements which are artificially archaized, borrowings from Tibetan penetrate the language... a new form of Uighur script is established and new letters invented—a real Mongolian script emerges; up to that time, the end of the XVIth century, the Mongols can be said to have employed Uighur letters."[2] The result of all this was to produce a language which can be called a "classical" written language.[3]

From the end of the XVIth and beginning of the XVIIth century the Tibetan language began to play an essential part in education and in the literary activity of the Mongols. A knowledge of Tibetan, as well as of other subjects, was considered to be an indispensable part of Buddhist education in Mongolia. This language begins to emerge in all the wealth of its great literature as a strong competitor of written Mongolian.

In the XVIIth century, however, the Tibetan language had still not won the commanding position which it attained in subsequent centuries.

An important new phenomenon in the cultural life of the Mongols in the XVI-XVIIth centuries was the establishment of a monasterial system of teaching in Mongolia. As there were no secular schools in the country, various religious schools were set up in monasteries and it also became a very common practice for Mongols to study in Tibetan monasteries. The Mongolian lama priesthood produced quite a large contingent of clerical-feudal intellectuals who devotedly served the interests of Mongolian feudalism. They included Undur-gegen Zanbazar (1635-1723), Zaya-pandita Luvsanprenlei of Khalkha (1642-1715), and Zaya-pandita the Oirat Namkhaizhamtso (1599-1662) and others.

They were not only leading lamas; they were also important figures in Mongol feudal culture. Undur-gegen was a talented exponent of Buddhist sculpture in Mongolia who has left examples of artistic castings of the XVIIth century. Luvsanprenlei and Namkhaizhamtso were engaged in literary activities. The works of Luvsanprenlei, written in Tibetan, form several volumes. The most important of them is the four-volume composition *Bright Mirror*, which contains valuable material on the history of Mongolia, India and Tibet. His autobiography constitutes a valuable source for the history of Lamaism in Tibet. He also compiled in Mongolian a biography of the Tushetu Khan of Khalkha but it has, unfortunately, not so far been discovered. Zaya-pandita of Oirat, spent most of his time translating Buddhist literature into the Oirat tongue. From the biographical details about Zaya-pandita, compiled by his pupil Randnabadra in 1690, it is clear that Namkhaizhamtso and his school made a translation of a large amount of Buddhist literature (over 200 titles). Some of these have come down to us in Oirat script.

The result of Namkhaizhamtso's philological work was the creation by him in 1648 of a new Oirat alphabet, based on Mongolian script. The alphabet of Zaya-pandita differs from the Mongolian in the tracing of certain letters and the additional diacritic signs which make it possible to convey exactly the sounds of Oirat speech. This is why the alphabet of Zaya-pandita was given by the Mongols the name *Tod bichig* ("Clear writing"). *Tod bichig*, however, was not widely used in Mongolia and even among the Oirats it enjoyed a comparatively short-lived success, as it was unable to hold out against the universal Mongolian alphabet and the Mongolian written language, which at that time had been adopted by all the Mongol peoples.

In connexion with the increased dissemination of Lamaism in Mongolia the translation of Buddhist literature into Mongolian began to occupy a specially prominent place in the literary activities of the Mongols in the XVIth century. In Ligdan-khan's time, and under the leadership of Gung-Odsor, a large group of translators made a translation from Tibetan into Mongolian of the Buddhist *Tripitaka* ("Gunjur"), a collection of ancient Indian Buddhist *sutras* comprising more than 100 volumes.

An idea of the art of this period can be obtained from certain examples, very few in number, which have come down to our day.

The most interesting memorial is the letter sent by the Tumet Altan Khan to the Ming Emperor, in which there is a reference to the despatch by the Tumets of the routine tribute to Peking. The text of the letter refers to the fact that Altan Khan is sending as a present to the Ming Emperor a gold saddle with inlay work, a gold bridle and a gold quiver, indicating that the working of jewellery was developed among the Mongols even in the post-Yuan period.

The letter of Altan Khan consists of a text and a picture, a large composition illustrating the route followed by the embassy bringing the tribute from the camping-grounds of the Tumets to Peking. This picture-map demonstrates the high level attained by the Mongols in painting at the end of the XVIIth century. The style of the drawing shows the influence of Chinese painters but, at the same time, the drawing is in many respects an original piece of work. The realistic way in which Altan Khan, his wife and retainers, also the riders and horsemen, are drawn, is particularly striking.

It is interesting to observe the very fine details in a number of places. The tracery of a bridge with seven arches, a wall with defensive bastions and the walls of the towns passed by the envoys bearing the tribute are carefully portrayed.

The painting is also interesting in that it gives a certain idea of the musical culture of the Tumets at the end of the XVIth century. At the spot in the composition which shows the official residence of Altan Khan, the court musicians are depicted. One of them is holding a string instrument, another a percussion instrument.

Another important painting—though, unfortunately, one that has been very badly disfigured by later inscriptions—is one dating to the middle of the XVIth century in the monastery-museum of Erdeni-tsu on the River Orkhon.

Specimens of artistic casting have also come down to our times. It is hard to say when this type of art began. Sources and documents furnish no answer to this question. In the XVIth century artistic casting was very widespread in connexion with the dissemination of Lamaism. Local skilled workers were employed by the lamas for making small images of little copper deities.

Since the Mongols had long been acquainted with forging and jewellery-making, artistic casting was considerably developed. Specimens of Mongolian artistic casting are elegantly shaped and carefully ornamented.

SECTION FIVE

MONGOLIA UNDER THE RULE OF THE MANCHU CONQUERORS (1691-1911)

CHAPTER I

MONGOLIA BECOMES A BORDERLAND
OF THE MANCHU EMPIRE

The defeat of the Mongols in the struggle against the Manchu conquerors resulted in the country losing its political independence. Mongolia became a borderland of the Manchu Empire, which had its base in China—finally conquered by the Manchu Khans by 1683.

The Manchu dynasty endeavoured to intensify the feudal disintegration of Mongolia and to avert the possibility of unification of the Mongol princedoms; it was afraid that the struggle of the Mongol people, a spontaneous, uncoordinated one, might, if unification succeeded, result in their emancipation. In order to consolidate their mastery of Mongolia and keep it economically and culturally backward, the Manchu conquerors followed the policy of isolating the Mongol from the Chinese and Russian peoples.

The Manchu Emperor proclaimed himself the *bogdikhan* of Mongolia and declared all its lands to be his property. The Manchu government extended its legislation to cover Mongolia. The so-called *Code of the Chamber of Foreign Relations* (published in 1789 and 1815) included a special section on the Mongols. The Manchu Emperors made the Mongol feudal nobles their vassals, arrogating to themselves the right to award the Mongol princes titles and ranks, to dismiss them from posts, to hand over to or take from them feudal domains.

The Chamber of Foreign Relations played a considerable role in the complex Manchu military-feudal bureaucratic system of administration. Set up to administer Mongolia and other borderlands, it began to handle all their affairs. In the case of Mongolia the Chamber of Foreign Relations was given the right to select candidates for appointment as imperial viceroys *(chang-chung)*, to staff their administrative apparatus, and to select candidates for the presidencies of the *aimak* assemblies and the *khoshun* governors or *dzasaks*.

The *chang-chung* was directly subordinate to the Chamber,

which was invested with military, administrative and political control over Mongolia and which it implemented through military and civilian assistants—*ambans* and *hupei-ambans*.

The Ching government abolished the rule of the Mongol khans in the *aimaks* but it retained the *aimakin chuulgan*—diets of the *khoshun dzasaks (aymagyn chuulgan)*. But the diets and their participants (*chuulgan darga*) were deprived of their independence and acted principally as intermediaries between the Manchu authorities and the Mongol *khoshun dzasaks*. The *aimak* diets had no real significance, especially as they were allowed to convene not oftener than once in three years, in specific places and, without fail, in the presence and under the observation of the *chang-chung* or his deputies.

The old division of Mongolia into *uluchi, tumens* and *otoki* was abolished and a single uniform system introduced under which the whole of Mongolia was divided up into *khoshuns*; the territorial borders of each *khoshun* and the *dzasak* for each *khoshun* were approved by the *bogdikhan*. The *khoshun dzasak* was given the right to deal with military, administrative and judicial matters within the borders of his *khoshun* or domain. He determined the borders of the *somons, bags* and *arbans* (tenths), appointed and dismissed their chiefs, regulated the use of the grazing grounds, and disposed of the *arat* serfs who were registered in his *khoshun*.

Although the authority of the *khoshun dzasaks* was recognized as hereditary, the Emperor Kansi, when he introduced the *khoshun* system, reviewed the hereditary rights of all the Mongol princes and their feudal domains and confirmed a specific number of princes as hereditary proprietors of the *khoshuns*. In so doing the Manchu Khan gave, as it were, title to the lands back again to the Mongol princes. The Manchu government made it a practice to suborn the Mongol princes as one way of holding them in subjection. This system expressed itself in different forms. Awards of new and higher titles and ranks or appointments to new positions, etc. were conditional on the degree of loyalty and submissiveness of the Mongol feudal nobles to the Manchu dynasty.

The Manchu government abolished the old Mongol titles and ranks and introduced Manchu and Chinese feudal ranks. These latter were laid down later on in the *Mongol Code*. In order of importance the princely ranks were subdivided as follows: *ching-wan, chung-wan, beylei, beysei, tusze-gung*, and *gung*. The majority of feudal nobles who were not landowners were given the rank of *taiji*. For princes who married princesses of the imperial house the rank of *tabunan* or *efu* was introduced. In the case of former *aimak* khans the title of khan was retained but in other respects they were placed on an equal footing with the *khoshun dzasaks*.

In 1733 the amount of salary payable to the princes of Mongolia was also defined. The higher the rank, the greater the salary the Mongol princes received. For instance, princes of the first grade, *ching-wans*, each received 2,000 *lan* in silver and 25 pieces of woven material per annum; princes of the sixth degree, *gungs*, received annually 200 *lan* and 7 pieces of material each.

In 1691, by an edict of the Emperor Kansi it was decided to bond *arat* families to landowning and non-landowning princes. The bonded *arats* were called *khamjilga*. Princes of the first degree were given 60 families and *taiji* of the fourth degree 4 families of *khamjilga*. At the same time the Manchu government fixed a salary for all *taiji*, depending on their degree, at 40—100 *lan* and 4 pieces of woven material each.

In addition to salary payments provision was made in the *Mongol Code* for presents to be given for various reasons by the Emperor to Mongol princes. For example the Mongol *aimak* khans and the Bogdo-gegen, when they offered tribute to the Emperor, were each given 25 pieces of silk and 15 pieces of cotton fabrics, and gold, silver and porcelain dishes. High-ranking princes were given the right to wear the same ceremonial dress and marks of distinction as were worn by the dignitaries of the Manchu court.

One of the methods used to link the Mongol princes closely with the Manchu dynasty was to give Manchu princesses in marriage to Mongol princes and, similarly, to marry Manchu dignitaries to the daughters of Mongol princes. In particular, the Emperor Szung-chih (1644-1661) was married to a Mongol princess. By means of all these sops and honours the Manchu *bogdikhans* gained influence over a considerable section of the Mongol feudal aristocracy which, for the sake of its mercenary class interests, betrayed the interests of the Mongol people and supported the domination of Mongolia by alien oppressors.

Depending on circumstances, the Manchu government sometimes extended and sometimes curtailed the rights and privileges of the Mongol *khoshun* princes by a combination of threats and promises. Relying entirely on the class of Mongol feudal nobles, the Manchu dynasty at the same time pursued a policy of disuniting these nobles in order to forestall the possibility of their taking joint action against the Manchu government.

Even under Manchu rule the Mongol princes continued to fight one another for feudal domains and for power in Mongolia. This no longer meant armed conflicts between the hostile feudal nobles but complaints against, and denunciations of, one another to the Manchu government. Mediation in the settlement of disputes between Mongol feudal nobles undoubtedly helped to strengthen the authority of the Manchu dynasty over Mongolia and to increase the dependence of the Mongol feudal nobles on the Manchu government.

In order to consolidate their authority the Manchu government recast the system of administrative and military organization in Mongolia. The aim here was to try to intensify feudal disintegration in Mongolia. For example, on the territory of Khalkha four *aimaks* were created instead of three. The fourth was formed in 1725 and consisted of 19 *khoshuns* taken from the *aimak* of Tushetu Khan. The new *aimak* was given the name of Sain-noyon-khan to correspond to the title of one Mongol prince who had done good service to the Manchu Emperor in wars against the Oirats.

The three former *aimaks* retained their old names: Tsetsen Khan, Tushetu Khan and Dzasaktu Khan. The number of *khoshuns* was constantly being increased by the Manchu government. In 1655 there were 8 in Khalkha and by 1725 the number was 74. Khalkha was split up in such a way that for each feudal domain—*khoshun* there were, on an average, not more than two *somons*. A special Manchu viceroy *(chang-chung)* was vested with the control and supervision of Khalkha, with a permanent residence at Ulyasutai—a Manchu military fortress in Khalkha.

The Manchu government turned the whole of the able-bodied Mongol population into soldiery for the *khoshun* armies. The landowning (sovereign) princes—*dzasaks*—were vested with the powers of army commanders. In the military sense the *khoshun*—"banner" was the basic military unit (about a division) and the *khoshun* prince was appointed commander. The *khoshun* was divided into *somons* (squadrons); several *khoshuns* (divisions) made up an *aimak* (corps). Though it represented a military organization, the *khoshun* continued to be the basic administrative unit and the feudal domain attached to one or other landowning (sovereign) Mongol prince.

The *khoshun dzasaks* of Khalkha were under obligation to assemble their troops annually for review. It should be noted that, though they set up an army consisting of Mongols, the Manchu government did not supply it with firearms, which were already supplied to the Manchu army, as they were afraid of the Mongols becoming stronger militarily. The Mongol soldiers continued to have, as before, only lances and bows.

The Manchu government made the Khalkha Mongols responsible for doing guard duty on the northern frontiers of their Empire.

In 1697, after the defeat of the Oirat-Mongol troops by the Manchu army and the withdrawal of those troops from Khalkha into the realm of the Oirat-Mongol khanate, Kansi sent back to Khalkha all the princes who had fled into Inner Mongolia in 1688 to escape from the invasion of Galdan Khan. He also suggested that the Khalkha Mongols who had fled at that time from Khalkha to Russia should return. Many of them, however, did not comply with his order. They had been given a friendly reception by the Russian and Buryat population of Transbaikalia and granted the use of grazing grounds, so they refused to return and adopted Russian citizenship.

Subsequently migrations by Mongols into Transbaikalia and Southern Siberia from Barga, Khalkha, Shin'sian and the district of Kobdo were fairly frequent. Among these who migrated to Russia from Khalkha was Prince Andakhai, with a thousand families of his subjects. His son Amor, who became a Russian interpreter (*tolmach*) was a participant in the negotiations between the Russian envoy Savva Raguzinski and the Manchu envoy when they concluded the Kyakhta Treaty in 1727.

After the meeting of the Dolon Nor diet, the Mongol princes in Khalkha tried for some time longer to pursue an independent policy. But in 1721 the Manchu Emperor restricted their rights to engage in any kind of direct negotiations with foreign states.

The domestic policy of the Mongol princes of Khalkha was decided by the laws adopted at the congresses held between 1709 and 1770 known as *Khalkha Jirum*. This code of laws consolidated the privileges of the feudal nobles, temporal and spiritual.

Even before Mongolia lost its political independence the khans of Khalkha were, from 1634 onwards, offering to the treasury of the Manchu khans, in the form of presents, the tribute of "nine white animals."[1] In the years of Khalkha's independence this tribute was a special diplomatic procedure observed in relations with the Manchu khans. As time went on, the Manchu khans made the Mongol "gifts" into a compulsory and burdensome tribute. After 1655, in accordance with an imperial edict, there was introduced, in addition to the annual tribute of the "nine whites" paid on behalf of the khans of Khalkha, a levy "on capital" imposed on all the other princes of Khalkha. The Manchu dynasty levied tribute in these two forms until the end of its rule. The "nine whites" tribute no longer represented a mere symbolic value; it included valuable furs, the hides of animals, the best domestic animals, principally horses, and also different kinds of valuables.

In order to deliver the tribute of the "nine whites" to Peking an embassy was constituted from eminent princes headed by the khans. This tribute was offered on solemn holidays to the *bogdikhan* himself on bended knees as a sign of submission. The levy "on capital" was presented in Peking by all the Mongol princes but this was done in turn and was handed over to any one of the Manchu dignitaries to be passed on to the imperial treasury. This tribute was levied on various pretexts including the occasion of a prince being confirmed in his post as *dzasak* or being raised to a new rank.

Popular Anti-Manchu Revolts in Outer Mongolia

In their long struggle against the Manchu conquerors the Mongols suffered defeat principally because of feudal disintegration and the perfidious policy of the higher ranks of the Lamaist priesthood. The Mongol people, nevertheless, continued to resist the oppressors even after the conquest of Mongolia by the Manchus.

After the death of Galdan the Djungarian state continued to exist, representing the last stronghold of the struggle against the Manchu conquerors. The Djungarian khans, Tsevan-Ravdan (1697-1727) and Galdan-Tseren (1727-1748), carried on an active policy of strengthening their positions in Kukunor and Tibet and also endeavoured to unite with the Khalkha princes in operations against the Manchus. In 1730 Oirat troops penetrated into Khalkha and, with the active support of the Khalkhans themselves, occupied its northern section. The Manchus, however, succeeded in driving the Oirat detachments out of Khalkha territory with the help of leading Mongol feudal nobles.

The rigorous occupation regime instituted by the Manchu troops and the systematic despoliation of the people by the Manchu usurpers aroused the deep indignation of the population and this erupted in 1755-1758 in a major popular uprising. Command of the uprising was taken over by the Oirat-Mongol Prince, Amursana, who had formerly been in the service of the Manchu government, had then broken with it and gone over to the side of the rebels. At first the rebellion of the Oirat Mongols developed successfully and they managed to defeat and annihilate the Manchu garrisons in Western Mongolia. However, the Manchu government sent a large army to put down the rebellion, the detachments of the rebels were defeated in bloody battles, and the Djungarian khanate was liquidated. Amursana fled to Russia.

After his flight individual detachments of the rebels still carried on the struggle until they were completely overthrown by the Manchu troops. The greater part of the Oirat population of Djungaria was massacred by Manchu punitive expeditions. Simultaneously with the rebellion of the Oirat-Mongols, precisely in 1755-1758, a major anti-Manchu movement began in Khalkha under the leadership of the Khotogoit Prince Chingunjav. Chingunjav formed rebel detachments which for a long time operated against the Manchu troops on the borders of Western Mongolia, helping the Oirat-Mongols to fight the

Manchu army. During this rebellion the *arats* of the *aimaks* of Dzasaktu Khan and Sanin-noyon Khan drove their herds deep into the steppes and ceased performing frontier-patrol duties and discharging *urton* servitudes, thus considerably hampering the operations of the Manchu punitive army against the Oirat-Mongols, and at the same time creating a certain threat to Manchu supremacy in Khalkha.

The brutal repressions and terror inflicted by the Manchu government on the population of Khalkha, the destruction of hundreds of *arats* and the execution of Chingunjav, who had been captured, aroused a new wave of indignation among the *arat* population of Khalkha. The liberation movement in Khalkha began to assume mass proportions; it was joined by many important feudal nobles who cherished anti-Manchu sentiments, among them Dzasaktu Khan Balzhir and Second *Khutukhta* of Urga, whose brother, Rinchindorzh, was captured and executed by the Manchus for having allied himself with Amursana. Acting on behalf of the Second *Khutukhta* of Urga, the Manchu government mobilized lama preachers to agitate for the cessation of the rebellion, convened an extraordinary diet of the *dzasaks* of Khalkha, and sent large armed forces into Khalkha. The rebellion was supressed.

Realising the enormous influence exercised by the Second *Khutukhta* over the population, the Manchu rulers did not dare to blame him openly for the obvious anti-Manchu stand he had taken during the Chingunjav movement; on the contrary, they preferred to win him over to their side by generous rewards and bribes. The Manchu Emperor gave the Second *Khutukhta* a golden seal, a charter and the title of "Benefactor of Animated Beings," but shortly after this the Second *Khutukhta* died suddenly. There is every ground for assuming that he was put to death by the Manchus.

The Manchu authorities rewarded the feudal nobles, religious and secular, who had helped the Manchu dynasty to suppress the uprisings in Khalkha and Western Mongolia, with various titles of honour. One of the princes of Khalkha, Tseren, at a time when very severe fighting was raging between the Manchu army and the Oirat-Mongols, forcibly mobilized the Mongols of Khalkha, formed punitive detachments and took the field with them on the side of the Manchu conquerors against the Oirat-Mongols. Tseren helped the Manchus to smash the Oirat-Mongols and, in return for his treachery and humble obeisance, was given by the Manchu government several degrees of promotion. In addition, he was given in marriage the daughter of the *bogdikhan*, which brought with it the rank of son-in-law of the Emperor—*efu*.

These and many similar facts of feudal nobles participating in the suppression of *arat* rebellions against the Manchus vividly testify to the treachery perpetrated by the feudal classes and to their betrayal of the interests of the Mongol people for the sake of their class advantages and privileges.

Shortly after the suppression of the rebellions of 1755-1758 the Manchu government completed the reorganization of the military and administrative system of Mongolia. A special district of Kobdo was set up in the northern part of the former Oirat-Mongol (Djungarian) khanate—in the neighbourhood of Khalkha. The Manchu dynasty instituted a dual control over the inhabitants of this district. In the Manchu fortress of Kobdo the Peking government appointed its plenipotentiary *(chan'-chan-dachen)* to exercise control over the population of the district and made the *chang-chung* of Khalkha responsible for supervising this plenipotentiary. In the frontier zone of Khalkha bordering on Russia the Manchu government created a special zone a little over 30 miles wide. The length of this zone between the frontier points of Abagaitu (on the east) and Shabin-Dabaga (on the west) amounted to more than 1,300 miles. Here the Manchus posted 87 Mongol border garrison patrols.

Service in this frontier zone was imposed on the *arat* population of Khalkha and the Kobdo district as a military servitude. Each patrol was composed of several "tenths" of *arats* under the command of Mongol chiefs but under the control and supervision of Manchu officers. In order to perform patrol service the Mongol *arat-tsiriks* had to migrate into the frontier zone, usually along with their families. The patrol servitude was one of the most onerous forms of the Manchu yoke.

The Lamaist Church Subservient to the Manchu Usurpers

Having asserted their supremacy in Mongolia, the Manchu conquerors realised the enormous influence of Lamaism and endeavoured to make use of the Lamaist church to divert the people from combating the alien yoke and feudal oppression.

The Lamaist church itself, headed by priests from the feudal classes, was, in its capacity as a feudal institution, no less interested in stifling the political consciousness of the labouring classes. During the rule of the Manchu the position of the Lamaist monasteries as feudal fiefs became stronger and stronger, the size of their landed properties increased and the number of serf-*shabinars* registered with them was multiplied. With the increase in the economic power of the monasteries the political influence of the higher ranks of the feudal church nobles increased also. Among the numerous lamas, who were divided into ranks and degrees, a special role was played by the *Chubil Khans* ("the re-incarnated"), who were at the head of the whole

Lamaist hierarchy. By social origin they belonged as a rule to the upper classes of the feudal nobles. They became abbots of the monasteries and were the feudal masters of the hundreds and thousands of *arat* serf-*shabinars* bonded to the monasteries. The *Chubil Khans*, who were considered by Lamaist believers to be "living gods" and enjoyed undisputed influence, were very sedulously cultivated by the Manchu Emperors.

In 1641 Gombo-Dordji, the son of the most important feudal noble of Khalkha, Tushetu Khan, was proclaimed *Chubil Khan* and head of the Lamaist church in Mongolia under the name of Undur-gegen (1635-1724). On the insistence of this *Chubil Khan* the great majority of the princes of Khalkha agreed to accept Manchu citizenship at the congress in Dolon Nor in 1691.

The Manchu Emperors maintained the Urga *khutukhtas* in their leading position amongst the Lamaist priests of Mongolia. The Manchu government paid them the same amount of salary as the Mongol khans. The Emperors often invited the Urga and other *khutukhtas* to Peking and entertained them with feasts in an endeavour to make them active champions of their policy in Mongolia.

The Urga *khutukhtas* proved themselves willing tools in the hands of the Manchu government and headed the reactionary anti-popular forces in Mongolia.

Under Manchu rule the position of the Lamaist church became so strong that it soon held a leading place among the feudal institutions of Mongolia. This was encouraged by the Manchu government's policy of favouring Lamaism. Not only the senior-ranking lamas but even the whole of the monastery lamas, were exempted from military, transport and other servitudes and from taxes. Lamas were given the right to travel free of charge, using the facilities of the *arat* population, for preaching purposes or for carrying out monastery business.

Feudal church nobles were allowed to judge their own lamas and punish them in accordance with monastery regulations. Many monasteries were subsidised by the Imperial Treasury.

The feudal church nobles became wealthy from the exploitation of the whole *arat* population. The exploitation took various forms, including "voluntary offerings," which were an important source of income for the monasteries and the lamas.

The lamas in higher-ranking posts controlled all the wealth in the monasteries. Lamas were not identical in origin or status. Only the higher-ranking lamas, most of whom came originally from the feudal nobility, belonged to the exploiter class. The bulk of the monastery lamas belonged to the class of pastoral *arats* and did not, as regards property qualification or legal status, belong to the class of the feudal nobility.

The lower-ranking *bandi*-lamas were completely dependent on the higher-ranking lamas but they too led a parasitic form of existence and took no part in socially-useful labour.

The many thousands of lower ranking monastery lamas were recruited mainly from *arats* and were maintained in the main by their own relatives. When an *arat* became a lama he was exempted from all obligations towards his secular *dzasak* or *taiji* and towards the Manchu government. These obligations were transferred to the *albatu-arats*. In order not to be left ultimately without serfs, the secular feudal nobles instituted a procedure which forbade *arats* to become lamas without the permission of the sovereign *khoshun* prince.

The Manchu government also issued an order in the second half of the XVIIIth century under which only lamas permanently resident in monasteries, who had no personal property in the steppe could benefit by exemptions. The total number of monastery lamas must not exceed one-third of the whole body of lamas. The remaining lamas, even though they were listed in the monastery registers, lived in their camping grounds. At the end of the XIXth century, in view of the increase in the number of ordinary lamas, the decrease in the number of *albatu-arats* and the exhaustion of their properties, lamas not permanently resident in monasteries were more and more frequently obliged to perform *urton*, partrolling and other servitudes.

Lamaism diverted a considerable proportion of the male population from productive labour, thus impeding the development of the national economy and holding back the growth of the country's population.

As a result of the enslavement of the *arat* masses and the growth of the economic power of the Lamaist monasteries the reactionary influence of the Lamaist church over the culture and way of life of the Mongols became stronger and stronger.

Utilizing the close relations between the lay population and the monasteries through the ordinary lamas who were family relatives and also through the "teacher"-lamas, the church maintained control over every Mongol family and interfered in the everyday life of the Mongols. It kept a close check on every individual from his birth right up to his death, constantly poisoning his mind with the narcotic of religion.

Under Manchu rule the Lamaist church became the weapon not only for the feudal exploitation of the *arat* population but also for the national oppression of the Mongol people.

CHAPTER II

THE *ARATS* INCREASINGLY EXPLOITED
AS FEUDAL SERFS UNDER MANCHU RULE

Relying on the Mongol feudal nobility, secular and religous, the Manchu conquerors reduced the bulk of the labouring Mongol population of *arat* serfs to a still more under-privileged situation than previously.

The laws of the Manchu government regarding Mongolia, as laid down in the *Mongol Code*, bore a clearly expressed class character. A harsh regime was instituted in the country under which all phases of the life of the Mongol working people were strictly regulated and subjected to control.

The *arats* were absolutely subject to the Manchu and Mongol authorities, the *taiji* and the senior-ranking lamas; they had to ask permission from their prince to move into another *khoshun*. Numerous servitudes and taxes were imposed upon them.

One of the important organs of military-feudal domination and compulsion was the court of law. The Manchu government extended the right of settling cases in the *khoshun* courts to the *khoshun dzasaks* who exercised both administrative and judicial functions. If a death sentence, however, was pronounced, principally in cases affecting the interests of the Manchu dynasty and also in all cases of offences committed by the Mongol feudal nobles themselves, the sentence was referred from lower to higher courts: the second higher court after the *khoshun dzasak* was the president of the *aimak* diet, the third instance was the *chang-chung* and the fourth the Chamber of Foreign Relations and the final instance the *bogdikhan*.

In addition to direct witnesses, large groups of *arats* from the *khoshun* concerned were summoned in turn to the *khoshun* courts to be present invariably during the inquiries, torturings and execution of the court's decisions. This was done in order to frighten the working people.

The principal forms of punishment under the *Code* were: sentence of death, deportation, enslavement, forced labour, *urton* service performed out of turn, corporal punishment, shackling in the stocks, imprisonment and varying fines. The *Code* limited punishment in the case of Mongol aristocrats in the main to fines, temporary loss of salary and, rarely, removal from appointment and loss of title or rank.

The class nature of the *Code* also found expression in the unequal measure of punishment meted out for the same offence.

For example, a prince who killed an *arat* was simply given a fine. The murder by an *arat*, on the other hand, of persons of any class was invariably punished by a sentence of death. Even the types of death sentence were fixed in accordance with the social position of the person killed. The most brutal punishment was appointed for *arats*. Insulting an ordinary person in word or deed was not considered an offence, but, if *arats* insulted "well-born" persons, to their faces or behind their backs, it entailed severe punishment.

Persons of all classes who committed so-called state offences, such as fleeing over the frontier or abetting such flight, were severely punished.

As the *Code* put it "All those who... flee abroad and who show resistance are to be killed without trial". For abetting a flight abroad a prince would be deprived of his title and his serfs taken from him; public officials were put to death by strangling and ordinary people had their heads cut off; the families of those executed were fined eighteen head of cattle in favour of the Manchu treasury.

During the period of Manchu rule, as previously, the practice of stock-breeding was combined, in the case of the *arats*, with various kinds of home handicrafts in each individual household. The *arats* made preserves of meat and milk products; prepared their own felt for covering *yurts* and ropes of hair and thongs, processed leather and sheepskin and sewed clothing and footwear from them. They made framework for *yurts* from wood, as well as chests, two-wheel waggons, saddles, bows, arrows, dishes and other articles of prime necessity for their households.

The *arat* economy continued to be a natural economy. Under the dual oppression Mongol craftsmanship could find no stimulus for further expansion or improvement.

The *arats* had no title to land and were dependent serfs personally of the temporal and spiritual princes. They were forbidden under pain of strict punishment to leave the territory of the *khoshun* voluntarily or to transfer from their own master to another. Within the *khoshun* the *arats* moved camp from one pasture ground to another as ordered by the princes, who were the feudal owners of the land. Land relationships in Mongolia constituted a vivid illustration of the Marxist-Leninist thesis on feudal ownership of land as the basis of feudalism.

Arat serfs were subdivided into *albatu, khamdjilga* and *shabinar.*

The predominant group of serfs was that of the *albatu-arats*, who were bonded to the rich feudal nobles, the *khoshun dzasaks*, and were bound to pay taxes and render services to their *dzasaks* and the Manchu government. During the period of Manchu rule the form of *alba* became more numerous. The basic forms were taxes paid in kind (rent paid in produce) and various kinds of corvée labour (rent paid by statutory labour). Altogether, there were more than 20 kinds of *alba*. As the amount of *alba* increased, the title of ownership of the *albatu-arats* to their property became more and more nominal in character. The rent payable in produce was levied for the upkeep of the *dzasaks* and their families, the *khoshun* officials and *aimak* administrations; for the routine tribute or non-routine "gifts" to the Manchu *bogdikhan;* for the offering of presents and bribes to the *chang-chung* and Manchu officials, who made frequent journeys through Mongolia; for the offering of "sacred gifts" to the Urga and other *khutukhtas* and *Chubil Khans;* for the journeys of princes to Peking and Lhasa, for military expenses, paying the debts of the *dzasaks*, etc.

The corvée labour of the *arat* serfs was utilized in the most widely differing forms. The principal form it took was the work done by *albatu-arats* in turn in the personal properties of the *dzasaks* who owned many thousands of flocks or herds. The whole job of looking after the feudal lord's cattle or livestock was done by the *arats*—including grazing the animals, rearing the young, arranging watering-places, shearing, milking, breaking in horses for riding, slaughtering livestock, laying in fuel, etc. They also dealt with the processing of the products of the feudal lord's stock-breeding economy and, as a rule, used their own tools for the job.

The *albatu-arats* also performed the duties of watchmen, stokers and did other service jobs in *khoshun* and *aimak* administrations, at the residences of princes and the offices of Manchu officials. The Manchu treasury did not expend a single *lan* for this.

The *albatu-arats*, as reservists, were registered with their *khoshun dzasaks* and reported annually at the military musters on their own horses, carrying their own weapons and provisions and were passed in review and given drill training. They had to be in a state of readiness for any campaign required. It was also principally the *albatu-arats* who were called up for service in frontier patrols.

On all the roads of Mongolia which were important as military or administrative lines of communication the *albatu-arats*, by order of the Manchu government, set up road and post stations *(urtons)*, provided them with their own means of transport, with drivers and guides, supplied the travelling Manchu officials, officers, government runners, etc. with accommodation for the night and food free of charge. In Khalkha in the second half of the XVIIIth century there were altogether 120 *urton* stations which had to be serviced by *albatu-arats*. At the end of the XIXth century there were twice as many *urtons*.

Dozens of *urtons* were established also on the internal routes of communication in Mongolia. The *urtons* deprived the *arat* economy of a large number of draught horses, oxen, camels and people for work.

The *albatu-arats* were also charged with transporting Manchu and Mongol officials from one camping-ground to another *(urga ula)* and for putting horses at the disposal of the headquarter offices of the *chang-chung's, ambanas,* etc. and also for *khoshun* and *aimak* administrations *(uya-agta).* As can be seen, the *urton* servitude was a particular form of rent, which combined in itself the elements of corvée rent and rent payable in products.

A still more diverse kind of rent was the rent in kind levied by the Manchu authorities. In addition to the two kinds of tribute laid down by Manchu legislation which have already been referred to, the Manchu government obtained from Mongolia whole herds of horses, large flocks of sheep and other animals, as special offerings from the Mongol princes who collected the livestock from the same *albatu-arats.* Quite a lot of valuables were exported from Mongolia to Peking to pay for the numerous fines imposed by the Chamber of Foreign Relations on the Mongol population.

According to documents in the state archives of the MPR relating to the XVIIIth century, the princes and the Urga *Khutukhtas* collected annually from the *albatu-arats* and sent to Peking, over and above the fixed tribute and in response to special demands by the Emperor, tens of thousands of head of livestock and different items of value: furs, felt, *yurts,* jewellery articles made by local craftsmen, etc., for all of which the *arats* received nothing from either the Manchu government of from the Mongol feudal lords.

The extent of extraordinary levies of this kind, according to data that are far from complete, can be gathered from the following individual examples. For the years 1715-1733 the princes of Khalkha presented on behalf of the four *aimaks* of Khalkha for the Imperial army: 222,000 horses, 25,000 camels, 400 head of cattle, 1,430,000 sheep and more than 238,000 goats. In 1753 the princes of Khalkha presented, additionally, 5,700 horses and 1,600 camels. In 1754 the *shabinar* administration of the Urga *Khutukhta* sent 5,000 horses and 350 camels for the army.

In 1819, over and above the "nine whites" tribute and the "tax on capital" the princes of Khalkha and the *Khutukhta* of Urga made offerings of 40,000 head of young cattle of various kinds by collecting 10,000 head of cattle each from the *arats* of each *aimak.* This rich gift was presented to the Manchu Emperor Tsiao-Ching on the occasion of his arrival in Dolon Nor.

According to official figures the principal Manchu servitudes in cash sums amounted to 619,350 *lan* in silver. A single *arat* tax-paying household had to pay more than 35 *lan* per year. In Khalkha-Mongolia there were altogether 21,015 *arat* tax-paying households.

The amount of movable property collected by the Imperial Treasury, mostly from tribute, special presents and fines, received from Mongolia and also from direct looting, in the first years of Manchu rule, is recounted in the evidence supplied by the French missionary, Fr. Gerbillon, a contemporary of Kansi. He claims that in 1696 the Emperor Kansi already possessed—between Kalgan and Peking—230 stud farms, each with 300 mares, all in foal, and 32 large herds of horses. A total of 40,000 head of cattle and 180,000 sheep grazed on Mongol pastures alienated to the Imperial Treasury. Moreover, almost all of the Emperor's cattle were attended and grazed by Mongol *arats* free of charge.

As time went on, in addition to the *bogdikhan's* flocks and herds, the *arats* in Mongolia were despoiled of many thousands of herds of horses for the benefit of the military department of the Manchu government.

The *khamdjilga-arats* were divided into two groups: the first belonged to the *khoshun dzasaks*, while the other was bonded over to the *taiji*. They were in complete subjection to the feudal lords, were obliged to follow them everywhere, to do service in their households, pay the personal debts of their masters, etc. When commodity and money relations began to develop in the country, the feudal nobles started making encroachments on the personal economy of their *khamdjilga* serfs, who displayed increasing opposition.

The *shabinar-arats* ("spiritual pupils" but not monastery novices) constituted a special group of working *arats*. In 1764 when, under the rule of the Manchus, they were officially bonded over to the *Chubil Khans* and the monasteries, this was already a sizable group of the *arat* population. With the consent of the Manchu authorities the *khoshun dzasaks* made many *arats* into "presents," which they offered to the *Khutukhta* of Urga and other *Chubil Khans*. As a result, there came into being a special group of *arat*-serfs who were bound by taxes and servitudes not to the *khoshun dzasaks* or *taiji* but to the higher-ranking lamas, the church feudal nobles.

Feudal exploitation of the *shabinar-arats* was the principal and permanent source of enrichment for the high-ranking monastery lamas. They paid an annual tax in kind, a rent in the form of produce. Furthermore, they were under obligation to graze the monastery livestock and they were also exploited by the church feudal nobles as porters, drovers, handicraftsmen, for building monasteries and other kinds of work. The *shabin-*

ars handed over a large part of their personal funds for the building of monasteries and the upkeep of lamas, for the mass pilgrimages of lamas to Tibet—to Lhasa—for the worship of different "holy ones," for inviting "famous" lamas from Tibet, etc.

Journeys by *Chubil Khans* to Lhasa and Peking cost the *shabinars* hundreds of thousands of *lans*. Thus, the regular journey to Peking of the fifth *Khutukhta* of Urga (1840) cost 50,000 *lan*, apart from the great cost of the gift presented by him to the *bogdikhan*, consisting of 9 "nines" of choice horses, silver foxes, sables, etc.

In 1889 the *Chubil Khan* Zain-gegen, in order to build a palace and travel to Peking, not only fleeced his *shabinars* but even obtained a large loan from Chinese firms. Because Zain-gegen failed to repay the loans of 20,000 *lan* on the due date, the Chinese usurers doubled the amount of the debt, i.e. raised it to 40,000 *lan* and added a further 13,000 *lan* for annual interest. This had all to be paid by the *shabinars*.

Slaves constituted a special, though a numerically small, group of the population. This group was formed in the period described, principally from *arats* sentenced to slavery by the courts. At this time slavery no longer existed as part of the economic structure. In practice the slaves reinforced the ranks of the *khamdjilga-arats* but they were even more underprivileged and oppressed.

The secular and religious princes were vested with the right of incomplete ownership of *arats* of all classes. The princes used to sell *arats*, make presents of them to the *Chubil Khans*, the monasteries, to their relatives and neighbours. By an edict of the Emperor Shang-lun of 1772 the Mongol princes were forbidden to sell *arats* to China but they retained the right to sell *arat* serfs within the boundaries of their own *aimak*. The only limitation on the power of the princes as regards *arats* was that they were forbidden to kill them at will, without a court hearing or enquiry, but the feudal lords often evaded this law.

* * *

From times of old Mongolia had trading connections with China and other countries. In the period preceding the invasion of the Manchu conquerors a lively trade was transacted between Mongolia and China, especially along the frontiers. After the conquest of Mongolia the Manchu government, to begin with, impeded the development of Chinese-Mongolian trade, which was consistent with its general policy, directed towards keeping the enslaved peoples of China, the Mongols and others apart, and isolating Mongolia from China and Russia.

The Chinese-Mongolian frontier was opened up to trade in the second half of the XVIIIth century after the anti-Manchu uprisings in Western Mongolia and Khalkha had been suppressed.

Nevertheless, trade between China and Mongolia was authorised only in three Mongolian populated centres—Kalgan, Khukh-khoto and Dolon Nor. Later on, Chinese merchants were allowed to enter other areas of Mongolia but subject to considerable restrictions. In particular, there was a restriction on the number of Chinese merchants staying at one and the same time in Mongolia.

The Chinese merchants were forbidden to enter Mongolia without special trading licences in which were shown the region, the time-limit for trading and the kinds of goods allowed to be imported. High customs duties were imposed on Chinese goods and there was a ban on giving Mongols loans in silver. The rengs of goods carried was limited and it was forbidden to bring in articles made of metal, except cast-iron pots and small wares. The ban was motivated by a fear that "evilly-disposed persons among the Mongols might re-make them into weapons of war."

The time-limit for traders to reside in Mongolia was limited to one year. The explanation given in the *Code* was: "This measure is necessary in order to prevent roaming hucksters, because of long-time residence in Mongolia, contracting any kind of unlawful connections and so damaging the peace of the community."

Chinese merchants who brought their goods in transit through Urga and Kyakhta to the Russian frontier were forbidden to trade *en route* with Mongols or in general to have direct relations with them. Chinese women were forbidden to enter Mongolia and Chinese men were not allowed to marry Mongol women.

The Manchu authorities imposed various measures of punishment on the Chinese who disobeyed all these regulations; they fined them, confiscated their goods in favour of the Manchu treasury and expelled them from Mongolia, forbidding them to enter the country a second time.

In a report by the Urga *amban*, Yundun-Dordji, it was stated that the Manchu officials, jointly with the Mongol *khoshun* authorities, annually checked the trading licences of Chinese merchants in Urga, Ulyasutai, Kobdo and Kyakhta. After one such chek, carried out in 1803 on the order of the Emperor Shia-shing (1796-1820), a large number of Chinese merchants were deported from the above-mentioned cities because they had no licences or their licences had expired.

In the course of time, especially after the beginning of the XIXth century, the interests of the Manchu feudal lords became more and more closely interwoven with the interests of the major trading and banking firms of China; the ruling clique of Manchu feudal lords was no longer able to disregard the trading interests of these firms in Mongolia and the Manchu government began to relax the restrictions on Chinese-Mongolian trade.

Many large firms operating in Mongolia secured in the XIXth century "high-placed protectors" (dignitaries of the Peking government).

The protection extended by senior Manchu officials to Chinese firms operating in Mongolia was seen with particular clarity in the case of a lengthy dispute between the Urga monastery of Ikh-Khure and Chinese merchants at the beginning of the XIXth century. By this time the Chinese *maimachen* at Urga had outgrown the boundaries of the territory allotted to it by the monastery and had approached very close to the latter with its stalls, warehouses and other buildings and so had aroused the discontent of the *Khutukhta* and the high-ranking lamas. In token of protest they arranged to move all the lamas of the monastery away to another place.

The manager *(stantszotba)* of the *shabin* department[1] complained to the Ulyasutai *chang-chung* about the actions of the Chinese merchants and asked for them to be sent away from Urga. At that time there were more than 1,000 Chinese traders living in the area of the monastery. The Manchu *chang-chung* in Ulyasutai, I-Huang, did not accept the complaint of the *shabin* department and supported the traders. True, when the *Khutukhta* of Urga protested, the Manchu government was obliged to review the decision of the Ulyasutai *chang-chung* and adopted a decision limiting the activities of Chinese merchants in Urga; these limitations, however, could only delay the penetration of Chinese traders and usurers into Mongolia but not halt it, more especially since by this time certain Mongol feudal lords, too, were beginning to join in the trading operations of Chinese firms; in particular, Deleg-Dordji, the *amban* of Urga, became a shareholder in several firms and had a shop in Urga.

Chinese merchants little by little penetrated into Outer Mongolia, settling in the larger populated centres: Urga, Erdeni-chu, Ulyasutai, Wan-khure, Kobdo and Mongolian Khyakhta. The leading position in trade between China and Mongolia was held by Urga, the religious centre of Mongolia.

As the number of permanent inhabitants of Urga increased—it was founded as early as the XVIIth century—and as it evolved into the military and administrative centre of the *aimaks* of Tushetu Khan and Tsetsen Khan, and also as trade between Russia and China developed, the trading activities of Chinese merchants in Urga expanded.

The trading settlements—*maimachens*—which had been formed in Urga, Kyakhta, Ulyasutai and Kobdo became large trading towns.

One of the leaders of the Russian religious mission in Peking, Sofroniy Gribovsky, who travelled through Khalkha in 1808, described Urga as a trading town that was large for its time. In spite of the restrictions imposed by the Manchu government Chinese traders established themselves firmly in Urga, They built there warehouses, shops and residences, they continued to rent premises from the lamas and they turned Urga into a wholesale and retail trade centre for the whole of Outer Mongolia.

Among the Chinese firms who developed their trading and money-lending operations in Mongolia the leading place was occupied by firms from Shang-shi. Before foreign capital invaded China they traded mainly in Chinese goods: silk and cotton fabrics, tea, tobacco, meal, metal, porcelain and pottery wares, articles for household use and for the Lamaist religion.

Russian goods also penetrated into Outer Mongolia, especially during the fur markets which took place in Kyakhta or Urga, where several thousand Chinese and Russian merchants and many Mongols congregated. The basic measure of value in trading transactions were sheep, sable skin, green tea brick, silver ingot, etc.

Wandering Chinese traders penetrated into *khoshuns* far away from the centre, as well as agents of larger firms or small independent traders. They exchanged their goods for cattle and furs or sold them on credit, charging high rates of interest on condition that the amounts owed would be settled for on their next visit. The Mongol *arats* were obliged to use this one-sided form of credit and, apart from their own debts, they had to pay up the debts of their feudal masters also.

As the turnover of the Chinese capitalist traders and usurers in Mongolia increased and their connections with the feudal-bureaucratic upper classes of the Manchu Empire became stronger, the laws which had restricted trade between China and Mongolia began to lose their effect and in the middle of the XIXth century the restrictions were removed, which helped to intensify still further the exploiting operations of capitalist traders and usurers in Mongolia.

The biggest Chinese firms in Mongolia, engaged mainly in lending money at usurious rates, were Ta Shen-khu, Tyang I-de, Huang Shen-de and Yun Chi-chen. The total annual turnover of all the Chinese firms in Outer Mongolia amounted by the end of the XIXth century to several tens of millions of *lan*.

The Mongols, in a figurative reference to the wealth of the firms Ta Shen-khu and Huang Shen-de, said that the former could pave the road from Urga to Peking (2,000 km) with 50-

lan silver ingots, while the latter could cover the whole of this road with camels two abreast.

The scale of the operations of the firms can be gauged, for instance, by the tea firm of Fin Tai-lun. It traded in Hankow, Kalgan, Urga, Kobdo and Kyakhta and had connections with Moscow. At the end of the XIXth century it sold in Outer Mongolia every year no less than 30,000 cases of brick tea.

The large Chinese merchant firms in Mongolia joined together to form trading companies headed by elders. These campanies fixed monopoly prices for Mongolian raw materials, and for unloading, loading and transport of goods. The *arats* were forced to hand over their camels—in payment of debts— to the ownership of the firms. To pay off debts the *arats* serviced the Chinese caravans and performed the jobs of loaders, teamsters, drovers, etc.

Chinese capital in the person of traders and usurers built up in Mongolia a flexible organisation which helped it to maintain a monopoly position on the Mongolian market. The basic method used by traders and usurers for enslaving and exploiting the *arats* was to sell goods on credit subject to the debt being paid off with a specific kind of raw material or cattle. High rates of usurious interest were charged on the debt. The high basic figure of 36% per annum fixed by the Manchu government was arbitrarily increased many times, rising to 400%. If the debt was not paid off on the due date, the merchants added the amount of interest to the debt and fixed a new rate of interest on the total amount. The firms tried not to accept payment of the debt in full so as to keep the debtor dependent on them and have a permanent source of profit. Moreover, sales of goods on credit were effected by the merchants at prices higher than market rates, while raw materials were bought from the Mongols at prices below the market level. At the same time, cheating, giving short weight and making wrong calculations were very common occurrences. Decades of this kind of "trade" turned many Mongol arats into insolvent debtors, into paupers or herdsmen of other persons' flocks.

The Mongol nomad fell under the thrall of the usurer. As Marx wrote "...In the case of small producers the retention or the loss of the ability to produce depends on a thousand accidental happenings; and each such accidental happening is tantamount to impoverishment and represents the moment when the parasite-usurer can get himself attached to the debtor. The small peasant needs only have a cow perish and he will already find himself unable to start up production again on the old scale. Consequently, he falls into the hands of the usurer and, once this happens, he will never again extricate himself."[2]

The Chinese usurers began to form close associations with the Mongol feudal nobles and officials and became the permanent creditors of the Mongol princes.

Furthermore, in the XIXth century certain leading Mongol princes and monasteries began to take a direct share in the trading and credit operations of Chinese firms. The Mongol princes, lay and religious, invested their capital in the operations of firms, became partners in them and received a specific share of the firms' profits.

As a result, the Mongol feudal nobles became increasingly dependent on the Chinese capitalist traders and usurers and began giving active support to the predatory trading and usurious operations of the bigger Chinese merchants in Mongolia. The traders and usurers began to make wider use of their connections with the local feudal authorities in order to intensify the exploitation of the *arat* population. In particular, if a debt was not paid and if the debtors made a protest, the firms would apply to the *khoshun* ruler, the *dzasak*, or to the representatives of the Manchu authority in Mongolia. Both the one and the other, in defence of the interests of the usurers, would force the *arats* to pay up the amounts owed by resorting to brutal excesses: they put them in the stocks, incarcerated them in prison, tortured them or put them to death.

In the XIXth century the *khoshun* princes farmed out the collection of taxes to the Chinese usurers who collected the taxes from the *arats* along with their own debts, thus resorting to methods of feudal exploitation.

There can be no doubt that the rapacious actions of the Chinese traders and usurers had grave consequences; they exhausted Mongolia's economy, held back the development of productive forces and contributed to the pauperization of the *arat* population.

The actions of Chinese working people temporarily or permanently resident in Mongolia had quite a different meaning for Mongolia; they helped to establish and develop friendship between the Mongols and the Chinese, and there was mutual enrichment of both peoples in the sphere of economic management and a cultural growth of both peoples.

CHAPTER III

MONGOLIA AT THE TIME OF THE PENETRATION
OF FOREIGN CAPITAL INTO CHINA. GROWTH
OF THE LIBERATION MOVEMENT AMONG THE MONGOL *ARATS*

The situation of the Mongol people and of the other peoples of the Manchu Empire became specially difficult as foreign capital made a forcible penetration of China.

When the capitalist powers began penetrating China in the 1830-1840s a radical change ensued in the international and the internal position of the Manchu Empire. The collapse of the system of "barbarous and hermetic isolation" (Marx) brought feudal China face to face with the capitalist world and with its powerful methods of attack. Decisive economic and political positions in the country began to pass into the hands of foreign capitalist states.

The armed irruption of the capitalist powers into China led to the seizure of markets and to the Manchu dynasty's policy being subordinated to their influence. The drawing of feudal China and its borderlands into the orbit of the capitalist markets of the world, the intensification of aggression by foreign powers led to the Manchu dynasty changing its methods of enslaving Outer Mongolia. The essential objective of the Ching government's policy in the second half of the XIXth and the beginning of the XXth century was to weaken Outer Mongolia further, economically and politically, to intensify its colonization and to isolate it from the outside world.

The new methods adopted by the Manchu dynasty to enslave Mongolia began to emerge extremely clearly at the turn of the century as the colonialist system of imperialism gained supremacy in the Far East and the predatory division of China into "spheres of influence" among the Great Powers was completed. While submitting to the will of the Western aggressors, the Ching government directed the principal spear-head of its policy on the north against Russia. While opposing a rapprochement between Russia and Mongolia and safeguarding its supremacy in Mongolia, the Manchu government, by laws enacted in the second half of the XIXth century, lifted all restrictions on the operations in Mongolia of capitalist traders and usurers, opened up the way for Chinese feudal nobles and traders to colonize Mongol lands and created favourable conditions for English, American and other foreign firms to despoil the Mongolian people both directly and through the intermediary of Chinese comprador capitalists.

This policy met with the support of the capitalists of the Western Powers, as it suited their aggressive interests. The capitalists of the USA, the United Kingdom, Japan and other countries reckoned that, with the support of the ruling feudal clique in China and through the intermediary of Chinese capitalist traders and usurers, they could seize Mongolia and make it a centre for selling their goods and a source of supply for stock-breeding products and other raw materials. The aggressive ambitions of the capitalist powers and the colonizing policy of the Manchu dynasty resulted in an extensive development of comprador and usurious operations by Chinese traders and a considerable growth in the number of their enterprises in Mongolia.

In the 1860s there were several dozens of large-and medium-size Chinese commercial and money-lending enterprises in Outer Mongolia, and at the outset of the XXth century their numbers had already grown to 500. Stores, shops and offices numbered: in the districts of Urga—160, Ulyasutai—86, Kobdo—65, Kyakhta—100, Wan-khure—30, Ulangom—20, Dzain-Shabi—12, etc.

After Chinese ports were "opened" for trade with foreigners many Chinese firms in Mongolia became dependent on foreign firms which had branches in Peking, Kalgan, Khukh-Khoto, etc. Chinese comprador traders began exporting from Mongolia different kinds of products of the Mongol economy—cattle, wool, furs, etc. and importing into Mongolia, in addition to Chinese goods, goods of foreign origin—groceries, haberdashery, grain products and fabrics of Japanese, American and English origin. These fabrics were imported into China through the port of Tsientsin and, after Chinese trade marks had been pasted on them, were put on the Mongolian market as Chinese *dalemba* or *tsuemba* (kinds of fabrics). A similar operation was done on haberdashery wares and other types of goods, to the point even of producing pictures of Buddhist *burkhans* which were prepared in very large quantities, particularly in Warsaw.

In 1909, 256,400 25-yard pieces of English and American cotton fabrics to the value of 1,400,000 roubles in gold were imported into Outer Mongolia and a considerable quantity of Japanese coarse calico. The whole of this import trade returned no equivalent benefit to Mongolian exports; it impoverished the national economy and gave the imperialist monopolies enormous profits. Not content with using the services of compradors, American, English and other firms began to open their own branch offices in Outer Mongolia. In 1907, for instance, the first English firm opened up in Urga and somewhat later an American firm followed.

The growing activities of foreign capital in Mongolia in the period of imperialism helped to increase the imbalance in trade and were ruining the *arat* population. The Mexican dollar which circulated in China, the Russian rouble and the old Chinese *lan*[1] all became accepted as currency units in Mongolia. The natural forms of trade exchange, taxes and levies were gradually replaced by money tokens. As a result both the *arats* and the Mongol princes began to find that their requirements for money advances were increasing in amount.

As money relationships increased, the exploitation of the Mongol masses became more and more intensified. The decline in the productive forces of the country continued. Though it was disturbing natural economic relationships, capital in the guise of traders and usurers did not, in view of the backwardness of Mongolia, basically change the feudal mode of production. As Karl Marx wrote: "In Asiatic conditions usurious money-lending can exist for a very long time without evoking anything but economic decline and political corruption."[2]

The indebtedness of the *arats* to usurers increased. At the beginning of the XXth century, quite apart from the general *khoshun* indebtedness to the usurers, each *arat* holding was indebted to the extent of 500 to 1,000 silver *lan* and the overall indebtedness of *khoshuns* amounted to 11 million *lan* in 1911. Such immense indebtedness reduced the *arats* to the status of slave debtors since it became impossible to pay off this indebtedness in full on account of the exhausted condition of the *arat* economy. For instance, the value of the whole property of the *arats* in the Kobdo district did not amount to even half of the total indebtedness to traders and usurers.

From the mid-XIXth century Chinese usurers began to become the real owners of large parcels of land in many of the *khoshuns* of Outer Mongolia. They seized the landed domains in lieu of "rent" or on account of payment for the debts of the *khoshuns*.

In the first decade of the XXth century the Peking government, in support of the colonizing ambitions of the usurers and to offset the increasing influence of Russia in Mongolia, carried through a series of urgent measures to speed up the complete colonization of Outer Mongolia.

A special office for migration questions in Mongolia was set up in 1906 in Peking and in 1909 it took a census of the population, cattle and lands in Outer Mongolia, assessed the arable land, drew up a colonisation scheme and drafted an agreement with the Mongol princes. The agreement and the plan were signed by the *khoshun dzasaks* of Outer Mongolia: Zorigtu Khan, Nointu-van and others who had been specially summoned for the purpose to a meeting in Peking. Under the agreement signed by them, all land suitable for agriculture was alienated in favour of the Peking government—subject to payment of 50% of the value of the land to the *khoshun dzasaks.*

After Peking had approved the "colonization plan" the traders and usurers started to seize land against debts owed, to utilize them for ploughing up, for vegetable growing and for pasture, on which they then began grazing cattle stolen from the Mongols, or to use the land for speculation.

This evoked sharp protests from the *arats.* When *khoshun* land in the Bator-van *khoshun, aimak* of Tushetu Khan, was handed over to one Chinese firm by the *khoshun* prince, the indignant *arats* lodged a collective complaint with the *aimak* administration and then, when no result followed, drove the firm's representatives out of the confines of the *khoshun.*

In 1909 the colonization office of the Peking government seized a large part of the best Mongol grazing-grounds. In the reports of Russian expeditions of the day we find the following comment: "There, where previously thousands of head of Mongol livestock once grazed and dozens or hundreds of *yurts* stood, now there is not one single *yurt* or one single herd. They have now been driven away from the wide valleys and rivers into the waterless steppe, where the Mongols are forced to use wells and poor pasture". According to the evidence of Kuropatkin, a representative of the tsarist government, in 1911 the area of land that had been alienated in the northern part of Outer Mongolia had risen to 4,905,000 *desyatinas.*[3] The mass alienation of grazing-grounds, together with servitude to the usurers, radically undermined the Mongol pastoral economy, ruined the *arat* population and at the same time injured the interests of the princes and high-ranking lamas by curtailing the basis of their feudal exploitation.

Apart from operating compulsory colonization, the Manchu government's Great Power policy took the form of intensifying the functions of the Manchu administration, limiting the rights of the local Mongol authorities and strengthening the Manchu garrisons.

The policy of the Manchu government, aimed at stepping up oppression of the Mongols as a nation and turning Outer Mongolia into a "barrier" against Russia, while at the same time intensifying inter-feudal exploitation at a time when Mongolia was being made into a raw-materials appendage to the world capital market, reduced the country to serious economic straits.

This situation, resulting from the despoliation of the masses of the people by the Mongol, Manchu and Chinese feudal nobles and by foreign capital, meant further impoverishment of the masses. By 1911, in many *khoshuns* of the Kobdo district up to 80% of *arat* livestock, and in the eastern *khoshuns* more than half, were owned by Chinese and other foreign firms. Some individual *khoshuns* were completely ruined and their population was scattered in all directions. This was the case, for instance, in the *khoshun* of the *dzasak* Tseren in the *aimak* of Tushetu Khan.

According to the evidence of Russian trade missions, the feudal exploitation practised the systematic alienation of Mongol livestock for debts and interest owed to Chinese and other firms, the fact of their pastures being beyond the borders of the country, and also the curtailment of grazing-grounds caused by alienation of land, led to a marked decline in the total numbers of the livestock population and the decay of the whole of Mongolia's economy. The situation was aggravated by a national disaster, due to the severe winters and the droughts experienced in the first decade of the XXth century.

The consequence of the long years spent under the yoke of the Manchu conquerors and the oppression of the Mongol feudal nobles, as well as of the predatory policy of the imperialist powers in Mongolia, was a great hold-up in the development of the country's productive resources, economic and cultural backwardness and the extreme impoverishment of the Mongol *arat* population.

At the outset of the XXth century, just as in the days of old, outdated pastoral and nomad stock-breeding practices continued to be the predominant feature of the whole economy of the country; industry failed to develop and agriculture among the *arats* was in rudimentary condition.

The reports of Russian expeditions to Mongolia at the beginning of the XXth century show that during the whole period of existence of the Manchu yoke in Mongolia the techniques and methods of economic management had not developed to any noticeable extent. As before, the Mongol economy was a raw material or semi-raw material economy. According to the evidence of a Moscow trading mission in 1911 an average *arat* holding with several dozen head of cattle was valued at 1,058 roubles.

At the beginning of the XXth century in four Khalkha *aimaks* there was an average of 60 head of cattle for each *arat* holding, 2,500 for each feudal holding, i. e. 40 times more head of cattle than for one *arat* holding, while a monastery holding would have on an average more than 5,000 head of cattle or 80 times more cattle than an *arat* holding.

At the end of the XIXth century large-scale pastoral and agricultural holdings of Chinese firms began to appear in Mongolia. The Chinese merchants and usurers realized the advantages of organizing such holdings on the basis of the cattle expropriated from the *arats* and with the free use of Mongol grazing-grounds. Under debt bondage conditions the *arats* were compelled to furnish labour for servicing these holdings, and to graze the cattle which had formerly belonged to themselves.

After the Manchus had brutally suppressed a popular uprising in 1755-1758 which extended over Djungaria and Khalkha, the *arats* did not abandon their fight against the oppression of the Manchu and Mongol feudal nobles and the Chinese merchants and usurers. At the end of the XVIIIth, and in the first half of the XIXth century there was a whole series of popular rebellions of a local character in Khalkha, more especially in the *khoshuns* of the Tushetu Khan and Tsetsen Khan *aimaks*. A special place among these *arat* rebellions is taken by the armed uprisings in the *khoshun* of Prince Togtokh-Ture in the Tsetsen Khan *aimak* in 1837-1840. These rebellions were not only anti-feudal but very definitely anti-Manchu in character. The *arats* openly declared their refusal to submit to the *khoshun* Prince and the Manchu Emperor.

It is common knowledge that the aggressive policy of the capitalist powers and the intensification of colonial and feudal oppression produced in China great popular uprisings such as the Taiping rebellion in 1850-1864 and the Ikhetuang rebellion in 1898-1901. These and other rebellions served as a signal for the development of a liberation movement even on the borders of the Manchu Empire. It was only with the help of foreign interventionists that the Manchu government was able to put down the rebellions. In order to combat the rebels the Manchu military command tried to mobilize men for the army by force, in Mongolia also. These measures, however, were unsuccessful.

In the liberation movement of the Mongol *arats* in the second half of the XIXth century, the Duguilan movement in Inner Mongolia was the most outstanding. It originated in 1852 in Ordos—in the *khoshun* of Ushin (province of Suiyuang) and was not only anti-Manchu but also anti-feudal in character. It took the form of popular conventions and meetings and was given the name *duguilan* from *ardin-duguilan*—"popular assembly". These meetings were based on the principle of full equality of the participants: they sat in a circle, on the same level, matters were decided in common, and decisions were signed by all the participants. At the beginning of the XXth century the Duguilan movement, headed by the popular hero Uldzey-Zhargal, assumed a mass character.

In the second half of the XIXth century the *arat* movement in Outer Mongolia began to assume increasingly differing forms. It was directed against the excessively onerous debt bondage system, the predatory actions of the Manchu *chang-chung*, the *ambans*, and the officials, and against the arbitrary behaviour of their own feudal lords. In the 1890s disturbances began in the Kobdo district. Attempts were made to take advantage of these disturbances by the adventurer Dambi-Djantsan, who announced himself a descendant and the *Chubil Khan* of Amursana, about whose "second coming" legends were then alive in the memories of the Mongol people.

Travelling through the Mongol *khoshuns*, Dambi-Djantsan summoned the Mongols to overthrow Manchu domination and expell from the country the usurers and officials. At the *aimak* diet where Dambi-Djantsan made an appearance, the *khoshun* princes supported him and suggested to the *chang-chung* of Ulyasutai that he should leave the diet.

In 1899, under the pressure of the *arats* and the ordinary lamas, a comprehensive petition was drawn up by a group of princes and addressed to the Manchu Emperor. It was signed by the most important princes and lamas. In this petition a demand was put forward for the immediate removal from his post of the *chang-chung* of Ulyasutai and his assistants and for a radical betterment of the situation of the Mongols. The petition wound up with the threat: "If matters continue to go on in this way, there will be nothing left for the Mongols but to take up arms". The Manchu government replied to this petition by intensifying repressions and sentencing the initiators of the petition.

In these years small groups of fugitive *arat* serfs were built up all over Outer Mongolia who, as a protest against the existing regime, set the steppes on fire at points where the headquarters of Manchu officials and Mongol princes were located and wrecked the shops of Chinese firms. There was no cessation of the *arats*' opposition, even in passive form. There are many facts that tell of this. For instance, large numbers of *arats* moved their camping grounds away and lodged complaints against Prince Dalai Khan Delger Namzhil, and as a result succeeded in getting him removed from his post as *dzasak*. In those years there were frequent cases of *arats* fleeing to the monasteries and taking advantage of the right of asylum. But even in the monasteries oppression by the feudal lords of the church awaited the *arats* and their debts to the usurers had to be paid off by their relatives. Protests by lower-ranking lamas who supported the *arat* movement began to occur more often. The numerous demonstrations made by the lamas of the Ulankom monastery may be mentioned as an example.

The Mongol people gave expression to their sympathies for the struggles of the Chinese people in every possible way. The Mongols refused to take part in the punitive expeditions organized by the Manchu government and the foreign aggressors against the Chinese working classes. In Outer Mongolia in 1900 the Manchu authorities tried to organize an army of 20,000 among the Mongols to march against the Ikhetuan but were able to muster only two thousand Mongols. And even this group, when handed over by the *khoshun* princes and put at the disposal of the Manchu *chang-chung* in Ulyasutai, rose up in rebellion under the leadership of the *arat* Enkhe-Taiwan. The rebels slaughtered the soldiers of the Ulyasutai Manchu garrison, wrecked the offices and shops of the merchants and then dispersed to their homes.

Almost simultaneously with the incident at Ulyasutai a new large-scale anti-Manchu rebellion broke out in the east of the country in the *khoshun* of Prince Sansar-dorzhi of the *aimak* of Tsetsen Khan. The rebel *arats* wrecked the offices and shops of Chinese traders, burnt the debt registers and drove the merchants and traders themselves—to the number of several hundreds—out of the area of their *khoshun*. After enveloping the whole population of the *khoshun* concerned, the movement spread over into the neighbouring *khoshuns*. Following their example, the *arats* of these *khoshuns* began to take action against the merchants and traders. However, the Manchu authorities immediately suppressed this movement and its participants were severely punished. The demonstrations of the Mongols gave the Manchu government a pretext for speeding up the military occupation of Outer Mongolia and for considerably reinforcing and strengthening the garrisons in a number of cities and inhabited centres with Manchus.

The 1905 revolution in Russia exerted a great influence on the expansion of the liberation movement in the East. In an article on "The Awakening of Asia" Lenin wrote: "World capitalism and the Russian movement of 1905 have finally awakened Asia. Hundreds of millions of downtrodden people, who have grown wild in mediaeval stagnation, have wakened up to a new life and to a struggle for the rudimentary rights of the individual and for democracy."[4] The Chinese people in their many millions rose up against the Manchu yoke, foreign oppression and feudal exploitation. They were followed by the oppressed national minorities of the Manchu Empire.

The revolution of 1905 and the revolutionary incidents connected with it in Transbaikalia, in the Minusinsk territory, the liberation movement of the Buryats, the formation of Soviets in Chita, Kranoyarsk, Verkhneudinsk and Irkutsk could not fail to influence the development of the liberation movement of the *arat* masses of Outer Mongolia.

At the beginning of the XXth century an *arat* liberation movement developed in a number of regions of Outer Mongolia. The best known of these are the *arat* rebellion under the leadership of the *arat* Ayushi and the disturbances in Urga and the Kobdo district. An element of organization was already observable in these demonstrations, which occurred almost simultaneously in different parts of Mongolia. The struggle of the *arats* was directed not only against the yoke of the Manchus but also against the oppression of the local feudal nobles. All these *arat* actions, which began in different parts of the country, merged in a general Mongol liberation movement in 1911, resulting in the overthrow of the Manchu dynasty's rule in Outer Mongolia.

The *arat* action under the leadership of Ayushi in the Tsetsegnur *somon* of the *khoshun* of Darkhan-baile of the aimak of Dzasaktu Khan began in 1903. Having refused to pay the routine *alba* tax on account of the debts of the *khoshun* prince Manibazar, the *arats*, headed by Ayushi, waged a struggle against their prince. At a joint meeting of *arats* and impoverished *taijis* a sharp protest was made against the debts to usurers and the arbitrary conduct of the prince, and a petition was drawn up recounting the complaints against his brutal exploitation. In the petition, which was a kind of political programme, demands were made for the whole population including even the princes, to be enlisted to do military service, for the abolition of the *alba* tax payable to the princes and for the formation of self-government for the *arats*.

Twelve men, with Ayushi at the head, were designated to hand over the petition to the president of the diet of the Dzasaktu Khan *aimak* and to conduct the litigation with Prince Manibazar. In response the *khoshun* prince and the Manchu authorities instigated brutal repressions. Ayushi and his comrades were arrested, tortured and fined. But, as soon as the *arat* Ayushi managed to get free, he again took command of the struggle begun against the oppressors.

The struggle of the *arats* in the western part of Outer Mongolia under the leadership of Ayushi broke out afresh in 1911 and became part of a general liberation movement of the *arat* population against Manchu rule and the Mongol feudal nobles. Having refused to acknowledge the authority of the *khoshun* prince and acting simultaneously against the Manchu authorities and the usurers, the *arats* organized a popular *duguilan* (of Tsetsegnur) on the lines of the *duguilans* of Inner Mongolia. The *arats* set up their own administration and, seizing what weapons they could find, moved their camps off into the mountains.

A petition consisting of 44 paragraphs was drawn up by the *arats* of this *duiguilan* under the leadership of Ayushi. In it the real meaning of exploitation and the arbitrary behaviour of the Mongol feudal nobles, the Manchu officials and the predatory greed of the usurers were grimly exposed.

The persecutions initiated by the Manchu and Mongol authorities failed to break the resistance of the *arats*, who boldly asserted their right to struggle against the *khoshun dzasak* Manibazar and others. Under the leadership of Ayushi the *arat* movement continued even during the years of Outer Mongolia's autonomy. Ayushi and his fellow fighters took an active part later on in the Mongolian people's revolution of 1921 and later in the construction of a new people's-democratic Mongolia. Ayushi died in 1939.

After 1909 active demonstrations by *arats* developed in Barga and in the Tsetsen Khan *aimak* of Khalkha. The *arat* rebel detachments formed under the leadership of Togtokho carried out raids on the offices and shops of traders and usurers, killed usurers, took away goods, drove the Manchu officials and Chinese estate-owners out of the Mongol *khoshuns*. In particular, they carried out raids on Sanbeise (present-day city of Choibalsan). In one of these raids the office of a firm of usurers which was the principal creditor of the *khutukhta* of Urga was wrecked. At the end of 1909 a large Manchu punitive detachment drove the rebels back to the Russo-Mongolian frontier. Togtokho and many of his fellow-fighters found asylum in Russia and settled temporarily in the territory of Transbaikalia. Individual armed groups of rebels, however, continued to carry out raids on the offices and shops of traders and usurers and on the headquarters of princes in Barga and Khalkha.

Besides the major armed actions, small spasmodic outbursts also occurred among *arats*, directed against Manchu officials and usurers. In 1906, for instance, there was a bitter fight between a group of *arat* debtors and Chinese usurers in which a large number of Mongols, including lower-ranking lamas, soon intervened.

In 1910 collisions occurred between lamas and usurers in Urga. When the Manchu police tried to arrest some Mongols the crowd rushed at the police and forced them to flee. The Mongols wrecked a number of shops and stores and compelled the *amban* Sando of Urga, who had come along to the scene of the incident, to leave by attacking him with stones and sticks. At this time also the movement of *arats* in the Kobdo district against usurers and Manchu officials gained in strength.

The growth of the *arat* movement of the beginning of the XXth century in Outer Mongolia proves that, as the struggle went on, the political consciousness of the *arat* masses increased. Under the influence of the Russian revolution of 1905 and the Chinese revolution of 1911, the struggle reached a higher level than in the previous period and the class content of the struggle became more profound. The *arats* turned to better organized forms of movement.

In 1911 the diverse *arat* actions merged in a single torrent of national-liberation struggle, directed against the Manchu rule. The leadership of this movement, however, was seized by the Mongol princes who were anxious to make use of it for their own narrow class interests. The liberation struggle, the main moving force behind which was the Mongol working *arat*, had developed in the context and under the influence of the 1911 Chinese revolution leading to the overthrow of Manchu rule in Outer Mongolia and to the formation of an autonomous Outer Mongolia.

The whole course of events in the period when feudal Outer Mongolia was under the rule of the Manchu conquerors, namely from 1691 to 1911, shows that this was an extraordinarily difficult period in the history of the Mongol people. The rule of the Manchu conquerors held back Mongolia's economic and cultural development.

Reactionary bourgeois historians represent Outer Mongolia as a country which had disappeared from the arena of history and the Mongol people as an inferior race dying a "natural death."

In reality, however, even in this difficult time of national and social enslavement, the Mongol people did not lose their freedom-loving spirit and fought heroically against the Manchu yoke and against feudal oppression for independence and freedom.

CHAPTER IV

DEVELOPMENT OF RUSSO-MONGOLIAN RELATIONS
(THE XIXth—THE BEGINNING OF THE XXth CENTURY)

It has been shown above that Russia sought to achieve peaceful economic collaboration with China and Mongolia and obtained considerable success in this direction. As time went on, many controversial questions were settled and the frontiers between Russia and the Manchu Empire were delimited. Economic links were strengthened by expanding caravan trade overland. In the XIXth century the activity of the Russian Religious Mission in Peking was widened. The heads of this Mission acted as diplomatic representatives. Many of the people working in the Mission made a study of China, Mongolia, Tibet and other countries of Central and Eastern Asia. *The Proceedings of the Russian Religious Mission* in this sphere have proved a very valuable contribution to Oriental studies. Particularly prominent among them are the works of N. Ya. Bichurin on the history of Mongolia and Tibet.

Up to the middle of the XIXth century Russo-Chinese and Russo-Mongolian relations developed on the basis of treaties concluded between the governments of the Russian and Manchu states—Treaty of Nerchinsk (1689) and those of Burin and Kyakhta (1727). Trade between Russia and China was conducted mainly in Kyakhta, Kalgan and Peking. The caravan trade route traversed Outer Mongolia from north to south.

In 1858 by the Treaty of Aygun and in 1860 by that of Peking the Russian frontier contiguous with Manchuria, Barga, Outer Mongolia and Sinkiang was once again delimited. It was proposed to establish here a special frontier belt extending about 35 miles on both sides of the borders. Subjects of Russia and the Manchu Empire were permitted to carry on duty-free trade in this belt.

In 1860 the Russian government sent its first consul to Outer Mongolia, to Urga. Russian privileges in respect of trade in Outer Mongolia were extended on the strength of the *Rules for Overland Trading* between Russia and China signed additionally on February 20, 1862, by both parties. Under this agreement, in addition to trade in the border strip, Russian trading firms and individual traders were given the right to carry on petty trade with Mongols free of customs duty in all the inhabited centres of Outer Mongolia. When Russian merchants travelled with their goods to the Chinese port of Tsientsin through Mongolia they were allowed to leave a fifth part of the goods in Kalgan for direct trade with the Mongols but not for wholesale sales and had the right to trade in Kyakhta and Urga where, as far back as the XVIIIth century, the first Russian fairgrounds were set up to serve merchants taking part in the caravan trade with China.

Notwithstanding the strict limitations and prohibitions imposed by Manchu Emperors, firm links were established between Russians and Mongols. A considerable part in this was played by the border population of Russia and Mongolia. Many inhabitants of Mongolia, in spite of the prohibitions, crossed the frontier at will in large and small groups and remained on Russian territory as temporary or permanent inhabitants. It is, for instance, known that a large group of Mongols from Khalkha, numbering several thousand, who did not wish to become Manchu subjects, fled from Mongolia to Transbaikalia at the end of the XVIIth century and stayed there as Russian subjects. Mongols crossed the frontier back and forth, in groups and singly, into Russian territory and later on, seeking to escape from the grievous oppression of the Manchu conquerors, from taxation, from frontier patrol and *urton* service and from other feudal servitudes.

Cases occurred, though in small numbers, of Russians also crossing into Mongolia. These were peasants—Old Believers who had been persecuted by the tsarist government and the Russian Orthodox church, fugitive peasants or political deportees and others. Russian travellers like N. M. Przhevalsky, P. K. Kozlov, G. N. Potanin and others have referred to the presence in Mongolia of individual groups of Russians who had migrated there in the XVIIIth and XIXth centuries. The Russians used to settle mainly in the valleys of the rivers Selenga, Onon, Orkhon and Tes. Here they engaged in small-scale agriculture, stock-breeding and hunting, and in various kinds of handicrafts, and they had friendly economic and social relations with the Mongol population, which considerably helped Russian popular culture to penetrate Mongolia.

Alongside this there was a penetration into Mongolia of Russian trade capital. Russian merchants, in agreement with local *khoshun* princes, built small trade factories in Mongolia, formed associations and traded with the Mongol population. Accordingly, by the time the Russian consulate in Outer Mongolia was opened in Urga in 1860 there were already a certain number of Russian peasant settlers, craftsmen and traders.

The Russian consuls in Urga, and later in Ulyasutai, and Kobdo, encouraged the activities of Russian citizens in Mongolia and paid special attention to expanding the trade of the Russian merchants. Russian consulates gave special support to the tea trade and to the export from Russia to China of furs, cloth and fabrics through Kyakhta—Urga—Kalgan—Peking.

To begin with, few Russian trading firms had settled in Mongolia but by the 1870s there were already several dozen.

Russian banks and industrial enterprises in Russia opened credits for Russian merchants trading in Outer Mongolia. A great role in the development of Russo-Mongolian trade was played by the Great Siberian Railway built by Russia in the 1890s; it brought the Mongol markets nearer to Russia, and helped to increase the volume of trade and the speedier inclusion of Outer Mongolia in the world market.

The main articles exported from Outer Mongolia to Russia were cattle on the hoof, furs and wool. Russia exported to Mongolia fabrics, cloth, flour, groceries and other commodities.

The total turnover of trade between Russia and Mongolia increased eighty-fold between 1861 and 1900. With the opening of the Siberian Railway the rates of the growth in trade augmented. For instance, in 1861 the total trade turnover of Mongolia with Russia amounted to 218,167 gold roubles, in 1885 to 1,700,000 roubles and in 1900 to 16,900,000 roubles. Great opposition to the further development of Russo-Mongolian trade was offered by the capital of imperialist powers who strengthened their competition on the Mongolian market and operated mainly through Chinese comprador firms. As they enjoyed the support of the Manchu government, the compradors secured considerable advantages on the Mongolian market. Whereas in 1880 they exported from Mongolia to the port of Tientsin 19 kinds of raw materials in 1899 there were exported about 40 kinds of different raw materials, mainly wool, furs, sheepskins and leather. In addition, the compradors held in their grip the trade in such items of prime necessity for the Mongols as tea and tobacco, *dalemba* and millet.

Unable to meet this competition, Russian merchants were obliged gradually to cut down their trade turnover in Outer Mongolia. According to the figures of the Koshagach customs house on the west frontier of Outer Mongolia, imports of textiles from Russia into Outer Mongolia between 1900 and 1909, i.e. ten years, fell to a tenth. The same tendency was noted also at other customs houses. Chinese comprador capital in trade and usury retained its dominant position on the Mongolian market right up to 1911 when the political situation in Outer Mongolia changed in Russia's favour.

Conflict between the imperialist interests of Japan and Russia in the Far East led to the Russo-Japanese War of 1904-1905 which ended in a defeat of tsarism. The tsarist government was obliged to conclude an agreement with Japan on spheres of influence. In particular, in 1907 a secret agreement was concluded under which Outer Mongolia was recognized as the sphere of influence of tsarist Russia and Inner Mongolia (except Barga) as that of Japan. The tsarist government next agreed to the annexation of Korea by Japan. Lenin called this imperialist act an "exchange" of Korea for Mongolia[1] and the Russo-Mongolian agreement of 1912 the "gentle embrace" of Mongolia by tsarism.[2]

In its relations with Outer Mongolia the tsarist government was, of course, motivated by the imperialistic, self-seeking interests of the exploiter classes of Russia. Nevertheless, the imperialist policy of the tsarist government could not upset the good-neighbourly and friendly relations between the mass of the Russian and Mongol peoples. Association with Russians and the influence of Russian culture had a positive and progressive meaning for the Mongol people.

Engels used to point out that Russia played a progressive role in the East. There can be no doubt that such a role on the part of Russia was especially significant as regards its neighbour, Outer Mongolia. Here the determining factors in Russo-Mongolian relations before the victory of the Great October Socialist Revolution in Russia were the influence of the Russian people's culture, which was more advanced than in feudal Mongolia, and of the progressive ideas and revolutionary movements of the masses in Russia.

Of great importance in this respect were the scientific trips into Mongolia made by such eminent explorers as N. M. Przhevalsky, G. N. Potanin, P. K. Kozlov, G. E. Grumm-Grzhimailo, B. Ya. Vladimirtsov and V. A. Obruchev. Their books helped wide circles of readers in Russia to become acquainted with the life of the Mongol people and strengthened the growth of sympathy between the Russian people and the *arats* of Mongolia.

By their scientific activities and their sympathetic attitude towards the difficult situation of the enslaved *arat* population the Russian scholars earned the respect of the Mongol people. Russian explorers helped the Mongols to discover the natural wealth of their native land and their historical monuments, to reveal the many-sided facets of the economic and cultural life and customs of the Mongol people.

CHAPTER V

THE CULTURE OF THE MONGOLS
IN THE XVIII-XIXth CENTURIES

The background to Mongolian cultural development during this period was Manchu rule and the further intensification of the influence exerted by the Lamaist religion on the spiritual life of the Mongols. This situation could not fail to leave a noticeable impress on the culture of the Mongolian people.

Buddhism held a leading position in the spiritual life of the Mongols and Buddhist education formed an essential part of all Mongol culture.

The consequence was that in Mongolia a situation arose similar to that in medieval Europe where, as Engels put it, "the clergy retained a monopoly of intellectual education... and education itself had acquired a predominantly theological character..."[1] In such circumstances the feudal-religious elements in Mongol culture were sharply intensified as a counterweight to popular tradition. The Buddhist religion sought to control all the intellectual activities of the Mongols. As Mongolia was completely isolated from the cultural world right up to the XXth century—the consequence of the predatory policy followed by the Manchu colonizers—Tibet, as the home of Lamaism, became for the Mongols a unique centre not only of religious but also of any other kind of culture. In these circumstances it was very difficult to develop Mongol culture.

Under the Manchus Lamaism, which had become a reactionary force in the history of the Mongol people, constituted a great obstacle to Mongol cultural development. During this time it lost certain cultural innovations which had accompanied the early stages of Buddhist penetration into Mongolia. Lamaism was, in the hands of the Manchu aggressors, a willing tool in the process of ideologically stupefying the nation.

In spite of all the difficulties the Mongol people continued to build up the cultural assets of their country. The more enlightened representatives of the Mongol people directed their efforts towards developing secular culture in the country as opposed to Lamaist culture, tried as far as possible to absorb all that was progressive and enlightened from the neighbouring cultured countries, to produce original works in some branches of knowledge, especially in Mongolian philology, national history, etc.

Developments in folklore acquired new scope and direction. Under the Manchu rule many works were written in a critical tone, which was directed against the Mongol feudal nobles and lamas and also their Manchu masters. Under alien rule wide popularity was gained by epic ballads which narrated the victory of the national hero *(batyr)* over the many-headed monster *(mangas)*. During the Manchu era folklore was enriched by a new form known under the name of *Badarchiny ulger* (pilgrim's tale). The *Badarchin* is an interesting figure of old Mongolia. He was constantly wandering around, keeping company with everyone and observing life in its various manifestations. It is very easy and convenient to associate such a person with all kinds of stories and adventures, and so a whole cycle of stories arose with *Badarchin* as their hero. Many of the tales in the *Badarchiny ulger* cycle are strikingly anti-feudal and anti-lama in character.

There is another series of stories also, closely resembling the *Badarchiny ulger;* their main hero is Balansengee. These often contain anti-feudal and anti-lama elements, too. Adroit, witty, resourceful, playing the fool now with lamas, now with traders, Balansengee enjoyed great popularity with the common people.

Talented folk story-tellers, writers and poet-improvisers *(yeroolch, magtaalch, ulgerchin)* were greatly loved by the simple people.

At the end of the XIXth and beginning of the XXth century a new current and a new trend arose in Mongol literature. Whereas, up to the middle of the XIXth century, the democratic elements were mainly contained in oral folklore and in some translations, in the second half of the XIXth century new writers appeared whose output was inseparably connected with the intensification of the liberation movement among the *arats*. Representatives of this trend were the *khuulch* Sandag, Gelegbalsan (1846-1923) and several others. The *khuulch* Sandag was a native of the *khoshun* of Govmergen-van of the *aimak* of Tushetu Khan and wrote in the second half of the XIXth century. His numerous poems, which circulated in manuscript form among readers, include such compositions as *Khavrin khailaad ursch baigaz tsasni khelsen n', Salkhind khiissen khamkhuulyn khelsen n', Botgonoos n' salgazh zhind khelselsen ingeniy khelsen n'* and *Sain muu tushmel bichech naryn khelsen n'*. Sandag was a talented poet admired by his contemporaries for his brilliant gift of instantaneous improvisation. Gelegbalsan, who was a native of the same *khoshun* as Sandag, was a leading representative of the popular poets and story-tellers of Mongolia. At thirty years of age he began his creative work. He lived the life of a working man, served as a caravan operator on the trade route between Mongolia and Peking, *Chulall-*

khaalga. Among his works *(yeruly)* which have survived are such examples of poetical creativeness as *Tengees boroo khur guizh tav'san yerool Naadmyn yerool, Guuniy sangiin yerocl,* and *Uchralyn yerool.* His writings vividly reflect the difficult situation of the masses.

One common special characteristic of the poetical works of most of the poet-improvisers of this period is that they often caustically ridicule the feudal nobles, lamas, merchants, usurers, extortionary officials and wealthy bloodsuckers.

The works of this type written by popular poets met with a lively response from the people at large and, as they were passed on by word of mouth and occasionally also in written form, they opened the eyes of the *arats* to many phenomena in the political life of the country and helped them to understand and comprehend a great deal.

A prominent poet who came from the Mongol lama class, was the *noyon khutagt* Ravzhai (1803-1856). Although Ravzhai wrote mostly on religious subjects, there are quite a few of his works, written on secular or civic subjects, which praise love, and happiness in life, or which keenly ridicule the defects of feudal society. It was precisely because of this feature of his writing that it enjoyed great popularity among the people. Such writings as *Uzemzhiyn chanar, Ur'khan khongor* and others circulated everywhere in Mongolia as folk songs, and they are sung even to this day. Many of his works have reached us written in Mongolian and Tibetan.

In the XVIIIth century, new works of artistic literature were produced. One of these is the *Legend of Geser Bogd Khan,* which represents a folklore work written and published in 1716 in xylographed form. Some of the chapter headings and versions of this *Legend* were revised by the feudal lamas and reflect the influence of Buddhist ideology. Nevertheless, the basic versions of the *Legend of Geser Bogd Khan* are popular in character and are widely known in Mongolia in oral and written form.

Another interesting memorial of the XVIIIth century is the *History of Amursana.* The fate of this work closely resembles that of the *Legend of Geser Bogd Khan,* since the *History of Amursana* also represents a record of one of the popular legends about Amursana who, in the middle of the XVIIIth century, headed a rebellion of the Oirats and Khotogoits against the Manchu feudal nobles. It is remarkable, primarily, because it tells about the heroic struggle of the people against the alien yoke.

In the XVIII-XIXth centuries, translations were made of a large amount of the literature of ancient India, China and Tibet. The translations from Tibetan were, principally, of Buddhist works but amidst this flood of religious literature works of secular and scholarly literature also appeared.

For instance, *Danzhur*, consisting of 220 volumes and well known, along with *Ganzhur*, as a basic Buddhist classic, really represents a very rich collection of the works of ancient Indian, and frequently also, Tibetan authors in various fields of knowledge: philosophy, philology, poetics, logic, medicine, art, astronomy, etc. The section on philological sciences in *Danzhur* includes the ancient Indian grammatical treatises of Panini (5th century B.C.), Kalapa, Chandrapa, Anubkhudisvarupa and others, and also a treatise on poetics: *Kavyadarshu* by Dandin (7th century A. D.), the poem *Megaduta* of the great Kalidas, etc. And in the section on medicine, there are many works devoted to almost all the branches of medical science in ancient India, including surgery and hygiene. As an example may be cited the medical treatise *Naiman gishuud*, composed on the basis of the ancient Indian shastra *Ayurved* and a medical work *Charakasamkhita*, compiled in the early years of our era.

Great popularity was enjoyed in Mongolia by such ancient Indian literary works as the tales from *Panchatantra*, the collections *Tales of the 32 Wooden Warriors*, *The Enchanted Corpse*, etc. Most of these works became completely acclimatized in the new terrain and were transformed, one might say, into original Mongolian works.

As they were completely isolated from the world of culture, and from the great scientific discoveries of the XVIII-XIXth centuries, the Mongols had no alternative but to be satisfied merely with what ancient India had given to mankind many hundreds of years before. Not only did they not prove humble followers of Buddhism, as the Manchu conquerors would have liked them to be, they were even jealous guardians of the cultural tradition of ancient Asian countries, especially ancient India and China.

Another extremely strong cultural trend, which penetrated Mongolia from abroad, came from China. In the XVIII-XIXth centuries, a large number of Chinese literary works were translated into Mongolian. They included, it is true, works intended to nurture feelings of loyalty among the Mongols, but most were old romances. Quite different in character are the works of the novella type by Pu Sun-lin, the collection of novellas *Tsing-hu-tsihuang* and certain others. They differ from the feudal romances in that they portray to the reader the life of simple people, their joys and sorrows, simple human feelings, anxieties and experiences.

During the period of alien rule educated people in Mongolia attached great importance to learning the native language and the history of the country. Several important works were written on Mongolian grammar, among which should be mentioned the *Commentary on the Cordial Cloak*, by Danzandagva, the *Ornamentation of Speech* by Agvan-Dandar, the works of Biligun Dalai, the *Lesson in Wisdom* by Togtokhtor, and the *Golden Mirror*, explaining the rules of Mongolian writing, by Lkhamsuren. A characteristic feature of most of these works is that their authors continued and developed the philological tradition of Choizh-Odsor, the author of the first Mongolian grammar. The value of the grammatical works of Mongol authors lies in the fact that they deal with the basic problems of Mongolian grammar, particularly orthography and phonology.

Mongolian philologists also made a study of other languages, principally Tibetan and Sanskrit, and compiled bilingual and multilingual dictionaries. Among the works written by Mongolian authors on Tibetan and Sanskrit grammar should be mentioned those of Zaya-pandita Sumba-Khamba, Agvan-Dandar, Luvasandash, and Bicheezh-tsorzh Agvan-Dorzh. The famous grammatical treatises of the Tibetan author Toimisambata (VIIth century A. D.) were studied all over Mongolia. Many works by Mongolian linguists are interpretations of these very treatises. The earliest of the large lexicographical works are the XVIIIth century four-language dictionary, the Tibetan-Mongolian dictionary *Merged garakhyn oron*—a collective work by a number of authors and an explanatory Manchu-Mongolian dictionary. A Chinese-Manchu-Mongolian dictionary *(Khuraasan bichig)* was compiled in the XIXth century. Other lexicographical works also appeared in the XVIII-XIXth centuries.

Mongolian men of letters wrote in Tibetan a number of works on poetical theory. They represent varying interpretations of an ancient Indian treatise on the theory of poetry—the *Kanyadarsha* of Dandin, translated in the XVIIIth century by the Mongolian translator Gelegzhamtso.

These include the works of Sumba-Khamba, Bicheezhtsorzh Agvan-Dorzh, Agvan-Dandar, Zhamyan-Garbo and others.

In the XVIII-XIXth centuries a number of major historical works appeared, including *The Flow of Gang* by the *gun* Gombozhav, the *Golden Wheel with a Thousand Spokes* by Shireetgush Darm, the *Crystal Beads* by Rashipuntsag, the *Precious Beads* by Galdan and the *Blue Book*. Among the Mongolian-Tibetan historical works may be mentioned the *Clear Mirror*, by Luvsanprelei, the historical works of Sumba-Khamba, the *History of Buddhism in Mongolia* by Tsembel-gush, the *History of Buddhism in Mongolia* by Darmadela, etc.

With the Mongols, history, like other branches of learning, served the cause of the Buddhist religion. One of the essential features of Mongolian historiography of this period is that its development was noticeably affected by the lengthy rule of the alien Manchu conquerors.

However narrow its religious outlook and however pro-Manchu the ideas it expressed, Mongolian historiography in the XVIII-XIXth centuries did, on the whole, signify a step forward as compared with what it had previously been. By this time there had been a considerable widening of the subjects treated by historical writers, the methods and techniques of writing history had been improved and there had been a great increase in the number of sources used by Mongolian historians.

The considerable achievement of Mongolian historiography in this period may be considered the appearance in it of a critical trend, an understanding of history as a subject designed to preserve folk memories of the historical past of the country under the conditions of alien rule.

An important representative of the critical trend is Rashipuntsag who in 1775 wrote a history of the Yuan Empire. In the case of this historian it is not difficult to notice the keenly critical attitude he adopts to his sources and the attempts, sometimes very successful, he makes to view with a critical eye and make a thorough analysis of particular historical events. Furthermore, at the end of the work Rashipuntsag gave his own personal views on the need to be critical and argumentative in the writing of history.

It is a fact that no overt action was taken by Mongolian historians against Manchu rule. In the difficult circumstances of Manchu rule this, of course, was hardly to be expected.

A positive feature in Mongolan historiography of this period was the striving of the historians to expand historical knowledge among Mongolian people. The Mongol chroniclers took up the study of the history of China, Tibet, India and other countries of Asia and showed themselves to be well acquainted with historical sources for these countries. As an example one may cite Sumba-Khamba Ishbalzhir and the *gun* Gombozhav, who wrote important works on the history of India, China and Tibet. Sumba-Khamba's works supply valuable historical information about the Turkish Empire, its capital Istanbul, the Moslem countries, Mecca, Russia and its capital Moscow, Germany, etc.

In the XVIIIth century one can also observe the beginning of the penetration into Mongolia of the exact sciences—in 1712 a translation was made from Chinese into Mongolian of the so-called *Treatise on Co-ordinates* ("Sol'bi-tsan-barikh bodrol bichig"). It should be noted that the authors of the translation did not confine themselves to mere translation but introduced their own amplifications and amendments. This work was important, too, in the sense that the Mongolian language was enriched by a new body of scientific expressions.

An interesting memorial of Mongol feudal culture of the mid-XIXth century are the ethical-economic precepts of To-Van, who has already been mentioned above as the author of a work on grammar. The *Precepts* of To-Van, a governor of one of the *khoshuns*, represent one of the first economic works in Mongolia.

As regards Mongol art of this particular period, folk artists had for centuries been perfecting their skill. Works from their clever hands could be seen in monasteries, in residences of feudal nobles and in a simple *arat's yurt*.

Here mention should be made of the emergence of elements of a Mongol style in architecture.

The origin of Mongol architecture is linked up with the construction of permanent temples and all kinds of monastery buildings. In erecting buildings of this type the lamas more often than not resorted to the Chinese and Tibetan styles. However, a simple imitation of foreign examples did not satisfy the builders; they sought to create something of their own, in the national style. The basic example for Mongol architecture was the nomad's *yurt*. This is why in the Mongol steppes *yurt*-shaped buildings appeared which were basically Lamaist temples.

The architects devoted a great deal of attention to the construction of the roof, which is one of the main architectural components of the whole building. They began to decorate roofs, sometimes with dormer windows and with a superstructure *(gokhon)* on the top. From the outside the *gokhon* looks like a small house in Chinese style.

Some of the pyramid-shaped roofs of square buildings are ornamented. On the very top of the roof so-called *khalz*, reminiscent of wheels, were erected. Along the edges of the roof three lines were drawn and discs placed on the centre line. These discs are called *erikh* (beads) or *tol* (mirror).

Elements of Mongol architecture formed a component part of buildings in a mixed style. Some temples have the lower part in Tibetan style, while the upper part ends in a *yurt*-shaped superstructure. Other combinations of Mongol style with Chinese or Tibetan may be seen.

Attempts to build *yurt*-shaped structures have been noted even in the contemporary period.

SECTION SIX

THE NATIONAL-LIBERATION MOVEMENT OF THE MONGOLIAN PEOPLE (1911-1912). DECLARATION OF MONGOLIAN STATE AUTONOMY

CHAPTER I

THE MOVEMENT FOR NATIONAL LIBERATION, 1911-1912

The beginning of the XXth century found Mongolia on the verge of complete impoverishment and ruin. Internal and external exploiters, namely, the Mongol feudal nobles, both secular and spiritual, the Manchu Chinese bureaucratic administration, foreign capitalist traders and usurers and finally, international imperialism vied with one another in intensively exploiting the Mongol people and destroying the productive forces of the country. This naturally resulted in the collapse of the basis of the economy—large-scale nomadic stock-breeding. Everywhere could be seen cases of *arat* holdings, whole *khoshuns* and regions being ruined; the country's basic wealth—livestock—became increasingly concentrated, principally in the hands of a small group of the leading feudal nobles and Chinese usurers. The *arats*, having been deprived of their source of livelihood—livestock—became shepherds or herdsmen for other people and eked out a beggarly, half-starved existence. Hunger and devastation were rampant everywhere and the country underwent a profound crisis.

There are numerous source materials, both official and those cited in the works of explorers and travellers, which vividly depict the depth and the acuteness of this crisis. One example is the *khoshun* of Tseren-Dzasak in the *aimak* of Tushetu Khan, the *arat* population of which was obliged in 1892 to pay the *khoshun's* debts to merchants and usurers, amounting to more than 100,000 *lan*, and to deposit in the *aimak djisan* (treasury) for various official needs an onerous quit-rent in goods and cash. The *arats* of this *khoshun* had, in addition, to acquire new weapons and equipment for the soldiers of their *somons* and equip military detachments to carry out frontier service. As the authorities of this *khoshun* themselves admitted, the entire property of the *arats* would not have sufficed for the discharge of the obligations imposed on them. Quite naturally, the *arat* population of this *khoshun* increasingly lost its economic independence. Twenty years later, in 1912, the *khoshun* was visited by a Russian traveller, Sveshnikov, who remarked that the *arats* here were merely the shepherds of the flocks of Chinese usurers and the carriers of their merchandise.

In 1912 in the *khoshun* Gonchik-Choindjon-dzasak of the *aimak* of Sian-noyon Khan a single *arat* holding had on an average only 2 head of cattle and 15 sheep and goats. Such a quantity of livestock could not possibly provide the *arats* with a livelihood, crushed as they were under the burden of feudal imposts and servitudes, and they were forced to obtain a livelihood for themselves from various earnings on the side. The miserable situation of the *arat* population was intensified still further by the fact that the indebtedness of this *khoshun* to Chinese firms amounted on an average to 100 *lan* for one *arat* holding. In the *khoshun* of Galdan-dzasak of the same *aimak* the *khoshun dzasak*, after exhausting all the usual sources of revenue, could find nothing better than to impose a special tax on beggars for the right to collect alms. Thenceforth, beggars had to allocate part of their "income" for the benefit of the governing feudal nobles. The situation of most of the other *khoshuns* of Mongolia was little different from that described above.

The unbridled and unlimited despoliation of the Mongol *arats* enriched the feudal nobles, temporal and spiritual, the traders, and the usurers, in whose hands enormous wealth was concentrated. This wealth, however, was not invested in the national economy, did not help to raise the subsistence level and the culture of the population and was not used to create a new and more progressive method of production.

In respect of its level of development Mongolia was, at the time described, an extremely backward country. The Manchu dynasty had done everything to deprive the Mongol people of the conditions necessary for social-economic and cultural development. As a result of the exceptional backwardness of the Mongolian economy and the low level of development of national handicrafts and industry, the *arats* became people whose labour could not be productively employed.

Colonialist oppression and the very brutal exploitation practised by the feudal nobles were a basic obstacle to the cultural development of the Mongol people, too. The natural result of such a policy was the practically universal illiteracy of the population and the low cultural level of the country. No newspapers or journals were published.

The yoke of the Manchus had a disastrous effect not only on the material conditions of life of the Mongol people, not only on their cultural level, but also on their physical condition and faced them with a direct threat of extinction. By the time Manchu rule ended almost one-half of the male population of the country were lamas. The existence of a hundred-thousand-strong army of lamas, bound by a vow of celibacy, inevitably resulted in a fall in the number of marriages and births. On the other hand, Mongolia had a numerous colony of Chinese merchants and usurers and their staffs, living temporarily in the country, without families. All this could not fail to have an undesirable effect on the Mongol family. Tibetan medicine, as the only form of medical help available to the people, could not safeguard the *arats* from the spread of diseases or from extinction. Doctors *(emchi)* were trained in Lamaist monasteries where the teaching given amounted merely to learning by heart the Tibetan texts of ancient Indian medical treatises *(Djud-shi)*, compiled some 2,500 years previously. These ignorant doctors "treated" the sick mainly by incantations and prayers. The insanitary conditions of the living accommodation and food and the low level of the whole structure of everyday life contributed to the widespread dissemination of social diseases and various epidemics.

The miserable conditions of life spurred the Mongol people on to fight for the abolition of the system which had brought them endless suffering and ruin. In the specific conditions of the end of the XIXth and the beginning of the XXth centuries the main obstacle blocking Mongolia's progress was the rule of the Manchu dynasty, and its overthrow was the basic task directly confronting the Mongol people. Unless the Manchu yoke was overthrown they could not hope to create the conditions requisite for overcoming their centuries-old backwardness and going forward.

Discontent increased more and more in the country and took the form of spontaneous outbursts by the *arats* against the Manchu authorities. These outbursts, which intensified considerably under the influence of the 1905 revolution in Russia, showed that ideas of a liberation struggle were beginning to get a hold over the *arat* masses. At the same time there was a growth in the sympathy felt by the *arats* for Russia, for the great Russian people who had heroically fought against tsarism. Nor even the predatory activities of Russian merchants, which differed little from those of the Chinese usurers, could stand in the way of this.

At the same time the development of a revolutionary consciousness among the *arats* was hampered to an extraordinary degree by the way they were split up and scattered over an enormous territory where there was on an average 2-3 square kilometres of land surface per person and no other means of communication or travel but horses and camels. Immense difficulties also arose in connection with the whole system of the ideological influence exerted by the lamas over the *arats* who, from childhood upwards, were imbued with religious mysticism and veneration for lamas, especially those of high rank, and also for their own feudal masters.

The class of *arat* serfs was the main driving force of the national-liberation movement in Mongolia, which developed under the influence of the Russian revolution of 1905 and in close connection with the revolution which had begun in China. The general conditions, however, in both domestic and international affairs, were unfavourable for the *arats*. Mongolia had no national working class which would have been capable of heading a national uprising and ensuring its victorious consummation. Nor did the *arat* population of Mongolia have any experience of organized struggle or any revolutionary political organisation of its own. The leadership of the movement, therefore, fell into the hands of the feudal nobles and the senior-ranking lamas, and it was they who at this stage reaped the fruits of the national struggle.

Relations between the Mongol feudal nobles and the Manchu dynasty began to change at the end of the XIXth century; from slavish servility to Manchu governors the feudal nobles began to move into positions of conflict with them. This was mainly due to a change in Manchu policy in Mongolia, aimed at colonizing Mongol lands, increasing the number of Manchu-Chinese troops in Mongolia, removing Mongol feudal nobles from the government of the country and strengthening the Manchu-Chinese administration. The growth of anti-Manchu feeling amongst the feudal nobles is also to a considerable degree explained by a general weakening in the foreign and domestic positions of the Manchu dynasty. The continuing devastation of the country and impoverishment of the *arats* contributed to this trend and as a result there were fewer possibilities for feudal exploitation of the *arats*. Finally, the Mongol feudal nobles were forced to follow the path of struggle against Manchu rule by the expansion and intensification of the spontaneous national-liberation struggle of the *arats* which threatened to develop into a struggle against the feudal nobles themselves. The Mongol princes were seeking to liberate the country from alien bondage, not because they were standing up for the interests of their people but because they wanted to place at the head of Mongolia their own Khan who would give them undivided control of the people and restore to them monopoly rights over the exploitation of the *arats*.

Realizing their weakness, the Mongol khans and princes looked for support to Russian tsarism with whose help they hoped to free themselves from the rule of the Manchu dynasty, keep the *arats* in submission and preserve their own privileges. But while the feudal classes rested all their hopes in tsarist Rusian and in Russian landlords and capitalists, the *arats* could obtain help only from the working classe of Russia.

CHAPTER II

THE OVERTHROW OF MANCHU RULE
AND THE FORMATION OF A FEUDAL-THEOCRATIC
MONGOLIAN STATE

In the era of imperialism Mongolia became the object of fierce struggles between imperialist forces. The very rich natural resources of the country and its strategically advantageous geographical situation attracted the attention of the imperialist plunderers of the Old and New Worlds. But the principal pretenders for domination in Mongolia were Japan and tsarist Russia.

Mongolia attracted the attention of the Japanese imperialists not only because of its riches but also as a jumping-off point for aggression against China and Russia. These were the ambitions which were subsequently used by imperialist Japan as a basis for the so-called Tanaka plan.

Tsarist Russia's interest in Mongolia stemmed, on the one hand, from considerations of defence against the far-reaching aggressive plans of Japan and, on the other hand, from the interest taken by Russian capital in the Mongolian market. Whereas, prior to the Russo-Japanese war, tsarist Russia had refrained from pursuing an active policy in Outer Mongolia because it lay outside the basic trends of its imperialist policy, after the war and the conclusion of a series of agreements with Japan concerning the division of spheres of influence the situation changed. Outer Mongolia began to occupy an important place in the policy of tsarist Russia.

Russian merchants and manufacturers, interested in exporting their products and in sources of cheap raw materials, began to pay special attention to Outer Mongolia. Their efforts to strengthen their positions in Mongolia met with opposition from Chinese capitalist traders and usurers who had become the servants of big American, British and Japanese firms. In reliance on these firms and with the support of the Manchu-Chinese authorities, Chinese merchants had a virtual monopoly on the Mongolian market and were displacing from it Russian goods and Russian capitalists. The result was that Russia's adverse balance of trade with Mongolia increased from year to year, and the Russian capitalists were compelled to cover it by exporting to Mongolia precious metals. In the years between 1891 and 1908 exports of goods from Russia to Mongolia rose by 22%, whereas imports into Russia of raw materials from Mongolia for the same years rose by 566%. Mongolia was an important source of raw materials for Russian industry. By 1909 Mongolia was supplying Russia with 12% of the leather raw materials she imported, 13% of the wool and furs, 25.5% of the horse hair, 10.5% of the cattle, 10.8% of the horses and 24.9% of the goats and sheep.

Russian commercial circles and manufacturers tried to set up a body capable of standing up to competition on the Mongolian market. In 1912 a Russian Export Association was organised in Moscow, headed by the well-known millionaire, merchant and manufacturer, Ryabushinsky, and it opened branches in Urga and Ulyasutai. But this was not enough. The big merchant and industrial circles began to call for tsarism to take a more active line, and also to demand effective measures for the "protection" of their interests in Mongolia. The nobility and court aristocrats who had an interest in colonialist ventures in their turn, exercised pressure on the foreign policy of the tsarist government and also insisted on active steps being taken in Mongolia. The new trend of Manchu policy towards the colonization of Mongolia evoked the displeasure of the ruling circles in tsarist Russia, for its implementation could seriously hamper Russian tsarism in its own expansionist schemes.

Nevertheless, the government of tsarist Russia was obliged to go cautiously, afraid that a policy of direct action might produce undesirable reactions from other imperialist states.

Even at that time imperialist Japan was seeking in every way possible to establish its supremacy in Mongolia. Its next task at this time was the enslavement of Inner Mongolia. The division of spheres of influence with tsarist Russia had put almost the whole of Inner Mongolia into Japanese hands. As a result greedy Japanese imperialism found itself the immediate neighbour of Outer Mongolia, to which Japanese military circles were dispatching their own agents and spies in small groups. The ruling circles of Japan, backing on the deep religious feelings of the *arat* masses of Mongolia, posed as protectors of Buddhism and Lamaism.

Thus the proximity of Japanese imperialism was for Outer Mongolia fraught with a constant threat of armed intervention and conversion into a Japanese colony.

In addition to Japan and tsarist Russia, other imperialist countries, especially the USA and Great Britain, were actively engaged in the struggle for supremacy in Mongolia, each seeking to take over the Mongolian market for itself. As a tool of their policy they exploited the government of the wholly decadent Manchu dynasty and, after the latter was overthrown, the various military cliques of reactionary Chinese generals, as well as Chinese capitalist traders and usurers. Through the medium of Chinese merchants and usurers Mongolian raw materials were beginning to come on to the market of Europe, America and also Japan in increasing quantities every year; through the same intermediaries, too, goods were exported to Mongolia from Japan, USA and Great Britain and successfully competed with the dearer goods from Russia.

In China the Manchu dynasty still continued to cling to power, although its days were clearly numbered. A revolution was brewing in the country and the ruling clique was no longer able to suppress it. On the other hand, however, because of the unfavourable international and internal conditions a revolution in China would not at this stage be able to solve the problem of transferring power to the people.

Such was the international position of Outer Mongolia on the eve of the events of 1911. In these circumstances the foreign policy best suited to the interests of the Mongol people would have been one that ensured reinforcement of its links with the great Russian people and which might have linked up its revolutionary struggle with the revolutionary struggle of the working class in Russia which, from the beginning of the XXth century, had been in the forefront of the international proletarian movement. At the time here described the prerequisites for a new revolutionary uprising were coming into being in Russia. The establishment of links with Russia opened the door into Mongolia for the progressive ideas of socialism and democracy and for friendship and co-operation between peoples. On the other hand, a policy directed towards establishing links with imperialist Japan or with other imperialist states held out no prospect for Outer Mongolia except reaction, fresh colonialist enslavement and ultimate ruin. Exactly the same result would have ensued for Outer Mongolia had policy of collusion with Chinese reaction been adopted. In this case Mongolia could not have avoided becoming a colony of one of the imperialist powers—Great Britain, America or Japan, depending on who was pulling the strings of the puppet militarist grouping which at the particular moment was in power in China.

The road to liberation of the Mongol people from the chains of colonialist and feudal oppression lay through strengthening the traditional friendship with the Russian people and also with the labouring classes of China who at this time had risen up in a revolutionary rebellion, which soon led to the overthrow of the Manchu dynasty.

The Manchu policy of the Great Powers in Outer Mongolia began to assume specially active form in the last few years of the rule of the Manchu dynasty. At the beginning of 1911 a special representative of the Ministry of War, Colonel Tan, arrived in Urga from Peking with a large number of officials. His main task was the reorganization of the military administration of Mongolia. On his orders barracks began to be built not far from Urga. The upkeep of all the newly-created departments, the innumerable journeys of officials and the cost of building barracks—all fell as an additional burden on the backs of the *arats*. The discontent of the masses grew and the situation in the country became more and more heated.

In July 1911 a meeting was held in Urga in secrecy from the Manchu authorities; it was attended by the most important feudal nobles, secular and religious, headed by the *Bogdo-gegen*. The meeting was also attended by representatives of Inner Mongolia and it discussed the situation in the country. Realizing the new trend in Manchu policy and the atmosphere prevailing among the *arats*, the participants in the meeting felt it was impossible to remain under the rule of the Manchu dynasty any longer. This decision was taken, following long discussions, by the majority of the participants, who pointed out that the revolution that had begun in China created a favourable situation for proclaiming the independence of Mongolia. The meeting took a decision to send a special deputation to Russia to negotiate for help.

The diplomatic representative of tsarist Russia was notified by the initiators of the meeting both of its having been convened and also of the decisions adopted. On July 28, 1911 he telegraphed to St. Petersburg and reported that a deputation would very shortly leave Urga for Russia to hand the Tsar a request that Mongolia be taken under the protection of Russia and that it would be given full powers to conduct negotiations for help by Russia to the new Mongol state, whose aim should be to unite Khalkha and Inner Mongolia.

After some hesitation, the tsarist government decided to receive the deputation on the understanding that "an effort would be made to put this matter in a desirable light for us," as the acting Prime Minister of the tsarist government, Kokovtsov, phrased it in his letter to the temporary head of the Foreign Ministry, Neratov.

Headed by the officer commanding the troops of the *aimak* of Tushetu Khan, the Ching-van Khanda-Dordji, the deputation of Mongol feudal nobles arrived in the Russian capital on August 15. A day later it was received by Sazonov, the Foreign Minister. Khanda-Dordji handed Sazonov a letter from the *Bogdo-gegen* dated July 30 and addressed to the Tsar of Russia containing a proposal to conclude a treaty acknowledging the independence of Mongolia, a trade agreement, an agreement for the construction of railways, for organizing postal communications, etc.; the *Bogdo-gegen* wrote that the khans and princes had decided to drive Chinese traders out of Mongolian territory and to transfer the trade into Russian hands. The letter explained in detail the reasons which had impelled the khans and princes to try to liberate the country from the rule of the Manchu dynasty and to request help from Russia. This part of the letter is interesting in that it reveals the real reasons which had prompted the ruling class of Mongolia to fight against those whom it had served loyally and faithfully for more than two hundred years.

Pointing out that Mongol khans had in the past themselves possessed unlimited rights to dispose at their own discretion of their inheritance, to enter into possession of the same and to appoint their successors and also to award titles and ranks, the authors of the letter wrote that at the present time "... the Chinese *tushemils* (officials) have arrogated this right and are levying tributes of thousands and tens of thousands of *lan* for transfer of inheritance and the award of titles. At the present time there are very many *dzasaks*... who, as they have not sufficient funds, are unable for years to get their titles. The Chinese *bogdykhan* has for many years not bestowed the annual gifts of silk materials to which we are entitled by law." It was further stated that the Manchu authorities "restrict and diminish the rights of many Mongol *dzasaks*."

In addition to the *Bogdo-gegen* this letter was signed by Tushetu Khan Dashi-Nima, Tsetsen Khan Navan-Nerin, Dzasaktu Khan Sodnom-Rabdan and Sain-noyon-khan Namnam-Suren. This document actually outlined the whole programme of the Mongol feudal nobles. As we see, the programme was based on narrow-minded selfish aims, mainly directed towards restoring the right of the feudal nobles to monopolize exploitation of the *arat* population. It was these interests which took priority over general national interests.

The proposals of the Mongol feudal nobles for the complete separation of Mongolia from China and for the proclamation of an official protectorate by Russia over the new Mongolian state were turned down by the tsarist government for fear of unfavourable reactions from the other imperialist powers; it did, however, agree to accept the role of intermediary between Urga and Peking with a view to inducing the Manchu government to abandon the colonization of Mongol lands, the introduction of Manchu-Chinese troops into Khalkha, the imposition on the country of its own administration and other similar reforms. In accordance with the decision adopted, the tsarist government sought to convince Khanda-Dordji and the other members of the deputation of the need to drop the plan of complete separation from China, promising in return to help in the forthcoming negotiations with the government of China. At the same time the tsarist government, through its representatives in Peking, brought pressure to bear on the Manchu government and demanded that it abandon its new course of policy in Mongolia. A powerful anti-Manchu movement by the Chinese people, which began at the end of summer in 1911, resulted, at the beginning of 1912, in the overthrow of the Manchu dynasty and this made it possible for the tsarist government to intervene more decisively in the relations between Urga and Peking. In October 1911 it demanded from the Manchu government a formal, written undertaking not to carry out in Outer Mongolia any reforms without prior agreement with the government of Russia. The government of the Manchus, which was on its last legs, was obliged to agree to this demand. On October 19, 1911, the Russian Embassy in Peking in a special letter stated that the Russian government had noted the declaration of the Manchu government to the effect that no repressions would be applied against the members of the Mongol delegation which had arrived in St. Petersburg. Wishing to reinforce its position vis-à-vis Peking and to show the Mongol feudal nobles that it was prepared to help them, the government of tsarist Russia, on the pretext of protecting the Russian consulate, sent to Urga a battalion of infantry and several squadrons of Cossacks.

In the middle of October 1911 the deputation of Khanda-Dordji returned to Urga. After discussing the results of the negotiations, and in view of the help promised by the tsarist regime and in the light of the revolution that was developing in China, the higher circles of the feudal nobles set about taking action. A committee of princes and senior lamas, formed for the purpose of leading the revolution, summoned to Urga on November 28, 1911, the Mongol militia from the nearest *khoshuns* and on November 30 presented a demand to the Manchu *amban* Sando-van that he leave the confines of Outer Mongolia.

On December 1, 1911, an appeal to the Mongol people was published, which stated: "Our Mongolia, when it was first founded, was a separate state and so, taking its stand on ancient right, Mongolia affirms that it is an independent state with a new government, with independent authority for handling its affairs. In view of the aforesaid it is hereby declared that we Mongols from now onwards will not submit to Manchu and Chinese officials whose authority is completely destroyed and therefore they must set off for home."

The Chinese garrison in Urga had no desire to defend the authority of the Manchu dynasty against which at this very moment the Chinese people had risen in rebellion. Rightly fearing the wrath of the masses and realizing the futility of resistance, Sando-van with his officials and their families sought refuge inside the walls of the tsarist consulate in Urga, which took them under its protection. On December 4, 1911, Sando-van and other officials left Urga for China under escort by Russian Cossacks. The tsarist consulate undertook the protection also of the Chinese merchants when the long-restrained hatred of the Mongol *arats* began to spill over into spontaneous action. The *chang-chung* of Ulyasutai who, like Sando-van, was helpless against the revolt of the people, also offered no serious resistance and at the end of December 1911 left Mongolia.

In the Kobdo region the situation developed on different lines as the Manchu *amban* had at his disposal a numerous garrison and large supplies of food and military stores. In the expectation of receiving help from Sinkiang, whence reinforcements had already been sent him, the *amban* refused to acknowledge the new Mongolian authority. He shut himself up inside the fort and began preparing for defence. At this point, however, the government of tsarist Russia stepped in and resolutely insisted that the Peking authorities should keep the troops from Sinkiang where they were. As a result the reinforcements from Sinkiang were halted at a distance from Kobdo, to which the rebel *arats* laid siege. On August 6, 1912, the city and fort of Kobdo were stormed and captured by the *arats*, whose military operations were commanded by Maksarzhav and Damdin-Suren. The population of Kobdo smashed up the shops and stores of the Chinese merchants and usurers and destroyed the debt records.

Thus, as a result of the powerful upsurge of the national-liberation movement of the Mongol *arats*, Mongolia threw off the Manchu yoke, which had lasted more than two centuries, drove the detested Manchu-Chinese bureaucracy out of the country and dealt a mighty blow at the positions of the Chinese merchants and usurers. But the government of the country did not pass into the hands of the Mongol people who had played a decisive part in the liberation struggle. Instead it went to the feudal nobles and the high-ranking lamas, who proclaimed the *Bogdo-gegen* Khan of the new Mongol state. On December 16, 1911, in Urga, in the Uzun-hure Monastery, a ceremony was held to celebrate the enthronement as Khan of the *Bogdo-gegen*, head of the Lamaist church, who was given the title "elevated by many." The *Bogdo-gegen* appointed a government in the first membership of which the portfolio of Prime Minister and Foreign Minister was given to one of the principal feudal religious nobles, Tseren-Chimid, the Foreign Minister was Khanda-Dordji, the post of War Minister was held by Dalai-van, that of Minister of Finance by Tushetu-van Gombo-Suren and of Minister of Justice by Namsarai-gun.

Thus, more than two hundred years after the destruction of Mongolian statehood, it was restored in the form of an unlimited feudal-theocratic monarchy. The creation of an independent Mongolian state, as the result of a powerful national-liberation movement of the Mongol people in 1911-1912, in spite of its being essentially feudal, was, objectively considered, a progressive phenomenon in the history of the country.

The new stage in the national-liberation movement was consummated by the liquidation of the Manchu colonialist regime in Mongolia and the restoration of national statehood. Nevertheless, this was not a complete solution of the tasks of the movement for whose sake the oppressed and freedom-loving Mongol people had fought. The Mongol feudal nobles, secular and religious, having taken charge of the struggle for liberation, exploited it in their narrow class interests and lost no time in turning the newly-created state into an instrument for exploiting the masses.

At this time the national-liberation movement in Inner Mongolia also was passing through a stormy phase of development. Uprisings occurred there in almost all the *khoshuns*. But, just as in Khalkha, the princes of Inner Mongolia seized control of the movement themselves. Such was the situation, too, in Western Mongolia. Thus, the wide sweep of the anti-Manchu movement which in 1911-1912 had encompassed Inner and Khalkha-Mongolia, was the only liberation movement of the Mongol people against whom, over a period of two hundred years, the Manchu authorities had pursued a policy of enforced isolation and artificial disunion. These efforts, however, could not halt the general aspiration of the Mongols to get rid of alien oppression and defend their liberty and the independence of their native land.

The movement reached its peak at the beginning of 1912 in Barga, which announced its accession to the Mongol state of Khalka. The majority of the *khoshuns* of Inner Mongolia (35 out of 49) declared that they were joining willingly. At that time in Inner Mongolia a most brutal colonialist policy was being pursued by the Manchu dynasty, as a result of which Mongol herdsmen were being driven out into the empty wastes to an ever greater extent. National oppression was intensified. All this stimulated the growth of the national-liberation movement in Inner Mongolia, which assumed various forms: armed uprising, migration into Khalkha, active assistance to the Khalkha troops, etc.

Numerous petitions, certified by signatures and seals, were sent to Urga from diets, *khoshuns* and also from individual persons.

The higher feudal circles of Khalkha and Inner Mongolia, in their efforts to unite the Mongol lands and to form a single national government, were motivated, of course, not so much by general national interests as by a desire to secure their right to monopolize the exploitation of the *arat* population.

The movement to unite the *khoshuns* of Inner Mongolia with Khalkha also had the active support of the government of the state set up by the feudal lords of Khalkha. Objectively, this policy of the *Bogdo-gegen's* government suited the interests of the masses, which were also trying to unite all the Mongol lands and create a strong national state.

The success of this policy depended primarily on the attitude of tsarist Russia. The government of the latter, however, guided by the interests of its own imperialist-minded middle classes, was opposed to the formation of a fully independent Mongol state; it also rejected the proposal to unite Barga and the *khoshuns* of Inner Mongolia with Khalkha-Mongolia. Japan and the other imperialist powers were also against the union of the two parts of Mongolia.

Taking advantage, however, of the difficult position of the government of the Manchu dynasty, the government of tsarist Russia started pressing for a wide degree of autonomy for Khalkha-Mongolia. In December 1911 the Russian Ambassador in Peking proposed to the government of China the conclusion of a formal treaty with Khalkha giving the latter extensive internal autonomy within the limits of the Chinese state. At the same time the tsarist government demanded official recognition of Russia's special rights in Khalkha-Mongolia and an agreement not to undertake any measures in the latter without the prior agreement of the government of Russia.

In January 1912 the Chinese people overthrew the detested Manchu dynasty, and the government of tsarist Russia opened negotiations regarding Khalkha-Mongolia with the new government of China, which dragged on unsuccessfully all through 1912. Voicing the views of the trading, usurer and bureaucratic circles of China, the government of Yuan Shih-kai categorically refused to recognize the separation of Mongolia from China. An equally decisive refusal was given to tsarist Russia's proposal that Mongolia be given internal autonomy.

Convinced of the impossibility of reaching agreement with the government of Yuan Shih-kai, the tsarist government decided to legalize independently the existence of Mongolia's autonomy and its predominating interest in it. As a result of lengthy negotiations between the representative of tsarist Russia, Korostovets, and the plenipotentiary of the government of the *Bogdo-gegen*, a Russo-Mongolian agreement was signed in Urga on November 3, 1912.

The very fact of the conclusion of such a treaty had an important political significance for the feudal-theocratic Mongol state. It meant that the government of the *Bogdo-gegen* had already entered into treaty agreements with such a great power as tsarist Russia and had begun to appear in the international arena as an independent force.

Russo-Mongolian negotiations began in Urga, and there were heated disputes which almost ended in their breaking down. Eventually, the parties agreed that in the text of the treaty the political independence of the Mongol state would be expressed in an indefinite formula, so that the Mongolian party could consider it as "full independence" and the Russians as "autonomy". This is the explanation of the utterance of the Minister of Foreign Affairs, Khanda-Dorji when, in conversation in St. Petersburg with the correspondent of the Vladivostok newspaper *Dalekaya Okraina* in January 1913, he remarked that, in concluding the Urga Agreement "we understood that by this document recognition is given to the full independence of Mongolia from China and we are firmly resolved to defend this..."

The preamble of this agreement noted that "in view of the desire of the Mongols to preserve the original structure of their country, Manchu troops and Manchu authorities have been removed from Mongolian territory and Djebtszun-damba-khutukhta has been proclaimed the sovereign of the Mongol people. The former relations between Mongolia and China have thus been removed from Mongolian territory and Djebtszun-damba-khutukhta has been proclaimed the sovereign of the Mongol people. The former relations between Mongolia and China have thus been ended." The agreement did not recognize Mongolia as an independent state and it evaded the question of the mutual relations between it and China. The agreement promised the Mongolian government Russia's help in the maintenance of autonomy, formation of armed forces, and prevention of Chinese colonization or the entry of Chinese troops. A protocol annexed to the agreement defining the rights of Russian citizens in Mongolia was phrased in blatantly imperialist terms; it gave Russian capitalists the right to travel throughout the country without let or hindrance, to engage in any trade they pleased, to be domiciled and to acquire immovable property, to import goods into Mongolia duty-free and export from it livestock and raw materials, to be exempted from all internal taxation and to enjoy exterritorial rights.

Prior to the conclusion of this agreement there had been stubborn struggles among the ruling circles of Mongolia who were seeking to implement their foreign policy programme. The higher ruling circles of Mongolia insisted that the agreement should clearly define the status of Barga and Inner Mongolia as integral parts of a single Mongol state. The representative of tsarist Russia objected to this. The single concession made by the government of tsarist Russia was that the expression "Outer Mongolia" would be replaced throughout the text of the agreement by the word "Mongolia". Even on this point, though, the tsarist representative, acting on instructions from St. Petersburg, explained in a secret note to the representatives of the Mongolian government that the tsarist government reserved the right to decide to what regions, apart from Khalkha itself, it would extend its guarantees to protect autonomous rights.

In pursuance of its imperialist aims in Mongolia, tsarist Russia was, in the objective sense, assisting in the progressive development of events in Mongolia. In actual fact, it recognized the existence of a Mongolian state.

A treaty between Russia and Mongolia, phrased in such highly ambiguous and veiled terms, aroused immediate reactions internationally. The imperialist competitors of tsarist Russia, fearing a strengthening of the positions of the latter in Mongolia and the whole of China behind the Wall, sharply criticized its foreign policy. The China of Yuan Shih-kai, which claimed Mongolia as an ordinary Chinese province, refused even to recognize the Russo-Mongolian treaty.

As for Mongolia proper, the refusal of tsarism to recognize Outer Mongolia and Barga being united to it aroused serious discontent among the bigger feudal nobles and high-ranking lamas. Even during the course of the negotiations there were cases of higher feudal nobles demanding the establishment of a link with Japan or the conclusion of an independent agreement with China. Korostovets, the representative of tsarist Russia, reported to St. Petersburg in October 1912 as follows: "Under the influence of agitation hostile to Russia Dalai Lamas, *shantszotbas* and some other dignitaries have recently shown themselves noticeably cooler to the agreement with us and are veering towards a rapprochement with China, with whom, as I know definitely, secret dealings are continuing".

Shortly after the signature of the Russo-Mongolian treaty the *Bogdo-gegen* sent the Dalai Lama, Tseren-Chimid, to Japan with a letter to the Japanese Emperor raising the question of giving "aid", i.e. practically speaking, of establishing Japanese protectorate over Mongolia. It is true that the Japanese imperialists, not being anxious at the time openly to spoil relations with tsarist Russia, held up the envoy of the *Bogdo-gegen* in Hailar, whence he was obliged to return to Urga, but the very attempt to appeal to the Emperor of Japan showed that the theocratic clique was ready to enter into collusion with the worst enemies of the Mongol people—the Japanese imperialists.

In 1912 a second mission, under Khanda-Dorji, was sent from Urga to St. Petersburg to negotiate with the government of tsarist Russia on frontiers, a loan, help in the organisation of an army, etc. The central topic in the negotiations was the problem of frontiers. As a result of the negotiations tsarism agreed to the Kobdo district being added to Outer Mongolia but rejected all the other territorial claims of Urga. In February 1913 a special agreement was signed for the formation of a

Mongol brigade, consisting of two cavalry regiments with machine-guns and an artillery sub-section, amounting altogether to 1,900 soldiers and officers. The Mongol government was to invite Russian instructors to train the personnel of the brigade. The agreement was concluded for a term of one year. The tsarist government also agreed to give the *Bogdo-gegen's* government a loan of 2,000,000 roubles and some armament.

With these results achieved Khanda-Dorji's mission left the capital of Russia in March 1913 and set out for home.

While conducting negotiations with tsarist Russia, the government of the *Bogdo-gegen* was simultaneously seeking opportunities of strengthening its position by establishing diplomatic relations with other states, in particular with the United States of America, the United Kingdom, Germany, Japan, France, Belgium, etc. A letter from the Foreign Minister of the feudal-theocratic state to the State Department of the USA, says that the Mongols "...having severed themselves from the Ching Empire, have set up an independent, sovereign state, have placed on the throne of the Khan of All-Mongolia Djebtszun-damba—the religious head of Khalkha-Mongolia, and have invested him with all the plenitude of governmental and religious power... In informing thereof your honourable government, we beg you to conclude a Treaty of Trade and Friendship. The ninth day of the first month of winter, 1912."

As we have already seen, Urga's attempt to obtain support in Japan had failed. The efforts undertaken by the *Bogdo-gegen's* government to establish contact with other countries were equally unsuccessful. This was hindered by tsarism, which had no desire for the newly-created Mongol state to secure recognition in the international field. Nor did the imperialist states themselves, to which the *Bogdo-gegen's* government had appealed, display any active concern in the question of Mongolia because of the inter-imperialist antagonisms that were becoming increasingly intensified in the Far East.

The conclusion of the Russo-Mongolian agreement of November 3, 1912, aroused great irritation in the Chinese reactionary camp which insistently demanded that Yuan Shih-kai take strict punitive measures against "mutinous" Outer Mongolia. The Peking government began to prepare a punitive expedition from Sinkiang against Outer Mongolia. In the summer of 1913 the government of tsarist Russia despatched Russian troops to the Kobdo area and this compelled the Peking government to recall its troops from the borders of Outer Mongolia.

By this time the situation in Inner Mongolia and Barga had become very heated. The liberation struggle of the people of Inner Mongolia and Barga was confronted with enormous difficulties. Punitive expeditions were sent from Peking. In reply to a request for help the government of the *Bogdo-gegen*, in spite of serious objections by tsarism, sent military units to the *khoshuns* of Inner Mongolia. At the beginning of 1913 bitter fighting broke out between Mongol and Chinese troops, with the pendulum swinging first one way then the other. As an imperialist power tsarist Russia, having restricted by its special treaties with Japan its "sphere of influence" in Inner Mongolia, could not support the *Bogdo-gegen's* claims. When the government of the *Bogdo-gegen* appealed to the government of tsarist Russia with a request to take the *khoshuns* of Inner Mongolia under its protection, it refused. The tsarist government wrote to the government of the *Bogdo-gegen*, saying that if the Chinese troops entered the territory of Outer Mongolia, Russia would immediately come to its help but that it could not give money or troops for conducting military operations outside Khalkha's borders.

This stand on the part of tsarism was known to Peking. Yuan Shih-kai became more and more convinced that he could not begin military operations against Outer Mongolia without clashing with Russia and he neither desired nor was in a position to enter into an armed conflict with her.

In view of the way circumstances had developed tsarist Russia and the Chinese Republic made arrangements, which substantially suited both their purposes, to settle the Mongolian question behind the back of the Mongols themselves—a characteristic feature of international relations in the era of imperialism.

In this fashion the way was prepared for negotiations, which ended on November 5, 1913, with the signature of a Russo-Chinese Declaration recognizing Outer Mongolia's autonomy, the territory of Outer Mongolia as part of the territory of China and the government of China as the suzerain of autonomous Outer Mongolia.

"Acknowledging the exclusive right of the Mongols of Outer Mongolia," the Declaration said, "to be responsible themselves for the internal administration of autonomous Mongolia and to decide all questions affecting this country in the spheres of trade and industry, China undertakes not to interfere in its affairs and accordingly will not maintain there any civil or military authorities and will refrain from any colonization of the said country... Russia, on her part, undertakes not to keep troops in Outer Mongolia with the exception of consulate guards, not to interfere in any branch of the country's administration whatsoever and to abstain from colonizing it."

The government of China agreed that Autonomous Outer Mongolia should consist of the 4 Khalkha *aimaks* and the district of Kobdo. It also agreed that territorial questions connected with Outer Mongolia would be settled only in agreement with the government of tsarist Russia. "As regards political and territorial questions, the Chinese government will settle them with the Russian government through the channel of negotiations in which the authorities of Outer Mongolia will take part."

The Russo-Chinese Declaration of 1913 gave Outer Mongolia a rather wide measure of internal autonomy. The government of Autonomous Mongolia was given the right to conduct negotiations, even with other states, on economic matters and to conclude appropriate agreements. It was only not allowed to conduct negotiations with other states on questions of a political nature or to conclude political treaties. Recognizing China's sovereign rights over Autonomous Mongolia was really an empty formality, as the Chinese government had neither the means nor the power to implement those rights.

In this fashion an attempt was made to decide the fate of Outer Mongolia in 1913 without the participation of the Mongols and behind their backs. The basic provisions of the Russo-Mongolian Treaty, imposed by tsarism on the Mongol people in November 1912, were in 1913 officially recognized and confirmed by the government of China.

The Russo-Chinese Declaration evoked an unfavourable reaction among the ruling circles in Mongolia. On December 2, 1913, the diplomatic representative of Russia in Urga was handed a note from the Mongolian government informing him that the latter categorically refused to recognize the Russo-Chinese Declaration as binding.

This was the official reply of the *Bogdo-gegen's* government to the 1913 Russo-Chinese Declaration on the question of Mongolia. But the Mongolian government as such continued to exist, regardless of what it was called by Russian tsarism and the Chinese Republic.

The government of the *Bogdo-gegen* expected that, if not tsarist Russia, then Japan or another power would come to its aid in defending its independence. Although such expectations were vain, it pursued as far as possible an active foreign policy in an endeavour to emerge into the world arena.

The publication of the Russo-Chinese Declaration of 1913 on the Mongolian question, providing for the formation of an Autonomous Mongolia under the *de facto* protectorate of tsarist Russia, seriously disturbed the imperialism powers—Great Britain, France, Germany, Japan and the USA. Those among them whose interests in one way or another bordered on Outer or Inner Mongolia adopted an equivocal policy. Japan, for instance, would have had no hesitation in enslaving the whole of Mongolia but could not do this as it was tied to tsarist Russia by secret treaties on "spheres of influence" in

Mongolia and so kept a close eye on every move of Russia's in the steppes of Mongolia.

American imperialism evinced great activity in Mongolia. Ever since the end of the XIXth century Mongolia had attracted keen attention from American monopolies which sought to penetrate into Mongolia by securing concessions for exploiting timber and mineral wealth. In 1910 representatives of American financial circles negotiated with the Manchu government to obtain a concession for building a railway from Kalgan to Urga. After the overthrow in Mongolia of the Manchu yoke the policy of American ruling circles, supporters of the reactionary regime of Yuan Shih-kai in China, was to bring Mongolia's autonomy to an end and hand it over to be ruled by China, where American capital held strong positions. After the conclusion of the 1913 Russo-Chinese Declaration the American diplomat Rockhill visited Urga in December 1913 to get acquainted with the situation in Outer Mongola. The representative of American firms in Urga, reflecting the official line taken by the American government on the so-called "Mongolian problem", gave every possible support in the *Bogdo-gegen's* government to the feudal nobles who took their guidance from Yuan Shih-kai China.

This reflected the expansionist policy of American imperialism with regard to Mongolia. At the same time it reflected the general intensification of imperialist antagonisms in the struggle for a repartition of the world.

The government of the *Bogdo-gegen,* taking advantage of the *status quo* in the Far East and exploiting the advances made to it by foreign powers, continued to develop an active foreign policy.

In November 1913 a new Mongolian mission headed by the Prime Minister, Sain-noyon-khan Namnon-Suren, set out for St. Petersburg. Its task was to reach an agreement with the tsarist government on a new loan to Mongolia, additional supplies of arms, etc. On December 4, 1913, Sain-noyon-khan informed the tsarist government in a special Note that the *Bogdo-gegen's* government, having received on November 7 the text of the Russo-Chinese Declaration and made a study of it and of the contents of the Notes exchanged between the representatives of Russia and China, was gratified to realize "...that China and Russia guaranteed and recognized the state structure now existing in Mongolia and its independence in all spheres of international administration, in matters concerning trade and industry, railways, telegraphs, and also financial and economic questions in the same connection, as regards mutual friendly relations with other powers...." "But at the same time," the Note went on, "it has already more than once been declared that Mongolia has finally broken off connections with

China and does not recognize that it is in any way dependent on the latter." "Accordingly," the Note concluded, "the Mongolian government will insist on the boundaries of the Mongolian state being so defined as to include within it all Mongols who have joined."

A similar note was handed by Sain-noyon-khan to the Chinese Embassy in St. Petersburg.

As will be noted, the problem of the union of Inner and Outer Mongolia continued to hold a central place in the foreign policy of the *Bogdo-gegen's* government. At the time when Sain-noyon-khan was negotiating in St. Petersburg with the tsarist government, the troops of Outer Mongolia, notwithstanding the urgings of the government of tsarist Russia, continued to fight, together with the rebel detachments of Inner Mongolia, against the punitive forces of Yuan Shih-kai. The local rebel detachments and the troops of the *Bogdo-gegen's* government that were sent to the spot were successfully battling with superior forces of the enemy and were being given active assistance by the local Mongol population.

Sain-noyon-khan was twice given an audience by the Russian Tsar, Nicholas II, and had many meetings with members of the tsarist government with whom he raised the questions of the future of Inner Mongolia, a loan, supplies of arms, the permanent diplomatic representation of Mongolia in St. Petersburg, etc. For its part, the tsarist government put forward the categorical demand that the *Bogdo-gegen's* government should recall its troops from Inner Mongolia and Barga. The tsarist government made its decision on a number of questions, including the loan and supplies of arms, dependent on Mongolia's complying with this demand.

Finally, the tsarist government agreed to give the *Bogdo-gegen* a new advance of 3 million roubles and to allocate for the needs of the Mongolian army additional arms and equipment. For his part, Sain-noyon-khan, in the name of the *Bogdo-gegen's* government, gave an undertaking to recall from Inner Mongolia and Barga the troops of Outer Mongolia and agreed to accept a Russian specialist proposed by the tsarist government to act as a counsellor to the Mongolian government. Sain-noyon-khan also agreed to take part in the forthcoming tripartite Russo-Chinese-Mongolian negotiations.

In compliance with the undertaking given, the government of the *Bogdo-gegen* withdrew its troops from the confines of Inner Mongolia. In the autumn of 1914 Russian troops, who had entered Mongolia in 1913, were withdrawn.

The *Bogdo-gegen's* government, however, though it withdrew its troops from the fields of battle, did not renounce its aim of uniting the country. It was decided to achieve this through diplomatic channels at the forthcoming tripartite conference.

The Kyakhta tripartite conference occupies a special place in the history of the feudal-theocratic state of Mongolia. The conference, which was attended by China, Khalkha-Mongolia and tsarist Russia, began its work in the autumn of 1914 and completed it eight months later in May 1915. The fact that the conference was so protracted shows the importance of the problem of the future of Mongolia, which was the subject under discussion. Each delegation brought along its own ready-prepared draft which differed radically from each of the other two drafts. The Chinese delegation arrived, firmly determined to reduce the sovereignty of the state of Mongolia to the level of an ordinary Chinese province.

The delegation of tsarist Russia upheld the idea of wide autonomy for Outer Mongolia under the suzerainty of China and completely ignored the question of the fate of Inner Mongolia.

The Mongolian plenipotentiaries, on the other hand, insistently sought for the recognition of Mongolia, including both Inner and Outer Mongolia, as a fully independent state. They did not succeed, however, in getting their views upheld. The Mongolian delegation was obliged ultimately to agree to accept the idea of wide autonomy, with which, after lengthy altercations, the Chinese delegation also concurred. All three parties to the agreement concurred in accepting that Khalkha-Mongolia would remain as part of China, would become an autonomous Mongolia, that China would not bring her troops into it, would not colonize its lands and would not interfere in its internal administration. The Agreement thus fully endorsed the principles laid down in the Russo-Chinese Declaration of November 5, 1913.

In signing the agreement the *Bogdo-gegen's* government thereby recognized as binding on it the Russo-Chinese decision on the future of Outer Mongolia as expressed in the 1913 Declaration.

As usually happens in the practice of international law in the era of imperialism, the outcome of the conference did not depend in the least on the arguments of any one party but on the general balance of forces of the party states, the strong dictating their will to the weak. The Kyakhta Tripartite Agreement was signed on May 25, 1915. According to the statement made by the diplomatic representative of tsarism, "by this document Outer Mongolia is finally recognized as an internally independent state occupying the position of a dependent vassal of China."

The Kyakhta Tripartite Agreement gnally determined the position in international law of the state of Mongolia, reducing it to the level of "Autonomous Outer Mongolia" and this was recognized and signed by the official representatives of the government of the *Bogdo-gegen*.

In this fashion the Mongolian feudal-theocratic state, which had proclaimed its independence following the national-liberation movement of the Mongol people in 1911-1912, existed as such until 1915 and it was only later that it became, *de facto* and *de jure*, Autonomous Outer Mongolia.

Nevertheless, Outer Mongolia continued to function as a state that enjoyed wide autonomous rights and depended on China as a vassal. Even the Chinese viceroys who arrived in Urga and other centres of Outer Mongolia in pursuance of the Tripartite Agreement could not exercise any influence whatever on the policy of the *Bogdo-gegen's* government and in those years merely symbolized the shadowy sovereignty of China. But even that proved to be sufficient for Chinese capitalist traders and money-lenders to start up their activities afresh in Khalkha soon after the conclusion of the Kyakhta Agreement and on the basis thereof.

As regards the masses of the Mongolian people, they were deeply indignant at the outcome of the Kyakhta Conference, which restricted the country's political independence and became a prelude for the intensification of national and colonialist oppression.

The history of the national-theocratic Mongolian state or the *Bogdo-gegen* monarchy, its rise, fall and abolition, as well as the inconsistent struggle, and at times betrayal of the country's national interests by the ruling feudal circles were a political lesson for the Mongolian people.

All this opened the eyes of the Mongolian people, who gradually came to realize that the feudal rulers, like the imperialists were the inveterate enemies of the real freedom and national independence of Mongolia.

CHAPTER III

SOCIAL AND STATE STRUCTURE
OF THE FEUDAL-THEOCRATIC MONARCHY

After throwing off the yoke of the Manchus, Mongolia became a feudal-theocratic empire. The head of the Lamaist church in Mongolia, the *Bogdo-gegen* Dzhebtszun-damba-khutukhta, became the sovereign of the Mongols, an unlimited autocratic monarch who concentrated in his hands all the plenitude of both spiritual and temporal authority.

The principal results of the national-liberation movement of the Mongol people were the rebirth of Mongolian statehood and the liquidation of the centuries-old rule of the Manchus.

The machinery of state set up after the revolution was entirely and completely at the service of the class interests of the feudal nobles and was the instrument used by them for exploiting the Mongol masses. The *arat* Mongols, as the main motive force behind the national-liberation struggle, took energetic action for social and national emancipation. They were, however, betrayed in their hopes. It should be pointed out that the overthrow of the Manchu authorities in Mongolia had as its direct consequence the liquidation of the national oppression operated by the Ching dynasty and this undoubtedly brought the country a certain amount of relief. It did not, however, signify complete freedom from national oppression in general. Chinese capitalist usurers stayed on in the country and began to intensify their activities again; the economic and political influence of tsarism grew in strength and the penetration of capital from the USA, Japan and other imperialist powers continued. The government of Outer Mongolia consisting of five ministers was responsible only to the *Bogdo-gegen*, appointed and dismissed by him. These ministers had charge of foreign affairs, internal affairs, the armed forces, finance and justice. The machinery created by the Manchus for oppressing and exploiting the *arat* population was retained and continued to function as in old times. The machinery of government was controlled entirely by the feudal nobles; they were the only persons permitted to exercise authority.

In 1914 there was established something rather resembling an Upper House, whose members included *dzasaks*, ministers, their deputies and other leading feudal nobles, and a Lower House with a membership of officials and less important feudal nobles. The Houses had deliberative functions only; they were convened at the order of the *Bogdo-gegen* and were dissolved when, in the view of the *Bogdo-gegen*, the need for them had ended.

The institution of a parliament, even though it played an insignificant role in the country's political life, was, nevertheless, a progressive phenomenon which had been brought into existence not so much by the desire of the ruling feudal nobles to use it as a lightning-conductor to deflect the wrath of the people in the event of any particular measures proving a failure, as by the demands of the middle-grade and the petty officials and traders to take part in the administration of the state.

In the *khoshuns* everything remained as in olden times. In the same way as under the Manchus *khoshuns* were divided into *somons* and "tenths". In Autonomous Mongolia, just as during the Manchu era, the *khoshun dzasak* had sovereign power to dispose of the lives of his serfs, whom he ruled with the help of the same *tuslakchi, dzakhirakhchi, meirens* and *dzasaks*. The Manchu *ambans* disappeared but their place was taken by the viceroys *(saitas)* of the *Bogdo-gegen* in Kobdo, Ulyasutai, i.e. the places where the *ambans* formerly had their residences.

The *Bogdo-gegen's* government kept in force the Manchu legislation and the class court established by the Manchus; there was one court for the khans, princes and *taiji* and another court for the *arat* serfs. As before, the *khoshun dzasak* combined in himself judicial, administrative and military power.

As they had been, so the *arats* continued to remain a class of serfs, obliged to maintain by their labour their masters, the feudal nobles, the lamas and a state based on serfdom. The *arats*, who had been deprived of rights under the Manchus, remained equally deprived during this period. As previously, they were divided into *khamdjilga, shabinars* and *albatu*. The lama priesthood continued to be a privileged class of parasites.

An essential characteristic of the social structure of feudal-theocratic Mongolia was its clearly defined theocratic character. The Lamaist feudal priests gained more than others from the overthrow of the Manchus and the formation of the Mongol state. Taking advantage of the fact that the head of the church sat on the throne of the khan, the feudal church leaders began to harry the khans and princes, seeking to snatch for their own benefit the bulk of feudal revenues. The first Prime Minister of the *Bogdo-gegen's* government and Minister of Internal Affairs was one of the most important feudal church nobles, the Da-Lama Tseren-Chimid. Under his direction, shortly after the overthrow of Manchu power, steps were taken to redistribute the livestock belonging to the Manchu Imperial

House which had been confiscated by an edict of the *Bogdo-gegen*. Thousands of camels and horses were distributed to princes and high-ranking lamas and the latter were given a very considerable part of the former imperial herds. Some months later, in 1912, Tseren-Chimid, as Minister of the Interior, sent a written request to Tushetu-van, who was the head of the Ministry of Finance, asking for material assistance to be given to the *Bogdo-gegen's shabinar* department which was "hard up". In the same year, the *Bogdo-gegen*, by special decree, exempted the *shabinars* from all taxes, the charges for conducting services of worship and for procuring images of the gods. In 1916 this decree was "explained" in this manner—that the costs of temple services had to be divided between the treasury of the *Bogdo-gegen* and the state treasury.

High-ranking lamas formed the closest and most influential members of the *Bogdo-gegen's* circle and played a considerable part in determining his foreign and domestic policy. They received from the state treasury enormous sums, completely intolerable for the devastated country, in the form of various subsidies and pensions. Take for instance the case of Lamain-gegen who owned an enormous area of 20,000 sq. km., had 2,000 serf families and, in addition, received from the treasury an annual "subsidy" of 15,000-18,000 roubles in gold. The senior lamas made wide use of state authority to increase the number of their serfs, taking them away from the secular feudal nobles.

At this time there was a particularly large increase in the rights and privileges of the religious feudal lords. On their insistence the government of the *Bogdo-gegen* transferred to the *shabinar* department the whole population of a number of *khoshuns*, thus giving the monasteries and the high-ranking lamas additional sources of enrichment.

The number of *shabinars* in the properties of the *Bogdo-gegen* alone increased during the years of autonomy from 55,479 to 89,362. According to some evidence, about one-third of the whole population of Khalkha in the years of the monarchy was dependent as serfs on the religious feudal nobles. The personal budget of the *Bogdo-gegen* amounted annually to as much as 900,000 *lan* and after him there came seven other leading *khutukhtas* and a great pack of petty *Chubil Khans, khambo, dedkhambo, tsordji,* etc., who under the monarchy had become the leading class in the country.

Such an acute intensification of the economic and political positions of the feudal priesthood could not fail to arouse the opposition of the secular feudal nobles. On this basis a struggle developed, and as time went on grew more acute, in Autonomous Mongolia between the secular khans and princes on the one hand and the senior lamas on the other. It was a struggle between two groups of feudal nobles for the share of each in the distribution of feudal revenues. This struggle found expression in problems connected with the foreign policy of Autonomous Mongolia. The clique of lamas which surrounded the *Bogdo-gegen* had, as we have seen, as early as 1912 embarked on the path of trafficking in the country's interests, offering its dependence, now to the Japanese imperialists, now to the Chinese militarists, in exchange for support for their great power plans. At the other extreme, most of the secular feudal nobles were looking towards Russia, which by then had already become the centre of a world revolutionary movement. In the struggle against its political opponents the *Bogdo-gegen's* clique did not hesitate to make use of poison. This was how it got rid of the Prime Minister, Sain-noyon-khan, and the Foreign Minister, Khanda-Dordji, who were following the policy of strengthening links with Russia.

The basic contradiction, however, in the social structure of Mongolia was the contradiction between the class of feudal nobles and the *arat* serfs. The overthrow of the Ching dynasty's yoke had brought some alleviation to the *arats* by partially freeing them from an enormous debt of fifteen million roubles to the usurers. Throwing off this yoke also freed the *arats* from the cost of maintaining the Manchu-Chinese bureaucracy, the Manchu-Chinese garrisons, etc., which alleviated the burden of taxation under which the *arats* had, up to 1911, been suffocating. The cessation of the colonization begun by the Manchu government removed the menace of pastoral starvation. Nonetheless, the general situation of the *arats* in feudal theocratic Mongolia had not improved; the oppression of feudal exploitation had not weakened. On the contrary, the feudal nobles, anxious to improve their affairs which had been in a shaky condition in the last period of the Manchu dynasty's rule, now exploited the *arats* to the hilt. Accordingly, the impoverishment of the *arat* economy, which had begun under the rule of the Manchus, continued even during the years of the existence of the *Bogdo-gegen* state. Convincing evidence in illustration of this process was submitted by a special expedition organized in 1915 by the Russian counsellor attached to the *Bogdo-gegen's* government. In its report the expedition, which made a study of a quarter of the country, stated "...the extremely small size of families, the small number of children, the relatively large number of the clergy class or lamas, the multiplicity of *shabinars* who do little towards performing servitudes of a general official character, the predominance of poor, weak holdings..." The expedition's report continued with the remark that "... it has been a usual, very common experience for it to come across a Mongol head of a household with no livestock of his own or only an insignificant number. The livestock registered with the family proved to be the property either of a Chinese firm or a monastery... from being a master the Mongol became a labourer or hired hand. In existing circumstances this phenomenon will in every likelihood quickly spread."

The expedition noted everywhere a picture of intolerably high taxes imposed by the *dzasaks* on the *arat* serfs and exacted at the most unexpected moments in the form of livestock or money. "The excessive taxes aggravate the burden of the Mongols' conditions of existence which, even without them, are hard enough. The general system of taxation in Mongolia exerts a powerful influence on the situation of stock-breeding and depresses it completely. Taxes are collected both in kind—livestock, and in money, which the Mongol can only obtain from the sale of livestock. Taxes, collected at short notice and without consideration, oblige the people to borrow the amount needed from traders against the future products of an occupation assessed at a very low amount or to obtain them from the sale of unfattened, low-priced livestock". As the expedition remarked, "Stock-raising in Mongolia is declining fast."

The expedition found that in the *aimak* of Tsetsen Khan in the *khoshun* of Darkhan-tsin-van the *arats* had been ruined by being obliged to pay the personal debts of the prince, that for a long time there had been no increase noted in the size of the population and depopulation was universal. In the *khoshun* of Dzoriktu-beise of the same *aimak* the expedition found that the total number of owners of *yurts* was 411, of whom 143 were beggars. The monsteries of this *khoshun* and the *dzasak* owned the same number of horses and one and a half times as many camels and cattle as all the *arats*. In the domains of the Ilagugsan-khutukhta out of 528 *shabinars* 153 were paupers or extremely poor. In the *khoshun* of the *tsin-van* Erdeni Dalai out of the whole population of 9,265— 5,740 were beggars. In the *khoshun* of the *tsin-van* Tsokbadarkho who at that time was the president of the *aimak* diet and deputy Minister of Justice all the *arats* had 6,200 head of cattle and 5,000 head of sheep and goats, whereas two monasteries alone in this *khoshun* owned 10,300 head of the former and 12,612 head of the latter.

In the *aimak* of Sain-noyon-khan the expedition visited the domains of the Erdeni-pandita khutukhta; his estate manager reported that 878 *shabinar* holdings had 3,124 horses, while the monastery and the *khutukhta* had 2,094 horses; camels numbered 4,619 and 4,011 respectively, sheep and goats 24,335 and 12,680. In the *khoshun* of Dashi-dordji there were 579 *arat* holdings. This *khoshun* had a total of 574 horses, 200 of which belonged to the prince; of 1,000 sheep 300 were owned by the prince.

The situation observed in almost all the *khoshuns* of Outer Mongolia was similar. The *Bogdo-gegen's* government suppressed any attempt at a protest on the part of the *arats*. When, for instance, the *arats* of one of the *khoshuns* of the Tushetu Khan *aimak* tried for the purposes of their holding to make use of a certain number of horses from the herd owned by a leading feudal prince of the church from the monastery of Choiren, the government immediately ordered severe punishment.

The grievous situation of the *arat* population during the monarchical period was the fundamental prerequisite for the aggravation of the class war in the country.

One of the clearest manifestations of the class war waged by the *arat* population in this period is the action of the *arats* in the *khoshun* of Prince Manibazar of the aimak of Dzasaktu Khan, known as the Aiyushi movement. This movement was not an isolated phenomenon of this period. Similar *arat* movements developed in other areas of the country, particularly in the *aimaks* of Tushetu Khan and Tsetsen Khan. Serious disturbances occurred also among soldiers in Outer Mongolia. The soldiers' movement formed part of the *arat* movement of that period.

In principle, the *arat* movement did not differ from the peasant movement of other countries. One of its characteristic features was that it was even more localized than in other countries. The nomadic mode of life, the extreme inadequacy of economic contacts, the sparse distribution of villages and the enormous expanses intensified the disunited character of the *arat* movements. In pre-revolutionary Mongolia there were no cities or towns, in the strict sense of the term; an *arat* movement out in the steppe could not expect any kind of support from the towns. Yet, despite all the barriers and hindrances the *arat* movement expanded.

The *arats'* struggle assumed varying forms—partial, passive resistance on the part of individual *arats*, the conducting of litigation with feudal nobles, leaving them or their camping or grazing grounds, the *duguilan* type of resistance or, finally, armed resistance. Passive resistance by individual *arats* was an everyday phenomenon in feudal Mongolia. It encompassed wide numbers of *arats* and took the form of refusal to pay taxes, to obey the orders of the feudal authorities, etc. In the circumstances of a pastoral economy one of the most widely practised forms of resistance was to conceal livestock from the feudal nobles. As feudal exploitation intensified, the *arats* moved on from partial and passive resistance to more active struggle. Such forms of struggle comprised litigation between *arats* and their princes and the removal of their tents to other grazing grounds. In Mongolian conditions the latter constituted an effective form of struggle. *Duguilan* was a more organized form of the struggle of the *arats* against the feudal nobles. Armed struggle and rebellions were the highest forms of the *arat* movement.

Besides the *arats*, lower-ranking lamas and *tsiriks* (soldiers) joined the movement, sometimes even acting independently. The petty *taiji* also took part in the *arat* movement but their interests were opposed to those of the *arats*. Whereas the *arats* fought against feudal oppression in general, the *taiji* sought only to re-establish their rights which had been infringed upon by the bigger feudal nobles. They fought to liberate themselves and their *khamdjilga* (domestics) from governmental and princely servitudes so that they themselves would have the opportunity to exercise undivided exploitation. The *taiji* played the part of reactionaries in the *arat* movement and held it back by their indecisiveness and conciliatory attitude. The *arat* movement had no formulated programme of struggle; its immediate aim was to try to achieve the maximum alleviation of the heavy burden of taxation. A characteristic feature of the *arat* movement was that it was spontaneously directed simultaneously both against the feudal nobles and against the alien oppressors in the persons of merchants and usurers. The feudal state acted as a machine of suppression in relation to the popular movement. Although the *arat* movement was spontaneous and unorganized, it was the genuine motive force of Mongol society. The historically progressive significance of the *arat* liberation movement consists in the fact that, by dealing shattering blows against the feudal system and undermining foundations, it facilitated the victory of the popular revolution.

The reactionary, anti-popular social structure of the *Bogdo-gegen* monarchy was matched by the reactionary, anti-popular economic policy of its government.

Year after year the budget of the government of Outer Mongolia continued to show a deficit. Invariably the deficit was covered out of so-called extraordinary revenue, i. e. from loans from tsarist Russia. During the years of the *Bogdo-gegen* monarchy's existence Russia on three occasions advanced money to the government of the *Bogdo-gegen*. The first loan, for a ten-year term, was advanced at the beginning of 1913 and was for an amount of 100,000 roubles for the organization of the army; the second loan, for a 20-year term, was given at the beginning of 1914 for 2,000,000 roubles to cover the cost of training the armed forces and for administrative requirements; the third loan for 3,000,000 roubles, for a term of thirty years, was made in the same year 1914. Tsarist loans were of the "strings attached" type and were always accompanied by fresh concessions on the part of the *Bogdo-gegen's* government.

The principal item on the revenue side of the budget was that of customs dues, which accounted for 70% and more of the total. The lion's share of these came not from the external custom-houses (Russian exports and imports were, under the Treaty of November 3, 1912, exempt from taxation), but from the internal custom-houses which levied duty on goods, raw materials and livestock moved from one region to another inside the country. Internal customs duty was paid by the Chinese merchants who had stayed behind in Mongolia and also by Mongols buying or selling livestock and raw materials (Russian merchants were exempted from these taxes). This system, while it was the outcome of feudal disunity, contributed in its turn to strengthening that disunity by obstructing internal trade and the formation of a single market. The 1916 customs tariff levied duty amounting to 5% of the market price on all goods imported and exported across the frontier by Chinese and Mongols and also on goods sold in the markets of Urga, Ulyasutai, Kobdo and the *maimachen* of Kyakhta (Russian merchants were also exempted from paying these duties).

It should be noted that internal customs duties were, for the first time in the history of Mongolia, introduced during the period of the feudal-theocratic state. Internal custom-houses were needed by the *Bogdo-gegen's* government as supplementary sources of official revenue; the government of tsarist Russia also had an interest in them as it regarded them as means of hampering the penetration of European, American, Japanese and other capital into the territory of Outer Mongolia.

The revenue derived from other items of the budget did not, over the whole history of Mongolia, play a role of great importance.

On the expenditure side of the state budget there was a complete lack of appropriations for public health. In contrast, pensions and grants to princes were two-and-a-half times greater than the amounts spent on education and veterinary treatment; the greater part of the state budget consisted of expenditure on the upkeep of the *Bogdo-gegen* and his court. Ignoring the real needs of the country and the people, the government of the *Bogdo-gegen,* as one of its first steps, restored the payment to all feudal nobles of a salary for rank and titles at the rates fixed in 1733 by the Manchu Emperor Yun-Cheng.

The state budget had, it is true, a so-called "reform fund," intended for financing measures for cultural and economic development. This fund was composed of receipts from the tax on forestry of timber, the revenues from telegraph and telephone services, the profits of the brickworks and the coal-mine in Nalaikha. In 1916 the fund had a revenue of 524,726 gold roubles, of which less than 20% was spent on measures of a social and cultural character and about 40% on economic measures. Over 40% of the fund was expended on the maintenance of the staff of the so-called reform committee.

It should be borne in mind that the undertakings (electricity plant, telephone network, brickworks, printing works) built by the reform committee had to serve principally the needs of the high-ranking aristocracy of the capital, that the measures taken in the sphere of public education were limited to the opening of one single school in Urga and of a number of elementary schools in individual *khoshuns;* that veterinary practice consisted mainly in organizing inoculations against plague in cattle intended for export abroad. These innovations, accordingly, did little to help the *arat* masses.

An analysis of the "local budgets" of the *Bogdo-gegen's* government also reveals their emphatically feudal, anti-popular character. The *khoshun dzasaks* squeezed out of their *arat* serfs as much funds as they considered necessary; they levied all kinds of dues on the *arats* without rendering account to anyone. As they were not limited or controlled by anyone, they expended the funds collected on purposes that had nothing at all to do with culture or progress.

The Russo-Mongolian Agreement of November 3, 1912, and the Russo-Chinese-Mongolian Agreement of Kyakhta of May 25, 1915, created exceptionally favourable conditions for Russian capital to capture the Mongolian market. Russian capitalists, however, failed to take full advantage of the results of the diplomatic victories won by tsarism; they could not take over the place of the Chinese merchants, most of whom had been driven out of Mongolia in 1911-1912. They did not become monopoly suppliers of industrial commodities and were unable to meet the Mongolians' demand for such commodities. The import of goods into Mongolia from Russia in 1912-1915 did not exceed 30-35% of the market's needs and, as there were no imports from China, this soon resulted in an acute commodity famine.

The First World War had the effect of weakening tsarist Russia's positions in Mongolia, as from 1916 onwards deliveries of Russian goods to Mongolia ceased completely. In these circumstances the Kyakhta Tripartite Agreement of 1915, which legalized the activities of Chinese merchants in Mongolia, though it did not place them on an equal footing, legally, with Russian capitalists, very soon led to the re-establishment of their predominance as suppliers of goods to Mongolia and as purchasers of Mongolian raw materials. The weakening of the economic position of tsarism, added to its military failures on the world war fronts, had the inevitable sequel of a gradual decline in the political influence of tsarist Russia in Mongolia.

The weakening of tsarist positions in the Far East did not, however, help to strengthen the positions of the Mongolian state. As the influence of tsarist Russia declined, the aggressive policy of Japanese imperialism became proportionally more active. Even before the First World War it had begun preparing to seize the whole of Mongolia. At the end of 1913, for instance, after the signing of the Russo-Chinese Declaration on an autonomous Mongolia, a Japanese government official, Kodama, arrived in Urga and conducted negotiations with the Foreign Minister, Khanda-Dordji, offering Japan's help in uniting Outer and Inner Mongolia into one state independent of China. In exchange for this "help" Kodama asked for Japan to be given "certain trade and territorial rights and advantages." Although Kodama's proposals met with a sympathetic reception from many influential feudal nobles and senior lamas, his mission was not successful; the government of tsarist Russia intervened and the Japanese government was obliged to dissociate itself officially from Kodama and his proposals. The Japanese imperialists had trustworthy agents in the persons of certain senior lamas in the entourage of the *Bogdo-gegen*. On their initiative the *Bogdo-gegen* wrote a second letter to the Emperor of Japan, on January 13, 1914, in which he expressed his regret that earlier attempts to establish relations between Mongolia and Japan had not been successful and voiced the hope that the Japanese Emperor would consent to help the "good cause" of uniting all Mongolians. But this attempt of the *Bogdo-gegen's* government to lean for support on Japanese imperialism also failed. The letter of the *Bogdo-gegen* fell into the hands of the government of tsarist Russia and as a result the Japanese government had to disclaim all connection with it.

In 1915 Japanese imperialism began a new offensive on a wide scale on the continent of Asia. The "Twenty-One Demands" presented by the Japanese government on January 18, 1915, to the government of China signified the beginning of this offensive. The policy of aggression pursued by Japanese imperialism in China was fraught with danger for Outer Mongolia, too.

The Great October Socialist Revolution and the formation of the Soviet state averted this threat from the Mongolian people, saving it once and for all from colonialist enslavement and helping it to break the shackles of feudal oppression.

* * *

During the period of the feudal-theocratic regime Russia had considerably strengthened its cultural influence over Outer Mongolia.

The revolutionary-minded workers and employees who arrived in Urga from Russia brought with them a progressive ideology and disseminated revolutionary ideas among the Mongolians with whom they were thrown into association. The social life and political struggle that went on in the Russian colony in Urga also exercised an effect on the progressively-minded *arats* and taught them methods of political struggle.

The influence of revolutionary ideology and of progressive Russian culture also made itself felt through young Mongolians sent at that time to Russia to be educated. Mongolian students had the opportunity of personally observing the class struggle and the development of the October battles in 1917. One of the students in Irkutsk was Kh. Choibalsan, the future organizer and leader of the Mongolian People's Revolutionary Party.

At this time the first small industrial enterprises were making an appearance in Mongolia. In particular, great cultural and political importance was attached to the printing shops set up in Mongolia by Russians.

The first Russo-Mongolian printing shop was organized as early as the beginning of the XXth century. It was a small press, equipped with several hand-operated presses, which were operated by a couple of dozen Russian and Mongolian workmen.

In the years of Autonomous Mongolia a second printing-shop was set up in Mongolia, attached to the Ministry of Foreign Affairs. It printed mainly official matter. At this time too a small typolithographic press was organized at the *shabinar* department, which printed chiefly departmental matter and all kinds of edicts and precepts of the *Bogdo-gegen*.

Sukhe Bator, the organizer and leader of the Mongolian revolution, worked for some time in a printing-shop, where he not only became a skilled compositor but also established relations with Russian workers. Later on, a mechanic of the Russo-Mongolian printing works, Kucherenko, gave Sukhe Bator quite a lot of help in organizing the Mongolian People's Revolutionary Party.

The existence of printing-shops made it possible to issue periodicals and to print books. During the years of the *Bogdo-gegen* monarchy the first Mongolian newspaper—*Niislel khureeniy sonin* ("News of the Capital")—started publication in Urga.

A major event was the opening of the first secular school, attached to the Ministry of Foreign Affairs. It was in this school that Kh. Choibalsan began his education. It should be mentioned that Danchinov, a political emigré from Russia, who was then working as a teacher in this school, helped Choibalsan to enter the school.

CHAPTER IV

CULTURE DURING THE PERIOD
OF THE MONGOLIAN MONARCHY (1911-1919)

Certain special characteristics mark the culture of this period, a time when the national-liberation movement of the Mongolian people was on the upsurge. A number of new phenomena are observable in the spiritual life of the Mongols connected with Mongolia's emergence from complete isolation from the cultural world and its entry into relations with other countries, above all with Russia. The traditional existence of the Mongols felt the breath of a fresh breeze which speeded the decay of the old and the birth of the new.

It was particularly important for the further development of Mongolia's national culture that by the time the monarchy was coming to the end of its existence in Mongolia the revolutionary ideas of the Great October Socialist Revolution in Russia were beginning to penetrate.

There was an intense desire among Mongols to learn from the cultured nations of the West, to govern their country on the example of the developed countries. This aspiration found expression in certain progressive measures adopted at the time in the sphere of culture and education.

First and foremost, steps were taken to open a secular school in Mongolia. In an application from the Ministry of Foreign Affairs addressed to the *Bogdo-gegen* in the 4th year of the rule of "By the many Enthroned" (1914) reference was made to the need for every person to be taught reading and writing, for the establishment in the country of a system of secular schooling as in Russia, France and England. Furthermore, the application stressed the extreme backwardness of Mongolia, pointing out that literacy in the country did not even extend to one person out of ten and that "Mongols up to the present time are still uneducated and have fallen into a state of poverty and backwardness."[1]

Under the monarchy a start was made in setting up a secular school in Mongolia alongside the numerous religious schools that already existed.[2] At that time schools came within the purview of the Ministry of Foreign Affairs.

In the regulations for elementary schools published in 1915 it was stated that "Children of government officials, *taiji* and of common people are admitted. At the end of elementary schooling the cleverest children will be selected for further education in high schools."[3]

On March 24, 1912 under the auspices of the Ministry of Foreign Affairs the first modern secular school was opened in Urga with an enrolment of 47 pupils taken from four *aimaks* and the *shabinar* department.

As a result of the rapprochement between Mongolia and Russia cultural relations between the two countries became more intensified.

The Ministry of Foreign Affairs established a Russian language school for Mongolian children in which teachers invited from Russia worked. According to June 1914 data the school had a director, two teachers, and three assistants, and the number of pupils was 46. This school played an important part in training some of the progressively-minded Mongolian intellectuals and also in disseminating advanced ideas in Mongolia. Young persons who had been pupils of the school in the capital were sent to study in Russian cities—Irkutsk and others, and some of them emerged subsequently as active participants in the Mongolian revolution.

In 1912 a military school was opened in Khuzhir-bulan with the participation of Russian instructors. Thirty graduates of this school subsequently became active fighters and commanders of the people's revolutionary troops.

The establishment of a number of bases for a secular school system under conditions where religious instruction was completely dominant in the country must be considered as a positive feature in the history of Mongolia's national culture. As a result of the steps taken in the sphere of education Mongolia began to a certain extent to come into contact with contemporary culture and the national self-awareness of the Mongolians developed considerably.

Many of those who obtained their education at this time worked in the early years of people's rule in the central and local state, party and social organizations, as well as in the cultural and educational institutions of the country.

It should at the same time be pointed out that, during the period of Mongolian monarchy, education was carried on in extremely difficult circumstances and so was not developed further. The ruling circles of the Mongolian monarchy made every possible effort to subordinate completely any cultural undertakings in the country solely to the narrow interests of the ruling feudal class. They were not concerned in the least about the people in general. In the first application of the Ministry of Home Affairs to the *Bogdo-gegen* concerning the organization of education stress was placed on the following main idea:

"The basis of religion and of the state lies solely in educated people capable of strengthening the authority of officials. These are the mainstay of the state. This must all begin with the organization of primary schools. It is, moreover, highly important to train educated persons fro mthe ranks of the hereditary princes and *noyons*. Accordingly, in the first instance education must be given to *noyons* and their children."[4]

The inception of the modern press in Mongolia must be considered as one of the important cultural achievements of the time since it paved the way for the appearance of a revolutionary newspaper in November 1920.

On March 6, 1913, there appeared the first number of the journal *Shineh tol* ("New Mirror") and in 1915 the newspaper *Niysleliyn khureeniy sonin bichig* was founded. These periodical publications sharply criticized the reactionary nature of the monarchical regime in the country and the extreme backwardness of Mongolia, and they also disseminated advanced, democratic ideas about the creation of a new, regenerated Mongol state. From their pages Mongolian readers learnt the news of the revolutionary events that were taking place at the time in Russia and China and also about the contemporary international situation.

Printing began to develop in Mongolia. Some books were issued in printed form, e.g. *Bukvar, Oyuun tulkhuur, Tsagaan shuvuuny tuuzh, Gadaad ulsyn tovch tuukh* ("Story of the Two Jumpers"), *Orchlongiyn sav shim* ("On the Structure of the Universe"), etc.

With the growth of the national-liberation movement of the Mongolian people and the increase in national self-awareness, there was a notable intensification of interest in the history of the country. Very intensive work was done to gather various kinds of material concerning the history and the genealogies of princes and *noyons*.

Steps were taken to compile a history of Mongolia. In 1918-1919 an official history of Mongolia was written under the title *Zarligaar togtooson Mongol ulsyn shastir*, in eleven volumes. The compilation of this history was shared by a group of authors which included the historians Tserendev, Gombotseren, Galsandonoi, Sh. Damdin, Sumya, Dashnyam, Togtokh and Namsraizhav.

This work propounds the view that Mongolia has from time immemorial been an independent state which, after emerging from being a part of the Manchu Empire, was revived in the form of a Mongolian monarchy. It is interesting to note that it contains a critical observation about the policy of the Manchus in Mongolia. It reads: "The representatives of the Manchu Emperor, in a deliberate refusal to respect and obey the laws and principles of the state and of religion, in that they indulge in bribery in respect of every matter, and are interested only in their own profits, have entirely violated the laws and lawful procedures and consider right as wrong and wrong as right. In view of the foregoing, all (people) without exception being driven to extremity, both physically and in regard to property"[5], have elected Bogdo Djebtszun-damba "By the many Enthroned" as the Kagan of the state of Mongolia.

The quotation shows that, although the representatives of the feudal class of Mongolia were very circumscribed in their criticisms of the policy of the alien oppressors, and despite the fact that the reasons for the establishment of an independent Mongolian monarchy were quite inadequately disclosed, it is still a noteworthy fact that the ideas of the national-liberation movement did find expression to some extent in Mongolian historical writing of that time.

Among the historians of the Mongolian monarchy period mention should be made of Sh. Damdin (1867-1937). He was a historian who had formerly been a lama, and wrote in Tibetan. Between 1900 and 1920 he wrote the following works: *Chronological Treatise, Short History of Buddhism in Mongolia*, a Tibetan translation of *Travel Notes of Fa-syang*, and others. In 1919 he began to write a history of Mongolia under the title *The Golden Book*. Although Damdin introduced a number of innovations by making use of contemporary historical data, nevertheless he was unable to free himself from the trammels of the feudal and religious ideology which were typical of Mongolian historiography of that period.

New trends were also observable in Mongolian literature of the period in question. Mongolian folklore reflects the yearnings and thoughts of a people that had entered on the path of a struggle for liberation. Popular oral productions sharply ridiculed the vices of the feudal class and at the same time extolled the courage and the talents of the ordinary people.

During the period under discussion such popular geniuses as Gelegbalsan, Luvsan and others continued their creative and fruitful activities. In the context of the liberation movement in the country the national feeling and critical trend inherent in their work stand out in even greater relief. The popular storytellers and poets of the period in question were the precursors of the writers of the revolutionary epoch. The person who "passed on the torch" from those times up to our day was the famous poet of the people, Luvsan Khuurch (1885-1943). He was a native of the *khoshun* of Vyizen-gun, *aimak* of Tsetsen Khan. Luvsan's ancestors had for three generations been gifted story-tellers.

A noteworthy feature of the art of that time is the intensive way in which some artists endeavour to depict actual life and to move away from the limitations imposed by religious subjects. A leading representative of the trend towards realism in Mongolian art is B. Sharav (Marzan) (1866-1939). He produced such major realistic works as *A Day in Mongolia*, portraits of Bogdo, Ekh Dagin, Bogdo's teacher, etc. Popular artists, in principle, worked for the *kagan* and *noyons*. For example, there was a group of master craftsmen in decorative art, artistic casting or moulding, appliqué work and embroidery at the court of the *Bogdo-gegen*.

The expansion of economic and cultural relations between Mongolia and Russia brought the Mongolians into contact with the achievements of contemporary culture and technical skills. A number of enterprises were established (a workshop for repairing weapons, a power station, etc.); a telephone center was instituted and a telephone system was opened in Urga with 50 subscribers. Some types of medical and veterinary services appeared and a small number of Mongolians worked as mechanics, fitters, technicians and drivers.

A Committee for the Exploration of Mongolia was instituted by the *Bogdo-gegen* government in conjunction with Russia. The Committee's charter stated that its aim was to make a study of the population and the economy, to survey the geological resources of the country, investigate regions for agriculture and haymaking, etc.

The emancipation of Mongolia from alien oppression gave a certain fillip to the development of Mongolian culture but conditions were unfavourable for an all-round advance in this sphere. The basic reason was that backward feudal relationships were still as dominant in Mongolia as before and the people were still not free.

PART II

SECTION ONE

THE MONGOLIAN PEOPLE'S REVOLUTION AND THE PROCLAMATION OF THE MONGILIAN PEOPLE'S REPUBLIC

CHAPTER I

UNIVERSAL HISTORICAL IMPORTANCE OF THE GREAT OCTOBER SOCIALIST REVOLUTION IN RUSSIA AND ITS INFLUENCE ON MONGOLIA

Influence of the October Socialist Revolution on Mongolia

The history of mankind is full of revolutionary uprisings of oppressed classes and enslaved peoples against oppressors and enslavers. Yet all these uprisings and bourgeois revolutions did not lead to the extinction of social oppression. Only the Great October Socialist Revolution—the first in the history to do so—abolished exploitation of man by man, finally and for ever destroyed exploiters and enslavers and established in Russia the dictatorship of the proletariat by completely emancipating the working class and the working peasantry and also the numerous non-Russian nationalities who had been oppressed and kept in submission by the ruling classes of land-owning, capitalist Russia.

Because of this special characteristic the significance of the October Revolution went far beyond the confines of the Russian state and exerted a powerful revolutionizing influence on the whole course of human history.

In defining the international significance of the Great October Socialist Revolution V. I. Lenin wrote that it was expressed in two forms: in its effect on the revolutionary movement in other countries and in the inevitability of the basic features of the Russian revolution being repeated on an international scale.

The victory of the Great October Socialist Revolution marked the beginning of a period of transition from capitalism and pre-capitalist relations to socialism.

Under the direct influence of the October Revolution the whole world of the exploited, who were languishing under the oppression of imprialism, went into movement. A series of revolutions—in Germany, Austro-Hungary and other countries—mass revolutionary action by workers in Europe and America shook the capitalist world to its foundations. The movement was joined by the enslaved peoples of the colonial countries.

The October Revolution showed the whole world, and above all the dependent and colonial peoples, who constituted more than half of mankind, the only proper way of solving the nationality problem.

From the first day of its existence the Soviet government resolutely broke away from the aggressive imperialist policy of old Russia. It annulled all the unequal treaties that had been forced upon colonial and semi-colonial countries by tsarism; it made public all the secret treaties of tsarist Russia with other imperialist states which were aimed at infringing the sovereign rights of the peoples of the East. It proclaimed as the immutable principles of its foreign policy the right of peoples to self-determination, peaceful co-operation and mutual respect for countries and peoples.

The objective course of history made Soviet Russia the centre of the revolutionary struggle of the peoples of the whole world in the fight against imperialism; the country of the Soviets became the trusty stronghold and ally of the oppressed peoples in their struggle against imperialist and feudal oppression.

The October Revolution was the starting-point for uniting the revolutionary actions of the workers and the national-liberation struggle into a single force capable of overthrowing imperialism.

The victory of the October Revolution, for instance, made it possible to put into practical effect an alliance between the working class of Soviet Russia and the *arat* revolutionaries in Mongolia. The historical roots of this alliance date back into the past when the Mongolian people, fighting against feudal and colonial oppression, sought and found support from the progressive representatives of the Russian people. Advanced ideas— ideas of democracy and socialism—penetrated into Mongolia from Russia. Association between the Mongolian and Russian peoples made it possible for leading members of the *arat* population to absorb the revolutionary experience of the Russian working class and its party. These leading representatives of the *arats* realized that the cause of liberating the long-suffering Mongolian people was indissolubly linked with the revolutionary struggle and the successes of the working class of Russia. Under the influence of the revolutionary events taking place there the class struggle of the *arats* against the feudal nobles and the *arat* liberation movement directed against foreign capitalists in the period of autonomous rule from 1911 to 1918 began to assume an increasingly bitter character, going over from isolated to group outbursts and sometimes developing into armed action. It was at this time that the struggle of the *arat* masses under the leadership of the famous popular hero, the *arat Ayushi*, broke out again with fresh force.

In the spring of 1914 serious disturbances occurred among military units on the western frontier and in Urga, and in January 1915 in frontier detachments on the south-eastern borders of the country.

During 1917, in a number of *khoshuns* of the *aimaks* of Tsetsen Khan, and Tushetu Khan, *arats* came forward with clearly expressed demands of an anti-feudal and anti-imperialist character. In view, however, of the absence of a leading organization and of a programme of action, these agitations met with no success.

The narrow class character of these demonstrations was reflected by the fact that they failed to pose the question of a revolutionary change in the social system and confined themselves mainly to protesting against the arbitrary behaviour of the feudal rulers and the predatory policy of foreign trading and money-lending firms.

It was only the triumph of the October Revolution and the emergence of the neighbouring Soviet socialist state that radically changed the situation and greatly facilitated the speedy ripening of subjective prerequisites for a people's revolution in Mongolia, ensuring the possibility of direct contact between the progressive sections of the Mongolian *arats* and the victorious working class in Russia. All this created favourable conditions for the successful development and triumphant consummation of the anti-imperialist and anti-feudal revolution, the principal motive force of which was the *arat* class, led by a revolutionary party of the Marxist type, closely allied internationally with the working class of Soviet Russia.

Consequently, the people's revolution in Mongolia was characterized by a whole series of special features.

The first of these was the fact that it developed under the direct ideological influence of the Great October Socialist Revolution and in close international association with the Russian working class.

The second special feature was that its attack was directed primarily and directly against imperialism, that the Mongolian people's war of liberation had, therefore, inevitably to be merged with the struggle of the peoples of Soviet Russia against world imperialism.

A third special feature of the people's revolution was that, from the very outset, the liberation struggle of the Mongolian people against imperialist oppression was very closely interwoven with the struggle against feudalism, that the anti-imperialist objectives of the revolution were indissolubly linked up with the anti-feudal tasks of transforming the country on democratic lines.

A fourth special feature was that, while it was by its nature anti-imperialist and anti-feudal, i.e. a bourgeois-democratic revolution of a new type, it had to result in the consolidation in the country not of a bourgeois, but of a people's democratic regime that would, with the help of the first socialist state in the world—Soviet Russia—set the country on the non-capitalist path of development towards socialism.

Due to these special features the people's revolution in Mongolia represented a new type of revolution—a people's democratic revolution.

The direct influence of the October Socialist Revolution on the national-liberation movement in Mongolia became more and more intensified as the Red Army made its successful advance in Siberia and the Far East against the White Guard hirelings of imperialism.

At the end of 1917 and the beginning of 1918, bitter fighting developed in the provinces bordering on Mongolia between the Russian, Tuva, Buryat and other working people on the one hand and the foreign interventionists, White Guards and local oppressors, on the other.

The *arat* population of Mongolia, more especially that part of it which had grazing grounds in the frontier areas, began to realize more and more clearly that the new rulers in Russia were protecting the interests of working people just like the *arats* themselves.

The struggle of the Russian settlers residing in Urga with the reactionary circles of the Russian colony also revealed the meaning of the events which were going on in Russia.

Having organized in 1919 an illegal revolutionary committee in Urga, Russian citizens favourable to the revolution secretly bought up arms and war supplies and transported them across to the partisan detachments which were fighting on the other side of the Russo-Mongolian frontier.

In the spring of 1918 Mongolia witnessed the arrival from Russia of refugee capitalists, landowners, White Guard officers, and kulaks whose malicious and scurrilous attacks on the Soviet regime and the Bolsheviks were interpreted by the progressive *arats* as fresh proof of the fact that the Soviet regime was combating the exploiters and protecting the interests of the oppressed and the have-nots.

At the end of 1918 when, with the help of foreign interventionists, the White Guard mutineers temporarily suppressed Soviet authority in the Far East and Siberia, families of Soviet activists and individual workers and peasants—supporters of the Soviet regime—also began to emigrate to Mongolia to escape from counter-revolutionary terror. They contributed to a large extent to enlightening the minds of the *arats*.

A considerable role in the further stimulation of the political activities of the masses in Mongolia was played by what happened when, under the leadership of the Communist Party, heroic partisan warfare developed in Siberia and the Far East between workers and peasants, on one hand, and the White Guard mutineers supported by the troops of Japanese, American and other imperialist interventionists, on the other.

Thus, the great liberating ideas of the October Revolution, and the experience of revolutionary struggle gained by the workers of Russia became the property of the working *arats*, awakened their class consciousness and their determination to fight for their own national and social liberation. It was precisely at this time that the first Mongolian revolutionary leaders, who played a prominent part in the people's revolution, began to group themselves together in the country.

In the summer of 1919 the Red Army of Soviet Russia began its triumphant advance on the Eastern front, foreshadowing the imminent liberation of Siberia and the Far East from the White Guard hirelings of imperialism. On August 3, 1919, the Soviet government addressed a special appeal to the government and people of Autonomous Mongolia stating that it completely renounced the advantages and privileges which had been seized by tsarist Russia under the unequal treaties imposed by the latter. "Mongolia," the appeal said, "is a free country. All authority in the country must belong to the Mongolian people. No single foreigner has the right to interfere in the internal affairs of Mongolia... The Soviet Government publicly announces this to the Mongolian people and proposes the opening forthwith of diplomatic relations with the Russian people and the dispatch of envoys of the free Mongolian people to meet the Red Army."[1]

The *Bogdo-gegen* clique not only made no reply to the Soviet government's appeal; it took every step to conceal it from the people. Notwithstanding, however, all its contrivances and police-type obstacles, news of the Soviet government's appeal reached the working people of Mongolia.

Fear of the liberating ideas of the October Revolution was what decided the feudal-theocratic government of the *Bogdo-gegen* to adopt the line of open collusion with the Japanese militarists and their agents, as represented by the Chinese militarists from the Anfu clique. Apprehensive of the stability of their regime and of losing their feudal privileges, the *Bogdo-gegen's* clique hoped, with the help of imperialist Japan and reactionary Chinese generals, to maintain feudal customs in the country and hold the *arat* population in subjection.

As a result of negotiations between the Japanese government and the Chinese militarists, held in March, April and

September 1918, agreements were concluded for the latter to join in armed intervention against Soviet Russia. The Chinese militarists undertook to introduce their troops into Autonomous Mongolia and, with it as a base, to begin an advance in the direction of Lake Baikal in order to cut off the Far East from Soviet Russia.

In 1918, with the agreement of the *Bogdo-gegen's* government in Urga, Chinese troops arrived on the pretext of protecting the north-western territory, i.e. Mongolia, from the "threat of Bolshevism." This was what later on led to the extinction of Outer Mongolia's autonomy. The counter-revolutionary struggle against Soviet Russia united in one reactionary camp Japanese, American, British and other imperialists, Chinese militarists, the *Bogdo-gegen* clique and representatives of the landowners and capitalists who had been overthrown in Russia. The active role in this block of plunderers devolved on Japanese militarism which was making its appearance in the Far East as the leader of the camp of world reaction. The Japanese militarists in their turn relied for support on the pro-Japanese Anfu clique which at that time held sway in Northern China.

The Japanese militarists reckoned that circumstances were favourable for the implementation of their plans to seize the whole of the Soviet Far East and Mongolia. As they were anxious, however, to disguise these agressive schemes, they first made an attempt to carry them into effect under the cover of a "Pan-Mongolian Movement." In devising the schemes for creating a so-called "Greater Mongolia" to include Buryatia, Outer and Inner Mongolia, Barga, Kukunor and other regions inhabited by Mongolian nationalities, the Japanese military clique decided to place at the head of the "Greater Mongolia" movement their paid agent, the White Guard ataman Semenov. If it succeeded, the plan for creating a "Greater Mongolia" state would open up the possibility for the Japanese militarists to transform into a colony for themselves an enormous territory extremely valuable to them in the economic and strategic sense.

Semenov, surrounded by Japanese advisers and lavishly supplied with money and arms, showed himself extremely active. He induced one of the influential hierarchs of the Lamaist church—Neise-gegen, several leading feudal nobles of Inner Mongolia and also a number of Buryat bourgeois nationalists to take part in the Pan-Mongolian venture. The *Bogdo-gegen* clique, however, which had been ruling Outer Mongolia refused to cooperate with Semenov from fear of losing their undivided domination over the Mongolian *arats*. The "Pan-Mongolian" venture of the Japanese militarists soon collapsed. The puppet government of "Greater Mongolia", recognized by no one, with no support from the mass of the people and torn by internal antagonisms, ended its inglorious existence at the close of 1919.

Establishment in Mongolia of a Regime of Occupation by the Chinese Militarists and Aggravation of the External and Internal Situation of the Country

The *Bogdo-gegen* government, the Prime Minister of which at the time was the *shantszotba* Badamdorzh, one of the most important clerical feudal nobles, apprehensive of the influence of the October Revolution on Mongolia, was prepared to hand over the country to the Anfu occupiers.

But the *Bogdo-gegen* clique could not abolish autonomy surreptitiously; there was bitter opposition to this not only on the part of the mass of the *arat* population but also from the lower- and middle-ranking officials of the central governmental institutions in Urga. Sukhe Bator and other representatives of the *arats* played a prominent part in the movement for the maintenance of autonomy.

In this connexion an acute struggle developed in Urga official circles in 1919. The leaders of the ruling feudal circles were prepared to agree on the abolition of autonomy, provided they retained their titles and privileges. The wider masses of the people, including the lower- and middle-ranking Urga officials, stubbornly opposed the attempt to abolish autonomy. The *arat* population had an interest in autonomy being maintained, as its place would have been taken by the domination of the imperialists and the grievous colonialist enslavement connected therewith. In these circumstances the only way in which the Chinese militarists could manage to abolish autonomy was by bribing the traitorous feudal nobles of the *Bogdo-gegen* government and by a military occupation of the country.

The summer of 1919 saw the beginning of direct action by the Chinese reactionaries to abolish autonomy. Chen Yi, the Chinese viceroy in Urga, persuaded the *Bogdo-gegen* and his government to renounce autonomy voluntarily by promising that the princes would retain all their advantages and privileges. Bargaining began over the conditions for renunciation of autonomy. The result was the appearance of a shameful document, known under the title "64 Paragraphs Concerning the Improvement of the Future Situation of Mongolia." Under these "Paragraphs" the government of Autonomous Mongolia was abolished. Mongolia was to be governed by Chinese viceroys and their assistants in Urga, Kobdo, Ulyasutai and Kyakhta; the rights of the Mongolian feudal nobles to exploit the *arats* remained as before; the *Bogdo-gegen* would retain the title of khan and was to receive an annual salary for himself and his wife amounting to more than 72,000 *lan;* the maintenance of the Chinese garrisons in Mongolia devolved upon the *arats*.

In July 1919 the Upper and Lower Houses were convened and given the task of discussing and approving the agreement for the abolition of autonomy. The Upper House approved the draft of this agreement but the Lower House, whose members included the lower- and middle-ranking officials, Sukhe Bator and other representatives of the *arats*, rejected the draft and voted for maintaining autonomy.

The failure of Chen Yi's policy to get agreement on the voluntary renunciation of autonomy forced the Chinese militarists to take more decisive action. In agreement with the Japanese militarists the Anfu clique governing China sent to Urga in October 1919 one of its leaders, General Sui Szu-chen, who in the course of a few days abolished the autonomy of Outer Mongolia. With the backing of his troops Sui demanded that Badamdorzh, the President of the Council of Ministers, should immediately submit a petition, signed by the *Bogdo-gegen*, the ministers and their deputies, unconditionally renouncing autonomy. The reactionary leaders of the feudal nobles, headed by the *Bogdo-gegen*, betrayed the interests of the country and people and complied with Sui Szu-chen's demand. On November 17, 1919, he was handed the petition as requested and five days later, on November 22, a decree of the President of China was promulgated, announcing the liquidation of the autonomy of Outer Mongolia.

Mongolia's autonomy, which had been gained by the struggle of the *arats* in 1911, was abolished. The rule of Chinese militarists was established in Outer Mongolia and, as a consequence, the already grievous situation of the *arat* population grew still worse.

Representatives and agents of Chinese firms which had "suffered losses" as a result of the events of 1911-1912 streamed into the country with demands that the Mongolians compensate them for the "damages" they had sustained. Sui Szu-chen issued an edict under which the Mongolian *arats* undertook to resume payments on the old one-sided agreements and deals, with extortionate interest for the 8-9 intervening years added on to the amount of the old debt. This amounted to an enormous sum which in many cases considerably exceeded the value of all the livestock of the *khoshun* debtors.

On Sui's initiative and with his active participation a branch of a bank was opened in Urga which called itself Chinese but the whole capital of which belonged to Japanese monopolies.

In addition to this, the whole burden of taxes and servitudes connected with the maintenance of the army, numbering several thousand, of the Chinese militarists who had occupied the country was borne by the *arat* population of Mongolia.

The sufferings of the people became unbearable, and the result was an unprecedented upsurge of the national-liberation movement.

Emergence of Revolutionary Groups in Urga and Establishment by Them of Links with the Comintern and Soviet Russia

Under the influence of the great ideas of the October Socialist Revolution the national-liberation movement of the *arats* assumed an increasingly acute character. It was directed primarily against the occupiers—the Chinese militarists and their lackeys, the Mongolian feudal nobles. In these circumstances two underground revolutionary groups were formed in Urga, the capital of Outer Mongolia, in the summer of 1919.

The first revolutionary group, which was called the Urga group, sprang up in the centre of the city. Its members included the representatives of the *arat* population, D. Sukhe Bator, and civilian and military employees of *arat* origin such as Danzan, D. Dogsom, M. Dugarzhav, Dendev, Galsan, Togtokh, Tsend, Dash and others.

Among the revolutionaries D. Sukhe Bator became pre-eminent as a hero and leader of the people.

Sukhe Bator was born on February 2, 1893, in the *aimak* of Tsetsen Khan in the family of a poor *arat* called Damdin. When he was about five years old his father and all the family removed to Urga in the hope of finding work there.

Sukhe had no hopes of obtaining an education. The difficult material situation of the family obliged him to look for a means of livelihood. At the age of 14 he took up work as a teamster of *urton* (transport) horses on the Urga-Kyakhta highway. As he mixed with a wide circle of people, Sukhe often found himself faced with examples of an unjust attitude towards *arats* on the part of feudal nobles, high-ranking lamas and Manchu officials.

In 1907 and 1908 Sukhe Bator worked as a day-labourer in Urga. In moments that were free from hard labour Sukhe worked stubbornly and persistently to learn to read and write Mongolian.

In 1912 he was called up into the army of Autonomous Mongolia. After successfully finishing the school for junior commanders, Sukhe Bator became squadron-commander. He frequently took part in battles against the Chinese militarists, was a skilful squadron-commander and exhibited personal bravery for which he was given several decorations and the honorary title of *bator* (hero), which later became part of his name.

Among the Russian instructors who were training Mongolian troops in Khudzhirbulun where Sukhe Bator was serving were officers who were sympathetic to the Revolution and to Soviet power. There is ground for the assumption that it was precisely from them that squadron-commander Sukhe Bator obtained his first detailed information about the Revolution in Russia.

As he was closely following developments in his country, Sukhe Bator reacted sharply to its occupation by Anfu troops. This was the time when his active revolutionary work began.

At the end of 1918 Sukhe Bator was demobilized from the army. He arrived in Urga and took up work there as a compositor in a printing-shop.

Somewhat later a second revolutionary group was formed; it was called the "Consul Group," as it sprang up in the consular quarter of the city. The membership of this group included: Kh. Choibalsan,[2] an *arat's* son, who had been brought back by the *Bogdo-gegen* government from studying in Irkutsk, Bodo, a teacher of the Mongolian language, the lama D. Losol, a private trader called D. Chagdarzhav, petty officials Zhamyan, Zhigmiddorzh, Altangerel, Babu and others.

At the outset the two groups had no organized form or programme, and operated separately. Group members distributed leaflets against the Chinese occupiers and their Mongolian myrmidons, checked on the exact numbers and dispositions of Chinese troops, bought arms, etc.

They expressed the interests of different sections of the population: *arats*, petty and medium-ranking feudal officials, and incipient capitalist elements, all of whom were united in the one aim to fight against the reactionary Chinese occupiers.

Gradually the revolutionaries realized the need for establishing links with Soviet Russia but this was hampered by the circumstance of the civil war in Siberia. Accordingly, Sukhe Bator's attempt to establish such a link in the spring of 1920 was unsuccessful. But the revolutionaries did not give up their attempts to link up with the Russian working class. This was greatly helped by the revolutionary work of Russian citizens—compositors in the Russian printing works in Urga, M. I. Kucherenko and Ya. V. Gembarzhevski.

At this time, on the other side of the Russo-Mongolian frontier, the heroic Red Army was beginning its powerful, triumphant advance. On January 7, 1920, at Krasnoyarsk, a crushing blow was dealt to the remnants of Kolchak's army. The victories of the Red Army contributed to a mighty upsurge of the partisan movement all over Siberia and the Far East. Partisan detachments of Russian and Buryat workers and peasants moved into the attack and liberated a number of towns and districts.

At the end of 1920 Soviet troops liberated Troitskosavsk and on March 2, Verkhneudinsk (Ulan-Ude). The hour had come for the complete liberation of Soviet territory from the imperialist interventionists and from the forces of the Russian bourgeois and landowner counter-revolutionaries.

The members of the revolutionary groups which had been operating very much underground realized clearly that the victories of the Red Army were creating a favourable situation for the revolutionary struggle of the Mongolian people. But, if the struggle was to be successful, it was necessary to combine their forces as quickly as possible, to make contact with the international revolutionary movement led by the Communist International and to enter into direct contact with the government of Soviet Russia. Before the two groups united there were frequent meetings between members of both.

Recalling his first meeting with Sukhe Bator, Choibalsan, in a speech given on February 3, 1942, at the Higher School for Party Cadres in Ulan Bator, told the audience: "In the autumn of 1919, when the Chinese militarists occupied Mongolia with the intention of abolishing our autonomy, I had my first conversation with Comrade Sukhe Bator about the difficult situation of the country. He talked about what had to be done to prevent Mongolia falling under the yoke of the Chinese militarists and to ensure that the Mongolian people obtained eternal freedom.... That was our first meeting; it has remained imprinted on my mind."[3]

On June 25, 1920, a joint meeting of the groups was held at which they were united into one organization under the name of the Mongolian People's Party.

A document called the "Oath of the Party Members" was agreed upon.

In the Oath there was a brief reference to the aims and objects of the future party, the chief of which were: "...to rid the country of bitter enemies... to strengthen the state.... to be adamant in protecting the Mongolian nation, to review and change the country's domestic policy, showing concern in every possible way for the interests of the *arat* masses, to safeguard their rights and put an end to the sufferings of the mass of the working people and the oppression of man by man."[4]

The Oath required that Party members be steadfast in carrying out the tasks of the Party, place the interests of the Party above their personal interests, be truthful to it and observe Party secrets.

"If any member of the Party is captured by enemies, he must not betray his comrades, must say nothing about Party matters and should die rather than become a traitor. In their turn, members of the Party who are at liberty must not grudge their lives to save arrested comrades."[5]

Realizing the extreme necessity for broadening the ranks of the Party, the Oath made it obligatory for Party members to work unceasingly to recruit new members.

"Every person," we read in paragraph 8 of the Oath, "who becomes a member of the Party, is obliged to bring into its ranks not less than 10 persons and, by forming them into a Party cell, direct it. Furthermore, the policy of the Party and its directives must be carried out everywhere in uniform fashion without any deviations whatsoever."[6]

The "Oath of the Party Members" reflects the organizational growth of the revolutionary struggle of the *arats* under the influence of the revolution in Russia in 1917. This document was of great importance in the struggle for the creation of a single Party organization with a single political platform, united by common objectives and strong in its consciousness and discipline.

The text of the Oath was discussed at a meeting of revolutionaries and approved. In accordance with the resolution adopted each of the members of the organization personally signed his name to the text, thus affirming his agreement with it. At the same time it was decided to make a seal with which all documents issued by the organization should be authenticated.

At the same meeting it was resolved to send a delegation to Soviet Russia to negotiate for assistance. For this purpose a delegation was approved consisting of Choibalsan and Danzan and subsequently the following were also appointed members of the delegation: Sukhe Bator, Losol, Dogsom, Bodo, Chagdarzhav. In June 28, 1920, the first group of delegates, headed by Choibalsan, left Urga for the north. A second group, headed by Sukhe Bator, was to set out a little later.

Sukhe Bator, however, stayed behind in Urga and continued to direct the work of the organization, which was working in exceptionally difficult conditions. The police regime and the terrorist policy of Sui Szu-chen demanded of the revolutionaries not only heroism but also great caution. For conspiratorial purposes meetings had to be held outside the city on the banks of the River Tola—on the pretext of pasturing horses or taking walks.

Meanwhile the situation in the country was becoming more and more acute. Sui Szu-chen stopped short of nothing in intensifying the terror against discontented elements. He even restricted freedom of worship by requiring the *Bogdo gegen* to ask permission of the occupation authorities to hold religious services. Unrest developed not only among the working people but also among some of the feudal official circles in Urga, who were afraid, however, to rely on the masses and call on them to take up arms. The feudal nobles visualized as the only alternative an appeal for help to the imperialist countries. One such appeal, signed by the Bogdo-gegen, was addressed to the US government and handed secretly to the American consul in Kalgan. A similar appeal was sent to Japan through the Japanese consul in Hailar.

Meanwhile, important events were unfolding in China itself, where a mass anti-imperialist movement had developed which went down in history as the movement of May 4, 1919. It was directed precisely against Japan and its Anfu agents.

In the summer of 1920 the Anfu clique was overthrown. Its place was taken by the so-called Chili clique of militarists, backed by Anglo-American capitalists. Following the defeat of the Anfu forces, Sui Szu-chen left Urga for Pekin, where he found refuge inside the Japanese Embassy.

In view of this situation, on July 15, 1920, a second group of delegates, with Sukhe Bator at their head, left Urga and set off northwards to Soviet Russia.

On July 22 it arrived in Verkhneudinsk where it linked up with Choibalsan's group. At the time described Verkhneudinsk was the centre of the Far Eastern Republic. In order to conduct negotiations with the representatives of the Soviet government it was necessary to travel westwards to the RSFSR. On August 15 the combined delegation, headed by Sukhe Bator and Choibalsan, arrived in Irkutsk.

Differences of opinion arose among the group members on the most important problems of revolutionary work. The spokesman of the interests of feudal officials, Bodo, and of the nascent bourgeois elements, Danzan, and others, strongly objected even to the idea of appealing to the Soviet government on behalf of the revolutionary organization. There was a lively discussion between the members of the delegation on the question whether to authenticate its appeal to the official organs of Soviet Russia with the seal of the *Bogdo-gegen* or the seal of the revolutionary organization. On the insistence of Sukhe Bator the members of the delegation decided to certify their documents with the seal of the revolutionary organization.

In Irkutsk the group members, on behalf of the Mongolian people, drew up an appeal to the government of the RSFSR in which it was stated: "We, the members of the People's Party, on behalf of our Party, appeal to mighty Russia and ask for help. In alliance with service elements (Mongolian military servicemen), on whom we count for military support, we seek to restore the autonomy of Mongolia, while retaining for the Khutukhta *Bogdo* the title of limited monarch. Next we desire to carry through the necessary measures for limiting the hereditary rights of the princes. Having achieved independence for the country, we, with the benefit of the experience of other countries, shall continue the struggle for the rights and interests of our people. The growth of the *arats'* national self-awareness will enable us in a year or two to advance the revolution further so as to abolish finally the rights of the ruling princes."⁷

Sukhe Bator and Choibalsan insisted that the text of the appeal should give clear expression to the aspirations of the Mongolian revolutionaries to establish friendly relations with the revolutionary organizations of Soviet Russia and China. It should be pointed out that even then, at the dawn of the Mongolian revolution, progressives in the country understood the community of interests linking the masses of Mongolia and China in their fight against imperialism.

On August 24, 1920, there was yet another meeting of the members of the delegation at which it was decided to split it into three groups: one group consisting of Danzan, Losol and Chagdarzhav would be sent to Moscow; another group, with Bodo and Dogsom as members, would return to Urga to intensify revolutionary work among the masses; Sukhe Bator and Choibalsan would remain in Irkutsk to direct the work of the revolutionary organization in Mongolia and act as liason with the delegation in Moscow.

While in Irkutsk, Sukhe Bator and Choibalsan worked hard to improve their political and military knowledge. Sukhe Bator attended a Party conference in Irkutsk and made a speech at it in which he voiced the determination of the *arats* and the members of the revolutionary groups to link up their struggle with that of the working class and of all the workers of Soviet Russia against the common enemy.

By this time the situation in Mongolia had taken a serious turn for the worse. After the flight from Urga of Sui Szu-chen, a representative of the Peking government, Chen Yi, arrived there as High Commissioner "for the pacification" of the northwestern province. The situation of the masses grew worse and worse. The Mongolian *arats*, as previously, bore the whole burden of the taxes connected with the maintenance of the army of occupation. There was no limit to the arbitrary actions, violence and plundering of the population. Terror was intensified against anyone who expressed the slightest dissatisfaction. The members of the revolutionary organization were subjected to a mighty wave of arrests and repressions. Khatan Bator Maksarzhav, Manlai Bator Damdinsuren and other sympathizers with the ideas of the revolution were arrested and anyone arrested was tortured.

Many of the revolutionaries had to leave the city and hide in the mountains in the environs of Urga, but in spite of all this, revolutionary work did not cease.

CHAPTER II

THE MONGOLIAN PEOPLE'S REVOLUTION OF 1921

Further Aggravation of the Situation of the Arats as a Result of the Irruption of White Guard Bands

When the Chinese occupation authorities got to know that a delegation of Mongolian revolutionaries had left for Soviet Russia to negotiate for help, they announced a reward of $10,000 for whoever captured Sukhe Bator and his fellow-fighters and handed them over. An announcement to this effect was posted up on the walls of Urga and other towns in Mongolia; measures were taken to make it widely known among the population of the countryside. Martial law was declared in Urga. But the occupiers were unable to halt the approaching popular revolution, inspired as it was by the ideas of the October Socialist Revolution.

The Japanese militarists, having failed in 1919 with their plan for creating a "Greater Mongolia" and been deprived in 1920 of their network of Anfu agents, decided to make use for their aggressive purposes of the Russian White Guards, remnants of which had fled into Mongolia and North-Eastern China after the defeat by the Red Army of the main forces of counter-revolution. They designated as leader of the White Guard army the adventurer and violent counter-revolutionary, Baron Ungern, assigning Japanese advisers to his staff and furnishing him with supplies and armaments.

On October 2, 1920, Ungern, with his "Asiatic cavalry division" consisting of four regiments with artillery, crossed the Mongolian frontier. The fighting core of the division were eight squadrons of Transbaikalian Cossacks.

With a view to transforming Mongolia into an anti-Soviet bridgehead Ungern decided to take advantage of the occupation regime created in Mongolia by the Chinese militarists, with which not only the *arats* but also the ruling circles of feudal nobles were dissatisfied, and represented himself as the champion of the liberation of Mongolia from the Chinese occupation authorities who intended to restore autonomy and all the rights and privileges of the feudal class of Mongolia under the leadership of the *Bogdo-gegen*.

Many of the Mongolian princes responded to Ungern's call. They were mainly feudal nobles who had personally suffered grievances at the hands of the Chinese militarists but at the same time mortally feared the revolutionary movement of the *arats*. They began to give active support to Ungern, supplying him with provisions, fodder, horses, etc. and mobilizing *arats* to serve in his forces.

With the help of the demagogic slogans "restoration of autonomy" and "protection of the yellow religion," Ungern succeeded in drawing over to his side new secular and clerical feudal nobles through whom to mobilize young Mongolians for his army. Thus, with the help of local feudal nobles he created detachments from the arats of the Tushetu Khan and Tsetsen Khan *aimaks* and *shabi* region. At this headquarters Ungern set up a puppet so-called provisional government of Mongolia headed by his protégés—the feudal nobles Luvsantseven and Zhamyan.

Fighting began between the Ungern forces and the troops of the Chinese militarists. In Urga a Chinese garrison of many thousand men was stationed under the command of General Ho Tsai-tyan. The White Guards' first attempt to occupy Urga on November 2, 1920, was repulsed. Ungern retreated to the east and took up positions in the valley of Tereldjin-gol where he made feverish preparations for a fresh advance on Urga by establishing liaison with the White Guard detachments which had fled from Russia into the western regions of Mongolia and bringing them under his command, taking livestock and other property away from the *arats* and, with the help of the feudal nobles and senior lamas, carrying through one mobilization after another.

Realizing the important part played in Mongolian life by the religious authority of the *Bogdo-gegen*, Ungern decided to bring the latter into his service. He managed to make contact secretly with the *Bogdo-gegen*, who was in Urga. At the end of January 1921 Ungern, with the full complicity of the *Bogdo-gegen* removed him from Urga and settled him at his own headquarters, thus gaining the possibility of posing as the executant of the "divine" will of the head of the church. After accumulating, with the help of the Mongolian feudal nobles and the *Bogdo-gegen*, sufficient forces, Ungern took the offensive in the beginning of February with the objective of occupying Urga.

On February 3-4 desperate fighting broke out between the troops of the Chinese militarists occupying Urga and detachments of the Russian White Guards, as a result of which the Chinese troops were defeated. The Ungern forces occupied Urga and the *Bogdo-gegen* arrived there shortly afterwards.

On February 21 a ceremony was held to celebrate the

reenthronement of the *Bogdo-gegen* on the throne of the Khan.

Some of the forces of the Chinese militarists which had been defeated by the troops of Ungern concentrated in the region south of Kyakhta. The rest of the Urga garrison withdrew to Kalgan (China).

After occupying Urga, Baron Ungern subjected the working *arats* to grievous spoliation and destruction, while at the same time sparing the property of the *vans, guns, khans,* and *khutukhtas.*

Terrible punishment began to be meted out to the population; reprisals were taken against anyone who evaded compliance with Ungern's orders. Progressively-minded Russian social workers living in Mongolia were hanged and shot. Among those killed were Kucherenko, Gembarzhevski and other members of the revolutionary committee of Russian citizens in Urga, as well as the physician Tsybyktarov.

Feudal circles in Urga, satisfied with the "help" given by Ungern, began to think that, as autonomy had been restored, there was no point in the masses continuing to fight. They tried in every way possible to prevent the revolutionary groups from establishing links with Soviet Russia. This met with a partial response from individual members of the revolutionary group whose views reflected a feudal or monarchical standpoint. For example, Bodo, one of the members of the united group, when sent to Urga to carry on revolutionary work, began to collaborate with Ungern supporters and this naturally caused the revolutionaries serious alarm.

However, Ungern's attempts to camouflage his criminal schemes and to deceive the Mongolian people were doomed inevitably to collapse. The idea of fighting against the peoples of Soviet Russia was sharply rejected by the people of Mongolia under the leadership of the revolutionary group.

The irruption of Ungern into Mongolia and the shift over to his side of the feudal clique in Urga, headed by the *Bogdogegen*, made it urgently necessary to organize the masses for the struggle against the two occuping forces—the Chinese militarists and the Ungern band.

In the meantime the delegates of the united revolutionary group who were in Soviet Russia began, under the influence of the ideas of the October Socialist Revolution, the Soviet regime and the counsels of Lenin, to gain an increasingly clear and more correct idea of the aim of the anti-imperialist and anti-feudal revolution and of concrete ways of carrying it through.

On November 16, 1920, the delegates returned from Moscow to Irkutsk. Here they gave Sukhe Bator and Choibalsan detailed information about the results of the negotiations with the government of Soviet Russia. Conveying the substance of their conversation with Lenin, they said that he had analyzed in great detail the international position of Mongolia. He had said that the only correct path for the working people of Mongolia to follow in their struggle for independence was an alliance with the workers and peasants of Russia, and had emphasized that this struggle could not be waged without coordination and therefore the creation of a party of Mongolian *arats* was an essential condition for success.

In sharply criticizing the nationalistic views of Danzan, a member of the delegation, Lenin indicated the need for international revolutionary solidarity on the part of the Mongolian *arats* with the workers and peasants of neighbouring countries.

Lenin's counsels formed the basis for the whole activity of the Mongolian revolutionaries and the MPR.

The Soviet government complied with the request of the delegates of the Mongolian people for assistance in the struggle against the common enemy—the Ungern bands.

As Choibalsan wrote: "The young Soviet Republic, having survived the difficult years of civil war, destruction and famine, stretched out the hand of fraternal assistance to the exhausted people of Mongolia and showed exceptional attention to and warm concern for its fate."[1]

On November 17, 1920, a meeting of members of the delegation was held in Irkutsk, at which Sukhe Bator proposed that a congress of the Party be convened as soon as possible, the revolutionary partisan detachments be formed and an armed uprising of the whole nation be prepared.

With this aim in view a delegation of Mongolian revolutionaries—the directing nucleus of the combined revolutionary group—was to return home immediately.

The return of Sukhe Bator and Choibalsan to Mongolia was, however, a matter of difficulty, as they were being hunted by the police of the Chinese occupation authorities and the Ungern bands.

Accordingly, on November 22 Sukhe Bator and Choibalsan arrived in Kyakhta in order to take charge of revolutionary operations temporarily from there.

At this time the situation of the masses was worsening more and more under the twofold oppression—of the Chinese militarists and the Ungern bands. Baron Ungern had become the real tyrant of Mongolia, with the *Bogdo-gegen* government eagerly carrying out all his orders. The Ungern bands and the Chinese militarists committed acts of violence and spoliation. The discontent of the masses with the Ungern regime grew more and more acute. Even some of the princes and lamas, who had previously looked upon Ungern as their saviour from the yoke of the Chinese militarists, gradually began to be irked by his crude interference in the administrative matters of Mongolia. Ungern riposted by resorting to harsh punitive measures. He executed Yesotu-beise Chultuma, the Minister for the Western Province, because of his inconsiderate attitude to the Whites. He removed from office the War Minister, Khatan Bator Maksarzhav, and sent him away to the distant province of Ulyasutai to act as commander of the Mongolian military forces which he was to mobilize. On Ungern's initiative the "government" of the *Bogdo-gegen* sent the Soviet government a hypocritical note offering to establish good-neighbourly relations, conclude a trading agreement, emphasizing all the while the "services" rendered by Ungern. This was a perfidious trick designed to cloak the preparations the Ungern bands were making to invade Soviet Russia.

At the same time the *Bogdo-gegen* "government" sent a note addressed to the Chinese government in which it pointed out that the Mongolians were not warring with the Chinese troops in order to sever relations with China but in order to re-establish their sovereignty.

While he was endeavouring to camouflage his intentions by means of these notes of the "government" of the *Bogdo-gegen*, Ungern went on accumulating strength. The White Guard bands of Kazagrandi, Kazantsev and of Kaigorodov who had occupied Kobdo city in March 1921, and also many other groups from the remnants of the troops of Kolchak, Annenkov, Dutov, Bakich and others, assembled under his command. Occupation by the Japanese and White Guard forces took the place of occupation by the Chinese militarists. The latter, retreating from Urga, Kobdo and other points in Mongolia, fled—some of them into China, and some concentrating their forces in the region of Maimachen (now Altan-Bulak) and preparing to resume the fight for the domination of Mongolia. Standing behind both the Russian White Guards and the Chinese militarists were the imperialist states, equally interested in throttling the liberation struggle of the Mongolian people, but torn apart by antagonisms. Whereas Ungern and his bands were serving the Japanese military imperialists, the troops of the Chinese militarists in Mongolia, led by the government of the Chili clique, were operating in the interests of the Chinese landowners and bourgeoisie, supported by Anglo-American imperialism which had no desire to see Mongolia become a sphere of exclusive interest for Japan.

The situation of the people became intolerable. Endless levies and requisitions on the orders, sometimes of Sui Szuchen, sometimes of Ho Tsai-tyan, Chen-Yi, or Ungern and also of the Mongolian feudal nobles, had finally ruined the *arats*. Terror and repression on the part of the interventionists, along with the treachery of the ruling classes of the feudal nobles, created an intense crisis in the country.

The masses of the people began their independent historic action at a time when not only the *arat* population had no desire to go on living in the old way but when the feudal nobles too were already unable to govern as before.

At the time described, i.e. at the end of 1920—beginning of 1921, Mongolia exhibited all the symptoms of a revolutionary situation.

Marxism-Leninism teaches that not every revolutionary situation leads to a revolution. A revolutionary situation will only lead to revolution "when, to the objective changes listed above, there is added a subjective change, namely: the ability of a revolutionary *class* is combined with mass revolutionary action sufficiently *strong* to break down (or undermine) the old government, which will never, even at a time of crises, 'collapse' unless it is 'overthrown'."[2] In order to ensure the triumph of the revolutionary class of the *arats*, it was necessary immediately to set up a People's Revolutionary Party as the guiding force of the revolution.

First Congress of the Mongolian People's Party.
Formation of a Provisional People's Government.
Triumph of the Nation-Wide Armed Uprising
in Kyakhta Maimachen

Sukhe Bator and Choibalsan, having arrived in the frontier zone began to take direct control of the revolutionary movement in the country and of the preparations for convening the first congress of the Mongolian People's Party. The revolutionary newspaper *Mongolyn unen* ("Mongolian truth") began to appear, printed in Irkutsk. This newspaper propagated the ideas of Marxism-Leninism, the ideas of the Great October Socialist Revoution.

In its first issue, which appeared on November 10, 1920, with an appeal "Workers of the World, Unite!", the aggressive policy of the imperialist states and the anti-popular actions of the Mongol feudal nobles were exposed. A clear exposition was given of the tasks involved if the Mongolian *arats* were to win control with the help of the working class of Soviet Russia. In addition to the newspaper, the Mongolian revolutionaries issued proclamations and leaflets which were distributed in Mongolia.

Sukhe Bator, Choibalsan and other revolutionaries who were residing illegally in the northern *khoshuns* of the country, carried on explanatory work among the masses, recruited volunteers for the partisan detachments and attracted more and more new people to the revolutionary organizations. Representatives of the lower and middle sections of the feudal-noble class and the lamas were drawn into the liberation movement of the *arats* because of their dissatisfaction with the regime of the occupiers.

Sukhe Bator performed a great job of organization and propaganda work. He organized the first partisan detachment made up of *arats* and *tsiriks* (soldiers) from the border posts of Chiktai, Kuder, Kuran, etc. B. Puntsag, a member of the organization, also carried out important revolutionary work. As a result of his efforts about 50 Mongolian border troops went over to the side of Sukhe Bator and constituted the nucleus of future partisan formations. Soon the first revolutionary regiment was formed from partisans, with B. Puntsag appointed as commander. A locality, Altan, situated at the confluence of the rivers Orkhon and Selenga, was chosen as a partisan base. The partisans fought several successful engagements with the troops of the Chinese militarists in the neighbourhood of the town of Maimachen.

On arriving in Urga, Choibalsan devoted much effort to organising explanatory work on a large scale with the object of unmasking Ungern as a Japanese hireling and the worst enemy of the Mongolian people. He conducted discussions in which he told of the results of the journey of the delegates to Soviet Russia, the forthcoming Party Congress and the coming people's revolution.

The chief concern of the revolutionaries under the leadership of Sukhe Bator was at this time to make preparations for the first Party Congress.

The first Congress of the Party was held on March 1, 1921, in Kyakhta.

The Congress was held at a time when the political crisis in the country was deepening, and the struggle of the Mongolian *arats* against the foreign occupiers and the local oppressors—the feudal nobles—becoming more intense.

The whole work of the Congress and its decisions clearly reflected the influence on Mongolia of the ideas of the October Revolution and the counsels of Lenin.

Twenty-six delegates were present at the Congress, most of them from *arat* circles.

At the first meeting they discussed the country's situation and the tasks of the Party. The Congress gave a detailed description of the international position of Mongolia, explained the position of Soviet Russia and its part in the struggle of the peoples for peace and freedom. After discussing in detail the problems of the internal situation, the Congress exposed the part played by Ungern as a Japanese hireling and the deadly enemy of the Mongolian people.

"We must," said Sukhe Bator, "wage an independent struggle for the liberation of the Mongolian people since the government in Urga is not only unable to deal with this matter but even complies submissively with all the orders of Baron Ungern. Our only alternative is to establish close touch with Soviet Russia and, with its help, fight against the worst enemy—Ungern and his supporters, the princes and the lamas."

The Congress defined the basic anti-imperialist and anti-feudal content of the forthcoming revolution, emphasizing that the leading role in the revolution must be played by the Party as spokesman for the interests of the oppressed class of *arats*, with assistance from Soviet Russia, and as being capable of leading the masses into the struggle for their complete national and social liberation.

The majority of the delegates favoured an orientation on Soviet Russia and an independent position in relation to the feudal nobles. Only a few of them, voicing the views of officials and lamas, sought to show that, inasmuch as autonomy had been restored with Ungern's help, there was no point in fighting against him, and these spoke out against the anti-feudal tasks of the Party. The upshot of two days' discussions was that the Congress adopted a resolution on the need for the Mongolian people basing themself, in their struggle, on the international workers' movement represented by the Comintern and Soviet Russia in order to be able to bring the anti-imperialist and anti-feudal revolution to a victorious conclusion.

It was then decided to combine all the partisan detachments into an army and to set up a controlling body—the staff of the People's Revolutionary Army. Sukhe Bator was appointed commander-in-chief and Choibalsan commissar of the People's Revolutionary Army.

The political programme adopted at the Congress was exceptionally important. The introductory part of the programme spoke from the Marxist standpoint of world imperialism and its aggressive colonialist policy, of the world proletarian movement and the role of Communist parties. The programme explained to the *arats* that only in alliance with the working class of other countries would the oppressed people achieve victory in the struggle against imperialism. Special emphasis was laid on the importance of the October Revolution and the role of the Comintern in the successful struggle of the oppressed masses for their freedom. The document exposed the colonialist policy of imperialism and the predatory actions of the "government" of the *Bogdo-gegen*. In an explanation of the situation of the oppressed peoples of the colonies, in particular of Mongolia, the programme pointed out that in such countries as Mongolia where pre-capitalist relations prevail, power must be transferred to the *arats*, that people's assemblies *(hurals)* must be set up. The programme also included an analysis of the international and internal position of Mongolia.

"At the present time when all the peoples of the world are endeavouring to win their freedom and the right to develop their culture and customs, the working *arats* and intellectuals of Mongolia, sparing neither their strength nor their property, have risen to fight for the return to the Mongolian people of power over lands that have been theirs since ancient times. In order to achieve this objective they have organised the Mongolian People's Party."[3]

In the first paragraph the programme declared that, by establishing the power of the people, the Party sought to destroy the bitter sufferings of the masses of the Mongolian people, to achieve their happiness, to "revive and develop the national might and culture on an equality with other peoples."[4]

This paragraph defined the basic task of the revolution—the task of winning power for the *arats*. When the people's rule had been consolidated and the country's independence restored, the People's Party would have to be guided in its policy by firm revolutionary principles.

The second paragraph was devoted to the more immediate and future tasks of the Party. "Whereas the peaceful existence of the Mongolian people and their acquisition of culture and education will be impossible so long as Mongolia does not achieve independence, the People's Party sees its ultimate aim in establishing an independent state of the Mongolian people, while the immediate aim of the Party is to liberate the Mongolians from the rule of the Chinese militarists and the Russian White Guards and to restore the recently-abolished autonomy of Outer Mongolia."[5]

The third paragraph referred to the class relationship of the Mongolian people to the Chinese militarists and the Chinese people. Agreement and friendship between the Mongolian and Chinese peoples, the document said, would help to protect them against danger from the imperialists, for "it is clearly to be seen that Japan and America are casting greedy eyes upon us..."[6]

The programme went on to point out that the Party "is anxious to establish friendly relations and contacts with the revolutionary organizations of Russia, China and other countries which are as equally concerned as our Party to destroy despotism, achieve progress and establish the power of the people on a basis of equality."[7]

In conclusion, the programme said that membership of the Party could be held by "all persons of Mongolian nationality, regardless of sex, who are desirous of devoting themselves to the great cause of liberating the Mongolian people and who accept the programme of our Party and submit to its rules."[8]

This was a programme aimed at a people's revolution.

The immense historical importance of the first Congress is that it created a really revolutionary Party and directed it towards the organization of an armed uprising and a war of liberation against imperialist oppression and for national independence.

The Congress agreed that wider action needed to be taken to explain the Party's programme to the working people.

The Central Committee elected by the Congress, its membership including Danzan, D. Losol and Ts. Dambadorzh, set about implementing the Congress directives. First of all, it was necessary to set up an authority capable of carrying on the fight against the hirelings of Japanese and Anglo-American imperialism—the Chinese militarists, the Ungern bands and their Mongolian hangers-on, to overthrow the rule of the feudal nobles and to establish democracy in the country.

The newspaper *Mongolyn unen* devoted extensive space to explanations of these problems. In an article "Basic Principles for the Creation of a New, People's-Mongolian Power" published on December 20, 1920, the newspaper gave a detailed elucidation of the democratic transformation of the country and criticized bourgeois democracy as the democracy of an exploiting minority. The article said: "Although the governing bodies of France or America are elected, the workers and peasants who form the bulk of the population have no rights there whatsoever and live in poverty. The reason for this is that in these and other countries, when state power and laws were established, the aristocracy and the capitalists grabbed all the advantages and thus made it possible to convert elected governmental power into the power of aristocrats and capitalists instead of people's power." The article went on to talk of the principal conditions required for establishing a really democratic state, namely, "...the government set up must be based only on elections held 'from the bottom upwards', since only elective power is not power vested in one person governing the country on a permanent or hereditary basis."

The article emphasized that "under a real government of the people, aristocrats and capitalists would be deprived of all opportunity to take part in matters of state or to exploit the masses... If people's power is established on these principles, statehood in Mongolia will be strengthened and the Mongolian people will really be able to live in freedom and with equal rights and their material and spiritual culture will be developed."

This was how the Party decided the question of the future form of state administration.

On March 13, 1921, a Congress of representatives of working people of the border *khoshuns*, partisan detachments and Party organizations was held in Troitskosavsk at which the first Provisional People's Government of Mongolia in the history of the country was elected; it consisted of Sukhe Bator, Chagdarzhav (President of the Government), Choibalsan, Bodo, Sumya, Bilegsaikhan and others. The Congress resolution states:

"The aim of the armed uprising of the people is, firstly, to free our country from the yoke of Chinese militarists and clear out from it the other aggressors who have invaded its territory; secondly, to set up a government capable of protecting the interests of the Mongolian people and developing their culture.

"In order to achieve the aims set forth we consider it necessary to elect a fully-authorised Provisional People's Government of Mongolia to convene a congress of representatives of Mongolian *arats*, to form a permanent government and approve a constitution of the state."[9]

In this elected government Sukhe Bator held the post of Minister of War and Commander-in-Chief of the armed forces, while Choibalsan became Deputy Commander-in-Chief for Political Affairs.

The young revolutionary government had to be backed by a well-organized armed force capable of ensuring the implementation of revolutionary measures, and it was decided to reorganize the partisan detachments into a regular army. Such a reorganization became possible because the numbers of partisans had increased, their battle training had improved, the first officer cadres had appeared and arms and equipment had improved.

Four cavalry regiments were formed to command which talented partisan leaders were appointed—B. Puntsag, B. Tserendorzh, Has Bator and Bazarsad.

On March 16, 1921, the Central Committee of the Party and the Provisional People's Government took a decision to liberate from the Chinese militarists the town of Maimachen, where some 10,000 Chinese troops were concentrated. The occupation of this town would give the Provisional Government an important base on Mongolian territory.

When preparations for the attack had been completed Sukhe Bator sent the Chinese command an ultimatum: lay down arms and surrender the town. As no reply was received, on the morning of March 18, 1921, fighting began between the Mongolian People's Army and the Chinese militarists and went on all day, with changing fortunes.

The battle ended on the night of March 18 with the complete victory of the People's Army, small in numbers but strong in spirit, over the numerous and well-armed enemy. March 18, 1921, the date of the liberation of Maimachen, subsequently renamed Altan-Bulak, is considered the birthday of the Mongolian People's Revolutionary Army. This historic victory of the uprising of the *arats* under the leadership of the People's Party resulted in the complete expulsion from the country of the Chinese militarists and created conditions for a successful struggle, jointly with units of the Red Army, against the common enemy—the White Guards.

On March 19 members of the Central Committee of the Party and the Provisional People's Government arrived in the town and on the same day a Manifesto from the Provisional Government was promulgated. It informed the population of Mongolia of the formation of the Provisional People's Government, which had set itself the aim of freeing the country from the domination of the Chinese militarists and the White Guards and of convening the Grand All-People's Hural. The Manifesto proclaimed that henceforth the country knew no power other than that of the people and that no one should comply with any orders or laws save those issued by the Mongolian People's power. The Manifesto called upon all Mongolians to rise and fight against the Russian White Guards. In conclusion, it solemnly declared: "The great moment has arrived for the rebirth of the Mongolian people, the moment for uniting thoughts, aspirations and actions for establishing a new people's administration in place of an obsolete despotism."[10]

After a few days a combined meeting of the Central Committee and the Provisional People's Government took a decision to set up three Ministries—of War, Finance and Internal Affairs.

On March 25 the Central Committee of the People's Party published an appeal "To the whole Chinese people, the Chinese Communist Party, trade unions, students and all revolutionary-democratic groups and true patriots of China." After explaining the meaning of the revolutionary struggle that had developed in Mongolia, the appeal said: "In the name of the common interests and solidarity of the workers of the whole world and, in particular, of dependent colonial Asia, and in view of the deep community of interests and ideals uniting the Chinese and Mongolian peoples, all equally exploited and oppressed by their own and by alien despoilers and violators, the Central Committee of the Mongolian People's Party categorically demands that the Peking government immediately stop sending troops into Mongolia and at the same time appeals to and sends friendly and sincere greetings to the Chinese people and to its best and noblest elements mentioned above, calling on them to support its demands. . ."

The above appeal proves clearly how correctly the People's Party understood the international solidarity of the workers of Mongolia and China in their struggle against oppressors.

The fighting for Maimachen marked the beginning of the armed uprising of the whole people and the beginning of the national-liberation war. The preparations for a revolution had ended, the revolution had become a fact.

The Spread and the Triumph of the People's Revolution

News of the revolutionary happenings in the north spread all over the country. The Party slogans summoning people to fight for the expulsion of the occupation authorities and their troops and the establishment of popular rule met with an eager response from the masses. The victory of Sukhe Bator's revolutionary troops over the numerically superior forces of the Chinese militarists filled the people with enthusiasm and raised their hopes for early emancipation.

The reactionary upper circles of the lay princes and the senior lamas of Mongolia and the Ungern bands united together in their struggle against the people in revolt, against their Party and the Provisional Government. These circles of the Mongolian feudal nobility extolled the role of Ungern and tried to prove that the aim of restoring autonomy had been achieved. They called upon the revolutionaries to end the struggle. Realizing the complete futility of their own appeal, they tried their utmost to discredit the revolutionaries, going so far as to declare them traitors and betrayers.

The Ministry of Internal Affairs of the Ungern "government" issued a special appeal on behalf of the *Bogdo-gegen* to the *arats* of the Tushetu Khan *aimak* where the Party's influence was especially strong. This appeal described services alleged to have been rendered by Ungern and criticized the leaders of the revolution—Sukhe Bator, Choibalsan and others—who, it averred, had on their own initiative established relations with Russia, created their own troops and were issuing appeals which talked about the rights of the *arat* masses, the ideas of their Party, etc. "This means struggle against the Khan's government. Such intentions cannot be realised even in large civilized states, let alone in our Mongolia."[11]

From the very outset the People's Party envisaged the possibility, in the interests of the revolution, of playing upon the antagonisms between the Mongolian feudal nobles and the foreign occupiers.

The Central Committee of the Party and the Provisional People's Government devoted their efforts to bringing the patriotically-minded feudal nobles over to the cause of freeing the country from alien domination. Consequently letters to this effect were sent out to princes and lamas. On March 23 one such letter was forwarded to Urga, addressed personally to the Prime Minister Jalkhanza-khutukhta. The letter called upon the head of the Ungern "government" to join in the liberation struggle of the people and suggested that he delegate representatives to proceed to Altan-Bulak for negotiations about unity of action.

The ruling circles of the Mongolian feudal nobles, however, did not respond to the invitations of the People's Party; they preferred the alliance with Ungern, the capitalists and the Chinese militarists to an alliance with their own people.

In these circumstances the Central Committee and the People's Government enlarged the ranks of the partisan army, reinforced their positions and continued to mobilize the masses for the struggle against the Ungern bands and the reactionary Mongolian feudal nobles, while drawing over to their side the patriotically-minded section of the officials, feudal nobles and lamas.

In order to explain the Party's policy and organize the population for the fight with the White Guards the Central Committee and the People's Government in March 1921 sent out their representatives to the most important regions of the country: Has Bator and Dambadorzh to the western *aimaks* of Mongolia, and Chagdarzhav to the northern ones. With the same aim in view Sukhe Bator, Choibalsan and Puntsag also travelled into the *khoshuns*.

In April 1921 the People's Government took a decision to call men over 19 up in the liberated part of the country into the ranks of the army.

On May 28 at a joint meeting of the Central Committee and the Provisional People's Government it was resolved to establish an institute *of khoshun* commissars— representatives of the Provisional Government with wide plenipotentiary powers and rights as defined in a special directive. Simultaneously, a decision was taken compelling *shabinars* to perform military service on the same terms as others.

Particular measures of the Central Committee and the People's Government bore a clearly expressed anti-feudal character. For instance, on May 21, 1921, the Provisional People's Government adopted a resolution revoking the right of private title to land. Rules were also laid down regarding the collection of taxes and duties. Plenipotentiary representatives of the Party and Government were given the right to control the actions of *khoshuns* and to remove counter-revolutionary princes from the office they held. The Central Committee and the People's Government issued appeals to the population exposing the aggressive and counter-revolutionary intentions of the Ungern bands and the traitors—the Mongolian feudal nobles.

Nevertheless, in spite of all this the forces were unequally matched. Ungern had an enormous numerical superiority; his army was plentifully supplied with experienced cadre officers and was superior in arms and equipment. Consequently, the Provisional People's Government, on a proposal made by Sukhe Bator on April 10, 1921, decided to appeal to the Government of Soviet Russia and ask for military help for the joint struggle against the common enemy—the Russian White Guards. The Soviet Government granted this request.

Meanwhile, the White Guard bands in the Far East made feverish preparations for new ventures. At secret meetings of the Japanese military clique and the White Guards, held in Port Arthur and Peking in March and April 1921, a plan was drawn up for a fresh large-scale advance on Soviet Russia from Mongolia, North-Eastern China and the Maritime Province (Primorye). These plans gave an important assignment to Ungern who was to suppress the revolutionary movement in Mongolia, strengthen the Mongolian feudal authorities under his orders and advance into the Soviet areas bordering on Mongolia.

Ungern's plan visualized a simultaneous advance by all his troops from different points in Mongolia. On May 20, 1921 Ungern, leaving a police guard in Urga, hurried forward with his main forces towards Altan-Bulak and Troitskosavsk. The general advance of the Ungern bands began. On May 22, 1921, Nemchinov's detachment occupied Manzu in the region of the Soviet-Mongolian frontier and on May 25 a cavalry regiment from Kazagranda's brigade—Molon-kul. At the same time General Rezukhin's brigade opened up military operations on the Soviet-Mongolian frontier in the region of Zheltura. The bands of General Bakich, as well as the detachments of Kazantsev and Kaigorodov prepared to attack the Soviet frontier from the western regions of Mongolia. On June 5 an advanced detachment of Ungern's, commanded by Bayar-gun, occupied the village of Ibitsik and on June 6 an advance began on the residence of the Provisional People's Government—the town of Altan-Bulak.

Units of the People's Revolutionary Army under the command of Sukhe Bator joined in stubborn battles with the Ungern troops in the region of Altan-Bulak, and smashed a detachment of Ungern's accomplice, Bayar-gun, whom they took prisoner. As a result of the powerful blows struck by units of the Red Army which had come to the aid of the Mongolian people, the main Ungern forces were thrown back from the frontier and seriously weakened. In these joint operations against the common enemy the soldiers of the young Mongolian People's Revolutionary Army commanded by Sukhe Bator and Choibalsan behaved like heroes.

This victory determined the success of the revolution. It gave a boost to the massive influx of volunteers into the ranks of the People's Revolutionary Army and signalized an increase in the partisan formation of *arats* joining in the struggle against the Ungern bands.

The entry of units of the fraternal Red Army into the confines of Mongolia radically altered the balance of forces in the country in favour of the revolution. It activated the revolutionary struggle of the *arat* masses while at the same time paralyzing the forces of reaction. The joint struggle of units of the Red Army and of the young People's Revolutionary Army against the White Guard bands strengthened the indissoluble alliance and brotherly friendship of the Mongolian and the Soviet peoples.

The Central Committee of the Party and the Provisional People's Government prepared to liberate the capital of the country—Urga—with the help of detachments of the Red Army.

The commanders of the units of the Red Army issued an appeal to the Mongolian population which read: "The Red Armies of Workers' and Peasants' Russia are entering the *khoshuns* of the Mongolian people as friends. The workers and peasants of Russia hold out the hand of brotherly help to the Mongolian people, who have hitherto been languishing under oppression. Aggressive intentions of any kind whatsoever are absolutely and definitely alien to them; they have no wish to force their domination on any people and desire to live in peace and friendship with all the other peoples of the world..."

The Provisional People's Government and the Central Committee of the MPPR also issued an appeal to the population which said: "Red Army soldiers of Soviet Russia are operating on the side of our People's Army... The Red Army puts the interests of the masses of the people above everything else; it is fighting in order to destroy completely the robber bands of the White Guards and will never allow sufferings to be inflicted on the *arat* masses of Mongolia."[12]

On June 27, 1921, the Mongolian People's Army under the command of Sukhe Bator and in co-operation with units of the Soviet troops began the historic march for the liberation of Urga. In accordance with the plan the Mongolian-Soviet troops moved in the following two directions: in the main direction towards the capital—the main forces of the Mongolian People's Army and units of the Red Army consisting of the 5th Kuban cavalry division, the 2nd Sretensk cavalry brigade, the 35th Siberian division; in a south-western direction, along the banks of the Selenga river—a special detachment commanded by Kh. Choibalsan, a mounted partisan detachment headed by the famous Siberian partisan P. E. Shchetinkin, the 105th infantry brigade, and the 35th mounted regiment commanded by K. K. Rokossovsky. The 104th brigade remained in reserve. The Soviet troops were commanded by the Chief of the 35th Siberian division, K. A. Neiman.[13]

The Mongolian population gave a warm welcome to the revolutionary armies. When they learnt of the approach of the Soviet and Mongolian troops, the working *arats* formed partisan groups and joined battle with the gangs of White bandits.

The organs of revolutionary authority enjoyed the full support of the population. With the help of the people the Government confiscated the property of those feudal nobles and officials who had fled with the White Guards.

The *Bogdo-gegen* was beginning to realize that the Ungern card was a loser and that the people's revolution was winning. Fearing the revolution but unable to prevent its triumph, the *Bogdo-gegen* and his entourage tried to stop, to hold back the revolution, to weaken its forces. In the *Bogdo-gegen's* name they issued appeal after appeal, urging the *arats* not to help the Red Army and the People's Revolutionary Army or join up with them. They also sent an appeal to Sukhe Bator and the Provisional People's Government containing lying assurances to the effect that the last remnants of the Ungern bands had fled from Urga and so peace and order were already established in the country and there was no reason, they alleged, to bring troops into the capital and organise a new government.

After a series of battles with the White Guards covering Urga, on the morning of July 6, 1921, the advanced detachments of the revolutionary troops entered the capital and two days later, on July 8, there arrived in Urga, along with the main forces of the army, the Provisional People's Government and the Central Committee of the Party. The population warmly greeted the Mongolian and Soviet soldiers.

Sukhe Bator made a speech in the War Ministry building:

"For the liberation of our country from foreign aggressors and for winning freedom and rights for the Mongolian people we have chosen a people's government and decided to establish state power on completely different principles.

"The people's government which had come to Urga could have behaved in a revolutionary manner. But, in view of the fact that you lamas and princes have offered no resistance and, bearing in mind also the situation in the country, the government have decided to set up people's power by proclaiming the *Bogdo* a limited monarch. The former ministers are dismissed from their posts and must hand over their business in complete order."[14]

On July 10, 1921, the Central Committee of the Party adopted a resolution handing over central authority to the people's government. In doing so the people's government was invested with the following tasks: firstly, to see that the *arats* became the owners of their own lands and water, secondly, to offer the *arats* rights and freedom and point out the way to the development and prosperity of the country. On July 11, 1921, the people's government requested the government of the RSFSR not to withdraw Soviet troops from Mongolia until the White Guard bands had been completely eliminated (on August 10,

1921, the Soviet government expressed its agreement to this request).

On July 16 a permanent people's revolutionary government was formed, consisting of the following members: Bodo, Prime Minister and Minister of Foreign Affairs, Sukhe Bator, Commander-in-Chief and Minister of War, Danzan, Minister of Finance, Maksarzhav-beis (Khurts), Minister of Justice and dalama Puntsagdorzh, Minister of Internal Affairs.

As military operations against the Ungern hands had not been completed and in view of the *Bogdo-gegen's* influence in clerical circles and among all believers, he was temporarily allowed to keep the title of limited monarch.

The transfer of power in the country into the hands of the Supreme People's Government marked the beginning of an important period in the first stage of the Mongolian people's revolution—the period of struggle for the final elimination of the Ungern bands, the reinforcement of people's power and the consequential carrying out of democratic reforms in the interests of the *arat* population— the motive force of the anti-feudal and anti-imperialist revolution.

Complete Destruction of the Ungern Bands and Agreement on Friendship Between People's Mongolia and Soviet Russia. Start Made on Solving Social Problems

Ungern had suffered a heavy defeat and for the time being evaded battle with the Soviet troops but he was still far from being utterly defeated. The White Guard occupying forces still held a large part of the country's territory—including the towns of Kobdo, Ulyasutai, Van-Khure, Sain-Beise (present-day Choibalsan) and others.

Fighting continued: Sukhe Bator's units were engaged in wiping out the Ungern bands in the areas around Urga; detachments of Kh. Choibalsan and B. Puntsag, together with Soviet troops, were battling with large Ungern forces in the northern regions. On July 18 and 21 battles took place on the banks of the River Selenga with the combined forces of Ungern and Rezukhin, who had reinforced his ranks in the region of Akhaigun Khure. In the east of the country Mongolian military units under the command of G. Bumatsende were pursuing the remnants of an Ungern band withdrawing into Manchuria, while in the west partisan troops led by Dambadorzh and Has-Bator, together with Red Army detachments under the command of Baikalov were wiping out other Ungern units located in this region.

On July 24, 1921, the bands of Ungern and Rezukhin again crossed into the RSFSR, counting on assistance from Japanese troops. On August 5 Red Army units defeated the White Guards in the region of Goose Lake. Ungern, with the remnants of his troops, again fled into Mongolia to escape being surrounded and finally smashed.

The Japanese-White Guard venture of Baron Ungern had suffered a political and a military defeat.

The Mongolian *tsiriks* in the ranks of Ungern troops, refusing to follow him into Western Mongolia, which was where he intended to go, seized and disarmed him. The captive Ungern, caught by the 35th cavalry regiment which was pursuing him, was taken to Novosibirsk, where he was sentenced by a revolutionary court and shot. Such was the end of the inglorious career of this hireling of the Japanese militarists who had tried to put down the Mongolian people's revolution and turn Mongolia into a base for war against Soviet Russia.

Some remnants of Ungern's and Rezukhin's troops were smashed by the People's Revolutionary Army and some fled into North-Eastern China. Thus, the eastern part of Mongolia was practically cleared of White bands. But the western part of the country still continued to be held by the White Guards. Detachments of the troops of Bakich, Sokolnitsky, Kazantsev and Kaigorodov were active there. On October 17, 1921, the people's government again appealed to the RSFSR government and proposed joint action to liquidate White Guard bands in Western Mongolia.

In May 1921 representatives of the Provisional People's Government, headed by Has-Bator, had already formed a regional committee of the Party in Western Mongolia and were conducting revolutionary work among the population and had formed partisan detachments. In June a regional government was formed there in which some princes of the Durbet *aimaks* participated. At the same time prince Khatan-Bator Maksarzhav, after making contact with the people's government, raised a rebellion in Ulyasutai during which Ungern's protégés, Shtein and Vandanov, were killed. On August 2, 1921, the regional government and regional bureau of the Party issued an appeal to the *arats* of Western Mongolia calling upon them to fight against the White bandits.

A combined detachment of Mongolian partisans and Red Army soldiers, under the command of Has-Bator and Baikalov, began the struggle against the Whites in Western Mongolia. There were slightly more than 300 men in the detachment. In September 1921, in the region of Lake Tolbo-nur, this detachment was surrounded by White bandits and remained surrounded more than forty days. The weather was cold and the soldiers had no warm clothing; provisions ran out and medicines were lacking. But the soldiers did not lose heart. They bravely beat back the attacks of the Whites, and resolutely refused invitations to surrender. Many of them, including the detachment's commander, the brave patriot Has-Bator, died a hero's death. On the 42nd day, when the soldiers still left alive decided to break out of the encirclement fighting or dying for the revolution, a Red Army regiment arrived to rescue them; it defeated the Whites and liberated the patriots.

As a result of protracted and stubborn fighting the White Guard bands in Mongolia were smashed up by the middle of 1922 and by the end of that year the whole country was virtually cleared of occupying forces and reunited under the rule of the people's government. The young People's Army of Mongolia, led by the talented commanders, Sukhe Bator, Choibalsan, Maksarzhav, Puntsag, Bumatsende and others, working in close fighting cooperation with the Soviet Red Army, brought its people a victory gained in armed struggle against the forces of imperialism—the Chinese militarists and the Russian White Guards.

The talented leadership of troops and the personal bravery exhibited by Sukhe Bator and his fellow fighters in the struggle against common enemies were highly esteemed by the Government of Soviet Russia. Sukhe Bator, Choibalsan and Khatan-Bator Maksarzhav were decorated in March 1922 with Soviet Orders of the Fighting Red Banner.

The Mongolian People's Government also marked the services of Sukhe Bator with a high decoration by designating him Zorikto-bator (Brave Hero).

The international situation of the country, however, still continued to be rather strained. Japanese imperialists and Chinese militarists were unwilling to admit that their plans for seizing Mongolia had been shattered. After Ungern's defeat the Chinese general Chang-Tso-lin endeavoured, with the help of Japanese imperialists, to throttle the people's revolution in Mongolia and bring the latter under his control. On July 1, 1921, a meeting organized by Chang Tso-lin was held in Mukden which was attended by representatives of the feudal nobility of Inner and Outer Mongolia. At the meeting plans were discussed for seizing Outer Mongolia. Chang Tso-lin made active preparations for a march on Urga; it did not take place, however, because of quarrels between the militarist cliques in China fighting for power in connection with the intensification of the anti-imperialist movement of the masses in China and the aggravation of disputes between imperialist states intriguing against one another and, finally because units of the heroic Soviet Red Army which had already demonstrated its strength to the whole world were still located on the territory of the young Mongolian people's state.

With regard to the imperialists of the USA, England and other countries, they were just as interested as the Japanese imperialists in putting down the revolution and making use of Mongolia as a base for counter-revolutionary war against Soviet Russia and against the liberation struggle of the peoples of China and the other countries of the East. At the same time they were endeavouring to drive their Japanese "allies" out of Mongolia in the interests of their own monopolies.

American imperialists, utilizing the Chinese militarists as a tool in their policy of aggression, were seeking to spread their influence in Mongolia. This was combined with intensive penetration of the country by American businessmen. For instance, at the end of May 1921 representatives of Anderson, Mayer and Company, an American firm, arrived in Urga to buy horses. In September 1921 the American consul in Kalgan offered the people's government his services as an intermediary in negotiations with China but the people's government in Mongolia rejected the services of the USA.

The people's government of Mongolia, born in the 1921 revolution, followed—from the very first day it came into being—a peace-loving and friendly foreign policy. As early as 1921 it made an offer to the people and to all the democratic forces of China to establish friendly relations on a footing of equality. The people's government also took steps to establish good-neighbourly relations with China in July 1921. However, the Peking Government and the militarist clique were not only unwilling to do anything in this direction but even did their utmost to complicate relations between the countries. Nevertheless, the government of People's Mongolia, continuing its efforts to organize friendly relations with China, gave permission to its trade organs to conduct an exchange of commodities with Chinese and other foreign firms on mutually advantageous conditions.

The people's government of Mongolia invariably observed international standards in regard to foreign nationals and trading firms, waged a struggle against the imperialists and their agents, strictly distinguishing between them and the peaceful Chinese, Russian, German, Hungarian, English, American and other private foreign nationals who were at that time resident in Mongolia.

On September 14, 1921, the people's government sent a declaration to all countries informing them that the Mongolian people had won their freedom and independence and announcing its peaceful desire to establish with all countries friendly and, in particular, trading relations. At the end of the declaration it stated that the government of Soviet Russia had renounced all previous privileges provided for in pre-revolutionary treaties and expressed the hope that the governments of other countries would follow this just and humane example.[15]

The governments of the capitalist countries did not respond to the repeated peaceful proposals of the Mongolian government.

The most important feature, however, of the foreign policy of the people's government was the strengthening of the fraternal friendship and co-operation with Soviet Russia which had been born and strengthened in joint struggle against world imperialism and its White Guard agents.

In October 1921 a delegation of the Mongolian People's Government arrived in Moscow, consisting of D. Sukhe Bator, B. Tserendorzh, Danzan and others, for negotiations on establishing friendly relations with the RSFSR.

On November 5, 1921, an agreement for the establishment of friendly relations was signed between the Mongolian People's Government and the Government of the RSFSR. This was Mongolia's first international agreement concluded entirely on a basis of equality. It pointed out that all earlier treaties and agreements concluded between the former tsarist government of Russia and the former government of Autonomous Mongolia were regarded as null and void. The Government of the RSFSR acknowledged the People's Government as the only lawful government of Mongolia. Both parties mutually undertook to give most-favoured-nation treatment in political and economic relations and also not to tolerate on its territory the activities of organizations inimical to the other party.

Faithful to the principles of socialist foreign policy, the Soviet government confirmed in a special article its renunciation of the exceptional rights and privileges in Mongolia which tsarist Russia had enjoyed, handed over without compensation to Mongolia certain property belonging to Russia and cancelled Mongolia's pre-revolutionary debt amounting to about 5 million roubles.

This agreement was immensely important in reinforcing the international and internal position of the Mongolian people's state, strengthening the positions of people's power, creating favourable conditions for the further development of the revolution and for constructing the bases of a people's democracy.

During the Mongolian delegation's stay in Moscow it was received by Lenin. In conversation Lenin expressed his satisfaction with the successful development of the revolution in Mongolia.

Lenin dwelt at length in conversations with the delegates on the idea of the non-capitalist development of Mongolia, and on the possibility and necessity of such development. He considered that the principal condition for the success of the movement towards socialism, by-passing capitalism, was to improve the work of the Party and the people's government; this should lead to a growth of co-operatives and the introduction of new forms of economic management and culture and to identifying the *arat* population more closely with the Party and people's power.

Some months later Lenin again talked with the Mongolian delegates, who were attending a congress of the peoples of the Far East. In this conversation he again reverted to the question of the non-capitalist path of development for Mongolia and remarked that co-operation was one basic form of such development.

Guided by the theory of Marxism-Leninism, the Party and the people's government held unswervingly to the policy of a further development of the revolutionary struggle against the economic and political attitudes of feudalism in the country. Only in this way and only by breaking down the feudal bases in economics and politics was it possible to prepare conditions for non-capitalist, i.e. socialist, development. Only along these lines could guarantees be created against a restoration of feudalism and colonialist oppression.

This was the path along which the Central Committee of the Party and the people's government led the working *arats*.

Against a background of struggle with the Ungern bands the people's government, under the guidance of the Mongolian People's Party, attacked such important revolutionary problems as extending the influence of people's power over the country, curtailing the political and economic privileges of the feudal noble class, making a start on solving the most important social and economic problems thrown up by the revolution.

On September 4, 1921, the People's Party published in the newspaper *Uria* an article on the policy of intensifying the anti-feudal revolution and reinforcing the authority of the people.

In compliance with the decisions of the Central Committee of the People's Party and People's Government adopted in the autumn of 1921, plenipotentiary representatives of the government were appointed to the *aimak* diets in order to explain to the workers the policy of the Party and the government, to carry out control over local government bodies and their democratization and to set up Party organizatons on the spot. Special government plenipotentiaries were also sent to the cities of Kobdo, Ulyasutai and Altan-Bulak. By the end of 1921, five local Party cells had been formed, with a total of 150 members.

The lack of more or less trained cadres among the *arats*, sabotage by officials of the old administration, the influence of the church on the people, the resistance of the reactionary members of the feudal nobility and remnants of the Ungern bands and of foreign capital were all factors that seriously hampered the implementation of revolutionary measures. But, under the leadership of the People's Party and by overcoming these and other difficulties, the People's Government inexorably, step by step, solved the problems of revolution as they materialized.

While utilizing the services of old officials the government systematically removed reactionary officials from the state apparatus, did everything to reinforce its supervision over the functioning of local government bodies and introduced the practice of electing persons to the post of *khoshun* governor. That was done on occasions when hereditary power was due to be handed over in the traditional way or where princes acted in a hostile manner towards the rule of the people.

The people's government abolished certain titles and ranks which had been conferred on influential Mongolian feudal nobles during the reign of the Manchu dynasty, the period of autonomy and the rule of the militarists and the Ungern bands. This applied also to the *Bogdo-gegen* and his wife.

The transfer of power in the country to the People's Revolutionary Government had to be given statutory force at a congress of representatives of the people.

Pending the convening of such a congress the Party considered it necessary to convene a consultative body of people's representatives. To this end the people's government on September 5, 1921, decided to set up in Urga a consultative body—the Provisional Little Hural, or pre-Parliament as it has sometimes been called by writers, consisting of 5 *arats* and one representative of the aristocracy from each *aimak* and *shabi*, as well as representatives of the army, the Party Central Committee and the Central Committee of the Revolutionary Youth League. This ensured that representatives of the *arats* would have 92% of the membership of the Provisional Little Hural.

The Provisional Little Hural expressed the wishes and interests of the mass of the people; it played a big part in drawing *arats* into state administration, encouraged the training of new managerial cadres and constituted an important preliminary stage towards the convening of the Grand Hural.

As authority in the country passed into the hands of the people's government the privileges of the feudal nobles began to be gradually curtailed, especially in the sphere of law and justice.

At the end of 1921 the government set up a special commission to prepare a democratic reform of the judicial system; torture was abolished and it was forbidden to apply Manchu laws.

The class and popular-democratic nature of these statutory measures lay in the elimination of the privileged status of the feudal classes in the eyes of the courts and the laws, in the enactment of stricter measures for punishing enemies of the people and of humane forms of punishment for working people, in the abolition of medieval methods of interrogation and in the introduction of the principle of labour education.

People's power curtailed the rights and privileges not only of the secular, but also of the eccelesiastical nobility. The sovereign powers of the *Chubil Khans* were abolished and later on the actual institution of *Chubil Khans* was done away with; the monastery herds were levied by taxation; the special privileges which, before the revolution, were conferred on Tibetan traders closely connected with the court of the *Bogdo-gegen* and with the big feudal nobles, were annulled; princes and monasteries lost their right to charge interest on loans in cattle or goods, etc.

In 1921, after Urga was liberated and during the fierce fighting with Ungern, the people's government devoted special attention to reducing the severest—and at the same time the basic—forms of feudal servitudes—the *urton* servitude on all the main highways and that of military service.

This was the policy inherently embodied in the decisions of the people's government promulgated on August 31, 1921, limiting the number of horses maintained for meeting the daily official requirements of the *Bogdo-gegen's* court; on September 13, 1921, concerning the allocation of horses belonging to *shabi* for *urton* service; on November 1, 1921, abrogating the right of princes and higher office-holding titled lamas to use *urton* horses when paying the traditional visits to each other at New Year and other such times.

The people's government also began to carry out a number of measures in connection with land problems and control was instituted over land leased to foreigners and private individuals.

On the directions of the Party's Central Committee the people's government put a stop to the payment of debts to foreign merchants and firms by both *arats* and *khoshuns* and subsequently declared a moratorium. This action by the People's Party and the people's government gave expression to the basic interests of the *arat* masses and consequently touched on one of the most important tasks of the anti-imperialist and anti-feudal revolution. New taxation and customs duty obligations, levied for the benefit of the state, were fixed for foreign firms.

The nationalization of industrial, agricultural and other enterprises which formerly belonged to private foreign entrepreneurs and the former tsarist government, and also to the former feudal government of pre-revolutionary Mongolia, and the creation of consumers' cooperative societies had one common aim—to weaken the economic position of foreign imperialism, get the country's economy in order and improve the situation of the *arats*.

In December 1921 the Mongolian Central Cooperative Society was instituted, its aim being to serve the interests of the people by driving out foreign capital and ensuring the possibility of the country's development along non-capitalist lines.

A great deal of work also started in the sphere of cultural construction. In September 1921 the first primary school was opened in Urga. Later on, several such schools were opened in *aimak* and some *khoshun* centres. A start was made to eliminate illiteracy among the adult population, especially among *tsiriks* in the People's Revolutionary Army. At the end of 1921 the printing shop in Urga, which had been destroyed by the Chinese militarists and the Ungern bands, was restored and began printing books and textbooks in Mongolian, the bulletin of MONTA (Mongolian Telegraph Agency) and the newspaper *Uria*. It was then, too, that the Mongolian scientific research organization—the Scholars' Committee, afterwards renamed the Committee of Sciences—was established.

In August 1921 the first meeting was held in Urga of leading representatives of the Mongolian youth at which a Central Committee of the Revolutionary Youth League consisting of five persons was elected. Choibalsan was unanimously elected Secretary of the Central Committee.

* * *

The measures taken to curtail the rights of the feudal nobles aggravated the class struggle. This struggle took highly diverse forms. The situation urgently called for a strict delimitation of the functions of the limited monarchy and people's government.

On November 1, 1921, the people's government, at a meeting attended by all the Ministers, their deputies, members of the Central Committee of the People's Party and members of the Central Committee of the Revolutionary Youth League, approved a decree curtailing the powers of the *Bogdo-gegen;* this has gone down under the name of the "Sworn Treaty".

All the basic paragraphs of this extremely important constitutional document were aimed very emphatically at expanding the role of the people's government and curtailing the rights of the monarch in all affairs of state. The *Bogdo-gegen's* loss of the right of veto was formally legalized and draft laws and legal regulations signed by him entered into force only after they had been approved by the people's government. In extraordinary cases the people's government had the right to enact laws and regulations without notifying the *Bogdo-gegen*. Paragraph 9 of the "Treaty" represents a reciprocal undertaking by the *Bogdo-gegen* and the people's government to comply with all the legislative regulations envisaged by this act.

By giving effect to this law the people's government provided for security and ensured protection of the gains won by the revolution.

The form of state structure instituted in the country made it possible to deprive the *Bogdo-gegen* of supreme power as head of the state and to limit his functions in the administration of church affairs.

The economic measures initiated by the people's government were aimed at introducing several very important limitations on the rights of the feudal nobles and on foreign capital so as to alleviate the situation of the liberated *arats*.

As the Party and government widened the front of their anti-feudal measures, the counter-revolutionary forces of feudal reaction became more and more active. Opposition began to be shown by the class that had been overthrown—secret activities of the *Bogdo-gegen*, an overt conspiracy by Bodo, the Prime Minister of the people's government, the da-lama Puntsagdorzh, the Minister of the Interior, Chagdarzhav, the spokesman of the budding middle-class elements and others. In 1922 they were all brought to trial and convicted.

The secular and clerical feudal nobles also began to organise anti-popular conspiracies one after another, seeking to re-establish the old feudal-theocratic monarchy. They made an effort to organise a counter-revolutionary mutiny with the help of Tibetan lamas and money-lenders, headed by Sachzhi-lama (Zhamyan-Danzan), an intimate of the *Bogdo-gegen's* and a former commander of a Tibetan detachment in the army of Ungern. The mutineers planned to attack Government House on the morning of December 21, 1921. However, on the night of December 20 soldiers of the People's Army arrested 48 members of this counter-revolutionary group.

At this time, too, there was discovered a conspiracy by Ochirov and Tuvanov, who had been commissioned by the Japanese counter-intelligence to destroy the people's government. A conspiracy by Tserempil was also unmasked and liquidated; through it the *Bogdo-gegen* was seeking to establish contact with Japanese imperialists.

The second half of 1921 was thus a very important period—a period when the Ungern bands were finally liquidated over the whole territory of the country by the combined forces of the Mongolian People's Army and the Red Army, a period of stabilization of people's power. It was at this time that a beginning was made, though cautiously and gradually, on the implementation of a number of social and economic reforms, which were entirely in the interests of the *arat* population and of the reinforcement of the democratic state structure.

CHAPTER III

DEMOCRATIC CHANGES AND PROCLAMATION
OF THE MPR (1922-1924)

Democratic Changes in the Country

The expulsion from the country of the Ungern occupation forces enabled the Mongolian people to tackle more radically many anti-feudal tasks in the first years after the revolution.

The difficulties and complications arising from historical causes were the reason why the democratic reforms preceding the proclamation of the Republic required a three-year period for their accomplishment. But, under the leadership of the Mongolian People's Revolutionary Party and, with the wholehearted support of the first Soviet socialist state in the world, the Mongolian people successfully overcame them and gradually and successfully solved the most important anti-feudal tasks designed to reinforce the structure of a People's Democracy.

In the years 1922-1924, in particular, extremely important revolutionary changes were, step by step, brought into effect: the dependent status of the *arat* serfs was abolished, feudal servitudes were abrogated, debts to foreign firms were cancelled, a start was made on limiting foreign capital by imposing customs dues and taxes and strengthening the national consumers' co-operative movement; the functioning of state enterprises and the state budget was put on a sound footing.

The abolition of serfdom among the *arats*, with all its political, economic and legal consequences, was one of the basic tasks of the anti-feudal revolution. The formation of people's power and the introduction of a number of political and economic measures in 1921 meant that a serious blow had been struck undermining serf relationships and these were later on entirely abolished.

One of the most onerous servitudes for the *arats*—military service rendered to the feudal state, with all the expenses it involved, was abolished. This problem had been partially solved in the course of the revolution itself but it was finally settled after the triumph of the revolution by annulling all the privileges of the feudal nobles in regard to military service.

As early as 1921 transport *(urton)* affairs were re-organised for the benefit of the *arats* and the state, and in 1922-1924 still further improvements were introduced on lines advantageous for the *arats*.

In the elaboration and implementation of taxation policy the Central Committee of the Party and the people's government took into consideration primarily the requirements of the revolution, the interests of the *arats* and the objectives of the struggle against the feudal class.

Taxes began to be levied on all sovereign and non-sovereign princes, clerical feudal nobles, courtiers, lamas, and also monasteries (the latter being given an allowance of 20 sheep to every 100 *bodo*).[1]

The imposition of taxes on feudal households, lamas, monasteries and the *shabi* population was in itself a great alleviation for the *arats*. The class nature of the taxation policy lay, further, in the fact that the tax was collected to meet the needs of the people's state.

Simultaneously with solving these social problems of primary importance, steps were taken for the gradual curtailment of the economic and legal privileges of important clerical and secular feudal nobles, starting with the *Bogdo-gegen* and ending with the non-sovereign princes and courtiers.

By reorganizing the *aimaks* and some *khoshuns* and by creating new *khoshuns* and *somons*, the state was also to a certain extent regulating pasturage, i. e. land problems. These measures deprived the *khoshun* proprietors of the right to control the movement of *arat* grazing grounds from one *khoshun* to another.

The adoption of the statute on local government bodies and the rights of sovereign and non-sovereign princes gave the measure depriving *khoshun* governors of hereditary property rights to land, i.e. to *khoshun* territories, the force of law.

The special rights of *shabinars* to move around freely on pastures that suited them were annulled, and they were in this respect placed on an equal footing with *somon arats*. This was extremely clearly expressed in the Statute on *shabi* approved by the government in 1923.[2]

The state budget was drawn up to cover the country's economy, defence expenses, cultural construction and other revolutionary measures.

In 1923 a mutually advantageous trading agreement was signed between the Governments of the USSR and Mongolia. From that time the proportion of trading transactions with the USSR in the aggregate external trade of Mongolia began increasing.

During those years the Mongolian Central Co-operative Society had mutual trading relations with American, Danish, German, English and other firms.

In 1924, at the request of the Mongolian Government, the USSR helped establish a trading and industrial bank as a joint stock company.

By all these political and economic measures the people's government helped improve the situation of the *arat* masses and to increase the size of livestock herds.

In 1923-1924 livestock-breeding in the country not only reached the pre-revolutionary level but even considerably exceeded it.

Favourable factors in this connection were:

the release from serfdom of the *khamjilga* and *shabinars* and alleviation of the situation of the *albatu arats;* abolition of the economic and political privileges of the secular and clerical feudal nobles and of their exemption from taxes; cancellation of debts to foreigners; attention paid by the People's Party and people's government to the poor and very poor sections of the population; extension of veterinary and other assistance to *arats.*

In 1923 the Central Committee of the Party worked out problems relating to the future development of the country's economy and these were reflected in the resolutions of the Second and Third Congresses of the Party.

Measures were taken to improve public education. In 1923 short-term courses began to function in Urga for teachers, cultural workers, and instructors as well as the People's University (opened in the summer of 1923).[3] In 1924 schools functained in the centres of *aimaks* and in a number of *khoshuns.* Several newspapers and periodicals began to appear in the country.

Along with these very important social and economic measures, in 1922-1924 a breach was made in the old state machinery, local government bodies being gradually replaced by *arat hurals* (popular assemblies).

In 1922 there was a wide extension of the control exercised by the people's government over the activities of local administrative bodies in order to reinforce contacts with the masses. Government plenipotentiaries played a great part in this connection.

In view of further democratization of the state structure the Mongolian people's government, on January 5, 1923, fully approved two very important pieces of legislation—the Statute on local self-government and the Statute on the rights of sovereign *(khoshun)* and non-sovereign princes *(vans* and *guns).*[4]

These statutes were immensely important for the final liquidation of the economic and legal bases of the feudal nobility class and for strengthening the organs of state authority in the form of *hurals.*

The two above-mentioned statutes supplemented one another and represented important constitutional instruments, aimed primarily against the feudal class and were thus in complete harmony with the vital interests of the *arat* masses and met with active support from them.

In 1922, for instance, *arats* in one of the *khoshuns* of the *aimak* of Dzasaktu Khan came out in protest against Prince Bayan-Zhargal and his son Lut-Ochir, who were trying to collect from the *arats* charges and duties which had been cancelled by the people's government. The *arats* appealed to the government representative in the Dzasaktu Khan *aimak* and asked him to remove Bayan-Zhargal and Lut-Ochir from the administration of the *khoshun*. Their request was granted by the government.

In the same year the *arats* of one of the *khoshuns* of the *aimak* of Tsetsen Khan took action against *gun* Luvsan-zhamba who, in spite of the fact that serfdom had been abolished, was compelling former *khamjilga* to work for him.

The *arats* came out in protest not only against the secular feudal nobles but also against the clergy. They refused to pay taxes in favour of the church and the monasteries. For instance, *arats* in the *khoshun* of Bator-van in the *aimak* of Tushetu Khan refused to provide hay for the *Bogdo-gegen's* horses and demanded the transfer to them of the piece of land which was set apart for this produce.

Encouraged by the policy of the Party and the people's government, the *arats* waged a struggle everywhere against the feudal nobles, the higher-ranking lamas and the representatives of foreign capital.

The abolition of the political domination of the feudal nobles and of serfdom, the restrictive policy of the people's government in regard to foreign mercantile capital, the emergence of the first state and co-operative enterprises in the country and the support given by the people's government to the *arats* with a view to improving output of their husbandries—all this had by 1924 considerably changed the character of the economy and had resulted in a regrouping of class forces in the country.

Under the leadership of the MPRP the working people of Mongolia waged a struggle against feudal reaction and the emergent capitalist elements which were supported by foreign capital.

Intensification of the Class Struggle and
General Line of the Party Aimed at Non-Capitalist
Development of the Country

In addition to direct counter-revolutionary activities, feudal reaction, relying on the very numerous sections of hostile officials left behind as a legacy to people's power by the old regime, was doing everything to frustrate the measures of the

Party and the government, undermine the confidence of the masses in them, discredit them in the eyes of the people, and organize sabotage of those decisions of the government which were detrimental to the interests of the feudal nobility and the church.

The exacerbation of the class struggle made it necessary to set up a special body for the suppression of reaction. In July 1922 a state internal security body was instituted which was subsequently reorganized into the Ministry of the Interior. The creation of this security body, a sharp weapon in the hands of the workers against the forces of counter-revolution and imperialism, played a large part in strengthening the people's revolutionary system.

A bitter struggle also developed in the ranks of the Revolutionary Youth League where agents of the feudal-theocratic reaction had also infiltrated and were trying to set the League in opposition to the Party and contesting its leading role.

On February 22, 1923, death plucked from the ranks of the Party a tried and trusted leader, the distinguished popular hero Sukhe Bator. Before his death he said: "I bid you, my friends, to cherish as sacred the freedom that has been won by the people, to subordinate the policy of the Party and the measures of the government to the interests of the *arat* labouring masses and that you should strengthen the liberation of the *arats* from the yoke of internal and external enemies."

On February 26, 1923, Urga, the capital of the country, paid its last respects to Sukhe Bator. The funeral procession became a tremendous demonstration the like of which Mongolia had never seen. Subsequently, the following words were engraved on the tomb of Sukhe Bator in Ulan Bator: "See to it that the freedom we have all fought for does not fall again into the hands of foreign invaders and the local feudal nobility. In order not to lose this freedom you must wage a merciless struggle against enemies and deepen the revolution."

The guiding force in the struggle of the Mongolian people to deepen the anti-feudal and anti-imperialist revolution was the Mongolian People's Revolutionary Party (MPRP). In all the measures carried out during the period we are considering (democratization of the state system, abolition of serfdom and of the political, economic and legal privileges of the class of feudal nobles, ensuring protection of the gains of the revolution, economic and cultural work) the organizing and mobilizing role of the People's Revolutionary Party was clearly visible.

During this time the Party developed ideologically and strengthened its organization. However, alien elements and enemies of the people who had infiltrated its ranks tried to change the Party line for their own counter-revolutionary ends.

In foreign policy they oriented themselves on the imperialist powers, and in domestic matters tried to hold up the development of the anti-feudal revolution. Some of them, too, tried to bring about a restoration of feudal ways while others, voicing the interests of the nascent bourgeoisie, sought to direct the country's development along capitalist lines.

Firmly cutting short the numerous onslaughts of the enemies of the people and the revolution the Party led the country forward on the path of revolutionary reorganization thanks to the strengthening of fraternal links with the Communist Party of the Soviet Union and the Comintern.

On July 18, 1923, the Second Congress of the MPRP opened which reviewed the programme adopted by the First Congress and made a series of amendments to it defining the Party's tasks in more exact and more concrete terms. At that time these tasks consisted in strengthening the rule of the people by a democratization of local self-government and convening the Grand People's Hural by bringing representatives of *arats* into the administration of state affairs both at the centre and locally, by making the courts democratic institutions, developing public education and public health, raising the wellbeing of the *arat* masses, strengthening co-operatives and weakening the positions of the feudal nobility class and of foreign capital in the economy of the country.

The Second Party Congress played a big part in deepening the anti-imperialist and anti-feudal revolution.

On August 4, 1924, the Third Congress of the MPRP opened.

The Third Congress unmasked the representatives of the nascent bourgeois elements headed by Danzan and for the first time adduced historical justification for the non-capitalist path of development for Mongolia, based on the teaching of Marx, Engels and Lenin on the possibility of previously backward countries developing on non-capitalist lines with the help of the proletariat of the advanced countries, the availability of support from the first socialist Soviet state in the world, the experience of the Central Asian Republics in building socialism and the experience of the Mongolian people themselves in the matter of revolutionary reforms.

The MPRP found in the teaching of Marxism and Leninism replies to questions about the prospects of the country's developing along the non-capitalist path.

The Grand People's Hural and the Proclamation of the MPR

The socio-economic measures carried through in 1922-1924 under the leadership of the MPRP helped to strengthen the people's state and created the necessary conditions for forming a republic.

The republic was set up against the background of further aggravation of the class struggle, which was expressed in serious resistance by the feudal nobles and the national bourgeois elements, supported by foreign capital. A favourable pretext for this was the death of the *Bogdo-gegen*.

The MPRP considered it a suitable moment for proclaiming a republic. On June 3, 1924, the Bureau of the Central Committee of the MPRP resolved to institute in the country a republican form of administration.[5] The convening of a widely representative congress became a practical necessity.

Preparations for convening the Grand Hural were carried out in accordance with the task of forming a republic and with the historic decisions of the Third Congress of the MPRP. The first Grand Hural had to discuss a report on the three years' activity of the people's government, give statutory expression to the proclamation of the republic, adopt its constitution and lay down the concrete political and economic tasks for a whole historical period in the light of the resolutions of the Third Party Congress on the non-capitalist line of the country's development.

Seventy-seven delegates were elected to the Hural—basically, representatives of the *arats* consisting principally of poor and middle peasants (92.2% of the total number of delegates elected) and six former noblemen. Among the delegates there were forty-six members of the MPRP and six members of the RYL.

The first Grand Hural opened on November 8, 1924.

It adopted a historic resolution on the political and economic tasks facing the country. Unanimously approving the foreign policy of the people's government, the Hural considered it necessary to reinforce in every possible way the friendship and economic co-operation with the Soviet Union.

On behalf of the working people of Mongolia the first Grand People's Hural once again affirmed that the USSR was the only friend and ally of the MPR. It unanimously considered that, with the help of the USSR, the MPR could by-pass the capitalist stage of development and move on to socialism.

On November 26, 1924, the Grand People's Hural approved the country's first constitution, which proclaimed Mongolia a people's republic. This date went down in history as a significant landmark in the life of the Mongolian people.

In drawing up the draft Constitution enormous attention was paid to the class direction and the state system of the Mongolian People's Republic; careful allowance was also made for the experience gained in winning power for the people. Many of the Chapters of the Constitution had as their basis the fundamental principles of the more important constitutional instruments: the Sworn Treaty of 1921, or the Statutes of the people's government on the curtailment of the rights of the *Bogdo-gegen*, the Statutes on the Provisional Little Hural (1921), on local self-government, on sovereign and non-sovereign princes, on the State Hural of the limited monarchy of Mongolia (1923); the decisions of the people's government of June 13, 1921, on the introduction into the country of a republican system and the Statute on the State Hural (Grand People's Hural) of the MPR (1924).

In this fashion the resolution of the MPRP and the people's government abolishing feudal and serf relationships and bondage to foreign capital, which were implemented in 1921-1924, were given legislative expression in the first constitution of the MPR. It reinforced the bases of people's democratic power and the independence of the Mongolian people.

The 1924 Constitution of the MPR [6] consists of a preamble and six chapters. The preamble confirms and reproduces in full the decision of the people's government of June 13, 1924, setting up a republic in the country without a president.

Chapter I—"Declaration of the Rights of the True Mongolian People," which sets out the general principles of the constitution; Chapter II—"The Supreme Authority"—talks about the powers and structure of the Grand People's Hural, the Little Hural, the Presidium of the Little Hural and the Government; Chapter III—"Local Self-Government," Chapter IV—"Electoral Law," ChapterV—"Budget Law," Chapter VI—"The State Seal, Coat-of-Arms and Flag of the MPR".

The preamble "Declaration of the Rights of the True Mongolian People", proclaimed:

"1. Mongolia is hereby declared an independent People's Republic in which all power belongs to the people themselves. The people exercise their supreme authority through the Grand People's Hural and a government elected by the latter.

2. The basic task of the Mongolian People's Republic consists in the extirpation of remnants of the old order and feudal world outlook, which existed under the enslavers and oppressors, and in reinforcing the foundations of the new republican order by a complete democratization of the state administration." [7]

Endorsing the resolutions of the people's government, the Constitution proclaimed that all international treaties and undertakings on loans concluded by the Mongolian authorities before the revolution were declared null and void as having been imposed by coercion.

The Constitution gave expression to the task of developing the country on non-capitalist lines for socialism with the help of the first Soviet socialist state in the world.

"Whereas people all over the world are seeking to extirpate present-day capitalism... and to achieve socialism and communism, the foreign policy of our People's Republic must correspond to the interests of the revolutionary masses and the basic tasks of the small oppressed peoples and the genuinely revolutionary peoples of the whole world." [8]

The Constitution proclaimed that the whole earth and its depths, the forests, waters and their riches within the confines of the territory of the MPR were the property of the whole nation and were entirely at the disposal of the people; private ownership of them, it declared, was not permissible.

The Constitution proclaimed equality of rights for all nationalities inhabiting the country, equal rights for men and women, freedom of speech, the press, trade unions, assembly and demonstrations. The right to elect and be elected to Hurals (Grand, Little and local) was given by the Constitution to all citizens of the Republic of either sex who had reached 18 years of age, and were earning a livelihood by their own labour, and also to soldiers of the People's Revolutionary Army.

According to the Constitution voting rights were denied to former lay and clerical feudal nobles and persons consecrated as lamas residing permanently in monasteries. The church was disestablished from the state and religion was declared a private matter for each citizen.

"The essence of the Constitution," as Lenin wrote, "lies in the fact that the basic laws of the state in general and the laws dealing with the right to vote in elections to representative institutions, their powers, etc. express the real relationship of forces in the class struggle."[9]

The state took over control of economic policy, implementing the gradual introduction of a monopoly in foreign trade.

In order to protect the Republic against external and internal enemies the Constitution decreed that everything be done to reinforce the Mongolian People's Revolutionary Army and that universal military training for the working people be introduced.

Under the Constitution the whole complex of supreme state power was vested in the people in the person of the Grand People's Hural, in the interval between its sessions—to the Little Hural, and in the period between the latter's sessions to the Presidium of the Little Hural and the government jointly.

Thus, the system of state power in the country became uniform. Power was exercised by the Hurals both at the centre and on the spot. This was brilliant confirmation of the principle put forward by Lenin at the Second Congress of the Comintern to the effect that "the idea of Soviet organization is simple and can be applied not only to proletarian but also to peasant, feudal and semi-feudal relationships."[10]

The Hurals were a variation of the rural Soviets, which were set up in the Republics of Soviet Central Asia where, up to the time of the October Revolution, pre-capitalist relationships prevailed. The People's Hurals established themselves as a form of power throughout the whole state system and became a permanent and unique political basis of the state administration of Mongolia, local and central. Statutory force was given in the country to a special form of dictatorship, dictatorship of the working people, to which Lenin made the following reference before the Russian bourgeois-democratic revolution: "A decisive victory for a democratic revolution can only take the form of a revolutionary-democratic dictatorship of the proletariat and the peasants."[11]

The Grand Hural elected a Little Hural of thirty members, including Kh. Choibalsan and Hatan-Bator Maksarzhav. In social composition, the Little Hural comprised twenty-three *arats* and six former princes, and of these twenty-nine Hural members twenty-three were members of the MPRP and the League of Youth.

On November 28, 1924, the session of the Little Hural elected a Presidium with a membership of five representatives of *arats*, and a government with a membership of twelve: the Prime Minister B. Tserendorzh, and army Commander-in-Chief Kh. Choibalsan. Only one member of the government was a former prince. The membership of the Little Hural and the government also testified to the enormous successes achieved in strengthening people's power, in particular its supreme organs.

Consequently, as a result of the leadership given by the People's Revolutionary Party, people's power in Mongolia represented at the first stage of the democratic revolution (1921-1940) a kind of revolutionary-democratic dictatorship of the proletariat and the peasantry. This is the standpoint from which one should approach the expression "dictatorship of the *arats*", bearing in mind the fact that, as regards their class make-up the organs of state power were *arat*. Actually, the people's government tackled such social problems as preventing the development of capitalism and creating conditions for the country's subsequent transition to socialism in an incomparably more thorough and more comprehensive fashion than any bourgeois democracy.

As a result of the victory of the Mongolian people's revolution and with the help and the support of the first country with a dictatorship of the proletariat, Mongolia's regeneration became possible, along with radical changes in its state system, in the economic sphere, and in class relations. The productive forces of the country now had opened before them wide scope for free and speedy growth. Favourable conditions were created for a continual advance in the material and cultural standards of the working classes.

SECTION TWO

THE MONGOLIAN PEOPLE IN THE FIGHT FOR DEVELOPMENT ON NON-CAPITALIST LINES (1925-1940)

CHAPTER I

STRUGGLE FOR THE LIQUIDATION
OF THE ECONOMIC POSITIONS OF THE FEUDAL CLASS
AND THE LIBERATION OF THE COUNTRY FROM
THE INFLUENCE OF FOREIGN CAPITAL
(1925-1932)

Consolidation of the External and Internal Position of the MPR

The proclamation of the Mongolian People's Republic and the adoption by the Grand People's Hural of the first Constitution of the MPR marked a further consolidation of people's power.

After the First Grand People's Hural the anti-feudal and anti-imperialist people's revolution developed in a relatively more favourable international situation than in 1921-1924. This was primarily the consequence of a further strengthening and development of friendship and co-operation between the MPR and the Soviet Union and the growth in the political, economic and cultural links between them. The Soviet Union extended to the MRP all-round brotherly help in consolidating the country's independence, in developing national industry, modern forms of transport and communications and in cultural advancement.

In the years 1925-1932 the people's government strove to strengthen the country's international position and put forward proposals for establishing diplomatic relations with other countries. In 1925 the government of the MPR recognized Tuva's independence and concluded a treaty of friendship with it.

In order to reinforce the external position of the MPR it was important to establish normal good-neighbourly relations with neighbouring China.

As a true friend of the Mongolian people, the USSR showed tireless concern for regulating the mutual relations between China and the MPR. However, the Chinese militarists not only refused to recognise the independence of the MPR but were also opposed to establishing diplomatic relations between China and the USSR. It was only under pressure of the revolutionary liberation movement developing in China and because of changed international circumstances (establishment of diplomatic relations between the USSR and a number of the most important capitalist states) that the government of China was obliged on May 31, 1924, to sign a Soviet-Chinese treaty on "General Principles for Regulating Problems between the Soviet Union and the Chinese Republic."

This treaty was also of great importance for the MPR since it meant a relaxation of the direct threat of intervention by Chinese militarists against the Mongolian People's Republic.

In 1925, as a result of the consolidation of the democratic system and an improvement in the international position of the MPR, the government of the Soviet Union raised the question of withdrawing from the MPR the Soviet troops brought into the country in 1921 on the request of the Mongolian people's government. In a note of the Soviet government dated January 24, 1925, the matter was referred to as follows: "Under the protection of Mongolian and Soviet army units, and as a result of the revolutionary actions of the people's government, real order was established in the country and conditions secured for its further democratization, for its proclamation as a Republic and for the convening of the Grand People's Hural. Consequently, and in view also of the definitive liquidation of White Guard bands, the government of the USSR considers that there is no further need for Soviet troops to remain within the borders of the Mongolian Republic."

The Government of the MPR agreed to the withdrawal of units of Soviet troops from the territory of its country and expressed its confidence that "henceforth, the people of the Union and of our Republic are linked together by an indissoluble common fate, by the interests and mighty ideas of real popular government and that in future the life of the two Republics will proceed in genuine friendship and mutual support in difficult moments generally. More especially, the people and the government of our Republic firmly rely on getting help from the Soviet Union and the Red Army should, contrary to expectations, conditions arise similar to those observed in 1921." In the same note the government of the MPR conveyed to the USSR government and the Red Army "the great gratitude of the Mongolian working people and the assurance of its eternal gratitude and undying friendship."[1]

The establishment of the republican system was extremely important for consolidating the independence of the MPR, for the further intensification of the people's revolution, for suppressing the resistance of the class of feudal nobles and of the nascent bourgeois elements.

Nevertheless, in its further development the MPR encountered a whole series of difficulties.

Among these difficulties were:

First, the rather strong position held by the class of feudal nobles in the country's economy. In 1925 more than 30% of the total livestock was in their hands.

Second, the existence of more than 700 monasteries with over 100,000 lamas and their reactionary influence on the *arat* masses.

Third, the country was still dominated by foreign, chiefly Chinese, capitalist traders and money-lenders who had a grip on almost all foreign trade and an overwhelming part of the internal trade. Some 480 Chinese, 12 Anglo-American and several firms from other capitalist states operated in the country; their trading centres, numbering thousands, were spread in a wide network all over the country.

Fourth, extensive livestock breeding with primitive labour technique remained as before the basic branch of the economy.

Fifth, industry, transport, communications and other branches of the national economy were poorly developed.

Sixth, the cultural level of the working people was still low, and public education was merely in the initial phase of its development. For example, in 1925 only 1,500 out of 79,000 children of school age were being taught. There was an acute shortage of new cadres devoted to the cause of the revolution, and in consequence state, economic and party organs were chock full of alien and enemy elements. Notwithstanding the difficulties enumerated above, the Mongolian People's Revolutionary Party firmly carried out its general line of policy, relying on the constant fraternal assistance of the Soviet people and taking advantage in its activities of the great experience of the Communist Party of the Soviet Union.

Socio-Economic and Political Measures and Their Significance

Implementation of the tasks set forth in the resolutions of the Third Congress of the MPRP and of the First Grand People's Hural was directed towards the definitive extermination of feudalism and to developing the country along non-capitalist lines.

In the further intensification of the anti-feudal and anti-imperialist people's revolution a great role was played by the Fourth Congress of the MPRP and the Second Grand People's Hural. The Fourth MPRP Congress, held in 1925, considered the next steps to be taken in implementing the tasks of developing the country on non-capitalist lines. The Congress emphasized that the most important task at that particular stage was the further consolidation of people's power and the concentration in the hands of the Government of the commanding heights of the economy. The Fourth Congress instructed the Central Committee to improve the work of the Party organizations by reinforcing their links with the mass of the working people. The Second Grand People's Hural, basing itself on the resolutions of the Party Congress, took important decisions on such matters as the abolition of the *shabinar* department and the institution of *shabi*, the levying of taxes on monastery properties, on carrying out judicial reforms, and the creation of a national monetary and state financial system.

In accordance with the decisions of the Party Congress and the Grand Hural the MPR government carried out a radical reform of the law courts by enacting in 1925-1926 the "Statute on People's Courts," a judicial code, criminal and civil codes and a number of other laws. This reform converted the court of law into an elective body of popular justice safeguarding the interests of the working people.

In 1925 with the aid of the Soviet Union a national currency was put into circulation. The introduction of a national currency—the *tugrik*—which was put into circulation on December 9, 1925, dealt a powerful blow at the positions held by foreign trading capital.

In 1926-1927 the people's government instituted a uniform national financial system. Local government bodies lost the right of fiscal initiative and there was a strict delimitation of functions between local and central budgets which were coordinated into a single general state budget. The full control gained by the people's government over the single budget greatly strengthened the role of the people's state in regulating economic and cultural development. Whereas in 1924, for example, appropriations for the national economy represented 10.7% of all expenditure, in 1926 the figure was 26%. The corresponding proportions for education were 3.22% and 6%.

With a view to weakening the economic basis of feudal ownership in 1926 the Presidium of the Little Hural adopted a law on the single tax. This law provided for differentiated progressive taxation of the properties of lay feudal nobles and monasteries and for complete exemption from tax of poor peasants' holdings up to 5 *bodo* and privileges for Government and co-operative concerns. As will be seen, the new single tax law transferred for the first time in the history of Mongolia the main burden of taxation on to the shoulders of the prosperous sections of the population and freed the poor people from taxes.

On September 3, 1926, in accordance with the Constitution, the MPR government enacted a law disestablishing the church from the state.

The senior lamas tried to recover their lost power by persuading the population of the need to find a ninth "reincarnation" of the Chebtzun-Damba-Khutukhta. As a reply to these intrigues of the senior lamas the MPRP Congress confirmed the decision already taken to abolish the institutions of the *Chubil Khans* in the MPR.

These measures dealt a serious blow to the clerical feudal nobles, resulted in a weakening of their influence over the masses and helped gradually to isolate the senior lamas from the rank-and-file of the lama clergy.

All these measures of the Party and government had enormous socio-economic and political importance and dealt an extremely powerful blow to feudalism.

During this period the country's economy comprised various forms of economic activity. Side by side with the individual working *arat's* economy which had predominated in the MPR, there still continued to exist large-scale monastery and princely properties, based on exploitation; a large role was also played by foreign mercantile capital and elements of a Mongolian mercantile bourgeoisie and a *kulak* class were emerging. Simultaneously, a start was being made to develop the state and co-operative sectors of the country's economy.

The Party and government being basically concerned with protecting the interests of the working people, with improving their material well-being and cultural level, waged a struggle to strengthen and develop the state and co-operative sectors of the national economy, to eliminate feudalism from the economy and to drive out foreign capital.

During the period under consideration the MPRP encouraged the development of the private economic initiative of the *arats* with the object of improving the commodity production of *arat* economies and increasing the numbers of livestock. At the same time, in order to improve livestock husbandry, the MPRP and the people's government implemented a number of measures to increase the network of veterinary services, the production of hay, and the construction of *khashans* and wells. Assistance was also given to the *arats* for the development of agriculture.

In 1925 a start was made in establishing industrial enterprises (brickworks, saw mills, cloth mills, etc.) and in 1926 a mixed Soviet-Mongolian shareholding company "Mongolstroy" was founded to produce materials for construction. In 1925 a state transport body was instituted which began to play an important part in transporting freight inside the country. Simultaneously, modern communication systems also began to develop.

Consumers' co-operatives began to grow at a fast rate; in 1925 the number of their members had already risen to 6,627 as compared with 1,596 in 1924, and the share capital rose to 225,000 *tugriks*. The turnover in retail co-operative trade amounted in 1926 to 4,334,000 *tugriks*.

The Mongolian people were greatly helped in their struggle to be economically independent of the capitalist countries by Soviet economic organizations which assisted in every way possible in developing and strengthening Mongolian consumers' and industrial co-operatives and in developing Mongolian state commercial and industrial organizations.

Defeat of the Right Deviationists

The policy of the MPRP directed towards ensuring a non-capitalist path of development for Mongolia and the practical measures taken by the people's government aroused stubborn resistance on the part of internal reactionaries and the foreign traders and usurers. The basic counter-revolutionary force inside the country was the class of the feudal nobility. In 1925-1928 they carried out a series of counter-revolutionary actions in the Khuren of Namnanul *khoshun* of the *aimak* of Tsetsenlik-Mandal and in other places.

In their struggle against the people's government the feudal nobles operated in alliance with foreign capital and with elements of the nascent Mongolian bourgeoisie. Foreign capital, struggling to hold its positions on the Mongolian market and anxious to weaken co-operation which was one of the most important economic levers in the hands of the people's government, tried to base itself on representatives of the Mongolian bourgeoisie. The existence in the country of small-scale commodity economies and the strong positions still held by foreign capital formed favourable soil for the growth of capitalist elements, primarily in the sphere of circulation and trade.

As the incipient elements of the Mongolian bourgeoisie had no large volume of capital or experience, they acted in the main merely as representatives of the big foreign capitalist firms, forming a mercantile bourgeoisie of the comprador type and acting as intermediaries between foreign firms and the local population.

Agents of all these forces hostile to the revolution tried to penetrate the ranks of the Party, state economic and social institutions and in fact rejected the Party's policy aimed at the constant intensification of the anti-imperialist and anti-feudal revolution.

The unmasking and defeat of the Danzan group at the Third MPRP Congress was a powerful blow to the right-opportunist elements inside the Party which represented the interests of foreign capital and the emergent comprador bourgeoisie. After some time, however, the right deviationists again redoubled their efforts against the general line of the Party. Right-wing elements in the MPRP, headed by Damba-Dorzhi and Dja-Demba aimed to switch the MPR to the capitalist path of development. They tried to delay and arrest the attack launched on the economic base of the feudal nobles, encouraged in every way the growth of capitalist elements, and gave assistance in the retention and reinforcement of foreign trading firms operating in the MPR.

The right deviationists tried to secure the abandonment of the non-capitalist path of development and a departure from Marxism-Leninism as the theoretical basic principle of the MPRP; they preached in favour of bourgeois nationalism and the reactionary idea of Pan-Mongolianism and tried to preserve and adapt Lamaism to the new conditions. With this aim in view one of the "ideologists" of the right deviationists, Zhamtsarano, tried to identify Buddhism with Marxism. The right deviationists opened the doors of the Party wide to lamas and other alien elements, which resulted in the ranks of the MPRP being cluttered up with socially alien and hostile elements.

The anti-Party activities of the right deviationists soon began to be reflected in the political and economic situation of the country. The economic positions of feudal elements and other exploiters began to grow in strength. The size of monastery herds of cattle rose by almost 30% during the two years of economic control by the rightists. The increase in the size of feudal herds of cattle, including those of the monasteries, was the result not so much of a natural increment in livestock as of the ruin wrought on small-scale *arat* farm-holdings. For instance, whereas in 1924 the holdings of poor *arats* covering from one to ten *bodo* represented 25% of all *arat* holdings in the MPR, in 1927 they amounted to more than 30%.

The rightists held up in every possible way the growth of national consumers' co-operatives and helped in maintaining in the country the positions of predatory foreign firms. In 1926 the share of foreign capitalist firms in the country's exports still amounted to 60.7%, and in the case of imports 77.6%.

The rightists tried to justify their policy of capitulation and the backwardness of social and economic development of Mongolia. In their foreign policy the rightists were patently heading for a breach in the friendship and alliance of the Mongolian people with their true friend—the great Soviet Union.

This policy of the deviationists evoked protest and sharp resistance from the mass of the Party members and all the working people. A powerful movement against the right deviationist policy emerged in the Party and in the country as a whole. Particularly active against the right deviationists were the lower-ranking Party organizations which resolutely supported the struggle for the general Party line.

This struggle was strikingly expressed at the Sixth MPRP Congress which lasted from September 22 to October 4, 1927.

The Sixth Party Congress showed that the mass of the Party members unanimously supported the general Party line.

Most of the Congress delegates expressed keen indignation at the policy of the right deviationists. In their speeches they exposed the anti-Party nature of the right deviation and vigorously criticized the efforts of the rightist leaders of the MPRP to switch the country to a capitalist path of development, one that involved breaking off friendly relations with the USSR.

Seeing that they had obviously failed, the right deviationists adopted the method of double-dealing by verbally admitting the anti-Party nature of their actions. Under the cloak of this hypocritical declaration they actually renewed, after the Congress was over, their struggle against the general Party line and their disruptive factional activity inside the Party.

At the April plenary meeting of the Central Committee of the MPRP in 1928 the rightists endeavoured to smash the leftists and to slander individual members of the Party who attacked them. A special commission set up by the plenary meeting to investigate the internal Party differences failed to unmask the rightists' policy of capitulation and its roots.

As a result of the actions of the right deviationists the forward advance of the anti-feudal revolution was held up and the position of the reactionaries temporarily strengthened. The mass of the Party members, faithful to the general Party line, attacked the criminal policy of the right deviationists and demanded their removal from the posts they held in the controlling organs of the Party.

The rightists were unmasked as anti-Party opportunists who had deviated from the general Party line at the October plenary meeting of the Central Committee and were defeated at the Seventh MPRP Congress held from October 23 to December 10, 1928.

The Seventh Party Congress, in an outspoken criticism of the anti-Party actions of the right deviationists, called on members of the Party and all the working people to intensify the struggle for a non-capitalist path of development for the country, based on still greater consolidation of the friendship with the Soviet Union. This Congress also expelled the right deviationists from the Central Committee. It should be mentioned that the use made by the MPRP of the CPSU's experience of combating opportunists and the direct assistance given by the Comintern were extremely important in defeating the right deviation. In this way the Congress, by defeating the rightists, both ideologically and organizationally, once again affirmed the stability of the general policy of the MPRP in ensuring a non-capitalist path of development for the MPR and in the further consolidation of Soviet-Mongolian friendship as a basic guarantee for the freedom and independence of the Mongolian people. This was the historical significance of the Seventh Party Congress.

Implementing the resolutions of the Seventh Party Congress, the Fifth Grand People's Hural, held from December 14, 1928, to January 14, 1929, adopted an exceptionally important regulation on the confiscation of the livestock and property of the feudal nobles and the transfer of this property to the poor peasant farmers, and also on reducing the taxes on poor peasant and middle peasant farmers, strengthening state and cooperative trade and instituting a foreign trade monopoly. The Fifth Grand People's Hural affirmed the immutability of the policy of consolidating friendship and brotherly collaboration with the Soviet Union.

Decisive Attack on the Economic Positions of the Feudal Class

The decisions of the Seventh Party Congress and the Fifth Grand People's Hural, warmly supported by the entire mass of the working people, marked the beginning of a decisive attack on the economic positions of the feudal nobles and thereby helped to create the conditions necessary for the non-capitalist path of development of the MPR.

In order to carry out the resolution of the Fifth Grand People's Hural on the confiscation of the property of the feudal nobles the MPR government set up a special state commission headed by the Chairman of the Little Hural Choibalsan, and also local branches of the commission. As a result of these commissions, supported by the enormous political upsurge of the *arat* masses and the direct participation of the *arats* themselves in carrying out confiscation, during the autumn of 1929 and the winter of 1929-1930 more than 600 properties belonging to important feudal nobles were confiscated out of 729 properties designated for expropriation. All the livestock and property thus confiscated, valued at approximately 4.5 million *tugriks*, were divided up between *arat* peasant farmers who owned no cattle or very few. Confiscation of the property and livestock of the secular feudal nobles and, in part, of the clerical feudal nobles continued even further in 1930-1931. By April 1932 property had been confiscated on altogether more than 11,000 secular and clerical feudal estates.

Another important measure which dealt a painful blow to the economic position of the feudal nobility was the organization in 1930 and 1931 of *jas* companies. These companies greatly weakened the economic power of the monasteries and liberated from exploitation by the latter *arat* proprietors who had formerly grazed monasteries' livestock on very onerous terms.

The formation of *jas* companies did not result in mass confiscation of monastery properties, although it was, in a way, an extension of feudal expropriation. This was due to the fact that the class and predatory character of the clerical feudal nobles was masked under the cover of religion and the Lamaist church still exercised a strong influence over the masses so that, before confiscating monastery livestock and property, it was necessary to carry out large-scale preparatory measures, such as forming a *jas* company; these steps were taken during the 1930s.

Confiscation of the property and livestock of the great feudal nobles dealt a crushing blow at the economic basis of feudalism, released from economic dependence on the feudal nobles tens of thousands of *arat* peasants who had hitherto been engaged in grazing the livestock of the feudal nobles on crippling conditions. From being the herdsmen of other people's livestock the *arats* had become the owners.

The *arats* saw with their own eyes that the revolution had given the working people not only political rights but also very appreciable material results on a large scale and had genuinely raised their standard of living.

Confiscations proceeded in face of the bitter opposition of the feudal nobles, who tried in every way to conceal and secrete their livestock and property to avoid confiscation. The success of the confiscation campaign was ensured by the active participation in it of the *arats*, who exposed the attempts made by the feudal nobles at evasion. This period constituted a great school of experience in the class struggle for the *arats*.

Along with the confiscation of feudal property a number of measures were carried out in 1929-1930 which had exceptionally great political and economic importance. After the purge in the Party, in 1929, state and economic institutions were thoroughly purged of alien elements hostile to the revolution. In 1931 the task of establishing new administrative areas in the country instead of the old feudal administrative divisions was carried through.

Fiscal policy was utilized as an effective weapon for crushing the economic power of the feudal nobles and curtailing the growth of capitalist elements. As a result of the stubborn struggle of the Mongolian people for liberation from economic dependence on foreign capital, the proportion of foreign capital in exports fell from 75.9% in 1925 to 26% in 1930 and in imports, correspondingly, from 80.5% to 9.8%. Thus, as a result of the attack made on the economic positions of foreign capital, the country came nearer to winning economic independence and got ready to introduce a monopoly in foreign trade which was instituted under the decision of the people's government of December 12, 1930. This period saw a great development in the MPR of consumers' co-operatives, operating in close economic collaboration with the economic organizations of the USSR and a beginning was made to create modern factory industries.

Thus, the implementation of the decisions of the Seventh MPRP Congress and the Fifth Grand People's Hural led to great social advances, to the redistribution of the national income and to the introduction of very important measures in extirpating feudal relationships and curtailing the growth of capitalist elements.

The confiscation of the property of the big feudal nobles and the other measures directed against feudal reaction aroused the furious opposition of the feudal-theocratic elements in the country and exacerbated the class struggle. The feudal nobles sought to secure at any cost the overthrow of people's revolutionary power and restore the old order of things. In this they had the active support of foreign capitalists.

The armed conflict which began in 1929 on the Chinese Eastern Railway (CER) and the resultant aggravation in the international situation were the stimuli which sparked off fresh counter-revolutionary plots but these were unmasked in good time.

Left Deviation Overcome

The intensification of the anti-feudal and anti-imperialist revolution was accompanied by an immense upsurge in the political activity of the mass of the working people.

By the confiscation of the property of the leading feudal nobles the MPR government was able to provide a considerable number of the farm-labourer and poorer groups of the *arats*, as well as some of the middle peasants, who had little property with livestock, chattels and other property. This led to an increase in the activities of the poor and middle-peasant sections of the *arat* population and there arose a tendency towards the joint operation of economies so as to be able to graze livestock, produce hay-crops, etc. in common.

The MPRP attached great importance to this very simple form of co-operation between *arat* farmers. The gravitation of the farm-labourer and middle-peasant sections, who had had the livestock of the feudal nobles placed at their disposal, towards co-operation in production did not, however, mean that conditions were now ripe for introducing collectivization in its higher forms—the communes.

The majority of those then in control of the MPRP Central Committee and the people's government failed to take this into account and started on a policy of mechanically copying the Soviet experiment of collectivizing agriculture without thoroughly studying the level of development of the country's productive forces, or considering whether a material base existed and without allowing for the socio-economic and special national peculiarities of everyday life in Mongolia. This was an incorrect policy which was in contradiction to the Marxist-Leninist principle of the need to make strict allowance, in carrying out any particular measure, for the concrete historical circumstances and special features of each country.

The "left" wing of the Party, overlooking the concrete circumstances and special features of the MPR, alleged that conditions in the country were ripe for moving on to direct socialist construction, and began introducing mass collectivization, substituting the method of crude administrative action for the principle of voluntary agreement.

At the Eighth MPRP Congress, held in 1930, the "leftists" succeeded in pushing through their adventurist policy for implementing wholesale collectivization. The operation of such a policy at a stage where the country was unprepared for the implementation of socialist construction was to put the cart before the horse.

The large numbers of "communes" and "kolkhozes" implanted by the "leftists" did not really represent, and could not in the current conditions represent, a socialist type of economy and they very soon dissolved, thus discrediting the collectivization idea in the eyes of the *arats*. In November 1929, for instance, in the Khan-Khukshin *khoshun* of the *aimak* of Tsetserlik-Mandal a commune was organized on the basis of livestock confiscated from the feudal nobles. There was no efficient organization of labour in the commune; labour discipline was extremely weak; all the members of the commune were given the same share of goods and produce regardless of how far they had played then part in productive work. As a result of the commune being thus turned into a consumers' co-operative its collectivized resources were exhausted in less than a year and, in addition, it accumulated a debt of 12,000 *tugriks* to the Mongolian Central Co-operative Society for goods and products received on credit.

The leftist excesses which were widely practised at this time not only inflicted immense direct damage on the country's national economy but, as they also discredited the collectivization idea, held back for a long time the development of the simplest forms of combined agricultural production among the *arats*.

Leftist elements instigated confiscation of the property of well-to-do *arats*, infringed upon the rights of private trade and transport and committed widespread excesses in fiscal policy.

The adventurist policy of the "left" deviationists deprived the *arats* of any incentive to increase the size of their herds of livestock.

As a result of leftist excesses and of direct sabotage by enemies of the people enormous damage was done to the livestock in a short space of time. The number of head of livestock, which in 1930 amounted to 23,500,000, had in the course of 1931 and 1932 fallen by 32%.

The "leftists" distorted the Party's policy on religion and failed to allow for the influence of Lamaism on a considerable section of the *arats*. These distortions took the form of replacing educational methods of combating religious prejudices by administrative methods. Yet the Third and Fourth MPRP Congresses had already pointed out that, as regards the attitude to be adopted towards Lamaism, it must not be forgotten that a considerable number of the lower ranks of the lama clergy were being exploited by the higher-ranking lamas—the church feudal nobles. The problem of associating the lower ranks of the lama clergy with labour for the benefit of the whole community was one of the most important problems in the Party and government policy in regard to the lama priesthood. The Party pointed to the necessity of allocating to the ordinary lamas in process of becoming laymen livestock and other property from the monastery possessions and of giving them an opportunity of joining cottage or home industry *artels*.

All these directives by the Party were ignored by the "left" deviationists and the lama clergy as a whole were regarded by leftist members as forming one single reactionary force.

The administrative measures applied by the local government bodies against the monasteries and the conditions laid down for handing over monastery livestock to *arats* for grazing purposes were such that they practically amounted to the confiscation of monastery livestock. This was an inopportune action.

Taking advantage of the leftist excesses the counter-revolutionary forces rallied themselves and won over to their side wide sections of the lama clergy and a certain number of *arats*. Bearing in mind, however, that the bulk of the working masses, in spite of leftist excesses, constituted the firm support of people's power, the counter-revolutionary elements rested their main hopes on intervention by the imperialists, with whose help they reckoned they could overthrow the rule of the people and restore the feudal-theocratic system.

Between 1929 and 1932 several counter-revolutionary groups and organizations were discovered and liquidated in the

MPR principally in monasteries. Nevertheless, feudal-Lamaist reaction continued its activity and in 1932 they succeeded in raising a counter-revolutionary rebellion in some of the western *aimaks* of the country. With the active support of the broad masses of the working people, organs of people's power succeeded in suppressing this rebellion. Simultaneously, it was necessary to take speedy and decisive action to put a stop to the leftist adventurist policy which was working against the interests of the masses and was contrary to the general line of the Party.

An extraordinary plenary meeting of the MPRP Central Committee, held in June 1932, bluntly condemned the policy pursued by the "leftists" and dismissed from the membership of the Central Committee Z. Shizh, O. Badarkho and other "left" deviationists. The Comintern and the CPSU gave the MPRP a great deal of help in this matter. A joint resolution of the Executive Committee of the Comintern and the Central Committee of the CPSU dated May 29, 1932, pointed out the serious mistakes committed by the majority of the leaders of the MPRP and indicated concrete ways of correcting them. In its resolution the plenary meeting pointed out that, as a result of leftist measures "that were not consistent with the economic and cultural condition of the country, as a result of ignoring the special national characteristics of the country's mode of life, and of following an incorrect policy, the Party had drifted away from its support—the working *arats*, had antagonized a considerable number of them and also driven the better-off sections of them into the arms of the counter-revolutionary feudal nobles and the reactionary upper circles of the Lamaist clergy."[2]

In defining the basic tasks of the Party at the time in question, the plenary meeting pointed out that: "The attention of the whole Party and its work should be directed towards consolidating the Republic as an independent, self-sufficing state of a new type, towards developing to the maximum the productive forces of the Republic, extirpating the remnants of feudalism, towards the gradual curtailment of the capitalist elements in line with the tasks of the economic development of the country, reinforcing its defensive capacity and laying the foundations for the gradual transition to the path of non-capitalist development."[3]

In order to solve these problems the plenary meeting laid down a programme of measures known as the "New Course". The plenary meeting pointed out that "the Party must mobilize the workers for the development and encouragement of private economic initiative, the gradual, cautious introduction of the simplest forms of co-operation and collectivization of the working *arats*, for a resolute struggle against the counter-revolutionary feudal nobles and the reactionary leaders of the lamas, for dissociating the working *arats*, as well as the better-off sections of *arats* and the lower-ranking lamas, from the counter-revolutionary elements and for the creation of a strong national army."[4] The censure of the leftist adventurist policy and the proclamation by the Plenary meeting of the "New Course" rallied the broad masses of the *arats* round the MPRP. Having surmounted the "left" deviation and purged its ranks of alien, opportunist and casual elements, the Party became more united and authoritative.

The "New Course" policy was not just a kind of new political Party line; it represented the restoration of the general line already laid down by the Third MPRP Congress, which had been distorted by the "left" deviationists.

In July 1932 the Seventeenth Extraordinary Session of the Little Hural and the First Republican Non-Party Conference were convened. Both of these unanimously welcomed and supported the decisions of the Second Plenary Meeting of the MPRP Central Committee. The session of the Little Hural discussed questions relating to the situation in the country, the steps to be taken to liquidate counter-revolutionary rebellions and a review of the laws enacted by the leftist leadership.

In order to explain to the masses of the people the decisions taken by the Third Plenary Meeting of the Party's Central Committee and the Seventeenth Session of the Little Hural and get them implemented, plenipotentiary commissions were sent into all the *aimaks* of the country. The commissions rectified on the spot the leftist errors which had distorted the general Party line, helped reorganize the work of the trading organizations and the taxation, financial and other local bodies to bring them into line with the decisions taken by the Seventeenth Session of the Little Hural.

The historic decisions of the Third Extraordinary Plenary Meeting of the MPRP Central Committee and the Seventeenth Session of the Little Hural were greeted by the masses with immense satisfaction as being completely in accord with their interests.

* * *

The intensification of the anti-imperialist and anti-feudal revolution in the MPR exacerbated the class struggle, strengthened the activities of the hostile, counter-revolutionary elements inside the country and also stimulated to greater activity the operations of foreign, especially Japanese, secret agents.

Having been defeated in the attempts it had made during the period preceding the proclamation of the Republic to reinforce the monarchy and restore feudalism, feudal reaction endeavoured, through the right deviationists, to steer the development of the Mongolian People's Republic on to the capitalist path by seeking to consolidate the positions of foreign capital in the country, preserve the economic positions of the feudal nobles and, more especially, break off the friendly relations between the MPR and the Soviet Union. Having been thoroughly routed in this attempt, too, the feudal reactionaries, by instigating and making use of leftist excesses, tried to provoke a counter-revolutionary uprising aimed at abetting imperialist intervention and destroying people's revolutionary power.

However, the MPRP, relying on the wide support of the working people and waging a stern, relentless inner-Party struggle for the general Party line against the right deviationists and the leftist adventurers, succeeded in finding the inner strength needed to uphold the revolutionary gains made by the Mongolian people and the independence of the MPR and to take the lead in building up the country's economy and culture to ensure its transition towards a non-capitalist path of development.

This was where the great vital strength of the People's Revolutionary Party and the people's democratic state lay—they were motivated in their actions by the teaching of Marxism-Leninism and relied, in their struggle to follow the non-capitalist path of national development on indissoluble brotherly friendship with the Soviet people and on all-round assistance from the Communist Party of the Soviet Union and the Soviet state.

In the period from 1924 to 1932 the Mongolian people, under the leadership of the Party and government and with the fraternal assistance of the USSR, overcame the resistance and the treacherous intrigues of enemies abroad and at home and achieved great success.

During this period, by upholding their own independence and consolidating economic links with the USSR, the MPR got rid forever of economic dependence on the imperialist countries which were seeking to turn Mongolia into a colony. The predatory foreign firms of traders and usurous money-leaders, which had pitilessly exploited and despoiled the Mongolian *arats*, lost all their positions in Mongolia which ceased to be a colonial market for imperialist monopolies.

During these years, and with the assistance of the USSR, national co-operation and state trading developed considerably; a national bank was founded and a national currency introduced.

The confiscation of the property of the lay feudal nobles, the implementation of class-angled fiscal and credit policy and also the transfer of monastery livestock for grazing to the poor and middle *arats*, all this revolutionary breach in feudal relationships radically undermined the economic basis of feudal reaction, led to a redistribution of the national income, improved the material well-being of the *arat* working people and strengthened the material basis for developing and consolidating the state and co-operative sectors of the national economy.

The events of this period and the whole course of the class struggle showed that the labouring classes of the MPR actively supported the general policy of the MPRP.

In the course of the class struggle the working masses of the MPR resolutely rebuffed the efforts of the deviationists to turn the country away from the path of non-capitalist development and demonstrated that in no circumstances would they surrender to anyone the gains made by the Mongolian People's Revolution, won by their own hands and their own blood.

The course taken by the class struggle in Mongolia once again demonstrated the absolute correctness of Lenin's statement that, despite all difficulties "...it is possible to stimulate in the masses a desire for independent political thinking and independent political activity even where there is almost no proletariat."[5]

CHAPTER II

THE MPR DURING THE COMPLETION OF THE STAGE
OF GENERAL DEMOCRATIC REVOLUTION (1932-1940)

The Mongolian People's Fight to Implement the "New Course" Policy. Ninth Congress of the MPRP

Further to the resolutions of the Third Extraordinary Plenary Meeting of the MPRP Central Committee and the Seventeenth Extraordinary Session of the Little Hural, the Council of Ministers of the MPR adopted a number of measures for remedying the leftist excesses, and for implementing the policy of the "New Course". On August 5, 1932, the Council of Ministers adopted a resolution which provided that collective farms, in the formation of which the voluntary principle had been violated, could be dissolved if their members did not wish to remain in them. Under this resolution the possibility was envisaged of reorganizing collective farms into the simplest forms of *arat* production associations with a view to joint action in harvesting hay, grazing livestock, building *khashans* (corrals for livestock), tilling the soil, etc.

It has, however, to be noted that the holder at the time of the post of Prime Minister, P. Gendun, distorted the meaning of this resolution and employed it to dissolve not only those communes and *artels* which had been forcibly set up but also the very simple *arat* voluntary production associations which undoubtedly, if they had been given proper organizational and technical assistance and had been correctly managed, could have eventually become stonger and developed. This tactic, employed by Gendun under the pretext of liquidating leftist excesses, did a great deal of damage to the national economy and to the cause of co-operative production among *arat* farmers. The Gendun anti-Party group was exposed and destroyed in due time.

A law was then enacted on the monastery tax and on the grazing of monastery livestock. Under this law monasteries were allowed to retain property title in herds but it provided that "the interests of the working *arats* employed in grazing monastery herds must be safeguarded against excessive exploitation on the part of the monastery."

In 1932-1934 the people's government carried through a number of important measures to develop stock-breeding—the basic branch of the country's economy. The network of veterinary services was considerably enlarged, improvements were made in water supplies and the provision of fodder for livestock and the construction of *khashans* was greatly increased.

In 1933 a new tax law was passed. Progressive income tax was replaced by a tax based not on the income derived from the livestock but on the number of head of cattle; moreover, the rate of taxation was considerably reduced for the smaller peasant holdings and poor farmers were completely exempted from it.

As a result of these measures the number of head of livestock began to increase rapidly.

Alongside the action taken to eliminate leftist excesses in stock-breeding and other branches of agriculture, the MPRP and the MPR government took steps to strengthen industrial construction and to train the national cadres of the working class.

Help from the Soviet Union played an enormous part in building up a national industry. The USSR invariably extended to the Mongolian People's Republic effective assistance with a view to ensuring a rapid increase in productive resources and the development of national industry. Thanks to this unselfish brotherly help from the Soviet people a national industry was set up in the MPR and began to develop successfully. For instance, in 1933 a mechanical wool-washing factory had already begun to function at Khatkhyl.

In March 1934 the first large-scale concern in the MPR was started up—an industrial enterprise manufacturing leather, woollen and other products. The growth of national industry was accompanied by the development of a fuel and power base. A power station, which supplied the capital and the industrial enterprise with electricity, was constructed in Ulan Bator.

The extraction of coal increased 5.5 times as compared with the 1928 figures.

The total number of workers in industry in 1934 was 10 times greater than in 1928.

The profitability of industrial enterprises in the MPR rose from year to year; the undertakings made quite a large contribution to the development of the country's new economy and culture. Laws were enacted with a view to developing producers' co-operatives, securing the voluntary associations of craftsmen and cottage-workers within such co-operatives and also at increasing the manufacture of consumer goods. In order to encourage the initiative of craftsmen and cottage-workers a change was made in the law on the business tax to reduce assessments for co-operative associations and enterprises. As a result of this, in 1934 there were already in the MPR 33 home-industry producers' associations with more than a thousand members. In 1934 producers' associations and craftsmen produced for *arat* requirements goods to the value of 5 million *tugriks* with a range of as many as 25 different sorts of goods.

The government took steps to settle in jobs rank-and-file lamas who had voluntarily left the monasteries: they were given assistance in joining producers' associations. It thus became possible for ordinary lamas to engage in socially useful work.

There was a considerable development of transport and communications. In the action taken to improve transport conditions, the MPR government was concerned to encourage transport by cart, and to create conditions that would give the *arats* an interest in such transport. For this purpose the "Mongoltrans" monopoly was wound up in 1933 and a system established of concluding goods transport agreements directly between trading organizations and *arats* on strictly voluntary lines.

During this period the government, anxious to improve the material position of the *arats*, rescinded the levy on road-building and assumed responsibility in the state budget for the cost of improvements to roads and bridges. Great attention was paid to the development of automobile transportation.

In 1934 the mileage covered by automobiles was more than twelve times the 1932 figure, while 35% more goods and passengers were transported than in 1932.

The development of national industry, transport, communications and construction works in the MPR generated a young working-class population which became the leading force of the Mongolian people in the struggle to create the material and spiritual prerequisites for the gradual transition to socialism. The first workers came from among the farm labourers, the home craftsmen, the lower ranks of the lama priesthood and *arat* herdsmen; their numbers quickly rose as manpower was released from employment in *arat* farming, not, however, at the cost of farming being ruined, as happens under capitalism, but as a result of improved farming conditions—the introduction of new equipment and greater knowledge.

The most important feature of the young Mongolian working class is that it was born under a people's-democratic regime and is free from exploitation of any kind. Another special feature of the working class in the MPR is that it developed with the help and under the benevolent influence of the working class of the USSR and in close co-operation with it.

From the early years of the emergence of the working class the MPRP and the people's government devoted enormous attention to educating the workers in political ideology, training them to adopt a socialist attitude to labour, familiarizing them with new machinery, etc. As a result, there was a rapid growth in the creative activity and consciousness of the workers and in their class organisation, striking evidence of which was the shock-worker movement which first emerged in 1934 in industrial enterprises in the capital of the Republic.

In 1937 the MPRP Central Committee adopted an important decision to initiate competition in state and co-operative enterprises and this met with a warm response from the workers.

At the end of the 1930s the MPRP and the people's government held a number of production conferences of shock-workers from state industrial and economic enterprises. The conferences encouraged workers to display creative initiative and inculcated in them a sense of responsibility for the work of a state and cooperative undertaking.

The MPRP and the government implemented a series of measures for eliminating the consequences of leftist excesses in the sphere of trade. In particular, with a view to speeding up the supply of goods to *arats* the number of itinerant trading organizations was more than tripled. Furthermore, the operations of private traders were authorised subject to certain limitations.

Permission to engage in private retail trade could not constitute an obstacle to the gradual transition of the country to the non-capitalist path of development, since all the basic levers of the MPR's economy, including trade, were held by the state. Furthermore, the proportion of private trading in the MPR did not exceed 17% of the total retail turnover. Simultaneously, everything was done to strengthen and develop consumer's co-operatives and to reinforce the regulating role of the state. In 1934 more than 80% of the country's commodity turnover was already being done through the state and co-operative trading systems.

In 1934 a trade agreement was concluded between the MPR and the Soviet Union the implementation of which helped to consolidate the foreign trade of the MPR and to improve its balance of trade.

It was also a valuable achievement to find the number of national personnel technically qualified in state and co-operative trading rising steadily. In 1932 such national cadres represented 76% of the total number of co-operative workers, while in 1934 they formed more than 95%.

In execution of the resolution of the Extraordinary Plenary Meeting of the MPRP Central Committee and of the Seventeenth Session of the Little Hural in the sphere of finance, the MPR government introduced such measures as a review of the structure of the state budget, a reduction of administrative and managerial costs and the placing of the MPR's currency circulation on a healthier basis.

Special attention was devoted to the problem of the credits structure of the economy of the MPR and of credits for *arat* herdsmen. Whereas at the beginning of 1932 the amount of credits extended to *arats* was 73,000 *tugriks*, in 1934 it rose to more than ten times; moreover, at least 50% of the advances were made to the poorest peasant farm-holders who had been exempt from tax.

All these figures show that, by following the "New Course" policy, the Party had rapidly eliminated the consequences of leftist deviation and made sure that the country would move forward along the path of non-capitalist development in accordance with its general line of policy.

The Ninth Congress of the MPRP was held from September 28 to October 5, 1934.

This Congress rescinded the erroneous decisions adopted at the Party's Eighth Congress, approved the decisions of the Third Extraordinary Plenary Meeting of the Central Committee and Central Investigative Committee and laid down the further tasks to be undertaken for consolidating the independence of the MPR and developing the economy and national culture. By the time the Ninth Congress met the basic work had already been done to eliminate the consequences of leftist excesses, and the Party's unity and its links with the masses of the working people had been consolidated. On this basis major successes were achieved in all branches of the national economy and culture. The local Hurals rallied round themselves the broad sections of the *arat* population, workers and intellectuals and became genuine organs of people's power.

In foreign policy the "New Course" was marked by a further strengthening of friendship with the Soviet Union.

The Ninth Congress noted with immense satisfaction that, as a result of the fraternal friendship with the Soviet people and the assistance of the Soviet Union, the MPR had succeeded in consolidating its independence and raising the level of its economy and culture. In a greeting adopted by the Congress and addressed to the Central Committee of the Soviet Communist Party (Bolshevik) it was stated: "The Mongolian People's Revolutionary Party, from the *arat* national revolution to the present day, has, thanks to the counsels of the Communist Party with its many years' experience of revolutionary struggle, and with the constant brotherly help of the Soviet Union, led the Mongolian *arats* along the path of anti-imperialist and anti-feudal revolution, strengthening national independence and developing in every way its productive forces. As a result of all this, during the past thirteen years of revolutionary struggle, the *arats* have, under the leadership of the Party and the government, achieved great revolutionary successes."

The agreements concluded at this time between the USSR and the MPR were a striking demonstration of the brotherly and unselfish assistance extended by the Soviet Union to the Mongolian People's Republic. In particular, under these agreements mixed enterprises—"Mongoltrans," "Mongolsherst", "Promkombinat" and others—were transferred to the full ownership of the MPR.

The "New Course" policy, by consolidating the internal and external position of the MPR, strengthened the links between the MPRP and the *arat* masses, increased the political activity of the masses and strengthened their aspirations for improving their cultural level.

The successes gained in economic development called for a higher cultural level. There had been a considerable lagging behind in this respect. The MPRP realized the importance of the problem of the cultural revolution and so the Ninth Congress made a special study of the problems of cultural development and took a decision to increase the number of schools in the country and to train teaching staff. It emphasised that the culture developing in the MPR must be revolutionary in content and national in form.

In connection with the emergence and growth in the MPR of a working class the question of a trade-union movement arose. Consequently, the Congress discussed the question of trade unions, defined their tasks in the organization and education of industrial and office workers, and in the development of revolutionary competition aimed at raising labour productivity and the quality of products. The Congress drew the attention of trade unions to the specially backward character of the work performed by farm labourers and herdsmen, who constituted an extremely low percentage of trade-union membership. At the time of the IXth MPRP Congress about 75% of industrial and office workers belonged to trade unions (out of 11,000 workers and employees about 8,000 were trade-union members).

Soon after the Ninth Congress the Seventh Grand People's Hural met from December 20 to 27, 1934.

The Grand Hural emphasized that "the 'New Course' policy, introduced in 1932 and given an enthusiastic welcome by the *arats*, is the only correct policy to create the conditions requisite for the successful development of our state. This policy is in full accord with the national political, economic and cultural conditions of our country, which is a nationally-independent, popular-revolutionary, anti-imperialist, anti-feudal, bourgeois-democratic republic of a new type, laying the foundations for a gradual transition to the path of non-capitalist development."[1]

The delegates of the Hural noted with satisfaction that, as a result of the elimination of the leftist excesses and the implementation of the "New Course" policy, the organs of the people's power had consolidated their ties with the masses and the authority of the government had increased.

The Grand Hural passed a new law disestablishing the church from the state. It was directed against any kind of interference by the monasteries in the political and economic life of the country; it instituted permanent control over the activities of monasteries and lamas by government bodies.

The disestablishment law eliminated the harmful consequences of leftist methods in combating the influence of religious ideology on the *arats*. The correct policy on this problem, as set forth in the law, was based on the view that lamas in the mass cannot be considered as a single whole, socially and politically, that a differentiated approach must be made to the lama clergy, bearing in mind that the ordinary lamas, although they are parasitic elements, nevertheless, do not, either by social origin or material condition, belong to the class of feudal nobles. Only the high-ranking lamas belong to the latter class. Accordingly, the problem was to isolate this clique of clerical feudal nobles from the bulk of ordinary lamas, wrest the latter from their influence and conduct a political and cultural campaign of work among the ordinary lamas to induce them to leave the monasteries and become involved in socially useful labour. The struggle with the influence of Lamaism on the mass of the *arats* was waged now by means of large-scale explanatory work and by taking steps to raise the cultural level of the population.

By means of day-to-day explanatory work, by isolating the counter-revolutionary higher circles of the lama clergy and exposing their anti-popular activities, the Party succeeded in considerably weakening the influence exercised by the Lamaist church and the monasteries over the *arat* masses.

The directives of the Ninth MPRP Congress and the resolutions of the Seventh Grand Hural formed a concrete programme of action for eliminating the remnants of feudalism and supplied a clear-cut plan for building the foundations of a new economy for the period of transition from feudalism to socialism.

Increase of the Menace Constituted by Japanese Imperialism. Intensification of the Class Struggle Inside the Country. Defeat of the Japanese Aggressors in the Khalkhin-Gol Region

The influence of the reactionary feudal elements, which had increased during the period of the leftist excesses, diminished sharply, but the class struggle continued with unabated intensity.

Having suffered defeat in their attempts to raise a rebellion in 1932, the reactionary elements continued to engage in subversive activities and to organize plots.

As regards international affairs at this time, various contradictions inherent in capitalism were becoming more acute as a result of the 1929-1933 world economic crisis. The imperialists sought for a way out of the crisis by unleashing another world war. Opposed to this aggressive, predatory policy of the imperialist states was the peace-loving policy of the Soviet Union—the policy of friendship between peoples.

The Soviet government strove constantly to establish businesslike, peaceful relations with all states. However, the reactionary circles of the capitalist countries did everything possible to oppose this. The bitterest and most implacable enemies of the USSR were the imperialist warmongers in Japan in the east and in Germany in the west. In their ambitions for world supremacy and for enslaving the peoples in the interests of securing maximum profits for German and Japanese capitalists, fascist Germany and militarist Japan made feverish preparations for an aggressive war.

In preparation for war with the Soviet Union the Japanese aggressors decided to begin first by attacking China, seizing North-East China (Manchuria) and the MPR, in order to make those territories their own colonies and a military bridgehead for further aggressive operations against China and the USSR.

Having seized North-East China and a considerable part of Inner Mongolia and while pushing on with their conquests in North China, the Japanese imperialists began sounding out the strength of the Soviet Union's frontiers, on the one hand, and preparing to seize the MPR on the other.

On November 27, 1934, therefore, at the request of the MPR government, a gentleman's agreement was concluded between the USSR and the MPR providing for "reciprocal support in every respect to avert and forestall the threat of a military attack, and also the extension to one another of help and support in the event of an attack by any third party whatsoever on the MPR or the USSR." This agreement was immensely important for safeguarding the independence of the MPR and maintaining peace in the Far East. Given this agreement, the Japanese militarists did not venture to start a war against the MPR but they went on provoking "incidents" on the frontier of the MPR and Manchukuo (the puppet state set up in 1932 by the Japanese aggressors in North-East China and abolished in 1945).

The MPR government replied to the provocations of the Japanese-Manchurian military clique by vigilantly guarding the frontiers and firmly pursued a policy of peaceful settlement of the frontier disputes provoked by the Japanese. For instance, after an attack by Japanese-Manchurian troops on the frontier post of Khalkhin-sume a Mongolian-Japanese-Manchurian conference was, on the proposal of the MPR government, convened at Manchuria station, at which the MPR delegation proposed setting up a mixed boundary commission to settle any border conflicts that might arise. In reply the Japanese military clique put forward a number of bare-faced, obviously unacceptable demands and threatened, in event of rejection, to use armed force.

In 1935-1936 the Japanese military clique intensified provocative actions in the frontier regions (Khalkhin-sume, Bulan-Ders, Adag-Dulan) but were duly repulsed. In defence of the independence of their homeland and the freedom of the people, the soldiers and commanders of the Mongolian People's Army, such as Sh. Gongor, the pilots D. Demberel and Ch. Shagdarsuren, Sodov and many others, gave remarkable displays of courage. In consequece of the aggravation of the tense situation on the eastern frontier the government took a number of important steps to reinforce the country's capacity for defence; military expenditure was increased. In 1934, for instance, it accounted for 34.7% of the total budget but in 1938 the proportion was 52.5%. There was an abrupt rise in the technical equipment of the People's Army, the term of military service was extended from 2 to 3 years, etc.

As the armed raids by Japanese troops on MPR frontier posts grew in intensity and assumed a more and more bare-faced character, they aggravated the tense situation on the eastern frontier of the MPR which had been created in 1936. The peaceful existence and national independence of the MPR became directly threatened. At this dangerous moment for the MPR there rang out all over the world a declaration by the USSR Government to the effect that in the event of Japan deciding to attack the Mongolian People's Republic by encroaching upon its independence, the Soviet Union would have to help the MPR.[2]

This declaration furnished fresh proof of the USSR's peace-loving policy and of the fraternal, friendly relations between the USSR and the MPR and of the readiness of the Soviet people to help the MPR protect its independence; it strengthened still further the friendship of the Soviet and Mongolian peoples, inspired the Mongolian people with new strength. The Protocol on Mutual Assistance between the USSR and MPR, signed on March 12, 1936, following this declaration, linked still more closely together the destinies of the two brother nations and formed a sure guarantee of the independence of the MPR.

In conformity with Articles 1 and 2 of this Protocol the two Contracting Parties, in event of a threat of an attack on the territory of the USSR or the MPR by a third State, undertook immediately to confer on the situation so created and to take all such steps as might be required to guard against the danger and to afford one another every possible assistance, including military assistance.

The Protocol on Mutual Assistance, which enlarged upon and put into legal form the gentleman's agreement of 1934, was exceptionally important for safeguarding the independence of the MPR. This document demonstrated the unshakable determination of the Soviet and Mongolian peoples to make joint efforts to defend peace in the Far East and protect the MPR against aggression by Japanese imperialism. The Protocol on Mutual Assistance was a striking expression of the peaceful foreign policy of both states, which was based on the principle of equality of rights, mutual respect and friendship of the peoples.

The Plenary Meeting of the MPRP Central Committee (March 1936) and Twentieth Session of the Little Hural laid special stress upon the growing danger of external attack and approved the steps taken by the government to reinforce the country's defence capacity and develop the economy. In order to intensify the struggle with counter-revolutionary elements inside the country, the Meeting approved the reorganization of Internal State Security as part of the Ministry of Internal Affairs.

In the spring of 1936 negotiations were resumed between representatives of the MPR and the Japanese-Manchurian command for a peaceful regulation of border disputes. However, because of the bare-faced and provocative demands put forward by the Japanese military clique, the negotiations again ended without any result.

The Japanese military clique responded to all the peaceable efforts of the MPR government with fresh provocations and a clear manifestation of preparations to invade the MPR.

The Japanese militarists established special military zones on the eastern frontier of the MPR, extending to them railway lines, highways, and lines of communication. Simultaneously, they augmented the number of secret agents despatched into MPR territory. The agents so despatched had the task of consolidating the forces of reaction inside the MPR and organizing counter-revolutionary plots, subversive activities and espionage.

The aggressive plans of the Japanese imperialists were aimed at seizing and enslaving the Mongolian Republic and turning its territory into a military bridgehead for a "great war" against the USSR.

Simultaneously with preparations for an attack on the MPR the Japanese imperialists conducted provocative military actions right on the Soviet frontier. In 1938 Japan attacked the USSR in the area of Lake Hasan with the intention of encircling Vladivostok. The Soviet troops successfully repelled this attack, routed the invading Japanese army units and the Japanese aggressors were forced to beat an ignominious retreat after suffering heavy losses.

Having convinced themselves of the strength of the Far Eastern frontiers of the USSR, the Japanese aggressors reinforced troop concentrations on the frontiers of the MPR, reckoning they could attack the USSR through the territory of the MPR. In liaison with the Japanese militarists, the last remnants of the class of feudal nobles and the reactionary higher-ranking lamas tried to create inside the MPR a situation favourable for a Japanese invasion. These elements, relying for support on the monasteries and playing on religious prejudices, endeavoured to frustrate the measures adopted by the people's government and discredit the general Party line in the eyes of the *arats,* and engaged in subversive activities against people's power.

The counter-revolutionary actions of the reactionary higher circles of the church were intensified from 1935 onwards in connection with the heightening of the aggressive intrigues of the Japanese imperialists on the eastern frontier of the MPR.

In 1935 and 1936 the official internal security organs of the MPR uncovered a big counter-revolutionary organization with a network that embraced about 20 monasteries located near the south-eastern state frontier of the MPR. The membership of this organization comprised more than one hundred senior lamas; its objective was to raise a rebellion inside the MPR and, with the help of Japan, to restore the old feudal order in the country under a Japanese protectorate. The reactionary monastery hierarchy sought to take advantage for their infamous ends of the deep-seated superstition and religious feelings of the population and in every possible way tried to undermine the friendly ties of the Mongolian People's Republic with the Soviet Union, striving to rupture Soviet-Mongolian relations.

Thus, the struggle to consummate the general democratic revolution was at this time being waged in difficult circumstances, both externally and internally. More specifically, in the course of implementing the "New Course" policy adopted by the Third Extraordinary Plenary Meeting of the Central Committee and the Central Investigative Committee of the MPRP there emerged within the Party leadership and the government "acute differences of opinion on radical, fundamental questions of Party policy."[3]

A right opportunist group headed by Gendun sought to belittle the Party's leadership role and to drive it off the only correct line of non-capitalist development for the country. This group also strove to undermine the friendship of the Soviet and Mongolian peoples and gave every possible encouragement to capitalist elements. This is one side of the story. On the other hand, Gendun's anti-Party group, taking advantage of the aggravation of the country's external situation as a result of the Japanese imperialist aggression and for its own mercenary and self-seeking motives, began committing crude breaches of revolutionary law and socialist democracy, initiated unjustified reprisals against innocent people based on various slanderous materials and staged the trumped up "Lkhumbo case". Thus, the line followed by the right oportunist group was very dangerous for the country and, if its aim had been achieved, it would have diverted the country from the non-capitalist path of development; friendship between the MPR and the USSR would have been seriously undermined, the country's defensive capacity would have been weakened, the forces of internal counter-revolution would have sprung into action and, ultimately, the Mongolian people would have found themselves helpless in the face of the danger threatening the country.

The Plenary Meeting of the MPRP Central Committee in 1936 exposed the anty-Party right opportunist activities of the Gendun group.

In January 1937 the case of the heads of the Yugotszar monastery came up for hearing in the Supreme Court of the MPR. This counter-revolutionary organization had links with Japanese agents and was preparing an armed uprising. A store of arms had been discovered in the monastery.

During 1937 the organs of the Ministry of Internal Affairs of the MPR discovered and liquidated a counter-revolutionary Lamaist conspiratorial organization headed by Enzon-Khambo and Ded-Khambo.

A major part in the unmasking and complete defeat of the counter-revolutionary forces in the country was played by Kh. Choibalsan who, together with other Party workers, fought energetically for the constant consolidation of the fraternal friendship between the MPR and the USSR, for strengthening the defence capacity of the country and for the protection of the interests of the people and the homeland. In this fight Kh. Choibalsan won still greater popularity in the Party, and became widely known among the people. However, Choibalsan's role was inordinately exaggerated, the great gains of the people's revolution being linked solely with his name. This ran counter to Lenin's principles of Party life and to the principles of socialist democracy, leading in practice to violation of legality. This was rightly condemned in 1962 by a Plenary Meeting of the Central Committee of the MPRP.[4]

Notwithstanding the growth of the personality cult, the MPRP and the people's government, with the active support of the masses of the working people and on their heightened consciousness and vigilance, completely defeated the reactionary elements, frustrated the attempts of the Japanese imperialists to form a fifth column in the MPR on whose backing they hoped to rely when they invaded the country. This circumstance was exceptionally important in ensuring the defensive strength of the MPR and in further reinforcing the solidarity of the masses round the MPRP and the government.

Noting the collapse of their subversive plans as a result of the failure of their network of agents, the Japanese imperialists speeded up preparations for a direct invasion of the MPR and intensified their provocative attacks on frontier posts.

In these circumstances the government of the MPR appealed to the Soviet government and asked for Soviet troops to be brought into the territory of the MPR. The Soviet government complied with this request in conformity with the Protocol on Mutual Assistance. In early September 1937 units of the Soviet Red Army entered the MPR and stood shoulder to shoulder with the soldiers of the Mongolian People's Revolutionary Army to protect the MPR's independence against Japanese imperialist aggression.

From January 1939 onwards the provocative actions of the Japanese military clique became especially frequent.

On May 11, 1939, Japanese troops attacked the state frontier of the MPR and penetrated as far as the River Khalkhin Gol. On May 28, 1939, the 64th Japanese regiment, two motorized detachments and a number of other units invaded the territory of the MPR in the Khalkhin Gol region and joined battle with frontier units of MPR troops. The aggressive actions of the Japanese military clique aroused the profound indignation of the working people of the MPR. It was the start of a just war against the Japanese imperialists for the national independence and territorial integrity of the MPR. In the battle area the Japanese command had at its disposal a powerful army group of several tens of thousands of officers and men, equipped with hundreds of tanks, aeroplanes and very heavy artillery. The Japanese troops had the tactical advantage of having at their disposal approach routes by road and rail and previously prepared supply bases. The Soviet-Mongolian units, on the other hand, were far away from their supply bases and did not have convenient routes of communication available.

But the Soviet-Mongolian troops were inspired by a belief in victory, since they were fighting for a just cause. The lofty morale of the Soviet-Mongolian troops, combined with their high level of skill in warfare, the superiority in strategy and tactics of the commanders of the Soviet-Mongolian troops and the superior quality of their battle tactics ensured the victory of the Soviet-Mongolian forces over the Japanese aggressors. After a series of crushing blows the Soviet-Mongolian troops at the end of August 1939 surrounded the Japanese group which had invaded MPR territory and completely crushed it, capturing huge spoils and a large number of prisoners. The Japanese forces lost about 60,000 killed and wounded in the Khalkhin Gol fighting; some 700 Japanese planes were brought down and more than 200 guns, 340 machine-guns, more than 12,000 rifles and about 2 million rounds of ammunition were captured.

In these valiant battles the Mongolian and Soviet soldiers covered themselves with undying glory and displayed a high level of bravery and courage in fighting for the cause of the MPR's independence. Among the units which specially distinguished themselves were the 6th and 8th Mongolian cavalry divisions and the 36th motorized rifle division, the 11th tank brigade, the 100th air brigade, the 24th motorized rifle regiment, 57th rifle division, motorized armoured brigades and the 149th rifle regiment of the Soviet Red Army. Great military skill was displayed in these battles by such eminent USSR army commanders as G. M. Shtern, G. K. Zhukov, M. P. Yakovlev, I. I. Fedyuninsky, M. I. Remizov, S. I. Gritsevets and G. P. Kravchenko. The names of the gallant sons of the Soviet nation, Yakovlev, Remizov and many others who fell in battle for the freedom and independence of the MPR will live eternally in the hearts of the Mongolian people. Whole-hearted gallantry in battles with the Japanese aggressors was displayed by soldiers and commanders of the Mongolian People's Revolutionary Army such as Zh. Lkhagvasuren, D. Nyantaisuren, L. Dandar, Ts. Olzvai, D. Khayankhyarva, Ch. Zhugdernamzhil, L. Gelegbator, Dorzhi, P. Chogdon, B. Sambu, B. Samdan, D. Baadai, S. Bataa, Turkhu, S. Nanzaidar, D. Luvsan, D. Sosorbaram, P. Degdekhe, A. Budhu, Zh. Myadag, Ts. Myrdenev, L. Sharav, Ts. Sodnom.

The blood spilt by the Soviet and Mongolian soldiers in joint battles with the common enemy set the seal still more firmly on the fraternal friendship of the Soviet and Mongolian peoples. The assistance rendered by the Soviet Union to the Mongolian People's Republic at its moment of mortal danger furnished still further striking proof of the Soviet government's loyalty to its undertakings under the treaties and agreements concluded.

The events at Khalkhin Gol also constituted a test of the stability and vitality of the people's democratic system in the MPR. This test was passed brilliantly. In that time of trial the Mongolian working people gave a remarkable example of patriotism and, rallying closely round the MPRP and the government, rose as one in defence of their country's independence, in defence of the gains won by their people's revolution. The rout of the Japanese aggressors at Khalkhin Gol was immensely important for consolidating the independence of the MPR, it deflated the arrogance of the Japanese *samurai*, demonstrated the solidity of the MPR's frontiers and the ability of the Mongolian people to defend their homeland heroically. The defeat of the Japanese army at Khalkhin Gol represented a serious blow not only to Japanese imperialism but also to the forces of international imperialist reaction which had assisted Japan in this aggression.

On September 15, 1939, an agreement was signed in Moscow between the MPR, the USSR and Japan for a settlement of the dispute in the Khalkhin Gol area under which all military operations were brought to an end at 14.00 hours on September 16.

To commemorate the fighting at Khalkhin Gol, a memorial was erected, on the decision of the MPR government, on the bank of the River Khalkhin Gol.

The memorial was unveiled on August 20, 1954 at the time of the 15th anniversary of the victory in this area. It is an imposing monument—a symbol of the friendship of the two fraternal peoples. Cut into the marble of the monument are the words: "Eternal glory to the soldier-heroes of the Soviet Army and the valiant *tsiriks* of the Mongolian People's Revolutionary Army who fell in battles with the Japanese aggressors in the area of the River Khalkhin Gol for the freedom and independence of the peace-loving Mongolian people, for the peace and security of the peoples against the imperialist aggressors."

Notwithstanding the desperate opposition of class enemies inside the country and the intrigues of the imperialists, including open acts of aggression on the part of imperialist Japan, the forward march of the MPR continued along the path defined by the general line of the MPRP steadily. The "New Course" policy fully justified itself. The targets set by the Ninth MPRP Congress had by 1940, when the Tenth Congress was held, been basically achieved.

*Completion of the General Democratic Stage
of the Revolution. Tenth Congress of the MPRP.
New Constitution of the MPR*

Major changes occurred in the internal life of the MPR.

The consolidation of the MPR, the economic and cultural progress achieved, the growth of political consciousness and patriotism among the *arat* masses—all of these created conditions under which the *arats* led by the MPRP, became firmly united constituting a force capable not only of resolutely resisting the remnants of the feudal class and other reactionary elements but also of moving into attack against them.

By 1938 almost all the reactionary organizations in Mongolia had been routed. The Lamaist monasteries which had been the centres of counter-revolutionary resistance, the centres of obscurantism and hotbeds of superstition, opposing all the measures of the Party and government for economic and cultural development, unmasked themselves in the eyes of the workers by their numerous hostile intrigues as an anti-popular force. As a consequence of this the lower-ranking lamas began leaving the monasteries *en masse* and the majority of the monasteries were left empty and ceased to function. This struck from the hands of the senior lamas and the feudal reactionaries generally a powerful ideological and organizational weapon for exercising their reactionary influence over the masses. The monasteries were no longer an obstruction on the MPR's path of development and its revolutionary evolution. The elimination of the feudal nobility, secular and clerical, was the most important result of the changes that ensued in the country during the years of popular rule.

The principal source of the *arats'* prosperity and the basis of the MPR's economy—stock-breeding—took a big step forward. During the period from 1934 to 1939 the numbers of livestock rose by 5.5 million head.

An increase of such considerable size in the number of livestock was the result, mainly, of the successes of the anti-feudal revolution and the liquidation of the class of feudal nobles. From being the herdsmen of other people's herds the *arats* had become owners of all the livestock in the country. This unleashed the productive forces which had in the past been fettered by feudal exploitation and induced the *arats* to take an interest in developing stock-breeding and improving the methods of operating a stock-breeding economy. On the strength of the *arats'* interest thus aroused in developing stock-breeding, and their increased consciousness and activity and the initiative and endeavours made by *arats* to improve their husbandry, the MPRP and the government carried out during this period a series of measures aimed at raising the level of stock-breeding and disseminating more advanced methods of operating this economy among the *arats*.

Considerable results were achieved in developing veterinary services. In 1940 the country had 237 veterinary and *feldsher* centres and the number of Mongolian veterinary surgeons and *feldshers* amounted to 244. A large plant for producing biological preparations, and reseach institutions were established which were able to supply the state's needs in medicines and biological preparations. As a result of the steps taken to set up a fodder base considerably larger quantities of hay were produced. For instance, whereas in 1924, during a dearth of fodder, hay was harvested in the republic over an area of 2,000 hectares, in 1940 the area under hay was 200,000 hectares.

Such a considerable increase in the area under hay crops became possible because in 1937, with the help of the Soviet Union, the first 10 mechanised haymaking stations were introduced and in 1938 there were already 24 of them. These stations became, as time went on, means of developing and replenishing the productive forces of the MPR's agriculture.

In order to protect livestock from snowstorms and frost the Party and the government gave every possible encouragement to the *arats* to construct heated premises for livestock in places suitable for the purpose as regards grazing, water supplies and hayfields, and to constructing light fencing for use when moving from place to place. The *arats* responded generously to the appeal of the people's authority and began to construct sheds for livestock on a large scale. Before 1932 there were hardly any such structures in the country but in 1940 they already numbered more than 200,000 but even this, compared with the number of livestock, was still not sufficient.

Whereas in 1932 official figures recorded about 9,000 wells, in 1940 there were already about 20,000. The MPRP and the government invited the *arats* to increase the number still more.

For the purchase of pedigree cattle, agricultural machinery and equipment, for the boring and construction of wells, the erection of heated sheds for cattle, the purchase of grain and other requirements of the *arat* herdsmen the state issued long- and short-term credits which in 1931 amounted to 73,500 *tugriks* and in 1940 rose to 2,500,000. After 1936 a start was made in supplying stock-breeding farms on credit with agricultural machinery and seeds. The area sown to grain and vegetables in 1940 doubled the 1934 figure.

There was a further expansion of the state sector of agriculture in the MPR. In 1931-1932 the republic had three state farms for breeding pedigree livestock and five crop-raising collective farms. As a result of the utilization of various types of agricultural machinery imported from the Soviet Union and also of the breeding and delivery of pedigree livestock, state farms constituted a base for disseminating scientific methods and the use of new technical aids in stock-breeding and agriculture.

In 1940 state farms and mechanical haymaking stations had in operation more than 160 tractors, about 1,000 mowers, hundreds of horse-drawn rakes, etc.

In 1940 the state farms and several of the mechanised haymaking stations were amalgamated into 19 large farms.

A new phenomenon which was immensely important in the socialist transformation of the agricultural economy in the period described was the emergence in 1934 of APA—*arat* production associations. In 1940 the republic had about 90 associations and organisations of various kinds set up on a voluntary basis.

With all its advances in agriculture the MPR was still developing slowly. This was due to the distortions and sabotage committed during the period when the "right" and "left" deviationists were in control in the country, and also to the existence of feudal survivals which could not be completely overcome in a short space of time.

During the period from 1932 onwards industry, too, was developing in the MPR. The output of coal and gold mines has considerably increased as well as the capacity of the power station combine; the construction of workshops and factories in the industrial combine was completed. Simultaneously there was more road and railway building, the railway from Ulan Bator to Nalaikha and a number of highways were built.

In 1938 a Ministry of Industry and Building was set up to be responsible for industrial development. Industrial enterprises began operating on a single state plan and became one of the most important levers in the economic policy of the Party and government. Equipped, with the help of the Soviet Union, with the latest machinery and mechanisms and working on home-produced raw materials, the industrial enterprises of the MPR laid a firm foundation for the non-capitalist path of development of the country. The following figures show the increase in industrialization: in 1927 the value of the output of industrial concerns amounted to 1,800 *tugriks*, in 1940 it was more than 52,100,000 *tugriks*, i.e. it had risen during the thirteen years almost 29 times or, as compared with 1934, almost six times.

With the growth of industry it became possible to utilize local raw materials and resources for the manufacture of a number of industrial commodities and products.

As industry developed there was a rise in the number of workers and qualified technicians. Wheareas in 1928 only 300 workers altogether were employed in the enterprises of the MPR, in 1940 there were more than 13,000 workers employed who were qualified in new production techniques, achieved high labour productivity, were striving for the economic and cultural progress of their country and, along with the *arats*, building up a new life in the MPR.

Side by side with state undertakings, producers' co-operatives developed in the MPR. The value of the output of producers' cooperatives increased to more than 4.5 times the 1934 level. The range of consumer goods produced by these co-operatives also increased from year to year and their quality improved.

Side by side with the cartage of freight by *arat* concerns, state transport developed successfully in the MPR. In 1940 air communications were opened between the MPR and the USSR, and also internal flights between different parts of the country.

Means of communication—postal services, telephones and the telegraph—began to acquire ever-increasing importance in the economy, and helped raise the political consciousness of the *arat* masses.

A communications medium developed during the years of the revolution was the radio. In 1940 almost all the *aimak* centres and other important points in the MPR had their own broadcasting stations and several thousand radio receivers.

Government and co-operative trading developed quickly. In 1940 the trading network had almost quadrupled as compared with 1934. There was also a successful development in foreign trade and in economic links with the friendly Soviet Union; total trade with the USSR rose from year to year.

Consumer co-operation in the MPR became an important factor in the national economy, trade and procurement turnover increasing more than twenty-four times as compared with 1924.

In order to improve supplies of goods to the inhabitants of *khudons* the number of trading posts was considerably enlarged: in 1934 they numbered 1,124 while in 1939 there were already 2,362. The extension of the trading network was extremely important, especially in view of the widely-dispersed nature of the camping grounds and the great distances separating them from *aimak* centres.

As well as providing the masses with consumer goods, co-operation in the MPR was very important in curtailing capitalist elements and creating foundations for the non-capitalist path of development of the MPR.

A striking indication of the growth in the economic capacity and well-being of the MPR as a result of carrying out the "New Course" policy and implementing the decisions of the Ninth MPRP Congress was the systematic growth of the MPR budget; in 1934 it showed on the revenue side a figure of 38,900,000 *tugriks* while the figure in 1940 was already 118,000,000 *tugriks*. There was a corresponding increase on the expenditure side of the budget.

Mongolia's budget expenditure was directed to developing and consolidating the country's defence capacity and raising the level of the culture and prosperity of the working classes.

The mass abandonment of the monasteries by rank-and-file lamas and the cessation of the operation of most of the monasteries had an immense bearing on the country's economy and its further cultural advance.

The victories won in all branches of the national economy and culture made it possible to raise considerably the living standards and prosperity of the *arat* masses.

All these achievements furnished striking evidence of the correctness of the general line of policy of the MPRP and the correctness of the "New Course" policy carried through on the basis of the directives of the Ninth MPRP Congress and the Seventh Grand Hural.

The correct policy of the Party and the government and the devoted struggle of the Mongolian people for its implementation ensured the successful termination of the general-democratic stage of the revolution and the gradual transition of the MPR towards constructing the basis for socialism.

In the difficult and complex circumstances of the twenties and thirties the MPRP was able to organize and carry through the destruction of the internal hostile forces, paralyse the hornets' nests of counter-revolution—the monasteries, mobilize the working people of the country to repel the external enemy and, finally, achieve the economic and cultural successes with which the MPR came to the Tenth Congress in March 1940.

The Tenth Congress is exceptionally important in the history of the MPRP and the Mongolian People's Republic.

The Congress summed up the results of the struggle of the MPR working people, under the Party's leadership, to complete the anti-feudal revolution and create conditions for non-capitalist development.

In summing up the overall results of the MPRP's work in guiding the Mongolian people in the building of a new, free life, and evaluating the significance of the successes achieved in the revolutionary development of the country, Kh. Choibalsan declared in his report to the Congress: "It can now be confidently asserted that we have firmly embarked on the path of non-capitalist development."[5]

These enormous changes in the whole image of Mongolia, the remarkable successes scored in the MPR's development along the path of progress were conditioned by the fact that the MPRP, guided by Marxist-Leninist teaching, has unswervingly followed the line of non-capitalist development of the country, with the backing of Soviet friendship and assistance, and by the fact that this policy of the MPRP was in complete accord with the basic interests of the MPR's working people.

The policy followed by the MPRP encouraged the growth of class consciousness in the Mongolian working classes and of their political activity.

In rightly stressing the decisive role played by the creative energy of the popular masses in building under the MPRP's guidance, a new kind of life, in achieving successes in taking the MPR along the non-capitalist path, the report to the Congress pointed out that "all these successes were won by the hands of the working people... of our country, by the hands of their new intellectuals, by the hands of people who love their country, people who do not grudge their efforts in the struggle for the interests of their people."[6]

In the sphere of foreign relations the MPR government consistently followed a policy of close friendship with the Soviet Union, profoundly realizing that friendship with the Soviet people represented a fundamental guarantee of the independence of the Mongolian People's Republic and of the freedom and happiness of the Mongolian people.

The Congress fully endorsed the foreign policy of the Central Committee and the government and noted that "the Party Central Committee and the government during the period under review succeeded in achieving still greater consolidation of the indissoluble fraternal friendship between the Soviet Union and our country.

"From the first days of our revolution the Soviet Union has extended to us political, economic and cultural assistance in the development and consolidation of the MPR."[7]

Productive forces continued to develop rapidly and there was a consolidation of the material basis of the social sector, represented in the country by state and co-operative industrial and transport enterprises, mechanised haymaking stations and *arat* associations. As industry developed in the country there was a rapid growth of the national working class and of worker intelligentsia.

Important though the development of industry was, the economy of the country continued to be based on stock-breeding. In the light of this fact, and attaching exceptional importance to the growth of stock-breeding, the MPRP Central Committee introduced for discussion at the Congress the question of the state of, and the tasks involved in developing stock-breeding in the MPR.

In its resolution the MPRP Tenth Congress emphasized that the development in every possible way of stock-breeding was decisive for the economy of the MPR, that growth of its economic capacity and successful progress in developing the country along the non-capitalist path depended on advancing stock-breeding to the utmost, increasing the head of livestock and improving commodity productivity in stock-breeding. The Congress pointed out that, while giving every possible encouragement to the private economic initiative of the *arat* masses in raising the level of stock-breeding, every possible assistance should be given in the organization and development of the simplest forms of *arat* production associations. It was also emphasised that *arat* production associations should be set up on a strictly voluntary basis. The Congress also enjoined the MPRP Central Committee to take steps to expand the network of mechanised haymaking stations.

In the report to the Congress attention was drawn to the importance of these stations: "These stations have been a firm foundation for rebuilding the backward pastoral, scattered, fragmented system of stock-breeding with its remnants of feudal relationships into a progressive, modern, intensive economy capable of ensuring the economic growth of the country. This is of very great political, economic and cultural importance for developing the country along the non-capitalist path."[8]

In the concluding section of the resolution the Congress, called on all Party organizations and members to take an active part in tackling the job of developing stock-breeding as the principal economic aim of the MPR. The Congress emphasized that a basic guarantee of the Mongolian people's successful advance along the non-capitalist path to socialism was the loyalty of the MPRP and all working people in the MPR to the victorious banner of Marxist-Leninist teaching.

The Congress adopted a new programme for the Party which defined very precisely and clearly the targets for the construction of the bases of socialism in the MPR. In the Party programme it is stated that "the policy of the Mongolian People's Republic is directed towards definitively extirpating the remnants of feudalism in the country's economy, to combating the survivals of feudalism in the minds of individuals, to ensuring the non-capitalist development of the country and preparing for the subsequent transition to socialism."[9]

Noting the radical changes that had taken place in the class composition and social structure of the country and the immense advances made in strengthening the people's-democratic system and in the growth of the national economy and culture, the Congress recognized the necessity of reviewing the constitution and holding a national discussion of the draft of a new constitution.

In June 1940 the Eighth Grand People's Hural was convened. The basic item on its agenda was the discussion and approval of the new MPR Constitution.

Kh. Choibalsan presented a report on the draft MPR Constitution at the Eighth Grand People's Hural. Addressing the delegates, he said: "...In our work we have been guided by the experience of the great country of socialism—the experience of the Soviet Union. Consequently, in drafting our Constitution the only example for us can be the Constitution of the Soviet Union."[10]

For the discussion of the most important amendments and additions put forward by the working people during the national discussion of the draft Constitution and for the definitive drafting of the text of the Constitution, the Grand People's Hural formed a drafting committee composed of thirty-five members.

The Eighth Grand People's Hural unanimously adopted the new Constitution of the MPR.

The new Constitution spelled out and legislatively consolidated the gains and successes scored by the Mongolian workers in the period between 1924 and 1940. The new Constitution marked a further democratization of the state administration. It reflected the successes gained in taking the MPR along the path to socialism.

Article I of the new Constitution gives a description of the Mongolian People's Republic: "The Mongolian People's Republic"—the Article says—is an independent State of the working people *(arat* herdsmen, workers and intellectuals), who have destroyed imperialist and feudal oppression and are providing a non-capitalist path of development for the country's subsequent transition to socialism".

Article 4 of the Constitution declares the basic objective of social production and development of the whole economy of the Republic to be a steady advance in the material prosperity and cultural level of the working people.

The Constitution of the MPR defines three types of property: state, co-operative and the private property of citizens based on personal labour; it is also laid down that "all the earth and the depths of the earth—the forests, waters and their riches, factories, works, mines, pits, etc.—are the property of the state, i.e. a national patrimony. They may not be owned by private individuals."

The Constitution lays down the basis of the state structure of the MPR and the basic regulations for the electoral or voting system.

The Constitution provides for full equality between citizens of the MPR, irrespective of property status, education, sex, nationality, religious beliefs, or whether they lead a nomadic or settled form of life.

The new Constitution emphasizes the leading role of the MPRP. Article 95 reads: "...The most active and public-minded citizens from the ranks of the workers, the *arat* working people and the intellectuals are united in the Mongolian People's Revolutionary Party, which represents the advance-guard of the working people in the fight to strengthen and develop the country along the non-capitalist path—a Party which represents the leading nucleus of all organizations of the working people, both voluntary and state organisations."

The Constitution establishes the unalterable rights of citizens of the MPR to labour, leisure and education, the right to elect and to be elected to all the organs of people's power in the country.

It should be pointed out that, alongside correct decisions, which were immensely important for the development of the people's economy, the Tenth Congress put forward an unrealistic, unrealizable target—to increase the head of livestock over 11-13 years by 200 million. This decision was the consequence of the personality cult and bore no relation to the practical possibilities of the country in view of the predominance of small-scale private *arat* husbandries.

The period 1932-1940 was one in which the basic targets of the anti-imperialist and anti-feudal revolution were triumphantly achieved. By combining the interests and initiative of *arat* peasant proprietors with the interests of the developing national state, the MPRP and the government carried out a series of very substantial socio-economic transformations which produced conditions conducive to the country's development along the non-capitalist path. It was precisely during this period that the Mongolian people, with the unselfish assistance of the USSR, carried through, under the leadership of the MPRP, the liquidation of the feudal nobility as a class and consolidated the decisive influence of the state and cooperative sectors of the MPR's economy over the course of the country's economic development.

The victory of the anti-imperialist and anti-feudal revolution in Mongolia was a striking demonstration of the power of Marxist-Leninist ideas, visible historical proof of the correctness of the Marxist-Leninist doctrine that it is possible for backward countries to develop from feudalism to socialism bypassing the stage of capitalism. The triumph of the Mongolian people in pursuing this type of development dealt a shattering blow to the racist "theory" that backward countries are incapable of independent development and that their peoples are doomed to extinction.

The experience of the MPR has shown in striking fashion that the non-capitalist path of development is realistic, that it is the only correct path for backward countries in their move forward to social progress.

SECTION THREE

THE FIGHT TO BUILD THE BASIS FOR SOCIALISM IN THE MPR (1940-1952)

CHAPTER I

THE MPR DURING THE YEARS OF THE SECOND WORLD WAR (1939-1945)

The attack launched by fascist Germany on Poland in September 1939 marked the beginning of the Second World War which continued until 1945. The Second World War arose between Germany, Italy and Japan, on the one side, and the USA, Great Britain and France, on the other, for sources of raw materials, for markets and spheres of influence. In antithesis to the camp of the imperialists stood the first state of workers and peasants in the world—the USSR. The Mongolian People's Republic, which was following the socialist path of development, took up a firm position of alliance with the USSR. International reaction looked upon German-Italian fascism and Japanese imperialism, which cherished a special hatred for the new social system—socialism, as a shock force which could rout and destroy the USSR and the MPR and restore capitalism in them. Accordingly, the British and American monopolies incited Germany and Japan to attack the USSR, encouraging them to take an aggressive line and hoping that in such a war the strength of both Germany and Japan and of the Soviet Union would be reciprocally weakened and exhausted and that as a result they would be able to establish their supremacy over the whole world.

For their part the ruling circles of the German-Italian-Japanese bloc sought to seize British, American and French colonies and spheres of influence in order to strengthen their might and then crush the USSR, subdue the revolutionary-democratic forces of peace and establish a fascist "new order" in every country. Both the imperialist groupings made thorough and persistent preparations for a bloody struggle. Accordingly, the Second World War, representing as it did the result of the exacerbation of imperialist antagonisms, assumed, to begin with, an imperialist character. The Soviet Union, realizing what a threat fascism represented for the whole world, had proposed to the British and French governments that there be mutual aid and a collective rebuff be organised to the fascist aggressors.

But the reactionary ruling circles of the Western Powers in fact rejected the proposal. The negotiations, begun in the summer of 1939, between the representatives of Great Britain and France, on the one hand, and of the Soviet Union, on the other gave no result. The imperialists of Great Britain and France simultaneously held secret negotiations with Hitler, offering to conclude with him a non-aggression pact and an agreement for the division of spheres of influence at the expense of the USSR and the other countries of Eastern Europe, while the reactionary circles of the USA and Great Britain encouraged the aggressive actions of the Japanese *samurai* and gave them generous assistance with deliveries of strategic materials. The Japanese imperialists, who had in September 1939 made a military attack on the MPR in the Khalkhin Gol area and been utterly routed by the Mongolian and Soviet troops, did not abandon their aggressive aims and awaited a suitable moment for an attack on the USSR and MPR. The threat of an attack on the USSR became ever greater and war drew nearer both from the West and from the East.

It was essential at all costs to free the first country of socialism from the threat of war hanging over it. The interests of socialism and the interests of the working people of all countries called for the preservation of the first socialist state in the world. Accordingly, in September 1939, the Soviet government concluded a non-aggression pact with Germany that had been proposed by Germany herself. In concluding this treaty the intention of Hitlerite Germany was to bring under its control first the countries of Western Europe and then, exploiting their resources, to fall upon the USSR. By this treaty the USSR was gaining time to prepare the country for defence and saving itself from the danger of having to wage war on two fronts in the circumstances of 1939. Thus, the conclusion with Germany of a non-aggression treaty represents a victory for the Soviet Union's diplomacy and a failure of the policy of "Isolate the USSR" followed by the Western Powers.

In spite of the endeavours of the imperialists of the Western Powers, the Second World War broke out not between the camps of socialism and capitalism, but inside the capitalist camp itself and between groupings of imperialist states. When Hitlerite Germany attacked Poland, the Western Powers—Great Britain and France—declared war on Germany on the pretext of "protecting" Poland. In point of fact they entered into war with Germany not for the sake of rescuing Poland but in order to safeguard their own imperialist interests and so they did nothing to help Poland. Poland fell in the course of some 14 days' fighting. Because the Polish government betrayed the interests of its people, Poland became nazi Germany's first victim. Under the leadership of their Communist Party the

Polish people began a difficult, unequal struggle to liberate the country from the nazi occupying troops.

The war that had begun between Great Britain and France, on the one side, and fascist Germany, on the other, was a "phoney war" because the Anglo-French troops did not begin military operations, for they anticipated a clash between Germany and the Soviet Union. Meanwhile, the peoples of the European countries occupied by the nazi forces began to rise and fight against fascism and for freedom and national independence. In this way the Second World War, which began as an imperialist and aggressive war, began to assume the character of a war of liberation of all peoples against fascism. The liberatory and just character of the Second World War was intensified when the Soviet Union entered the war against Hitler's Germany.

A situation arose where the imperialists of the USA, Great Britain and France found that they had one enemy—German fascism—in common with the masses who had become the victims of fascist aggression.

In the first stage (from September 1, 1939, to June 22, 1941) when the war was raging between imperialist groupings and bore an imperialist character, the foreign policy of the MPR was one of further strengthening the friendship with the Soviet Union, waging the fight against fascism and for peace, and extending all possible support to the antifascist peaceloving forces headed by the USSR.

In the report to the Tenth MPRP Congress it was stated that the Mongolian People's Revolutionary Party and the government were under an obligation to pursue a foreign policy which would guarantee the peaceful existence of the Republic and the strengthening and preservation of its national independence. To this end "...we have achieved... still greater consolidation of friendship with the one and only country which is really fighting for the maintenance of peace throughout the world, which really recognizes the freedom and independence of all peoples, with our friend—the USSR."[1]

In pursuance of its peaceful foreign policy, the government of the MPR, acting together with the Soviet Union, was defending peace in the Far East and blocking the path of aggressive Japanese imperialism.

The Tenth Congress and the Eighth Grand People's Hural summed up the results of the immense historical victories won by the Mongolian people along the path of revolutionary changes between 1921 and 1940.

The new Constitution of the MPR, reflecting the changes that had occurred in the country's social and economic life, gave them statutory force.

The main attention of the MPRP Central Committee and the MPR government was upon the planned growth of the country's productive forces. To begin with, there was the problem of increasing the head of livestock and also raising the level of other branches of the economy needed to ensure the transition to socialist construction. Accordingly, the problems of national economic planning in the socialisation stage of development of the Mongolian People's Republic became exceptionally important.

In order to compile plans for the development of the national economy and supervise their implementation, as well as the execution of the most important decisions of the government, on May 24, 1941, there was set up a department for planning, accounting and inspection attached to the Council of Ministers of the MPR.

On December 29, 1940, the Plenary Meeting of the MPRP Central Committee adopted a resolution on "the National Economic Plan for 1941." The Plenary Meeting noted the enormous economic and political importance of a national economic plan for advancing the MPR along the non-capitalist path and for a further improvement of the political self-awareness of the working people of the MPR. Essentially, this was the first plan in the history of the MPR for national economic, social and cultural development which made provision for a further advance in the various branches of the economy and a substantial expansion of capital investments not only in the republic as a whole but also in individual *aimaks* and *somons*.

On the basis of the decisions of the December Plenary Meeting all the *aimak* and municipal committees of the MPRP descussed the national economic plan at their own plenary meetings, and the plan was widely discussed at meetings of *arats*, and industrial and office workers. In this way the economy and culture of the MPR began to be developed on the basis of one year planning. The plan was not a long-term plan; it could not make provision for the development of the country's economy and culture for several years ahead. One year planning could exist until the country was able to move on to long-term planning. In spite of everything, one-year planning was a step forward from the old system of planning.

In accordance with the decisions of the Plenary Meeting and in connection with the beginning of national economic planning the MPR government envisaged labour legislation for the MPR directed towards "strengthening labour discipline and raising labour productivity and the qualifications of workers, reducing waste and costs of production, and eliminating fluctuations of manpower, etc."[2]

The Labour Law of February 14, 1971, adopted by the Twenty-fourth Session of the Little Hural of the MPR, defined the procedure for engaging and discharging hired workers, their rights and obligations and also the rights and obligations of managements of departments and private individuals employing hired labour. The Labour Law made provision also for the basic conditions of employment, i. e. working hours, rest periods, wages and labour protection. Social insurance was introduced for persons working for hire, regulations for protecting mothers and children, prohibition of employment of juveniles, social and welfare services for the workers and employees at factories and offices, etc.

The old Labour Law of August 3, 1934, was no longer suited to the country's level of development; it made no provision for punishing shirkers and other persons transgressing labour discipline.

The new Law indicated measures for strengthening labour discipline, improving labour productivity, eliminating instability of the labour force and attaching factory and office workers more firmly to their places of employment.

On the basis of this Law a uniform system of labour cards was introduced for all factory and office workers and this helped to introduce order at places of work as regards keeping a check on employees and on their engagement and discharge.

The new Labour Law was adapted to the country's level of development and to the new tasks envisaged. It was immensely important from the political, the practical and the educational standpoint.

In conformity with the new tasks ahead a new Code of the Republican Council for Consumers' Co-operatives, a Code for the MPR State Building Trust, and also plans for developing stockbreeding and livestock purchasing, for developing state purchases and procurements of wool was adopted.

Of great importance for the development of stock-breeding in the MPR was a Law approved at the Twenty Fourth Session of the MPR Little Hural (February, 14, 1941) on a "single tax on the stock-breeding farm" under which the earnings of *arat* farmers from agriculture, haymaking, hunting, grazing cattle for hire and from personal employment in domestic industry were exempted from taxation; similarly exempted were income derived from pedigree breeding of all types of domestic animals, as well as from livestock owned by state and co-operative stock-breeding and agricultural concerns; and income from communal livestock in *arat* production associations.

The MPR government took a decision to build a number of new establishments, including the state theatre and the meat-packing plant, the most important concern in the state food industry. On January 4, 1941, the MPR Government enacted laws "On the Compulsory State Conveyance of Loads by Cart

Transport in the MPR" and "On the *Urton*-Horse Transport Service in the MPR."

The introduction of these laws was called for by the targets set for defence, economic and cultural development and also by the growth of internal trade.

All these measures ensured the transition to a planned system of running the economy and to the development of the culture of the MPR.

Under the leadership of the MPRP and the people's government the working people of the MPR joined in an active fight for further economic and cultural advances. But the peaceful work done by the Mongolian people in building the basis for socialism was interrupted when fascist Germany made its flagrant attack on the Soviet Union.

The MPR During the Years of the Great Patriotic War of the Soviet Union

At dawn on June 22, 1941, fascist Germany and her satellites attacked the USSR without a declaration of war.

A total of 190 technically well-equipped and well-trained divisions of Germany and her satellites were concentrated on the frontiers of the Soviet Union. These formations comprised more than 3,500 tanks, more than 50,000 guns and mortars and more than 3,900 aircraft.[3] The attack was carried out by land, sea and air along the western frontier of the USSR from the Arctic Ocean to the Black Sea.

Strong forces of nazi bombers subjected many peaceful cities in the Western Republics of the Soviet Union to barbarous bombing.

This was the beginning of the Great Patriotic War of the Soviet people against fascist Germany which went on for about four years. From the very first days of the war the whole Soviet people, answering the call of the Communist Party and the Soviet Government, rose as one to defend their homeland.

The Soviet people were obliged to take up arms in order to defend themselves, to save the lives of their children, to defend their right to independence and political and national existence and to preserve the great gains won by the socialist revolution.

In defining the aim and the tasks of Soviet people in this war, the Communist Party and the Soviet Government gave prominence to the task of helping all the peoples of Europe to throw off fascist slavery and thereby gave the workers of the countries occupied by the nazis inspiration for the struggle. The fight of the anti-fascists and the national-liberation struggle in the occupied countries acquired a broader character.

The news of the treacherous attack on the USSR by Hitler's Germany aroused the immense indignation of the Mongolian people and evoked a national movement to gear the national economy to the tasks of war-time and extend material assistance to the Soviet people in their Great Patriotic War.

On June 22, 1941, a joint meeting was held of the Presidium of the MPRP Central Committee, the Presidium of the Little Hural and the Council of Ministers of the MPR which clearly defined the attitude of the MPR to this war. In a declaration adopted at the meeting it was stated that German fascism had thrown down a challenge to all progressive mankind by daring to attack the homeland of the workers of the whole world, a source generating the light of true freedom for oppressed and exploited peoples—the Union of Soviet Socialist Republics.

"The whole population of our freedom-loving and independent Republic," this historic document stated, "linked by ties of blood and indissoluble friendship with the Soviet people, with the deepest contempt brands this perfidious act on the part of fascist Germany, will respond by strengthening in every way the friendship of the Soviet and Mongolian peoples, will be faithful to the obligations assumed under the Mutual Assistance Treaty concluded between the MPR and the USSR on March 12, 1936."[4]

In its resolution the government of the MPR and the Presidium of the MPRP Central Committee assured the government of the Soviet Union that the Mongolian people "are ready hand in hand with the Soviet people, to rise in defence of their freedom and independence, and to safeguard their gains." The Party and the MPR government called upon the *arats*, industrial and office workers, and intellectuals of the MPR to rally still more closely around their people's government and the People's Revolutionary Party, and by increasing labour productivity and the quality of the work done "steadfastly to consolidate the economic and defence might" of its homeland.

In reply to this appeal a mighty wave of meetings and gatherings of working people of Mongolia swept the country, expressing the warmest sympathy for their great friend, the Soviet people and their Army and assuring them of their readiness to help with all their strength in the fight with the common enemy. The Mongolian people, at the call of the MPRP, joined the united anti-fascist front of the struggle.

In a telegram sent on June 25, 1941, by the MPR government to the Soviet government it was stated: "the gains won by the Great October Socialist Revolution are as dear to us as the gains won by our own national-democratic revolution. Our people are ready, hand in hand with the Soviet people, to stand staunchly in defence of the sacred frontiers of the great socialist power, the homeland of the working people." One of the basic tasks of the MPR now was the task of extending all possible assistance to the people of the Soviet Union valiantly fighting fascist Germany, victory over whom constituted the guarantee of the further free and successful development of the MPR.

At a Plenary Meeting of the MPR Central Committee held in November 1941 an important decision was adopted "on utilizing the local resources of the MPR and increasing the output of consumer goods and commodities," on the basis of which the Twenty-fifth Session of the Little Hural (January 1942) outlined a series of concrete measures. On the basis of the decisions of the Plenary Meeting and the Session a start was made on reorganizing the whole national economy and subordinating it to the task of giving every possible help to the peoples of the Soviet Union and strengthening the defence capacity of their own country.

The tasks of increasing the head of livestock and the greatest possible collection and procurement of wool continued to be important and decisive tasks. Besides this, it was necessary to achieve a serious advance in the development of industry, especially industry producing consumer goods.

From the very first days of the Great Patriotic war of the USSR there was a wide expansion all over the country of collections of funds for assisting and sending gifts to Soviet soldiers. By the time the 24th anniversary of the Great October Socialist Revolution came round tens of thousands of sheepskin coats, felt boots, fur-lined gloves and other necessary items had been sent to the front as gifts to soldiers and officers of the Soviet Army.

In conformity with war-time conditions and the organisation of help to the USSR, Patriotic War fronts against the fascist agressors, the November 1941 Plenary Meeting of the MPRP Central Committee and the Twenty-fifth Session of the Little Hural drew attention to the need for increasing in every possible way the head of livestock, making wide use of the country's internal resources, especially in the output of livestock produce, strengthening the country's defences and increasing help to the Soviet Army. One of the important indices of the development of livestock-breeding in the country was the increase in the number of young animals born and reared. During the period of 1940-1941, for instance, the number of young animals born and reared rose on the average from 54 to 62 per 100 dams. In the case of particular types of livestock the success was even more marked. Whereas in 1940 the number of young sheep born and reared per 100 sheep amounted to 56, in 1944 this figure rose to 67; the figures were 55.5 to 64 in the case of cattle, 43 to 54 in the case of horses. Progressive *aimaks*, *somons* and individual *arat* farms achieved even bigger successes.

A summer drought in 1944 and a particularly frosty and blizzard-swept winter created unfavourable conditions over a large part of the MPR's territory for its agriculture and primarily for stock-breeding.

In order to avert loss of livestock on a mass scale the MPRP Central Committee and the people's government carried out a number of measures: they arranged for the *arats* and their livestock to be shifted to areas with more favourable conditions, to clear away snow from pastures and also to issue free, at the expense of state funds, fodder for livestock and provisions for *arat* victims and their families, to supply medicinal and veterinary help free of charge and help in the restoration and erection of livestock premises, etc.

These measures by the MPRP and the MPR government, organized in the winter of 1944-1945 to help *arat* herdsmen who were in trouble because of a dearth of fodder, enabled the *arats* to maintain the basic numbers of their herds and in subsequent years to create conditions for the normal development of the stock-breeding industry.

During this period much attention was paid by the Party and government to improving the use made of the products of stock-breeding and increasing its profitability. Milk, which had formerly been consumed by the *arat* farmers themselves, now went largely into manufactured products. Between 1940 and 1944 the volume of products made from milk increased more than five times and hundreds of tons of butter and other dairy products began to be made from it.

In 1941 the first 85 creameries were built in the MPR and thereafter their number increased year by year until by the end of 1943 their output not only covered the country's requirements in animal fat but even made it possible to export a certain quantity of butter abroad.

In 1942 the Ministry for the Food Industry was created. Starting in 1941 there was an increase in the procurement of meat, and especially of wool, leather and furs, the production of butter, fats and other products of stock-breeding and also in the yield of fisheries. In 1942 the collection and procurement of wool in the MPR was more than $2^1/_2$ times higher than in 1940 and this had a favourable effect by increasing the profitability of *arat* farming.

In pursuing a policy of consolidating the country's food-supply base and thereby solving the problem of mobilizing internal resources, the Party and the government set the *arat* farms and the state farms the task of developing agriculture.

As a result the areas of the Republic under cultivation in 1942 rose to nearly 70,000 hectares, as against 27,000 hectares in 1941. In 1942 about 40,000 tons of grain crops and 6,000 tons of vegetables were harvested in the MPR. By 1945 the area under vegetables was icnreased considerably and the yield quadrupled as compared with 1941.

The state and co-operative industry of the MPR expanded the output of consumer goods and of products needed by the front.

Operating on local raw materials, industry, from 1941 onwards, not only manufactured large quantities of industrial goods which were formerly imported from the USSR but it even started producing items which were needed by the front.

Existing industrial capacities and transport concerns were enlarged and new ones built. The Soviet Union, notwithstanding difficult war-time conditions, continued to help the MPR in developing industry, transport, agriculture and culture.

Capital investments in industry during the period of 1941-1944 amounted to more than 100 million *tugriks*. The value of the MPR's industrial output during the war rose from 91.5 million *tugriks* in 1941 to 141.2 million *tugriks* in 1944, i. e. during those years it increased by more than 54%. The number of workers in industry rose during the same period by almost 30%.

Thanks to the successful growth of industry in the country it was possible in 1942 to create certain reserves of goods and foodstuffs.

The successful growth achieved in stock-breeding, industry and other branches of the economy during this period was made possible primarily because the overwhelming majority of working people in the MPR—*arats*, industrial and office workers and intellectuals—laboured honestly and conscientiously, increasing labour productivity, consolidating labour discipline and seeking to fulfil the national economic plan.

The second republican conference of leading cattle-breeders, which was held in November 1943, and the first republican conference of shock-workers in state industry, cottage industry co-operatives and transport in the MPR, convened at the beginning of May 1943, summed up the results of the experience of leading *arat* farms, *bags*, *somons* and *aimaks* in agriculture and the experience in industry and transport of the best shock-workers and intellectuals qualified in production techniques.

Responding to the appeal of the Twenty-fifth Session of the Little Hural, the Mongolian people extended still more widely the collection of funds and gifts to help the front.

The gifts were produced in factories and works, in the workshops of domestic craft industry co-operatives, on state farms, in *arat* encampments and in schools. All the working people in the country, from the lowest to the highest, helped collect for the Soviet Army Aid Fund, contributions to which comprised money, gold and silver articles, warm clothing, foodstuffs, etc. The movement for organizing every kind of help for the front embraced the whole country. At its head was the young working class of the MPR. At assemblies and meetings held in enterprises engineers and technicians undertook to produce goods beyond the target set by the state plan, to organize assistance in money for soldiers of the Soviet Army and to collect warm clothing as gifts for frontline soldiers fighting heroically against the fascists. Workers in the industrial combine were among the leaders in the organisation of aid for the Soviet Army and in fighting for fulfilment of the state plan. For the self-sacrificing and honest work accomplished and for over-fulfilling state targets the MPR government in 1942 conferred the Order of the Red Banner of Labour on the industrial combine.

A patriotic movement in support of a new labour upsurge developed also among the Nalaikha miners, the workers in domestic craft industry, the Khatkhil wool-washing works, the state printing works and other enterprises in the country. All the country's workers exerted themselves to the utmost under the slogan "Everything for the front, everything for victory."

In the country's enterprises there arose a wave of revolutionary emulation, a powerful stimulus to increased labour productivity, better labour discipline and greater industrial production. In its leading article the newspaper *Unen* ("Truth") wrote that every industrial and office worker should clearly know that he was bound today to produce during working hours as much as possible, "not putting off till tomorrow what could be done today." As a result of this campaign there were numerous cases in enterprises of people working three or four times harder and producing per day 300% and even up to 600%, of the day's quota.

Many of the workers in the industrial combine and the cottage industry co-operative in the city of Ulan Bator regularly overfulfilled their monthly and quarterly targets by 300-500%. Ts. Tsembel, a woman shock-worker in the shoe factory of the industrial combine, G. Dolzhin, a woman worker in the cottage industry co-operative of Ulan Bator, O. Gunchin, a military worker, and many other leading workers overfulfilled annual plans by 500-1,000%. As a result of all this the output of state industry in 1945 was twice as much as in 1940 and now accounted for 30% of the domestic good turnover. Whereas at the beginning of the war (1941) the share of the gross output of all state industry amounted to 60.9%, by the end of the war it amounted to 77%.

Up to March 1943, i.e. in 20 months of the Patriotic War eight troop-trains laden with gifts had already been despatched to the front, including 60,000 personal gifts to soldiers and officers of the Soviet Army. The train-loads of gifts despatched in 1942 by the Mongolian people were escorted by four groups of delegations.

On their return from the USSR the delegates told the Mongolian people about the heroic fight of the Soviet Army and all the Soviet people on the front and of the selfless work being done in the rear for victory over the fascist aggressors, of the unforgettable meetings the MPR delegates had had with soldiers and officers of the Soviet Army, with Soviet workers and with leading figures of the Soviet Union.

Simultaneously with the collection of funds for gifts to the front, purchases of horses and livestock were made in the country for the needs of the front. Over the war years Mongolian stock-breeders sold the Red Army more than 480,000 horses and donated more than 30,000 of their finest horses.[5]

The workers of the MPR collected large amounts for the purchase of a tank column "Revolutionary Mongolia", which on January 12, 1943, was handed over, along with individual gifts, to the Soviet Army by a delegation of the Mongolian people. In the same year, on a decision taken by the Twenty-sixth Session of the Little Hural, an air squadron, "Mongolian Arat", was purchased out of funds voluntarily contributed by enterprises, departments and individual workers of the MPR and handed over to the USSR Air Force.

During the war years the Mongolian people collected and sent to the Red Army gifts to the value of 65 million *tugriks* and undertook to maintain the personnel of the tank brigade and the air squadron until the end of the war. Moreover, considerable funds were collected to help in the restoration of property in Soviet areas liberated from German occupation.

Every victory won by the Soviet army on the Great Patriotic War front aroused great joy among the Mongolian people and still further intensified the endeavours of all the workers of Mongolia to give help to the front in order to achieve the speediest possible defeat of the enemy. The MPRP and MPR people's government, in the difficult war-time conditions, by their organizational and political work increased the political activity of the great mass of the working people so that they extended all possible help to the front. At the same time the MPR strengthened in every possible way its own armed forces which were protecting the frontiers of the Republic from the threat of attack by Japanese imperialists. The numerical strength of the People's Army was increased 3-4 times. With the Soviet Union's help it was continually being supplied with the most up-to-date and modern equipment and weapons. The tank and motorized troops, the artillery and air force were reinforced.

New military academies and training courses were organized to give instruction in the latest technical methods. During the Second World War the military school where ordinary army officers were trained was expanded. In 1943 the "Sukhe Bator" officers' school was opened for the training of junior officers. As a result of the improved military-political training given in the army military discipline was strengthened. In view of this a resolution of the MPRP Central Committee and the MPR Council of Ministers, passed in June 1943, abolished the posts of army commissars who ranked equally with officers, and complete unity of command was introduced. The soldiers and officers of the Mongolian People's Revolutionary Army made a close study of the fighting experience gained by Soviet troops and of such military operations as the battle on the Volga which is an example of the military art of surrounding, breaching defences, outflanking, encircling and destroying an enemy. Under a resolution of the MPRP Central Committee and the Council of Ministers adopted on March 16, 1943, men called up had to report for active military service with their own horses.[6]

In 1944 the Presidium of the Little Hural adopted a resolution re-naming the commanding and senior personnel of the Mongolian People's Revolutionary Army as officer personnel, instituting personal military ranks and new distinguishing badges. Simultaneously, the senior ranks of the officer personnel were re-registered and a new compulsory military service law was adopted (September 20, 1944). Under the new law "all men, citizens of the MPR, without distinction of nationality, religion, education, social origin or status are obliged to do military service in the armed forces." During the war years state loans amounting to 80 million *tugriks* were issued for the defence of the country. The best Party and state executives were sent into the ranks of the Mongolian People's Revolutionary Army to act as political workers. The growth in political consciousness and sense of international duty is shown by the fact that a large number of applications were received from officers and men of the Mongolian People's Revolutionary Army asking to be sent to the Soviet front to fight fascism.

Under a decision of the Party and government detachments of people's militia were created in the spring of 1942 and played a great role in giving the population military training.

All these and other measures ensured the further consolidation of the international and internal position of the MPR and aroused a powerful upsurge of patriotism in the country. Following a series of major decisive victories won by the Soviet troops over the fascist army and the armies of its satellites, the international situation in Europe underwent a radical change in 1944. The fascist aggressors began to be driven out *en masse* beyond the confines of the Soviet Union.

In pursuit of the enemy the Soviet troops marched into the territory of the countries occupied by Hitler's troops—Poland, Romania, Bulgaria, Finland, Norway, Hungary, Yugoslavia and Czechoslovakia—in order to liberate the peoples of these countries from the nazi aggressors. The military and political alliance of fascist Germany and its satellites was decisively defeated.

The victory of the Soviet armed forces encouraged the growth and consolidation of the anti-fascist people's movement and anti-fascist coalition. On being liberated, Romania, Bulgaria and then Hungary broke off their links with Germány and entered the war against her on the side of the Soviet Union. The struggle of the peoples of the countries seized by the nazis against the "new order" in Europe began. The victory of the Soviet troops made the allies, the USA and Great Britain, open a second front in Western Europe in June 1944.

In the countries liberated by Soviet troops—Bulgaria, Poland and Romania—people's democratic governments were formed and all pro-fascist organizations and institutions dissolved. In the spring of 1945 the Soviet army dealt a blow that finished off fascist Germany and her armed forces. The German troops covering Berlin were surrounded by the troops of three fronts of the Soviet army. On the morning of May 1, Berlin, the capital of Hitlerite Germany, was occupied by Soviet troops and the Banner of Victory fluttered over the Reichstag.

On May 2, 1945, the Berlin garrison capitulated and on May 8 a representative of the German command signed the instrument of unconditional surrender of Germany. The Mongolian people with great joy celebrated, along with the Soviet people, May 9, 1945, as the day of victory over fascist Germany.

At a meeting of the workers of Ulan Bator on the occasion of the Day of Victory over fascist Germany, Comrade Yu. Tsedenbal, Secretary-General of the MPRP Central Committee, said: "The whole progressive world, including our Mongolian people, is immeasurably delighted with the full and complete victory of the Soviet people over the German fascists. Who, if not we, who, if not the Mongolian people, should rejoice on this great and solemn day."[7]

Such meetings went on all over the country.

The MPR's Part in the Defeat of the Armed Forces of Imperialist Japan

In February 1945 a conference of the leaders of the three Allied Powers, the USSR, the USA, and Great Britain was held in Yalta, in the Crimea. The three Powers agreed to liquidate German militarism, nazism and all fascist organisations and institutions in order that Germany might never more disturb peace all over the world. For the maintenance of peace and security the Allies decided to set up an international organisation—the United Nations. Another question also discussed at the conference was that of the Soviet Union entering the war against imperialist Japan two or three months after the surrender of Germany.

On the proposal of the Soviet delegation the representatives of the USA and the United Kingdom at the Crimea conference agreed to maintain the status quo of the Mongolian People's Republic after the Second World War. In so doing the USA and the United Kingdom in actual fact acknowledged the independence of the MPR which was the result of the outstanding victory won by the Soviet armed forces, the result of the Mongolian people's fight for independence and the consolidation of the people's democracy. With the surrender of fascist Germany the war in Europe ended. The fascist "new order" was destroyed but, as a whole, the Second World War still continued. Imperialist Japan—the ally of fascist Germany in the Second World War—continued the war in the Far East against the allied nations. The demand by the three Powers—the USA, the United Kingdom and China—made on July 26, 1945, for Japan's unconditional surrender was rejected by the Japanese government. Urgent and decisive measures had to be taken to put an end to the Second World War and to liberate the peoples of the Far East who had been enslaved by Japanese imperialism.

Relations between the USSR and Japan were governed by the Neutrality Pact which had been concluded by them on April 13, 1941, i.e., before Germany attacked the USSR and before the beginning of the war between Japan, on the one hand, and the USA and Great Britain, on the other. After fascist Germany had perfidiously attacked the USSR, Japan not only did not observe neutrality in the war begun between the USSR and Germany but, on the contrary, followed a policy hostile to the Soviet Union and gave every kind of help to the German fascists. Japan concentrated in North-Eastern China (Manchuria) a very large army. This army, which had been brought up to more than one million men and was armed with more than 5,000 guns, 1,000 tanks and up to 1,500 aircraft, plus a detachment of several thousand police, gendarmerie and troops of the puppet government of Manchukuo,[8] was stationed, fully prepared for battle, on the frontiers of the USSR and MPR. There were numerous instances of Soviet vessels being fired upon, sunk and illegally detained and of the state frontiers of the USSR and the MPR being violated. Furthermore, at the court proceedings held in Khabarovsk (1949) in the case of former members of the Japanese army it was established that the Japanese military clique was preparing to wage bacteriological warfare against the USSR and the MPR. Special bacteriological detachments and formations were being created in the Kwantung army located in Manchuria, a plan had been worked out for attacking the USSR and the MPR, large quantities of bacteriological weapons had been manufactured, experiments carried out in their use, and special bacteria and viruses for utilisation against the population of the USSR and the MPR were being cultivated in the factories.[9]

An expedition was mounted to organize a bacteriological diversion against the MPR. Even just before the complete collapse of Hitlerite Germany in the spring of 1945, Japan did not change its hostile policy towards the Soviet Union and the MPR. The Soviet government, considering that "in such a situation the Neutrality Pact had lost its meaning and continuation of this Pact had become impossible", denounced it (notified its intention to disown it) on April 5, 1945.

When Germany surrendered Japan made a formal "protest" in reply and, demonstratively breaking the military and other treaties with Germany, continued to wage war in the Pacific Ocean.

In the obvious desire to gain time for regrouping its forces and hoping for difference of view to arise among the members of the anti-fascist coalition, Japan in July 1945 hypocritically asked the USSR Government to act as an intermediary in peace negotiations with the USA and Great Britain. The Soviet government brought this to the notice of the representatives of the USA and Great Britain at the Berlin conference of the Three Powers which was being held at the time.

On July 27 in Potsdam a declaration was published on behalf of the USA, the United Kingdom and China in which the Allies proposed that Japan declare her unconditional surrender and warned her of the consequences of refusal. The government of Japan paid no attention to this proposal, thereby indicating her intention to continue the war.

On August 8, 1945, the government of the Soviet Union notified the government of Japan that the USSR associated itself with the Allied Powers' declaration of July 27 of that year and that, as from August 9, i.e. the following day, the Soviet Union would regard itself as in a state of war with Japan.

The decision of the Soviet Union was very strongly endorsed not only by the people of the USSR but also by the working people of the whole world, including Mongolian people.

In an expression of the thoughts and desires of the masses of the people the Little Hural and the MPR government issued a declaration on August 10, 1945, in which it was announced "that the Little Hural and the government of the MPR, faithful to their undertakings under the Treaty of Mutual Assistance between the MPR and the USSR, concluded on March 12, 1936, inspired by the single desire of the democratic states and freedom-loving people of the world to achieve universal peace more speedily, and also in order to make their contribution to the cause of the United Nations," declared war against Japan, fully associating themselves with the declaration of the Soviet government made on August 8, 1945, in Moscow.

On the same day the Prime Minister of MPR, Kh. Choibalsan, addressed the whole population of the MPR by radio. In this address mention was made of the decision adopted by the Government to declare war on Japan and of the reasons which had led the Government to take this decision. In his address to the soldiers, sergeants, officers and generals of the Mongolian People's Revolutionary Army, Kh. Choibalsan summoned them to display courage, bravery and heroism in a war for a just cause, for their people and their native land.

The Soviet Army's military operations against the Japanese troops were commanded by Marshal of the Soviet Union Vasilevsky and developed simultaneously along an immense front of more than 4,000 kilometres. Taking part in the fighting were the troops of the Transbaikal and the 1st and 2nd Far East Fronts, as well as the river, naval and air armed forces of the USSR in the Far East. The troops of the Mongolian People's Revolutionary Army, under the command of Marshal Choibalsan, conducted operations in close co-operation with the troops of the Transbaikal front.

During their rule in North-Eastern China the Japanese had set up a network of military communications, dozens of large aerodromes and a number of fortified regions equipped with the most up-to-date fortification devices. All the natural resources of the country were utilized for military purposes. The finest armed forces of Japan were concentrated in North-Eastern China.

Notwithstanding all this, the heroic troops of the Soviet Army moved into attack on August 9, 1945, breached the enemy's defence lines and in a short time routed the famous Kwantung Army and the other armed forces of the Japanese aggressors.

The conditions during the advance of the Soviet Army were extraordinarily difficult. They had to break through a defence that had been long prepared and was set up in great depth, force their way across mountain ranges covered with impenetrable forests which, for instance, were as wide as 200-300 kilometres on the Great Khingan mountains. The enemy troops resisted desperately and used the most perfidious fighting tricks, poisoning water in wells and setting fire to the steppe grass but nothing could halt the powerful pressure of the advancing Soviet troops. The Mongolian army, acting in cooperation with the troops of the Soviet army, began an advance in the direction of Dolonnor-Kalgan in order to reach Liaotung Bay.

Overcoming the great difficulties of crossing over the Gobi desert, the Mongolian army dealt a series of blows to the enemy's fortified points; it liberated the town of Dolonnor and continued its advance southwards to Liaotung Bay.

The Mongolian troops displayed ability and skill in changing over from operations in one set of conditions to fighting in a completely different situation. For example, Mongolian cavalry units, when advancing in joint operations with light tanks and armoured cars and moving from the flat plains into mountain regions where it is particularly important to employ the flexible tactics of small groups and fight for individual roads, etc., exhibited their complete ability to solve problems on new and complicated terrain. Units of the Mongolian People's Revolutionary Army, too, tackled similar difficulties on the approaches to the town of Jehol.

A heroic raid carried out by units of the Mongolian People's Revolutionary Army in the direction of Liaotung Bay once again displayed the great skill and tactical training of that army, and the gallantry and boldness of its officers and men and proved the Mongolian People's Revolutionary Army to be a worthy comrade-in-arms of its fighting friend, the Soviet Army.

A great part in the defeat of imperialist Japan was played by the 8th and the New 4th revolutionary armies of China and by partisan detachments which were commanded by the Communist Party of China.

The population of North-East China, Inner Mongolia, and Barga which had been ruined and reduced to poverty under the Japanese colonial yoke, greeted with the greatest delight the liberating Soviet Army, and its allies, the MPR troops.

On August 10, 1945, i.e. on the second day of the victorious advance of the Soviet Army deep into North-East China the Japanese government announced to the USSR and the Allied Powers that it was prepared to accept the conditions of July 26. But it gave no order to its troops to cease military operations. On the contrary, the counter-attacks of Japanese troops in North-East China were intensified.

On August 14 the Japanese government announced its acceptance of the conditions of the Potsdam Declaration and its readiness to execute all the orders of the Allied Command. But even after this notification of surrender the resistance of the enemy continued. It was only after the Soviet Army had dealt the Japanese troops a series of further shattering blows that the Japanese command was forced on August 23 to cease resistance and lay down arms.

During the period from August 9 to 23 the Soviet Army, in a headlong rout of the troops of the Japanese aggressors, liberated the whole of North-East China, South Sakhalin and the islands of Syumusyu and Paramushir in the Kurile Islands group. In these battles the Japanese aggressors suffered over 80,000 men casualties—killed and wounded. The Soviet and Mongolian armies captured more than 594,000 Japanese officers and men and enormous quantities of spoils of war were also seized.

On September 2, 1945, the representatives of Japan, as in the case of nazi Germany, signed an act of unconditional surrender. With the surrender of imperialist Japan the Second World War came to an end and peace was established in the Far East. By defeating Germany the Soviet Union saved European civilization and saved the peoples of Europe from enslavement by the German fascist aggressors; by dealing a decisive blow to Japanese imperialism, a blow which reduced Japan to complete surrender, the Soviet Union saved the peoples of Asia from the danger of becoming enslaved. The Soviet Union's victory in the Second World War is of universal historical importance. It is, above all, the victory of socialism and of democratic forces over the forces of reaction. The victory of the Soviet Union radically changed the international situation and the balance of forces in the world arena. A mighty world socialist system of society, confronting the capitalist system, took shape.

The MPR made its own contribution to the fight against German fascism and Japanese imperialism and helped the peoples of China and Inner Mongolia to free themselves from the oppression of Japanese imperialism. At an internationally difficult moment the MPRP and the MPR government successfully mobilized all the resources of the Mongolian people for the country's defence, for the fight against imperialist aggressors, for extending assistance to the heroic Soviet Army and bringing to light and making use of the country's internal resources. The threat of imperialist intervention and the war against the fascist aggressors impeded the development of the productive forces, and the country's economy and culture. The war diverted great material resources, strength and time from the tasks of socialist construction in the country. During the period of 1935-1945 Japanese imperialists and their agents, as documentary evidence shows, violated the frontiers of the MPR more than 500 times for the purposes of sabotage and provocation. Thousands of Mongolian Army soldiers died the death of the brave in the struggle with Japanese aggressors fighting for the freedom and independence of their native land. The material damage done to the Mongolian people and their state by the Japanese imperialists during this time is estimated to amount to hundreds of millions of *tugriks*.

In a speech made at a meeting of *arat* workers and army units of Ulan Bator on September 3, 1945, the Secretary-General of the MPRP Central Committee, Yu. Tsedenbal, remarked that the Mongolian people had succeeded in defending their independence and taken part in eliminating this last aggressor, thus making their own contribution to the great cause of the struggle of the peoples against the enemies of peace and freedom.

In a telegram to the Soviet government adopted at this meeting the workers of the MPR wrote: "We have devoted all our strength and abilities to the welfare of our independent homeland, to the further consolidation of fraternal friendship between the Soviet and Mongolian peoples, a friendship which has stood up to all the trials endured during the present war and has been still further reinforced in the joint struggle with our common enemy."

The government of the Soviet Union had a high appreciation of the fighting services rendered by the Mongolian People's Revolutionary Army. In an order of August 23, 1945, on the occasion of the final victory won over Japan, the Supreme Commander-in Chief of the Soviet armed forces mentioned, side by side with the heroic troops of the Soviet Army, the units of the Mongolian army which had distinguished themselves in battle. For their skilful handling of military operations by the troops of the Mongolian People's Revolutionary Army in the fight against the common enemy, imperialist Japan and for the gallantry and bravery displayed therein the Presidium of the Supreme Soviet of the USSR in September 1945 awarded the Order of Suvorov, first grade, to Marshal Kh. Choibalsan, the Order of Kutuzov, first grade, to Lieut.-General Yu. Tsedenbal, the Order of Suvorov, second grade, to Lieut.-General Lkhagvasuren, and other USSR orders to a further twenty distinguished generals and officers of the MPRA, among them Major-Generals Damdinkha and Erendo, and Colonel Nyantaisuren.

Under a resolution of the Presidium of the Little Hural of of the MPR the title of Hero of the MPR was awarded to Sengiyn Dampil, machine-gunner of an armoured brigade, and to Danzan-Vanchig, a mortar-man. The title of Hero of the MPR was posthumously awarded to scout Luvsantserengiyn Ayushi who, fighting until his last round when surrounded by the enemy, destroyed a considerable number of enemy soldiers and fell in hand-to-hand fighting. About two thousand men who took part in the battles against Japan were awarded military orders and medals of the MPR.

CHAPTER II

MPR's TRANSITION TO PEACEFUL PLANNED
ECONOMIC DEVELOPMENT (1946-1952)

*Consolidation of the International Status
of the MPR in the Post-War Years*

As a result of the victorious completion by the Soviet Union of the Second World War the balance of forces in the world arena changed over in favour of democracy and socialism. The aggressor states, Germany, Italy and Japan, suffered defeat, while Great Britain and France emerged from the war considerably weakened. True, the USA, the strongest capitalist state in the world emerged from the war much strengthened economically and militarily, but the world capitalist system as a whole was rocked to its foundations. Democracy and socialism had won a victory. The second stage in the general crisis of capitalism had begun.

The Soviet Union, which had proved to be the decisive force in defeating fascist Germany and imperialist Japan, which had suffered immense material and human losses, came out of the war greatly strengthened; its might and international authority had increased. The attraction of socialism for the working people of the world was increasing. Favourable conditions arose for the development of democracy and socialism. The people of Czechoslovakia, Poland, Hungary, Romania, Bulgaria, Yugoslavia and Albania, liberated with the Soviet Army's help from fascist enslavement, under the leadership of their own communist and workers' parties overthrew the rule of landowners and capitalists.

After setting up a people's democratic system, the workers of these countries set about socialist construction. In October 1949 the German Democratic Republic was proclaimed. The emergence of the GDR in the middle of Europe constituted an important event in international life. The people's governments formed in these countries carried out democratic changes; the peoples obtained democratic rights and freedoms; as a result of the implementation of land reforms the peasants received land, the landlords' ownership of the land was abolished, reactionary forces were routed in an intensive class war.

Simultaneously the colonial system of imperialism was in a state of disintegration. As a result of the defeat of fascism and Japanese militarism and the general crisis of imperialism the national-liberation movement of colonial and semi-colonial peoples and of dependent countries grew apace. Important events occurred in Asia. The long-drawn out heroic struggle of the Chinese people against foreign imperialists and internal reaction ended in final victory. Under the leadership of the Communist Party the Chinese people overthrew the Kuomintang government and took power into their own hands. On October 1, 1949, the Chinese People's Republic, a state of workers and peasants, was proclaimed.

A number of new independent states emerged in Asia. In 1945, as a result of the stubborn and protracted liberation struggle of the Vietnamese people against the French colonisers in Indo-China, the Democratic Republic of Vietnam was formed. In North Korea, after its liberation by the Soviet army, the Korean People's Democratic Republic was proclaimed. The peoples of these countries took the path of socialist construction. Independence was proclaimed in the Indonesian Republic, Burma, India and Pakistan. The peoples of Ceylon and Cambodia won independence. The whole continent of Africa was swept up in a movement for national liberation. Two opposing systems, socialist and capitalist, were formed in the world arena. On the one side, there was the capitalist system headed by the USA, having as its basic objectives the establishment of world supremacy under the aegis of American imperialism and the destruction of democracy, and on the other side, the socialist system, headed by the Soviet Union with the basic aims of strengthening democracy and ensuring security and co-operation between the peoples, in the cause of peace, democracy and socialism.

These great events, and also the successes of the Mongolian people in building up a people's democracy were the basic factors in strengthening the MPR's international status in the post-war years.

The Soviet Union, the liberator and best friend of the Mongolian people, invariably defended the interests of the MPR.

Following negotiations held in August 1945 in Moscow between the Soviet Union and Kuomintang government of China, the latter agreed to acknowledge the Mongolian People's Republic as a sovereign and independent state within its existing frontiers, if a plebiscite confirmed the desire of the Mongolian people to retain their independence.

The declaration of the Kuomintang government of China recognising the independence of the MPR on condition that it was confirmed by a plebiscite represented a forced and belated acknowledgement of a *fait accompli*, especially since the *status quo* of Outer Mongolia—the MPR—i.e. its *de facto* status as a state independent of China, had been confirmed by the Crimea Conference of the Heads of the three Great Powers, the USSR, the USA and Great Britain. The demand by the Kuomintang government for a plebiscite to be held in the MPR was clear evidence of the insincerity of the Kuomintang rulers and of a desire to make still another attempt to drag out formal recognition by them of the MPR's independence. In addition, the Kuomintang government of China wished to make it appear that it was making a present of independence to the MPR, an independence which had really been won by the Mongolian people in struggle against the foreign aggressors. Nevertheless, the declaration of the representative of the Kuomintang government of China made in the note had a definite significance.

Having fallen under the rule of the Manchu dynasty and lost their independence several centuries back, the Mongolian people dreamt of the time when they would again become free and independent. It was only after the victory of the Great October Socialist Revolution in Russia and with the fraternal and unselfish assistance of the Soviet people that the Mongolian people's fight for freedom and independence was crowned with success.

On September 21, 1945, the Presidium of the Little Hural of the MPR, in conformity with the content of the agreement concluded by representatives of the governments of the USSR and China through an exchange of notes on August 14, 1945, concerning the independence of the MPR, resolved that a vote by all the people—a plebiscite—must be taken throughout the republic simultaneously on October 20.

The Presidium of the Little Hural resolved that all citizens of the MPR holding the franchise should take part in the plebiscite by voting on lists drawn up by local government bodies.

The plebiscite proved a striking demonstration of the unity, lofty patriotism and political consciousness of the masses of the MPR. More than thirteen thousand meetings and gatherings were held throughout the country which were attended by hundreds of thousands of people—*arat* herdsmen, workers and intellectuals.

In their speeches and resolutions the people taking part in all these meetings and gatherings referred in immensely patriotic terms to the achievements of the MPR, declared their loyalty to the MPRP and the MPR government and voiced their complete unanimity in voting for the independence of their native land.

The Central Commission for holding the plebiscite received 1,525 letters and declarations as well as 83,789 greetings, messages and wishes assuring it of people's readiness to cast their votes and, if need be, give their lives, for the state independence of the MPR.

October 20, 1945, the day of the plebiscite, became a national holiday, a triumph for democracy and the independence of the MPR. At many of the polling stations there were spontaneous demonstrations. People arrived carrying slogans, banners and portraits of the leader of the Mongolian people, Sukhe Bator. In the centre of the *aimak* Bayan-Khongor, to celebrate plebiscite day, voters erected an obelisk called the "State Independence Column."

In favour of state independence for the Mongolian People's Republic 487,409 votes were cast, i.e. 100% of all the citizens of the country who took part in the plebiscite. Not one single vote was cast against.

In pointing this out the Central Commission, in its formal report "On the result of the plebiscite held on the question of the independence of the MPR," drew the conclusion that "the plebiscite fully confirmed the desire of the people of the Mongolian People's Republic for an independent state existence which must be accepted by the Chinese Republic in accordance with the Chinese government's declaration of August 14, 1945."

By a decision of the Presidium of the Little Hural, the Central Commission's report was published and on November 10, 1945, it was forwarded to the governments of the Soviet Union and the Chinese Republic.

While the plebiscite was being held plenipotentiaries of the government of the Chinese Republic were present in the Mongolian People's Republic to observe the course of the plebiscite.

On January 5, 1946 the Kuomintang government of China, having been informed of the results of the voting, was obliged to recognize the independence of the Mongolian People's Republic.

On February 13, 1946, diplomatic relations were established between the Mongolian People's Republic and the Chinese Republic. Although the Chinese government had recognized the independence of the Mongolian People's Republic and established diplomatic relations with it, reactionary right-wing circles of Kuomintang China continued, by acts of armed aggression, to violate the state frontier of the MPR in the region of Baitag-bogdo in the south-west of the country. It was only after the triumph of the people's revolution in China in 1949 and the overthrow of the reactionary Kuomintang government that friendly and good-neighbourly relations were first established between the Mongolian and Chinese peoples.

On October 6, 1949, the government of the Mongolian People's Republic recognised the Chinese People's Republic.

On February 15, 1950, a Treaty of Friendship, Alliance and Mutual Assistance was concluded between the Soviet Union and the Chinese People's Republic.

In a Soviet-Chinese communiqué published on the signing of the Treaty and of Agreements between the Soviet Union and the Chinese People's Republic it was stated that in this connection the representatives of the governments of both countries had exchanged notes in which, as stated in the communiqué mentioned, "...both governments take note that the independent status of the Mongolian People's Republic has been fully ensured as a result of the referendum held in 1945 and the establishment of diplomatic re lations with the Chinese People's Republic."

The achievement by the Mongolian people of their state independence is the result not only of their many centuries [1] struggle for their own liberation but also of the intensive labour of the Mongolian people during the years of building up the Mongolian People's Republic. It is also due to the friendly and selfless assistance given to the Mongolian people by the great country of socialism—the Soviet Union.

When the validity of the Soviet-Mongolian Protocol of 1936 on friendship and mutual assistance expired, on February 27, 1946 the Protocol was converted into a ten-year Treaty of Friendship and Mutual Assistance. At the same time an Agreement was signed on economic and cultural co-operation. These documents were immensely important for the further consolidation of the friendship of the peoples of the Soviet Union and the MPR and for guaranteeing peace in the Far East.

In its telegram to the MPR government on the occasion of the anniversary of the signing of the Treaty and Agreement on Economic and Cultural Co-operation between the MPR and the USSR the Soviet government wrote: "these historic instruments constitute a valuable contribution to the cause of peace and security in the Far East and serve as a sound foundation for the further development of mutual friendly relations between our countries."

The Mongolian people, having extended moral and material support to the heroic Korean people in their struggle against the American interventionists and to the struggle of the workers of Vietnam against the French colonialists, reinforced still further the friendship and co-operation with the Korean People's Democratic Republic and the Democratic Republic of Vietnam. Between 1948 and 1950 the MPR established diplomatic relations with the Korean People's Democratic Republic, the German Democratic Republic, the People's Republic of Poland, the Bulgarian People's Republic, the People's Republic of Czechoslovakia, the Hungarian People's Republic and the Romanian People's Republic.

Under the leadership of the Communist Party the Soviet Union in an incredibly short space of time, unthinkable in capitalist countries, not only restored areas of the country which had suffered from the war but even exceeded the pre-war level of development of industry and agriculture. The powerful socialist economy of the Soviet Union is the firm economic basis for all-round assistance to the countries of people's democracy and for co-operation with them.

The economic and political links between the USSR and the countries of the socialist camp, including the MPR, and also the links of these countries between themselves, constitute a new type of mutual relationships between peoples. Representing the complete opposite to the relations of capitalist countries, which are based on the policy of imperialist suppression of independence and enslavement of the peoples, relations inside the socialist camp are based on the full and genuine equality of rights of all the peoples, on recognition of the sovereignty of the state and the inadmissibility of interference in the internal affairs of each of them.

The peoples of the world and all peace-loving forces in all the countries who support the foreign policy of the Soviet state—the policy of peace and friendship between peoples—are united together in a wholehearted struggle to strengthen world peace.

Delegations of the Mongolian people, by taking an active part in the work of all the three world congresses of peace fighters and the congress of peace fighters of the countries of Asia and the Pacific Ocean, have participated and are participating in the work of the World Council of Peace, the Women's International Democratic Federation, the World Federation of Trade Unions, the World Federation of Democratic Youth and the International Union of Students and other international organisations.

The young people and the students of the MPR take an active part in international festivals. The representatives of the MPR, acting as spokesmen for their people at international congresses and conferences, stand up for the cause of friendship and cooperation between peoples.

The Mongolian people resolutely support the movement of peoples in favour of relaxing international tension and strengthening peace.

In April 1950 the Presidium of the Little Hural of the MPR adopted a Declaration expressing its agreement with an Appeal by the Standing Committee of the World Peace Congress.

"By the present Declaration the Presidium of the Little Hural of the MPR associates itself with the peace proposals of the Standing Committee for the ending of the arms race by cutting down military budgets and the number of military contingents, for an unconditional ban on atomic weapons, the cessation of interventionist wars in Indonesia, Malaya, Vietnam and the conclusion of a treaty of Friendship between the Big Powers, supports the proposal of international democratic organizations to combat the militarization of Japan and West Germany."

In October 1950, at the First All-Mongolian National Peace Congress a Mongolian Peace Committee was formed.

The whole of the adult population of the Mongolian People's Republic unanimously signed the Stockholm Appeal and the Appeal for the Conclusion of a Five Power Peace Pact.

On February 27, 1951, the Presidium of the Little Hural enacted a Law for the defence of peace which lays down a term of 10-25 years imprisonment for war propaganda, plus loss of civil rights and confiscation of property.

The MPR, by its peaceful policy, and its people, by their energetic fight for peace, earned the right to a legitimate place in the United Nations. In June 1946 the MPR government made an application to the United Nations. However, the forces of aggression, headed by the American imperialists, in disregard of the Charter of the UN and of international law, for 15 years maliciously obstructed the admission of the MPR into the United Nations. These actions of the ruling circles of the USA and certain other powers evidenced the profoundly reactionary and adventurist character of their foreign policy. The Mongolian people were firmly confident that the time would come when the intrigues of the reactionaries would fail and the MPR would occupy its lawful seat in the United Nations and this came about, thanks to the support of the USSR and other peace-loving countries, in 1961.

Waging an active fight for peace together with its friend, the USSR, and with all the countries of people's democracy and the peace-loving forces of the world, the MPR has been working for the establishment of lasting peace and friendship between the peoples.

The consolidation of the international status of the MPR and in particular the establishment of fraternal relations with the countries of the socialist camp, have helped to promote the rapid development of the country's economy and culture and a further consolidation of the people's-democratic system.

Transition to Peaceful Construction. First Five-Year Plan for Economic and Cultural Development

At the end of the Second World War all countries returned to peaceful reconstruction, and the MPR started work on the peaceful development of the national economy and on overcoming the consequences of the Second World War.

It is common knowledge that the MPR is a country which is proceeding from feudalism to socialism, by-passing capitalism. In the first general democratic stage of the revolution it successfully tackled the anti-feudal and anti-imperialist problems of the revolution. It was at this stage that the prerequisites for a future socialist society were basically created in the country. But the constant threat from imperialist Japan and the Second World War for a long period diverted the Mongolian people's attention from the problems of peaceful socialist construction. The need now was to switch the country's economy back on to the lines of peaceful construction by reorganizing the whole work of the Party, the state and the economy.

The country met with serious difficulties in following this path. The first difficulty lay in the fact that the Second World War had done great economic damage. In the war against Japan alone, in 1945, the national economy of the MPR suffered losses amounting to more than 200 million *tugriks.* Many economic, cultural and organizational problems raised by the decisions of the Tenth MPRP Congress and the Eighth Grand People's Hural, which should have been dealt with at the beginning of the 1940s, had been deferred indefinitely. For instance, the war held up the construction of the Ulan Bator railway linking the capitals of the Mongolian People's Republic and the Soviet Union, as well as a number of other industrial projects.

A second difficulty was that a predominant part in the country's economy was played by the small-commodity, individual husbandry of the *arats,* which depended on the vagaries of nature and were incapable of developing stock-breeding at fast rates of growth. The expansion of the economic and defence capacity and the prosperity of the people of the MPR depended on increasing the head of livestock. And yet, over the years 1940-1945 the total number of livestock had fallen by more than 6 million. The socialist sector (state farms, haymaking stations, production associations, etc.) in agriculture had still not managed to consolidate itself economically or organizationally and there were practically no large-scale industrial or transport firms with adequate technical equipment. In order to reconstruct, expand and re-equip the existing industrial and transport concerns and establish new ones and also to expand the fuel and electricity supply base the country needed large material and financial resources. *Arat* transportation facilities by caravan, carts and pack-animals still played a big part in the conveyance of official and local freight.

A third difficulty lay in the fact that there still existed survivals of the past in the economy and in the minds of people which powerfully affected the functioning of the state and economic apparatus. After the war, having overcome these difficulties, the workers of the MPR began in real earnest to implement the decisions of the Tenth MPRP Congress and the

Eighth Grand People's Hural for the development in every possible way of the national economy on socialist lines.

The Mongolian People's Revolutionary Party and the people's government drew up measures of an economic, political and cultural character to ensure the development of the country's productive forces and to raise the material and cultural level of the workers. The Mongolian People's Revolutionary Party devoted special attention to improving the economic, educational and organizational functions of the state authority, to strengthening the state and economic apparatus and to educating and training national personnel.

In 1946 the Plenary Meeting of the MPRP Central Committee, discussing the problem "The condition of the state and economic apparatus and measures for improving its functioning," pointed out that, in order to make a radical improvement in the work of the state and economic apparatus it would be essential to intensify the check kept on the execution of decisions, reorganize work in all the sections of the Party, state and economic apparatus, raise the level of official and labour discipline, improve supervision and the selection, distribution and training of personnel, develop criticism and self-criticism more widely, disseminate improved methods, planning and efficiency in working, wage a campaign for economy, for strengthening economic and financial discipline and for simpler and cheaper forms of administration.

With a view to safeguarding and consolidating state, communal and co-operative property the Presidium of the Little Hural of the Mongolian People's Republic adopted on February 4, 1947, a special regulation for the protection of such property and made it obligatory on all official state bodies to take resolute measures against persons found embezzling or plundering public property.

On December 27, 1947, the Council of Ministers of the Mongolian People's Republic adopted a resolution on "Measures for improving the organizational work of the presidiums of *aimak* Little Hurals and *somon* administrations." The resolution called for resolute action to strengthen and improve the work of local government bodies and transform them into militant organs of state authority which would be able really to ensure mobilization of the masses for the fulfilment of the national economic plan.

Another important step was the decision of the Council of Ministers and the MPRP Central Committee, taken on January 16, 1948, on "Information on the progress of the fulfilment of the five-year plan targets." This regulation provided for a regular check to be made by higher bodies of the records kept by organizations and undertakings on the progress made by them in carrying out their plans for each quarter. As an outcome of the measures taken there was an expansion in the functions of local Party and state bodies and an improvement in their working, which in turn had a positive effect in intensifying the activity of the masses.

During these years the Party's attention was centred on problems of ideological work. It led a resolute fight against the remnants of feudal superstitions in people's minds, against displays of nationalism and other forms of hostile ideology impeding the growth of the creative activities of the masses, and the forward advance of society towards socialism.

The MPRP Central Committee adopted a number of important decisions on ideological problems. In December 1949 the Central Committee of the Party adopted a resolution on the teaching of history and literature in educational institutions in which it was pointed out that the teaching of history and literature was not being conducted on a high enough level, that bourgeois-nationalist views still prevailed—in particular, Genghis Khan was still being extolled, the role of the masses in the MPR was being belittled and little attention being paid to the problems of social and economic relations. The resolution vigorously demanded that ideological errors and distortions be done away with, a systematic effort made to improve and perfect the ideological and theoretical training of teaching staffs and to see that the teaching of history and literature was based on Marxist-Leninist methodology.

In January 1950 the Plenary Meeting of the Central Committee of the Mongolian People's Revolutionary Party discovered a number of defects in the way mass political work was being organized and called for a vigorous fight against defects and for a raising of the ideological level of mass political work. The Plenary Meeting pointed out that the political consciousness and the activities of the masses had a decisive bearing on the successes won and the rate at which the MPR would evolve towards socialism.

All these measures taken by the Party and the Government of the Mongolian People's Republic had a very important bearing on the problem of eliminating shortcomings, improving the work of Party, state and economic establishments, educating personnel, making the masses more active and overcoming difficulties.

The most important undertaking of the MPRP and the people's democratic state was the elaboration of the Five-Year Plan for the development of the national economy and culture of the MPR.

In December 1947 the Eleventh MPRP Congress met and in February 1949 the Grand People's Hural.

The Mongolian people came to the Eleventh Party Congress with great successes to record in the sphere of economic and cultural construction and in the consolidation of the country's international standing.

The profound socio-economic and cultural changes which had occurred in the post-war years had created a situation which made it easier for the Mongolian people to lay the foundations of socialism. By entering the united family of socialist countries the Mongolian People's Republic obtained new opportunities of speeding up the rate of its advance towards socialism. The all-round fraternal assistance received from the Soviet Union and the other countries of people's democracy was a powerful factor in developing the economy and culture of the MPR and in raising the living standards of its working people. At the time of its Eleventh Congress the Party was still more closely united and strengthened, organisationally and ideologically, and its authority among the wide masses of the workers was immeasurably enhanced.

The Eleventh Party Congress, after summing up the results achieved during the period since the Tenth Congress, adopted the First Five-Year Plan for the development of the MPR's national economy and culture for 1948-1952.

The basic economic and political targets of the 1948-1952 Five-Year Plan were: "To develop in every way the productive forces of the MPR on the basis of maximum utilization of the country's resources and, in particular, to develop steadily the basic branch of its economy—stock-breeding; to develop to a further extent culture, education and public health services so as to ensure the subsequent speedy economic and cultural growth of the MPR; to increase in every possible way the well-being of the Mongolian people and also the political consciousness and labour activity of the working masses and induce them to take an active part in implementing the Five-Year Plan; to continue the struggle with the remnants of feudalism in the economy and its survivals in the minds of the people."

In 1949 the Ninth Grand People's Hural, after discussing a number of very important questions about a further democratization of the state system and of the problems involved in the economic and cultural construction of the country, endorsed the Five-Year Plan for the development of the national economy and culture of the Mongolian People's Republic for 1948-1952.

The Ninth Grand People's Hural laid down, from 1949 onwards, an obligatory annual plan for an increase in the number of livestock for each *arat* husbandry. Under this law, as from 1950, all *arat* husbandries were liable to a stock-breeding tax and had to make deliveries of meat, wool, fats and milk, not expressed in actual figures but based on the number and types of livestock as laid down in the state plan for each year. Any numbers of livestock bred by the *arat* farmers over and above the statutory plan were completely exempted from liability to tax and from compulsory deliveries of wool, meat and other stock-breeding products. In the case of *arat* farmers owning up to 21 head of livestock no compulsory state plan for numerical increase was fixed. However, these husbandries were liable to pay the stock-breeding tax and to make all the types of deliveries at the current rates applying to them but with an allowance for the number of beasts registered as owned by them in 1948.

For the Mongolian working people the Five-Year Plan was a mobilising force in their effort to build a socialist society. A movement for implementing on schedule the targets of the Five-Year Plan began to spread widely in all enterprises and in all the *aimaks* and *somons*. Members of the MPRP, of the Revolutionary Youth League, and workers, engineers and technicians at their meetings came forward and declared that they would fight for the implementation of the Five-Year Plan, that they would devote their strength and energy in order to achieve this objective. There was a wide expansion of competition between enterprises, workshops, participants and individual workers, under the leadership of the Party, Revolutionary Youth League and trade unions. The years of the First Five-Year Plan saw the Mongolian working class going all out to fulfil and overfulfil the First Five-Year Plan, as a result of which the working class strengthened its role as leader in the socialist transformation of society.

A major positive part was played by the Fifth Congress of the Trade Unions of the MPR and the Eleventh Congress of the Revolutionary Youth League, which were held in February and May 1948 and which defined the tasks of the trade union and Revolutionary Youth League organizations in the fight to fulfil the First Five-Year Plan. The decisions adopted by these Congresses pointed out that the principal task of trade unions and the Revolutionary Youth League was to mobilize the energies of the workers and youth workers for the execution of the targets of the Five-Year Plan, the development of competition and shock-worker techniques, the struggle to raise labour productivity and to reduce production costs.

During the years of the First Five-Year Plan there was a wide expansion of revolutionary competition in enterprises. In the course and as a result of competition progressive labour methods were introduced, there was a steady rise in the labour productivity of workers, costs were reduced and the quality of the goods manufactured was improved. A characteristic feature of competition in the final period of the First Five-Year Plan was the endeavour to move forward from records of individual producers to collective shock-working and to the creation of shock brigades, shock sections and workshops.[1]

The transition from records made by single individuals to a general increase had great significance as regards inculcating new methods of labour, training workers to adopt a new socialist attitude to labour. Competition opened up to the Mongolian working class wide possibilities for developing initiative and, as a result, the talents and energy latent within the masses began to reveal themselves very clearly. From year to year competition gained the interest of increasing numbers of workers. Whereas in 1948 little more than 70% of the workers were engaged in competition, by the end of the Five-Year Plan (1952) there were about 90%.

Socialist competition helped to raise the moral outlook of the Mongolian workers to a new level and stimulated their ideological development. In the campaign to increase production the study of the wealth of experience gained by the workers of the Soviet Union and the people's-democratic countries was immensely important, as well as the direct assistance given to the Mongolian workers by Soviet production innovators. During the years of the First Five-Year Plan leading figures in production and construction, drivers, mineworkers and others began to make a thorough study of and to apply the working methods of well-known Soviet innovators. As a result multi-lathe operatives appeared who operated simultaneously two or three lathes, and drivers who drove for one hundred thousand, and subsequently two and three hundred thousand kilometres without having to take their vehicles in for major repairs.

Many workers in the first four years of the Five-Year Plan fulfilled 6-14 times their annual individual norm. Among these were Ts. Tsembel, D. Sambu and G. Puntsag-Endon, workers at the Industrial Combine, Eryan, T. Kuderbergen and D. Davazhav, timberers in the Nalaikha coal-mine, B. Choigombo and L. Dolgorzhav, workers in the Ulan Bator cottage industry association, T. Gelegzhamts, D. Zhamyan and Tsedev, transport drivers, Namsrai, Sansraidorzh, building workers, S. Tsaganshukhert, tractor driver, Sh. Sembreldorzh and M. Sundui, drillers in the Chonogol mine and many others.

The year 1952 was the final one of the First Five-Year Plan. Conscious of the responsible tasks facing the country, the working class and all the working people of the MPR intensified the struggle to fulfil the targets of the Five-Year Plan. The mineworkers of the Chonogol mine launched an appeal on May Day 1952 to all the workers of the Republic to engage in the first socialist competition for the complete fulfilment of the Five-Year Plan targets.

The appeal of the Chonogol miners was supported by all the working people of the country. In June 1952, the MPRP Central Committee, in support of the proposal made by the

Chonogol miners, adopted a decision on the expansion of socialist competition in all the industrial and transport enterprises of the country on the basis of the undertakings given by the Chonogol miners. The appeal launched by the Chonogol workers was extremely important for the further expansion of socialist competition, for the development of creative initiative among the workers and for expanding the ranks of advanced workers and rationalizers. Socialist competition played an extremely important role in fulfilling and over-fulfilling the production plan. Workers who worked with particular efficiency and success began to be awarded honorary titles such as "production shock-worker" and "MPR shock-worker," and over ten thousand workers were so honoured. A start was made in organizing competition between *aimaks, somons* and *bags* and between individual *arat* farmholdings in increasing the numbers of livestock, improving their productivity and fulfilling the plan for state deliveries.

Despite great efforts by advanced workers and herdsmen, however, the Five-Year Plan as a whole for the Republic was not quantitatively fulfilled. The head of livestock did not reach 31 million, as laid down in the Five-Year Plan. This was due, firstly, to post-war difficulties and also to unfavourable climatic conditions which resulted in great losses of cattle and, secondly, to over-estimation of the possibilities of private *arat* farming by the planning organizations and, thirdly, the fact that certain measures, in particular deliveries to the state of meat, milk, wool and other products of stock-breeding and the system of taxation and procurement operative in those years did not conduce to an increase in economic initiative on the part of *arat* farmers and did not give them an economic interest in developing stock-breeding. The attempt by the state to introduce planning control of private individual *arat* farming did not prove effective either. Nevertheless, during the years of the First Five-Year Plan the Republic, on the whole, achieved successes in economic and cultural development and the country moved forward towards socialism. For the Party and the people the First Five-Year Plan represented the first experiment in long-term economic planning and its implementation.

*Results of the First Five-Year Plan
and Further Democratization
of the Electoral System*

In reliance on the whole-hearted unselfish fraternal assistance of the Soviet people, the MPRP and the MPR government carried through a number of very important measures for a further improvement in economic development and a further rise in the material and cultural standards of the working people.

A g r i c u l t u r e. Development of stock-breeding and greater productivity in this sphere constituted the basic, central task of the Five-Year Plan. Accordingly, the MPRP and the MPR government adopted a number of measures for this period aimed at increasing the head of livestock and improving the well-being of the people; compulsory provision of horse transport facilities *(urton)* was abolished, considerable rebates were given to *arat* husbandries on the tax on cattle; new horse-powered haymaking stations were organized; veterinary services were considerably expanded and a large number of qualified personnel were trained for all branches of the economy.

The number of horse-powered haymaking units was increased 5 times and the construction of all types of livestock sheds was increased $3^1/_2$ times. More than twice as many mechanized wells were constructed at state expense as were laid down in the plan.

All these and a number of other measures taken by the government created favourable conditions and opportunities for increasing the head of livestock, raising the material welfare and cultural level of the people.

In 1952 the total number of livestock had increased, however, to only 8.7% above the 1947 figure, of which 7.1% was accounted for by *arat* husbandries; on state farms the increase was 112.5 per cent while in the case of *arat* production association the increase was 6.5 times.

The socialized sector of agriculture, represented by state farms, horse-powered haymaking stations and *arat* production associations was reinforced. The total number of livestock in these three categories of economic activity rose by 43% during 1953.

Preparation of fodder by *arat* husbandries rose by 44.8%, by horse-powered haymaking stations an average of 2.6 times per station and by *arat* associations 246% and state farms 114.8%.

The Five-Year Plan for increasing the area under cultivation on state farms was overfulfilled by 51.1%, the harvest of grain crops by 12.5% and areas under hay-crops by 5.5%.

I n d u s t r y. In the development of industry during the post-war period and, more especially, during the years of the First Five-Year Plan, the Mongolian people, thanks to the assistance of the USSR, achieved major successes. On the basis of the Agreement on Economic and Cultural Co-operation between the MPR and the USSR large-scale mining and oil-refining industries were established in the MPR during these years.

Average annual industrial output growth was about 10% during this period. Total industrial output (taking into account output of newly-created enterprises) amounted in 1951 (calculated in 1940 prices) to 151% as compared with 1947 and was 2¹/₂ times greater than the 1940 figure.

During the Five-Year Plan period labour productivity rose by 28.8% and costs of production fell by 17.5% The average wage per industrial worker was 22% higher in 1952 than in 1947, while the amount spent on labour protection rose by 24.4% during the Five-Year Plan period.

The increase in coal production and power generating capacity was of great significance for the development of industry in the MPR. In 1953 the central power station in Ulan Bator produced 13 times as much power as in 1934.

The biggest state industry enterprises, the motor works and the Industrial Combine in Ulan Bator, were expanded and re-tooled. The Industrial Combine expanded its range of products to 140 types of cloth, woollen, leather and other items.

During the period from 1948 to 1952 seven new pits were opened in the Nalaikha region and several old pits reconstructed. Improvements were made in the mechanization of coal mining work requiring considerable labour; scraper transporters began to be used in the pits, and also powerful conveyor-lines, etc. During the years of the First Five-Year Plan a start was made on the construction of the "Nalaikha-Kapitalnaya" coal-mine and extensions were made to the Ulan Bator district heating plant.

The greatest development during the period 1941-1952 was recorded by the food industry. In 1940 the country had only 24 small food-processing enterprises whereas in 1945 there were already 423 and by 1952 more than 2,000, i.e. their number had increased more than 80 times as compared with 1940.

The number of creameries rose during the Five-Year Plan period alone from 164 in 1947 to 264 in 1952. In 1951 a total of 16 times more butter was processed in these creameries than in 1941 and in 1952 twice as much as in 1947. Output of flour rose during the Five-Year Plan period by 15.2% and that of sausages by 51.3%.

In 1952, at the end of the first five-year period, the volume of foodstuffs produced under the Ministry of Industry system was 17.1% more than in 1947. A meat processing combine equipped with modern machinery was constructed with the USSR's assistance.

In all *aimaks* food combines, based on local resources, were established for the manufacture of foodstuffs, alcohol distilleries, bakeries, canteens, etc.

There was a notable expansion of the printing and publishing industry; the state printing-works, which in 1945 had 87 up-to-date, improved printing-presses with an output of 30 million sheets, had in 1952 already 100 printing presses and produced more than 70 million sheets. Small local printing shops were set up in all the *aimaks*.

Civil construction and the production of local building materials continued to expand.

Over the period 1940-1951 dozens of industrial objects, schools, hospitals, cultural and educational institutions and dwelling houses were constructed and handed over for use in Ulan Bator and in *aimak* and *somon* centres. Among the largest of these are the Ulan Bator State University, the State Drama Theatre, the Ulan Bator Eldeb-Ochir Cinema and the State Library.

A large amount of work was done in erecting communal buildings in industrial plants, on state farms and *arat* production associations. Altogether, over 1 million square metres of floor space of building were constructed during this period.

Alongside state industry, cottage industry co-operation also continued to expand, creating in different regions of the country more and more new branches of production needed to meet the needs of the population. By the end of the First Five-Year Plan more than 200 *artels* in the system of MPR producers' co-operatives were turning out a wide range of consumer goods, especially building materials and foodstuffs. A number of industrial concerns in co-operative industry were equipped with modern technical machinery.

The Five-Year Plan for gross output, as amended by the MPR Council of Ministers, was fulfilled by the Union for Cottage Industry to the extent of 101.7%. Compared with 1947, the output of ready-made clothes and overcoats (Europan style), including civilian suits, was increased 6.9 times. The production of top-boots rose by 73.8% and of stoves for *yurts* 6 times, etc.

The development of state industry in the Mongolian People's Republic, insofar as its enterprises are equipped in the main with modern machinery, proceeds considerably faster than that of co-operative industry; in terms of output it has far outstripped the latter. For example, in 1950 the relative share of state industry in the gross value of output amounted to 75.9% and that of co-operative industry to 24.1%.

In the period since 1940 the industry of the Mongolian People's Republic has held an important place in the country's economy. In 1950 the share of its output in internal trade already amounted to 46%, as compared with 25% in 1938. It was this which enabled the state, holding control over the banks, foreign and domestic trade, transport, communications, haymaking stations and state farms and relying for support on assistance from the Soviet Union, to develop the national economy on planning principles to begin with, from 1941 onwards on the basis of annual plans and then, after 1948, on the basis of a Five-Year Plan.

Transport and Communications. In the post-war period considerable advances were also made in transport and communications in the Mongolian People's Republic. It was a major event, one of the greatest importance not only in the development of transport but also in the development of the whole national economy and culture, when the Ulan Bator railway, built with the assistance of the USSR, started operating. The Ulan Bator railway fulfilled the freight transport plan for 1951-1952 by 110%.

The introduction of motor-vehicle transport in place of *urton* transport considerably improved passenger travel all over the country, particularly between *aimaks*, *somons* and other administrative and economic centres of the MPR.

The fleet of motor vehicles operated by the Ministry of Transport increased by 67% over a five-year period and by $2^1/_2$ times as compared with 1952. Labour productivity during the Five-Year Plan improved by 13.9%, the cost of transportation fell by 18.4% and the number of mechanical transport depots steadily rose. During this period motor transport depots were opened in all *aimak* centres with a considerable number of motor-vehicles operating and passengers being conveyed between the *aimak* centres and Ulan Bator, as well as within the *aimaks*.

A direct telephone line, 1,500 kilometres long, was laid between Ulan Bator and Kobdo and telephone and telegraph communications in *aimaks* were considerably expanded; one-third of all the *somons* in the Republic were linked up direct by telephone with *aimaks*. Radio receivers were installed in all somons. Several radio stations were built in *aimaks* and over ten radio relay centres in *somons*.

Commerce and Finance. As a consequence of the growth of industry and agriculture there was a continuous expansion in the post-war period of trade, both internal and external.

The relative share of private trade, permitted only on the home market and regulated by the state, had by the end of the Five-Year Plan dropped to 6% of the country's gross goods turnover. The remaining 94% of the trade turnover was accounted for by state and co-operative trading, the turnover in state trading being about 40% of this internal section of the trade turnover of the Mongolian People's Republic, while co-operative trading accounted for about 60%.

After the Second World War, as the various branches of the national economy developed and strengthened, as labour productivity rose, costs fell and commodity resources increased, the Party and government carried through measures for a systematic reduction of retail prices. For example there were price reductions in 1946, 1947, 1948 and 1951.

In April 1950 the Council of Ministers of the Mongolian People's Republic and the Central Committee of the Mongolian People's Revolutionary Party adopted a resolution "On the complete abolition of the system of rationed sales of goods to the population, the system of merchandizing procurements of wool and raw materials and the transition to the free sale of foodstuffs and manufactured articles to the population." This highly important resolution opened up new possibilities for the development of trade. It helped to encourage the development of trading inside the country. Starting in May 1950, free trading at uniform state prices was resumed throughout the country.

The MPR's trade with the USSR also increased. Thus, during the Five-Year Plan period the import figures rose by 26.4% and for exports by 15.6%. There was also an increase in the range of goods exported to the Mongolian People's Republic by the Soviet Union. Between 1940 and 1950, there was a 90% increase in deliveries of consumer goods and a 79,5% increase in deliveries of industrial equipment and materials.

There was a noticeable increase in internal trade, particularly in consumer goods. In 1952, 30% more flour was produced than in 1947, 6 times more millet, 42% more textiles, 37% more tobacco (*dunzi*). Between 1940 and 1950 the consumption of flour more than doubled, tea consumption more than tripled (3.2 times) and the consumption of cotton textiles increased by 1.3 times, etc. Over this period there was a particularly large rise in the demand by the population for goods for cultural purposes. In 1950, for instance, the amount of cultural goods purchased by the population was four times as much as in 1945.

In 1952 after the five-year period, the state budget was 26.2% higher than in 1947.

The Five-Year Plan for capital investments in industry was fulfilled 104.5%. Capital investments in agriculture in 1952 increased to more than 10 times above the figure for 1947.

Capital investments in all branches of the economy rose from year to year, as can be seen from the rapid increase in the national wealth of the country. Whereas in 1948, 40.6 million *tugriks* were invested in the national economy, in 1952 the figure was 49.5 million. The total figure for the first five-year period amounted to 203.7 million *tugriks*.

P u b l i c   H e a l t h   a n d   C u l t u r e. The Five-Year Plan was successfully fulfilled in the sphere of public education, public health and culture.

The plan for expanding the network of general schools was fulfilled to the extent of 101.9%, that for technical secondary schools 100% and that for higher educational institutions 100%.

The plan for expanding the network of hospitals and medical centres was fulfilled to the extent of 110.2%, the number of doctors was more than tripled and that of *feldshers* increased by 47.7% as compared with 1947. During the five-year period the number of pupils attending primary schools rose by 84.4% and those attending seven-year schools by 33.3%, while in ten-year schools the number was quadrupled, pupils attending technical institutes were 27% more numerous and students of higher educational institutions doubled in numbers. As a result of all this the number of specialists and of persons with higher and secondary education increased considerably.

Over the five-year period the problem of abolishing illiteracy among the population was solved in the main; in 1952, 99% of the adult population of the country were able to read and write in their native language. This is one of the biggest triumphs of the Mongolian people during the years of people's-democratic rule and was gained under the leadership of the MPRP. For the first time in their thousands of years of history the Mongolian people left behind such a grievous survival of the backward feudal past as illiteracy.

Over the five-year period, and with the help of the USSR Academy of Sciences, a great deal of work was carried out in investigating the problems of stock-breeding, pastures, haymaking and in studying the country's mineral wealth. Much work was done in the field of studying the history, literature and economy of the MPR. There was a rise in the number of scientific workers holding a scientific degree. During the years of the First Five-Year Plan the industrial base of the Republic was considerably widened, the socialist sector in the national economy was reinforced, the working people were stimulated to become more active, the people's-democratic system was consolidated and the country made a major advance along the path of socialism.

Growth of the Working Class. With the development of industry, transport and communications and the introduction of ever newer branches thereof, fresh contingents of the Mongolian working class made their appearance and grew in strength. Over the Five-Year Plan period alone the number of workers in the enterprises of the Ministry of Industry of the Mongolian People's Republic increased by 25.9%. In the Ministry for the Food Industry the number of workers during the Five-Year Plan period more than doubled, in the Transport Ministry by 23%, in the state printing works by 14%, etc. During this period new detachments of workers in the mining and oil industries, in building and rail transport emerged and consolidated. In 1952 there were already over 70,000 people working in industry and transport, i.e. about 14% of the whole able-bodied population of the MPR. The quantitative growth of the working class was accompanied by a qualitative growth. Its political level, general education and production qualifications were higher. The MPRP and the MPR government displayed constant concern for the steady growth and improvement of the qualifications of the national personnel in industry, transport and communications.

In addition to the training and improved qualifications gained by workers in state and co-operative industry directly in enterprises and *artels* by means of individual and team apprenticeship and the organization of technical societies, special schools and technical colleges based on factories were established in Ulan Bator and other industrial centres of the country during the years of the Five-Year Plan.

Qualified workers—miners, drillers, engine-drivers, fitters, turners, electricians, stonemasons, plasterers, etc., were given training. Between 1940 and 1948 the number of engineers and technicians in industry increased 2.5 times.

The Mongolian working class fulfilled the targets set for industry by the Mongolian People's Revolutionary Party and the government of the Mongolian People's Republic. These targets included raising labour productivity, lowering production costs by the strict observance of economy, getting the workers to adopt modern techniques and improve their qualifications, all of which was necessary in order to provide the country's population with industrial goods and foodstuffs.

The working class and the technically-trained intellectuals of the MPR assimilated the experience of industrial innovators in the Soviet Union and successfully learnt from the Soviet working class.

Along with the increase in the general educational and technical accomplishments of the working class there was a rise in the political level and in the level of its ideological education. This was reflected, more particularly, in the growth of the working class element in the Mongolian People's Revolutionary Party and the Mongolian Revolutionary League of Youth, trade unions and other voluntary organizations.

The working class continued to take an active part in the social and political life of the country, was a builder of socialism and the leader of all the working people of Mongolia. In this period the social composition of the Mongolian People's Revolutionary Party and the people's government benefited by the emergence of advanced workers, working *arats* and working intellectuals.

Whereas in 1947, at the time of the Eleventh Congress, the working class element inside the Party amounted to 4.7%, herdsmen 54.1% and intellectuals 41.2%, by the time the Twelfth Congress met in 1954 workers made up 14.9% of Party members, herdsmen 38.6% and intellectuals 46.5%. During these years the percentage of the worker element inside the Party almost doubled, intellectuals rose by 5% and the number of herdsmen members by 15.5%. During the five-year period the number of workers in the League of Youth rose to 83% above the 1947 figure and that of trade-union members to 10.8% above the 1947 figure. The proportion of working-class representatives in higher governmental bodies and in the membership of the Grand People's Hural rose from 5.4% in 1949 to 10.3% in 1951. A similar example was offered by the social composition of local hurals.

All these changes and improvements in the social make up of the Party and people's power in favour of the working class and working intellectuals reflected a profound change in the class structure of the MPR and a speeding-up of the rate of the country's socialist development over the years of the First Five-Year Plan. Evidence of the consolidation of the social and state structure of the Mongolian People's Republic was furnished by the decision of the Ninth Grand People's Hural in February 1949 on the further democratization of the electoral system by replacing not entirely equal voting rights by direct and equal voting at the various electoral stages, and replacing open polling by secret polling for all governmental bodies. This further democratization of the electoral system was only possible as a result of the enormous changes and the successes achieved in the socio-political, economic and cultural life of the country, as a result of the growth in the political consciousness and activity of the working class and of all working people of the MPR and as a result of the unity and solidarity of the Party and people.

In June 1951 elections to the Grand People's Hural were held in the Mongolian People's Republic for the first time on the basis of the new electoral system. Altogether, 99.92% of voters took part in the voting, of whom 99.67% voted for candidates of the block of Party members and non-Party candidates. The best representatives of the workers, herdsmen and intellectuals were elected to membership of the Grand People's Hural.

The elections constituted a fresh demonstration of the moral and political unity of Mongolian people and of their solidarity round the MPRP and people's power.

In October 1952 elections were held for local government bodies throughout the country, in which a total of 49,641 deputies were elected to local hurals. As a result of these elections thousands more workers, herdsmen and intellectuals—the finest people in the country—were drawn into state administration. The elections demonstrated the feelings of love and the loyalty felt by the people for their Party, for people's power.

The further democratization of the electoral system ensured the reinforcement of the alliance between the working class and the *arat* population, in which the working class played the leading role.

SECTION FOUR

THE FIGHT OF THE MONGOLIAN PEOPLE FOR THE VICTORY OF SOCIALISM

CHAPTER I

THE SOCIALIST TRANSFORMATION OF THE ECONOMY OF THE MPR

Prerequisites for the Socialist Transformation of the Economy

The years which followed on the First Five-Year Plan, i. e the years from 1953 to 1960, were a most important period ir which decisive steps were taken in the socialist constructior of the MPR and when a victory was won for socialist produc tion relations in all departments of the economy.

The further consolidation of the world socialist system anc the strengthening of the country's foreign policy created favourable conditions for economic development, specifically for tackling the historical tasks of transforming agriculture or socialist lines.

This period was also marked by a further consolida tion of the MPR's international position and by a widening oi its friendship and co-operation with all peoples and states.

The consistent foreign policy of the MPR, based on the suc cesses achieved in extensive socialist construction and based or the unalterable principles of peace and peaceful co-existence has earned the MPR the respect and approval of the whole oi progressive humanity and formed a guarantee of the steady growth of its prestige and its position in world politics.

The consolidation of the MPR's international position is further explained by the fact that, as a result of the consolida tion of the world socialist system, in latter years the balance oi power in the world arena has continued to change in favoui of peace, democracy and socialism.

The activity of the MPR government in foreign affairs, direct ed to the preservation and consolidation of a stable peace on earth, derives from the very essence of the socialist structure of the MPR and accords with the interests of the Mongolian people, engaged in the building of socialism.

In times when world reaction, headed by the USA, is pursu ing a mad armaments race, accumulating stocks of nuclear weapons and continuing to follow the policy of exacerbating the international situation, the socialist countries and all peace-loving states consider it necessary to wage a stubborn fight for world peace.

In recent years the USA and the other imperialist states have more than once pushed the world to the brink of a new war. The Suez crisis, the counter-revolutionary revolt in Hungary in 1956, the Congo tragedy, the blockade of Cuba, the events in Vietnam—these are the basic events which have exposed the aggressive policy of world imperialism. The centres of a new war which have emerged in a number of regions of the world through the fault of the neo-colonialists and imperialists have been extinguished in good time thanks to the judicious policy of the Soviet Union and the other socialist countries and to the efforts of all the peace-loving peoples. But to this day, the flame of colonial warfare is still glowing in South Vietnam, as it has for more than ten years, and events are happening in various parts of the world which aggravate the international situation.

In a situation where the forces of reaction and war, of imperialism and colonialism, are pursuing a policy of provocation, it is essential to continue still further intensifying the struggle for the peace and security of peoples, for solving all international problems through peaceful negotiations, to seek out ways and means of strengthening confidence between states with different social structures, to create conditions for establishing a peace without weapons and wars and to take in this direction decisive action.

This is the position taken by the MPR now as in the past. As Yu. Tsedendal has said: "The MPR is an inseparable, integral part of the world socialist system, is carrying on a foreign policy directed towards the consolidation of peace, the deepening of fraternal friendship and unity with the great Soviet Union, the Chinese People's Republic and all brotherly socialist countries, for the systematic implementation of the principles of peaceful co-existence with states of a different social structure."[1]

One of the cornerstones of the MPR's foreign policy is the steady consolidation of friendship and co-operation with all socialist countries on the principles of Marxism-Leninism and of proletarian internationalism, and a good deal of work has been done in this connection.

Motivated by the growth of socialist construction within its country, the MPR steadfastly advocates the unity and solidarity of the socialist camp and the world Communist movement.

It stands for the purity of Marxist-Leninist doctrine and fights resolutely against revisionism, dogmatism and sectarianism and all displays of bourgeois nationalism.

The decisions of the Party Congresses and Plenary Meetings of the MPRP Central Committee lay down the line to be followed in home and foreign policy at any particular stage of development, the MPRP being an active outpost of the world Communist movement of which the generally-recognized leader is the great Party of Lenin—the CPSU. The wealth of experience of the CPSU is of enormous international significance. In the historical resolutions of the Twentieth, Twenty-first and Twenty-second Congresses of the CPSU and in the CPSU Programme new practical and theoretical principles have been drawn up concerning contemporary world development, and this constitutes an immense contribution to the treasure-house of Marxism-Leninism.

The MPRP is guided in its activity by the principles laid down in collectively produced documents—the Declaration and the Statement, adopted at the Moscow Conferences of Communist and Workers' Parties in 1957 and 1960.

During the last ten years, on the invitation of the MPRP Central Committee and the MPR government, the Mongolian People's Republic has received friendly visits at different times from Party and government delegations of fraternel countries—the Soviet Union, Czechoslovakia, Romania, the German Democratic Republic, Poland, the Democratic Republic of Vietnam, the Chinese People's Republic, Hungary, the North Korean Democratic Republic, Bulgaria, Yugoslavia and Cuba. The eminent guests, representatives of fraternal peoples following the path of socialism and communism, were given an exceptionally warm and hospitable reception by the Mongolian people.

In their turn the Mongolian Party and government delegations have travelled to most of the socialist countries, in particular to the Soviet Union, Czechoslovakia, Poland, and Hungary, where they have familiarised themselves with the life of fraternal peoples, with their experience and with the successes gained in socialist construction.

These visits, and also the maintenance of contacts through other channels, have helped to promote the further development of friendship and all-round co-operation between the MPR and other socialist countries.

It should be noted that the agreements and treaties concluded with friendly socialist countries have real strength and are always scrupulously embodied in the everyday socialist construction of the country. Examples of this are the various agreements concluded by the MPR with fraternal countries. Mention may be made of the agreement on the provision by the USSR of technical assistance to Mongolia in the construction of industrial and communal public-utility establishments, concluded in August 1955. The Agreement and Treaty on the further expansion of economic co-operation between the MPR and the

USSR signed in February and September 1960 respectively, envisaging in particular USSR assistance in building the new town of Darkhan with its industrial and fuel supply complex, the trade agreements for 1961-1965 concluded in 1961 with the German Democratic Republic, Czechoslovakia, Bulgaria, Poland, Hungary, etc. The Mongolian people are constantly conscious of the beneficial results of these agreements.

Admission to membership of the Council for Mutual Economic Assistance (CMEA) in July 1962 was immensely important for the MPR. In contrast to the various associations of capitalist monopolies, such as the European Common Market, where uncontrolled competition and the law of the jungle predominate, the Council for Mutual Economic Assistance is an international organization of a completely different type.

It accepts as its task the intensification of economic collaboration and mutual fraternal assistance between socialist countries so as to enable them to utilize with the maximum degree of profit the advantages of socialism in ironing out differences in the level of their development and their joint progress forward to Communism.

At the request of the Mongolian government the relevant CMEA bodies are carrying out a great deal of work to study the country's economic situation; they draw up plans for helping Mongolia in agriculture and in the geological study of natural resources. The countries of CMEA are helping the MPR to draw up a general long-term plan extending to 1980.

Friendly relations with the new young states which have been freed from colonialist oppression and are following the path of national independence are developing satisfactorily. These relations are based on the international principles of the MPR's foreign policy, directed towards giving the utmost help to the national-liberation movement in the fight against colonialism and imperialism.

At the present time the MPR has diplomatic relations with several developing states such as Indonesia, Guinea, Ceylon, Afghanistan, Nepal, Cambodia, Burma, Pakistan, Algeria, the ARE and Mali.

In conformity with the principles of peaceful co-existence, the MPR endeavours to establish and expand friendly links with the capitalist world on a basis of equality and mutual benefit, respect for sovereignty and non-interference in one another's affairs. Here it should be emphasised that until recently certain capitalist countries such as the USA, the United Kingdom, and France, did not wish to recognize the MPR as they were pursuing an unfriendly policy towards it.

However, the consolidation of the freedom and independence of the MPR, the achievements of socialist construction and the successes of the country's peace-loving foreign policy have still further enhanced its prestige and authority in the world arena and resulted in certain capitalist states which, in the past, did not recognize the sovereignty of the MPR, finding themselves obliged to change their policy. Thus, in recent years Mongolia has established diplomatic relations with a number of capitalist countries, including the United Kingdom, Austria, Switzerland, Finland, Sweden and France. The establishment of diplomatic relations by the biggest Western Powers with the MPR testifies to the growth in the MPR's prestige in international affairs, as well as to the bankruptcy of the imperialist policy of discrimination. Trade is an excellent indicator of the expansion of foreign political links. The foreign trade of the MPR increases every year. In addition to the socialist countries the MPR carries on trade with Japan, Switzerland, France, Finland, Sweden, the ARE, India, the United Kingdom, etc. In recent years trade organizations of the country have participated successfully in international fairs in Leipzig, Brno, Plovdiv and other cities.

Foreign links have also been expanded considerably in the case of social, cultural, trade union, youth, athletic and other organizations and also through the Peace Committee.

The representatives of the Mongolian National Committee for the Defence of Peace took an active part in the Peace Congresses held in 1954-1964 in Helsinki, Stockholm and Moscow, advocating the consolidation of the unity and solidarity of all progressive mankind in the fight for universal peace and security and against the threat of a new world war.

The steady expansion of foreign links through voluntary organizations helps workers in foreign countries to learn of the Mongolian people's achievements in socialist construction.

The admission of the MPR to membership of the United Nations on October 27, 1961, was a major triumph for the peace-loving foreign policy of the MPR. Thus, the fifteen-year struggle of the MPR for the establishment of its legitimate rights in the United Nations was crowned with success.

Admission to the United Nations widened the field of the MPR's foreign policy activities and gave it an opportunity to co-operate with peace-loving forces in this international body whose function it is to defend peace between the peoples.

The government of the MPR, both in the United Nations and outside it, firmly upholds the interests of peace and progress in the fight against colonialism and imperialism.

The MPR's attitude on basic international problems is clear and intelligible. The Mongolian Government is in favour of a constructive solution of such topical international problems as general and complete disarmament, the prohibition of the testing and use of nuclear weapons, the definitive liquidation of the colonial system, the conclusion of a peace treaty with Germany, the end of American aggression in South Vietnam.

The attitudes of the MPR in regard to foreign political problems have been precisely and clearly outlined in its government's declarations published during the years 1954-1964, in particular on the Three-Power aggression against Egypt, the aggressive plans of NATO, the situation in the Straits of Taiwan, the conclusion of a peace treaty with Germany, general, complete disarmament, accession to the Moscow Treaty banning nuclear weapon tests in three media, West Irian, the second conference of Afro-Asian countries, etc.

As evidence of this there are the numerous statutes adopted by the Grand People's Hural and its executive bodies on international problems as well as the declarations of the Ministry of Foreign Affairs of the MPR.

All these MPR foreign policy documents reflect the fight waged by the MPR government and people to avert the danger of war and to maintain universal peace on earth.

By its active and consistent struggle in the international forum the MPR makes its appropriate contribution to the common cause of maintaining and reinforcing peace on our planet.

The consistent strengthening of the international position of the MPR in consequence of the correct foreign policy followed by its government signifies an expansion of the economic and cultural ties with foreign countries, thus promoting the successful construction of socialism within the country.

On June 13, 1954, new elections were held for the Grand People's Hural. All the electors cast their votes for the candidates of the block of Party and non-Party candidates. The results of the elections once again demonstrated the great solidarity of the Mongolian people and their profound confidence in the MPRP and people's government.

The first session of the second convocation of the Grand People's Hural, held in July 1954, elected Zh. Sambu Chairman of its Presidium and formed a government with Yu. Tsedenbal as its head. In November of the same year there took place the Twelfth MPRP Congress which, while summing up the results of the fulfilment of the tasks of the First Five-Year Plan, confirmed the directives for the Second Five-Year Plan for economic and cultural development for 1953-1957. The basic objective of the new Five-Year Plan was to ensure a substantial advance in all branches of the national economy along with a steady growth and consolidation of the socialist sector, a further development of stock-breeding by giving all-round support to *arat* farmers and considerably improving on this basis the material and cultural level of the working people.

In the Second Five-Year Plan concrete targets were fixed for increasing the head of livestock and the output of stockbreeding, for reinforcing the socialist sector (*arat* production associations—APA, producers' co-operatives—PC, and state farms) in agriculture and also for expanding industry, building and other branches of the national economy.

In order to achieve the successful execution of the objective of the Second Five-Year Plan the MPRP and the people's government carried out a series of political, economic and organizational measures.

In 1955 the MPRP Central Committee and the MPR Council of Ministers adopted a resolution on measures for the organizational and economical consolidation of state farms under which managerial specialization was introduced in state farms—the production team became the basic form of labour organization on farms.

Following the principle of the socialist transformation of argiculture, the MPRP speeded up the co-operative movement among *arat* farmers. The first congress of leading representatives of *arat* production associations, held in March 1955 on the decision of the MPRP Central Committee and the MPR Council of Ministers, generalized the results of the socialist transformation of agriculture and adopted Model Rules for Agricultural Associations (AA). In October 1955 the MPRP and the people's government adopted a decision on the organizational and economic consolidation of the AA. A great role in the organizational and economic consolidation of the socialist sector in agriculture was played by the decisions of the December Plenary Meeting of the MPRP Central Committee held in 1955 on the "Tasks of Party, governmental and agricultural bodies in the organizational and managerial consolidation of the AA, PC and state farms" and raising the level of Party and governmental work in them. In conformity with the decisions of the Plenary Meeting of the MPRP Central Committee the Party drafted into work in the AA more than 300 volunteer-activists from Party, governmental and economic departments in order to provide the socialist sector of agriculture with experienced, highly-qualified cadres capable of managing a large-scale socialist economy. With a view to helping increase the production of the fodder supplies and expand land cultivation in the socialist sectors of agriculture and in order to consolidate the socialist sector, the distribution of land among farms was settled during the Second Five-Year Plan and from 1957 onwards the honorary title of "Hero of Labour of the MPR" began to be conferred upon AA members, workers on state farms and machine and stock-breeding stations (MSS) who achieved high indicators.

Along with the socialist sector of agriculture the Party and government did everything to boost the personal interest of the *arat* farmers in increasing the number of their livestock. The fourth meeting of leading herdsmen of the Republic convened for this purpose mobilized the *arats* in order to achieve a further advance in stock-breeding; to encourage *arat* herdsmen who increased the head of their own livestock in the course of two years by not less than 15% through rearing young beasts, the title of "Leading Herdsman of the Republic" began to be awarded in 1957. To assist *arat* farmers to increase the size of livestock herds, the Party and government in 1955 and 1956 offered a 10% rebate on compulsory deliveries of meat to the state and the indebtedness of AA members and *arat* farms in respect of state deliveries of meat, wool and milk for 1954, 1955 and 1956 was written off. *Arat* farms were given fresh rebates under the Law on the Stock-breeding Tax. Short-term and long-term credit facilities for *arat* farms were increased.

As a result of such measures taken by the Party and government for the expansion of agriculture the rate of increase in the head of livestock was speeded up during the years of the Second Five-Year Plan and the socialist sector in agriculture became a great force. Eight new state farms and dozens of producers' co-operatives were set up and in 1956 these co-operatives were reorganized into mechanized stock-breeding stations (MSS).

In order to implement socialist construction successfully and improve its management the MPRP adopted a series of measures for perfecting the operation and reducing the cost of governmental, central and local bodies, economic organizations and cultural institutions. The elimination of the effects of the personality cult played a large part in consolidating local government bodies and in the further progress of democratization. The decisions of the Twentieth Congress of the CPSU condemning the personality cult were welcomed with great enthusiasm by the MPRP. The Plenary Meeting of the MPRP Central Committee in 1956 sharply criticized the Kh. Choibalsan personality cult in the MPR, exposed actual cases of fragrant breaches of revolutionary legality in the 1930s and adopted important resolutions on eliminating the harmful effects of the personality cult and strengthening the Party's control over the actions of the law courts, the public prosecutor's office, the organs of state security, etc.

Thanks to the devoted efforts of the working class, the *arat* herdsmen and working intellectuals and also to the organizational and political measures of the MPRP and the people's government the targets set by the Second Five-Year Plan were, in the main, successfully fulfilled.

The Thirteenth MPRP Congress, held in March 1958, after noting with satisfaction the decisive steps taken by the country during the years of the Second Five-Year Plan for the construction of socialism, approved the directives for the Three-Year Plan for the development of the national economy and culture for the years 1958-1960. The basic objective of the Three-Year Plan was to ensure a further rise in the country's productive forces, to develop and consolidate in every way the socialist structure in agriculture, bring about a further expension of all branches of the national economy and ensure on this basis a steady rise in the material and cultural standards of the workers.

The targets set in the Three-Year Plan were to increase the head of livestock by 7.2% and the gross output of industry by 53.2%, and bring the volume of capital investment up to 1,300 million *tugriks*. Taking into account the tendency of the bulk of individual arat farmers towards collective farming, the Thirteenth Party Congress felt it was necessary to complete the introduction of co-operative methods in the bulk of *arat* husbandries during the forthcoming three years.

The most important achievement of the MPR's national economy during the years of the Three-Year Plan was the expansion of land cultivation. The Third Plenary Meeting of the MPRP Central Committee, held in March 1958, put forward as a target a steep rise in land cultivation by bringing under cultivation in the years 1959-1961 300,000 hectares of virgin lands in order to meet the country's requirements in home-produced grain. The USSR gave great help in implementing this programme, sending the MPR hundreds of specialists, and supplying 3,000 motor-vehicles, 2,500 tractors, 500 combines and other agricultural machinery.

In 1959, in the regions where virgin land was being brought under tillage, several new state grain farms were organized and the area under crops on already existing state farms was greatly expanded. As a result, in 1959-1960, 260,000 hectares of virgin land were brought under cultivation and a rich grain harvest gathered: 7 million *poods* in 1959 and 16 million *poods* in 1960.

Thus, the target set by the Third Plenary Meeting of the MPRP Central Committee was achieved in two years. With the expansion of land cultivation agriculture became an independent branch of the national economy.

In the years of the Second Five-Year Plan and the Three-Year Plan considerable success was achieved by industry, transport and other branches of the economy.

I n d u s t r y. On the basis of the level of industrial development reached in the First Five-Year Plan the MPRP and people's government during the years of the Second Five-Year Plan and the Three-Year Plan concentrated their attention on the further development of all branches of industry and, above all, of those branches which could work economically and most profitably on local raw materials.

In 1953-1957 several measures were put into effect for the more efficient utilization of machinery and equipment, for making savings in raw materials, for improving the qualifications of labourers and engineering and technical workers, for drawing factory and office workers into socialist competition and disseminating the experience gained by leading workers in production, for bettering the economy and improving economic estimating, accountability, etc. Steps were taken to eliminate excessive labour turnover and to raise workers' standards of living.

Thanks to the devoted efforts of the working class under the leadership of the MPRP and with the unselfish assistance of the USSR and other fraternal socialist countries, the industry of the MPR fulfilled the targets of the Second Five-Year Plan by 107%. The gross output of industry over the five-year period rose by 69%, including a rise of 73% in state industry and of 55% in co-operative industry. During this period the average annual rate of growth in industrial output amounted to 13.1% instead of the planned target of 7.8%. As a result of the mechanization and electrification of industrial processes and the adoption of new techniques and of rationalisers' suggestions there was a significant increase in labour productivity; in the case of state industry the increase amounted to 57.6% and in the co-operative sector 38%. Enterprises in state and co-operative industry learned how to manufacture a number of new agricultural implements and equipment and their spare parts, as well as consumer goods.

During the Second Five-Year Plan enterprises such as the Ulan Bator heating and power station, meat-packing plant and the furniture factory were expanded or reconstructed. During this period a soap factory, a matchworks and several locally important coal-mines were opened and a potters' producers' co-operative was set up.

During the years of the Second Five-Year Plan there was a considerable consolidation and expansion of the oil and mining industries, in the development of which a decisive role was played by the Soviet-Mongolian joint stock company "Sovmongolmetall" and the "Mongolneft" trust.

There was also rapid development in construction and building. The total volume of the output of building materials had, by the end of 1967, risen to almost 8 times higher than in 1952, instead of the target increase of 3.7 times. As the production of building materials and capital construction expanded the building industry became an independent branch of heavy industry.

The basic reasons for the comparatively high rate of industrial development were the considerable growth in capita investments and the steady rise in labour productivity. During the years of the Second Five-Year Plan capital investments (excluding the help given by the USSR and other socialist countries) amounted to 141.8 million *tugriks* or 4.4 times more than the figure for the First Five-Year Plan.

The fraternal assistance given by the Soviet Union played an important part in the development of industry. For example, in 1957 the Soviet Union handed over to the MPR free of charge the oil wells and oil refineries built at its own expense and costing 300,000,000 roubles and transferred, on specially advantageous terms, the whole of its shares in the "Sovmongolmetall" joint stock company, to the value of 40 million roubles.

The targets fixed under the Three-Year Plan for industry were successfully achieved. The total rise in gross industrial output for the years 1958-1960 amounted to 63.8% instead of the planned target of 52% and the average annual rise in industrial output over the three-year period amounted to 17.9%. Thus, the rates of industrial production in the MPR over the years of long-term planning gradually rose. Whereas in the First Five-Year Plan (1948-1952) the annual rise in industrial output was 2.4%, in the Second (1953-1957) it was 13.1% and in the years of the Three-Year Plan (1958-1960) 17.9%.

During the Three-Year Plan period, with the economic assistance of the USSR, the Czechoslovak Socialist Republic, the German Democratic Republic new industrial concerns were built and handed over for operation, including the "Nalaikha-Kapitalnaya" coal-mine producing 600,000 tons of coal per year, a creamery, and a printing works intaglio presses.

As a result of the construction of new undertakings and the completion of the reconstruction of old installations the technical re-equipment of industry was carried out on the basis of the most up-to-date techniques. In this connection there was a considerable increase in capital investment in industry, which in the three-year period showed an increase of 49% as compared with the Second Five-Year Plan.

The equipment of industrial concerns with up-to-date plant and the introduction of progressive technology made it possible to increase greatly labour productivity, which in 1960 was 21% higher than in 1957.

During this period, as a result of the rapid and successful expansion of land cultivation, a new branch of the foodstuffs industry—flour milling—was set up. In 1959, with the help of the Soviet Union, mechanized mills were built in Ulangom, Bulgan and Choibalsan, a milling combine in Ulan Bator with a capacity of 31,200 tons of flour per year and a confectionery works with an output capacity of 5,000 tons of products per year.

There was also a successful expansion of light industry during the years of the Three-Year Plan; a felt-fulling mill, footwear and leather goods factories were rebuilt and a wool-combing mill and other factories erected.

Cottage industry co-operative enterprises considerably expanded the output of consumer goods, various types of agricultural implements, building materials, etc., as a result of making better use of industrial waste, sub-standard raw materials and local raw material resources.

As a result of the successful fulfilment of the Second Five-Year and Three-Year Plans for the development of the national economy, the MPR changed from an agrarian into an agrarian-industrial country. In 1957 the share of industrial production in the overall output of industrial and agricultural production amounted to 41%. In 1960 the volume of industrial output rose 7.4 times as compared with 1940, which includes an increase of 6.6 times in the volume of output of heavy industry. In level of industrial development the MPR has caught up with such countries as Pakistan, Turkey, and Iran.

Transport and Communications. The period under consideration was marked by a further expansion of modern forms of transport and communications. At the end of 1955 the railway line Ulan Bator—Dzamyn-Ude stretching for more than 700 kilometres, started operations. By this time the total length of broad-gauge railways line in the MPR had doubled as compared with 1952 and transports of freight by rail increased to 17.4 times the 1952 figure.

The railway has become one of the principal forms of transport in respect of volume of freight conveyed. At the end of 1960 the railways carried 42% of all internal and external transportation in the country and the share of the railways in external freight transports amounted to 93% of the total freight turnover.

There was a considerable expansion also in motor-vehicle transport. Freight conveyed by motor transport in 1960 increased to threefold the 1957 figure and transport of passengers rose $1^1/_2$ times.

Air transport also assumed great importance. The transfer free of charge by the Soviet Union of airport and civil aviation facilities, valued at more than 20 million roubles, laid a firm foundation for civil aviation in Mongolia.

The Five-Year and Three-Year Plans for the development of communications facilities were also carried out before the target date in respect of all indices. The number of telephone stations rose by 16% and the number of wireless centres by 31%.

Direct telephone communication was established between Ulan Bator and many state farms and agricultural associations, all the *somons* were connected by telephone with the *aimak* centres.

The Soviet Union gave enormous assistance in developing all types of modern communications. In 1957 it handed over free of charge for the use of the MPR the multi-channel telephone line connecting Ulan Bator with Moscow and Peking, built at the expense of the USSR, and in April 1960, with the USSR's help, a powerful central radio station named in honour of V. I. Lenin was built in Khonkhor which provides reliable reception of transmissions from Ulan Bator in every corner of the country.

T r a d e. The expansion of the external and internal trade of the MPR depended on the successful development of the country's industry and agriculture and also on a further extension and consolidation of the MPR's economic collaboration with the socialist countries.

\ During the years of the Second Five-Year Plan and the Three-Year Plan the MPRP and the MPR people's government took a number of important steps to develop and consolidate state and co-operative trading and give better service to the working people. In 1954 and 1958 prices were reduced for certain consumer goods, while state purchasing prices for livestock and the products of stock-breeding were frequently increased.

A decision taken by the November Plenary Meeting of the MPRP Central Committee (1958) was essentially important for the further development and extension of socialist trading and for strengthening trade organizations. The Plenary Meeting, after considering the problems of state and co-operative trading adopted important decisions for further improving trading services to the population and increasing the retail turnover of goods in the country. With a view to greater satisfaction to the constantly increasing material and cultural needs of the population and centralizing the management of trade and procurements, the meeting decided to alter the organizational structure of trade. On the basis of this decision a Ministry of Trade and Procurements was established at the beginning of 1959 and the Mongolian Co-operative Association was reorganized as a voluntary consumer's company for the promotion of trade and procurements. State trading began to play a leading part in the country's retail trade turnover; its share rose from 47% in 1957 to 92% in 1960. The share of co-operative trading fell correspondingly from 39% in 1957 to 7.6% in 1960.

As a result of the successful expansion of the socialist sector in trade, i.e. state and co-operative trade as a whole, the share of private trading fell considerably. Whereas in 1952 it amounted to 22.2% of the aggregate retail goods turnover, in 1957 the figure was 14.8%. Thanks to the measures taken by the

MPRP and the MPR people's government to encourage the voluntary association of private traders in *artels*, by 1958 the private sector in trade ceased to exist. This was still another great achievement of the Mongolian people in socialist construction.

As a result of the successful implementation of the national economic plan for the years 1953-1960 and the steady growth in the incomes of the working people and the rise in the purchasing power of the population, there was a steady increase in retail goods turnover which, in 1957, was 95% greater than in 1952 and in 1960 12.7% greater than in 1958. There was a big change also in the nature of the population's consumption. A demand appeared for such goods as washing machines, vacuum cleaners, motor-cars, motor-cycles, etc.

There was a considerable rise in the annual consumption of goods per head of population. For instance, between 1955 and 1959 sales of bread per head of population almost doubled, sales of meat products and butter almost tripled and sales of sewing machines increased 17 times, while sales of cotton textiles, ready-made clothing, leather footwear and goods for cultural purposes doubled, etc.

Along with the rise in internal retail turnover the MPR's foreign trade turnover increased from year to year. In the Second Five-Year Plan it showed a rise of 57% on imports and 30% on exports, while the corresponding figures for the Three-Year Plan years were 40% and 26.5%. Substantial changes occurred in its structure. In the country's imports the share of industrial equipment, machinery, mechanisms and technical goods rose to 40% in 1958 as against 24% in 1952, while the share of such goods as ready-made clothing, woollen fabrics, leather manufactures, ceramic ware, oil-derivatives and others fell considerably. In the years 1953-1959 the MPR established trade relations with all the countries of the socialist system. In recent years there has also been some development in the MPR's trade with capitalist countries.

Further Development of the Working Class and Peasantry. In connection with the successful development of socialist industry, transport and communications the national working class increased quantitatively and its qualitative composition improved. In 1958 there were 3 times as many workers as in 1940, while in 1960 there were 5.8 times as many. At the beginning of 1958 workers employed directly in production constituted 14% of the country's total population, while factory and office workers together with their families, amounted to 28.6% in 1958 and 36.1% in 1960. There was a considerable heightening of the leading role played by the working class in the whole social and political life of the country. The number of workers who were members of the MPRP increased. Whereas in 1954 the workers had accounted for 14.9%, in 1958 the figure was 19.4% and in 1961—26.2%. An ever-increasing number of workers are elected deputies to the Grand People's Hural and local government bodies. In the membership of the Grand People's Hural, first convocation (1951), workers constituted 12% of all the deputies, while in the membership of the Third convocation (1957) the figure was 25%.

The alliance between the working class and the *arats* who had become co-operative farmers was strengthened. The working class gives great help to these *arat* co-operative members. The best representatives of the working class are voluntarily transferring to work in agriculture, workers' collectives in industrial enterprises are acting as patrons of AAs; deductions are made from the profits of industrial enterprises in order to strengthen agricultural associations organizationally and economically, etc.

There was a considerable rise in the level of the technical knowledge and the culture of workers. When industrial enterprises equipped with the latest technical facilities began operations and when the reconstruction of older concerns was successfully completed, a demand arose for large number of highly-qualified workers and engineering and technical personnel. The answer was—and still is—to train cadres in secondary technical and in higher educational institutions in the country, in the USSR and in other fraternal socialist countries and to encourage workers to improve their qualifications at part-time courses. During the years of the Second Five-Year Plan alone the number of national cadres with higher education in industry increased 18 times and of cadres with secondary education 8 times. Many Mongolian workers have been given practical training in production in the USSR, the CSR and other socialist countries.

During the campaign for successful fulfilment of the targets of the Five-Year and Three-Year Plans there has been a wide expansion of the rationalisation and invention movement. In expanding the production rationalisation movement a great role was played by the first (1955) and second (1959) Republican meetings of foremost workers in industry, construction, transport and communications. During this period a large number of workers were found to have overfulfilled planning targets; among these were such advanced production workers as the first MPR Heroes of Labour— D. Davazhav, coal-miner, D. Sharav, a worker at the Industrial Combine, and others.

In the course of the socialist competition practised during the years of the Three-Year Plan there was born a movement, which became very widespread, for earning the right to the title of socialist labour team, with the basic slogan: "Study, work and live as a socialist." This movement, which sprang up in 1959 in the team of locomotive depot repairers at Ulan Bator Station, spread in a short time to encompass all branches of the economy and wide sections of the workers. By the end of 1960 there were already 20 socialist labour teams in the country and 600 people involved in competition for this lofty title.

In close association with the successful construction of a socialist economy there was a rapid development of socialist culture, arts and science and a rise in the cultural level of the working people.

In the middle of the 1950s, as a result of the expansion of the country's economy and culture, realistic conditions were generated for accelerating the process of introducing co-operation in agriculture.

The socialist transformation of agriculture is one of the general laws of development for any country that is building socialism. On the basis of this natural law, taking as guidance Lenin's plan for co-operation and employing a creative approach to the experience in the collectivization of agriculture gained in the USSR and other countries of socialism, the MPRP and the people's government, making due allowance for the national peculiarities of its country, organised the transition from small fragmented *arat* husbandries to large-scale associations of *arat* producers. A good deal of time and hard work on the part of the Party and people was required for carrying through the socialist transformation of agriculture.

In the early years of the country's revolution the land which belonged to the feudal class was, as we have seen, nationalised. The transfer of land into public ownership, i.e. ownership by the whole people, was one of the most important prerequisites for the emergence of a socialist structure in agriculture. This, however, was far from constituting a solution of the problems of the socialist transformation of agriculture. The principal wealth of the country, livestock, remained in the hands of small producers; the state gave every kind of encouragement and assistance to improving these husbandries in order to prepare the necessary material conditions for transferring them to public ownership.

As a result of the ever-increasing material, technical and organizational assistance given by the people's state the economy of *arat* husbandries improved and they reached the level of middle peasant husbandries. In 1956 middle peasant husbandries constituted 63% of all *arat* farms in the country. Wealthy and poor husbandries disappeared.

The most important feature in the development of *arat* husbandries, particularly those of the middle peasants, was the gradual transition from a natural economy to commodity production. The volume of the commodity output of *arat* husbandries grew both absolutely and relatively. In 1957, for instance, procurements of livestock in the country were 33%, and of wool 35% higher than in 1952. All this, however, did not cover the country's requirements in stock-breeding products.

As stated above, one of the leading branches of the Republic's economy—stock-breeding—was still in the hands of small producers. According to the figures of the MPR population census held in 1956, individual *arat* herdsman constituted 61.4% of the total population of the country; they owned 80.9% of the livestock in the country. The predominance of individually-owned husbandries made it impossible for the state to bring the whole of agriculture under planned control. Consequently, it was essential for the economic development of the country to accelerate the co-operative movement among *arat* farmers.

In introducing the co-operative principle into agriculture a great role was played by the creation and development of the country's own industry, transport and communications, a state finance system, state trading, the socialist agricultural economies of state farms and mechanised stock-breeding stations.

Special attention should be drawn to the importance of state farms and MSS in demonstrating to the *arats* the advantages and benefits of large-scale socialist agricultural production.

For the small *arat* husbandries they served as a school and an example of how to operate a large socialist farm. These were the circumstances under which the transition from small *arat* husbandries to the co-operative form of development was achieved.

The Completion of Arat Husbandries' Cooperation

As a result of the great organizational and political work done by the Party and state in the years of the First Five-Year Plan the APA achieved considerable successes in developing management of public property and attracting the *arat* masses into associations.

In the years 1948-1952 the number of APA in the country rose by 52.7%, the number of APA members by 100% and the head of publicly-owned livestock increased six-fold. By the end of the First Five-Year Plan 5% of *arat* husbandries had become co-operative associations and the share of APA-owned livestock constituted 1.2% of the total head of livestock in the Republic.

At the Plenary Meeting of the MPRP Central Committee (March 1953) for the first time a discussion was held on the problem "The organizational and economic consolidation of *arat* production associations in the Republic."

The Meeting noted that, as a result of the organizational and financial help given by the people's state, *arat* production associations in the Republic had in recent years achieved substantial successes in expanding and consolidating the commonly owned enterprise. However, the process of turning *arat* husbandries into cooperative associations and consolidating the joint land holdings of the APA was proceeding extremely slowly.

The existence of a large number of livestock in personally-owned husbandries had an unfavourable effect on the growth and consolidation of common ownership and the consolidation in every way of joint holdings in the APA. Since the bulk of the members of the APA were engaged in operating their own holdings, they had very little time left for working on jointly-owned holdings. This prevented members of associations from taking an active part in communal production and deprived them of taking an interest in developing and consolidating in every way the jointly-owned land-holdings.

The slow increase in the proportionate number of jointly-owned livestock and in the number of APA members is explained also by the absence in the regulations of a clear definition of the meaning of a jointly-owned holding and of social labour performed by APA members in the further development and consolidation of the newly-established AP associations.

In 1954 the MPR Council of Ministers adopted a resolution on "Measures for improving the organization and payment of work done in *arat* production associations." In this resolution the government recommended all APA bodies to organize labour on the team (brigade) system, to fix approximate norms for output and to evaluate the jobs performed in terms of work-days. It was also pointed out in the same resolution that, as common ownership continued to develop, it would be necessary to introduce planning control of collective activities in the APA. The state gave great assistance in training accountants and managers for associations, organizing at state expense a series of courses for training book-keepers, team-leaders and chairmen of APA. From 1954 on, in response to an appeal from the Party, many envoys sent by the Party, government and voluntary organizations, and also agricultural specialists, were transferred to work in the APA. As a result the collective activities of the APA improved. Following a resolution of the Party Central Committee and the government, two meetings were held during 1953 and 1954 of APA chairmen in the Republic, which were attended by leading workers in local and central Party and government bodies.

Many APAs became important public properties. Individual associations achieved real successes in the organization of labour. Permanent teams became the basic models for the organization of collective labour in first-line farms. A start was made in arranging for accounts to be kept of labour-input and social-output. Collectively owned farms started operating according to the plan. Estimates of income and expenditure began to be compiled.

The areas under cultivation on APA farms were expanded. Whereas in 1953 the total APA area under cultivation in the Republic amounted to 1,397 hectares, in 1954 it amounted to 2,193 hectares. In some associations the income from cultivated land rose to 10-15% above the 1953 figure. The consolidation and development of branches of collective farming and the participation of many members of associations in collective production resulted in an increase in APA revenues in cash and in kind. In 1954 the cash revenues of APA in the Republic were 56% higher than the revenues for 1952.

These facts conclusively prove that the existing APA had accumulated a certain amount of experience in the development of farm-holdings; some outstanding farmholdings emerged.

At the end of the First Five-Year Plan *arat* production associations had won the confidence of a considerable part of the *arat* population and, as a type of collective ownership brought into prominence by the practice of socialist construction in the *khudon*, had proved its ability to survive.

In 1954 the country had 198 associations with 15,400 members. Communal livestock in the associations numbered 979,500 head.

During this period, as the existing APAs grew in strength, new associations were also set up, the number of their members rose and there was a rapid increase in the number of head of commonly-owned livestock.

During the years of the Second Five-Year Plan the Party and the government carried out substantial economic measures for improving and strengthening the economy of APAs. The most important economic measures taken by the Party and the government include financial policy in the field of agriculture and the policy of procurements of agricultural produce and taxation policy in respect of *arat* husbandries and AP associations.

One of the forms of economic assistance given to AP associations by the state were and are short-term and long-term credits. Financial assistance by the state, given in the form of bank advances, was immensely important for the organizational and economic consolidation of associations and for ensuring the rapid growth of their jointly-owned properties, including a rise in the number of jointly-owned livestock, improvement of breeds and raising the productivity of livestock, extension of haylands and development of land cultivation, introduction of cultural and technological developments into agricultural production, an increase in the cash income of associations and, consequently, an improvement in the material welfare and cultural level of their members.

The amounts of financial credits issued by the State Bank to meet the needs of AP associations increased yearly. In 1957 the total amount of these advances was five time as high as in 1952, with long-term credits showing a four-fold and short-term credits, an eleven-fold increase. In 1957 members of agricultural associations in the Republic (AA) were given loans of 700,000 *tugriks* for building individual dwelling-houses. As from 1955 the MPR Council of Ministers increased the extent of each association's credit plus balance to 100,000 *tugriks* in the case of long-term credits and to 10,000 *tugriks* for short-term credits. This made it possible for APAs to make more extensive use of bank loans and utilize them for the rapid development of publicly-owned property.

Taxation policy and the policy for procurements were used by the Party and state as the most important regulators for the economic strengthening of the farms of workers, for restricting *kulak* elements and for putting *arat* farms onto co-operative lines.

Take, for example, the system of the stock-breeding tax in *arat* farms after 1954. This tax was first computed on the basis of the head of livestock on the farm according to the previous year's registration. The total amount of the tax on livestock was reduced by roughly 25%. Under the 1954 Law new rates of tax were fixed on more differentiated lines, depending on the economic strength of the farm. Farms owned by poor *arats* were given large rebates. For instance, farms with up to 20 head of livestock were completely exempted from payment of the tax. The lowest rates were fixed for livestock on farms which had between 21 and 50 head of livestock. As the farms of poorer owners enjoyed big reductions on the stock-breeding tax they were enabled to develop their property independent of pressure from the bigger more prosperous farmers.

A second important result of the new Law on the stock-breeding tax was the sliding scale fixed for livestock on farms which had large numbers of livestock. Those with between 51 and 100 head of livestock paid the stock-breeding tax at the following rates per head of the various types of livestock: 4 *tugriks* per camel, 3 *tugriks* per horse, 2 *tugriks* per head of cattle, 0,7 *tugriks* per sheep and 0.25 *tugriks* per goat, while larger farms paid correspondingly: 8-10 *tugriks* per camel, 7-9 *tugriks* per horse, 6-8 *tugriks* per head of cattle, 1.75-2.30 *tugriks* per sheep, 1,25-2 *tugriks* per goat.

The Party and the government pursued a policy of restricting *kulak* elements and of converting a considerable proportion of the *arat* population into members of co-operatives. The rates of tax fixed under this Law for jointly-owned APA livestock and for the personally-owned livestock of their members were considerably lower than the rates for livestock on personally-owned *arat* farms.

In reliance on the growth and consolidation evinced by the national economy and on the alliance between the working class and the working *arats* (herdsmen)—the basis of the people's democratic system, the people's state set itself the task of speedily completing the voluntary transformation of agriculture into a co-operative economy with a view to creating socialist production relationships in all branches of the national economy.

The new system of procurements (March 1954) played a certain part in accelerating the process of introducing voluntary co-operation into agriculture. Under this Law the norm for deliveries of stock-breeding products was fixed for APA members at 10% below the norm for *arat* farm-holdings and in the case of *arats* joining associations the amount of production to be delivered was reduced to correspond with the numbers of livestock which became jointly-owned property. In the case of *arat* farms progressive, differentiated norms were fixed for delivery of stock-breeding products depending on the strength of the farm.

Farms covering 11-30 *bodo* delivered 20 kilograms of meat and 60 litres of cow's milk per head of cattle, 0.8 kilograms of wool per sheep, and the largest farms, with more than 260 *bodo*, 45 kilograms of meat and 100 litres of milk and 1.5 kilograms of wool, correspondingly.

In the case of the commonly-owned livestock of APA uniform proportional norms were fixed for deliveries of stock-breeding products regardless of the size of the commonly-owned farm. For instance, the APA norm for delivery of meat to the state amounted to 24 kilograms of beef per head of cattle, 4 kilograms of mutton per sheep, 3 kilograms of goat's meat per goat. APA farms had to supply 1.2 kilograms of wool per sheep, 4.2 kilograms per camel, 0.2 kilograms wool and 0.22 kilograms down per goat.

For APA farms the milk supply norm per cow was fixed at 65 litres, irrespective of the number of commonly-owned cattle.

This system of deliveries of produce to the state was aimed at the utmost development and strengthening of the APA economy and the improvement of the material and cultural standards of their members.

The system of deliveries and taxes operated during this period also facilitated the voluntary movement of a considerable number of *arat* farms into APA associations and blocked the development of capitalist elements in agriculture.

In the twelve years from 1942 to 1954 after the adoption of the APA model rules serious changes of socialist character occurred in their existence. These changes were reflected in the new Model Rules.

The new Model Rules were drawn up by the Party and the government with the active participation of wide sections of the rural population and of the active members of central and local Party and governmental bodies and of leaders in industry and APA managerial workers. This marked the conclusion of the first stage of the co-operative movement.

The First Republican Congress of leading figures in agricultural associations (March 1955) was extremely important for the creation and consolidation of collective farming. The new Model Rules for agricultural associations were adopted at this Congress and APA were renamed and were called Agricultural Associations (AA).

The new Model Rules introduced much that was new into the problems of creating and developing AA, as can be seen from the following basic points from the Rules. Membership of an association covers, in addition to the head of the family, all the other members who have attained 16 years of age. Every member of an association is bound to work on the common holding or farm and must put in not less than 75 work days a year. Thus, the Rules clearly express the role played by the labour of every able-bodied member of the association in collective production and emphasize the role of labour as one of the principal factors in the existence and consolidation of the common enterprise of the AA.

The Rules specify the extent to which an *arat's* holding of livestock becomes common property when he becomes a member of an AA—it is based on the particular farm's capacity. Under the new Rules non-divisible funds were set apart annually from the common income, as well as from the common means of production. 25% to 30% of the communal livestock and property is credited to the non-divisible fund— the whole of the entrance fee. Other funds are opened for collective utilization. The Rules define in concrete figures the number of livestock which an AA member is entitled to keep on his individual holding. This varies in different parts of the country. For example, AA members in the Khangai zone may have up to 100 head of livestock on their own personal farm while in the Gobi zone they may have up to 150.

The Rules confirm the status of the permanent production team or brigade as the basic model for the organization of labour in the AA. Income earned by a collective farm was distributed in proportion to the work-days. Thus, the new

Rules represent a higher level of development of cooperative production; an AA differed completely from an APA in the way it was instituted, in its economic functioning and in the labour contribution made by each member to collective production. The adoption of the new Rules signified new qualitative changes in the APA economy. From being groups for mutual labour assistance among *arats*, the APA, changed over to co-operative bodies of a higher type—the AA. It was precisely from this date (March 1955) that the second stage of the co-operative movement began in the MPR.

In the new stage of development of the co-operative movement the AA, under the leadership of the MPRP and the people's state, achieved fresh successes in strengthening collective farming and raising the living and cultural standards of their members.

The numbers of collective livestock speedily increased as the level of collectivization of the livestock of members of old associations rose to the figures laid down in the Model Rules.

The increase in the number of head of collective livestock was due also to the voluntary collectivization of the livestock of *arats* newly admitted to AA membership. The umbers of commonly-owned livestock herds were found to have increased considerably both as a result of the herds' own reproduction and, to some extent also, as a result of purchases of pedigree and improved breeds of animals. At the end of the Second Five-Year Plan, i. e. in 1957, the AA in the Republic had 5,223,600 *bodo* of commonly-owned livestock or 28 times more than in 1952.

At the end of 1957, 33% of *arat* farms in the country had joined the AA and collective cattle amounted to 22.5% of the livestock herds in the country.

In individual *aimaks* the co-operative movement offered the following kind of picture. In the Bulgan *aimak* in 1957 the AA embraced 40% of all *arat* farms and 63% of the *aimak* livestock. In the Bayan-Khongor *aimak* in the same year 38% of *arat* farms became co-operatives and communalized livestock represented 44% of the total. At the same time 74.3% of all *arat* farms in the Bogd-*somon* of the same *aimak*, 77% of the whole population, 90,9% of all the head of livestock in the *arat* farms of the *somon* went over to co-operation. In the Zereg-*somon* of the *aimak* of Kobdo the change-over of the *arat* population to co-operation in the same year was expressed in the following figures: 80% of *arat* households, 70% of the whole population and 79% of all the livestock of *arat* farms.

At the end of 1957 between 50% and 65% of all the *arat* farms in individual *somons* of the Ara-Khangai *aimak* joined the AA. New associations were formed in all the *aimaks* of the country.

After the adoption of the new Rules (1955) and of the new Laws on the stock-breeding tax and on state deliveries (1955) well-to-do and middle sections of *arat* farmers began to join the AA.

The co-operative movement enveloped all sections of the *arat* population, penetrated into every corner of the country and assumed the character of a mass movement.

As a consequence of all this the MPRP and people's state were enabled, while consolidating in every way the existing associations in the country, to raise the problem of accelerating the process of inducing the *arat* population to adopt co-operation voluntarily, basing themselves on the experience accumulated by APA bodies in operating communal farming and on the confidence felt by members of associations and a large proportion of the *arat* population in collective forms of farming, and taking advantage also of the necessary prerequisites created in preceding years by the labour and struggle of Mongolian people for the successful development and consolidation of AA communal farming.

The Thirteenth MPRP Congress (March 1958) found that, in the matter of securing the voluntary accession of *arat* farmers to the co-operative movement, the targets of the Twelfth MPRP Congress had been largely over-fulfilled—more than one third of the *arat* farms had joined agricultural associations and their collective wealth was steadily increasing. The Thirteenth MPRP Congress, in summing up the progress of co-operation among *arat* farmers and considering that a radical improvement in all branches of agriculture was possible only if it were transformed on socialist lines, laid down as a target the completion within three years of bringing the main bulk of *arat* farms into co-operative associations on a voluntary basis and at the same time consolidating and expanding the existing AA. Taking this decision of the Congress as a directive and with the backing of the main mass of the *arat* population, the MPRP and the people's state ensured the transition of *arat* farming to co-operative production. During the years 1958-1959, i. e. in two years of the Three-Year Plan, co-operative farming in the Republic was an accomplished fact.

In 1959, 99.3% of all *arat* farms in the Republic were being worked as co-operatives. Instead of 200,000 small individual *arat* farms 389 large collective farms were created. Each of them had, on an average, 13,000 head of collectivized livestock (expressed in terms of *bodo*), 475 *arat* husbandries and a population of 1,161 of whom 744 were able-bodied adults.

The correct economic policy of the MPRP and people's state, and the stubborn struggle and the devoted efforts of the Mongolian people had resulted in full and final victory for socialist production relations in agriculture.

In its content and results socialist co-operation constituted a major political event comparable to the 1921 people's revolution. Petty-bourgeois production relations were replaced by socialist relations and the roots of economic inequality, private property—the basis of exploitation of man by man—were extirpated. The *arat* population with its large numbers of working people turned irrevocably towards socialism. As a result of the victory of the co-operative system the alliance of the working class and *arat* co-operators was still further consolidated.

As a result of the successful completion of the process of placing agriculture on a co-operative basis a uniform socialist national economy was created. The objective economic laws of socialism, particularly the law of the planned and proportional development of the national economy, the law of extended reproduction, etc., began to operate in agriculture as well. This in turn opened up great opportunities and prospects for a rapid development of agricultural output.

The completion of the transformation of agriculture on co-operative lines coincided with the amalgamation of some small-scale AA. As a result the number of the latter in the country fell sharply and in 1959 they numbered 389 as compared with 675 in 1958. During the same period there was also a recurrence in many *aimaks* of the process of communalizing AA livestock. At the end of 1959 individual AA members' farm had 33 head of livestock as compared with 62 in 1958. In individual *aimaks*, during the second phase of livestock communalization there were cases of directive instructions being disregarded but these were rectified in good time.

In connection with the consolidation and expansion of the common enterprises of AA, a number of steps were taken to improve and reduce the costs of the local government apparatus. The *bag* sub-division was abolished and the *somon* became the basic administrative unit of government. A large number of workers and specialists were trained and sent out to localities to manage AA.

The victory of the people's revolution, the establishment and consolidation of the socialist system in the country's national economy, the further strengthening of the alliance between the working class and the working *arats* and also the experience of the victory of collectivization in the USSR and the completion of the process of making agriculture co-operative in a number of countries in the socialist camp constituted a most important prerequisite and socio-economic condition for the successful completion of the co-operativization of agriculture in the Mongolian People's Republic.

Thanks to the triumph of co-operation in agriculture the country embarked on a new phase of its development—a period of expanded socialist construction.

The victory of co-operation marked a new stage for the AA—a stage in the further consolidation and development of a collective economy.

The Fourth Plenary Meeting of the MPRP Central Committee (December 1959) discussed the question of "The results of transforming *arat* farms into co-operatives and certain very important measures in the organizational and economic strengthening of the AA." Summarizing the successes gained in making *arat* farms into co-operatives, the Central Committee Plenary Meeting outlined a number of new organizational and economic measures for the further consolidation of AA collective farming and for a rapid advance in the material and cultural level of AA members. At the end of 1959 the Second Congress of AA leading members was held, which introduced a number of substantial changes and additions to the AA Model Rules. In view of the rapid development and consolidation of co-operative farming and of the experience of the foremost farms under the new Rules considerable reductions were made in the number of livestock permissible on the individual farms of AA members. Under the new Model Rules a single household (family) may keep the following number of livestock for personal use: in the Khangai zone—10 head of livestock for each member of the family but not more than 50 head on the farm, in the Gobi zone—15 head of livestock for each member of the family but not more than 75 head per farm.

The Congress increased the extent to which AA communal funds might be set up. In the new stage of AA development the Party and the government introduced and implemented extremely important measures for strengthening the economy of the AA. In 1958 a resolution of the MPRP Central Committee and the MPR Council of Ministers was adopted concerning the further development and consolidation of AA communal farming and improving the productive activity of MSS in servicing the AA.

During the three years from 1957 to 1959 the output of wool, milk and meat in the AA of the Republic rose from 2.5 to 3.4 times and the gross yield of grain crops rose fivefold and that of the hay-crop 2.5-fold.

In 1959 AA farms had 5,049,000 head of commonly-owned livestock as compared with 1,642,000 head of livestock (in terms of *bodo*) in 1957.

It is, however, necessary to emphasize that the rise in the output of basic livestock produce in the AA was basically the result of a further communalization of livestock. As regards land cultivation there was almost no such cultivation done on *arat* farms and accordingly the introduction and development of land cultivation was the consequence of an increase in areas under tillage and also in crop yields on AA farms and proof of the unquestionable superiority of collective production. When the organizational period was over the increased output of produce on AA farms after 1959 followed as a result of extended reproduction in the sphere of communal farming.

At this time noticeable improvements of a qualitative character occurred in the development of collective stockbreeding. Work continued on AA farms to mechanize the production and procurement of forage, bore and operate wells, process milk, etc. More accommodation was built for livestock and modern veterinary advances were introduced into stockbreeding and the number of agricultural specialists on AA farms was increased. Steps were taken to improve the quality and productivity of animals. AA farms became large-stock farms. During this period each AA farm had on an average 15,000 head of livestock (expressed in terms of *bodo*). Leading AA farms not only increased the head of cattle but they also secured qualitative improvements in local livestock and raised its productivity.

The AA expanded land cultivation and subsidiary branches of activity and soon overcame the one-sided development of agriculture which had been a feature of ordinary *arat* farms. Over the five-year period (1955-1959) the area under cultivation on AA farms rose more than sixfold and formed 22.5% of the total area under tillage in the Republic. There was a steady rise in the gross yield of their grain crop.

In many AA there was a successful development of enterprises for the processing of agricultural produce and of all kinds of subsidiary concerns (brickworks, lime kilns, salt pans, game-hunting, mechanical and joinery workshops, saw mills, etc.) and of various workshops for making and repairing clothing.

The development of auxiliary branches on AA farms not only made for the fuller utilisation of a farm's labour resources throughout the whole year but was also valuable in helping to increase the commodity production and income-earning capacity of a farm. In 1960 the proportional share of cash income earned by auxiliary branches amounted to 21.6% of the total cash earnings of the AA. During this period (1958-1960) cooperation between the AAs and the joint enterprises created by them increased; many AAs combined their efforts and funds to produce supplies of building timber, dig irrigation channels and carry out joint sowing campaigns.

The development and consolidation of AAs and the increase in output were greatly assisted by the steps taken at the time by the MPRP and the MPR government, by the change made in the procurement system for agricultural produce (1960), by the organization and considerable improvement in the work of MSS in servicing the AA, by the greater assistance in financial and technical matters received from the state and the larger credit facilities offered to the AA, by the writing-off of the indebtedness of the AA and their members in respect of deliveries to the state of stock-breeding produce and of the arrears incurred in respect of the tax on stock-breeding. The latter tax was replaced by an income tax and a great reduction was made in the over-all volume of the taxes levied on associations (1960). During this time (1958-1960) several increases were made in the procurement and purchasing prices paid by the state for basic AA produce, as a result of which the AA and their members earned 200,000,000 *tugriks* more.

In the years 1957-1959 the state carried out land distribution. The AA were allotted 120 million hectares of land.

As a result of all these measures the AA became economically stronger and constituted the basic producers and suppliers of stock-breeding products in the country. The AA of the Republic are producing and supplying three-quarters of the products of stock-breeding in the country.

The constant growth of production and the considerable improvement in the material and cultural standards of AA members testify to the unquestionable advantages of the AA over small-scale *arat* farms and also to the existence of enormous reserves for increasing production still untapped.

At the same time it is impossible not to mention the special features and the serious difficulties connected with the emergence and development of a new system of managing agriculture. The period we are considering is a period in which AAs have become a collectivized economy, a period in which new production relations emerged and in which old relations collapsed.

The organizational period, with its well-known inherent difficulties, has been developing against the background of a poorly-developed material base. The non-divisible funds of the AA were not large and consisted mainly of the *arat's* rather primitive means of production which had been collectivized—low-yield livestock, primitive working tools and simple peasant structures for livestock. The AA did not have sufficient material or financial resources to make radical changes and improvements in methods of carrying on agriculture. During the period under consideration the AA had available considerable reserves of labour but these were still not being fully utilized for the development of collective farming.

The socialist transformation of agriculture in the MPR also had its own special features. In Mongolia the country was engaged in the transition from feudalism to socialism, by-passing capitalism. This is the main special feature of the socio-economic development of the MPR. The co-operativization of agriculture in the MPR took place in historical circumstances differing from those in other socialist countries.

In the early years of the revolution the land was nationalized.

This, however, did not solve the basic problems of the co-operativization of agriculture, which in other countries usually begins with the collectivization of the peasants' land. In the specific conditions obtaining in the MPR this did not happen. The one-sided development of extensive pastoral stock-breeding in pre-revolutionary Mongolia, the consequence of the backwardness and natural forms of farming practised by the *arats* is an important feature of the development of Mongolia's agriculture in general. The basic trend of *arat* farming in Mongolia was towards pastoral stock-breeding, not to the cultivation of land; there were still stretches of territory, mainly unirrigated, which had still not been brought under cultivation.

The transformation of *arat* stock-breeders into co-operators meant the collectivization of livestock and the creation of collective farming with a trend towards stock-breeding. This is the basic characteristic of the co-operativization of *arat* farms and the creation of AA collective farming.

Because of the survivals of a natural economy the *arats* usually kept on their farms different types of animals of both sexes and various ages. This is because small *arat* farms could not carry on rational farming on the basis of a correct distribution and specialization of production because of the poor development of social division of labour and the low level of growth of productive resources.

The development of communal farming in the AA created favourable economic conditions for the rational location and specialization of farming.

Before state farms were set up and *arat* farms joined co-operative associations land cultivation in the country was poorly developed. It had still not emerged as an independent branch of agriculture and was not combined with stock-breeding. In their turn, the various types of livestock were located all over the country on individual *arat* farms. Stock-breeding not only continued to be a backward branch of agriculture but it also retained in very marked fashion a natural, consumer character.

When the AA were set up the state handed over to them for their use specific farmland. In utilizing the latter the AA began to develop land cultivation alongside stock-breeding. This had serious repercussions in eliminating the survivals of the natural form of stock-breeding. This was the second special feature of the co-operativization of agriculture in the MPR.

In connection with the successful development of land cultivation as an independent branch of agriculture and the further intensification of stock-breeding there was a noticeable intensification of the trend of the rural population to adopt a settled way of life.

Realizing these special features of agriculture in the various stages of the country's economic development, the MPRP and the MPR government fixed concrete targets for the extent and level of the communalization of livestock with a view to creating collective farming at various stages and ensuring a proper combination of personal and collective interest in the AA.

The communalization of livestock in the AA was carried through twice. This is another example of the special form taken by the co-operativization of individual *arat* farms.

The process of completing the reorganization of agriculture in the MPR and in many countries of socialism proceeded almost simultaneously; advantage was taken of the great historical experience of the Soviet Union in building up collective farming. This greatly facilitated the solution of the complicated problems of co-operativization. The victory of socialism and the rapid growth of agricultural production in a number of countries in Europe and Asia exercised a beneficial influence and effect on the co-operativization of *arat* farms in Mongolia.

Because of the specific historical circumstances and special features of Mongolia's economic development the co-operativization of agriculture in the MPR was carried into effect, despite the fact that the country was without its own agricultural machinery industry.

Nevertheless the existence of the world socialist system and the all-round help given by it to the Mongolian people greatly facilitated the victory of socialist production relations in Mongolian agriculture.

Ratification of the New Constitution

After the Constitution was adopted in 1940 immense changes occurred in the MPR; basic revolutionary socio-economic and political transformations were carried through which resulted in the completion of the transition from feudalism to socialism.

In the socialist stage of the revolution the Mongolian people achieved enormous successes in all departments of the socio-political, economic and cultural life of the country. National industry and modern methods of transport were successfully developed. Very important branches of industry such as mining, oil-extraction and oil-refining were created.

From being a predominantly stock-breeding country the MPR became an agricultural-industrial country. The outstanding event and achievement in the history of the Mongolian people is the completion of the socialist collectivisation of individual *arat* farming, based on Lenin's doctrine of voluntary co-operativization of agriculture, which led to the creation of a new socialist economy and the victory of socialist production relations in the whole of the country's economy.

At this stage the Mongolian people's culture developed greatly and big successes were achieved in raising the material and cultural standards of the workers.

The most profound changes occurred in the field of ideology. Buddhism was successfully and completely displaced from the political forum of Mongolian society as the ideology of the exploiting classes. Marxism-Leninism had now been finally established as the ideology of the working class and of a socialist society.

Basic qualitative changes occurred in the MPR in the class structure of society.

There was a steady increase of the working class and of its role in the industrial-economic and socio-political life of the country; it emerges as the most decisive force in the transformation of society, as the builder of socialism, as the leader of the workers of the MPR. In the course of the socialist co-operativization of agriculture the *arat* community, from being a class of small individual proprietors, became a new socialist class of *arat* co-operators. The outstanding triumphs of the Mongolian people consist in the practical implementation of Lenin's doctrine of the possibility of formerly backward peoples following the non-capitalist path of development from feudalism to socialism. The position and prestige of the MPR on the international scene grew immensly. The formation of a world socialist system, the development of friendly relations between socialist countries, the growth of a national-liberation and revolutionary movement among the peoples of Asia and Africa, the disintegration of the colonialist system of imperialism, the intensification of the general crisis of capitalism—all this created extremely favourable conditions for the MPR in the construction of socialism. All these achievements and the successes of the Mongolian people needed to be formulated in legislation and consolidated.

In July 6, 1960, the first Session of the Grand People's Hural, fourth convocation, unanimously adopted a new Constitution of the MPR.

The new Constitution is the organic law of the Mongolian People's Republic as it entered the period of the completion of the socialist transformation of society. The preamble to the Constitution stated that "The Mongolian People's Republic poses as its target the completion of socialist construction and the eventual building of communist society."

The new Constitution gave statutory force to the socialist principles of the social and economic organization of the MPR, extended the constitutional rights of citizens of the Republic and strengthened the guarantees of those rights.

In its class nature, objectives and functions the MPR is now "a socialist state of workers, *arats* in co-operative associations (*arat* herdsmen) and worker-intellectuals, based on an alliance of the working class and members of *arat* co-operative associations."

With the completion of the co-operativization of individual *arat* farms the economic prerequisites for dividing society into antagonistic classes and exploitation of man by man were completely eliminated. The Mongolian society consists of two friendly classes—the working class and the class of *arat* co-operative members, and also worker-intellectuals. In the new circumstances the alliance of the working class and the *arat* co-operative members becomes increasingly strong and is developing on a new basis. This alliance represents the supreme principle of the dictatorship of the proletariat—the principal weapon for the revolutionary transformation of Mongolian society.

The task of building socialism in the MPR now becomes the universal aim of all classes and workers in the MPR. In the MPR the workers exercise governmental authority through the state governmental bodies—the hurals of people's deputies. At the centre and locally all deputies are elected by the people and are representatives of the whole working people. The social composition of the deputies to the Grand People's Hural of the last four convocations—1951, 1954, 1957 and 1960—is as follows: herdsmen AA members accounted for 38.3%, 34.2%, 33.3% and 35.2% of the total number of deputies at each convocation, workers—13.6%, 19.3%, 24.9% and 23.3%, and intellectuals—48.1%, 46.5%, 41.6% and 41.5%. These figures show that the proportion of the working class in the membership of the Grand People's Hural is steadily rising. The economic basis of the MPR is furnished by the socialist system of farming and by socialist ownership of the means of production, created as a result of the abolition of private ownership of the means of production and the elimination of exploitation of man by man.

In the MPR there are two forms of socialist ownership: state ownership, i.e. property owned by the people as a whole, and co-operative ownership, property owned by agricultural associations and other types of co-operatives. Today the socialist sector occupies the leading position in the whole national economy of the MPR. The role played by the people's-democratic state in the economy is steadily increasing.

The new MPR Constitution reflects the role and the functions of the Mongolian socialist state. Inside the country the basic functions of the socialist state are its activities in the field of economic organization and cultural education, while outside the country it has to consolidate friendship and collaboration with the countries of the socialist system, ensure peace and friendship with all peoples, based on the principles of peaceful co-existence, and protect the country from imperialist encroachments. The new Constitution states that "the socialist state safeguards and strengthens common socialist ownership, ensures active participation by members of the public in economic and cultural construction, reinforces in every way the socialist discipline of labour and organizes the country's defence against imperialist aggression." A people's democratic state has at its disposal powerful regulators and effective methods, one of which is the planning of economic and cultural construction. In managing the national economy the state keeps a check and control over production and distribution, over the amount of work done and the volume of consumption. In the MPR the national income is divided between members in proportion to the quality and quantity of the work done and on the basis of the socialist principle: "From each according to his ability, to each according to his work." Approximately 75% of the national income goes on satisfying the personal needs of members of the socialist society and 25% is spent on social needs. The state gives workers different kinds of free services and assistance in the form of free medical help, free education, pensions, student scholarships, grants to mothers of large families, paid holidays and material assistance.

The social and governmental structure of the MPR, based on socialist production relations and devoid of any exploitation of man by man, has created favourable conditions for an all-round development of the personality, and wide opportunities for the working people to participate in the country's social and political life. All citizens of the MPR who have reached the age of 18, irrespective of nationality, have equal opportunities to take part in all spheres of the governmental, economic, cultural and socio-political life of the country; women have equal rights with men in every respect.

The state strictly safeguards the rights of citizens. A major victory won by the Mongolian people during the years of the people's power is the separation of the church from the state and of the school from the church. Under the Constitution citizens enjoy freedom of religious belief and of anti-religious propaganda.

Thus, the 1960 Constitution has given statutory force to the triumph of socialism in the MPR.

CHAPTER II

THE MPR IN THE FIGHT TO COMPLETE
THE CONSTRUCTION OF THE MATERIAL
AND TECHNICAL BASIS OF SOCIALISM

*The Tasks of Creating the Material
and Technical Basis of Socialism in the MPR.
Fourteenth MPRP Congress*

Historical changes occurred in the life of the country as a result of the complete victory of socialist production relations, and the Party and the people were faced with new tasks. At this time the MPRP held its Fourteenth Congress from July 3 to 7, 1961, in Ulan Bator.

The Congress discussed the report of the MPRP Central Committee and the report on the Third Five-Year Plan for the development of the MPR's national economy and culture for the years 1961-1965, and historic decisions were adopted on these questions.

With the complete victory of socialist production relations in the country the period of transition from feudalism to socialism in the MPR came to an end. This was reflected in the MPRP Central Committee's report to the Fourteenth Congress in which it is pointed out that in the MPR "the basic contradiction of the transition period has finally been settled in favour of socialism." [1]

The Fourteenth Congress of the MPRP noted that, from 1960, the country embarked upon a new period of its development—the period of completion of the construction of a socialist society.[2] The Congress pointed out that "the basic problem in this period is to develop in every way and to complete the process of creating the material and technical basic of socialism." [3] The victory of socialist production relationships created favourable conditions for accelerating the development of the country's productive forces, especially for completing the creation of a material and technical basis for socialism.

The importance attached to the problem of the material and technical basis of socialism does not mean that nothing had so far been done in this direction or that it was the first time the question was being raised.

The MPR had advanced immeasurably far beyond the level of the productive forces of a feudal society. All the successes achieved during the years of the people's rule in the technical and economic field amounted precisely to the beginning of the creating of the material and technical basis of socialism and the basis for widespread socialist construction. After socialist production relations had completely prevailed, the task of completing the construction of the material and technical basis of socialism became the key point in socialist construction in the MPR.

In view of this the Congress pointed out that "the principal factors in the creation of a material and technical basis for socialism are the industrialization of the country and the mechanization of agriculture so as to ensure its intensification." [4]

The industrialization of a country is one of the main problems in constructing a material and technical basis for socialism.

In solving the problem of industrializing the country it is extremely important for the MPR to collaborate with the countries of the socialist system. At the present time when there exists a single world system of socialist economy there is no need to develop all branches of heavy industry in each individual socialist country. The heavy industry of the whole socialist system is jointly called upon to act as the material and technical basis of socialism for each country in the socialist system. This circumstance relieves the MPR of the need for the comprehensive development of all branches of heavy industry.

Industrialization in the MPR will be carried out by developing new branches of industry corresponding to the specific natural and economic features of the country and its essential requirements, taking into account the interests of the socialist system as a whole, by expanding in every way technical progress, steadfastly introducing into production up-to-date advanced technology and making production processes automatic and on this basis steadily increasing labour productivity.

The problem of creating the material and technical basis for socialism as far as it relates to agriculture consists in introducing into agricultural production scientific and technological improvements on a wide scale, mechanizing the principal operations involved in tilling the land and in stock-breeding—gradually converting the *arat* herdsmen into permanent settlers.

To create the material and technical basis for socialism it is necessary to train an adequate number of qualified cadres needed for all branches of the national economy and culture and to raise the cultural and technical level of the working people.

With the accomplishment of the historical tasks involved in

creating the material and technical basis of socialism the MPR will become an industrial-agrarian country.

In its decisions the Fourteenth MPRP Congress pointed out that: "The most important task for our Party and for all the workers of the country consists in converting the MPR in the immediate future from an agrarian-industrial country into an industrial-agrarian country."

The Congress took a decision to draw up as speedily as possible a long-term plan for the development of the MPR over the next 15-20 years which embraces the immense tasks facing the country during the period in question.

The general long-term economic development plan takes in the period in which the construction of a socialist society, with its material and technical basis, is to be completed and the period for preparing the conditions for a gradual transition to the construction of a communist society.

The Fourteenth MPRP Congress pointed out that the time was fully ripe for considering the problem of drawing up a new Party programme in which the historical experience of the MPRP's activities should be reviewed from the Marxist-Leninist point of view, and the prospects outlined in advance for the further development of the country along the path of socialism and for the gradual transition to communism.

The Third Five-Year Plan (1961-1965) represented an immense step towards completing the construction of a socialist society. This plan for developing the national economy and culture would result in accelerating the development rate of all branches of the economy and a tremendous advancement of the country's productive forces. A special place was allotted in the plan to the development of agriculture—the basic branch of the MPR's economy.

The Third Five-Year Plan differed from its predecessors in that it was based on the principle of developing the cooperative type of socialist agriculture, not individual *arat* farms. The new Five-Year Plan envisaged stock-breeding and land cultivation developing proportionally.

\ During the Third Five-Year Plan the gross output of agriculture was to increase 1.8 times. The head of cattle was to be increased by 11% and by the end of 1965 would amount to 22,900,000.

Pedigree breeding was the basic measure designed to ensure a rise in the productivity of stock-breeding. For this purpose plans were outlined for developing sheep-breeding with concentration on the production of fine-fleece, semi-fine-fleece sheep and types of sheep producing both lean mutton and fat and coarse fleece, and for breeding dairy, beef and dairy-beef types of cattle.

In 1965 the number of cross-bred stock was to be increased to 7.2 times the 1960 figure and of pure pedigree high-producer animals to 2.5 times.

Great attention was paid to improving pedigree types of livestock and to bettering the organization of campaigns for the mating of livestock. In the years of the Third Five-Year Plan 42 stations were established for the breeding and artificial insemination of livestock and about 2,000 similar centres. In addition to developing the traditional five types of livestock during the years of the Third Five-Year Plan, almost new branches of agriculture such as pig-breeding, poultry-farming and the breeding of fur-bearing animals were also widely developed.

One of the basic conditions for the intensive development of animal husbandry is the ensurance of reliable fodder supplies. In 1965 the output of all types of fodder was to be increased to 33% above the 1960 figure. Alongside the procurement of natural fodder there was to be a considerable rise in the production of artificial fodder which in 1965 was to amount to 500,000 tons.

The Party gave first priority as an economic target to the irrigation of arid pastures. The total area under pasture in the country amounted to 137 million hectares, of which 38% or about 50 million hectares had no water supply. By the end of the Third Five-Year Plan 75% of all pastures were to be irrigated.

In the years of the Third Five-Year Plan there was a target fixed for providing pens or sheds—roofed and heated accommodation—for livestock. This would mean that the difficult problem of providing all the country's livestock with the necessary accommodation would be basically achieved.

The Third Five-Year Plan envisaged the creation of veterinary-surgeon centres in each agricultural association, a veterinary-*feldshers* centre in each livestock "brigade", since the campaign against infectious diseases in livestock plays a most important part in ensuring the normal development of stockbreeding.

In accordance with the Third Five-Year Plan the following basic targets were laid down in regard to land cultivation: further assimilation of virgin lands, increasing the harvest yield per hectare, providing the population with vegetables and increasing the proportion of fodder crops in fodder procurements for livestock.

An important step was envisaged with regard to the introduction into agriculture of the achievements of modern science and technology and in the mechanization and electrification of agriculture. In 1965, for instance, there were to be 2.8 times as many tractors as in 1960 and 2.2. times as many combines. In the years 1961-1965, 15 machine and stock-breeding stations would again be established. The Fourteenth MPRP Congress drew attention to the need for further improvements in the organization of labour in agricultural associations and for switching agricultural associations over to paying cash wages for labour and it forecast that the volume of long-term credits issued to such associations would be 5 times as high in 1965.

The task of the Third Five-Year Plan in relation to industry was to ensure, on the basis of a further increase in the industrial processing of agricultural raw materials and of utilization in every possible way of the country's very rich natural wealth, the development as a first priority, of a fuel and power industry and the utmost development of light and food industries. The Five-Year Plan envisaged increasing gross industrial output to 2.1 times the 1960 figure; to this end, 32% of the total amount of capital investments in the national economy would go to industry. The average annual growth in the gross industrial output was to amount to 16%.

In the interests of creating the material and technical basis for socialism in the MPR basic attention is being paid to developing, as a first priority, the production of the means of production. As a result, in 1965 the share of group "A" in industrial output was to amount to 57%, and of the total growth in industrial output to 54% as a result of increased labour productivity.

The Third Five-Year Plan also provided for dozens of new industrial enterprises to be brought into operation, for the creation of completely new branches of industry, for the rational location of industrial enterprises so as to bring them closer to raw material supplies and consumers, for the large-scale introduction into production of modern scientific and technological methods, for a basic improvement in material and technical supplies, for production and the training of engineering and technical staff, for an improvement in the quality of the products manufactured and for a reduction in production costs.

During the years of the Third Five-Year Plan there was to be a marked improvement in the mechanical transport of freight. During this period transport of freight by all forms of transport was to be increased by 90%.

During this period the centres of all agricultural associations and large centres of population were to be linked up with local administrative centres by modern systems of communication, including radio and telephone networks.

The volume of capital investment in the development of the national economy was to amount in the years of the Third Five-Year Plan to 446,000 million *tugriks*.

Geologists were given an immense task—to accomplish a new and important advance in discovering the natural wealth of the country and to prepare a long-term plan of geological surveys for the next 10-15 years.

Considerable progress was to be made in raising the level of the workers' material welfare and culture.

Targets have been fixed for the reorganization of the system of public education based on strengthening the link between learning and life and switching over to compulsory incomplete secondary education of all children of school age. In the decisions of the Fourteenth MPRP Congress it was stated that "...the Communist education of workers, above all, of the young generation, is a highly important task..."[5] There was to be a considerable increase in the number of theatres, cinemas, houses of culture, clubs and libraries which were to become real centres of culture.

In the directives of the Five-Year Plan attention was drawn to the necessity for improving record- and book-keeping in all branches of the economy, for the practical introduction of progressive methods of managing a socialist economy, the reduction of production costs, the expenditure of both material and cash resources and an increase in socialist accumulation.

The organized management of socialist construction is based on popularizing progressive experience, on giving every kind of support to all that is progressive, on working correctly with cadres and improving the control over the fulfilment of tasks.

The accomplishment of the Third Five-Year Plan represented an immense step forward to creating the material and technical basis of socialism in the MPR.

The Mongolian People in the Campaign to Fulfil the Third Five-Year Plan for Developing the National Economy and Culture

Under the guidance of the Mongolian People's Revolutionary Party the Mongolian people were working energetically for the successful fulfilment of the tasks of the Third Five-Year Plan.

The tasks advanced by the Fourteenth Congress and the Second Plenary Meeting of the MPRP Central Committee for radically improving the management of economic and cultural construction and for mobilizing the organizational and ideological work of the Party in solving the basic problems of developing the economy were successfully fulfilled.

The problem of reorganizing and improving agricultural management became particularly critical because of the completely new conditions that had arisen as a result of the completion of the co-operativization of *arat*-farms, which made it necessary completely to replace the old method of managing individual *arat* farms by a method for managing a single socialist farm.

Important steps have been taken by the Party and government to strengthen the economy and improve the organization of agricultural associations to increase the material interest of association members, and to raise the material and cultural level of people working in agriculture on the basis of utilizing the advantages of large-scale collective farming. On this problem the MPRP Central Committee and the MPR Council of Ministers took a number of important steps to change the state system of procurement, to extend the system of inter-association production, improve record-keeping and book-keeping systems and the supervision of agricultural associations, expand operations for the irrigation of pastoral holdings, improve repairs to, and conservation of, agricultural machinery and mechanical installations, the operations of mechanized stock-breeding centres and the organization and payment of labour in agricultural associations.

In May 1963 a resolution was adopted by the MPRP Central Committee and Council of Ministers of the MPR on "Measures for the development of inter-association production." [6] The resolution indicated the main directions in which agricultural associations should develop joint production: procurement of fodder, organization of land-cultivation operations, processing of certain types of stock-breeding products and waste materials, local manufacture of building materials, etc. Management of joint operations in combined production devolved on a Council for Combined Production. Revenues from production were to be distributed according to the size of the assets contributed to the association.

This measure opened up wide possibilities for utilizing the concealed reserves of each association which it was difficult to achieve within the framework of individual farms because of the shortage of manpower and low profitability. This measure was designed to strengthen the economy of the associations and to expand their productive forces.

On the basis of the decision of the MPRP Central Committee and MPR Council of Ministers regarding "Measures to improve the organization of labour and payment of labour in agricultural associations," [7] adopted in August 1963, better work was done to introduce a new procedure for the organization and remuneration of labour in agricultural associations.

The basic feature was the organization of labour in teams, sectors and branches with a clear differentiation between these three production sectors. Positive results were achieved by issuing labour cards to association members.[8]

Under the new procedure the amount of the assets contributed, the amount of work done per month and the payments due were entered on the labour card.

In order to increase an association's interest in developing land cultivation lower prices have been introduced for the high-grade seeds supplied to associations and higher prices (compared with those fixed for state farms) for the grain handed over to the state. The state gave the associations every kind of assistance to acquire machinery and pedigree livestock and to expand construction work in their farms.

In the years 1961-1963 internal land distribution was carried out on these farms, which was extremely important for the rational utilization of land-holdings.

Effect was also given to such measures, aimed at improving farm management and supplying agriculture with qualified specialists, as sending out about 600 managerial workers on Party assignments to agricultural associations and building sites, inaugurating two-year courses for Party organisers and team-leaders of agricultural associations, which were held in 1962 at the Higher Party School attached to the MPRP Central Committee, and inaugurating in 1963 a school for young stockbreeders with a view to the organised training of stockbreeders. In four years 726 agricultural specialists with higher education and 1,888 with special secondary education were trained. In stimulating the material interest of members of agricultural associations, in increasing the head of livestock and improving material welfare of the people an important part was played by the decision of the Party and government to raise procurement prices for meat and wool, exempt the members of agricultural associations from obligatory deliveries of meat, milk and livestock from their personal subsidiary farms and lay down a new procedure for rewarding the foremost agricultural associations.

The introduction into production of progressive experience and of the suggestions of innovators gave corresponding results in the sphere of improving production techniques, increasing labour productivity, detecting and making use of internal reserves and economizing in the use of cash funds.

The organizational management of the introduction of innovatory proposals and progressive experience into production was carried out by a special State Commission which had about 900 sub-committees in the centre and the provinces. In 1962-1965 Mongolian innovators in production, whose number had risen to more than 17,000, put forward about 13,000 proposals, 11,000 of which were acted upon. This brought the state 43.5

million *tugriks* clear profit. In 1963 the first republican conference of production innovators was held and the results of the experience accumulated were reviewed.

All over the country there was a wide development of a mass movement taking the form of socialist competition to fulfil the Third Five-Year Plan; the patriotism and creativeness of the workers rose to unprecedented heights. The movement to earn the title of "brigade of socialist labour", one of the factors stimulating people to take an active part in the fight for the construction of socialism, also spread very widely. The first republican conference of collectives and shock-workers of socialist labour was held in November 1961.

Workshops, enterprises and farms were becoming socialist labour collectives. This signified a new phase in the development of the popular movement for the title of socialist labour brigade. This new, higher form of socialist competition became an important economic and moral factor in speeding up an advance towards the creation of a material-technical basis for socialism.

In 1964 there were reckoned to be 2,500 brigades fighting for the title of socialist labour collective, 1,488 socialist labour brigades, more than 900 societies of intellectuals for cultural assistance, 70 enterprises competing for the title of socialist labour collective, 12 industrial enterprises and farms of socialist labour, the total number involved in this movement being 72,000. Not only individual groups of people but whole collectives of industrial and farming organizations joined the movement for socialist labour, which speaks for the mass appeal and scope of this movement at the higher level of its development. The country had 72 MPR Heroes of Labour.

As a result of all this, between 1962 and 1965 considerable changes occurred in the development of all branches of the country's economy and culture and in the raising of the material well-being of the people.

In the years 1961-1965 great successes were achieved in the development of stock-breeding. Extensive work was done to introduce into stock-breeding the achievements of progressive experience and science.

The Party and the government did a great deal of work to disseminate and apply in practice the progressive methods and procedures of a well-known herdsman, Ochir, Hero of Labour of the MPR, in grazing livestock for fattening. It is extremely important to see that livestock are thoroughly fattened in order to improve their productivity, enable them to withstand successfully the natural calamities that are often met with and get through the winters safely. This is exactly why it has become an excellent tradition to organize a campaign for fattening livestock at pasture and since 1961 this campaign has been conducted in the country annually during the period May-November.

As official statistics show, in the years 1963-1964 alone the fattened weight of herded livestock was increased by 39,500 tons by arranging for fattening at pasture. This is equivalent to the live weight of 1,000,000 head of sheep.

The main source of an increase in the number of livestock is the progeny they breed and so very great attention is paid to organized mating and to bringing the young animals into the world successfully and rearing them to full growth. The use of artificial insemination, along with other methods, has done away with haphazard mating at breeding-time and given the breeding campaign a more organized character on a nation-wide scale. For these purposes, in 1961-1964, 34 artificial insemination centres were set up out of the 42 originally planned. The application of the "foster-group" method of rearing lambs and the foster rearing of calves constituted an important advance in the conservation of progeny. As a result of implementing the measures for increasing in every possible way the proportion of female animals in the total herd, females in 1964 amounted to more than 47% of the total head of livestock.

Success was achieved in introducing into agriculture the achievements of science and technology. A new semi-fine fleece Orkhon breed of sheep was developed which is very productive and well-adapted to rigorous climatic conditions. A new Orkhon type of wheat was also created.

An experiment in producing combined, mixed and mineral fodder of a concentrated type gave good results. A start was made in building factories for making combined fodder.

A number of systematic steps were taken by the veterinary bodies of the country to improve the health services available for treating animals and veterinary prophylactic facilities and as a result the target fixed by the Third Five-Year Plan in this field was fulfilled in 1964, i.e. a year ahead of schedule.

In the 1962-1965 important results were achieved in solving the problems of fodder and water supplies which were the principal factors conditioning the growth in head of livestock and improving its productivity. An essential factor in the procurement of fodder for livestock is the cultivation and production of fodder crops. In 1962-1965 the area under fodder crops was increased 2.5 times. A great deal of work was done in that period in irrigating grazing grounds, especially in the Gobi region. During this time, both in the centre and locally, technically well-equipped water works were constructed, prospecting work was done in order to discover sources of water, some 5,400 wells were dug and more than 560 borehoe wells sunk; in the localities of Bayan-Nur and Gulinskaya steppe new irrigation works were built. Capital investment in irrigation operations amounted to 54.3 million *tugriks*. Some 30 million hectares of pasture lands were irrigated.

During this period great successes were achieved in creating a material and technical base for agriculture. In the main, labour-consuming processes in land cultivation were mechanized. The number of tractors and grain combines used in agriculture rose respectively 2.3 and 1.6 times in 1964 as compared with 1960. The natural calamities of 1964 which affected certain regions of the country exceeded in strength and severity the *dzut*—the winter dearth of fodder of 1944 and 1945. Nevertheless, as a result of the measures taken by the Party and government, the help received from the Soviet Union and other socialist countries, and the self-sacrificing efforts of and the stubborn fight waged by, the *arat* population the damage and consequences suffered from *dzut* proved to be only about 28 per cent of those suffered during previous natural calamities.

As a result of all this, in 1964 the total head of livestock was 4% higher than in 1960.

In four years more than 300,000 hectares of virgin soil were brought under cultivation and the gross yield of the grain harvest was increased by 50% as against 1960. In output of grain per head of the population the MPR outstripped the United Kingdom, Italy, West Germany, and other capitalist countries.

In 1965 there were 293 AA, with an average of 477 households, and more than 900 able-bodied persons; a single AA had about 72,700 head of livestock and more than 420,000 hectares of farmland. The AA were growing stronger in the economic sense, their collective property was increasing, and also their cash income, the overwhelming majority (90%) of which ran into millions of *tugriks*. In 1964 the cash remuneration of associations was 2.9 times as much as in 1959 and the average payment per member 4.4 times as much. The payment received by members of associations for their labour became their basic source of livelihood.

The Party and government encouraged the development of personal subsidiary farms on which the head of livestock rose by 14.3% in four years.

These successes of AA were very closely bound up with their provision with agricultural machinery and the introduction of scientific advances into agriculture.

In 1965 the country had 39 mechanization and stock-breeding stations which assisted the AA with machinery and specialists. The MSS were equipped with machinery and had the requisite repair facilities. With their help the most labour-consuming farming operations were completely mechanized.

The co-operativization of agriculture helped to change the appearance of rural regions. Modern amenities were provided at centres of rural associations and their teams. These are important centres of population equipped with electricity, radio and telephone communications, hospitals, schools, kindergartens, day nurseries and clubs.

The results achieved by agricultural associations prove that the co-operative system offers enormous possibilities for developing the productive forces of agriculture and for increasing the well-being and cultural level of the workers.

The country's 29 state farms owned at that time 764,300 head of livestock and accounted for 71.5% of the country's cultivated area. In 1962-1965, alongside the increase in the head of livestock and the expansion of the crop area, the productivity of livestock rose and the volume of crops harvested per hectare increased. Procurement of wool rose by 12%. The number of crossbreed cattle in state farms increased 5 times and the number of cross-breed sheep—4 times.

In the Third Five-Year Plan period industry achieved great successes. In 1965 the gross figure of industrial output was 1.6 times the 1960 figure and the average annual growth in production comprised 10.3%. In 1961-1965 about 90 new manufacturing enterprises and workshops were brought into operation and their technical equipment increased. Thanks to the fraternal assistance of socialist countries and, above all, of the Soviet Union, in the years of the Third Five-Year Plan many collective establishments were built and started working; they included the fifth section of the Ulan Bator Thermal Electric Power Station, a kid-leather tannery, a house-building combine, an extension to the Ulan Bator elevator, a thermal electric power station in Tolgoita, a poultry farm in Bukhega, a woodworking combine in Tosontsengel, shops for repairing agricultural machinery, the first section of the Ulan Bator airport, etc.

During that period a large meat-packing plant and a big motor repair works in Ulan Bator, two motor-repair works in *aimaks*, a bakery, a pig-fattening farm, a kid-leather tannery, a clothing factory, a light-weight concrete works, and a number of workshops for repairing agricultural technical machinery were built; water-works, hydro-technical installations and ferro-concrete bridges were under construction.

A great deal of industrial construction was under way in the north of the country—in the Darkhan region, where such highly important industrial projects as the Sharingol coalmine, an electrical heating plant, a cement works, a silicate brick works, a plant making ferro-concrete structures, a woodworking and an oxygen plant, mechanical repair shops, a high-voltage electricity transmission line, branch railway lines, etc., were built.

The Darkhan region was becoming the country's second industrial centre.

As a result of the measures taken for the priority development of electricity production, which is a source of technical progress, in 1964 the capacity of electrical power stations was 43.5% higher than in 1960 and the increase in output of electricity exceeded the overall increase in the gross output of industry by 19.5%. Whereas in 1960 the output of electric power amounted to 142 kilowatt-hours per head of population, in 1964 this figure reached 242 kilowatt-hours.

In the *aimaks* of Middle Gobi, Ubur-Khangai, Bayan ulgei, Ubsunur and Sukhebator, a number of coal-mines were brought into operation and gross coal output was increased to 29-88% above the 1960 figure. A wolfram mine was opened at Ikh Khairkhan. In 1964 the output of wolfram increased by 30% above the 1960 level, that of fluorspar by 88.6% and output of the metal-processing industry by 66.7%.

Big advances were made in construction. In 1961-1964, 180% more assembly-work was carried out in capital construction than in the preceding four years. The Party and the Government took steps to expand and develop construction work and as a result this became an independent branch of the national economy. The Fifth Plenary Meeting of the Central Committee of the MPRP pointed out there had been a considerable increase in construction work, and that the building industry had become an independent branch of the economy. It stated that "the major tasks in capital construction were to cut completion periods, put buildings into exploitation at a rapid rate, concentrate attention on the most vital projects and see that construction work be organized on an economic basis."[9]

In addition, quite a number of successes were achieved in the light and food industries. The production of large-size hides was increased; a new enterprise was set up for producing 1.3 million sheepskins per year.

In the years 1961-1964 flour mills started operation in Sukhe Bator, Muren, Khar-Khorin and Under-Khan, and as a result, in 1965 the production of flour exceeded that of 1960 by 3 times and more than 1,000 tons of casein were manufactured. In 1965 the light and food industries accounted for more than 50% of industrial output.

During these years considerable successes were achieved in the technical reconstruction and automation of communications, and in providing rural localities with radio and postal facilities. As a result of the expansion of the telephone and telegraph main line between Ulan Bator and Sukhe Bator by utilizing the country's twelve-channel systems, permanent communications were organized with the Soviet Union and other countries of socialism. During this time the total number of telephone exchanges rose by 62%; 77% of all telephone stations in Mongolia were automatic.

In 1964 radio reception centres were set up in 91 *somon* centres. *Somon* centres, state farms and large centres of population had, in addition to postal services, telephone and radio links with *aimak* centres. In this way one of the basic targets set by the Third Five-Year Plan in the sphere of communications was fulfilled.

The transport plan for the first four years of the Third Five-Year Plan was successfully accomplished. The amount of freight conveyed by motor transport in 1964 showed a 120% increase on the 1960 figure.

Considerable successes were achieved in the geological prospecting of the country with a view to accelerated development of industry and the rational location of industrial establishments in the country, and also to increasing the number of minerals for export; 70% of the country's territory was covered by geological survey, many mineral deposits were discovered and their exploration began. In the years 1961-1964 108.4 million *tugriks* were spent for geological survey and exploration. In 1964 the Council for Mutual Economic Assistance gave great help in the carrying out of geological work in Mongolia.

Thanks to the rapid growth of the economy and the concern and attention shown by the Party and government the material welfare of the country's working people steadily increased.

Striking confirmation of the rise in the working people's well-being and their level of culture and a concrete result of the immense attention paid by the Party and government to improving the health of the people is the high population growth rate. The MPR occupies one of the first places in the world for population increase.

During the years of the people's power the population has almost doubled, and is by January 1, 1973 1,339,000. The rise in the urban population reflects the development of industrial production and the consequent redistribution of population between the two most important branches of the national economy—industry and agriculture.

This also means that a considerable section of the Mongolian population has adopted a settled form of life. Nearly 40% of the population of the MPR live in towns and more than 60% in rural localities. During the first three years of the Five-Year Plan the number of workers and office employees increased by 17% and their wages fund by 283%; the cash incomes of AA members rose by more than 60% and the total amount of state pensions and allowances paid to workers over the same period rose by 2.4 times. Since April 1964 rates of income tax on the wages of workers and office employees have been reduced and wages rates of the lower-paid workers and office employees have been raised.

As regards the development of socialist trading it was proposed in the Third Five-Year Plan to increase the average annual retail trade turnover in the state and co-operative net work by 7.6% but in actual fact it was increased by 9.2% in the first four years. Sales to the public of sugar, green tea, cotton textiles, high boots and other goods in 1963 reached the figure planned for 1965.

In the first four years of the plan period goods turnover rose by 41%. Foreign trade was expanded. Whereas Mongolian export trade formerly consisted exclusively of the products of stock-breeding, the position underwent a change and as a result of the development of industry and agriculture the sources from which export commodities are derived increased. Feldspar, wolfram, rock crystal, woollen and leather goods, casein and grain began to be exported to world markets.

The entry of the MPR into the Council for Mutual Economic Assistance in June 1962 was an event of extreme importance for the country's social and economic development.

The involvement of the MPR in the sphere of multilateral co-operation between socialist countries and of the international socialist division of labour enabled Mongolia to ensure high rates of development for its national economy on the basis of maximum utilization of the country's domestic resources and the advantages of the fraternal friendship, collaboration and mutual assistance with the countries of socialism. Thanks to this the MPR would be able in a short space of time to overcome successfully its relative backwardness as compared with some socialist countries in level of economic development and to create the prerequisites for a more or less simultaneous transition along with the other socialist countries to Communism.

The countries belonging to the Council for Mutual Economic Assistance will be taking an immense step forward in their development by 1980. They will increase their industrial and agricultural output six- and three-fold respectively as compared with 1960 and at the same time the MPR will increase its industrial and agricultural output by fifteen- and four-fold respectively as compared with 1960.

In January 1962 the Second Plenary Meeting of the MPRP Central Committee was held and special stress laid on the tremendous importance of the scientifically-based programme for the construction of Communism adopted at the Twenty-Second Congress of the CPSU—the first time this was done in history.

"The programme of the CPSU reveals our immediate future and draws a picture of the happy tomorrow of the Mongolian people."

The Plenary Meeting pointed out that the ending of the Stalin personality cult and the elimination of its consequences were of great importance not only for the USSR but also for the whole international communist and workers' movement, including the Mongolian People's Revolutionary Party.

The Meeting discussed the problems connected with the Choibalsan personality cult and the consequences of the mistakes and distortions committed at the time and outlined measures to exclude the possibility of similar phenomena ever arising again.

The Meeting pointed to the backwardness prevailing in agriculture, especially in stock-breeding, which was expressed in the slow growth in the head of livestock over a lengthy period.

The view was taken that the reason for the serious backwardness of agriculture was the inadequate disclosure and utilization of the reserves of socialist agriculture, the unsatisfactory situation with regard to increasing the material incentive for the *arats* to develop animal husbandry, the slackening of attention to animal husbandry and the low standard of land cultivation; it pointed out the necessity of eliminating these defects and making radical changes in the development of animal husbandry.

The MPRP and the MPR government had been taking important action to combine Party and governmental work with economic construction, to develop still further democracy in the Party and state, to strengthen collective management, raise the militancy of Party organizations, intensify supervision and checking in the work of the Party and state apparatus and extend criticism and self-criticism and unite the Party's ideological work more closely with life and practice.

At the end of 1961 cuts were made in the staff complements of state, Party and voluntary organizations. About 10,000 persons were discharged and found employment for themselves in other branches of the national economy.[10]

The MPRP and the government took a number of important measures to eliminate superfluous centralization in the national economy and to extend the rights of local government bodies. The MS stations were taken over by the executive boards of the *aimak* hurals of people's deputies. This helped to bring the management of local government bodies closer to the MSS and improve supervision to ensure better utilization of agricultural machinery. In view of the great importance of local government bodies in the advancement of agriculture a special water board was formed in January 1961 under the Council of Ministers, and also special agricultural boards attached to the *aimak* hural executive boards with departments for agricultural associations, land cultivation, haymaking, veterinary medicine, etc.

In the years of the Third Five-Year Plan there was a further development of socialist legality on the basis of which there was an intensification of the struggle to protect collective property, to strengthen labour discipline and to educate the masses in the spirit of full respect for socialist laws.

In the years of the Third Five-Year Plan certain functions of governmental executive bodies were transferred to voluntary collective organizations. People's courts run by the public, volunteer brigades for assisting organs of the militia, etc., began to function.

On January 5, 1963, a Decree of the Presidium of the Grand People's Hural was promulgated on reinforcing the fight against squanderers of state and collective property, against robbery and embezzlement, and on the basis of this Decree amendments were made to the relevant articles of the MPR Criminal Code.

The new Civil Code was ratified on February 9, 1963 by the Fourth Session of the Grand People's Hural, fourth convocation, and represented a noteworthy development in the history of the socialist law of the MPRP. The basic content of the new Civil Code was aimed at creating the material and technical basis for socialism and at the further development of socialist democracy.

The need for the adoption of the new Code arose from the great changes that had occurred in the social and economic life of the country since the Criminal Code was enacted in 1952, a subject which had been fairly fully discussed when the Constitution was reviewed in 1960. The new Civil Code had 88 new articles. Of these 26 were devoted to property rights alone and new articles were also inserted on authors' rights, the rights of rationalizers in production, etc.

In the process of socialist construction socialist democracy became still more firmly entrenched, more and more working people were drawn into state administration; the links between state bodies and the masses became closer. An increasing variety of forms emerged for workers, engineers and technicians in industrial concerns, and AA members, workers and office employees of state farms and MSS to share in administering the state and the affairs of their enterprises. In addition to the part played by workers in management through Party, trade union, youth league and other voluntary or collective organizations, closer co-operation was arranged with Party control bodies; there was increasing participation in the work of commissions of trade-union committees, and various councils and societies, in discussion of the vital tasks involved in the development of production in a socialist society.

Democracy was strengthened in the agricultural associations. An AA is not merely an economic enterprise for production but a specific social unit. Democracy in the AA is an integral part of the socialist democracy of the state.

In February 1963 a special resolution was adopted by the MPRP Central Committee and the MPR Council of Ministers on "Measures for strengthening democracy in agricultural associations."[11] This resolution disclosed serious shortcomings in the work of a number of associations and also violations of democracy inside the AA.

The Party and the government called upon members of AAs to fight for strict observance of the democratic requirements of the regulations and for improving the activity of all members in the life of agricultural associations.

The state machinery was strengthened by the intensification of the alliance of the working class with those working in agriculture. Thus, the main principle of alliance between the working class and the peasantry was being enriched by new forms of communication and mutual assistance between the two friendly classes.

The working class helped the *arats* by setting up state farms and MSS, by providing finance for agriculture and also special training of cadres for stock-breeding and land cultivation.

Industrial enterprises accept AA members for production training and for acquiring the different trades needed in the mechanization of agricultural work.

An important form of direct participation by the mass of the workers in strengthening the co-operative structure of the *khudon* was the patronage extended by industrial enterprises to agricultural associations. The patrons extend material assistance in production to the *arats:* a certain proportion of the profits earned in excess of the Plan is handed over to the AA and workers and office employees take a hand in the harvesting, in procuring forage for the winter, building farm premises, wells, etc. The strengthening of socialist ownership is guarantee of the further strengthening of the union between the working class and the *arats*. The stability of this alliance was proved by the result of the elections to the Grand People's Hural.

In June 1963 elections were held for the Grand People's Hural of the MPR and for local government bodies, at which 99.9% of the electors cast their votes for the candidates of the block of Party and non-Party candidates.

A reform of public education has been carried through on the basis of strengthening the links between school and life. The introduction of the new system of public education entailed changes in the direction of combining studies with labour and ensuring the education of a rising generation with all-round development.

Faithful to the teaching of Marxism-Leninism, the Declaration of 1957 and the 1960 Statement of the Communist and

Workers' Parties, the MPR continued to wage a fight for the strengthening of friendship, brotherhood and unity between the countries of the world socialist system and for rallying the ranks of the international Communist and workers' movement.

The constant consolidation of the unity and solidarity of the countries of the whole socialist commonwealth and the international Communist movement on the basis of the principles of Marxism-Leninism and of proletarian internationalism constitutes the basic condition for the triumph of world socialism and the further growth of its forces.

The MPR has always fostered in all the working people the spirit of proletarian internationalism, the spirit of Marxism-Leninism, constantly repudiating dogmatism, revisionism, nationalism, nihilism and all the other ideas alien to Marxism-Leninism.

At the Plenary Meetings of the Party's Central Committee the anti-Party activities of T. Tumur-Ochir and L. Tsend were exposed and defeated. Their nationalistic and nihilistic attitudes did a certain amount of damage to the Party cause and their disorganizing work contributed to the apolitical attitude and laxity of belief among certain backward elements and to the weakening of Party and labour discipline.

The Sixth Plenary Meeting of the MPR Central Committee, held in December 1964, is specially important for the country's development. The Meeting discussed the questions: "Measures for further improving Party, state and collective control" and "The introduction of certain changes in the 1961-1965 Plan for the development of the national economy and culture of the MPR."

At the Plenary Meeting urgent decisions were adopted for the further improvement of Party, state and collective control and checking: measures were outlined for drawing the masses on a wider scale into work in Party and state control on the basis of the Leninist principle of checking up on the fulfilment of decisions.

The Meeting considered that in order to improve control it was necessary to give the control bodies wider and more concrete tasks and, correspondingly, to carry through a certain amount of reorganization of control bodies.

It was decided to retain the Party Control Committee attached to the MPRP Central Committee and the State Control Commission attached to the MPR Council of Ministers, as two independent control bodies, delegating to the Party Control Committee general responsibility for the organisation of control in the country and establishing in *aimak* (and town) committees of the Party *aimak* control commissions and public control committees directly on the spot. The immediate duty of Party, state and voluntary organizations is to check on the carrying out of directives of the Party and government, to combat plundering of socialist property and breaches of socialist legality and Party and state labour discipline; to help further improve and reduce the cost of the administrative apparatus; to combat bureaucracy, abuses of official position, whitewash and falsification of returns.

The improvement of Party, state and public control played an important part in combating the harmful phenomena encountered in the course of social development and also in speeding up socialist construction.

At the Sixth Plenary Meeting the anti-Party factional group of Ts. Lokhuz, G. Nyamba and V. Surmazhav, who had opposed the domestic and foreign policy of the Party and the government, was exposed and defeated. The Meeting pointed out that: "All Party organizations and MPRP members shall constantly increase their political vigilance, expose and suppress any actions likely to harm the unity of Party ranks, take resolute steps to strengthen the principles of democratic centralism, repudiate any symptoms of nationalism and other views inconsistent with Marxism, intensify the education of the working people in the spirit of Marxist-Leninist principles, in the spirit of the principles of proletarian internationalism."

The workers, *arat* co-operative members and the working intellectuals of the country continue to wage an active fight to carry out the task—one posed by history—of creating the material and technical basis for socialism, improving socialist production relationships and educating the new type of man, under the wise guidance of the MPRP and the people's government, and with the international assistance of the great Soviet Union and the other fraternal socialist countries.

SECTION FIVE

CULTURAL CONSTRUCTION IN THE MPR

From the very beginning of its activity the MPRP has been guided by the Leninist doctrine of the cultural revolution—a doctrine which forms an integral part of the Marxist theory of socialist revolution. The whole experience of cultural construction in the MPR has confirmed the correctness of this doctrine in Mongolian conditions. V. I. Lenin regarded the cultural revolution as one of the most important and decisive conditions for the victory of socialism, as a radical revolution in the development of the intellectual life of society and as the most effective means of giving the mass of the people access to the achievement of culture.

Implementation of the basic tasks of the cultural revolution was especially necessary in Mongolia which in the past had been one of the most backward countries in the world. From the earliest days of the people's revolution in Mongolia development of the national culture represented one of the most important tasks in the construction of a new life along non-capitalist lines. In carrying out this task, however, the people had to overcome enormous difficulties, due mainly to the extreme economic backwardness of pre-revolutionary Mongolia and the survivals of feudal relationships in Mongolian society. A major obstacle in the development of the new culture was Lamaism, which had ruled supreme for many centuries in the spiritual life of the people. These peculiar historical and economic conditions determined the specific features of the cultural revolution in Mongolia.

The cultural revolution in Mongolia passed through two stages in its development, the revolutionary-democratic stage (1921-1940) and the socialist stage (post-1940). Because of its extreme backwardness Mongolia could not make an immediate start on the direct implementation of the basic tasks of a socialist cultural revolution, but was obliged to begin at the beginning, with the most elementary problems of the cultural revolution. In the initial stage of Mongolia's cultural revolution the paramount tasks were a persistent campaign against mass illiteracy, the creation of a basis for a system of public education, the training of a national intelligentsia, the development of a new revolutionary literature and art, etc. At this stage Mongolian culture was entirely a revolutionary democratic culture, which had been freed from the shackles of feudal and religious ideology and was laying the foundations for a genuinely socialist culture.

The 1940s saw the opening of a new socialist stage of the cultural revolution in the MPR. Cultural construction in Mongolia, is becoming an inseparable, integral part of the process of socialist transformation of the whole of society. This is the stage of the blossoming out of the Mongolian people's culture, socialist in content but national in form. The second stage of the cultural revolution is closely linked with the successful building up of the basis for socialism, with the development of national industry, the socialist transformation of agriculture and the entrenchment of the socialist economy in the MPR. Nowadays culture in Mongolia is developing on a solid material basis, the creation of which V. I. Lenin regarded as an essential condition for the consolidation of a socialist cultural revolution. As a consequence of the completion of the socialist cultural revolution in Mongolia the country will attain the cultural level of the foremost socialist countries.

The whole history of cultural construction in the MPR has proceeded in the context of relentless struggle of a progressive scientific world outlook with a feudal Lamaist ideology and bourgeois nationalism, against the background of the formation and triumph of Marxist-Leninist ideology, which constitutes the theoretical basis of present-day culture in Mongolia. The new upsurge of culture in the MPR of recent years is imbued with the creative spirit of the very important decisions adopted by the MPRP on ideological problems.

Public Education

One of the great achievements in the development of postrevolutionary culture in the MPR is the successful solution of the difficult problem of establishing a system of public education. The country now has an extensive network of institutions for pre-school education, general educational and professional schools, courses of various types, higher educational institutions and cultural and educational organizations for workers.

All this was not created at one fell swoop but gradually, as the country's material possibilities permitted. In organizing public education the government had to overcome enormous difficulties. Before the revolution there was no system of secular public education in the country. There were only the church schools *(datsan)* attached to Buddhist monasteries. These schools were attended by the bulk of children of school age. Teaching in the monastery schools was formal, scholastic and completely isolated from life. The student lamas were taught only Buddhist dogmas and the Tibetan language, the basic language of the church in Mongolia. The native Mongolian language, the history and culture of the country were alien to them.

After the victory of the revolution the Lamaist church was the principal ideological enemy of progressive culture and science. Over and above all this there were not sufficient financial resources for schools, teachers or literate persons generally who could be enlisted in the cause of popular education. It was in this situation that the MPRP and the people's government set to work to organize schooling throughout the country.

In August 1921, i. e. a month after the triumph of the revolution, the people's government adopted decisions for the organization of schools. On November 2 the first new type of primary school for 40 pupils was opened in Urga. The next year more than 10 new schools were opened in different populated centres and in 1924 a further 13 schools with 501 pupils. From 1922 onwards, in addition to state-supported schools, so-called *khoshun* schools paid for by the local population began to be established. In 1924 there were altogether 23 such schools with 419 pupils.

In the 1922-1923 school-year teacher training and refresher training courses were organized for training teachers for senior posts. In 1928 these courses were reorganized as the Higher People's School which, however, was little different from the previous courses and could not fully solve the problem of cadres. Special secondary institutions of the teacher-training type were needed. In 1925 a teacher's training college was established which has played a big part in the development of public education and culture in the country.

The same year saw the opening of a school of finance to train cadres of financial workers for economic and governmental institutions.

The creation of a Ministry of Public Education in February 1924, based on the reorganization of the former national education department attached to the Ministry of the Interior was an important departure in the development of national education.

The establishment in the country of a people's republic created still more favourable conditions for a further expansion of the national culture and popular education. The new Constitution, adopted at the First Grand People's Hural, provided all the workers of the country with a broad right to free education and freedom of religion, and separated the church from the state, the relevant statute adopted by the First Grand People's Hural being of great importance of principle. All these measures of the Party and the government continued to play a decisive role in overcoming the pernicious influence of the Lamaist church over the school, over the education and the upbringing of the rising generation. In the ten years from 1924 to 1934 considerable successes were achieved in the development of public education. In 1934 the country had 59 primary schools for 3,125 children, 5 seven-year schools for 600 pupils, 1 teachers' training college for 250 students.

The foundations of public education had been laid. However the influence of the Lamaist church over the spiritual life of the country has not been overcome. According to the 1933 figures, 3,725 children or approximately 2.7% of all children between 8 and 17 years of age were being taught in 64 schools. In the monasteries, however, 18,000 children were being taught, i. e. 13% of all children of that age-group, i. e. four and a half times as many as in schools. The monasteries absorbed enormous national resources which could have been spent on public education. The overwhelming majority of the population still continued to be illiterate. Accordingly, the question of developing national culture and public education was specially discussed at the Ninth MPRP Congress and the Seventh Grand People's Hural. The congresses adopted a comprehensive programme on all problems of culture and education. In particular, one of the first places in this programme was allotted to the development of schooling and the abolition of illiteracy. The period between 1934 and 1940 was marked by a campaign for attaining the targets fixed by these Congresses.

It was very important for the further development of school building to secure the active participation of the mass of herdsmen in establishing the so-called voluntary people's schools. Whereas in 1934 there were only two schools for 40 pupils, by 1939 more than 100 schools with a total number of 4,300 pupils had been established in the country. In 1940 there were 331 primary and secondary schools operating in the country, in which 24,341 children were being taught and 7 specialised secondary schools with enrolment of 1,332 pupils. Cultural collaboration between the MPR and the Soviet Union played a big part in achieving successes in the field of public education. Soviet assistance was of great importance in developing education in the MPR. From the first years of people's power it became a practice to send young Mongolians on missions to the USSR to receive pedagogical, medical and other training. The number of young Mongolians studying in the USSR increased from year to year. In 1937, for instance, 314 people were studying in the USSR, whereas in 1940 the number was 739.

After 1940 a new phase in the development of culture and public education opens up. With the country embarking on the path of direct socialist construction, cultural and educational work becomes of paramount importance. From this time on the country set about implementing the grand tasks of socialist cultural revolution. These tasks were indicated by the Tenth Party Congress and the Eighth Grand People's Hural. The Tenth Congress pointed out: "If we wish to move forward, we must accomplish a real revolution in the development of culture and enlightenment." The Eighth Grand People's Hural issued a directive on the introduction of primary schooling in the years immediately ahead. The new MPR Constitution adopted by the Eighth Hural offered the people the widest rights to education. Article 90 of the Constitution reads: "Citizens of the MPR have a right to education. This right is guaranteed by free teaching, the development of a network of schools, technical institutes and higher educational institutions, by giving instruction in schools in the native tongue, by a system of state grants in higher schools."[1]

The period from 1940 to the present has been one of rapid development of culture in all fields, including public education. Even in the difficult war years the Mongolian people, with the help of the Soviet Union, continued to expand construction for cultural purposes. The big successes achieved in developing public education, in particular, and in cultural construction, in general, made it possible for the state to set about organizing higher education, which is the final link in a public education system. The founding in 1940 of a two-year pedagogical institute marked the beginning of higher education in the country. Following this, a Higher Party School, named after Sukhe Bator, was organized in 1941, based on the former Party courses which had been set up back in 1924. A major event in the country's cultural life was the opening in 1942 of the country's first state university. The Soviet Union, which was going through the grim years of the Patriotic War, gave great assistance to Mongolia in organizing higher education.

Hundreds of specialists and professors worked in the higher educational institutions of Mongolia helping the Mongolians to make the riches of modern science and technology their own.

After the war there was a further acceleration of tempoes in the battle for culture. The whole system of public education attained a higher level of development. In this effort the successful fulfilment of the targets of the First, Second, and Third Five-Year Plans played a very important part. During these years the target of universal, compulsory, primary education was completely fulfilled and the decisions of the Party and government for implementing universal, compulsory seven-year education were successfully executed.

In the school year 1964-1965 there were 523 general educational schools with an enrolment of more than 157,600 pupils; the number of teachers in these schools was 4,800.

Major successes were achieved in developing specialized and higher education. Agricultural, economic and medical institutes and a number of technical colleges were set up. Whereas in 1952, 2,143 people were studying in four higher educational institutions, in the 1964-65 educational year there were more than 11,000 students at eight higher educational institutions; 9,700 people were being taught in 18 specialized schools.

At the present time 1,677 out of every 10,000 persons are studying in schools of various grades, including 104 in higher educational institutions, 91 in secondary specialized schools and 1,482 in general educational schools. In 1962-1965 the higher and specialized educational institutions have given the state 11,000 specialists.

One of the most important results of the all-round development of public education in Mongolia during the years of the people's power is the creation of a great army of intellectuals who have come from among the people and constitute a decisive force in the cultural revolution.

In a country which, until quite recently, had only very few people who were even barely literate there are nowadays large numbers of scientists, qualified engineers and technicians, teachers, workers in culture and the arts. According to 1969 figures the number of teachers has risen to 10,000 and that of medical workers to 200,000. In 1967 there were 13-15 veterinary surgeons in every *aimak*.

Cultural and Educational Activities

One of the first-priority tasks of cultural construction in the MPR throughout all the periods of the Mongolian revolution has been cultural and educational work to raise the general cultural level of the masses. The revolutionary transformation of Mongolia's feudal society into a socialist one made it imperative to radically remould people's thinking. All the cultural and educational work done in the country was directed against the Lamaist religion, the survivals of medievalism, the "birthmarks" of Mongolian feudalism. It was always inseparably bound up with the revolutionary struggle of the working people for the radical transformation of the whole social life of Mongolia on new socialist principles.

From its very inception, the MPRP attached the greatest importance to political and cultural-educational work among the herdsmen. It viewed this as a powerful means for making the people more politically conscious and rallying them to take an active part in the revolutionary struggle and work constructively in the cause of building socialism in Mongolia.

One of the main problems of cultural and educational work after the victory of the revolution in Mongolia was the removal of the pall of illiteracy that covered the country. Lenin used to point out: "...so long as there is such a thing as illiteracy in our country it is too much to talk about political education. This is not a political problem, it is a condition without which it is useless talking about politics. An illiterate person stands outside politics; he must first learn his ABC. Without that there can be no politics—without that there are rumours, gossip, fairy-tales and prejudice, but not politics."[2]

Immediately after the victory of the revolution the MPRP and the government set about the task of wiping out illiteracy and organizing the trade training of the adult population through a network of various courses and clubs. In carrying out this highly important task of cultural development the Mongolian people had to grapple with enormous difficulties. In the first place, there were not enough literate people to be drawn into the job of eradicating illiteracy. There were no teaching manuals or books designed for teaching adults to read and write. Even the actual business of getting the mass of the people to learn to read and write was quite a difficult problem. At the outset a great deal of work had to be done to explain to the *arats* the value of learning and literacy.

Another difficulty consisted in the imperfections and the difficulty of assimilating the old written Mongolian language which had been borrowed from the Uighurs many hundreds of years back. All the numerous endeavours made by the Party and government to teach the population the old form of writing failed for a long time to yield the results desired. The efforts made to eradicate illiteracy in the country fell far short of the requirements of life. In the period between the victory of the revolution and 1940 only 20.8% of the population were literate.

The further development of the country urgently called for a steep rise in the cultural level and literacy of those building a socialist society. On the other hand, the old script was not suitable for the further development of the Mongolian literary language. It became more and more clear that this form of writing did not accord with the literary, phonetic and special grammatical and lexical features of contemporary Mongolian. It became necessary to change the system of writing Mongolian, and the Tenth MPRP Congress took a decision to change over to a new alphabet. A large-scale campaign was organized throughout the whole country for eradicating illiteracy on the basis of a new Mongolian alphabet differing from the old one primarily in being easier to learn and more accessible to the wider masses of the people. General state and local commissions for the eradication of illiteracy were responsible for the direct control of this campaign. Every possible device was employed to secure the participation of the widest circles of the population in the job of eradicating illiteracy. All state departments, economic and industrial enterprises, Party and voluntary organizations had to join in the task of eradicating illiteracy as one of the most important problems of mass cultural work. A really national movement developed for the attainment of literacy. The principal slogan employed by the movement was the Party's appeal: "Every literate person must teach at least three people."

As a result of the numerous and varied measures taken by the Party and government the work of eradicating illiteracy on the basis of a new Mongolian alphabet progressed incredibly fast.

By 1947 the literate population amounted to 43.3%, by 1956 it was 72.2% and by 1963 90%. Illiteracy, the grim legacy of the past, has now been abolished in Mongolia. In this fashion practical experience has shown the vital importance and the great advantages of the new alphabet.

Along with the abolition of illiteracy a great deal of work was done to create a network of cultural and educational institutions in the country. From the 1920s onwards clubs, so-called "Red Corners," "Red Yurts" and various courses in political education, etc. began to come into being. The organization of cultural and educational institutes started with the founding in 1924 of the Sukhe Bator Club. The variety of the organizational forms of cultural and educational work in Mongolian conditions made it possible to extend the benefits of mass cultural work on the widest possible scale to the whole population. Through a broad network of cultural and educational institutions the Party and government proceeded to organize the most varied types of work for raising the cultural and political level of the population. Talks were held and lectures given on varying subjects to wider sections of the people; amateur entertainment groups were organised and other cultural work carried out among the masses.

In the early years of the people's power, when the lamas and monasteries still wielded considerable power, anti-religious and atheistic propaganda was exceptionally important. The MPRP followed Lenin's instructions about the need to combat the "fog of religion" with purely ideological weapons and only with such weapons, using the Press and its ability to take to the masses a scientific, materialist world outlook. It was the cultural and educational work done in the years of the people's rule which played a decisive role in liberating the *arats* from the opiate of religion, bringing progressive culture to them and heightening the political consciousness and activity of the *arats*.

Since the establishment of people's power the number of cultural and educational institutions has increased year by year. Nowadays there are more than 200 clubs, over 1,100 libraries and about 500 stationary and mobile cinema film projectors operating in the country. Every *aimak* has a fine arts department and centre for regional studies.

Great attention is devoted to improving the general and specialized education of the mass of the people. Some 800 persons are now being taught in 50 evening schools for general and specialized education and more than 11,000 attend the numerous schools of culture.

In the period from 1961 to 1963 more than 17,000 persons were given primary education and out of the 21,000 persons studying in evening schools for adults, 9,000 finished classes IV, VII and X.

Throughout the country a widespread movement developed under the slogan: "Live, work and study like socialists." This movement plays an important part in the development of socialist relationships between people and in the formation of the socialist way of life and morality in Mongolia.

In Mongolia an important role is played in ideological work by the periodical press and book publication. The birth of a new, revolutionary press was associated with the commencement of the activity of the MPRP The first Party documents, leaflets and appeals, which were published by the Party even before the revolution was won, laid the foundations for the Mongolian revolutionary press.

After the triumph of the revolution, publishing began to expand at a rapid rate in the country; newspapers, periodicals and books began to come out. In place of the newspaper *Mongolyn Unen*, published before the revolution, in 1921 the newspaper *Uria* ("Appeal") began to appear as the organ of the MPRP Central Committee and the government.

In 1923 the newspaper *Ardyn erkh* ("People's Right") began publication as the organ of the MPRP Central Committee and the government and appeared up to April 1925 when it was renamed *Unen* ("Truth"). Since then the newspaper *Unen* has appeared without a break and is the leading organ of the press in the MPR. From 1924 until September 1927 a special newspaper, *Ardyn tsereg*, ("People's Warrior") was published for army servicemen by the political department of the army from 1927 to 1930, similarly, a newspaper called *The Cultural Path of the Revolutionary Red Army*. Since September 1930 the army newspaper *Ulaan od* ("Red Star") has appeared.

In 1930 a newspaper *Zaluuchudyn unen* ("Young People's Truth") began to appear as the organ of the Central Committee of the Revolutionary Youth League, which also publishes one for Young Pioneers, *Pioneryn unen* (Pioneers' Truth").

In the 1930s the trade unions began publishing their own periodical — *Khudulmur* ("Labour"). Since 1955 the newspaper *Literature* has been appearing but has changed its title several times and is now published under the name *Literature and the Arts*. A newspaper called *Road of Friendship* is published for railway workers; *Socialist Agriculture* for workers in agriculture and for workers in the capital *Ulan Bator News*.

In addition to newspapers published in the centre, there are *aimak* newspapers. With the publication of the latter there has been a still further expansion of the social role of the press and a broadening of its links with the masses.

Magazines also began to be published in the early years after the revolution. The first revolutionary magazines to appear were *Mongol ardyn nam* ("Mongolian People's Party"), the organ of the MPRP Central Committee and *Manai zan* ("Our Path"), the organ of the Revolutionary Youth League Central Committee. Both began publication in 1922. *Mongol ardyn nam* has been renamed several times and since 1933 has been called "Party Building." *Manai Zam* was published during 1922 and 1923. The Revolutionary Youth League Central Committee later resumed publication of its journal in 1925 under the title *Khuvsgalt zuluuchudyn evlel* ("League of Revolutionary Youth"). Since 1925 the journal *Zalgajlagch*, subsequently re-named *Pioneer*, has been published.

The first socio-political and literary periodical *Mongol ardyn undesniy soyelyn zam* ("Path of National Culture of the Mongolian Peoples) was published from 1934 to 1942.

Of the magazines which sprang up in the 1940s mention should be made of the satirical *Matar* ("Crocodile") which at the present time is published under the title *Khumuuzhil zhigshil* and the literary-political journal *Tsog* ("Light").

In 1944 the journal *Sain duryn uran saikhanchuudad tuslamzh* ("Help for Members of Amateur Entertainment Groups") appeared, which subsequently changed its name to *Uran saikhanchdad tuslamzh*. In 1950 writers obtained still another platform—the socio-political and literary-artistic monthly *Tuyaa* ("Dawn"). In 1954 this journal became the organ of the MPR Writers' Union. Among the most important periodicals that have appeared recently mention should be made of *Orchin uein mongol* ("Modern Mongolia") which is published in Mongolian, Russian and English, *Ediyn zasag, erkhiyn asuudal* ("Problems of Economics and Law"), *Eruul mend* ("Health"), *Surgan khumuuzhulegch* ("Pedagogics"), *Oyuun tulkhuur* ("Key to Knowledge") and "Science and Engineering", the organ of the society for the dissemination of scientific knowledge, etc. Altogether 50 titles of newspapers and periodicals are now being published in the country.

Considerable successes have been achieved in the sphere of publishing. In recent years, especially, work on the translation of Marxist-Leninist classics has been greatly extended. At the present moment the publication of a complete collection of Lenin's works in Mongolian is nearing completion. A Mongolian translation of Marx's *Capital* will shortly be brought out.

The publication of a series of the Marxist-Leninist classics and of political literature is extremely important for the ideological education of the masses and helps the working people to assimilate rapidly the victorious ideas of Marxism-Leninism.

Every year increasing numbers of works of fiction of the fraternal socialist and other countries of the world are translated and published in the Mongolian language. While more than 1.500 such works of art and 150 folklore works of 39 countries were published between 1921 and 1955, in the years from 1956 to 1960 a total of 1,369 literary works and 212 popular folklore works from 57 countries were published in Mongolia. The translation of the literature of other countries, especially of the socialist countries, plays a major role in educating the working people of Mongolia in the spirit of proletarian internationalism and friendship between the peoples.

An important place is occupied by the publication of works by Mongolian writers and scholars, and teaching manuals for various schools.

The development of publishing is very closely linked up with improvements in the country's printing industry. The most important publishing centre in the country is the Sukhe Bator Central State Printing Works, which is equipped with the most up-to-date printing machinery, especially for intaglio printing. In addition to the State Printing Works, the MPR has now more than 20 large and small printing works operating.

Along with the press an extremely important role in the ideological education of the people has been played since 1934 by the Mongolian radio service. Nowadays, radio has become an indispensable part of the everyday life of the working people of Mongolia. A powerful wireless station, equipped with the most modern technical devices, operates in the capital and every centre of population has its own broadcasting or radio centre.

Science

The people's revolution opened up before the Mongolian people a broad highway to advanced science.

In the MPR science sprang from, and is developing on the basis of, the theory of Marxism-Leninism and conflicts with feudal-lamaist and bourgeois-nationalist ideology. It derives from the interest of the people and is placed at the service of the people.

On November 19, 1921, a Scientific Committee was created which was subsequently re-named the Committee of Sciences. The first chairman of the Scientific Committee was the well-known worker in Mongolian culture, O. Zhamyan (1864-1930).

At the outset the Committee of Sciences which at that time had modest resources and funds at its disposal, confined its activities to collecting archival materials, manuscripts and historical monuments, materials for regional studies and to the translation and publication of popular science literature. In 1921 the Committee of Sciences had a language study room, which also dealt with history, and a library in the reading-room of which popular science lectures were given. In 1924 a museum for regional studies was organized. In the same year study-rooms were opened for history and geography.

In 1927 the Committee of Sciences inaugurated the State Archives, thus initiating archival research in the MPR. In the 1930s branches were set up in the Committee of Sciences system which had direct links with economic development. In 1937 an agricultural laboratory was organized, which also dealt with stock-breeding problems, and in 1938 a geological laboratory. In 1938 stock-breeding specialists were selected from the agricultural laboratory to organize a laboratory for stock-breeding studies. As a result of the creation of all these laboratories the Committee of Sciences was able to expand research work with a view to the comprehensive development of the Republic's economy and culture.

Scientific and cultural collaboration between the MPR and the Soviet Union played a decisive role in the inception and development of advanced science in the MPR. The USSR gave the Mongolian people great help in training scientific cadres, in organizing scientific research centres and in conducting a comprehensive survey of the country, etc.

Close contacts were established between Mongolian and Soviet scientists. Such Soviet scholars as V. A. Obruchev, V. L. Komarov, P. K. Kozlov, S. F. Oldenburg, F. I. Shcherbatskoi, B. Ya. Vladimirtsov and S. A. Kozin assisted as foreign members of the Committee of Sciences. The conclusion in October 1929 of the first agreement between the USSR Academy of Sciences and the MPR Committee of Sciences on joint research was highly important for the development of science in the MPR. As early as the 1920s joint Mongolo-Soviet expeditions had begun work on the territory of the MPR. Later on, the study of the Mongolian People's Republic by expeditions of

Soviet scientists was concentrated in the Mongolian Commission of the USSR Academy of Sciences, which carried out a systematic and comprehensive study of the Republic. The work it did was a valuable contribution to scientific knowledge about Mongolia. The commission worked in close touch with the MPR Committee of Sciences. This kind of collaboration facilitated the exchange of experience and knowledge between Mongolian and Soviet scholars.

During the years of its existence the MPR Committee of Sciences accomplished a great deal of work. Mongolian linguists produced a number of works under the general title "For the improvement of the Mongolian language", published a series of reference works on terminology and compiled a large Russian-Mongolian dictionary and a number of grammars.

The 1920s and 1930s saw the appearance of works by the Mongolian philologists O. Zhamyan, S. Shagzh, Ch. Bat-Ochir, Sh. Luvsan-vandan and others. Many of the works of these philologists formed the first textbooks in the native language for primary and secondary schools. The work done by Mongolian linguists in creating the new script was exceptionally important. The commission for the reform of the written language was headed by Yu. Tsedenbal, while the scholar Ts. Damdinsuren drew up the draft alphabet and orthography and compiled a number of manuals on the new script.

Literary experts put in a lot of work collecting and editing items of folklore, and rendered great services in making translations of world literature, prominent among which are the works of Russian classical and Soviet writers.

Considerable successes have also been achieved in the field of history; a new Mongolian science of historiography came into being. Radical changes are being made in Mongolian historiography in the sense of a complete secularization of history, an intensification of the understanding of history from the standpoint of the class struggle and finally of the gradual redevelopment of Mongolian historical literature along Marxist lines. Mongolian historians saw the main practical importance of their work in putting history at the service of the revolution and the national interests of the country. These were the objectives which motivated the appearance of the first historical works produced by Mongolian authors after the revolution (Ch. Bat-Ochir, L. Magsarzhav, A. Amar, L. Dendev, D. Natsagdorzh, B. Buyanchulgan, and others).

As a result of work done by the geography laboratory a large number of maps were compiled (a geographical atlas of the Mongolian People's Republic, physical and administrative maps, etc.), and a textbook on the geography of the MPR was published. The work done by the geographers was useful to the MPR government in carrying out the new delimitation of districts in 1930 and subsequent years.

MPR geologists made a survey of the Mongolian People's Republic and drew up a geological map. The geology section of the Committee of Sciences has been giving great help to industrial enterprises by placing at their disposal information on sources of raw materials and fuel.

The agricultural laboratory began work by studying the history of agriculture in Mongolia and then proceeded to produce a soil survey and set up experiments in growing various crops under varying agrotechnical conditions. The result of the laboratory's work were charts showing the vegetative cover and a series of works summarizing the scientific facts for introducing modern techniques in agriculture.

The specialist on stock-breeding in the MPR Committee of Sciences started off by studying the vegetative cover, the experience gained by *arats* in breeding livestock and the pedigree qualities of Mongolian livestock. The research workers then set up experiments on improving the breed and increasing the productivity of Mongolian livestock.

A major landmark in the development of scientific thought in Mongolia was the transformation of the former Committee of Sciences into the Academy of Sciences of the MPR in 1961 in accordance with a decision of the Central Committee of the MPRP and the Council of Ministers of the MPR. It was at that time that a start was made to set up research institutes as collective teams dealing with branches of social, agricultural and natural sciences of primary importance to the country. The Academy of Sciences and other research institutions have over the past five year period grown stronger in both the scientific and the organizational respect, and have made big advances in building up their material base.[3]

Today scientific research is being conducted not only within the system of institutes and laboratories of the Academy of Sciences but also in institutes for separate branches of the economy under the Ministry of Agriculture, the Ministry of Construction and Construction Materials, the Ministry of Education, the Ministry of Health and higher educational institutions. This organizational pattern of research work, which has become firmly established in practice in scientific affairs in almost all the fraternal socialist countries, has without any doubt been proved justified by the needs of the socialist system. More than one thousand people are engaged in research work in the Mongolian People's Republic. Working to raise their theoretical qualifications, and assimilating the experience of scientists in the USSR and other socialist countries, they are thus making a significant contribution to the country's economic development.

Since the foundation of the Academy of Sciences in 1961 its research activity has been carried out on the basis of five-year and one-year plans, depending on the availability of a laboratory base and qualified researchers, having regard to the priority tasks dictated by the development of the economy and also by the state of science in the country and the tasks of scientific and technical progress.

The work done on individual problems of Mongolian history, Mongolian language and literature, the economy of the country, in particular livestock farming, crop-raising, biology, medicine, physics, chemistry and geography, is an important result of the scientific activities carried out by the establishments of the Academy of Sciences of the MPR during the period of its First Five-Year Plan, 1961-65. During the five-year period more than eighty monographs, 216 other types of work, and more than 200 recommendations and proposals of direct significance to production have been published.

The plan for research to be carried out by the Academy's institutions in 1966-1970, compiled on the basis of the experience of the previous five-year period, with account for the tasks involved in scientific and technical advance in the national economy, was successfully fulfilled.

The theoretical level and practical significance of the results of research works carried out by scientists have risen substantially.

The scientific research conducted within the Academy of Sciences system combines both theoretical and practical questions. Under the heading of theoretical, one may quote, in the first place, certain research done in the sphere of history, language and literature, philosophy and also in nuclear physics according to the programme of the Joint Institute of Atomic Research in Dubna, of seismology, terrestial magnetism, and the study of phenomena on the sun, and the works of the Institute of Biology on genetics and geobotany and the Institute of Geology on stratigraphy and tectonics.

At the same time the research done at practically all the institutes of the Academy of Sciences concerns in one degree or another a study of the mineral resources, flora, a qualitative definition of natural and raw material resources in the country; natural soil and climatic conditions within geographical zones and the present-day distribution of forces in the country; the application of physical analyses and mathematical methods in research.

During the five years the staff of the Geology Institute carried out considerable work to discover certain laws governing the spatial distribution of important minerals—rare non-ferrous metals, rare trace elements, phosphorite, fluorite and others, and to study the origins and certain petrological and geochemical features and the ore content in granitoid formations. Geologists have compiled a number of geological, tectonic and stratigraphic charts, and all this enables prospecting to be carried out in the most promising areas.

The results of the research done by biologists provides the basis for the correct utilisation, conservation and reproduction of the country's plant, fur and other resources.

Of great practical interest is the geobotanical and biological research conducted with regard to pastures and ways of raising cereal yields and combating rodents and other pests, and also recommendations on the principles to be followed in introducing the sowing of perennial grasses to increase fodder resources, and on the need to ensure the reproduction of timber resources by sowing seeds and planting out sets.

A biological and a chemical study of medicinal herbs, in which the country is rich, is of both scientific and practical value. If certain varieties of plants, such as adonis and milk vetch can be made more biologically effective there can be a significant increase in the production of valuable medicinal preparations from local raw materials.

Concentrating, above all, on a study of various types of agricultural and mineral raw materials, the chemists have provided the country's economic institutions with a number of standard technological specifications, one of them being for the processing of common salt, of which there are vast amounts in the MPR's many lakes and have evolved standards for the chemical composition of different varieties of wheat, barley, and so on.

On the basis of earlier research and additional study, geographers have produced a number of monographs, among them *A Physical Geography of the MPR,* and *An Economic Geography of the Principal Branches of the MPR Economy,* and also dozens of maps which have found practical application.

The above-mentionel research in physical and economic geography is likely to provide valuable basic material for scientific descriptions of the soil and climatic conditions of various zones in the country, of the geographical environment and the distribution of natural and raw materials in relation to factors of soil-geography, climate and hydrology.

The economists have carried out a great deal of work with a view to estimating potential manpower resources, and also made a study of questions linked with the specialisation and distribution of agricultural production, the economic assessment of pasture and agricultural land and improved agricultural planning.

Apart from their research in theoretical physics and astrophysics, the physicists and mathematicians have been working on a number of matters directly connected with the country's economic development.

The practical application of just a few of the results of the research carried out in the first and second five-year plans has already been of substantial economic benefit. What has been accomplished along these lines in 1966-1970 has not only recouped the money allocated by the state for the requirements of the Academy of Sciences of the MPR over the period but brought in profits amounting to millions of *tugriks*.

Considerable investigations have been carried out by the MPR's historians in the fields of archaeology, history and the study of sources. The results of their work have been published in the one-volume *History of the Mongolian People's Republic*, in a three-volume work of the same name, and dozens of important monographs. These works trace the history of Mongolia from ancient times to our day from the standpoint of historical materialism, devoting considerable attention to the half-century that began with the victory of the People's Revolution in 1921.

The publication of *A Short Course in the History of the MPRP* and the preparation of the more profound *A Full Course in the History of the MPRP* are of great importance.

Philologists have concentrated upon a scientific study of the grammar of the Mongolian language and the history of the literature of the Mongolian people. A number of fundamental monographs have been published on Mongolian grammar, as have several volumes on the history of Mongolian literature, and various dictionaries.

All the works listed above have the aim of deepening the theoretical study of the country's thousands of years of history, of Mongolian culture and present-day problems arising from the needs of socialist society, and of securing a scientific evaluation of the country's natural, raw materials and manpower resources so that they may be wisely used.

Valuable results have been obtained by the staffs of research institutes and by scholars teaching at colleges and universities, in connexion with the tasks involved in developing agriculture, industry, construction and education. These scientists and scholars are also endeavouring to define what should be the main trend in research and are working on the chief questions arising in the organisation of scientific work as a whole in the country. At the same time scientists follow the achievements of world science and ensure that where applicable they are applied with regard to conditions in Mongolia. They also take into consideration the international division of labour and scientific and technological cooperation with the fraternal socialist countries.

In the drafting of long-term plans for research in the MPR attention is focussed upon: problems of general theoretical importance which in the long run will have a substantial influence in practice; problems whose solution will have a direct effect on the advancement of the economy; problems linked with the tasks of the cultural revolution, especially with the education of the working people in a Communist spirit.

The fact that complexes of scientific problemes are considered together is one of the most effective forms of organisation of research work, leading to more productive results and cutting the time taken to apply those results in production. The Mongolian Academy of Sciences makes provision in its plans for both the next five years and for the more distant future for the study of such wide problems as manpower resources, the development of the power industry, the genetic basis for pedigree and selection work, specific problems associated with the intensification of agriculture, especially the use of chemicals on an increasing scale, but always with an eye to soil and climatic conditions, the use of the resources of the forests, their reproduction and conservation, the reasonable use of pastures and haylands, the economic application of results attained by Soviet and other scientists and technologists and the dissemination and mastering of scientific and technological information.

All these questions are directly connected with economic plans for many years ahead, which serve as a point of orientation in the constant efforts of the people to perfect the material and economic base of socialism and the system of controlling the national economy. In long-term plans for research a significant place is assigned to the social sciences, which have a tremendous role to play in the life of socialist Mongolia.

Literature

The emergence and successful development of Mongolian socialist realist literature offers striking proof of the flourishing condition of culture in the MPR. Present-day Mongolian literature is developing on the basis of the Mongolian people's progressive literary heritage and under the fruitful influence of the literature of socialist realism of the USSR.

The new Mongolian literature was already emerging during the period of the revolutionary battles—in the partisan detachments fighting for the freedom and national independence of the Mongolian people. The fighters of the 1921 revolution were the composers of such remarkable songs, the first revolutionary marching-songs, as *Shive khiagt, Magnag usegteitug, Ulaan tug, Agaar nissdeg aeroplan*, etc., which called on the people for revolutionary exploits.

After the victory of the revolution the first literary centre was formed in the Sukhe Bator club. Future poets and writers worked there, supplying the club's arts group with literary texts and songs. The club premises witnessed the beginnings of the creative careers of D. Natsagdorzh (1906-1937), S. Buyannemekh (1901-1937) and others.

The most remarkable works, which laid the foundations for the new revolutionary school of Mongolian poetry, are the verses and songs of D. Natsagdorzh, such as the songs "Turning Blue" written in 1923, "Song of the Young Pioneers" (1925), the verses "From Ulan Bator to Berlin" and others. Among the budding poets of the early 1920s S. Buyannemekh deserves mention. His "Mongolian Internationale" (written in 1922), "Song of the Revolutionary Youth," and "Red Sun" gained wide popularity among the people.

On January 9, 1929, under the auspices of the MPRP Central Committee, a Mongolian writers' organization *Khuvsgalyn uran zokhiolchdyn bulgem* ("Group of Revolutionary Writers") was formed on the basis of a decision of the Seventh MPRP Congress. Among the members of this group were such Mongolian writers as D. Natsagdorzh, S. Buyannemekh, G. Navaannamzhil (1882-1931), Ts. Damdinsuren, B. Rinchen, Ch. Yadamsuren (1904-1937) and others. The basic task of the organization was to unite the efforts of Mongolian writers in developing new revolutionary literature.

Among the first members of the literary group were promising writers holding different points of view on literary work. The ideological training and professional skills of these writers were on an extremely low level. In the writing of S. Buyannemekh, Ch. Yadamsuren and others there were serious ideological and artistic defects which found expression in naturalist themes and nationalistic tendencies. Among the first writers of the post-revolutionary period a group headed by D. Natsagdorzh stood out prominently.

In their literary significance the works of D. Natsagdorzh occupy an outstanding place in Mongolian literature and he is rightly regarded as the founder of modern Mongolian literature.

Very important for the formation of revolutionary literature in Mongolia were the direct contacts and business connections of Mongolian writers with the Soviet literary world in the person of the great proletarian writer, Maxim Gorky, who displayed the liveliest interest in the first successes achieved in the development of the new Mongolian culture and especially its literature. As early as 1925 E. Batukhan (1888-1948), who then held the post of MPR Minister of Education, wrote a letter to Gorky, in which, after telling the great writer in detail about the country's cultural life, asked for his advice on the principle to be followed in translating Russian literary works into Mongolian. In a letter dated May 19, 1925, Gorky expressed deep appreciation of the work of the new Mongolian intelligentsia. He wrote: "There is no more important or more difficult work in the world than the work that you, the intellectuals of Mongolia, have so courageously begun."[4] In the same letter the great proletarian writer recommended that the Mongolian intellectuals "translate just those European books which give the clearest expression to the principle of activity, of mental exertion, striving for active freedom, not for the freedom of inaction."[5] In his advice Gorky neatly defined the basic direction for the development of the new Mongolian literature, as a literature destined to liberate the minds of the Mongolian people from the influence of Lamaism and awaken the creative energies of the masses of the people for building a happy life. Later on the links between the Mongolian and Soviet writers grew stronger and stronger.

At the end of the 1920s and 1930s works of considerable importance were produced which indicated still further successes of the young Mongolian writers in creating an original national, realistic literature. These works include *Gologdson khuukhen* ("The Rejected Maiden") (1929) by Ts. Damdinsuren, the tales of D. Natsagdorzh, *Malchin Toovudai* ("Herdsman Toovudai") (1932), *Tsagan sar, khar pulims* ("White Month, Black Tears") by S. Buyannemekh, "The Young Couple" (1934), *Gurvan khuukhen* ("Three Maidens") (1935) by M. Yadamsuren, *Chaban Naidan* (1935), *Bold Sambu* (1935) by D. Tsevegmid, etc. The story of "The Rejected Maiden," written by the well-known writer and great scholar Ts. Damdinsuren, marked the beginning of present-day Mongolian prose.

The important successes achieved in the new poetry are evidenced by the appearance of D. Natsagdorzh's verses *Miniy nutag* ("My Native Land") and Ts. Damdinsuren's *Buural eezh min* ("My Dear Grey-Haired Mother"). These works are the first-born of modern Mongolian poetry.

The foundations of modern dramatic writing were laid in the 1920s and 1930s. In this period there appeared the plays of S. Buyannemekh, D. Natsagdorzh, Sh. Ayush and D. Namdag, which form the main repertoire of Mongolian theatres and clubs. The most important plays of Buyannemekh are *Unen* ("Truth"), *Zhanzhin Sukhbaatar, Kharankhui zasag, Maral shar,* etc. Sh. Ayush is the author of such works as *Yag 18, Kharts Damdin, khatan Dolgor*, etc. D. Namdag wrote *Sureg chono* ("Pack of Wolves"), *Temtsel ("Struggle")*, etc. In 1934 the first musical drama *Uchirtai gurvan tolgoi* ("Three Sad Hills") was staged with a libretto composed by D. Natsagdorzh. After the 1930s realistic methods of artistic composition took firm root in Mongolian dramatic writing. The principal subject of Mongolian drama was contemporary life.

The literature of the MPR achieved considerable heights in the 1940s. In the years of the Second World War historical and heroic themes predominated in Mongolian literature, on the one hand, and the theme of Soviet-Mongolian friendship and the Great Patriotic War, on the other. The first theme found expression principally in dramatic writing and the second in poetry and prose. Historical-revolutionary plays about the partisans' war were produced, such as *Talin baatar* ("The Steppe Knights") by E. Oyuun and *Tsogiyn ider nas* ("Tsog's Youth") by B. Baast and Ts. Tsedenzhav. The poem *Khar mangasig darsni ulger* written by Ch. Lkhamsuren, deals with the subject of the Great Patriotic War of the Soviet Union against Hitler's Germany.

The prose writers devoted a large number of works to the heroism of the Soviet people; among these may be mentioned *Salkhin Zeerd* by Tsevegmid, *Malgaitai chono* by Ch. Lodoidamba and others.

The heroic work done by the Mongolian people during the years of the Second World War is the subject treated in such works as Ts. Damdinsuren's *Soliig Solson n*, B. Rinchen's *Ikh goviyn zorigt khumuus*, etc.

The post-war years were a period of further advance by Mongolian literature in creating of highly artistic, faithful images of people of the socialist era and boldly picturing the heroic romanticism of the labour exploits of the Mongolian people.

Even in the period when the unwarranted exaggeration of Choibalsan's personal role was having an adverse effect on creative work, literature and arts as a whole continued to advance, together with the life of the people and the country. Literary works in Mongolian continued to follow the correct line. This is proved by the important successes achieved in the development of Mongolian literature in recent years.

Contemporary Mongolian literature has taken a firm stand on the basis of socialist realism as the main method for Mongolian writers to follow in their artistic work. This is the fundamental and decisive achievement of Mongolian literature during the years of people's power. In the MPR literature has recently seen a further consolidation of the principle of closeness to the people and Party commitment in literature, a wealth of new forms, a perfecting of the artistic skills of the writers, a considerable reinforcement of the ranks of literary intellectuals by new young forces, and an expansion of the range of subjects dealt with in creative works. The new Mongolian literature is now successfully serving the interests of its own people and is loyally helping the MPRP to build up a socialist society in Mongolia. The Party is waging a relentless fight against everything that hinders the development of the literature of socialist realism in Mongolia, and, above all, against nationalism in all its manifestations and the pernicious influence of bourgeois ideology. The MPRP gave a timely and well-merited rebuff to certain manifestations of nationalistic trends in literature and safeguarded the ideological purity of Mongolian literature.

The rapid development of all types of prose, signifying the elimination of a certain one-sidedness in the development of Mongolian literature which had until quite recently been basically dominated by poetry, must be regarded as the most important achievement of literature in the MPR of recent years. The first Mongolian novels, a number of major stories, numerous new novellas, sketches, etc. have been written. Among the new Mongolian novels mention should be made of B. Rinchen's *Uuriyn tuyaa* ("Dawn in the Steppe"), D. Namdag's *Tsag teriyan uimeen* ("People and Years"), Ch. Lodoidamba's *Tungalag tamir* ("The Transparent Tamir"), Ch. Chimid's *Khavar, namar* ("Spring, Autumn") and others. Namdag's novel *People and Years* was awarded a State Prize. In his work the author has very skilfully contrived to reproduce a picture of the revolutionary struggle of the Mongolian people.

Among the more important stories mention should be made of *Ayuush* by D. Senge, *In the Altai Mountains* by Ch. Lodoidamba, *Zhil ongorokhod* ("A Year Later") by S. Erdene, *Khuniy chanar* ("A Man's Quality") by Ts. Ulambayar and many others. Mongolian story-telling has not only increased quantitatively, it has undergone a qualitative change. It has become more varied in its subject matter and in the artistic methods used for picturing real life. The socialist contemporary life of Mongolia is the centre of attention of Mongolian story writers.

The considerable development of the most militant and operative form of artistic creativety—stories, sketches and journalism—must be regarded as a great achievement of Mongolian literature of recent years. The representatives of the older generation, masters in the production of short stories, have been joined by a whole galaxy of young writers who are working successfully in this field.

Mongolian poetry has embarked on a new phase of its development. It has been enriched by new forms and the professional skill of Mongolian poets has considerably improved and the subject matter of the poems produced has greatly widened. Mongolian poets have written a number of important poems on historical-biographical, lyrical and socio-political subjects. These poems include the poems of Ch. Lkhamsuren *(Khuren Mor)*, Ts. Gaitav's *(D. Sukhe Bator)*, S. Dashdoorot's *(Mongol)*, Akhtanaa's *(The Falcon)*, S. Dashdendev's *(Three Alls)*, etc.

The successes achieved by Mongolian dramatic writing are evidenced by the appearance of a large number of new works by Mongolian playwrights and screenplay writers.

At the present time theatres in Mongolia are giving successful performances of plays written by the Mongolian dramatists L. Vangan ("Doctors", "In the Steppe of Arvaikher", "Chauffeur Tozhoo"), by Ch. Chimid ("Signal", "On the Threshold"), by Ch. Logoidamba ("Believable"), etc. Among the important film scenarios written by Mongolian authors mention should be made of *Serelt* ("Resurrection") by L. Vangan, Ch. Oidov's *Ardin elch* ("The People's Envoy"), "Daddy who is in Ulan Bator" by Ts. Nadmid and Do. Zhodorzh, etc.

Literary criticism, which had for long been a backward sector of the literary front, has of recent years found its true path. Marxist literary criticism is being created in the Mongolian People's Republic and is battling with the ideology of bourgeois nationalism for the literature of socialist realism.

In recent years the increasing attention of world opinion was attracted to the productions of Mongolian writers. Whereas, until recently, only certain works of old Mongolian literature were known to individual scholars, nowadays the verses, stories, tales and novels of Mongolian writers are being translated into foreign languages. For example, Russian translations have been published of the works of D. Natsagdorzh, Ts. Damdinsuren, Ch. Chimid, Ts. Gaitav, S. Erdene, D. Namdag, Ch. Lodoidamba, B. Yavukolan. Many works of Mongolian writers have been translated into Chinese, Czech, Albanian, Polish and other languages.

In the history of contemporary Mongolian literature translations rightly occupy an honourable place. The first translations of works from West-European, Russian classical and Soviet literature go back to the beginning of the 1930s.

Mongolian writers began by translating the works of Alexander Pushkin back in 1930. In 1935 Tolstoy's "The Prisoner of the Caucasus" appeared as a separate publication and then followed translations of individual works of Lermontov and Nekrasov, Gogol and Turgenev, Krylov and Saltykov-Shchedrin, Chekhov and other Russian writers. It was approximately in these years that Mongolian readers began to become acquainted with the works of the Soviet writers M. Gorky, D. Furmanov, Dzhambul, N. Ostrovsky and others.

In addition to the works of Russian classical and Soviet literature translations have been made into Mongolian of a number of works of West-European and American literature, in particular, the plays of Goldoni and Lope de Vega, the novellas of Boccaccio and Guy de Maupassant, Daniel Defoe's *Robinson Crusoe*, Swift's *Gulliver's Travels*, *The Gadfly* by Ethel Voinich, the works of Beaumarchais, Daudet, Edgar

Allan Poe, Victor Hugo, Anatole France, A. Barbusse, Jack London, Jules Verne and other writers.

Mongolian literary translation has acquired particularly great importance in recent years. Mongolian readers now read in their own language many works of almost all the most important Soviet writers: Mayakovsky, Fadeev, Tikhonov, Alexei Tolstoy, Ehrenburg, Sholokhov, etc.

A large number of works from many countries, especially the socialist states, have been translated into Mongolian. For instance, translations have been made of the works of Fučik, Hašek, Petöfi, Lu Sing, etc. World classics which have been translated into Mongolian include the works of Shakespeare—*Othello, King Lear*, etc., Victor Hugo—*Notre Dame, The Man who Smiles, Balzac's Gobsek*, etc., Charles Dickens's *David Copperfield*, Rabelais' *Gargantua and Pantagruel*, Duma's *The Count of Monte Cristo* and *The Three Musketeers*, Stendahl's *Rouge et Noir*, Theodore Dreiser's *An American Tragedy*, etc.

The works of contemporary progressive writers of many countries are published in Mongolian (Louis Aragon, Tagore, Nazim Hikmet, Pablo Neruda, Georges Amadu, etc).

The Third Congress of Mongolian Writers, held in 1962, was a major event in the history of Mongolian literature. The Congress summed up the successes achieved by Mongolian literature in recent years and indicated the concrete tasks facing Mongolian literature during the years of the people's power. A fully-valid modern literature of socialist realism has been created in Mongolia, a literature such as was never produced in the thousand years of Mongolian culture.

Theatre, Films, Circus

In the 1920s the Mongolian theatre was completely non-professional. In its development it was based on popular tradition and on the experience of the Soviet theatre.

Immediately after the victory of the Revolution the MPRP took concrete steps to lay the foundations of theatrical art in Mongolia. By February 1922 a theatre studio company *Shiy Zhuzhgiyn bulgem* had been organized, consisting of 26 persons and an artistic-political commission of 7 members set up under the Revolutionary Youth League's Central Committee. This was the basis of the new revolutionary theatre in Mongolia. To begin with, the theatre studio was accommodated in the building of the so-called People's Palace, built in July 1921 at the cost of the Mongolian Ministry of Finance and of social and trading organizations of foreigners living in Mongolia. At that time the People's Palace was an international club where evening entertainments and concerts of the various nationalities resident in the capital of Mongolia were organized, Soviet films were shown, Russian and Mongolian entertainments were staged by Russian and Mongolian amateur groups. Plays by Ostrovsky and Pushkin—*From Rags to Riches, Overnight, Hard Times, Rusalka*—were performed in the People's Palace. Thanks to the People's Palace activities Mongolian audiences were able for the first time to become acquainted with modern theatrical art and early Soviet films. But for the members of the first Mongolian theatre studio the People's Palace constituted a creative school where they gained an idea of genuine, popular, realistic theatrical art. The first artistic performance staged by the studio theatre was a representation of *Sando amban*, which was given on the stage of the People's Palace on March 28, 1922. This play portrayed the anti-Manchu struggle of the Mongolian people. It was remarkable for its political acuteness and the appeal it made to the mass of the people.

The new type of life called for the creation of a new repertoire. In the 1920's good literary productions were scarce; there were no playwrights and the actors themselves supplied the repertoire. This gave rise to the production of plays written by the actual people performing the work. Incidentally, these productions can hardly be called plays. What the actors wrote was more reminiscent of a short libretto—supplying merely the groundwork for the performance about to be given. The rest was added by the actors while the play was going on—by improvising as best they could. Naturally, not all the plays were of good quality and the improvisations were not always successful. But performances of this type were redeemed by the topicality of the subject treated and the enthusiasm of the performers. In the whole of the theatre's work there could be felt a craving for realism in art, a desire to serve a liberated people with all one's strength.

In October 1924 the Sukhe Bator Central Club was founded and it soon became the centre of amateur entertainment activities in the first years of people's power. In this club began the productive careers of the People's Actors O. Dashdeleg and D. Ichinkhorloo, the veteran actor L. Damdinbazar (1889-1937), Ch. Luvsansodnom (1900-1931), the woman musician D. Ishdulam (1869-1947) and others. On the stage of the club successful performances were given of plays with a new revolutionary content such as *Sumya noen, Ushandar* and *Sakhilaa martagch lam*. From 1926 onwards a great role in the history of founding a Mongolian national theatre was played by the People's Palace of Culture *Ardin Tsengeldekh khureelen*, in which dramatic and musical sections were organized with a permanent staff of artists.

In these years an obvious search was being made for ways of creating a new theatre and the first burgeonings of realistic theatrical art began to appear.

The 1930s saw the opening of a new page in the history of the Mongolian theatre. In September 1930 a studio company was organized and began, under the leadership of a producer invited from the Soviet Union, to lay the foundations of a professional theatre. There followed for the amateur participants a period of concentrated study. The first public rehearsal presented by the group was given in February 1931. Subsequently, such rehearsals were given regularly.

In November 1931 the studio group was transformed into a state theatre. Thenceforth, members of the studio, working in different localities, became professional actors. The state theatre inaugurated its productions with the staging of the play *Unen* written by S. Buyannemekh. The play narrated the revolutionary heroism of the Mongolian people, who had risen up against their enemies under the influence of the Great October Revolution.

A weak feature of the work of the budding theatre continued to be the repertoire. The theatre had few good plays. In order to solve this problem the MPR government set up in March 1933 an artistic-political council attached to the theatre. In 1935 this council was abolished and in its place a new one was instituted under the MPR Council of Ministers.

These measures of the government created favourable conditions for the creative work of the theatre. In 1933 the theatre participated in Moscow in an International Olympiad of Revolutionary Theatres. The performances of the Mongolian theatre both at the Olympiad and before the public in the capital of the Soviet Union were successful; a number of Soviet and European newspapers and the jury of the Olympiad gave a favourable assessment of its work. In the same year the Mongolian State Theatre gave performances to the workers of the Buryat ASSR. Here again the performances given by the Mongolian actors met with success.

Encouraged by the warm reception in the Soviet Union, Mongolian actors set about studying to try and improve their skills with redoubled energy. They staged a number of interesting plays which testified to the growth both of acting and of literary cadres in the country. Among these performances were the musical drama *Uchirtai gurvan tolgoi* ("Three Sad Hills"). This drama, like many of its predecessors, dealt with the Mongolian people's past, and the conditions of life under feudalism. In this production D. Natsagdorzh showed an *arat* fighting for his freedom. The musical drama *Uchirtai gurvan tolgoi* was, unquestionably, a realistic production. This initiative by D. Natsagdorzh was taken up by other dramatists.

Along with national plays the theatre performed classical Soviet plays. One of the first Soviet plays staged by the State theatre was *Armoured Train No. 14/69* by V. Ivanov (1938).

The West European classics performed by the theatre included *Sheep's Fountain* by Lope de Vega, *Servant of Two Masters* by Goldoni, Molière's *Les Fourberies de Scapin* and several others.

Thus, the 1930s in the history of theatrical art were characterized by the fact that during this period a professional theatre was organized, a correct course for its development was outlined and initial successes were achieved in founding a new theatre of realism. The formalistic and naturalistic plays which had previously been staged gradually disappeared from the scene and were replaced by productions which were basically realistic; the theatre's repertoire was expanded and enriched. At this time a number of dramatists emerged in the country and produced a number of very interesting plays.

During the years of the Second World War the theatre produced many excellent plays dealing with historical, revolutionary and epic subjects.

Plays depicting the heroic past of the Mongolian people also met with great success. Audiences saw defile before them a whole series of heroes (Mandkhai, Amursana, Tsokto-taiji, etc.).

The subject of Mongolian soldiers' heroism during the war against the Japanese imperialists was reflected in the theatre's repertoire. Among the plays devoted to this subject may be mentioned Ch. Oidov's *Birthday* and E. Oyuun's *Brothers*. The latter play was awarded a State Prize in 1946.

The play *Miniy bayasgalan* ("My Joy") by Ch. Oidov depicts the brotherly assistance rendered by Mongolian herdsmen to the heroic Soviet Army.

The transition of the country to peacetime conditions faced the theatre and dramatists with the problem of depicting the peaceful creative labour of the Mongolian people. The first play to be staged was Ch. Oidov's *Zam* ("The Road") dealing with the construction by the *arats* of one *somon* of a macadamized highway and telegraph line connecting the *somon* with the centre. The theatre also repeated the performance of E. Oyuun's play *Stoibishche* about the humdrum labours of *arat* herdsmen.

Plays of this kind, however, were few in number and they depicted only the work of a herdsman. There were no plays about workers, intellectuals, cultural construction, etc. in the theatre's repertoire.

With the help of the MPRP and the people's government the theatre and the writers' organization succeeded in overcoming this difficulty and plays devoted to contemporary problems in all their variety began to make their appearance one after another on the stage of the theatre.

The spectator saw on stage the life and work of Mongolian workers (*Erdeniyan Dorzh* of Ts. Zandr and Ch. Lodoidamba, *Yandangiyn duu* of Ch. Chimid, *Tozhoo Zholooch* of L. Vangan and others), of agricultural workers (*Arvijikh Family, Believable* of Ch. Lodoidamba, *The Individualists, In the Arvaikher Steppe* of L. Vangan, *On the Threshold* by Ch. Chimid and others), and of new Mongolian intellectuals (*The New Generation* of D. Namdag and Sh. Natsagdorzh, *The Doctors* of L. Vangan and others).

In this fashion the Mongolian theatre has succeeded in making the transition to modern subjects. Historical and epic heroes have given way to a new hero and the theatre has begun to depict the new man born of the revolution and the people's democratic system.

Many productions of world classics and of Soviet dramatists have become firmly installed in the Mongolian theatre's repertoire. Successful performances are given on the stage of the State Drama Theatre of *Othello, King Lear,* Schiller's *Perfidy and Love,* Ostrovsky's *Thunder,* Gorky's *The Lower Depths,* Sholokhov's *Virgin Soil Upturned,* Korneichuk's *The Thicket of Guelder Roses,* Popov's *The Ulyanov Family,* Arbuzov's *The Irkutsk Story,* etc. All this testifies to the maturity of the Mongolian theatre.

Of recent years the Mongolian theatre has grown considerably stronger in the organizational sense also. By the end of the First Five-Year Plan the theatre represented an important body with a large group of theatrical workers at its disposal. The theatre consisted of drama and opera companies, a folk instruments orchestra, a symphony orchestra, a choir and a ballet company. Independent theatrical sections have been set up by the State Drama Theatre.

In 1948 puppet and children's theatres were instituted and since 1963 a State Opera and Ballet Theatre has been functioning.

Alongside the central theatres, music and drama theatres are now functioning in the towns of Choibalsan, Kobdo, Bayan Olgiy. Amateur entertainment activities continue to develop. The centres around which lovers of the arts converge are the numerous palaces of culture and clubs. Clubs have amateur orchestras and choirs, with amateur musicians working away devotedly at improving their skill. A large number of actors and professional musicians began their career in amateur groups. Amateur activity is an important factor in the country's cultural life and constitutes a reserve from which art derives fresh professional strength.

The MPRP and the MPR government have done a great deal of work to provide film-showing facilities throughout the country and to develop a national film industry.

In 1929-1930 club-screens began to be fitted up in the MPR (at the People's Palace, the Sukhe Bator Club, Palace of Culture, the V. I. Lenin Club, etc.) on which Soviet films were displayed.

In 1933 a mobile cinema department was organized under the Ministry of Education. The first Mongolian cinema, the *Arat*, was opened in 1934 in Ulan Bator.

In 1936 a studio for making artistic and documentary films was opened in Ulan Bator. It proceeded to put out news films depicting the MPR's successes in different sectors of the country's economic and cultural construction. National cadres of film personnel were trained here under the guidance of Soviet specialists.

Mention should also be made of the gift presented in 1936 by the Soviet Government to the workers of the Mongolian People's Republic—12 mobile cinemas with a supply of sound films. In the same year, with the assistance of Soviet cinema film organizations, the first artistic sound film *Son of Mongolia* (in Russian and Mongolian) was produced. Soviet producers and cameramen took part in making the film and the roles were taken by actors of the Mongolian theatre.

In 1940 Mongolian and Soviet cinema workers embarked on the production of a full-length feature film *They Call Him Sukhe Bator*. In 1941 the Ulan Bator film studio issued the feature and documentary films *Gongor*, about the hero of the battles in the Khalkhin-Gol region, and *Twenty Years of the Mongolian State*, followed by the film *A Frontier Happening* (about the heroic frontier guards) and the shorts *The Tank Soldiers* and *The Cavalrymen* (about the military training of troops).

In 1944 Mongolian and Soviet cinema workers jointly produced the feature film *Tsog taij* (Russian version *The Knights of the Steppes)* dealing with a Mongolian political figure of the XVIIth century. The film was made in Russian and Mongolian.

For the twentieth anniversary of the Mongolian revolution a film entitled *Independent Mongolia* was produced. A film on the International Festival of Democratic Youth in 1947, made by Zhigzhid, Honoured Artist of the MPR, one of the participants in the Festival, enjoyed great success in the MPR.

In recent years Mongolkino has been at work learning the technique of producing colour films. The first attempt on these lines was made in connection with the celebration of the 30th anniversary of the Mongolian revolution, and the colour film *Mongolian People's Republic* was issued. During the years of their existence Mongolfilm makers have made more than one hundred films depicting the life and work of the people. In recent years there have appeared such full-length films as: *The People's Envoy, I'd Like a Horse, Oh! These Girls, One in a Thousand, Daddy, Who is in Ulan Bator, The Rejected Maiden, On Life's Threshold, Khokho Will Soon be Marrying, The Taste of the Wind, Fair Shares, Nugel-Buyan, Tus bish us.*

At the present time the film studio is issuing annually five full-length, two documentary and more than 40 sections of short-length films and news films.

The success of Mongolian cinema productions is proved by the fact that a number of films have been awarded prizes at international cinema festivals. For example, the films *What is Preventing Us* and *I'd Like a Horse* were awarded prizes at the Film Festival in Karlovy Vary and the colour documentary picture *Present-Day Mongolia* received the Grand Lumumba prize at the Film Festival of Asian and African countries held in 1964 in Indonesia.

At the present time the task of providing film-showing facilities throughout the country is being successfully accomplished. Numerous cinemas and permanent and mobile film projectors are operating in all the cities and populated centres of the country. Thus, firm foundations for a national cinema industry have been laid during the years of people's power.

The art of the circus is developing successfully in the MPR.

The decision to organize a State Circus dates back to 1940. Invitations were extended to Soviet artists who then undertook the task of training national cadres.

The first art director of the new circus was Honoured Artist of the MPR Randnabazar (1912-1947), who did a lot to develop the national circus art. The State Circus gave its first performance during the celebrations of the twentieth anniversary of the Mongolian revolution.

In 1942 the Circus left for a two-month tour of the Buryat ASSR where they gave successful performances.

In the summer of 1952 the MPR State Circus again left to tour the USSR, giving performances in Moscow, Zaporozhye and Kiev. The Soviet press commented on the great skill of the circus artists, especially of Honoured Artists Zh. Damdinsuren, L. Natsog and Zh. Danzan.

The State Circus met with great success on tours abroad in the Chinese People's Republic, the Korean National Democratic Republic, the Democratic Republic of Vietnam, India and other countries of the world. The skill of the Mongolian artists was highly appreciated by world audience. The Mongolian State Circus artists are now ceaselessly perfecting their professional skills and mastering new types of circus art.

Music

The first productions of the new Mongolian music were the songs of the partisans, which gave a stimulus to the composition of new musical works. The first remarkable Mongolian revolutionary march *Shivee Khiagt* was composed by a partisan, the popular musician and flute-player Gavar, from Dzasagtu-Khan *aimak*. This song about the expulsion of the foreign occupiers from a small frontier village in the north of Mongolia sprang up literally in the first battles of the Mongolian revolution.

One of the pioneers of contemporary Mongolian music was one of the first members of the MPRP, the well-known folk-singer and partisan, M. Dugarzhav (1893-1944). He composed *Ulaan tug* ("Red Flag"), *Ider zhinchin, Bayan mongol, Ukherchin khuu, Uezesgelen goe* and other songs which are even now popular. The *Song of the First Party Congress* composed by a group of musicians headed by M. Dugarzhav, opened a new chapter in the history of the Mongolian revolutionary song. The typical characteristics of the early Mongolian revolutionary songs are their joyously uplifted tone, their sense of excitement, the majestic beat of the cavalry march and the melodiousness of the traditional tune.

In their works the composers of these songs based themselves on the musical traditions of the Mongolian people. Their forerunners and teachers were the popular poets—*khuurch, tuulch, yeroolch* and more especially the familiar Ya. Luvsan-*khuurch*. He was not only the guardian of the people's heritage of song but also the creator of new works. During the years of the revolution he composed a large number of new songs.

Following the songs of the partisans there appeared the songs of the first years of the revolution: *Lenin ba Sukhbaatar* ("Lenin and Sukhe-Bator"), *Pioneryan duu* ("Song of the Pioneers") *Arvan zhil* ("Ten years") and many others.

The songs of the first years of the revolution are remarkable in that they denoted the birth of an entirely new revolutionary type of subject in Mongolian music. The sentiments of happiness and pride of a people born anew by the revolution rang out for the first time in the simple, radiant motifs of these songs.

The basis for the development of a new musical art in Mongolia was laid by the establishment in the autumn of 1922 of an amateur national music society on the initiative of the women's section of the MPRP Central Committee. The first decade was the period of formation of contemporary musical culture in the MPR. The origin of professional music dates back to the 1930s. In this a great part was played by the Mongolian State Theatre in which a music studio and a symphony orchestra were organized. Until recently the State Theatre was called the Mongolian State Music and Drama Theatre. Various amateur courses and also the school of music and choreography in Ulan Bator played a big part in training national cadres. Many leaders in the Mongolian arts obtained their higher musical education in the conservatories of the USSR.

The successes achieved in recent years by Mongolian music are especially noteworthy. The great work done in preceding years in developing music in Mongolia produced the conditions essential for organizing an independent national music theatre as well as orchestral, dance and choral groups. At the present time the MPR has a State Opera and Ballet Theatre, two symphony orchestras, a State Folk-Song and Dance Ensemble, Folk Instruments Ensemble, a People's Army Song and Dance Ensemble, numerous orchestras of national instruments and choirs. The major centre of musical art in the MPR is the State Opera and Ballet Theatre whose repertoire includes Mongolian and classical operas and ballets.

There has been a considerable increase in the musical output of Mongolian composers, whose ranks are being reinforced year after year by new youthful talents. The formation of national Mongolian symphony, operatic, ballet, choral, chamber and mass-performed music should be esteemed a major achievement of musical art in the MPR. Among the symphonic works of Mongolian composers should be mentioned the symphony "My Native Land" by L. Murdorzh, which is the first major production of Mongolian instrumental music, the symphonic sketch "Khasbaatar" and "In the Khentei Mountains" by Damdinsuren, the "Symphonic Poem on the Party" by S. Gonchigsumla and other works. The first Mongolian national opera is "Among the Three Sad Hills," written by the Mongolian composer B. Damdinsuren, Honoured Artist of the MPR, State Prize Winner. After the first opera other national operas also appeared, such as "The Way to Happiness" by B. Damdinsuren, S. Gonchigsumla's "Truth", L. Murdorzh's "Khokho Namzhil", etc.

The successes of Mongolian choreography are evidenced by the appearance of national ballets. In 1954 a one-act ballet was staged, composed by Honoured Musician of the MPR G. Zhamyan, and entitled "Our Union" on a subject taken from the life of one agricultural association. This was the first successful attempt to create an original Mongolian ballet.

The composer S. Gonchigsumla has written the ballet "Gankhuyag" which has been awarded a State Prize. The State Opera and Ballet Theatre stages very successful performances of the "Fountain of Bakhchisarai" of B. Asafyev, A. S. Dorogomizhsky's "Rusalka", N. A. Rimsky-Korsakov's "Schahrazade," F. Yarullin's "Shurale," etc. Particularly notable are the successes achieved in choral and massed-group music. Mongolian composers of melodic music have composed a large number of songs which have gained widespread acclaim among the people.

The successes of Mongolian professional musical art are inseparable from the cadres of performers, talented musicians and singers, many of whom have been awarded the title of Honoured Artist of the MPR. The State Opera and Ballet Theatre has a friendly working group comprising well-known artists—the singers G. Khaidav, P. Purevdorzh and A. Zafdcuren, the composer Ts. Namaraizhav, and the conductor Ch. Chuluun, the choir conductor and the composer D. Luvsansharav, the musician D. Tserendolgor (1932-1965), the *morinkhur* player G. Zhamyan and others.

In addition to the development of professional music, amateur music has experienced a rapid growth in the country. Numerous groups and clubs of musical amateurs are now operating with thousands of music-lovers playing an active part in them. Another remarkable phenomenon in the country's musical life is the increasing area of activity and the rapid growth in the general musical culture of the ordinary herdsmen, workers and from among the people's intellectuals.

A major event in the history of the development of musical art in the MPR was the founding of the Union of Mongolian Composers in 1957. The first congress of Mongolian composers was held in 1964. The congress summed up the successes achieved in developing contemporary Mongolian music and defined its further tasks and prospects.

Fine Arts

After the people's revolution Mongolian fine arts slowly and gradually freed themselves from the grim canonical directives and modes of Buddhism and religious ideology and made a decisive swing over to life. The inception of new contemporary Mongolian fine arts was very closely linked up with the tasks and the needs of revolutionary Mongolia. The appearance of the first revolutionary propaganda posters of the MPRP at the very outset of the people's revolution signified the birth of a completely new type of art in Mongolia, one destined to serve the interests of the people and the aims of its revolutionary struggle.

One of the professional artists and pioneers of the new school of realism was Baliaryn (Marzan) Sharav (1866-1939). He produced a number of original works on revolutionary subjects which were a new phenomenon in the history of

Mongolian national painting. His work is characterized, in general, by an ability to combine lofty revolutionary ideas with expressiveness and the adaptability of artistic means of realistic representation of actuality. His paintings are also notable for their naturalness and originality. Among his best works are an original portrait of Lenin which he described as "The invincible teaching of Lenin", the "Portrait of Sukhe Bator," the revolutionary posters "Stable and Unstable Yurt," posters depicting the friendship between Mongolian and Soviet soldiers, etc.

Along with Sharav a great role in creating the new Mongolian pictorial art was played by such popular artists as Zhungder, Zhalsrai, Tsagaan-Zhamba, D. Manibadar (1889-1963) and others. D. Manibadar was an outstanding artist and a great connoisseur of the traditions of folk art. From his childhood he showed an interest in folk ornamentation and made a very rich collection of specimens of ornamentation. During the years of the people's rule D. Manibadar created a whole series of patterns of national ornamentation and taught young people the art of ornamentation. The works of Manibadar nowadays decorate the interior of the Pioneers' Palace in Ulan Bator, of the State Opera and Ballet Theatre, of the government building in Ikh-Tengere, etc.

The first two decades after the people's revolution were the period of the inception and formation of contemporary Mongolian fine arts as well as the period of training professional masters. From the early 1930s onwards the first amateur art clubs organized at the state theatre and the teachers' training college in Ulan Bator played an important part in developing Mongolian pictorial arts. In these schools many future Mongolian masters had their lessons in realistic art. From the first clubs there emerged such well-known Mongolian artists as O. Tseverjav, D. Choidog, N. Chultem, L. Gava, O. Odon, Sanzhzhav and others. Many of these artists subsequently completed their education at higher schools in the USSR.

The 1940s marked a new phase in the development of contemporary Mongolian art. At the end of 1942 a Mongolian board of administration for the fine arts was organized with branches in 18 of the country's *aimaks*. This organization, which was subsequently re-named the Union of Mongolian Artists, is the centre of the creative and productive work of fine arts in Mongolia.

The success achieved in the development of the fine arts was demonstrated at the first exhibition of the works of Mongolian artists held in 1944. It showed that the MPR has a national school of painting and cadres of masters in this form of art.

In the period of expansion of socialist construction Mongolian fine arts developed still further. The most important achievement of Mongolian art in recent years is the fact that it has adopted as its principal subject the socialist aspect of present-day life in Mongolia. The professional skill of artists has considerably improved and there has been a great enrichment of the genres and types of Mongolian fine arts.

The best pictures of many artists are devoted to the heroism in the work of the people, to personifying the images of labourers in socialist agriculture and of the workers and intellectuals of the new Mongolia. Among them may be mentioned the series of line engravings of the young artists D. Amgalan, "Socialist Ulan Bator", exalting the inspired work of the builders of the capital, O. Odon's pictures "Coalmine Kapitalnaya" and "Oilworkers", N. Chultem's "Portrait of a Brigadier", Gava's "Portrait of the People's Actress Dashdeleg", O. Tsevegzhav's "Union Members", Ts. Budbazar's "Advent of the Water", M. Tsembeldorzh's "Land Tenure", S. Natsagdorzh's "The Young Tractor-Driver", etc. These works, distinguished as they are by their delicacy of execution, depict the life and labour of our contemporaries—the builders of socialism.

Mongolian artists are interested in historical-revolutionary subjects such as the heroism of the Mongolian people in the revolutionary struggle. Among recent works dealing with this subject may be mentioned N. Chultem's "Sukhe Bator's meeting with Lenin", A. Sengetsokhio's "Revolt of the Uliasutai troops" and "Portrait of Tsingunzhav", O. Tsevegzhav's "Return from the War" and "The Feat of the Heroes", O. Odon's "Partisan Khasbataar", L. Namkhaitseren's "Against War", O. Mayagmar's "On the Way to Da-Khuree", etc.

Mongolian artists are also producing successful work in the field of painting. With great affection and skill they reproduce the beauty and majesty of nature in the lap of which the workers of the homeland find inspiration for labour. The boundless, flowering steppe, transformed by the hands of our contemporaries, the majestic snow-clad mountains—all of this is depicted on the canvases of such Mongolian landscape painters as N. Chultem ("Khamtyn khudulmur", "Aduuchin"), L. Gava ("Altain magtaal"), O. Odon ("Goviin bagana", "Tsaagan els"), Ts. Dorzhpalam ("Khashir Malchin"), Sanzhaa ("Ogloo"), Ts. Zhamsran ("Sangiin azh akhuid tuslakhar"), Ts. Budbazar ("Kherlen"), G. Tserendondog ("Zerengiin khendiy"), S. Rinchin ("Sukhe-Bator khot"), ("Brigadyn tov"), etc.

Graphic art, as the most militant and popular form of figurative art, has occupied a worthy place in Mongolian fine arts. Among the important works produced in this sphere mention should be made of D. Amgalan's "Motherland Morning", "Going to School", "Mother, the Sun and I", and S. Natsagdorzh's "The Flute-Player" and "My Country".

The large number of political posters and caricatures produced by Mongolian artists in recent years testify to the close ties linking them with the contemporary life of the country. Among recent works which have enjoyed success with the country's workers may be mentioned Luvsanzhamts' posters on the subject of peace, "Mongol" by S. Natsagdorzh, "Fortieth Anniversary of the Revolutionary Youth League" by Amgalan, "Peace" by Gombosuren, "Nakhoigoo khor" and "Get Out of the UN" by Nyamsuren, "Obligations and Execution" and "Greetings to All" by Gursed and many others.

One of the important achievements of Mongolian fine arts during the years of the people's rule is the creation of national sculpture. Talented national sculptors have appeared. A major role in the development of the professional art of sculpture in Mongolia has been played by the sculpture studio organized in 1945 under the leadership of the veteran Mongolian sculptor, laureate of a State award, S. Chaimbol. From this studio have emerged many Mongolian sculptors (A. Davatseren, L. Makhbal, etc.).

A memorial to Sukhe Bator, designed by Ch. Choimbol, was erected in 1946 on the main square of Ulan Bator. The same artist has also created a number of monumental memorials (sculpture of Kh. Choibalsan sited near the building of the State University, etc.).

Among the best works of N. Zhamba mention should be made of the memorial to a popular leader of the Ayushi revolt, "The Untamed Steed", "The Horseherd of the Agricultural Association", "Coalminer Davazhav", "Dugar-zaisan", etc. A. Davaatseren has made a sculpture "A Father's Commendation" in which, with the profound internal penetration of an artist, he has depicted the parting message of the ailing father to his son, the future leader of the Mongolian people, Sukhe Bator, as he sets off on a far journey. Among the works of L. Makhbal should be mentioned the monumental memorial to D. Natsagdorzh, the founder of contemporary Mongolian literature, "Partisan", etc. In recent years the ranks of Mongolian sculptors have been joined by new youthful talents.

One of the special features of contemporary art in Mongolia is the way in which the Mongolian people's national tradition of applied art continues to develop in creativeness.

The professional ranks of artists and sculptors are, with every year that passes, being swelled by the gifted natural works of the people. Chased work, wood-, bone- and stone-carving, embroidery and rug-making have become widely practised in the MPR.

The work done by the goldsmith Baldan-Osor, the steel engravers Sumya and Chultem, the embroiderers Mazhig, Tserma and Norolkoo, the engravings of the Honoured Artists D. Gelegdandar, L. Dorzh, Gund, Gevshehu, B. Zhamyansharav, S. Sengee, the artistic casting experts Kh. Dagvadorzh, Azaibural and other talented craftsmen, enjoy a wide reputation.

The productions of Mongolian artists are becoming well-known not only inside the country but even far beyond the borders of Mongolia. The works of Mongolian artists, sculptors and craftsmen are being displayed more and more frequently at exhibitions in the fraternal socialist countries and at international youth festivals. The work of Mongolian artists shown at exhibitions has been favourably commented on by the world public.

* * *

The whole history of cultural construction in the MPR shows very clearly that the people's revolution has opened up wide access for the working masses of Mongolia to all forms of social and cultural creation, has awakened enormous creative forces in the people and ensured the complete flowering of all its abilities and talents. This constitutes the great creative and productive strength of the Mongolian revolution. The practical experience of the revolution in Mongolia refutes completely one of the principal concepts of bourgeois sociology, which claims that any revolution carries with it nothing but destruction and the ruin of civilization. Quite a few people in the bourgeois world have asserted and still assert that, after the revolution, in Mongolia, there was a collapse of the national culture, the disappearance of the specific national features of the Mongolian people. Historical facts, however, prove that it was precisely during the years of the people's power that the Mongolian people managed to put an end to the centuries-old backwardness of the country and to escape from a medieval mentality and obscurantism. The experience of cultural construction in the MPR confirms the correctness of the postulate in the CPSU Programme which asserts that "socialism is the path that leads peoples to freedom and happiness... Socialism provides the working class and all the workers with a high material and cultural level of life. Socialism extricates the masses of the people from darkness and ignorance and brings them into contact with contemporary culture."[6]

In place of a medieval, feudal Mongolia with hundreds of monasteries and a great army of lamas constituting a half of the total male population of the country there came a new, re-born Mongolia with an advanced socialist culture. Judging by certain data indicative of its cultural growth the MPR stands away ahead of individual capitalist countries. In the number of students per head of the population the MPR now stands higher than Western Germany, Italy, Japan, Turkey, Pakistan and Iran And the number of people per doctor in Mongolia is very much less than in Turkey, Iran, Pakistan and South Vietnam.

The fact that socialism brings the Mongolian people a happy prosperous life is proved by the steady increase in the material welfare of the workers of the MPR. The people have now got rid forever of the threat of ruin and impoverishment and the former age-old hardship and ignorance, the injustices and the squalor of a herdsman's life have vanished into oblivion. The successful completion of the co-operativization of agriculture in the MPR has opened up the widest possibilities for an unbroken rise in the material welfare of the main bulk of the workers. As a result of the adoption by the Party and government of numerous measures for raising the material well-being of the *arats* life in the agricultural associations improves from one day to the next. The central farmsteads of many associations are gradually being transformed into well-built, well-planned villages which have cultural institutions for the masses, schools, medical and veterinary centres, clubs, libraries, permanent and mobile cinemas, wireless broadcasting points, telephone exchanges, etc. In 1963, 40% of all the associations changed over to paying for work-day units in cash. In the years 1960-1964 alone the cash revenues of associations' members rose by 90%.

An important indicator of the growth in the well-being of a population is the steady rise in the nominal and real wages of workers and employees. During the years of the Second Five-Year Plan the real wages of workers and employees rose by 40% and in the first three years of the Third Five-Year Plan (1960-1963) there was a rise of 30% in the wages fund. As a result of the decrease in the income tax levied on workers and employees in 1963 alone money incomes rose to 18 million *tugriks*. In recent years the wages earned by lower-paid workers and employees were increased in towns and populated centres by 14-19% and in rural localities by 21-22%.

The most generalized expression of the steep rise in the living standards of the workers of the MPR, as of other socialist countries too, is the rapid and steady rise in the national income which constitutes the only source of an increase in the incomes of the population. In the last five years the gross national income of the MPR has risen by 50%. In 1960-1964, the national income in the country was distributed as follows: 74-80% was appropriated to consumption and 20-26% to savings or accumulation.

The MPR is a practical example of the implementation of the supreme principle of socialism: "From each according to his ability, to each according to his work," in accordance with which the material benefits of a society are distributed between its members. At the same time a considerable part of the material and cultural benefits is distributed between the workers without payment being required regardless of the quantity or quality of the labour expended. The State defrays all the costs of medical services for the whole population and also of educating the workers. Pensions and scholarships are paid for by the community; part of the expenditure on organizing public meals and worker's holidays is defrayed and the state expends large amounts on social insurance benefits, on helping large families, expanding the network of children's institutions, providing the population with well-planned housing accommodation, etc.

One of the striking indications of the increasing prosperity of the population is the way public health is organized in the MPR. It is common knowledge that, before the revolution, Mongolia had not been aware of modern medicine; the backward medical science of India and Tibet exercised complete sway in the country and was powerless to meet the threat of extermination of the Mongolian population. One of the greatest triumphs of the people's revolution must be esteemed the organization of medical services for the population and the rapid growth of modern medical science in the MPR. As a result of the large-scale ameliorative, prophylactic and other social and cultural measures introduced there has been a great reduction in the country of the death-rate and an increase in the birth-rate. Before the revolution 48 out of every 100 new-born children died before reaching 3 years of age. Nowadays, infant mortality is low and, in general, the death-rate among the population has fallen during the years of the people's rule to a fifth of the former figure and amounts to 10 per thousand. In relative increase of population the MPR occupies one of the first places in the world. A total of 43.5% of the population of the MPR are persons under 18 years of age. During the years of the people's power the population of the MPR has almost doubled.

The housing conditions of the workers are improving every year. In recent years especially there has been a considerable increase in the volume and speed of housebuilding in the MPR. Large amouts are appropriated annually from the state budget for building living accommodation. In this sphere great help is being given by the USSR and other countries of socialism. In 1964 there was an 80% increase in the living space available as compared with 1960 and the number of towns and residential localities had doubled. The appearance of the cities and populated centres in the MPR has changed out of all recognition. The best example of the new town-planning in

Mongolia is the capital itself—Ulan Bator, which improves in appearance with every year that passes.

From what has been narrated above it is clear that the successes achieved in cultural construction during the years of the people's rule are really immense. This is a matter of pride not only for the Mongolian people themselves; many foreign representatives from the capitalist world also acknowledge the successes of the Mongolian people in developing the national culture.

AFTERWORD

Only a few years have gone by since the translation from Russian into English of the "History of the Mongolian People's Republic". During those years, however, there have been a considerable number of important events in the life of the Republic providing evidence of its continued all-round advance. The Fifteenth Congress of the Mongolian People's Revolutionary Party, held in June 1966, summed up the creative work done by the Party and the Mongolian people to carry out the decisions of the Fourteenth Congress; it laid down specific tasks for the country's development in the new, Fourth, Five-Year Plan period, and adopted a new Party programme.

The main results achieved in the fulfilment of the Third Five-Year Plan for the economic and cultural development of the MPR in 1961-1965 demonstrated that the country had taken a big new step forward in building up the material and technical basis for socialism. During that period the basic production assets of the national economy increased by 80 per cent, including industry 90 per cent, agriculture 120 per cent, construction 110 per cent, and transport and communications 20 per cent; the aggregate national product grew by more than 30 per cent.[1]

The tasks of the Third Five-Year Plan in industrial development were successfully fulfilled. For example, total industrial output in 1965 amounted to more than 1,000 million *tugriks*, or 60 per cent more than in 1960. Average annual growth rate of industrial output during the five years amounted to 10.5 per cent. In 1965 production of the means of production accounted for 42.7 per cent of all industrial output, and the production of consumer goods to 57.3 per cent.[2] With the fraternal help of the Soviet Union and other socialist countries, in 1961-1966 the MPR built more than 90 industrial objectives, including the Ulan Bator house-building plant, a woodworking plant in Tosontsengel, a power station and a construction materials works in Darkhan, the Sharyngol coal mine, etc. A further impetus to the development of the flourmilling industry, a new branch which came into being at the end of the fifties and beginning of the sixties, was given by the construction and putting into operation of flour mills in Sukhe-Bator, Muren, Under-Khan and Kharkhorin. Hundreds of hospitals and clinics nurseries and kindergartens were also built in the same period and extensive road and bridge building was carried out. Total capital investments under the plan came to 3,862 million *tugriks*.[3] Particular note should be made of the successful construction, with the help from the USSR, Czechoslovakia and Poland, of a new industrial complex in the vicinity of Darkhan which has become a symbol of the international friendship and cooperation among these countries.

An important feature of agricultural development under the plan was that for the first time it took place within the context of a unified socialist system of economy. In the period of the Third Plan the cooperative system in agriculture proved its superiority over farming by individual *arats*. Total agricultural output in the five years increased by 20 per cent and the plan for adding to the numbers of cattle over that period was fulfilled by 104 per cent.[4]

The cultivation of virgin lands made it possible to raise the crop area in the country by 80 per cent. The total grain harvest in 1965 was 22,100,000 *poods*, 38 per cent more than in 1960 Consequently the share of crop-farming accounted for almost one third of the total agricultural output.[5] High growth rates in the development of land cultivation enabled the MPR to satisfy all its own grain requirements. The Fifteenth MPRP Congress noted this as being one of the most important achievements in Mongolia's economic development.[6] Altogether total agricultural output in 1965 showed an increase of 187 per cent over the 1940 figure, which included a 152.3 per cent increase in animal products and an 81,6 times increase[7] in crop farming. Machinery began to be widely introduced into agriculture—here the formation of large cooperative farms facilitated the process. On average an agricultural association received four tractors and five or six lorries. State farms were also supplied with more machinery: by the opening of the Fifteenth Congress of the MPRP state farms had an average of 155 tractors (in conventional 15 h.p. units), 44 combines and 19 lorries.[8]

The Fifteenth Congress set new tasks which were specified in the Directives for the MPRP's Fourth Five-Year Plan for economic and cultural development, covering the period 1966-1970. In determining the basic tasks of the new plan the MPRP took as its starting point the country's real possibilities and the level attained by her productive forces. The new Plan assumed observance of fundamental economic proportions and better coordination of the development of separate branches in accordance with the country's material, financial and manpower resources. Particular attention was given to the most burning problems facing Mongolia's economy. Specifically, the plan directed the efforts of leading economic bodies to bringing to light, calculating and fully utilising the country's manpower resources and also to the rational organisation of labour and to making greater use of both fixed and circulating assets of the economy. It also envisaged that higher national income would be assured by increasing the efficiency of social production and labour productivity. The increasing of efficiency in production was one of the central economic tasks. In this connexion an intensification of the process of industrialisation was noted, together with a rising level of mechanisation in agriculture and the supply of greater numbers of machines to individual branches of the economy. Overall, the economic tasks of the MPR for 1966-1970 accorded with the historical prospects which were defined in the new programme of the MPRP adopted at the Fifteenth Party Congress—a programme for the completion of socialist construction in the MPR. The programme states: "The main task of the MPRP during the period of completing the construction of socialism in the MPR is the all-round development of the productive forces of socialist society on the basis of the achievements of modern scientific and technological progress, the ensurance of high growth rates in the economic might of the country and an upsurge of socialist culture, the perfection of socialist social relations, further progress in communist education of the working people and the achievement of a further rise in the material well-being and cultural level of the people".[9] The programme stated that during the period of completing socialist construction the MPR would take a significant step nearer to the level of the leading socialist countries in volume of national income and in important types of industrial and agricultural output per head of population. The planned development of the country's productive forces was linked in the programme with the development and perfection of socialist social relations, with the successes in communist education of the working people, an essential condition and component part of building socialism. The new programme clearly formulated the foreign policy line and international tasks of the MPRP. "The MPRP, like other Marxist-Leninist parties, sets itself the aim of ensuring peaceful conditions for building socialism and communism, strengthening unity, friendship and cooperation between the countries of the peaceful socialist system, supporting the national-liberation movement of the peoples and the revolutionary struggle of the working class in the capitalist countries, encouraging the uniting of all revolutionary forces of our time and preserving and reinforcing world peace and the security of the nations."[10]

The Mongolian people endorse the policy of the MPRP for further reinforcing friendship and cooperation with the peoples of the Soviet Union and other socialist states. With deep satisfaction they took note of the programme of the Communist Party of the Soviet Union, worked out by the 24th Congress, for building communism in the USSR. The friendly visit to the MPR of a Party and government delegation from the Soviet Union headed by Leonid Brezhnev, General Secretary of the Central Committee of the CPSU, in 1966 was of great significance for strengthening Mongolian-Soviet friendship. During the visit a new Treaty of Friendship, Cooperation and Mutual Assistance was signed between the MPR and the USSR. Another striking expression of the unbreakable friendship and effective cooperation between the two countries was the results of the talks held in October 1970 in Moscow between Party and government delegations of the USSR and the MPR, at which the main lines of economic cooperation were agreed and a decision taken by the Soviet government to render further big assistance available to the MPR for economic development.

For the Mongolian people 1971 was a noteworthy year—on July 11, 1971, the Mongolian people, together with the peoples of the USSR and the fraternal socialist countries and progressive forces throughout the world, celebrated the fiftieth anniversary of the Mongolian People's Revolution, which had brought the country complete national and social liberation.

At the anniversary session of the Central Committee of the MPRP, the Presidium of the Grand People's Hural, the Council of Ministers, the Ulan Bator City Committee of the MPRP and the Executive Committee of the Hural of Working People's Deputies, Comrade Y. Tsedenbal said that, "advancing along the road indicated by great Lenin, the Mongolian people have in a short historical space of time made a gigantic stride from the remote middle ages to the socialist social system. In this the strength and invincibility of socialism—our Marxist-Leninist ideology—has been clearly revealed".[11]

At the same session A. N. Kosygin, head of the Soviet Party and government delegation, member of the Political Bureau of the Central Committee of the Communist Party of the Soviet Union and chairman of the Council of Ministers of the USSR conveyed warm fraternal greetings and hearty congratulations from the Soviet people, the Central Committee of the CPSU and the Soviet government to the Mongolian people, the Mongolian People's Revolutionary Party and the Mongolian government on the occasion of the fiftieth anniversary of the victory of the People's Revolution: "Mongolia has accomplished the transition from backwardness to progress in close co-operation and with the support of the Soviet Union, and later of other socialist countries. This has enabled it to take a way forward which does not, as in capitalist countries, involve tossing aside thousands upon thousands of people. The MPRP has taken the path of raising the material and cultural standards of its working people.

The viability of the non-capitalist way of development is confirmed by the experience of the Mongolian people, and this represents an outstanding contribution on their part to the history of mankind. The theoretical possibility of the non-capitalist road of social development was demonstrated by Karl Marx, Frederick Engels and Vladimir Lenin, the great teachers of the Communists. But in practice the correctness of this brilliant vision of the future has been confirmed only by the experience of modern social development".[12]

The celebrations of the fiftieth anniversary of the MPR were a striking demonstration of the traditional friendship between the Soviet and Mongolian peoples, the unity of the countries of the socialist commonwealth and of all progressive, anti-imperialist forces.

The Sixteenth Congress of the MPRP, held in the anniversary year, took cognizance of the successes achieved by the working people of the republic in the building of socialist society and noted with satisfaction that the Mongolian People's Revolutionary Party, "having gone through half a century of struggle and victories, has come to its Congress still more united and monolithic, still more confident of its strength and the correctness of its political line, which is directed to ensuring the complete victory of socialism on Mongolian soil."[13]

An important indication of the steady growth in the role and prestige of the MPRP, of its unity with the mass of the working people is the quantitative and qualitative increase in the Party's ranks. At April 1, 1971, the MPRP had 58,048 members and candidate members, of whom workers accounted for 30 per cent, members of agricultural associations for 20.4 per cent, and white collar workers and intellectuals for 49.6 per cent.[14] The many-thousand-strong army of Mongolian communists is in the vanguard of the fight to build socialism.

During the Fourth Five-Year Plan economic contacts between the MPR and fraternal countries continued to grow and gain in strength, particularly those with the members of the Council for Mutual Economic Assistance. Joint inter-governmental commissions were set up for economic, scientific and technical cooperation with the USSR, the People's Republic of Bulgaria, the Hungarian People's Republic and the German Democratic Republic. Mongolia's active participation in CMEA's work has enabled it to accelerate rates of economic development, and to make more profound and rational use of the advantages of international socialist division of labour. This acquires even greater significance at a time when the CMEA member countries are following a course of socialist integration, which should facilitate a general upswing of the economic potentials of the socialist countries. Coordination of economic plans is one of the main lines along which socialist integration is proceeding. The 1971-1975 plan for the economic and cultural development of the MPR was coordinated with those of the other CMEA members, and the successful fulfilment of the tasks of the Fifth Five-Year Plan is being made easier by the MPR's participation in CMEA. Within the country the achievements of the Fourth Five-Year Plan provide a jumping-off ground. In 1966-1970 fixed assets in production increased by 50 per cent. In 1970 the production assets of agricultural associations were on average 63 per cent higher per farm than in 1966, and were in all valued at almost 5 million *tugriks*. Despite considerable losses of cattle in the severe winter of 1967-1968, the head of cattle showed an increase of 1,800,000 in 1969-1970. The Ninth Plenary Meeting of the Central Committee of the MPRP held in February 1971 outlined concrete tasks for ensuring a steady development in agriculture and above all in animal husbandry: the strengthening of the material and technical base for agriculture and the taking of measures to increase manpower resources and to stimulate an increase in the production of agricultural associations and state farms.[15] The Directives of the Sixteenth Congress of the MPRP for the Fifth Five-Year Plan envisaged a rise in total agricultural output by 22-25 per cent, including 14-16 per cent in animal husbandry and 40-50 per cent in crop-farming. An increase in the head of cattle is planned: from 22,600,000 in 1970 the figure will rise to 25 million in 1975, i.e. by 11 per cent.[16]

During the Fourth Five-Year Plan period the country made a substantial advance in carrying out the programme tasks of the Party—the transformation of the MPR into an industrial-agrarian country. Total industrial output in 1970 amounted to 60 per cent above the 1965 figure, and the average annual growth rate was 9.9 per cent. At the same time production of the means of production developed at faster rates than production of consumer goods, and by 1971 the former made up 52.6 per cent of total industrial production (in terms of 1967 prices). The Fourth Five-Year Plan period saw a further increase in capital investments in industry, which made it possible to build or reconstruct about 90 industrial enterprises or shops.[17] All this facilitated an improvement in the territorial distribution of industry and its pattern of organisation according to branches of industry. In the last Five-Year Plan period a new industrial complex was built in the east of the country—in the city of Choibolsan. There the Adunchulun coal mine, a thermal power station and a number of light industrial enterprises, and enterprises of the food industry, went into operation.

Changes in the pattern of Mongolian industry were expressed in a rise in the share of the fuel and power industry. Under the Fourth Five-Year Plan the capacity of power stations increased 20 per cent, a central power grid was set up covering territory in which one third of the MPR's population live. As a result the level of electric power available for industry showed a rise of 60 per cent between 1965 and 1970. The overall role of industry in the MPR's economy also increased: by the beginning of the Fifth Five-Year Plan industry was producing 34 per cent of the aggregate national product and more than 60 per cent of total agricultural and industrial output.[18] The 1971-1975 plan has set industry new tasks, including the further strengthening of the fuel and power base, the greater use of mineral and raw material resources, the development of consumer industries, the raising of production efficiency and quality of output. In the new, Fifth, Five-Year Plan it is proposed to increase industrial production 53-56 per cent and to bring up the share of industry in the production of the national income to 27 per cent.

In recent years there has been a steady rise in living standards of the working people in the MPR. In 1966-1970 alone social consumption funds increased by 24.6 per cent and the wages and salaries fund by 27 per cent. On average old age pensions went up by 20 per cent and the minimum was raised to 150 *tugriks* a month. The people's growing well-being was reflected in the expansion of goods' turnover. In 1965 total retail trade showed an increase of 163 per cent over the 1961 figure, while in 1970 it was 195 per cent higher than in 1966.[19] Figures for sales of flour per head of population in 1965 and 1969 were, respectively, 72.4 *kg* and 75.7 *kg*; for bread the figures were 15.5 *kg* and 16.1 *kg*, for rice 3.8 *kg* and 5.2 *kg*, meat and meat products 16.8 *kg* and 26.1 *kg*. In the same years the following sales were made per ten thousand of population: refrigerators 4.1 and 4.8, motor cycles 10.3 and 24.7, 41.2 television sets were sold on average per ten thousand people (in 1969).[20]

A major role in raising the incomes of those working in agriculture was played by the increasing of state purchase prices for the main types of animal products and the establishment of incentives in the form of higher prices for above-plan sales of products to the state. Under the Fifth Five-Year Plan it is proposed to increase incomes of the population by about 22-23 per cent and social consumption funds by 36-40 per cent.

The growth of the working people's living standards is facilitated by the development of a unified system of public education. In the new Five-Year Plan the transfer to general eight-year secondary education of school age children, begun under the Fourth Five-Year Plan, is continuing. By the end of the current plan, 80 per cent of the *somons* will have eight-year secondary schools. In recent years a polytechnical institute has been opened in Ulan Bator and a number of technical schools in the *aimaks*.

Substantial measures are being taken to extend the network of medical institutions and medical services for the population. By the end of the current Five-Year Plan 70 per cent of all *somons* had hospitals and medical centres. According to 1965 data the total number of physicians was 1,511 and in 1970 there were 2,259, that is, 13.5 and 17.7 respectively per ten thousand of population.[21]

Today the Mongolian people, carrying out the decisions of the Sixteenth Congress of the MPRP and the tasks of the Fifth Five-Year Plan for economic and cultural development in 1971-1975, have considerable successes to their credit. In 1971, for instance, 11,000 million *tugriks* were invested in the economy, and basic assets rose by 9.6 per cent. In 1971 most *aimaks* showed a further growth in the head of cattle in their possession. A total of 25,800,000 *poods* of grain was the splendid harvest for that year. The 1971 plan was overfulfilled for growth of industrial output, total profits increased by 43.5 per cent and the increase in labour productivity led to a more than 60 per cent growth in the national income. In 1971-1972 almost 9,000 specialists completed their higher or secondary special education in Mongolia. More than 22,000 people who finished trade and technical schools and general educational schools started work in the national economy.[22] The present epoch is a time of swift-moving scientific and technological revolution. In the Mongolian People's Republic the utmost importance is attached to the use of the achievements of science and engineering in the interests of society. The Second Plenary Meeting of the Central Committee of the Mongolian Revolutionary Party (1972) drew attention to the need for a constant rise in standards of education, skilled and scientific guidance of the economy.

In summer 1972 local authority elections were held in the MPR, the results of which bore witness to the strengthening of socialist democracy in the country and once again demonstrated the monolithic unity of the Party and the people.

The prestige of the Mongolian People's Republic is growing in international affairs. In their foreign policy, the MPRP and the Mongolian People's government, constantly reinforcing their ties with the socialist countries, continue to follow the line of establishing friendly relations with countries outside the socialist system. In 1971 the MPR opened diplomatic relations with Japan, Chile, Bangla Desh and other countries, and today it has such relations with 60 countries altogether.

The Mongolian People's Revolutionary Party played an active part in the preparation and holding of the Moscow Meeting of Communist and Workers' Parties in 1969. Together with fraternal parties it continues to work for the unity and cohesion of the Communist movement, for the purity of Marxism-Leninism, combating right and "left" opportunism, reactionary ideology, anti-communism and anti-Sovietism.

The Mongolian people have immense successes to their credit in all economic and political spheres precisely because just over half a century ago they took into their armoury the invincible teaching of Marxism-Leninism and are confidently going ahead under the leadership of the Mongolian People's Revolutionary Party, in borterly cooperation with the USSR and other socialist countries.

BASIC DATES IN THE HISTORY OF THE MONGOLIAN PEOPLE'S REPUBLIC

IV-III centuries B.C.—Formation on the territory of Mongolia of the tribal alliances of the Huns.
III century B.C.—Formation of the Hun state.
I century B.C.—Formation of the Syan'pi state.
III century A.D.—Break-up of the Syan'pi state.
III century A. D.—Strengthening of the power of the Toba tribes; conquest by them of Northern China and formation on its territory of the early feudal state of Toba.
V century A.D.—Formation of the early feudal state of Zhuzhan.
VI century A.D.—Strengthening of the tribes of the Orkhon Turks, defeat by them of the Zhuzhan Kaganate and formation of the Turkic Kaganate.
End of VI century A.D.—Break-up of the Turkic Kaganate into two parts—Eastern and Western.
630 A.D.—Weakening of the East-Turkic Kaganate.
680—700 A.D.—Re-establishment of the power of the East-Turkic Kaganate.
693-716 A.D.—Rule of the Kagan Mocho.
745 A.D.—Defeat of the East-Turkic Kaganate by the Uighurs and creation on the territory of Mongolia of the Uighur Khanate.
840 A.D.—Defeat of the Uighur Khanate by the Yenisei Kirghiz.
X century A.D.—Strengthening of the Khitans. Seizure by them of Northern and North-Eastern China and formation of the Khitan State.
1125 A.D.—Defeat of the Khitan Empire of Liao by the Churchens and establishment on the territory of Mongolia, Northern and North-Eastern China of the Churchen Ching State.
1162 A.D.—Birth of Temuchin.
XII century—Intensification of the struggle between the family-tribal associations of Mongols. Elevation of the competing tribal leaders—Temuchin, Jamugha and Wang-Khan.
1204-1205—Completion by Temuchin of the struggle with the competing tribal leaders and unification of the Mongol tribes.
1206—Proclamation of Temuchin as Genghis Khan and formation on the territory of Mongolia of a feudal state.
1207—Genghis Khan begins his campaigns of conquest.
1211-1215—Conquest of Northern China.
1218—Capture of Eastern Turkestan and Semirechye.
1219-1221—Conquest of Khwarezm.
1221—Invasion of Azerbaijan.
1223—Campaign against Russia; battle on the River Kalka.
1226—Campaign against the Tanguts.
1227—Death of Genghis Khan.
1228—Ugadei proclaimed Khan of Mongolia.

1235—Completion of the construction of Karakorum and transfer to it of the capital of the Mongolian Empire.
1236-1240—Batu's campaigns against Russia.
1241-1242—The Mongol conquerors invade Poland, Hungary and Moravia.
1241—Death of Ugadei.
1246—Guyuk proclaimed Khan of Mongolia.
1248—Death of Guyuk.
1251—Munke ascends the Khan's throne.
1252—Conquest of Iran.
1258—Capture of Baghdad.
1258—Death of Munke.
1260—Kublai proclaimed Khan of Mongolia.
1271—Establishment by Kublai of the Chinese title "Yuan" for the Mongol dynasty.
1274—Kublai's first campaign against Japan.
1279—Completion of the conquest of the whole territory of China.
1281—Kublai's second campaign against Japan.
1289—The Mongol princes rebel against Kublai. Transfer of the capital to Peking (Daidu).
1294—Death of Kublai.
1368—Rebellion of the Chinese people against the yoke of the Mongol conquerors and fall of the Yuan dynasty.
1380—Chinese troops march into Mongolia; destruction of Karakorum.
1380—Rebellion of the Russian people against the Mongol-Tartar yoke. Battle of Kulikovo.
1409—The Oirat princes march into China.
1414—Defeat of the Oirat armies by the Chinese.
1434—The whole of Mongolia subject to the authority of the Oirat prince Togon.
1466—Dayan Khan ascends the Khan's Throne in Mongolia.
1551—Conclusion of peace between the Tumet Altan Khan and China.
1574—Opening by the Chinese Government of a market in Gansu for barter trade with the Mongols.
1577—Adoption by Altan Khan of Lamaism.
1577—Adoption of Lamaism by Abatai Khan of Khalkha.
1586—Erection of the monastery of Erdeni-tsu.
1616—First Russian Embassy in Mongolia.
1618—Arrival in Russia of the first Embassy from Mongolia.
1635—Batur-Khuntaiji proclaimed Khan of all the Oirats.
1636—Negotiations between the princes of Khalkha and the Manchurian prince Abakhai.
1640—Congress of the Mongol princes in Djungaria and adoption by this Congress of the so-called "Mongol-Oirat Laws". The son of Tushetu Khan (Undur-gegen) proclaimed Chubil Khan and head of the Lamaist church of Mongolia.
1671—Galdan-Boshoktu ascends the Oirat Khan's Throne.
1688-1697—War between the Oirat princes and Khalkha Khans.
1691—Congress at Dolon-nor and inclusion of Khalkha in the Manchu Empire.
1697—Defeat of the Oirat-Mongol troops by the Manchus.
1755-1758—Anti-Manchu popular rebellion of the Oirat-Mongols under Amursana. Rebellion in Khalkha under the Khotogoit Prince Chingunjav against the Manchus.
1860—Treaty of Peking between Russia and China.
1878—The Ching Government revokes the restrictions on the activities of Chinese trading firms in Mongolia.
1881—Treaty of St. Petersburg between Russia and China.
1893, February 2—Birth of Sukhe Bator.
1895, February 8—Birth of Choibalsan.
1900—Anti-Manchu rebellion of the Mongolian *tsiriks* in Ulyasutai.
1903-1911—Liberation movement of the *arats* under Ayushi.

1907—Signing of the Russo-Japanese agreement on division of spheres of influence in the Far East.
1910—Armed collision between *arats* and the Manchu garrison in Urga.
1911, December—Expulsion of the Manchu *amban* from Urga.
December—Overthrow of the Manchu authority in Outer Mongolia and declaration of an independent Mongolian feudal-theocratic State. Proclamation of the Bogdo-gegen as Khan of all Mongolia.
December—Expulsion from Ulyasutai of the Manchu *chang-chung*.
1912, June—Conclusion in St. Petersburg of the Russo-Japanese convention affirming and enlarging the spirit of previous treaties of 1907 and 1910.
August—Liberation by the *arats* of Kobdo from the Manchu garrison.
November 3—Signing in Urga of the Russo-Mongolian treaty under which tsarist Russia factually acknowledged the Mongolian feudal-theocratic State.
1913, November—Signing in Peking of the Russo-Chinese Declaration on the autonomy of Outer Mongolia.
November—Opening in Urga of the first secular school.
1915, May 25—Signing in Kyakhta of the Tripartite Russo-Chinese-Mongolian Agreement under which the Mongolian feudal-theocratic State was forcibly obliged to accept the status of an autonomous Outer Mongolia under Chinese suzerainty.
1917, 7 November—The Great October Socialist Revolution.
1918, September—Beginning of the occupation of Outer Mongolia by the troops of the Chinese militarists.
1919, May—Formation in Dauria of a pro-Japanese puppet government of a so-called "Great Mongolia".
August—Appeal by the RSFSR Government to the Mongolian people and to the Government of Autonomous Outer Mongolia.
August-December—Decisive advance by the Red Army on the Eastern front. Liberation of Siberia; beginning of the liberation of the Far East. Defeat of Kolchak.
November—Arrival in Urga of the Anfu General Sui Szu-Chen and occupation by his troops of Mongolia. Autonomy abolished.
November-December—Organisation of the first revolutionary groups in Urga.
1920, June 25—Union of revolutionary clubs. Adoption of "the Oath of the Party Members".
June-July—Sukhe Bator and Choibalsan leave for Soviet Russia.
October—White Guard bands of Ungern invade Outer Mongolia.
November—Appearance of the first number of the newspaper *Mongolyn Unen* ("Mongolian Truth").
1921, March—First Congress of the Mongolian People's Party. Formation of a Provisional People's Government. Creation of Staff of the Mongolian People's Army. Liberation of Maimachen (Altan-Bulak) by the revolutionary Mongolian troops.
April—Appeal of the Provisional People's Government to the Government of the RSFSR asking for assistance for joint struggle against the White Guard bands occupying Mongolia.
June—Defeat in the region of Troitskosavsk—Kyakhta by the Soviet and Mongolian troops of the Ungern bands.
July—Liberation of Urga by the Red Army and the Mongolian revolutionary troops.
July—Formation of a permanent People's Government of Mongolia.
August—Creation of the Revolutionary Youth League of Mongolia.
October—Opening of the Provisional Little State Hural.
October—Arrival in Moscow of the Mongolian Government delegation, headed by Sukhe Bator.

November—Signature in Moscow of an Agreement on mutual recognition and friendship between the Governments of the RSFSR and the Mongolian State. Talk between V. I. Lenin and Sukhe Bator.
December—Enactment by the People's Government of the laws revoking serfdom; revoking mutual guarantees; abolishing feudal servitudes.
December—Creation of the Central People's Co-operative *(Montsenkoop)*; organization of committee of science; organization of Department of Education under Ministry of the Interior.

1922, July—First Congress of the Revolutionary Youth League of Mongolia.
July—Formation of State Internal Security Body.
December—Abolition of the institution of hereditary feudal rulers.
December—Organization of the first courses in the country for the retraining of teachers.

1923, January—Enactment of the law on elections of local government bodies.
February 22—Death of the Leader of the Mongolian Revolution, Sukhe Bator.
July-August—Second Congress of the Mongolian People's Party.

1924, February—Creation of the Ministry of National Education.
March—Organization of the Ministry of National Economy.
May—Death of the Bogdo-gegen—last Khan of Mongolia.
June—Resolution of the Central Committee of the People's Party and the People's Government to abolish the monarchy and introduce the republican system into the country.
June—Adoption of the law on nationalization of the property of the Bogdo-gegen.
June—Formation of the State Bank.
August—Third Congress of the People's Party. The Mongolian People's Party renamed the Mongolian People's Revolutionary Party (MPRP).
August—Exposure and liquidation of the Danzan counter-revolutionary conspiracy.
Novemberf—I Grand People's Hural. Proclamation of the Mongolian People's Republic and approval of the Constitution of the Mongolian People's Republic.
November—Urga re-named Ulan Bator.

1925, March—Plenary Meeting of the Central Committee of the Mongolian People's Revolutionary Party.
July—Creation of the MPR transport board for conveyance of freight in the territory of the MPR.
September—Fourth Congress of the MPRP.
October—Opening in Ulan Bator of the first hospital.
November—II Great People's Hural.
November—Abolition of the *shabi* department.
November—Democratization of the judicial system; introduction of elected judges.
December—Beginning of currency reform; issue of national currency—*tugrik.*

1926, April—Decision of the People's Government to levy taxes on livestock owned by monasteries.
September—Fifth Congress of the MPRP.
September—Enactment of law on separation of the Church from the State.
October—III Grand People's Hural.

1927, January—Elections of *khoshun* and *aimak* courts. Formation of Supreme Court of the Republic.
June—Opening in Ulan Bator of the first veterinary technical college.
June—Formation of Departments of National Education under *aimak* administrations.
August—I Congress of Trade Unions.
September—Sixth Congress of the MPRP.

October-November—IV Grand People's Hural.
1928, October—Seventh Congress of the MPRP. Defeat of right deviationists.
December—V Grand People's Hural.
December—Decision to confiscate the large-scale feudal property.
1930. August—VI Grand People's Hural.
February—Eighth Congress of the MPRP.
November—Formation of mixed Soviet-Mongolian road transport company "Mongoltrans".
December—Adoption of the law on State monopoly of foreign trade.
December—Organization of school of finance.
1931, February—Adoption of the law on economic organization of regions (abolition of *khoshuns*, breaking-up of *aimaks*).
August—Opening of the State Theatre in Ulan Bator.
1932, June—Third Extraordinary Plenary Meeting of the Central Committee of the MPRP.
June—Defeat of "leftist" deviation in the Party.
July—17 Extraordinary Session of the Little People's Hural.
July—First Republican Conference of *Arats*.
July-December—Enactment of new laws designed to eradicate the consequences of the "leftist" deviation in all spheres of national economy.
1933, February—Beginning of wireless broadcasting in the country.
December—Wool-washing mill starts operations in Khatkhila.
1934, April—Industrial Combine starts operations in Ulan Bator.
September-October—Ninth Congress of the MPRP.
October—Organization of the Department for the *Arats* attached to the MPR Government.
November—"Gentleman's" agreement between the USSR and the MPR on mutual assistance.
December—VII Grand People's Hural.
1935, January/December—Adoption of new laws on the *arat* tax, the war tax, measures for introducing lamas into productive labour, the laws on trade.
January—Beginning of the construction of the narrow gauge railway Nalaikha—Ulan Bator.
1936, March—Signature of the Protocol on mutual assistance between the governments of the MPR and the USSR.
August—Opening of the schools of agriculture and medicine and the communications technical college.
1937, September—Arrival in the MPR of equipment for 10 tractorised mechanical hay-harvesting stations offered by the Government of the USSR as a gift to the MPR Government.
1938, January/December—Formation of the MPR Ministry of Industry and Construction.
1939, May/August—Troops of the Japanese aggressors invade the MPR. Battles in the Khalkhin-Gol region. Defeat of the Japanese aggressors by the Soviet-Mongolian troops.
1940, March—Tenth Congress of the MPRP. Approval of the Party's Programme and Charter.
June—VIII Grand People's Hural. Approval of the new Constitution of the MPR.
October—Formation of the Ministry of Transport.
December—Resolution of the MPR Council of Ministers to set up a State University.
1941, February—Transformation of "Kustpromsoyuz" into the Central Council of Cottage Industries Co-operatives.
February—Adoption of new laws on labour, a single tax on livestock farms and machinery-hire centres.
March—Decision of the MPRP Central Committee and Council of Ministers to introduce a new Mongolian alphabet.

June—Resolution of the MPRP Central Committee, Presidium of the Little Hural and Council of Ministers in connection with the criminal, treacherous attack of Hitlerite Germany on the USSR.

July/December—National collection of funds for the defence of the country and gifts to the heroic army of the Soviet Union.

September—Organization of the Higher School for Governmental and Party cadres (Higher Party School).

November—Plenary Meeting of the Central Committee of the MPRP. Resolution on the question of the utilization of local resources and the development of the production of consumer goods.

November/December—First Republican Conference of foremost workers in stockbreeding.

1942, October—Opening of the Mongolian State University.

November—Formation of the Ministry for the Food Industry.

1943, April—Organization of the State Farms Trust.

May—First Republican Conference of shock-workers in industry and transport.

August—Adoption of the law on the protection of public property.

November—Second Republican Conference of foremost workers in stockbreeding.

1944, May—Reorganization of the Ministry of Industry and Construction into a Ministry of Industry.

May—Formation of a Ministry of Communications.

November—Adoption of the new electoral law.

1945, January—Transformation of the Department of Planning, Registration and Control into the State Planning Commission under the MPR Council of Ministers.

February—Agreement of the three Powers, USSR, USA and UK to maintain the *status quo* of the MPR.

August—The Government of the USSR declares war on the Government of Imperialist Japan. The MPR proclaims a state of war with Japan.

September—Signature of the instrument of unconditional surrender of Japan.

October—Plebiscite on the question of the State independence of the MPR.

1946, January—Recognition by Kuomintang China of the independence of the MPR.

February—Treaty of Friendship and Mutual Assistance between the Governments of the USSR and the MPR.

February—The meat combine starts operations.

November—Decision of the MPR Government to lower the prices of goods and products.

1947, August—Decision of the MPR Government to lower prices of goods and products.

September—Creation of the Mongolian-Soviet Friendship Society.

December—Eleventh Congress of the MPRP. Approval of the First Five-Year Plan for the development of the national economy and culture.

1948, February—Decision of the MPR Government to lower prices of goods and products.

October—Establishment of diplomatic relations between the MPR and the Korean People's Democratic Republic.

December—Third Republican Conference of shock-workers in stockbreeding and agriculture.

1949—February—IX Grand People's Hural.

October—National Conference of MPR Fighters for Peace.

October—Formation in the MPR of Permanent Committee of Fighters for Peace.

November—Railway line Naushki—Ulan Bator starts operations.

1950, January—Participation of Mongolian Delegation in the Conference of the Women's International Democratic Federation in Moscow.
April—Establishment of diplomatic relations between the MPR and GDR, MPR and PRP, MPR and PRB, MPR and Czechoslovakian Socialist Republic, MPR and VPR, MPR and RSR.
October—Participation of Mongolian Delegation in Conference of Trade Unions of the countries of Asia and Oceania in Peking.
October—Participation of the Mongolian Delegation in the Second Congress of Fighters for Peace in Warsaw.
1951, February—Adoption of the law against war propaganda.
June—Elections to the MPR Grand People's Hural under the new electoral law.
July—Opening of the Pedagogical Institute.
1952, January 26—Death of Marshal Choibalsan, Prime Minister of the MPR.
1952, May—Appointment of Yu. Tsedenbal as Prime Minister of the MPR.
December—Participation of the Mongolian Delegation in the Vienna Peace Congress.
1953, March—Plenary Meeting of the MPRP Central Committee. Results of fulfilment of the First Five-Year Plan for the development of the national economy and culture of the MPR.
1954, January—Adoption by the MPR Council of Ministers of a resolution "On the regulation of model standards of output and evaluation thereof in terms of 'labour-days' in *arat* production associations".
March—Decision of the MPR Council of Ministers and MPRP Central Committee to raise the State procurement and purchasing prices for livestock.
April—Resolution of the Plenary Meeting of the MPRP Central Committee on measures for the further development of stockbreeding.
June—Decision of the MPR Government to lower State retail prices on foodstuffs and industrial goods.
June—Elections to the MPR Grand People's Hural.
August—Erection of the monument to the heroes of the battles on the shore of Khalkhin-Gol River.
November 19-24—Twelfth Congress of the MPRP. Approval given to the Second Five-Year Plan for 1953-57.
1955, March 11-16—First Congress of foremost workers of Agricultural Associations. (AA).
December 31—Opening of Ulan Bator—Dzamin-Ude railway.
1956, October—Adoption by the MPR Council of Ministers of a resolution on introduction of land reform on State farms and agricultural associations.
1957, May 11-15—Soviet-Mongolian negotiations between intergovernmental USSR and MPR delegations. Publication of joint Soviet-Mongolian Declaration.
June 16—Ordinary elections to the Grand People's Hural.
November—Conference of representatives of Communist and Workers' Parties in Moscow.
1958, January 5—Coal mine "Nalaikha-Kapitalnaya" started up.
March 17-22—Thirteenth Congress of the MPRP. Approval given to the directives for the MPR Three-Year Plan for the development of the national economy and culture for 1958-1960.
1959, March—Second Republican Conference of shork-workers in industry, transport and communications.
March 27-30—Third Plenary Meeting of the MPRP Central Committee.
December 16-17—Fourth Plenary Meeting of the MPRP Central Committee. Definition of the problems involved in the further organizational and economic consolidation of agricultural associations.
December—II Congress of AA and adoption thereat of AA Model Rules.

1960, March—Adoption of resolution of MPRP Central Committee and MPR Council of Ministers on "transfer of managing of MSS to an *aimak* executive administration".
April—Inauguration of the V. I. Lenin Central Broadcasting Station in Khonkhor.
June—Meeting of representatives of Communist and Workers' Parties in Bucharest.
July 6—I Session of the Grand People's Hural, IV convocation. Adoption of new Constitution of the MPR.
November—Conference of representatives of Communist and Workers' Parties in Moscow.
1961, May—Foundation of the Academy of Sciences of the MPR.
July 3-6—Fourteenth Congress of the MPRP.
October 27—Admission of the MPR to membership of the UN.
1962, January—Second Plenary Meeting of the MPRP Central Committee. Results of the XXII CPSU Congress and tasks of the MPRP.
May—Third Congress of Mongolian Writers.
June—Entry of the MPR into CMEA.
September—Third Plenary Meeting of the MPRP Central Committee.
1963, January 8-10—Republican Conference of ideological workers met in Ulan Bator.
August 8—The MPR Government signed in Moscow and London the Treaty on the prohibition of nuclear weapon tests in the atmosphere, in space and under water.
December 20-22—Fifth Plenary Meeting of the MPRP Central Committee. On the results of the July 1960 Conference of First Secretaries of Central Committees of Communist and Workers' Parties and the Heads of Governments of CMEA member countries. On the situation and measures for improving capital construction in the MPR.
1964, June 24-27—Congress of Mongolian Women held in Ulan Bator.
June—Holding of Republican Conference of Social Science Teachers.
November—VI Plenary Meeting of the MPRP Central Committee. On measures for improving Party and collective control.
November—I Congress of Mongolian Composers.
1966, January—Conclusion of a treaty of friendship and mutual assistance between the USSR and the MPR.
June 7-11—Fifteenth Congress of the MPRP.
1971, March 1—Celebration of the 50th anniversary of the MPRP.
July—Sixteenth Congress of the MPRP.
July 11—Celebration of the 50th anniversary of the People's Revolution.
November 19—Celebration of the 50th anniversary of the first scientific institution, the Committee of Science, and the 10th anniversary of the Academy of Sciences of MPR.

BIBLIOGRAPHY

Introduction

[1] V. I. Lenin, *Collected Works*, vol. 31, p. 244.

Brief Survey of the Sources for, and Basic Literature on, the History of the Mongolian People

[1] "Transactions of the Orkhon Archaeological Expedition", vols. I, IV, VI, St. Petersburg, 1892-1899.

[2] See A. P. Okladnikov, *Primitive Mongolia*,—"Studia Archaeologica", vol. III, facs. 10, Ulan Bator, 1962. Same author, *New Matter in the Study of the Earliest Mongolian Cultures*,—"SE" Journal, 1962, No. 1.

[3] V. V. Volkov, *History of the Study of Bronze Age Memorials in MPR*,—"Studia Archaeologica", vol. III, facs. 10, Ulan Bator, 1962. N. Ser-Odzhav, D. Dolgosuren, *Dundgov' aimag khurliyn usd* ("The Bronze Age on the Territory of the Central Biy *aimak*",—"Studia Archaeologica," vol. IV, facs. 9, Ulan Bator, 1964.

[4] "Short Reports of the Expedition for the Exploration of Northern Mongolia in Association with the Mongolian-Tibetan Expedition of P. K. Kozlov", Leningrad, 1925; K. V. Trever, *Finds Made in Mongolia, 1924-1925*.—"Communications of the State Historical Academy of Material Culture," 1931, Nos. 9-10.

[5] Ts. Dorzhsuren, *Umard Khunnu*, Ulan Bator, 1961.

[6] "Collection of the Proceedings of the Orkhon Expedition," Part III, UK, St. Petersburg, 1895; S. E. Malov, *Memorials of Ancient Turkic Literature*, Moscow-Leningrad, 1951; same author, *Memorials of Ancient Turkic Literature of Mongolia and Kirghizia*, Moscow-Leningrad, 1959; S. Klyashtorny, *Ancient Turkic Inscriptions*, Moscow-Leningrad, 1963.

[7] N. Ser-Odzhav, *Turkic Inscriptions from the Burial Edifice of Ton'yukuk*,—"Studia Archaeologica," vol. 1, facs. VI, Ulan Bator, 1958.

[8] N. Ser-Odzhav, *Building Material from the Burial Edifice of Kul-Tegin*,—"Nauka", Nos. 5-6, 1959; Lumir, *Explorations of Archaeological Memorials in MPR*,—"Archeologicke Rozhledy," 1961, vol. XIII, p. 49.

[9] "Card Index of Archaeological Memorials of MPR". The manuscript is kept in the archives inscriptions of the Institute of History of the USSR Academy of Sciences. Kh. Perlee, *Short History of Ancient and Mediaeval Towns and Settlements in MPR*, Ulan Bator, 1961.

[10] "Ancient Mongolian Towns," Moscow-Leningrad, 1965.

[11] "Proceedings of the Members of the Russian Religious Mission in Peking," St. Petersburg, 1966, vol. IV, pp. 1-258.

[12] For more details see *Bibliography*.

[13] The manuscript is preserved in the archives of the State Library, Ulan Bator. The text has been published by V. Khaissik in the book: "Dit Familien und Kirchengeschichtsschreibung der Mongolen 16-18 Jahrhundert," I, 1959, Otto Harrassowitz, Wiesbaden.

[14] B. Ya. Vladimirtsov, *Social System of the Mongols*, Leningrad, 1934, p.6.
[15] "Rashid ad-Din", Collection of Chronicles, vol. I, book I, Moscow-Leningrad, 1952; vol. I, book II, Moscow-Leningrad, 1952; vol. III, Moscow-Leningrad, 1946.
[16] V. G. Thiesenhausen, *Collection of Materials on the History of the Golden Horde*, St. Petersburg, 1884, vol. 1, pp. 1-45.
[17] Ata Malik Juvaini, *The Conqueror of the World*, 1961, vols. I-II.
[18] P. Pelliot, L. Hambis, *Notes on Marco Polo*, vols. I-II, 1960.
[19] A full translation from English, collated with a Japanese translation by Ch. Gombozhab, was published in Inner Mongolia during the Second World War. A short translation from German was made by D. Natsagdorzhi and an incomplete one by B. Rinchen. The translations are kept in the manuscript collection of the Historical Institute of the MPR Academy of Sciences.
[20] "History of the Mongols by the Monk Magakiy, XIIIth century, with translation and explanations of K. P. Patkanov," St. Petersburg, 1871; "History of the *Archars* (Mongols) by Grigor of Ajang," edited, with an English translation and notes by Robert P. Blake and Richard N. Frye, Cambridge, Massachusetts, 1954.
[21] "General History of Vardan the Great", trans. N. Emin, Moscow, 1891.
[22] "Chronological History, compiled by Father Mkhitar, Vardanet of Erivan", with translation and notes by K. P. Patkanov, St. Petersburg, 1869.
[23] "History of the Mongols Based on Armenian Sources," translated by K. P. Patkanov, book 1, St. Petersburg, 1873.
[24] "History of the Mongols Based on Armenian Sources," book 2, translated by K. P. Patkanov, St. Petersburg, 1874.
[25] For the works of recent authors see A. Galstyan.
[26] "History of the Mongols Based on Armenian Sources," Book II, p. V.
[27] The most important of these are "Historical Notes", "History of the Early Hang Dynasty," "History of the Dynasty of Northern Wei," "History of the Sui Dynasty," "History of the Khitan Empire" and "Northern History."
[28] "Collection of Material about the Huns," "Collection of Material about the Zhuzhans," "Collection of Material about the Turks," and "Collection of Material about the Uighurs."
[29] N. Ya. Bichurin, *Collection of Information about the Inhabitants of Central Asia in Ancient Times*, 3 vols, Moscow 1950-1953; A. V. Kyuner, *Chinese Information on the Peoples of Southern Siberia, Central Asia and the Far East*, Moscow, 1961.
[30] The manuscripts are preserved in the collection of the State Library of the MPR.
[31] "Sheng-wu Tsin-Ch'en-lu. Description of the Personal Campaigns of a Holy Warrior." Translation, Preface and Notes,—"Eastern Collection," I, St. Petersburg, 1877; "Histoire des Campagnes de Genghis-khan Cheng-wou-tsintscheng-lou". Traduit et annoté par P. Pelliot et L. Hambis, vol. I, Leyden, 1951. The Mongolian translation is preserved in the manuscript collection of the MPR State Library.
[32] See E. Bretschneider, *Medieval Researches from Eastern Asiatic Sources*, vols. I-II. London, 1888.
[33] Ibid., pp. 25-34.
[34] Ibid., pp. 35-109; "Proceedings of the Members of the Russian Religious Mission in Peking," vol. IV, St. Petersburg, 1866.
[35] V. P. Vasiliev, *Note on Mongolian Tartars*,—"Proceedings of the Eastern Section of the Russian Archaeological Society (ESRAS)," vol. IV, St. Petersburg, 1859.
[36] N. Ts. Munkuev, *The Chinese Traveller on the Ancient Mongols*, "Men-da-bey-lu" ("Full description of the Mongolian Tartars"). Translation and research notes. (In course of publication).
[37] "China and Japan (History and Philology)," Moscow, 1961.
[38] "Travel Notes of the Chinese Ch'an-de-khoi During a Journey to Mongolia in First Half of XIIIth century,"—Siberian Section RGS, 1867, books IX-X.
[39] P. Savelyev, *Mongolian Paidze Found in Trans-Baikal Province*,—"Pro-

ceedings ESRAS," vol. II, 1856; D. Banzarov, *Paidze or Metal Plates with Portrayals of Mongol Khans*,—"Records of Archaeol. Society," vol. II, 1848; "Mongolian Inscription of Genghis Khan Period, Found in Eastern Siberia, Read and Translated by Archimandrite Avakuum,"—"Journal of Ministry of Interior," vol. 12, 1846; In: Klyukin, *The Most Ancient Mongol Manuscript on a Kharkhiras ("Genghis") Stone*, "Proc. State Far East. Unity," series VI, No. 5, Vladivostok, 1927; Kh. Perley, *Chingissiin chuluuny bichgees* ("Three Articles"),—"Studia Mongolica," vol. III, facs. 13, Ulan Bator, 1962.

[40] Russian translation and study made by N. Shastina, is being prepared for publication in Moscow.

[41] K. F. Holstunsky, *Mongolian-Oirat Laws, 1640, Supplementary Edicts of Galdan-khun-taidzhi and Laws Compiled for the Volga Kalfyks under the Kalmyk Khan Donduk-Dashi*, St. Petersburg, 1880.

[42] D. Pokotilov, *History of the Eastern Mongols during the Ming Dynasty, 1368-1634*, St. Petersburg. 1893.

[43] Syao Ta-syan, *Mongolchuudyn zan zanshlyn temdeglel ("Khel, sokhiol, tuukh")*, 1960, No. 2. A Mongolian translation of the second work is being prepared for printing in Ulan Bator by the Sinologist L. Zhamsaran.

[44] N. P. Shastina, *Russo-Mongolian Ambassadorial Relations in the XVIIth Century*, Moscow, 1958; I. Ya. Zlatkin. *History of the Dzhungarian Khanate*, Moscow, 1964.

[45] V. A. Ryazanovsky, *Mongolian Law, Primarily Common Law*, Harbin, 1931.

[46] "Zhalan-aazhav. Khalkh-zhuram bol mongolyn khuul tsaazni dursgalt bichig men", Ulan Bator, 1961.

[47] "Qalg a Jirum." Translated into Russian by Dr. Lamcarano; edited by Prof. Dr. Rintchen, Ulan Bator, 1959. "Khalkha Dzhirum" (Memorial of Mongolian Feudal Law of the XVIIIth Century). Summarized text and translation of Ts. Zh. Zhamtsarano, publication prepared, translation drafted, introduction and notes by S. D. Dylykov, Moscow, 1965.

[48] "Shabi Yamun-u ulagan-khatsarty atsa khagulugsan durim," Ulan Bator, 1959.

[49] S. Lipovtsev, *Code of the Chinese Chamber of Foreign Relations*, vol. 2. St. Petersburg, 1828; N. Ya. Bichurin, *Notes on Mongolia*, St. Petersburg, 1828, P. IV containing the *Mongol Code*, pp. 203-339.

[50] "Documents on the Oppressed Position of Mongolian women in the Period of Manchu rule (1764-1833)." Compiled by U. Chimid, Ulan Bator, 1956. "Fight for the Independence of the Mongolian People under Chingunzhaba in Northern Mongolia," compiled by U. Chimid, Ulan Bator, 1963.

[51] "Dereven aimgiyn alba tegshitgesen dans, 1962" and "Khariyatu khoshigunu dotura dagazhu yavugulura togtagan tushiyagsan ukhagulakhu bichig—un ekhi", 1959, et alia.

[52] Sh. Bira, *Mongolian Historical Literature in the Tibetan Tongue (XVII-XIXth centuries)*, Ulan Bator. 1960.

[53] N. Ya. Bichurin, Notes on Mongolia, vols. I-II, St. Petersburg, 1828; Same author, *Description of Dzhungaria and Eastern Turkestan in Their Ancient and Present Day State*, translated from Chinese, St. Petersburg, 1820; same author, *Historical Review of the Oirats or Kalmyks from the XVth century to the Present Day*, St. Petersburg, 1834.

[54] E. Timkovsky, *Journey to China via Mongolia, 1820-1821*, St. Petersburg, 1824.

[55] I. M. Przhevalsky, *Mongolia and the Country of the Tanguts. 3-years' Journeying in the Eastern Highlands of Asia*, vols. I-II, St. Petersburg. 1875-1876.

[56] G. N. Potanin, *Sketches of North-Western Mongolia—Results of a Journey made in 1876-1877*, vols. I-II, St. Petersburg, 1881-1883; same author, *The Tangut-Tibetan Borderland of China*, St. Petersburg, 1898.

[57] M. B. Pyevtsov, *Sketch of a Journey through Mongolia and the Northern Provinces of Inner China*. Omsk, 1883.

[58] P. K. Kozlov, *Mongolia and Kam*, St. Petersburg, 1905-1907.

[59] A. M. Pozdneev, *Mongolia and the Mongols*, vols. I-II, St. Petersburg, 1896-1898.

[60] "1921 ony ardyn khuvsgalyn tuukhend kholbogdokh barimt bichuguud (1917-1921)," Ulan Bator, 1957; "Oron nuttagt ardchilsan zasag zakhirgaany baiguulaguudyg baiguulsan n Ts. Nasanbalzhir emkhtgev:" Ulan Bator, 1958, etc.

[61] "Mongol ardyn zhuramt tsergiyn durtgaluud, D. Gongor, G. Tserendorzh har emkhetgev," Ulan Bator, 1961.

[62] "BNMAU-yn zasag zakhirgaany erkhtey kholbogdokh khuul chilsan aktuudyn sistegilsen emkhtgel," No. 1, Ulan Bator, 1961; "Khedee azh akhuid (negdlees busad) kholbogdokh khuul chilsan aktuudyn sistemchilsen emkhtgel," No. 1, Ulan Bator, 1962; "Soel-gegeerliyn baiguullaguudyn azhlyn talaar kholbogdoltoi zarlyg, togtool, zaavruudyn sistemchilsen emkhtgel (1940-1961)", Ulan Bator, 1962; "BNMAU-yn khedelmeriyin erkhiyin talaar garsan khuul chilsan aktuudyn sistemchilsan emkhtgel," Ulan Bator, 1962; "Teever kholboony talaar gargasan khuul chilsan aktuudyn sistemchilsen emkhtgel (1940-1962)," Ulan Bator. 1963; "Bugd nairamdakh Mongol Ard Ulsyn gadaad khariltsaany barimt bichuudiyin emkhtgel", 1 bot' 1921-1961.

[63] Ch. Bat-Ochir, *Mongol ulsyn ertnees ulamzhlan irsniyig temdeglesen bichig ("Short Outline History of the Mongolian State")*, Ulan Bator, 1927; Kh. Magsarzhav, *Khurts Mongol Ulsyn shine garsan tuukh*. Bichmel ("New History of Mongolia") (manuscript), 1927; L. Dendev, *Mongolyn tovch tuukh ("Short History of Mongolia")*, vol. 4, Ulan Bator, 1934; A. Amor, *Mongolyn tovch tuukh* ("Short History of Mongolia"), vol. 1, Ulan Bator, 1934; G. Navannamzhil, *Gadaad Mongolyn avtonomit yein tuukh* ("History of Autonomous Outer Mongolia"), 1927. The manuscript is kept in the State Library of the MPR.

[64] Translations were made of the *Manifesto of the Communist Party* of Marx and Engels, 1925,—"Communism"; F. Engels, *Origin of the Family, Private Property and the State*, 1928; V. I. Lenin, *Three Sources and Three Component Parts of Marxism*, 1931; V. I. Lenin, *Socialism and Religion*, 1931; V. I. Lenin, *Socialist Revolution and the Right of Nations to Self-determination*, 1931; K. Marx, *Wage, Labour and Capital*, 1935.

[65] Kh. Choibalsan, D. Losol. D. Demid, *Mongolyn ardyn undesehiy khuv sgalyn ankh uusen baiguulagdsan tovch tuukh ("Short Outline of the History of the Mongolian People's Revolution")*, books I, II, Ulan Bator, 1934.

[66] B. Buyanchulgan, *The Period of Manchu Rule in Mongolia*, Ulan Bator, 1934; same author, *The History of Four Oirats*, Ulan Bator, published in 1935-1937 in the journal *Shine-Toli*. Same author, *Materials on the History of Mongolia of the Manchu Period*, 4 vols., 1936. Manuscript is kept in the State Library, Ulan Bator.

[67] Kh. Choibalsan, *Khatan baatar Magsarzhan*, Ulan Bator, 1946; Sh. Natsagdorzh, *Manlai baatar Damdinsuren*, Ulan Bator, 1946.

[68] G. Navaannamzhil, *Zorigt baatar Togtokh*, Ulan Bator, 1946.

[69] Ts. Puntsagnorov, *History of Mongolia during the Autonomous Era*, Ulan Bator, 1955.

[70] Sh. Natsagdorzh, *The History of Khalkha, 1691-1911*, Ulan Bator, 1963.

[71] Sh. Natsagdorzh, *The Arat Movement in Northern Mongolia*, Ulan Bator, 1956.

[72] Ts. Nasanbalzhir, *The Servitudes Rendered to the Ching Dynasty*, Ulan Bator. 1962.

[73] N. Ishzhamts, *The Armed Struggle of the Mongolian People Against the Manchu Yoke for Freedom and Independence in 1755-1758*, Ulan Bator, 1962; M. Sanzhdorzh, *The Penetration of Chinese Capitalist Merchants and Usurers into Khalkha-Mongolia and its Expansion*, Ulan Bator, 1963; Ts. Sodnomdagva, *The Administrative Structure of Northern Mongolia during the Period of Manchu Rule (1901-1911)*, Ulan Bator, 1961; S. Purevzhav, *Pre-revolutionary Ikh Khure (Urga)*, Ulan Bator, 1961; D. Tsedev, *Shabinars of Bogdo-gegen*, Ulan Bator, 1964.

[74] "Oktyabriyn sotsialist ikh khuv sgal ba MAKH Ham. Oguulluudiyn

[75] B. Shirendyb, *The People's Revolution in Mongolia and the Formation of the Mongolian People's Republic*, Moscow, 1956.

[76] B. Shirendyb, *Mongolia on the Frontier of the XIXth and XXth Centuries*, Ulan Bator, 1963.

[77] L. Tudev, *From the History of the Growth of the Working Class*, Ulan Bator, 1963.

[78] "BNMAU—yn tuukh," Negan bot, Ulan Bator, 1954.

[79] "MAKHN—yn tovch tuukh" ("Short Outline History of the MPRP"). General editors—A commission of the MPRP, Central Committee consisting of B. Lkhamsuren, corresponding member of the MPR Academy of Sciences, Academician B. Shirendyb, B. Baldo, L. Sanzh and B. Tudev.

[80] Yu Tsedenbal, *Selected Speeches and Addresses*, vols. I-II, Moscow, 1961.

[81] See Karl Marx, *Secret Diplomacy of the XVIIIth Century*, vol. V of Marx and Engels Archives, Chronological Extracts, pp. 219-232.

[82] See V. I. Lenin, *Talks with the Delegation of the Mongolian People's Republic, November 1921*,—Works, vol. 44, pp. 232-233.

[83] I. E. Fisher. *Siberian History from the First Discovery of Siberia to its Conquest by Russian Arms*, St. Petersburg, 1774 (translated from the German edition published in Petersburg in 1768).

[84] G. F. Miller, *Description of the Siberian Empire and Everything that Occurred in It, Especially from its Subjugation by the Russian State up to the Present Time*, St. Petersburg, 1750, 2nd edition; "History of Siberia", vols. I-II, Moscow-Leningrad, 1937-1939.

[85] Pallas, *Sammlungen historischer Nachrichten über die Mongolischen Volkerschaften*. Vol. I-II, St. Petersburg, 1776-1801. Russian translations of separate parts. "Collection of Historical Data on Mongol Peoples",—"Vestnik," St. Petersburg, 1778, parts I-V; "Classification of Peoples of Mongol Origin,"—"Monthly Review of History and Geography for 1797."

[86] De Guignes, *Histoire générale des Huns, des Turcs, des Mongols*, Paris, 1756-1758; Visdelou, *Histoire de Tartarie*, Paris, 1779; M. Mailla, *Histoire générale de la Chine ou annales de cet Empire*, vols. IX, X, XI, Paris, 1777-1781.

[87] N. Ya. Bichurin, *Collection of Information on the Peoples Who Inhabited Central Asia in Ancient Times*, in 3 parts. St. Petersburg, 1851; 2nd edition, vols. I-II, Moscow-Leningrad, 1950.

[88] N. Ya. Bichurin, *Notes on Mongolia*, p. 157.

[89] D'Ohsson, *Histoire des Mongols depuis Tshingis-Khan jusqu'à Timour Beg ou Tamerlan*, vols. I-IV, La Haye et Amsterdam, 1834-1835.

[90] H. Howorth, *History of the Mongols*, pt. I-IV, London, 1876-1888.

[91] A. M. Pozdneev, *The Mongolian Chronicle Erdeniyn Erikhe*, St. Petersburg, 1883.

[92] Ibid, p. 97.

[93] V. V. Bartold, *The Formation of the Empire of Genghis Khan*,—"Notes in WORAS," vol. X.

[94] G. E. Grumm-Grzhimailo, *Western Mongolia and the Uryankhai Territory*, vol. II (Historical sketch of these countries in connection with the history of Central Asia), Leningrad, 1926.

[95] B. Va. Vladimirtsov, *Social System of the Mongols. Mongolian Nomadic Feudalism*, Leningrad, 1934.

[96] B. D. Grekov, A. Yu. Yakubovsky. *The Golden Horde*, Leningrad, 1937; B. D. Grekov, A. Yu. Yakubovsky, *The Golden Horde and Its Downfall*, Moscow-Leningrad, 1950.

[97] I. M. Maisky, *Mongolia on the Eve of the Popular Revolution*, Moscow, 1959.

[98] I. Ya. Zlatkin, *Sketches of the Modern and Contemporary History of Mongolia*.

[99] "The Mongolian Peoples' Republic," Collection of articles, Moscow, 1952; S. K. Roshchin, *Socialist Sector in the Economy of the MPR*, Moscow,

1958; G. S. Matveeva, *Socialist Changes in the Rural Economy of the MPR*, Moscow, 1960; "The Mongolian People's Republic, 1921-1961," Collection of articles, Moscow, 1961; "40 Years of People's Mongolia," Collection of articles, Moscow, 1961; L. M. Gataullina, *The Mongolian People's Republic in the Socialist Commonwealth*, Moscow, 1964.

[100] B. Tsybikov, *The Defeat of the Ungern Invaders*, Ulan Ude, 1947.

[101] A. Kislov, *The Defeat of Ungern*, Moscow, 1964.

[102] G. Kumgurov and I. Sorokovikov. *The Arat Revolution*, Irkutsk, 1947; N. T. Vargin, *The Mongolian People's Republic*, Economic essay, Moscow, 1950; S. S. Demidov, *The Mongolian People's Republic*. Moscow, 1952; D. B. Ulymzhiev, *The Mongolian People's Republic Builds Socialism*, Ulan Ude, 1959.

[103] M. V. Meshcheryakov, *Essays in Economic Collaboration between the Soviet Union and the Mongolian People's Republic*, Moscow, 1959; E. P. Bavrin, M. V. Meshcheryakov, *The Mongolian People's Republic. Economy and Foreign Trade*, Moscow, 1961; V. I. Pisarev, *The Mongolian People's Republic on the Way to Completing the Construction of Socialism*, Moscow, 1964.

[104] O. Lattimore, *Nationalism and Revolution in Mongolia*, New York, 1955; same author, *Nomads and Commissars. Mongolia Revisited*, New York, 1962.

[105] D. R. Phillips, *Russia, Japan and Mongolia*, London, 1942.

[106] P. Tang, *Russian and Soviet Policy in Manchuria and Outer Mongolia, 1917-1931*, Durham, 1959.

[107] D. Friberg, *Outer Mongolia and its International Position*, Baltimore, 1949.

[108] G. Murphy, *Planning in the Mongolian People's Republic (1947-1958)*,—"Journal of Asian Studies," vol, 18, 1959, No. 2, pp. 241-158; same author, *The Mongolian People's Republic: a Dual Economy*,—"Proceedings of the XXVth International Congress of Orientalists," vol. V, Moscow, 1963, pp. 343-351, et alia.

[109] I. Tayama, *Shin zhidaini Okery Mokoko sakai sei do*. Tokyo, 1955; M. Ume Hara, *Moko Noin Ula Khakken no ibuzu*, Tokyo, 1960.

[110] R. Rupen, *Inside Outer Mongolia*.—"Foreign Affairs," vol. 37, 1957, No. 2; same author, *Mongolian Nationalism*,—"Royal Central Asian Journal," vol. XLV, April, July-October, 1958.

[111] W. B. Ballis, *The Political Evolution of a Soviet Satellite*,—"Western Political Quarterly," vol. IX, 1958, No. 2, pp. 293-328; same author, *Historical Perspectives on the Formation and Development of the Mongolian People's Republic*,—"Proceedings of the XXVth International Congress of Orientalists," vol. V, 1963, pp. 306-313.

[112] O. Lattimore, *Nomads and Commissars. Mongolia Revisited*, New York, 1962.

[113] R. Rupen, *The Mongols of the XXth Century*, vols. 1, 2, Bloomington, 1964.

[114] A. Park, *The Non-Capitalistic Path of Development*, New York, 1949.

[115] D. Knutson, *Outer Mongolia. A Study of Soviet Colonialism*, Hong Kong, 1959.

[116] Ivor Montagu, *The Country of Blue Sky*, London, 1957.

[117] G. Vernadsky, *The Mongols and Russia*, vol. II, New Haven, 1953.

[118] H. Desmond Martin, *The Rise of Genghis Khan and His Conquest of North China*, Baltimore, 1950.

[119] Ch'ou Lien-hsiao, *On Genghis Khan*,—"Li-shi yan'tseyu," 1962, No. 4; Khan-Ju-lin, *On Genghis Khan*,—"Li-shi yan'tseyu," 1962, No. 3; Yui Bayan, Chen tsei sy khan (*Genghis Khan)*, Peking, 1955, et alia.

[120] Introductory speech of Yu. Tsedenbal and report by B. Lkhamsuren at the Republican Conference on Problems of Ideological Work, January, 1963; Records of the Conference of Teachers of Social Sciences, June, 1964; I. Maisky, *Genghis Khan*,—"Problems of History," No. 5, 1962; N. Ya. Merpert, V. T. Pashuto, V. Cherepnin, *Genghis Khan and His Legacy*,—"History of the USSR" No. 2, 1964.

PART 1

Section One

Chapter I

[1] A. P. Okladnikov, Primitive Mongolia,—"Studia Archaeologica," vol. III, facs. 8, p. 16.
[2] From the place where the first finds were made of these nuclei.
[3] The Ordos man was found in Southern Mongolia at Salaa-us in 1920.
[4] Geologically, world history is divided into eras which in turn are subdivided into shorter periods of time, to each of which correspond specific sedimentary rocks or layers. The Tertiary began about 60 million years ago and ended one million years before our time. It was followed by the Quaternary period which includes the present era.
[5] Sh. Tsegmid, *Khentiyn uularkhag orny fizikgazar zuyn ba ertniy mostlogiyn tukhai todorkhoilolt*, Ulan Bator, 1955.
[6] Epi—a Greek word meaning "on" or "above."

Chapter II

[1] XIII-XIIth centuries B. C.
[2] F. Engels, *The Origin of the Family, Private Property and the State*, p. 230, Moscow, 1948.
[3] Ibid, p. 226.
[4] Ibid., p. 228.
[5] Ibid.. p. 229.

Section Two

Chapter I

[1] In Chinese historical chronicles of the first millennium B. C. there are references to tribes under the general designation of Jung, Di and Hu as inhabiting Central Asia.
[2] F. Engels, *The Origin of the Family, Private Property and the State*, page, 233, Moscow, 1948.
[3] Ibid.
[4] Ibid.

Section Three

Chapter I

[1] The present day Cis-Angara territory.
[2] K. Marx, *Forms Precedent to Capitalist Ownership*,—"Ancient History Gazette," 1940, No. 1, p. 21.

Chapter II

[1] Tax on cattle at pasture.

Section Four

Chapter I

[1] V. I. Lenin, *Works*, vol. 3, Moscow, 1960, p. 192.
[2] Ibid., pp. 192-193.
[3] K. Marx, *Capital*, vol. III, Moscow, 1959, p. 774.
[4] K. Marx, *Capital*, vol. III, Moscow, 1959, p. 776.

Chapter II

[1] South-west of the town of Huailai in Chakhar province.

Chapter III

[1] V. I. Lenin, *Collected Works*, vol. 10, p. 83.
[2] K. Marx and F. Engels, *Works*, vol. V. p. 173.
[3] F. Engels, *The Peasant War in Germany*, London, 1927, pp. 40, 41.

Chapter VI

[1] Syao Da-syan, *Mongolin zan Zanzhilin temdeglel khel, zokhiol, tuukh*, 1960, p. 8.
[2] B. Ya. Vladimirtsov, *Comparative Grammar...*, pp. 23-24.
[3] Ibid., p. 24.

Section Five

Chapter I

[1] A tribute which originally bore a symbolic character and consisted of nine animals of a white colour—eight horses and one camel.

Chapter II

[1] Shabin department— the *Bogdo-gegen's* administration dealing with *arat* serfs.
[2] K. Marx, *Capital*, vol. III, p. 613.

Chapter III

[1] *Lan (lyan)*—a specific measure of the weight of silver ingots, equal to 37,301 grammes.
[2] K. Marx, *Capital*, vol. III, 1953, p. 611.
[3] *Desyatina*—2.7 acres.
[4] V. I. Lenin, *Works*, vol. 19, p. 56.

Chapter IV

[1] See V. I. Lenin, *Notebooks on Imperialism*, 1939, p. 621.
[2] See V. I. Lenin, *Works*, vol. 18. pp. 371, 387.

Chapter V

[1] F. Engels, *The Peasant War in Germany*, London, 1927, p. 52.

Section Six

Chapter IV

[1] "Ulsyn Archiv", 6 *angi*, 31 *buleg* 1 *bus*.
[2] For schools of the period, see N. Ser-Odzhav, *Mongolian avtonomit ueyin soyolin zarim asuudluud*—SHU, 1855, No. 3, 13-18; Sh. Bira, *Mongolyn avtonomit zasgiyn ued teriyn surgulliyn khergiyg khegzhuulekh talaar avch yavuulsan zarim devshilt arga khemzheeniy tukhai*, Ulan Bator, 1950; L. Dugersuren. *Ulaanbaatar khotyn tuukhees*—"Niyslel khuree", Ulan Bator, 1956, pp. 65-66.
[3] For regulations on elementary and high schools, see "Ulsyn Tov

Archive," 1 *angi*, 29 *buleg*, 8 *bus*.; B. Rinchen, *Mongol bichgiyn khelniy zuy*, Ulan Bator, 1964, pp. 44-57.

[4] "Uslyn Archiv", 1 *angi*, 29 *buleg*, 1 *bus*.

[5] "Mongol ulsyn shastir", vol. 11 (pages not indicated).

PART II

Section One

Chapter I

[1] See "History of the Mongolian People's Republic" (Russian edition), Moscow, 1954, p. 32.

[2] Kh. Choibalsan was born on February 8, 1895, in Tsetstn Khan (now Eastern) *aimak* in the family of a poor *arat* woman, Khorlo. His childhood was difficult. As she was unable to feed the family the mother decided to hand over Choibalsan to a monastery. After spending two years in the monastery Choibalsan ran away from it and in 1912 came to Urga where, after lengthy tribulations, he got into the school attached to the Foreign Ministry. Choibalsan was an excellent student and in 1914 he and other good students were sent to Irkutsk to continue their education.

The stay in Russia did a lot for Choibalsan. He learnt Russian, familiarized himself with the culture of the great Russian people. The revolutionary struggle of the Russian working class, the overthrow of autocracy, the class and party struggle in Russia after the February bourgeois-democratic revolution—all this had a great influence on the young Choibalsan and the other young Mongolians who were studying at the time in Russia.

[3] Kh. Choibalsan, *Sukhbaator bol chukhamkhuu mapai khairt udirdaych mon*, Ulan Bator, 1944, p. 4.

[4] Kh. Choibalsan, *Short Outline of the History of the Mongolian People's Revolution*, Moscow, 1952, pp. 21-22.

[5] Ibid., p. 22.

[6] Ibid.

[7] Ibid., pp. 25-26.

Chapter II

[1] Kh. Choibalsan, *Short Outline of the History of the Mongolian People's Revolution*, p. 28.

[2] V. I. Lenin, *Works*, vol. 21, p. 190.

[3] Cited from: Kh. Choibalsan, *Short Outline of the History of the Mongolian People's Revolution*, p. 42.

[4] Ibid.

[5] Ibid.

[6] Ibid.

[7] Ibid., p. 43.

[8] Ibid.

[9] Ibid.

[10] "Revolutionary Measures of the People's Government of Mongolia in 1921-1924," Moscow, 1960, p. 12 (in Russian).

[11] "History of the Mongolian People's Republic" (Russian edition), p. 256.

[12] "Revolutionary Measures of the People's Government of Mongolia in 1921-24," Moscow, 1960, p. 19 (in Russian).

[13] The former commander of the second Sretensk cavalry brigade, Litvintsev, had been placed at the disposal of Sukhe Bator and was first Chief of Staff of the PRA.

[14] Cited from the book: Kh. Choibalsan, *Short Ourline of the History of the Mongolian People's Revolution*, p. 73.

[15] The Russian text was published in the *Izvestia* of Oct. 6, 1921, and in condensed form in the *Vlast Truda* of Oct. 8, 1921.

Chapter III

[1] *Bodo*—a conventional unit, equivalent at the time to ¹/₂ camel or one ox or seven sheep.
[2] "Ardyn zasgass 1921-1924 onuudad avsan khuvsgalt arga khemzheenuud," Ulan Bator, 1954, p. 66.
[3] *Vlast Truda*, August 2, 1923.
[4] "Ardyn zasgass 1921-1924 onuudal avsan khuvsgalt arga khemzheenuud."
[5] For details, of the formation of MPR see book of B. Shirendyb "The People's Revolution in Mongolia and Formation of MPR."
[6] See "Basic Law (Constitution) of the MPR" and appendices in book: "Mongolian Legislation," 1 ed., Ulan Bator, 1928.
[7] "Bugd Nairamdakh Mongol Ard Ulsyn undsen khuul," Oros mongol khevleliyn khoroo, Ulan Bator, 1924, p. 5.
[8] Ibid., p. 12.
[9] V. I. Lenin, *Works*, vol. 15, p. 308.
[10] V. I. Lenin, *Works*, vol. 31, p. 218.
[11] V. I. Lenin, *Works*, vol. 9, p. 281.

Section Two

Chapter I

[1] Quoted from the newspaper *Izvestya Ulan-Bator Hoto*, March 15, 1925.
[2] "MAKHN-yn Tov Khoroony ba Tov khyanan baytsaah komissyn khamtarsan onts buyd khurlyn iltgel ba togtooluud," 1932, pp. 66-67.
[3] Ibid., p. 68.
[4] Ibid., pp. 68-69.
[5] V. I. Lenin, *Works*, vol. 31, p. 218.

Chapter II

[1] "Sovremennaya Mongolya," 1935, No. 1, p. 35.
[2] "Pravda," March 1, 1936.
[3] "Informatsionniy bulleten," 1962, No. 1 (15), p. 12.
[4] Ibid., p. 36.
[5] "Reports and Speeches of Kh. Choibalsan," vol. II, p. 406.
[6] Ibid.
[7] "Sovremennaya Mongoliya," 1940, No. 12, p. 77.
[8] Ibid., p. 9.
[9] Ibid., p. 80.
[10] "Sovremennaya Mongoliya," 1940, No. 3, p. 4.

Section Three

Chapter I

[1] "Sovremennaya Mongoliya," 1940, Nos 1-2, p. 5.
[2] "Collection of Laws and Basic Resolutions of the MPR Government," Ulan Bator, 1941, p. 29.
[3] "History of the Great Patriotic War of the Soviet Union 1941-1945," Moscow, vol. II, 1961, p. 9.
[4] "BNMAU, Zkhu-yn ekh orny ikh dainy yed," Ulan Bator, 1954, pp. 5-6.
[5] MAKHN-yn tovch tuukh — "Namyn amdral," 1964, No. 4, p. 22.
[6] "Collection of Laws and Basic Resolutions of the MPR Government," 3rd ed., Ulan Bator, 1943, pp. 103-104.
[7] Yu. Tsedenbal, *Selected Articles and Speeches*, Moscow, 1962, p. 39.
[8] "History of the USSR," Moscow, 1957, p. 636.
[9] "International Relations in the Far East (1870-1945)," Moscow, p. 598.

Chapter II

[1] B. Tudev. *BNMAU-yn azhiichi angiyn tuukh,* Ulan Bator, 1963, pp. 107-121.

Section Four

Chapter I

[1] Yu. Tsedenbal, Report of the MPRP Central Committee to the Fourteenth Party Congress. Selected articles and speeches, Moscow, 1963, p. 313.

Chapter II

[1] "XIVth MPRP Congress," Ulan Bator, 1961, p. 11.
[2] Ibid., p. 176.
[3] Ibid.
[4] Ibid.
[5] Ibid., p. 196.
[6] "Unen," May 29, 1963.
[7] "Unen", November 12, 1963.
[8] Ibid.
[9] "Information bulletin," No. 1-2, Ulan Bator, 1964, p. 32.
[10] "Unen", January 6, 1962.
[11] "Unen", November 16, 1963.

Section Five

[1] "BNMAU-yn ikh, baga Khurlyn togtool, undsen khuul, Tunkhaguud," 348 ta!.
[2] V. I. Lenin, *Works,* vol. 33, p. 78.
[3] "XIVth Congress of the MPRP," p. 53.
[4] "Materials for the History and Philology of Central Asia," Ulan-Ude, 1962, p. 141.
[5] Ibid.
[6] "XXIInd Congress of the CPSU," vol. III, Moscow, 1962, p. 163.

Afterword

[1] "Fifteenth Congress of the MPRP", Moscow, 1966, pp. 81-82.
[2] Ibid., pp. 83-84.
[3] Ibid., p. 96.
[4] Ibid., p. 82.
[5] Ibid., p. 83.
[6] Ibid.
[7] "50 Years of the MPR. Statistical Handbook", Ulan Bator, 1971, p. 70.
[8] Fifteenth Congress of the MPRP," p. 37.
[9] Ibid., p. 117.
[10] Ibid., pp. 195-196.
[11] "Pravda", July 11, 1971.
[12] Ibid.
[13] See Yu. Tsedenbal, Report to the Central Committee of the MPRP, Ulan Bator, 1971, p. 6.
[14] Ibid., p. 67.
[15] "Unen", 28.2.71.
[16] "Unen", 8.7.71.
[17] "Unen", 8.7.71.
[18] "Unen", 8.7.71.
[19] "Fifty Years of the MPR. Statistical Handbook", p. 197.
[20] Ibid., pp. 203-204.
[21] Ibid., p. 225.
[22] "Unen", 8.7.72.

Printed in the United States
119223LV00001B/83/A